W9-BVH-125

United States Foreign Policy and World Order

United States Foreign Policy and World Order

Third Edition

James A. Nathan
James K. Oliver
University of Delaware

Little, Brown and Company

Boston   Toronto

Library of Congress Cataloging in Publication Data

Nathan, James A.

  United States foreign policy and world order.

  Includes bibliographical references and index.
   1. United States—Foreign relations—1945–
  2. United States—Foreign relations administration.
  I. Oliver, James K.   II. Title.
  E744.N34   1984   327.73   84–21805
  ISBN 0–316–59870–4

Library of Congress Catalog Card No. 84–21805

ISBN 0-316-59870-4

9 8 7 6 5 4 3

MV

Published simultaneously in Canada
by Little, Brown & Company (Canada) Limited

Printed in the United States of America

The authors gratefully acknowledge permission to reprint from the following copyrighted
works.

Portions of the Introduction are published by permission of Transaction, Inc., from James
A. Nathan and James K. Oliver, "Diplomacy of Violence," in *Society*, Vol. 11, No. 6.
Copyright © 1974 by Transaction, Inc.

Excerpts from Dean Acheson, *Present at the Creation*, are reprinted by permission of W.W.
Norton & Company, Inc., and Hughes Massie Limited. Copyright © 1969 by Dean Acheson.

Portions of Chapter 8 are from James A. Nathan, "The Cuban Missile Crisis: His Finest
Hour Now," *World Politics*, Vol. 27, No. 2 (January 1975). Copyright © 1975 by Princeton
University Press.

Portions of Chapter 10 are from James A. Nathan, "Commitments in Search of a Roost: The
Foreign Policy of the Nixon Administration," *Virginia Quarterly Review*, Vol. 50, No. 3
(Summer 1974). Reprinted by permission.

(continued on page 486)

Preface

U.S. foreign policy in the 1980s shows a remarkable continuity. The cold war is now a forty-year-old struggle, marked by familiar contours, policy repertoires, and rhetoric. The dialogue between the great powers has been marked by a now-routine absence of civility; the common idiom still employed by both powers remains that of coercive diplomacy buttressed by the final implication of nuclear weapons. Today's contest between the Soviets and the United States would be recognizable to the founding generation of the cold war. Indeed, not a few of them are still involved in the policymaking of both nations.

The massive buildup of U.S. forces—which began under the last years of the Carter administration—has been not only the Navy and the Army and other forces preparing themselves for sustained battles and placing themselves in "harm's way" but, more important, the enormous buildup of nuclear weapons systems.

Perhaps not since the "new look" of President Dwight David Eisenhower have nuclear weapons been so thoroughly integrated into virtually every level of national security planning. Tactical nuclear weapons, or "dual use" weapons, are essential features of all segments of the U.S. military. For instance, there are huge numbers of cruise missiles now being placed on U.S. surface ships. Some are nuclear armed. Some are conventionally armed. It is impossible for an observer to distinguish which are nuclear and which are conventional. Moreover, the effect of the explosive power of a sea-launched nuclear cruise weapon can be of the same order of intensity as a conventional sea-launched cruise weapon. The distinction between the potential damage of a sea-launched cruise missile and that of a sea-borne strategic nuclear weapon is academic and hypothetical. The American strategic nuclear warhead inventory has undergone a 100 percent expansion.

The idea of "vital interests"—interests worth fighting for—has been expanded. Hence, Defense Secretary Caspar Weinberger has instructed the U.S. military to be prepared to fight "in wars of any size and shape and in any region where we have vital interests." The markers of this policy of undifferentiated globalism can be seen in the form of the refurbished and vastly expanded fleets now on guard in the Mediterranean, off the coasts of Central America, in the Red Sea and Indian Ocean and Straits of Hormuz, as well as in the far Pacific and North Atlantic.

The result of the great expansion of nuclear weapons of all kinds has been to make nuclear war more viable to some policymakers. The distinction between conventional and exotic ordnance is breaking down. Thermal weapons produce the heat of nuclear weapons. Land-based anti-aircraft Patriot missiles are now capable of ballistic missile defense. Conventional artillery shells now use expended nuclear material for their armor-piercing functions. Low-yield nuclear weaons are all but indistinguishable from higher-yield conventional munitions. Increasingly effective and destructive conventional weapons have blurred the distinction between conventional and nuclear explosives.

The confusion between strategic and theater weapons, and the expansion of "vital interests" combined with a new bellicosity in American politics and planning,* has found a correspondence in obdurate Soviet diplomacy. The widening definition of national interests and the new delicacy in superpower relations find the great nuclear rivals in unchartered arenas of hostility.

The dollar cost to the United States may not be calculable. Some economists believe that perhaps two-thirds of the current budget deficit can be attributed to defense spending. In any case, the new emphasis on defense casts real doubts on the United States' economic future. It is uncertain how the current defense program can be sustained. Further, it is unclear whether U.S. demographics can fulfill current and projected military manpower needs.

The portents are disturbing. Both the Soviet Union and the United States are prepared to use military force in areas where interests have expanded. There has come about a more explicit intimacy among force, politics, and nuclear weapons. However, nuclear weapons are antipolitical, for in a real sense they do not serve policy. Nonetheless, there is an increasing tempo of superpower involvement in the third world. Power projection in the third world has been facilitated by unprecedented technological advances. Renewed great-power interest in the third world, combined with superpower dependence on nuclear weapons, is a matter for profound disquiet. All this is not entirely novel; it does not spring unexpected like Athena from the head of Zeus. But although the course of events may have come to seem natural, the result may prove to be startling.

*Especially *current* U.S. military doctrine. Current U.S. plans would have NATO strike deep within Warsaw Pact territory and even well into European Russia. Control of violence, or even the management of its threat, has frayed. Indeed, the new doctrine, in the words of Harvard analyst John Mearsheimer, "comes very close to calling for preemptive strikes." Cited by Michael T. Klare, "Conventional Arms, Military Doctrine and Nuclear War: The Vanishing Firebreak," *Fordham University Quarterly*, Vol. 59, No. 232 (March 1984), p. 6.

The Soviet experiment and the Soviet Union's legitimacy are in constant devaluation, challenged from Afghanistan to Poland to Africa. The irrelevance of the Soviets' model to the 1980s does not diminish the danger of their weapons, nor their sullen distemper hardened by storms of invective. The few remaining tools of classic diplomacy languish from disuse.

This third edition of *United States Foreign Policy and World Order* has been edited, tightened, and updated. Nonetheless, it is a linear child of the second edition. A theme has been elaborated here, new historical information has been incorporated there. The response to the new book has been a joy. Unfailingly, our editor at Little, Brown and his staff have provided yet again the holding of hands and the cheers and frowns that bestir what craftsmanship we have been able to muster. Numerous colleagues have shared their ideas with us over the years. In the earlier editions, and in this one, we have tried to acknowledge our intellectual debts in the annotations.

In the course of creating this edition, Nathan suffered a sudden, bitter incapacitation which meant that Oliver had to carry more than his share of the usual struggles with galley proofs and copy editors. It is today a better book, however, and James K. Oliver deserves a salute and more.

J.N.

Contents

Chapter 5: Conserving Containment   157

Chapter 6: Crisis and Salvaging the Status Quo   199

Chapter 7: Containment on the New Frontier   236

Chapter 8: The Apotheosis of Containment   271

Chapter 9: Containment "Turns the Corner" . . . into the Swamp   306

Chapter 10: The Nixon Doctrine and Beyond   347

United States
Foreign Policy
and World Order

Introduction

International relations as a distinct mode of inquiry—separate from history, government, philosophy, or law—has achieved independent status and recognition only within the last thirty or forty years. Before this period there were historical narratives of wars or diplomatic machinations, texts and analyses of international law, and philosophical treatments of how people and states should relate to one another. But only the press of the great conflcits of the twentieth century, combined with the rapid rise of universities to a place of prominence in public life, has allowed for the creation of a separate discipline complete with a vast literature, separate schools of thought—even heretics.

So vast has this study of international relations become that simple divisions and distinctions about the study seem facile or incomplete. Yet for all the complexity of the subject matter, it seems that there have arisen clearly defined alternative frameworks for viewing people's international political behavior and the foreign policy of states. Each of these frameworks emphasizes and illuminates some kinds of activity and passes over and distorts others. These concepts of international relations are like a geographer's map that cannot be true to spatial relations, distance, and shape at all times, but can be fairly accurate to two of the three.

TWO VIEWS
OF WORLD POLITICAL REALITY

The "picture in the head," as Walter Lippmann used to say, of most political leaders concerned with international affairs has been to see international relations as if they consisted almost solely of the interaction of nation-states. From this traditional perspective, international society is a separate and dangerous domain of human activity, in contrast to the orderly processes of Anglo-American domestic political life. Wolfers and Martin have explained that

> domestic political conditions stand in striking contrast to the conditions . . . nations face in their external relations; the domestic conditions are characterized by order, lawfulness and peace arising from popular con-

1

sensus on principle—a consensus so marked that some believe coercion has practically ceased to play a role here; but the external relations continue to be full of bitter struggle, violence, and Machiavellian practices.[1]

The classic conception of traditional statecraft is that in international relations, where there is no force able to regulate disputes, wars occur because there is little to stop them, aside from self-restraint. Foreign policy is conducted in an arena of politics where there is no reliable mechanism for regulating disputes except self-help. This condition of anarchy necessarily stimulates competition for military power. Military capability is sought to secure states in a domain of threat—international society. This society is such a cockpit of hostility and danger that alliances, conventions, and treaties are all made with the understanding that the ability to defend oneself is never given away. A state must always be sovereign or independent in order to protect its customs, institutions, and inhabitants. As Henry Kissinger once intoned, "No nation can make its survival dependent on the good will of another state if it has any choice about it."[2]

The nature of an international system that is marked by the absence of a superior public monopoly of force is commonly understood by leaders and analysts as a society at the edge of war. Force, in this society, is the common medium of exchange; and power is the only means of gaining interest. It is a realm of politics that recalls Cicero's lament, "What can be done against force without force?"[3] Foreign policy, in such an environment, is above all to protect national interests against the dangerous and hostile forces at loose in a world where there are no international police and no courts with binding authority.

An alternative view of international relations, while not dismissing these traditional concerns, nonetheless urges attention to a host of new forces in world politics that have in some measure made most states more interdependent with one another.[4] In these circumstances military power does not now seem to bring benefits commensurate with its cost; nor does force usually seem an especially useful tool to deal with world economic and social crises. Military power, moreover, does not always serve its historic function by which states traditionally won their legitimacy. Even the most awesome nuclear power can no longer protect citizens against enemies. Indeed, every American president since Harry Truman has warned that the United States cannot survive an onslaught of nuclear weapons. The state used to be the citizen's fortress against capricious violence. The state would provide for the conditions of order and stability in which citizens could plan for their children or undertake their own livelihood. In this sense, the state used to be a precondition of society's benefits: health, wealth, rectitude, or justice. In previous eras, a good life was impossible without a sound, viable state. In turn, the inhabitants of states agreed, at least in theory, to be citizens, to profess allegiance, to pay taxes, and to participate, if necessary, in the state's common defense. But if the state can no longer be counted on to serve as the agent of defense; in fact, if the state becomes an agent of society's ills, then an ancient agreement is shattered as the "roof has been blown off" the historic shelter that nation-states once provided.[5]

The monopolization of military force gave historic states their definition. It was also an instrument of their will. The ability to direct violence against foreign states was a critical element of national greatness. Diplomacy and force were inextricably related. Yet the rise of irregular warfare (both urban and rural) and the expansion of force to the point where the use of force implies suicide has largely paralyzed the greatest military machines. Nuclear weapons have great destructive power; but because world order is delicately balanced, the threat of force seems foolish if the other side can, with assurance, retaliate. To use nuclear weapons and nuclear blackmail seems more and more unreasonable as the threat is disproportionate to almost any conceivable gain. Nuclear weapons have become impotent except as symbols of national greatness and as grim reminders that all humanity is grouped together under the same dark shadow.

Historically military power either begot economic wealth, or economic strength purchased military power. Today, however, there are vast discrepancies between wealth and power. Some countries are all but impoverished yet possess tremendous military potential; others are fabulously wealthy yet militarily feeble.

From this interdependence perspective, the nation-state is seen as caught in a surge of technological change that has brought most aspects of human interaction into closer proximity. There has been an internationalization of social and economic life. In America, for example, the economy has become sensitive to world commodity markets. Economic sovereignty has been breached through the vulnerability of American energy resources. And although in the early 1980s the dollar regained its position as one of the world's strongest currencies, the trading competitiveness of the United States diminished. By 1984 the prospect was for a $100 billion trade deficit and the loss of 1.2 to 1.5 million American jobs.[6]

For years economists and politicians were confident that national measures taken by central governments could control inflation and unemployment by priming the national budgetary pump or by changing the costs of borrowing money. Now, however, national remedies are highly dependent for their success on being harmonized with compatible actions in other nations. Complicating such efforts are significant concentrations of private economic power whose activities inevitably link the U.S. economy to the international economy. Thus by the late 1970s U.S. merchandise exports constituted 10 percent of all the goods produced in the United States, twice the level of the 1950s. The foreign subsidiaries and branches of U.S. multinational corporations were producing 25 percent of the parent firms' production. Americans in foreign countries held some $350 billion in assets while foreigners had invested in the United States $275 billion.[7] Furthermore, by the end of the 1970s, international banks held some $666 billion in foreign currency deposits "denominated in a currency other than that of the host country,"[8] of which $436.6 billion were dollars.[9] At the same time, however, high interest rates in the United States in the early 1980s, combined with sluggish economies elsewhere, increased the attractiveness of the United States to foreign investors.[10] By early 1984, foreign investment in the United States—most of it in United States government liabilities such as Treasury securities or U.S. securities sensitive to U.S. interest rates—was increasing at a faster rate than U.S. investment abroad. This combination of high interest rates in the United States and sluggish foreign economies raised the prospect that the United States might become in the mid-1980s a debtor nation for the first time since the early twentieth century.[11]

These circumstances necessarily place much of the U.S. business world in an interdependent relationship with a global economic system separated from easy national control. Today great corporations nominally based in Delaware, London, or Zurich may have operations in one hundred countries. No one national headquarters will contain more than a fraction of its activities. Several such corporations or banks, by shifting their reserves, for instance, out of one currency and into another (this can be done in a paper transaction by calling practically any bank) can cause the value of national currencies to plummet or ascend. Nor are such effects confined to the third world. As many in the United States have noted, including Paul Volker, chairman of the Federal Reserve Board, a rapid withdrawal of foreign investment here could end American economic recovery.[12]

In this way, the United States and most other nations have in some measure become captive to an international financial system from which they can disentangle themselves only at great risk. As Bergsten noted, the old refrain, "Let trade wars come, we'll win them," now sounds as ludicrous as Mao Zedong's famous dictum that China would emerge victorious from the ashes of a nuclear holocaust.[13] Increasingly, therefore, all states in international society find themselves in the same leaky craft.

Finally, economic instruments are not readily available for other political or strategic uses. Thus the attempt by the Reagan administration to limit the economic ties of Europe to the Soviet Union, as part of American economic warfare against the Soviets, was a failure and probably damaged the alliance more than it hurt the Soviets.[14] Similarly, when the United States in 1979 and 1980 sought to mobilize its European and Japanese allies to impose economic sanctions on the revolutionary regime in Iran, to compel the release of American diplomatic hostages, these forces of interdependence proved to be major constraints. The Europeans and especially the Japanese, being more dependent upon Iranian oil than the United States, were extremely reluctant to move decisively against the Iranians. Furthermore, the presence of a large American naval task force and a bungled military effort to free the hostages in early 1980 had not secured the release of the hostages by mid-1980 and only underscored the problem of using force in the contemporary world system. In neighboring Afghanistan the Soviet Union, despite the insertion of more than eighty thousand troops in an effort to suppress an anticommunist insurgency, was faced by the mid-1980s with a situation sometimes described as similar to the American intervention in Vietnam more than a decade earlier.

Yet surely, one might retort, security policy—wars and those who threaten them—dominate our attention and the media. If we concentrate on the newer features of interdependence, do we not miss the critical questions of national life and death? Those who maintain that a global systems perspective is useful would not deny the urgent questions of foreign policy—the politics of war and peace. But the interdependence view of the globe moves our attention to some of the interactions that are no longer contained or controlled by national policy. Of course, a view of international politics that looks to a kind of primitive global society has limits. It seems best used to illustrate economic, social, and political transnational behavior. The global systems view does not help as much in understanding Henry Kissinger's secret trip to Beijing in 1971, the 1973 or 1982 Middle East wars, or the strategic arms negotiations. These politics of power, balance, and strategy are much better illuminated by the classic world view. But the vision of an increasingly complex and interdependent political economics on a global scale does help capture some of the rapidly changing complexities of the last quarter of this century. If we recognize that these elements of interdependence have grown out of and coexist with elements of the traditional international politics of the first half of the century, we will have an even more complete image of the context within which American foreign policy has operated during the period surveyed in this book.

THINKING ABOUT
UNITED STATES FOREIGN POLICY

Thus the student of international relations and the making and conduct of foreign policy is confronted with different though connected conceptions of the structure and dynamics of world politics in the late twentieth century. On the one hand, there is a "traditional" or "realist" framework which emphasizes the interaction of nation-states in a quasi-anarchical environment. "Neo-realists" accept the new salience of economic interdependence, but for them the preparation for and use of force are the dominant and controlling realities for foreign policy makers and the societies within which they act. In contrast, there is an "interdependence" or "transnational" framework which, while acknowledging the continuing importance of the nation-state and its strategic concerns, nonetheless emphasizes the new importance of political economic forces and conditions which penetrate nation-states and give rise to new actors and forces which now constrain the foreign policies of even the most powerful of states.

But the analyst and student of American foreign policy is confronted with still other analytical debates and choices. Undoubtedly one of the most intense of these conceptual arguments during the last several decades involves those who see the course of American foreign policy as determined by the exigencies of the bipolar struggle between an America intent upon establishing an open, liberal capitalist world order and an aggressive, expansionist Soviet Union intent upon establishing a closed, totalitarian communist world state. This "orthodox" or "traditional" view of the motivation of American foreign policy maintains that American behavior since the end of World War II has been essentially a defensive reaction to the unremitting expansionism of the Soviet Union. In contrast, the "revisionists" tend to view American policy and behavior as largely responsible for the cold war. In its economic determinist form, revisionism sees in American foreign policy the operation of institutional imperatives growing out of capitalism and its purported need for international dominion to secure markets, raw materials, and cheap labor.[15]

In a variant of revisionism somewhat closer to the position adopted in the analysis to follow, greater emphasis is placed on the sense of moral, social, cultural, and historical as well as economic "exceptionalism" which has informed so much of the American view of itself and its role in the world. With its roots undoubtedly extending back to the colonial and revolutionary experience, but, in any event, full-blown by the turn of the nineteenth into the twentieth century and most eloquently and forcefully articulated by Woodrow Wilson, this American "exceptionalism" has tended to define American security interests broadly and in terms of a world order which excludes virtually all other notions of security. When confronted in the early twentieth century with an alternative and no less mutually exclusive conception of world order—communism—cold war would become likely. Insofar as the seat of that competitive order was in a state—Soviet Russia—whose historical situation was defined, not only by communist revolution, but also by authoritarian rule, cultural isolation, periodic invasion resulting in a historical sense of insecurity, and pride in having persevered in its position on the "edge" of Europe, it would have been surprising if bipolar conflict over the future of world order had not occurred.

The analytical approach adopted in this study is eclectic. We have no desire to demonstrate the truth or error of the many philosophical and analytical perspectives contending for the attention and allegiance of the student of American foreign policy. Where the traditional or orthodox analysis seems valid to us, we employ it, but where a revisionist perspective appears reasonable and warranted by documentation, we are not averse to bringing such analysis to bear. In any event, we have tried to make our analytical posture explicit within the range of possible interpretive positions.

Similarly, regarding the various models of policy making and the other accoutrements of contemporary political science and policy analysis, we have searched for and tried to apply those that explain and enlighten. Here again, the student and analyst are confronted with several possibilities as to the level of analysis at which one might work. One might, for example, simply conceive of the United States and its foreign policy processes as a kind of black box from which "policy" emerges and interacts with the actors and conditions that the international political system comprises. From this perspective the United States can be regarded as a "rational actor" seeking to devise courses of action which maximize its interests and minimize the costs associated with the pursuit of the national interest. On the other hand, much contemporary analysis of American foreign policy insists that one must shift the level of analysis to that of the political system operating within the black box. But here one encounters still more levels or potential foci of analysis.[16]

Concentrating on "bureaucratic politics" has assumed much prominence among students of foreign policy in the last decade. In this view foreign policy is best understood as the outcome of a complex intragovernmental bargaining process involving career bureaucrats, political appointees, and, of course, the president, all seeking to maximize their personal interests, their organization's interests, or both within the policy process. The "national interest" is, therefore, defined in specific policy terms as the result of the pulling and pushing of the bureaucratic process over which presidents and their closest advisers seek to extend their control. A variant of this approach concentrates on the group dynamics of close presidential advisers and their interplay with the president.[17] Even more focused is analysis that concentrates on the psychology and the cognitive and administrative styles of presidents and high officialdom.[18]

Yet another approach suggests that this concentration on bureaucratic politics, personal psychology, or small group dynamics ignores a much broader, but no less important, political interaction within American society as a whole.[19] Thus foreign policy is constrained by, and must be understood in terms of, such diverse factors as executive-legislative relations, electoral politics, the interplay of public attitudes and opinion with the governmental decision-making process, as well as the activities of the many concentrations of private power in the American political system.

We have not applied, for we do not find universally applicable, a single framework, model, perspective, or level of analysis that encompasses these many dimensions and implications of American foreign policy. The careful student will observe, however, a tendency for analysis to focus on the perceptions (insofar as these can be determined), actions, and rationalizations of presidents and their chief advisers. We are concerned primarily with the perceptions of international relations and America's role in world politics that seem to have dominated American foreign policy since World War II and the consequences of those perceptions becoming policy. Inasmuch as the process whereby these perceptions are translated into policy has focused on the president and the presidency during the period under study, our focus seems warranted. At the same time, however, we find it essential to place such analysis in the rich context of bureaucratic and executive-legislative politics, public opinion, the exercise of private power, and ultimately the interaction of American policy with the constraints imposed by a dynamic international system. Our approach has as its objective understanding the origins of the American image of international reality, the resultant policies, and the global consequences of these policies. Finally, we hope to shed some light on the extent to which the dominant perceptions of America's interests and policy have reached the outer limits of utility.

THE CONTEXT OF WORLD POLITICS
AND THE COURSE OF AMERICAN POLICY

The chapters which follow trace the attempt by the United States to fashion and apply its conception of world order in the increasingly turbulent and interdependent post–World War II world. This complex international context of new forces and traditional political forms and concerns has frustrated any simple resolution of the problems of world order. American foreign policy has sought for four decades to build an international order predicated on American military and economic superiority. From the outset of the postwar period, American policymakers postulated a relationship between American national security and some form of world order. In late 1945, American policymakers confronted the tasks of reconstructing a world order shattered by three decades of global war, economic dislocation, depression, and political and social revolution. The United States possessed seemingly limitless military power with its monopoly of atomic weapons and was the only national economy of significance to have come through World War II intact. There was apprehension about inflation and postwar adjustment, but whereas Europe lay in ruins, the American economy had grown and even prospered as the arsenal for the wartime alliance.

But the postwar international system has been resistant to American political, economic, and military capability. The cold war between the Soviet Union and the United States concerning the political, military, economic, and social structure and dynamics of Europe immediately took the place of World War II. The origins of this conflict lie in the chaotic end of World War I and the American, European, and Japanese attempts to crush the Russian communist revolution of 1917. That intervention failed, but the resultant Soviet anxiety with respect to the capitalist world and Western preoccupation with the purported global designs of communist ideology festered throughout the interwar period and were not really suppressed even when a common enemy threw the two worlds together in a superficial alliance between 1941 and 1945 (see Chapter 1).

In the West the greatest threat to international order after World War II was the political and economic chaos of Western Europe. These conditions seemed to provide the opportunity for Soviet expansion beyond the hegemony over Central Europe gained through the defeat of Nazi power in that region during 1944 and 1945. Inasmuch as the immediate postwar European problem was deemed to be primarily economic in origin, economic remedies seemed most appropriate (see Chapter 2); however, because American economic assistance was predicated on the twin necessities of a strong, essentially capitalist Europe and a reconstructed Germany (see Chapters 2 and 3), the Soviets' long-standing fear of a capitalist encirclement on the one hand and the possibility of renewed German aggression on the other could not help but be exacerbated by American policies (see Chapters 1 and 3). The result of this conflict between Soviet security concerns and superior American arms and economic strength directed toward an open, liberal world order was a sustained period of crisis beginning with the Berlin Blockade of

1948–1949. As crisis followed crisis, the apparent necessity for employing in some fashion—either by threat or demonstrations of "will"—the instrumentalities of force and the American sense of responsibility for the military imperatives of world order came to override an earlier interest in the international economic order and the economic instrumentalities of the Marshall Plan (see Chapter 3). That a successful diplomacy had to be predicated on military power was a lesson subsequently confirmed by the Korean War (see Chapter 4).

The psychological and material burdens of the Korean conflict seriously eroded domestic support for American conventional military interventions in furtherance of U.S. global activism. But the Eisenhower administration successfully deflected this frustration and built an even larger structure of international obligations. Massive retaliation, the dependence on the threat of ultimate nuclear force, was the temporary response of the Eisenhower administration to uphold far-flung commitments at a reduced cost (see Chapter 5). During the late 1950s and early 1960s, the Soviet Union's apparent acquisition of a global nuclear capability and the appearance of nationalist upheaval throughout the third world seemed to neutralize this conjoining of nuclear force with an American interest in global order (see Chapters 6 and 7). To meet this challenge, a coalition of scholars and analysts who feared that the possession of nuclear weapons by the Soviet Union and the United States had robbed the threat of force of its credibility developed a conception of limited war. The problem, wrote Henry Kissinger in the late 1950s, was that "since diplomacy which is not related to a plausible employment of force is sterile it must be the task of our military policy to develop a doctrine and capability for the graduated employment of force."[20] A great edifice of strategic theory on how to make military force relevant to diplomacy was subsequently incorporated into the Kennedy administration's concepts of "flexible response." The upper ranges of this strategic doctrine were employed in Cuba in 1962 (see Chapter 8), and the lower ranges were used throughout the third world—especially in Vietnam from the mid-1960s until the end of the decade (see Chapter 9).

By the mid-1960s "graduated response," in the Defense Department's argot, became an article of faith. The *Pentagon Papers* show the Joint Chiefs of Staff and civilians in the executive branch debating varieties of "squeezes" on Vietnam. There were intervals of "pain" proposed, each with "pauses" that varied in tempo from "low" through "moderate" and proceeded to a fast, "full squeeze" and then to a "blitz" or a "crescendo."[21] Maxwell Taylor, the most prominent military theoretician of the late 1950s and 1960s, echoed the prevailing policy consensus—that "too much" coercion is as bad as "too little."[22] But by the 1970s it was still an open question whether enormously expanded military power, no matter how "flexible," could be effectively managed to support American security interests (see Chapter 10). More than a decade of American policy had been predicated in large measure on the assumption that force could be productively wedded to diplomacy. It is now apparent, however, that this vast undertaking was perhaps too simple in formulation and too complex in execution.

In the meantime, the conditions of world politics seemed to change significantly. Prior to the mid-1960s it was at least plausible to view the world as remaining within the traditional image of world politics with its emphasis on military security. By the mid-1960s, however, the newer forces emphasized by the interdependence perspective had begun to emerge, and by the decade of the 1970s they were, if not ascendant, then certainly of no less importance than traditional security problems. The latter had by no means disappeared, for the Soviet Union's achieving of strategic parity or, by some measures, superiority to the United States meant that the context of American national security policy was profoundly changed. At the same time, however, new problems—the Arab oil embargo of 1973–1974, the persistence of global inflation, and an international economic and financial system dominated by concentrations of economic power outside the traditional framework of the industrialized world—confronted American foreign policy of the 1970s and early 1980s with challenges for which the lessons of the cold war seemed inappropriate (see Chapter 11).

But no consensus concerning the lessons of the 1970s emerged. Instead, the cumulative impact of the Vietnam failure, the economic crisis at mid-decade, and the difficulties experienced by the United States in protecting or pursuing its interests in the late 1970s intensified the fragmentation of the pre-Vietnam consensus on American foreign policy. By the late 1970s and early 1980s, students of American public and elite opinion discerned a fragmented set of belief systems about America's role in the world.[23] One set of beliefs sought to retain the central elements of the old cold war consensus and apply them to the world of the 1980s. These cold war, or "conservative," internationalists believed, therefore, that the world remained essentially bipolar and was dominated by the strategic threat to American interests and world leadership posed by an aggressive and expansionist Soviet Union. The "new forces" in world politics were, in this view, ultimately secondary to the "old" realities of the cold war era.

A second set of beliefs and attitudes constituted a "liberal" or post–cold war internationalism that rejected the traditional emphasis on a bipolar cold war in which the threat and use of military instruments was dominant. For this group the new forces and conditions of Soviet-American strategic parity, international political economics, third world nationalism and upheaval, and diminished capacity for American leadership comprised the essence of world politics. These circumstances required not less but a different form of international commitment and activism than the conditions of cold war, for the interests and objectives of American policy were seen as necessarily more restrained and subtle than in the 1950s and 1960s.

Yet a third position—the "noninternationalists" or "neo-isolationists"—was itself split. On the one hand, there was a belief, largely on the part of mass publics, that the United States should avoid and minimize the interdependencies of world politics, seek peace, but also retain its strength. Others, for the most part within the policy elite, went even further and doubted the efficacy and utility of military force and preferred a concentration on domestic economic, environmental, and social priorities.

The Carter administration tried and failed to straddle these positions in its approach to the world of the late 1970s. By 1980, it had reverted to the strenuous commitments of cold war internationalism, but its conversion was too little and too late to stave off the ascendency of a Reagan administration whose leader and members had never strayed from the verities of the cold war approach to international relations (Chapters 12 and 13). As the Reagan administration entered into its reelection effort, the appropriateness and efficacy of its conservative internationalism remained open to question, for neither American strategic superiority nor economic hegemony—the essence of the original American primacy— had been reestablished or seemed within reach. The eagle was indeed defiant, but it remained no less entangled than in the 1970s.[24]

NOTES

1. Arnold Wolfers and Lawrence W. Martin, eds., *The Anglo American Tradition in Foreign Affairs* (New Haven, Conn.: Yale University Press, 1966), pp. xv–xvi.
2. *Washington Post*, February 5, 1973.
3. Cited by Kenneth W. Waltz, *Man, the State and War: A Theoretical Analysis* (New York: Columbia University Press, 1959), p. 159.
4. The literature on these new forces and on the notion of interdependence is fast becoming unmanageably vast. A useful introduction (and bibliographies) are found in Seyom Brown, *New Forces in World Politics* (Washington, D.C.: The Brookings Institution, 1975), and Robert O. Keohane and Joseph S. Nye, *Power and Interdependence: World Politics in Transition* (Boston: Little, Brown, 1977). Proponents of the more traditional view are not unaware of the importance of these new forces. See, for example, Robert Gilpin, *War and Change in World Politics* (New York: Cambridge

University Press, 1981). They do feel, however, that these new forces are of less importance than the more traditional forces.

5. John H. Herz, "The Rise and the Demise of the Territorial State," *World Politics*, Vol. 9, No. 4 (July 1957), pp. 473–494.

6. "U.S. Trade Deficit Sets a Record," *New York Times*, 1 March 1984, p. D1.

7. W. Michael Blumenthal, "Steering in Crowded Waters," *Foreign Affairs*, Vol. 56, No. 4 (July 1978), p. 729.

8. Ronald I. McKinnon, "The Eurocurrency Market," *Essays in International Finance*, No. 125 (Princeton, N.J.: International Finance Section, Department of Economics, Princeton University, December 1977), p. 1.

9. *50th Annual Report, 1979–1980*, Geneva Bank for International Settlements, 1980.

10. See International Monetary Fund, *World Economic Outlook*, Occasional Paper No. 21 (Washington, D.C.: IMF, 1983), esp. pp. 39–43.

11. Peter Kilborn, "U.S. Nears Status of Debtor Nation," *New York Times*, 20 February 1984, p. A1.

12. See Raymond Vernon's lucid summary, "Multinationals: No Strings Attached," *Foreign Policy*, No. 33 (Winter 1978–1979), pp. 121–135. See also: C. Fred Bergsten, Thomas Horst, and Theodore Moran, *American Multinationals and American Interests* (Washington, D.C.: The Brookings Institution, 1978) and Robert Gilpin, *U.S. Power and the Multinational Corporation: The Political Economy of Foreign Direct Investment* (New York: Basic Books, 1975), as well as the earlier and more critical Richard J. Barnett and Ronald E. Muller, *Global Reach: The Power of Multinational Corporations* (New York: Simon and Schuster, 1974). On the effects of investment flows on the American economy of the early 1980s, see Kilborn, op. cit.

13. C. Fred Bergsten, "The Response to the Third World," *Foreign Policy*, No. 17 (Winter 1974–1975), p. 14.

14. See Chapter 12.

15. Perhaps the most straightforward statement of this thesis remains that of Harry Magdoff, *The Age of Imperialism: The Economics of U.S. Foreign Policy* (New York: Monthly Review Press, 1969). The most comprehensive development of the thesis is to be found in Joyce and Gabriel Kolko, *The Limits of Power: The World and United States Foreign Policy, 1945–1954* (New York: Harper and Row, 1972).

16. Justifiably the most important exploration of these levels of analysis as well as the original exposition of the "bureaucratic politics" approach to analyzing foreign policy is Graham Allison, *Essence of Decision: Explaining the Cuban Missile Crisis* (Boston: Little, Brown, 1971). See also Morton H. Halperin and Arnold Kanter, eds., *Readings in American Foreign Policy: A Bureaucratic Perspective* (Boston: Little, Brown, 1973); Halperin, *Bureaucratic Politics and Foreign Policy* (Washington, D.C.: Brookings, 1974); and Allison and Halperin, "Bureaucratic Politics: A Paradigm and Some Policy Implications," in Richard Ullman and Raymond Tanter, eds., *Theory and Policy in International Relations* (Princeton: Princeton University Press, 1972). For the authors' critique of this approach see James A. Nathan and James K. Oliver, "Bureaucratic Politics: Academic Windfalls and Intellectual Pitfalls," *Journal of Political and Military Sociology*, Vol. 6 (Spring 1978), pp. 81–91.

17. Irving Janis, *Groupthink*, 2nd ed. (Boston: Houghton Mifflin, 1982).

18. James David Barber, *The Presidential Character*, 2nd ed. (Englewood Cliffs, N.J.: Prentice-Hall, 1977); see also Alexander George, "Assessing Presidential Character," *World Politics*, Vol. 27 (January 1974).

19. See James A. Nathan and James K. Oliver, *Foreign Policy Making and the American Political System* (Boston: Little, Brown, 1983).

20. Henry Kissinger, *Nuclear Weapons and Foreign Policy* (New York: W. W. Norton, 1969), p. 54.

21. Neil Sheehan, Hedrick Smith, E. W. Kenworthy, and Fox Butterfield, *The Pentagon Papers* (as published in *The New York Times*) (New York: Bantam Books, 1971), pp. 365–371, especially documents nos. 85 and 87.

22. Ibid., pp. 294–298, 340–344, 366–367, 369, 377, 392; and Richard C. Barnett, *Roots of War: The Men and Institutions Behind U.S. Foreign Policy* (Baltimore: Penguin Books, 1972), p. 104.

23. Ole Holsti and James Rosenau, "Vietnam, Consensus, and the Belief Systems of American Leaders," *World Politics,* Vol. 31 (October 1979), pp. 1–56 and "U.S. Leadership in a Shrinking World: The Breakdown of Consensus and the Emergence of Conflicting Belief Systems," *World Politics,* Vol. 35 (April 1983), pp. 368–392. See also William Schneider, "Conservatism, Not Interventionism: Trends in Foreign Policy Opinion, 1974–1982," in Kenneth A. Oye et al., *Eagle Defiant: United States Foreign Policy in the 1980s* (Boston: Little, Brown, 1983), pp. 33–64.

24. See Kenneth A. Oye, Robert J. Lieber, *Eagle Defiant: United States Foreign Policy in the 1980s* (Boston: Little, Brown, 1983) and, by the same authors, *Eagle Entangled: U.S. Foreign Policy in a Complex World* (New York: Longman, 1979).

Chapter 1
Prelude to the
Cold War

Just prior to the outbreak of World War I, Woodrow Wilson[1] identified American ideals and aspirations with those of all mankind:

> My dream is that as the years go by and the world knows more and more of America it . . . will turn to America for those moral inspirations which lie at the basis of all freedom . . . and that America will come into the full light of day when all shall know that she puts human rights above all other rights, and that her flag is the flag not only of America, but of humanity.
>
> I do not know that there will ever be a declaration of independence and of grievances for mankind, but I believe that if any such document is ever drawn it will be drawn in the spirit of the American Declaration of Independence, and that America has lifted high the light which will shine unto all generations and guide the feet of mankind to the goal of justice and liberty and peace.[2]

Yet there was more to this vision than patriotic rhetoric, for it was part of a larger conception of world order which continues to shape American foreign policy.

To Wilson, the internal order of states was a major determinant of state behavior and, hence, world peace. If a state's domestic politics were not marked by democratic institutions and processes, then that state was a potential threat to world peace. For states characterized by undemocratic domestic institutions almost invariably turn to aggressive behavior for the aggrandizement of their rulers or to deflect the attention of the ruled from their domestic plight. Wilson's beliefs about world politics supported an interventionist policy in two ways: First, the exceptional purity of the American purpose and power allowed America to contribute to the creation of an international order among states. But, second, the Wilsonian vision was necessarily concerned with the undemocratic internal order of those states that might become a threat to the larger international order. Both dimensions are captured in Wilson's famous statement at the time of World War I:

> We are glad . . . to fight thus for the ultimate peace of world and for the liberation of its peoples . . . for the rights of nations great and small and the privilege of men everywhere to choose their way of life and of obedience.

The world must be made safe for democracy. Its peace must be planted upon the tested foundations of political liberty.[3]

There is, however, an important paradox in this vision. People were "to choose their way of life and obedience," but there was the strong implication that unless the outcome of this act of self-determination conformed to Wilsonian standards, intervention would follow. How could it be otherwise if one believed that those "moral inspirations which lie at the basis of all freedom" were somehow uniquely American? Denial of what was to Wilson a self-evident truth necessarily placed the offending state in the camp of the enemy. Wilson, moreover, was prepared to use force in pursuit and protection of his vision. In the case of the Mexican intervention in 1916 and again in World War I, Wilson fought— presumably for some higher notion of the "ultimate peace." And in his conception of the League of Nations after World War I, force was deemed essential to the maintenance of world order.[4] Only now it was to be the "concerted force of the combined action of mankind through the instrumentality of all the enlightened governments of the world."[5] But through all the rhetoric one assumption remained constant and unchallenged: "the tested foundations of political liberty" were self-evident, and they were "drawn in the spirit of the American Declaration of Independence." To deny this—to deny that America's flag was indeed "the flag of humanity"—marked a state as one of the unenlightened and hence the legitimate target of intervention.

The Soviet view of international politics and Russia's place in the international system that emerged from the Bolshevik Revolution in 1917 challenged Wilson's vision. Yet, curiously, Lenin's understanding of world politics paralleled some features of American foreign policy. For instance, the Leninist view of world politics carried traces of the traditional Russian sense of mission, which was similar to the American and Wilsonian vision. The sixteenth-century idea of Moscow as a "third Rome" and the nineteenth-century Pan-Slavic movement both saw Russia as possessing a destiny and a duty larger than the mere frontiers of Great Russia. But whereas Wilson viewed consensus as the natural scheme of things, Marxism saw class conflict as the path of social and political development. Where democracy was seen in the liberal tradition as a means for giving expression to the people at large, Marxists thought democracy in the West but an expression of dominant economic and class interest.

Lenin, moreover, felt that his regime was not secure while capitalist values flourished in Europe. He and his followers felt that European leaders would be profoundly hostile to a Soviet Russia. The Soviet Union stood for social revolution; the West stood for orderly progress. As the West questioned the very validity of the political, moral, and intellectual foundation of the Soviet state, the Soviets denied the validity of the Western order. Furthermore, Lenin and his followers believed that the West would attempt, in Churchill's metaphor, to strangle the Soviet infant in its crib (he called it a "monster"); and therefore the best protection for the October Revolution was an expanding system of states based on the revolutionary principles propounded by the Bolsheviks. As Lenin said in March 1919:

> We live not only in a state, but in a system of states, and the existence of the Soviet Republic side by side with the imperialist states for a prolonged period of time is unthinkable. In the meantime a series of frightful collisions will occur.[6]

Wilson's reaction to the Bolsheviks was predictable—they had established, he felt, an illegitimate government. As Wilson proclaimed in July 1919, "The men who . . . control . . . the affairs of Russia represent nobody but themselves. . . . They have no mandate from anybody. . . . [A] group of men more cruel than the Czar himself is controlling the destinies of that great people."[7] The loathing of the West for the kind of regime that had come to power in 1917 was intensified by Lenin's successful extrication of Russia from World War I and Trotsky's negotiation of a quick peace favorable to the Germans. The most fundamental source of Wilson's antipathy, however, was the communist vision of humanity's political, economic, and social order that emerged from the revolution of 1917. Wilson therefore sought to interpose American military and economic power against the Communists even as they, and all of Russia, were engulfed in civil war.

INTERVENTION IN
THE RUSSIAN CIVIL WAR

Some seventy thousand Czechoslovak soldiers,[8] deserters from the Austrian army, were left in the Soviet Union after the Bolsheviks signed the Treaty of Brest-Litovsk ending hostilities with the Germans. The Czechs, though isolated in Siberia, retained their discipline and organization and represented an important organized military force in Russia during the chaotic civil war that followed the revolution and Russia's departure from World War I. The plight of the Czechs helped fuel anti-Bolshevik sentiment in the West and served as a rationalization for Wilson to contribute to the intervention by Allied troops ostensibly to aid the Czechs to reach the European front. But the Czechs had been joined by

Russian anti-Bolshevik forces, so the decision to intervene was known to support the anti-Bolshevik factions in the Russian civil war. In Wilson's words, the intervention would "steady any efforts of the Russians at self-defense, or the establishment of law and order."[9] Such "self-defense" assistance to aid the Russians regain "self-government" left little doubt that the dispatch of troops to help the brave Czechs who had attracted so much attention would also buttress anti-Bolshevik factions.

In the end there were two American interventions in alliance with the British and French, who were as appalled by initial Bolshevik successes as Wilson. One was in European Russia, in the north, above the Arctic Circle. In the summer of 1918, five thousand men went to Murmansk and Archangel in order to see that the vast Allied stores of war goods might not fall into German hands. The American troops were to join an Allied expedition that had already battled Bolshevik troops in an attempt to gain authority over the two important port cities. On arrival, the American troops, plagued by dysentery, confused leadership, and clothing ill-suited for the harsh climate, were placed in the position of defending White Russians and breakaway Bolsheviks against Lenin's regime. As temperatures fell to –50°F and casualties rose to more than five hundred, the Americans neared mutiny.[10] A second American troop contingent entered Siberia in 1918 at just about the same time that the troops destined for Murmansk and Archangel had arrived. There were more than nine thousand men in Siberia under the command of General Graves, who divided his loathing for Russian politicians equally between Whites and Bolsheviks. The American presence in Siberia was related to Japanese designs on Siberia.[11] But once American troops were in place in Siberia, their presence tended to favor the reactionary anti-communist forces. Indeed the Russian embassy in Washington, representing the provisional White Russian government, campaigned vigorously to get the American people to support the intervention, including sending speakers on tour in the United States and even suggesting logistics to the State Department.[12]

The Intervention and Its Consequences

Although Wilson reached his decision to intervene in the Soviet Union because of his wider image of American interests, he had support from large sections of public opinion. When the Bolsheviks seized power, "most Americans reacted as if the impossible had happened."[13] The Bolsheviks were considered, in Secretary of State Robert Lansing's words, a "usurping gang" of lunatics, anarchists, and Jews. Since they were considered illegitimate in every sense by Americans, it was generally predicted that they would not last. In one study by Walter

Lippmann, the demise of Soviet rule was predicted ninety-one times in the years from 1917 to 1919.[14] If the impossible had happened, it was comfortable to predict that it would soon cease happening. The vilification of the new regime in the press was intense. The *Saturday Evening Post* was typical. It editorialized that German despotism was at least practiced by an elite. But Bolshevism was a "despotism by all the lowest."[15] The Bolsheviks came to be characterized as veritable freaks and monsters. *The New York Times,* for instance, reported that in Soviet areas, every eighteen-year-old girl had to register at a "bureau of free love" and was then given a husband without her consent.[16]

Thus American involvement in the intervention had enormous consequences domestically. It froze American attitudes toward the Soviet Union into a kind of hostility that can only be described as bizarre. The famous journalist Lincoln Steffens wrote privately that "Bolshevism means chaos, wholesale murder, the complete destruction of civilization."[17] Senator Henry Lee Myers of Montana spoke for many Americans:

> They have utterly destroyed marriage, the home, the fireside, the family, the cornerstones of all civilization, all society. They have undertaken to destroy what God created and ordained. They defy alike the will of God, the precepts of Christianity, the decrees of civilization, the customs of society. It is hard to realize that such things exist and are tolerated by the civilized world.[18]

The atheism of Bolsheviks repulsed the vast majority of Americans. The influential *Literary Digest* reported that the Soviet government had sponsored ceremonies in which young men dressed as devils and danced about bonfires containing effigies of Jesus, Moses, and Mohammed.[19]

It is important to note the degree of isolation and disruption the Soviets experienced in this period. Their only port, Petrograd, was blockaded by the Allies; foreign trade was reduced to smuggling; even gold was embargoed. In 1919, the only foreign official in the Soviet Union was a Danish representative of the Red Cross.[20] It is not, therefore, hard to see how the intervention confirmed the suspicion of the Bolsheviks that the West was implacably hostile to the Soviet regime. The nature of these interventions and America's involvement in them are well remembered by Soviet historians. Yet they are all but ignored by Western scholarship. The scholarly former U.S. ambassador to the Soviet Union, George F. Kennan, confessed that he did not understand the reasons for the contempt and resentment borne by the early Bolsheviks toward the Western powers until he unearthed the details in his own research.[21]

In the American and Allied intervention Lenin and the Bolsheviks saw the fulfillment of the communist prophecy of capitalist enmity and aggression. It did not matter that Wilson's aims in the intervention, although undeniably anti-Bolshevik, were pursued with some reluctance. The Americans were clearly part of the range of forces arrayed against the Bolsheviks. Huge sums of money were spent on this adventure. But its cost continued to mount long after Western troops had left. Very probably this intervention aided the coup d'état of October 1917 in becoming a permanent regime, for as the Russian civil war and the intervention coalesced, the communist leaders played the role of national leaders fighting foreigners. During the struggle, the Communists were able to forge an army, a police force, and a party apparatus that enabled them to expand from a very weak base. This power was to become so early entrenched that very soon the Soviet regime was able to undergo the tremendous strain of social transformation under the brutal leadership of Stalin. And the early isolation and encirclement of the new communist state became absorbed in the Soviet mentality. The heroic theme of being subjected to the onslaught of world capitalism and repulsing it was a useful forge on which to build the foundations of a new Soviet order.

The intervention failed because of pro-Bolshevism in much of the Russian population and because the cost of imposing a Western solution was disproportionate to any immediate security interest. Troops in the Russian intervention never quite understood what their purpose was, and by mid-1919 outraged parents who had sent their sons to fight the Kaiser caught the ear of Congress, and the troops were withdrawn. But the expansive Wilsonian concept of world order based on a comprehensive political capitalism was a precursor of later years and later administrations and, as such, forms the opening phrases of the dialogue of distrust that characterizes the cold war.

Nonrecognition

Throughout the 1920s Soviet-American relations were frozen by an American policy of nonrecognition of the communist regime. Wilson's secretary of state, Bainbridge Colby, explained that

> the existing regime in Russia is based upon . . . the negation of every principle of honor and good faith upon which it is possible to base . . . relations. . . . [S]pokesmen of this power have declared . . . the maintenance of their role depends . . . upon the occurrence of revolutions in all other great civilized nations . . . and set up Bolshevist rule in their stead . . . [w]ith a Power whose conceptions of international relations are so entirely alien . . . so utterly repugnant . . . we cannot hold official relations.[22]

The United States pressed for Soviet acknowledgment of Czarist debts. It was clear, however, that the Soviet conception of world order and the internal regime of states were the dominant bones of contention. Even as Russia experienced a terrible famine in the spring and summer of 1921, the emergency relief organized by Secretary of Commerce Herbert Hoover was tied to preconditions. "It was his view that the Allies should insist, as part of the price [for food] . . . that the Bolsheviki cease hostilities against their opponents in Russia and stop their propaganda abroad."[23] These conditions, concluded Kennan, although "moderate and reasonable," would be such as to place before the Soviet government the choice of falling in with the general Western desideratum or accepting the onus of denying food to the Russian people.[24]

Despite Lenin's death and Stalin's break with Trotsky over, in the dictator's words, "the idiotic slogan, 'The World Revolution,'"[25] lurid reports of Soviet activity in China and Britain, as well as the beginnings of Latin American revolutions purported to be Soviet inspired, were sufficient cause for restricting contact with the Bolshevik regime. Thus, in spite of the emerging "peace offensive" of Soviet foreign minister Maxim Litvinov and the expulsion of Trotsky, the Russians were not invited to sign the Kellogg-Briand agreement, which outlawed war as an instrument of state relations. Only global economic depression brought the United States to a reversal of more than a decade of nonrecognition. In 1933, Litvinov was reportedly talking of placing orders of more than an incredible $1 billion with the West.[26] Whereas American editors appeared five to one to oppose recognition in 1931, a poll in late 1933 showed editors almost three to one favoring relations.[27] There were objections when Roosevelt and Litvinov exchanged terms of agreement in November 1933, but the view of most Americans had become, according to the *Literary Digest*, an agnostic willingness to "see how it all works out."[28]

THE COMING OF WORLD WAR II

American and especially Western European cooperation with the Soviet regime never moved beyond these tentative contacts. The United States remained preoccupied with the Depression, and the Europeans, especially the British, persisted in a distrustful, even hostile ambivalence toward Stalin. Nowhere was this posture more evident and with greater consequence than regarding the rise of Adolf Hitler in Germany.

Stalin was initially ambivalent—perhaps believing that Hitler was not much more than the anti-Western "national socialist" he (Hitler) proclaimed himself to be. Moreover, Hitler's natural adversaries in Germany, the Social Democrats, were not pro-Soviet in their sentiments. Indeed, they seemed sympathetic to similar regimes in the West, thereby raising the possibility of a formidable alliance against Russia. Stalin was, therefore, passive if not actually supportive of the Nazis' destruction of the Social Democrats.

It became increasingly difficult to ignore, however, that the Nazis were a real menace to the Soviet Union. German officials had begun advocating giving Germany "space for the settlement of its vigorous race" in Russia where "war, revolution and internal decay had made a beginning" and must be stopped.[29] Words like these and the increasing militarization of Germany led Stalin to seek allies in the West, as in the Franco-Russian mutual assistance treaty in 1935. Furthermore, when the Spanish civil war broke out in 1936, Stalin attempted to enlist the West in aiding the Republican forces against the Fascists led by Franco and equipped by the Italians and Germans. Stalin's intervention in the Spanish civil war resulted, in part, from communist ideology; but Stalin also sought to induce Britain and France to intervene and thus join in containing Germany. The British, however, feared antagonizing the Fascists and hoped for a Western settlement that would, by implication, have thrown Hitler against the East and Russia. The unsuccessful effort to enlist the West to aid antifascist forces in Spain and the emerging Western policy of appeasement convinced Stalin that he should make preparations to deal independently with Hitler.[30] For if collective security had not tempted the West, neither was it apparent that Hitler would be interested in a deal; thus, in Kennan's view, Stalin's diplomacy was increasingly one of "watchful waiting."[31]

Further evidence of Russia's isolation was recorded in Moscow when Hitler moved on Austria in March 1938, raising an obvious security threat to Central Europe. France, however, declined to consult with its nominal ally, Russia. Hitler next denounced the Czech government as a staging area for Bolshevism in Central Europe, and charged that Germans living in Czechoslovakia were being oppressed by the Czechs. But when the Soviets urged a multilateral "firm and unambiguous stand," Neville Chamberlain, the British prime minister, told the House of Commons that such a "mutual undertaking" was unacceptable because it would handicap the British government's freedom to maneuver. Paris and London seemed more interested in accommodating themselves to a German plan for partitioning the Czech state than in entertaining the Russian suggestion of concerted resistance to German expansion. Only when Hitler demanded an "international guarantee" of the new Czech boundaries and German occupation of Czechoslovak districts did Chamberlain become alarmed. But his response was a continuation of past policy.

"How horrible, fantastic and incredible," he told a British radio audience, that "we should be digging trenches and trying on gas masks here because of a quarrel in a far-away country between people of whom we know nothing."[32] Hitler gave respite to Chamberlain by inviting him, the French premier, Edouard Daladier, and Mussolini to confer at Munich. The Czechs and the Soviets were noticeable by their absence even as Chamberlain agreed to all of Hitler's demands. The Soviets protested the Munich agreements as "monstrous," knowing that the remaining Czech state would be a virtually indefensible vassal of Hitler. The British prime minister knew, however, that the Munich settlement pointed Hitler eastward, and he declared that the agreement signaled "peace in our time."[33]

When, in March of the next year, the German army moved to occupy all of Czechoslovakia, Chamberlain finally became aroused. Chamberlain had staked his reputation on divining the dark corners of Hitler's mind, but now he was convinced that he would have to be more forceful. When it appeared that Poland would be the next victim of Hitler's aggression, Chamberlain, together with Daladier, guaranteed Polish independence. The Poles, however, did not want the Soviets included in this declaration, harboring a historic anti-Russian and, now, an anti-communist orientation. However, the exclusion of Russia once more from Western security arrangements was hardly encouraging to Moscow and moved Stalin to pursue actively his own arrangement with Hitler. His short-run objectives were not unlike those of Lenin at the end of World War I—to gain a territorial buffer in Eastern Europe and, hence, time.

Russia initiated feelers to Germany while continuing attempts to make security arrangements with the West.[34] In May 1939 London and Paris languidly made an overture to Moscow to discuss a tripartite security pact. But the formula submitted for negotiation contained such caveats as excluding the invasion of the Baltic states by Germany as sufficient cause for France and England coming to the aid of the Soviet Union.[35] On the other hand, Russian demands for transit rights through Poland in the event of war were understandably rejected by the Poles, and the talks stalemated. Moreover, it was known that Stalin was now in formal contact with Hitler. In sum, it might be said, the Allies were less than forthcoming and the Russian negotiating style was ponderous and opaque as Stalin sought to extract the best terms possible from the negotiations.

Finally, in the last days of August 1939, the courtship of the West ended as Stalin wired Hitler to send Foreign Minister Joachim von Ribbentrop to Moscow, where a Nazi-Soviet pact was announced and the Anglo-French mission sent home. Through the agreement Hitler sought to dissuade the West from standing by Poland, now wedged between the so-called German and Soviet allies. This was, of course, Hitler's major miscalculation—the miscalculation that brought on the war. In the short run, however, he had prevented the Soviet opposition to his pending move into Poland. The price was a Soviet sphere of influence in eastern Poland and Soviet control of the Baltic states under the guise of Moscow as their guarantor. In addition, the two dictators agreed that the Balkan states were to be viewed in a disinterested manner. To the extent that Stalin believed that Hitler would allow him a free hand in this area, he miscalculated as grievously as Hitler concerning Western intentions. In the meantime, however, Stalin now felt that he had bought time to prepare for any future German aggression whether the West assisted or not.

The degree of animosity in the West stemming from the blinding shock of the Nazi-Soviet pact cancelled whatever marginal improvement of Soviet-Western relations might have been garnished by the Litvinov period of diplomacy. The Russians were blamed, with justification, for encouraging the Nazi attack on Poland that brought on the full measure of World War II. Finally, the image of a cynical Soviet Union was fixed in the Western mind—an image that was confirmed as Stalin hastily embarked on a course of strategic consolidation that involved the occupation of the Baltic states of Latvia, Lithuania, and Estonia. Similar moves were initiated against Rumania (with the consent of the Nazis) as well as a clumsy invasion of Finland. By November of 1940, Stalin was demanding of Hitler formal recognition of Soviet control of these areas. No doubt Stalin was buoyed by the success of the British in the air battle of Britain and the possibility that the Germans would be preoccupied in the West until well into 1941. Stalin probably figured that even if Hitler, not wanting to fight on two fronts, would not concede a Southeastern European buffer to the Soviets, the Germans would at least proceed cautiously with their·claims in the area. But Stalin miscalculated. For instead of continuing the air assault on Britain, Hitler turned to planning a strike on Britain's Mediterranean lifelines. This stratagem required German pressure in the Balkans and an absence there of Hitler's ally, the Russians. By attempting to give himself more of a buffer in the Balkans, Stalin may have hastened Hitler's preparation of his attack on the Soviet Union, which eventually came in 1941.

The German attack on Russia in the spring of 1941 was greeted with disbelief by the Russians and relief by the West, especially the British, who had stood alone since the collapse of continental resistance after Dunkirk. Roosevelt's personal reaction to the German attack on Russia was equally unambiguous. He was delighted, and told Churchill that he would support "any announcement that the Prime Minister might make welcoming Russia as an ally."[36] But Roosevelt's policy had considerable opposition in the American government, especially among the foreign service officers who had watched the unpleasant paroxysm induced by Stalin's purges in the 1930s and did not want to be associated in the same moral universe as Stalin.[37] Nevertheless, Roosevelt promised more than $1.5 million to Russia by the fall of 1941, and succeeded in the not inconsiderable feat of moving a balky bureaucracy and garnishing Congressional consent to the extension of "lend-lease" aid to Russia.[38] In his letter to the lend-lease administration Roosevelt confirmed that "the defense of the Union of Soviet Socialist Republics is vital to the defense of the United States."[39]

The emergence of the common enemy in the spring of 1941 was not, however, a sufficient basis for overriding the dismal history of distrust of the previous twenty-five years. Russia and the West fought a common enemy simultaneously, and tens of millions of dollars in assistance and materiel were extended to the Russians by the West, but the diplomacy of East-West interactions during the war reveals a continuation of the misunderstandings and real differences that separated Russia and the West before Hitler struck across the Niemen in June 1941. Stalin's objectives and diplomacy during the war were consistent with his efforts before 1941 in that he sought from his new allies what he had sought from Hitler: Soviet influence and control in Eastern Europe and the Balkans.[40] But during and after World War II, Stalin's efforts to construct and gain legitimacy for a Soviet presence in Central Europe were resisted by the West, and Western resistance to Soviet consolidation of their objectives in Europe was to be the central politico-strategic issue of the early cold war.

CONFLICTING STRATEGIC CONCEPTS

The slaughter of World War I seared the memories of the British. They had lost a generation in Flanders, the Marne, and the Somme in a ghoulish holocaust that drained Britain's treasury and enervated its society. A repetition of such sacrifice would not be countenanced by Churchill. He favored, not surprisingly, the use of Britain as if it were a massive aircraft carrier to launch Allied bombers at German industry. Indeed, 50 percent of British production was allocated to the bomber command. Yet he knew that wars are won and lost on the ground.[41] At the first meeting of the combined chiefs of staff, Churchill presented his view of a gradual encirclement of Germany; then, when Germany was bled white, the last dagger would be inserted in a continental assault from the west. Churchill pushed for a landing in French North Africa in cooperation with a large American expedition. Germany was to be engaged at a distance in 1942, in a classic grid that guarded historic British interest in the Mediterranean and India while eventually wrestling the weakened Germans to defeat.[43]

Churchill's attention to the periphery of battle was prompted by the bogey of a Japanese-German division of India and the Middle East as a mortal peril, "a measureless disaster." Roosevelt was skeptical of such joint action by the Axis powers,[43] and the American military questioned Churchill's strategy. General George C. Marshall thought that Churchill's policy was fraught with risk and was never convinced that the Russians could withstand Hitler unaided by Allied reinforcements. Furthermore, if the Russian army of eight million were defeated, then the war would be lost. Even if the Russian army withstood the formidable Wehrmacht, Marshall believed that the war would drag on until 1944 or 1945 if a second front were not launched, and the result would be higher, not lower, Allied costs.

Clearly, these two conceptions of how to proceed with the war were incompatible. It fell to Roosevelt to resolve the issue, for it could only be with American assistance that any strategy would succeed. Roosevelt's decision was in favor of the British concept, thus the invasion of Europe was deferred. Among the factors influencing Roosevelt were British opposition and his own views concerning the as yet incomplete American mobilization and also the inevitability of very high casualties resulting from a frontal assault on Germany's continental bastion. The Russo-German theater of the war remained, therefore, disconnected from the Anglo-American engagement of German power on the periphery of Europe for more than two years. However, eventual Soviet victory in the struggle between the two former totalitarian allies was to be the central factor in the postwar configuration of power in Central Europe. The nature of the victory no doubt intensified Soviet conviction that they alone should structure politically and economically what had been largely their conquest of the eastern portion of the Nazi empire. In the meantime, the issue of Anglo-American assistance to the Soviets by wasy of a second front poisoned East-West diplomacy.

The Issue of the Second Front

Even before Pearl Harbor, when Britain was weathering a furious air onslaught, Stalin pressed Churchill to open a second front. Churchill turned the pleas aside,[44] perhaps believing that Russia could not hold out, and that a second front would make little sense if he had to face the full might of the German army alone. British military intelligence concurred with the German estimates that Russia would be beaten before the famous Russian winter set in. The Germans had fielded 175 divisions and soon raised the number to 232. But they had badly miscalculated, for although Germany gave an initial appearance of success, it was more apparent than real. Hilter's supply lines were badly extended; and when the Russians stood their ground and mobilized remarkable numbers, German casualties assumed staggering proportions. Nevertheless, the Russian situation was grave. By October the Germans stood at the bus stops in the outer suburbs of Moscow only five miles from the city center.[45] The effect of the initial joyous proclamation of Churchill that the British and Russians were partners in the same glorious enterprise was shaken. But a number of factors conjoined to vitiate the effect of Churchill's obvious reluctance to commit troops to the Russians. First, the vicious Russian winter overtook German troops ill equipped for temperatures that reached −40°F.[46] Second, the Western allies committed themselves to substantial military aid for the Soviets by the middle of the next year.[47] Finally, the Japanese attack on Pearl Harbor and the consolidation of their conquests in Southeast Asia diverted their attention from the Soviets' Asian front and allowed for the transfer of Russian forces to the European front.

Perhaps as important, Roosevelt did not have the abiding dislike of the Soviets that Churchill maintained. He believed that his own personal winning charm could bridge great historic and ideological cleavages. He wrote somewhat arrogantly to Churchill, "I know you will not mind my being brutally frank when I tell you I think I can personally handle Stalin better than either your Foreign Office or my State Department. Stalin hates the guts of all your top people. He thinks he likes me better, and I hope he will continue to do so."[48] Nor did Roosevelt have the same history of anti-Bolshevik efforts and statements that had motivated Churchill since his days as First Lord of the Amdiralty in World War I. While many Americans shared Senator Harry Truman's view, "If we see that Germany is winning we ought to help Russia and if Russia is winning, we ought to help Germany and that way let them kill as many as possible . . . ."[49] Roosevelt had somewhat daringly proclaimed: "I think the Russians are perfectly friendly; they aren't trying to gobble up all the rest of Europe or the world."[50]

On the other hand, Churchill's conception of how to proceed with the war ultimately won over Roosevelt; hence the United States was inevitably a target of Soviet distrust during and after the war as a result of the issue of the second front. This distrust was deepened by what must have appeared to the Russians to have been Churchillian duplicity in 1942. When Vyacheslav Molotov came to Washington in May 1942, he elicited a joint declaration that "full understanding was reached with regard to the urgent task of creating a second front in Europe in 1942."[51] Churchill reluctantly endorsed this document and handed Molotov a memorandum that claimed that Britain was "making preparations for a landing on the continent in August or September, 1942."[52] But by July 1942 the British had vetoed the idea of a second front in favor of a North African one followed by an Italian invasion. Marshall threatened to resign; Eisenhower feared that a North Africa campaign would "not materially assist the Russians in time to save them,"[53] and concluded that this decision could go down as "the blackest day in history."[54]

Roosevelt, understandably, suggested that Churchill himself relate the change of plans to Stalin.[55] Churchill complained, "It was like carrying a large lump of ice to the North Pole."[56] Churchill again promised Stalin that there would be a second front in 1943. But Stalin was skeptical and claimed to an associate after Churchill's departure, "A campaign in Africa, Italy . . . they want us bled white in order to dictate to us their terms later on. . . ."

The landings in North Africa allowed, by Stalin's estimate, more than 27 German divisions—confident that the Allies would not invade that year in Europe—to move to the Eastern front.[58] By Churchill's own embarrassed estimate in early 1943, the West was engaged with, at the most, 12 German divisions, the Russians with 185.[59] The net effect of the North African campaign was to limit the amount of materiel that could be conveyed to the Soviet Union[60] and increase Soviet suspicions of the West. The rearrangement of manufacturing in preparation for the desert campaign cut into the production of landing craft and artillery shells, prerequisites for a large landing in France, and the West did not regain its 1942 production levels for this materiel until 1944. In short, the North African campaign precluded a landing in France in 1943 as had been promised.

Stalin was enraged. He noted that there was not a single German division in France of any value, a fact confirmed by British intelligence. The German policy was to station those in the West who suffered disabilities and could not be sent East.[61] Against this rather motley effluvia of the German war machine, Churchill unconvincingly related to Stalin that the British guns and aircraft were keeping the "Germans pinned in Pas de Calais" across the English Channel.[62] Stalin's lack of appreciation was evident in his reply: "That, I hope, does not imply a renunciation of your Moscow promise to open a second front in Western Europe in the spring of 1943."[63] But the North African campaign could not lead to a landing in France as the West had promised.[64] Instead, the invasion was directed at Italy by the way of Sicily. The net result of the landings in Sicily and southern Italy—predicted by Eisenhower—was an early Italian surrender; but the Germans stayed on doggedly in central and northern Italy, and the Allies were bogged down in Italy for almost two more years.[65]

The invasion of France would not come until June 1944, less than one year before the war ended and well after a Russian victory in Central Europe became inevitable. Of more immediate importance, it would not come until the Russians were convinced that it was Allied policy to bleed them white. The Allies, for their part, saw themselves as moving with all prudent speed. The gap in mutual perceptions became an open breach by late 1943 as Stalin withdrew his ambassadors from London and Washington.

Fears of a Separate Peace

Exacerbating the distrust generated by the second front issue were persistent rumors and occasional indications that one side or another would seek a separate peace with Hitler. Stalin may have deliberately manipulated the situation in his eagerness to encourage more Anglo-American assistance. On the other hand, in view of the Molotov-Ribbentrop Non-Aggression Pact, one can understand that the Americans and British were not prepared to place the best interpretation on Soviet maneuvering. Furthermore, during 1942 and 1943 there were reported low-level contacts between German and Soviet agents concerning a break-off in the fighting and some form of frontier agreement. And in June 1943, according to some historians, a meeting of foreign ministers Molotov and Ribbentrop was held behind German lines to discuss a separate peace and the postwar Russian-Polish frontier.[66] However, all talks were broken off in late 1943 after the Soviet successes at Stalingrad and then at Kursk had signaled the beginning of the Soviet offensive that would end the war in the East.

From the Soviet standpoint, the most suspicious developments were at the end of the war when German, British, and American intelligence and military officers met in early 1945 in Berne, Switzerland, to negotiate the surrender of remaining German troops in Italy. The talks expanded to include all German troops in Western Europe. The Russians, however, were not invited to these talks, and they reached the conclusion that the Western Allies were conspiring with the Germans so as to allow rapid movement of Anglo-American forces to the East. The American ambassador to Moscow, Averell Harriman, counseled against letting the talks be broadened. Harriman, with long bitter experience in negotiating with Russians, thought that such a stand would teach the Russians a salutary lesson that they could not always get what they asked for.[67]

Churchill, himself, was later to admit that these talks treaded close to actual negotiations. But Allen Dulles (former head of OSS and CIA), in his memoirs, *Secret Surrender,* while confirming Churchill's observation, also notes that the full extent of these conversations was not at all clear to Roosevelt.[68] Roosevelt, faced with harsh Soviet suspicions,[69] promised that if details of a surrender were talked about, then Soviet leaders would be invited. These were, he emphasized, preliminary discussions and not negotiations.[70] Nevertheless, Russian fear of a separate peace or settlement primarily or even exclusively beneficial to the West ran throughout the war and was particularly intense at the end of the war. Soviet suspicions intensified and poisoned the atmosphere in which important substantive issues were coming to a head, most notably the interrelated questions of Eastern Europe and the postwar disposition of Germany. In the disputes surrounding these political and strategic issues we find the immediate antecedents to the cold war.

POLAND AND EASTERN EUROPE: THE TURN TOWARD COLD WAR

Eastern Europe and Poland were the incubus in which old distrusts festered. The issue of Poland was, perhaps, the most critical in the wartime and immediate postwar dialogue between the West and the Soviet Union. Poland provided the sharpest challenge to Allied unity because of the seemingly unreconcilable ambitions and interests—a conflict that anticipated and contributed to what was to follow.

The Poles had suffered great privations under the czars and the Soviets. They had suffered partition, absorption, and various efforts at colonization and, of course, the Soviets had attempted to extinguish Poland in league with the Nazis in the Molotov-Ribbentrop pact. In the West sympathy was high for the Poles; many refugee Poles fought bravely with the British, and about 20 percent of the pilots who fought the battle of Britain were Polish.[71] Moreover, urban Polish-Americans were an influential minority that merited considerable attention in American electoral politics. For example, there were and are more Polish-speaking persons in Chicago than in Warsaw, and more Polish radio stations and newspapers in the United States than in Poland. For the Americans at the end of the war, the Polish question had become a factor in domestic politics and a symbol of Soviet-Western cooperation.[72] The Soviets' claims in Poland had an entirely different justification. As Stalin noted:

> In the course of twenty-five years the Germans twice invaded Russia via Poland. . . . The invasions were not warfare but like incursions of the Huns. . . . Germany had been able to do this because Poland had been regarded as part of the *cordon sanitaire* around the Soviet Union and that

previous European policy had been that Polish governments must be hostile to Russia. In these circumstances either Poland had been too weak to oppose Germany or had let the Germans come through. . . . Poland's weakness and hostility had been a great source of weakness to the Soviet Union and had permitted the Germans to do what they wished in the East and also the West. . . . It is therefore in Russia's vital interest that Poland should be both strong and friendly.[73]

Thus the postwar political future and a territorial configuration of Poland, based on 1941 borders, was a central concern of Russian wartime diplomacy. Soviet insistence on a different geography for Poland also strained their delicate, newly formed relationship with the London-based Polish government in exile. The London Polish government was recognized by the Soviet Union in July 1941, but the London Poles were in a precarious position. Except for whatever influence they might have with the British or Americans, they were practically powerless. Moreover, the British were less than completely supportive, as the Polish question stood between the Soviets and the British in reaching other understandings and was therefore something of an embarrassment.[74] Yet the Poles refused tenaciously to yield to the Russians their eastern territories. They harbored little good will for the Russians in view of the 1939 pact with the Nazis. The fate of some fifteen thousand captured officers and more soldiers as well as about one and a half million Poles deported from the zone the Soviets occupied after the Molotov-Ribbentrop pact greatly concerned the exile government.

The West, not able to deliver a second front and watching the rapid advance of the Soviet army, began to move toward placation of Stalin. As the West began to waver in support, the Poles felt abandoned[75] and became increasingly unyielding toward Soviet claims in the face of the ever-apparent Russian designs in Poland. The actual break between the London Poles and the Russians occurred in April 1943, when the Germans discovered the graves of fifteen thousand Polish officers in the Katyn Forest of Poland. The Germans claimed they were slaughtered by Russia in 1940—a claim accepted by the London group. Stalin's fury at this immediate Polish acceptance of the Nazi version of the massacre prompted him to break diplomatic rlations with the London Poles.

There were, by now, two distinct issues involved. One was the future composition of the Polish government, and the second was the geographic boundaries of Poland. The Soviets argued for an eastern limit of Poland that coincided with the frontier of 1941 resulting from the Molotov-Ribbentrop pact. At Tehran in late 1943 Churchill and Eden initiated a proposal that this line be adopted in the east and Poland be compensated in the west out of former Prussian territory to the Oder

River. Roosevelt did not demur in the massive territorial or population adjustments that Stalin had conceded. But, he added, "he could not publicly take part in any such arrangement" because he could ot prejudice the "six to seven million Polish-American votes in the upcoming election."[76] Roosevelt's concern about his domestic flank was well taken, for the Republicans would build much of their campaign around charges that Roosevelt's labor support tied him to communist influences. Such Republican "Red-baiting" would become commonplace and more effective over the next decade. But even in 1944 its effect was sufficient to undercut Roosevelt's seemingly impregnable position to the point that his electoral margin would be one of the smallest in decades.[77] To have publicly associated himself with the Polish boundary decision, therefore, might well have been disastrous. There was probably no alternative available to Roosevelt and Churchill, but by this action they conceded to Stalin both the dominant voice in the future government of Poland and the territorial aggrandizement he desired.

The Tehran plan envisaged a population movement involving at least six million people who would have to find homes in Germany. The territory to be taken from Germany stretched two hundred miles into Prussia. A future government that displaced so many Germans and held such a vast tract of former German territory could not but be fearful of German claims in the future and dependent on Moscow. As for the new regime to be established in postwar Poland, Stalin now demanded that it comprise primarily those Poles acceptable to the Soviet Union. As Soviet troops were marching into Poland, Stalin created the Polish Committee of Liberation that was clearly the prototype government of Poland. When Soviet troops entered Lublin, this group was installed, and Lublin was made the administrative center for all of Poland.

But the meaning and full consequences of Soviet policy became clear as the Soviet military action in Poland revealed a kind of record for cynicism. As the Russians reached the banks of the Vistula within sight of Warsaw in August 1944, Moscow radio urged the Polish underground, or home, army to revolt. The Poles did, yet the Russians did not advance to drive out the Germans; rather, they watched until January 1945 as the Nazis liquidated the last vestiges of any potential opposition to Soviet domination of the future government of Poland. A quarter of a million Poles were to die in Warsaw fighting Nazis, alone, and the city was destroyed, blown up block by block. Stalin even refused landing rights to Western planes to drop supplies to the beleaguered Poles.

The Allies were horrified but could do little more than tacitly support the Soviet territorial claim in Poland legitimized earlier at Tehran. The British and the Americans had been presented with an accomplished fact of Soviet power in Poland and Soviet recognition of the

Lublin government in spite of protestations that the decision to recognize a Polish government be left until the summit conference at Yalta in February 1945.

Yalta

At the Yalta Conference Roosevelt extracted vague and ambiguous assurances from Stalin concerning reorganization of the Lublin government and free elections in Poland. Similar weak commitments were made by Stalin concerning all of Soviet-controlled Eastern Europe. Overseeing these elections was left vague and elastic, and when the Soviets later interpreted matters to their advantage, many in the United States would denounce the Yalta agreements as a sellout. But Roosevelt's biographer James McGregor Burns has concluded otherwise:

> He had reached the limit of his bargaining power at Yalta. His position resulted not from naivete, ignorance, illness, or perfidy, but from his acceptance of the facts: Russia occupied Poland. Russia distrusted its Western allies. Russia had a million men who could fight Japan. . . . And Russia was absolutely determined about Poland and always had been.[78]

Moreover, Roosevelt believed—and he may have indulged his vanity to the point of self-deception here—that his personal charm could cut through the ideological differences, accumulated distrust of the preceding decades, as well as the historic Russian interests in Central Europe to capture Stalin's trust and cooperation. If successful, the Wilsonian ideal of an institutionalized world order might yet be fulfilled in the new United Nations, in which case the compromises of Yalta would be mere footnotes on the opening pages of a new era.

On the other hand, the presentation of the Yalta accords to the American people led most Americans to believe that there would be free democratic elections in Eastern Europe. At the same time, Roosevelt understood enough of the realities of the situation to know that in the free hand he had allowed the Soviets since 1943 in Poland and in his acceptance of the "friendly" governments—no matter how cloaked in electoral procedure—he had acknowledged the Soviets their ambitions. Also, he must have known that the military realities of the postwar situation conflicted with what the American people had been led to expect in terms of a new liberal order promised to arise out of the ashes of the war.[79]

It was Harry Truman who was to try to resolve the dilemma of public and private expectations in favor of America's aspirations, rather than acknowledge what increasingly seemed inevitable in the face of Soviet guns and tough interpretations of their security interests. Truman and his advisers were to argue the issue as a breach of faith.[80] There was never explicit agreement, however, on the procedure or meaning of free elections or international supervision. These items were kept ambiguous because it was apparent that the declaration of Yalta concerning Poland satisfied different purposes for the West and Stalin. To the West, it helped keep up appearances, and to the Russians it confirmed the obvious. As Stalin was to remark: "This war is not as in the past; whoever occupies territory also imposes his own social system as far as his army can reach. It cannot be otherwise."[81]

THE ADMINISTRATION OF LIBERATION

The issue of the administration of former enemy and enemy-occupied states in Europe was a consistent element of the growing distrust between Russia and the West. It is commonly held that the cold war was a contest between a Western vision of an open, liberal political order and a narrow Soviet definition of security in terms of spheres of interest.[82] But the West accommodated itself to having its own security spheres when military convenience allowed it in Europe or when historical ambition demanded it in Latin America. The first evidence of a lack of deep Western commitment to its liberal rhetoric and aspirations was in North Africa, where the United States and the British worked out a surrender deal with the anti-Semitic, collaborationist commander of the Vichy French forces. In return for his surrender, Admiral Jean Darlan was allowed to maintain his political position.[83]

The squalid arrangement with Darlan was viewed as being an unfortunate expediency. Unhappily, it was repeated in the Western action in Italy of negotiating with the rightist regime of General Pietro Badoglio. By dealing with the leader of Italy's brutal Ethiopian campaign and leaving much of Mussolini's governmental structure intact, the West indicated the possibility that the Allies would deal with anyone when the time came. But just as important, the West, by managing to arrange for a sphere of influence in areas in which Western troops were placed, became poorly positioned to argue against the harsher but functionally equivalent strategy that the Soviets employed in Eastern Europe.

In Greece, German withdrawal touched off fighting between communist and left-wing partisans on the one hand and collaborationists and monarchists on the other. The British army supported the rightists, actively attempted to root out the left opposition, disbanded the partisan resistance by extreme methods, and tried to reinstate the king; reportedly 80 percent of the population was opposed to such moves.[84] It was a blatant and unpopular exercise in reclamation of the British Empire, which brought protest to the House of Commons and from some Americans who saw liberal principles desecrated. Nevertheless, Roosevelt acquiesced in Churchill's attempt to impose a British solution on Greece.[85]

In spite of the fact that the British army was aimed at the "communistic elements in Greece [who] plan to seize power by force,"[86] not a word of reproach was uttered by the Soviet press, and Stalin was completely silent on the subject. In this, Stalin was conforming to the agreement worked out between Churchill and himself in October 1944 in which Rumania and Bulgaria were conceded to the Soviet sphere of influence and Greece to the British. Yugoslavia and Hungary were to be divided equally. Churchill wrote appreciatively, "I am increasingly impressed, up to date, with the loyalty with which . . . Stalin has kept off Greece in accordance with our agreement."[87] The Russians did nothing to help their ideological brethren in Greece and everything possible to discourage them. Stalin even aided the British occupation by offering the British reconstituted monarchist Greek government Soviet recognition in December 1945. The move caused extreme consternation among the left in Greece; but it was impressive evidence that the Soviets understood the language of power and interest. They had, after all, their own fish to fry in Germany and Eastern Europe.

In Greece, Italy, and North Africa, the Soviets had precedent for their conduct in Eastern Europe. But the West would not concede that spheres of interest could cohabit the same planet. If they had, then the Soviets and the West might not have undergone the frightful postwar tension that was rapidly strangling the slim neck of wartime amity. But the Western powers were unable or unwilling to reciprocate Stalin's behavior regarding Greece. The harsh Soviet interpretation of their own security needs and Anglo-American resistance to this interpretation (while pursuing a similar policy wherever practicable) became, therefore, the focus of dissension and distrust from which other issues proliferated.

Americans emerged from the war in Europe supremely confident that they could exact the leadership of a new order. Although planning for the postwar period had not been systematic, the State Department envisaged a world where the judicious use of postwar rehabilitation loans would break down trade barriers and establish a prosperous global economy free from imperialism and free from revolutionary socialism. By late 1944, Ambassador Harriman was suggesting that postwar economic reconstruction aid be used to influence Soviet behavior in Eastern Europe. The U.S. Air Force and military planners saw a world where American military power would be so imposing that threats to the peace would have little choice but to yield.[88] The Soviet vision was clearly different. Although the Soviet Union was in ruins, with three-quarters of its industrial plant destroyed and twenty million dead, it nonetheless possessed an immediate challenge to the American vision by the presence of its troops in the heart of Europe and by the affinity of armed partisans for collectivist principles. This, in Stalin's view, could become the basis of a Soviet-controlled Central European barrier to future aggression from the West.

TRUMAN AND THE ORIGINS OF THE COLD WAR

In this context, Harry Truman came to power following President Roosevelt's death little versed in foreign affairs and, in contrast to Roosevelt, heavily dependent on his advisers. Indeed, given Roosevelt's personal diplomacy, Truman had been excluded from major decisions and was relatively ignorant of what had transpired previously. His closest foreign affairs advisers had long and bitter distrust of Soviet ambitions and chafed at Roosevelt's view that good will and yielding to the strongest of Soviet security claims in Eastern Europe could beget a condominium of great powers. They had witnessed the purges and the undeniable excesses and dark features of Soviet life and Stalin's character for long years.[89] The majority of these officials concurred with Kennan's analysis that the Soviets were "Never—neither then nor at any later date . . . a fit ally or associate, actual or potential."[90]

Ambassador Averell Harriman left the Moscow embassy to George Kennan's care and returned to Washington to advise Truman. Harriman had spent months attempting to resolve the question as to which parties actually constituted "democratic and anti-Nazi parties"[91]—those agreed to by the Soviets at Yalta as acceptable in a new Polish government. Neither Roosevelt nor Churchill had frankly faced up to the fact that truly free elections might have returned governments manifestly unfriendly to the Soviet Union; and the Soviets were reluctant to provide a structure on which all parties whom the West supported might stand. Harriman was exasperated and told Truman that Russia confronted Eastern Europe with a "barbarian invasion." They could be responded to firmly for, he held, they needed reconstruction credit for their decimated industry. The tough approach to Russia was seconded by most of Truman's foreign affairs advisers, although some broached the fear that too unyielding an attitude over Poland would break Soviet-American relations completely and endanger the entrance of Russia into the Pacific war.

. Truman responded to Harriman that he understood "the Russians need us more than we need them" and though we cannot "expect 100 percent of what he proposed," he did feel "we would be able to get 85 percent."[92] The first step in the march toward 85 percent of U.S. claims was to be taken with Molotov, who was coming to San Francisco in a gesture of good will to the fledgling United Nations Conference and the new American president. In meetings with the Soviet foreign minister, Truman pointed out in "words of one syllable" the American desire for immediate free elections. Truman stated that Poland had become the symbol of U.S. foreign policy. The terse but correct conversation turned into a very undiplomatic diatribe. Truman spoke to the foreign minister as if he were a simple-minded recruit, demanding that elements of the London Poles join the Polish government and that elections be held immediately. Molotov protested, "I have never been talked to like that in my life." Truman snapped, "Carry out your agreements and you won't get talked to like that."[93]

Stalin seemed both puzzled and bitter. In a letter following Truman's April 23, 1945, meeting with Molotov, the Soviet premier protested that "Poland, unlike Great Britain and the United States, had common frontiers with the Soviet Union. . . . 'I do not know whether a truly representative government has been set up in Greece or whether the government in Belgium is truly democratic.' The Soviet Union was not consulted . . . and claimed no right to interfere, 'as it understands the full significance of Belgium and Greece for the security of Great Britain.'"[94]

Truman did not see his policy as the reversal of previous agreements. Instead he seemed to fear that the political closing of Eastern Europe would presage its closure economically. In the view of Truman and his advisers, such a political and economic division of East and West would threaten economic chaos in Europe. Moreover, Truman's most fervently held belief was that a "breach of peace anywhere in the world, threatens the peace of the entire world."[95] In contrast, the Russians concluded that the West, because of its concern and claims in Eastern Europe, was involved in a resurrection of the old course of encirclement.

It is not clear that security meant expansion for the Russians. To the contrary, there were going to be momentous difficulties in holding the areas where their armies stood. The "iron curtain" was a protective shell masking Stalin's concern that the relaxation of ideological control Russia experienced in the "great patriotic war" would accelerate. Moreover, it was feared that the extent of the internal devastation, if it were known, would be an invitation for the West to press its claim. If the Russians had been ready to advance they would not have demobilized nor torn out the rail connetions between the Soviet Union and Germany that ran through

Poland. The extent of this winding down is even more impressive if one considers the very considerable state of tension in Central Europe in this period and the enormous amount of police supervision required. Yet the West understood the Soviets' fierce defense of their acquisitions and political tactics as preparation for expansion.[96]

Truman increased the pressure. Shortly after Truman's decision to search for 85 percent Soviet agreement with the American understanding of the political future of Eastern Europe, lend-lease was abruptly cancelled. Ships already unloading cargo were packed up and others in the mid-Atlantic turned around in an effort to use economic leverage against the Soviets. As the assistant chief of lend-lease observed, this "decision was taken deliberately and probably was a part of a general squeeze now being put on the USSR."[97] Stalin protested, "the American attitude toward the Soviet Union had peceptibly cooled once it became obvious that Germany was defeated. . . ."[98] Although the decision was partially reversed,[99] the damage already done was exacerbated by Truman's decision to implement a "more realistic policy": an approach minimizing financial help to the Russians while agreements were yet to be reached on Eastern Europe to Truman's satisfaction—a satisfaction that demanded a great deal from the Soviets.

THE ATOM BOMB, ASIA, AND EUROPE

Economics were only one part of the strategy of convincing the Russians that they needed to cooperate in Eastern Europe. There was the potential of the atomic bomb, which Secretary of State James F. Byrnes told Truman "might well put us in the position to dictate our own terms."[100] Or, as Truman himself explained just before the news of the first test reached him, "If it explodes . . . I'll certainly have a hammer on those boys."[101] The Polish issue and the atomic bomb were conjoined, if not, as some have argued, "inextricably bound together."[102]

In the meantime, Truman called on Harry Hopkins, well known as an associate of Roosevelt and a symbol of more cordial times, to go to Moscow, although Hopkins was gravely ill. In Moscow, Hopkins made a substantial concession that granted that the Lublin Poles be formally recognized as the basis for a postwar government in Poland in return for the admittance of a few London Poles. On July 5, 1945, pleased with Stalin's promise to insert five independent Poles and the Poles from London into a nucleus of a Warsaw (Lublin) cabinet and pleased with Stalin's reaffirmation of his pledge to hold free elections, Truman extended diplomatic recognition of the Polish provisional government.

Nevertheless, this agreement over the composition of the Polish government was not considered final by Truman and his advisers.[103]

There were indications that Stalin, having received a Polish government compatible with Soviet interest, relaxed some controls in most of Eastern Europe. There were concessions granted to the West in the Allied commissions of Hungary and Rumania, and in Hungary the West was even given a veto in the Allied Control Commission. Coalition governments were accepted in Hungary and Czechoslovakia. Stalin probably pursued this policy for three reasons. First, it was a conciliatory gesture toward the West. The territory in which he was interested was under the control of Soviet troops, Poland had been accorded recognition, and there were other matters in Central Europe and of economic assistance to which he now felt he could turn. Second, he had, no doubt, no desire to provoke the further ill will of the West. Third, there were administrative limits to the Soviets achieving effective control over such a vast area—if indeed that was their strategy. The nature of that control became quite harsh; but the most unpleasant features of Eastern European life were not established until after the defection of Yugoslavia in 1948. Whether or not totalitarian domination was the long-range vision of Stalin, the immediate tactics of gaining Soviet control were gradualist and unprovocative to center leftist parties in Eastern Europe and conciliatory of Western sensibilities. Stalin requested that Truman recognize leftist regimes in Eastern Europe; but the Americans refused—stating that the governments were neither representative nor responsive to the will of the people.

Truman and Churchill arrived in a devastated Berlin for their meeting with Stalin at Potsdam, a suburb of Berlin, on July 16, 1945. Truman said that his "immediate purpose was to get the Russians into the war against Japan as soon as possible."[104] But the need to substitute Russian casualties for Americans became less apparent when a message arrived from the heat-fused desert of Alamogordo, New Mexico, that the atom bomb had been tested successfully. The success at testing the bomb signaled to the West, in Churchill's words, that "we should not need the Russians. . . . We had no need to ask favors of them."[105] Truman became both confident and visibly more rigid with Stalin after the news of the New Mexico test arrived. He no longer negotiated with the Russians; rather there occurred a sharply barbed exchange of views. As Churchill recalled, "[Truman] stood up to the Russians in a most emphatic and decisive manner, telling them as to certain demands that they absolutely could not have and the United States was entirely against them. . . . He told the Russians just where they could get off and generally bossed the whole meeting."[106] In short, the bomb buoyed the

West, for as Churchill told the House of Commons, "we possessed powers which were irresistible"[107]—or so it seemed.

Truman, his advisers, and Churchill determined that the bomb could have several diplomatic and military purposes. First, if it was used quickly, the shock might prompt an immediate surrender of the Japanese and thus be, in Churchill's words, "a merciful abridgement of the slaughter."[108] Second, it could keep Russian participation in the Asian war and hence postwar claims against Japan and China to a minimum. As Navy Secretary James Forrestal recalled in his diary, "Byrnes [the secretary of state] said he was most anxious to get the Japanese affairs over with before the Russians get in. . . . Once in there, he felt, it would not be easy to get them out."[109] Third, a significant Russian voice in the internal order of the postwar Japanese government by means of the occupational control agreement might not come into force if Japan could be forced to surrender before Russia managed a significant participation in the war. Truman recalled: "I would not allow the Russians any part in the control of Japan. . . . I made up my mind that General MacArthur would be given complete command and control of Japan."[110]

Finally, it was hoped, especially by Secretary of State Byrnes and probably by President Truman as well, that the bomb could be exploited to political advantage in Eastern Europe. As Byrnes explained in relation to Eastern Europe in late July, the "New Mexico situation had given us great power, and that in the final analysis, it would control."[111] After the bomb was dropped, Byrnes became increasingly rigid, as Henry L. Stimson's diary relates:

> I took up the question . . . how to handle Russia with the big bomb. I found that Byrnes was very much against any attempt to cooperate with the Russians. . . . He looks to having the presence of the bomb in his pocket.[112]

The official American justification for dropping the bomb has always been in terms of a calculus of military necessity and humanitarian concern. President Truman explained that the bomb was dropped "to shorten the agony of war, in order to save the lives of thousands and thousands of young Americans."[113] But historical evidence suggests that there were alternatives to dropping the bomb. First, was the bomb necessary to save lives? The Japanese may have wanted to surrender anyway. In mid-June 1945, Foreign Minister Hideki Tojo approached the Russians "with a view to terminating the war if possible by September."[114] These overtures became more intense throughout the summer, others were intercepted, and still others were being made directly to the West.[115] The Americans, who had broken the Japanese code years earlier, had easy access to Japanese communications, which were alive with efforts to convince the Russians to intercede on their behalf. In fact, Hopkins advised that these peace overtures be explored, but they were not. Instead, on July 26, 1945, only thirteen days before Russia was scheduled to enter the war, China, the United States, and Britain issued an ultimatum to the Japanese to surrender unconditionally or face "prompt and utter destruction."

This insistence on unconditional surrender in the face of Japanese attempts to quit if only the future status of the emperor was clarified is confusing in view of Truman's contention that his sole motive was to end the war with the least bloodshed. If the complete humiliation of Japan was desired, then one can only note that the terms finally offered and accepted did allow for the retention of the emperor and were the same as an important faction of the deeply divided Japanese cabinet was prepared to accept in mid-summer 1945. If the minimizing of human suffering alone was the motive, then those terms could have been at least explored; instead, they were ignored until after the bombs were dropped.

Moreover, the bomb was not universally perceived as a military necessity. The fire raids on Tokyo destroyed as much life. American air strikes came and went with no interference—imposing fire storms that incinerated up to one hundred thousand human beings a raid. Much American military analysis was in agreement with General Curtis LeMay that "even without the atomic bomb and the Russian entry into the war, Japan would have surrendered in two weeks. . . . The atomic bomb has nothing to do with the end of the war." The authors of the U.S. Strategic Bombing Survey concluded that

> it is the Survey's opinion that . . . in all probability prior to November 31, 1945 Japan would have surrendered even if the atomic bomb had not been dropped, even if Russia had not entered the war, and even if no invasion had been planned or contemplated.[116]

Finally, contemporary critics of the decision to use the bomb have noted that there were other options available to the president the use of which either alone or in combination could have brought Japanese surrender. These included: (1) diplomatic negotiations especially on the terms of surrender; (2) a naval blockade; or (3) the Russian action of declaring war. The use of force, including the bomb itself, could have taken a different form as well. For example, conventional air strikes could have continued given total American air superiority. It has been suggested that Truman might have threatened its use or even demonstrated the bomb rather than use it on civilians with no warning.[117] In each case, of course, these options would have required time and thus increased the possibility or even ensured greater Russian participation and presence in the structuring of postwar Asia. Herbert Feis has concluded:

> It is likely that Churchill, and probably also Truman, conceived that besides bringing the war to a quick end, it would improve the chances of arranging a satisfactory peace both in Europe and in the Far East. Stimson and Byrnes certainly had that thought in mind. For would not the same dramatic proof of western power that shocked Japan into surrender impress the Russians also? . . . In short, the bomb, it may have been thought or hoped, would not only subdue the Japanese aggressors, but perhaps also monitor Russian behavior.[118]

The bomb seemed to yield benefits: Japan surrendered and the Americans moved quickly to build a "sympathetic Japan . . . in case there should be any aggression by Russia in Manchuria."[119] The attempt to contain Soviet influence in Asia was furthered by the order to the Japanese in Korea, the Philippines, Indochina, and East Asia to surrender only to forces that General Douglas MacArthur would designate. The order was calculated to minimize the possibility that the Japanese would surrender to partisan resistance forces under Mao Zedong, Ho Chi Minh, or others fighting in Indonesia, Korea, and the Philippines, and thereby strengthen the influence of left-led partisans who would presumably have been sympathetic to Russian power. The Russians protested, but they had not been able to establish much of a presence in Asia by dint of arms and, more important, their major concern was Central Europe. Thus, although the Russians largely respected the West's claims in Asia, the bomb had probably less to do with it than the balance of Soviet and American capability deployed in the Far East at the end of the war. This was, of course, a mirror image of the situation in Central Europe; but in Europe Truman would concede nothing.

Potsdam and Beyond

In the meantime, at Potsdam, Truman proceeded to push claims against the Soviets that denied to the Russians the kind of exclusive arrangement the West had pursued in Greece, Italy, and North Africa. The discussion became increasingly sharp and Truman soon wearied of it, thinking it futile—and, perhaps, believing that soon the great demonstration of American power over Hiroshima and Nagasaki would give the Soviets second thoughts. The issue of whether Eastern Europe was to be open or closed to Western influence remained, however, unaffected by the bomb. This issue turned instead on the disposition of forces during and immediately after the war. The question of postwar Germany's political and economic future became therefore the most frequently debated issue in the Potsdam conference.

Early in the war Roosevelt had approved of the plan of his secretary of the treasury, Henry Morgenthau, to fragment Germany, "pastoralize it," and bring to Germany the forceful lessons of a Carthaginian peace. When the plan was originally proposed to him, the president endorsed it enthusiastically: "We have to castrate the German people or you have to treat them in such a manner so they can't go on reproducing people who want to go on the way they have in the past."[120] Roosevelt's advisers and Churchill, however, did not fully support this vision, fearing that it would bankrupt European reconstruction, encourage nationalist irredentism, and open the way for communism. By Yalta, the president was also becoming wary of some of the implications of this plan; Roosevelt did not want mass starvation to occur; nor did he want a repetition of the reparations experience after World War I which had contributed to the economic instability of Germany in the 1920s and 1930s. Subsequently, therefore, Roosevelt rejected the harsh "planned chaos" of the initial Morgenthau proposal, while accepting other implications of the plan concerning some reduction of the German standard of living. Hence, at Yalta, Roosevelt became committed, as a basis of discussion, to the figure of $20 billion or 50 percent of German wealth drawn from all of Germany as the basic reparations payment. Thus, although divided politically into occupation zones, Germany was to be treated as a single economic unit.

At Potsdam, however, the Americans demanded that there be no specific figure set for reparations. It was a harsh blow for the Soviets, who had been promised a $20 billion talking figure. The Russians knew that the action of cutting off lend-lease and of procrastination on Soviet loan requests left reparations drawn from Germany as the only reasonable recourse, in terms of outside assistance, for postwar reconstruction of Russia. In part, Truman's decision to withdraw reparations from the Russians was prompted by concern that, eventually, Americans would wind up subsidizing German reparations payments to the Russians. Second, Truman proposed that any reparations paid to the Allies should be drawn from their respective zones of occupation, rather than from Germany as a whole as envisioned at Yalta. A zonal approach to reparations, it was argued by the Americans, would minimize conflict about what the Germans could or could not afford. The Russians protested, however, that such an arrangement would deprive them of access to the industrialized Western zones, especially the Ruhr. Soviet-controlled East Germany was largely agricultural, and the Russians had removed in a draconian fashion almost all its rolling stock, cattle, a good deal of industrial plant, and even toilets before the Big Three convened in Berlin. It was, they declared, "war booty" and not part of the reparations calculation.

More important: would not this mean, Molotov asked, "that each country would have a free hand in their own zone and would act entirely independent of the other?"[121] In other words, the American proposal outlined a divided Germany in which Four Power control would be minimized if not eliminated in the respective zones. In view of the Soviet desire to maintain access to and influence on any and all facets of German political and economic reconstruction, this turn of events could not be viewed with optimism in Moscow. The Russians were aware of the need for a German economic reconstruction sufficient to maintain reparations. But they were concerned primarily with the security implications of a Germany, or any part of it, not open to their influence and, if possible, an administrative veto over German policies. At Yalta, Churchill had remarked to Stalin, "If you want a horse to pull a wagon, you have to give it fodder." The Soviet dictator replied, "But care should be taken to see that the horse did not turn around and kick you."[122]

At Potsdam, therefore, the contentious nature of the German question—the pivotal issue of the next crucial five years—was drawn. Germany was the key variable in opposing Soviet and American conceptions of a secure and stable Europe. On the other hand, the conference did seem to offer the Soviets a softening of the Western position on Poland. It was not inconceivable, therefore, that the German problem could be worked out by the foreign ministers in the fall of 1945.

Atomic Diplomacy Proves Inadequate

The mushroom clouds from the bombs exploding in the Orient reached silently over the shoulders of the statesmen who sat at the London foreign ministers' meeting, discussing Eastern Europe in the fall of 1945. It was not mentioned in the conference proceedings, but cartoonists drew pictures of it perched on the conference table. As *Time* magazine commented: "at the . . . conference, U.S. diplomats had been reluctant to talk about the bomb. When the subject came up in private conversation they would say something like 'of course, the world knows that the U.S. would never. . . .' Such sentences usually trailed off in inaudible mumbles."[123] But in the end, the bomb only served to exaggerate the reactions of both sides. Secretary Byrnes's whole negotiating strategy seemed infused with a sense of atomic omnipotence.[124] At London, the tenor of the coming cold war was in evidence as diplomacy turned vitriolic. The conference degenerated into a series of alternating press conferences in which the two sides explained their own positions and castigated each other concerning their respective policies in their European spheres of influence. The atomic threat was always present if unarticulated, but Molotov and the Russians were unmoved—the existing balance of forces in Europe, not the vague if ominous threats of atomic diplomacy, moved the Russians. The conference stalemated.

Byrnes decided to shift his tactics in the next foreign ministers' conference, to be held in Moscow in December 1945. Rather than pursue his London tack of public diplomacy, he undertook a more secretive style and approached Stalin and Molotov with offers of recognition for the Rumanian and Bulgarian regimes if the Russians would agree to a German peace treaty as well as a general set of agreements covering all of Eastern Europe. In Byrnes's scheme, all of these issues would be resolved in a large peace conference which would negotiate the political agreements as well as provide economic access to Central Europe.

The Soviets seemed satisfied[125] but President Truman was not. He was more than a little miffed at Byrnes's secrecy and the latitude exercised by the secretary of state in his negotiations. From all appearances in Washington, Byrnes was free-lancing and making vague concessions to the Russians without presidential approval. Moreover, such diplomacy opened Truman to attacks from conservative Republicans who were labeling Roosevelt's actions at Yalta and Democratic party diplomacy in general a sellout. Senator Arthur Vandenberg, ranking member and then chair of the Senate Foreign Relations Committee, grumbled that the conciliatory language of the Moscow meeting and the lack of progress reminded him of "Chamberlain and his umbrella appeasement." House Leader Joe Martin called it a "betrayal of the small nations of the world in the making of peace."[126] Under such attack an already tough Byrnes was pushed even further to the right and into a more inflexible policy line as the postwar conferences began again in 1946.

From the Soviet perspective, the American course in Germany was unacceptable. Indeed, it was potentially dangerous, for it implied a reconstituted Germany perhaps ruled by the very class of people who had directed the destruction of twenty million Russians during the preceding five years. All in all, it was not a prospect that would win Russian favor or evoke Russian confidence and trust. Western proposals in Germany—an area regarded by the Soviets as the very core of their security interests—were, predictably, rejected. Instead, the Soviets and the Americans turned to the imposition of greater control of their respective zones of occupation. The Allied Control Council for Germany became merely an administrative shell as the military commanders in each occupation zone assumed supreme political as well as military authority. The division of Germany seemed assured when, in May 1946, General Lucius Clay informed the Russians that no more reparations would be paid to them from the Western zones. Similarly, the Soviets, at about the same time, stopped removing machinery from East Germany and apparently decided to regenerate industrial production within the East German zone.

In a highly publicized speech in Stuttgart, on September 4, 1946, Secretary of State Byrnes announced that Germany needed to develop a "self-sustaining" economy and a capacity to export. "Germany is a part of Europe, and European recovery . . . will be slowed with her great resources turned into a poor house," Byrnes explained.[127] Germans, he declared, should be given primary responsibility for running their own affairs. Moreover, the United States would never recognize the Oder-Neisse as the eastern boundary that separated Poland and East Germany. There were over three and a half million Germans expelled from Poland, living in Western zones. Byrnes's speech gave them hope that they would return, and tied the future German government to that assumption for twenty-five years. Byrnes's speech also implied that the United States would keep its troops in Germany for "a long time to come," but a provisional government would be set up to manage German contributions to its own and general European recovery. Such a state of affairs, a reconstituted Germany administered by those who had lost the war, could be held up to the Eastern Europeans as a bogey of revenge—and tie the whole area to the Russians.

The East Germans made little pretense at being self-governing. They would be only a hypothetical security threat to Russia's satellites; they had no refugees and were "satisfied." Still, the specter of American troops guarding the Western sectors of a divided Germany with claims to the East promised no immediate reconciliation of the partitioned Germanies. The Americans did not recognize Soviet security interests in Central Europe and feared Soviet designs and Soviet power. Soviet actions were almost without exception interpreted as challenges to the West that had to be met with stern resolve. Unity became an imperative, and the recovery of Europe was only a part of the larger need for sustained resistance to the Soviet threat. In this way a set of conditions were established that were to serve as a persistent flashpoint of East-West contention for the next twenty-five years.

NOTES

1. N. Gordon Levin, Jr., *Woodrow Wilson and World Politics: America's Response to War and Revolution* (New York: Oxford University Press, 1968).
2. Ray S. Baker and William E. Dodd, *The Public Papers of Woodrow Wilson, III* (New York: 1927), pp. 147–148, as cited by Robert E. Osgood, *Ideals and Self-Interest in*

America's Foreign Relation: The Great Transformation of the Twentieth Century (Chicago: University of Chicago Press, 1953), p. 178.

3. Albert Shaw, ed., *President Wilson's State Papers and Addresses* (New York: George A. Doran Co., 1918), pp. 380–381.

4. A good summary of the literature of Woodrow Wilson's view of world order can be found in Lloyd E. Ambosius, "The Orthodoxy of Revisionism; Woodrow Wilson and the New Left," *Diplomatic History*, Vol. 1, No. 3 (Summer 1977), especialy pp. 209–211.

5. Cited by Inis Claude, *Power and International Relations* (New York: Random House, 1962), p. 101.

6. G. H. Stern, "The Foreign Policy of the Soviet Union," in F. S. Northedge, ed., *The Foreign Policies of the Great Powers* (New York: Praeger Publishers, 1962), p. 77. An exhaustive review of the "Soviet diplomatic method" can be found in Joseph G. Whelan's *Soviet Diplomacy and Negotiating Behavior: Emerging New Context for U.S. Diplomacy*, Special Studies on Foreign Affairs Issues, Congressional Research Service for the Senate Committe on Foreign Relations, July 11, 1979.

7. Woodrow Wilson, Speech at Kansas City, Mo., September 6, 1919, reprinted in Thomas G. Paterson, ed., *Major Problems in American Foreign Policy: Documents and Essays*, Vol. 2 (since 1914) (Lexington, Mass.: D.C. Heath, 1978), pp. 96–97.

8. The figure is from Betty Miller Unterberger, "President Wilson and the Decision to Send Troops to Siberia," *Pacific Historical Review*, Vol. 24 (February 1955), pp. 63–74. A good review of the documents and literature is Unterberger, ed., *American Intervention in the Russian Civil War* (Lexington, Mass.: D.C. Heath, 1969).

9. Levin, op. cit., p. 107.

10. One soldier penned a bit of doggerel which captured their misery: "It's the land of the infernal odor, the land of the national smell. The average United States soldier would rather be quartered in L." *Literary Digest*, Vol. 60 (February 8, 1919), p. 99, cited in Thomas A. Bailey, *America Faces Russia* (Ithaca, N.Y.: Cornell University Press, 1950), p. 242.

11. See Linda Killen, "The Search for a Democratic Russia," *Diplomatic History*, Vol. 2, No. 3 (Summer 1978), p. 241. Alongside the American military effort, Wilson directed American grains to be sent to the White controlled area since this was a "most effective means of limiting the spread of Bolshevism." The wheat never arrived, however, because its destination, Petrograd, fell to the communists before American ships could deliver the consigned grain.

12. Ibid, p. 251.

13. John G. Stoessinger, *Nations in Darkness* (New York: Random House, 1971), p. 116.

14. Walter Lippmann and Charles Merz, "A Test of the News," *New Republic*, Vol. 2 (August 4, 1920), pp. 1–42. For an excellent recent summary of the literature on the public's attitudes toward the Soviet Union as a function of official policy, see Ralph B. Levering, *The Public and American Foreign Policy 1918–1978* (New York: William Morrow, 1978).

15. Stoessinger, op. cit., p. 119, citing the *Saturday Evening Post*, July 6, 1918.

16. Ibid.

17. Ibid., p. 120

18. Ibid., p. 133.

19. Ibid., p. 141.

20. Stephen Pichon, "Allied Policy in Russia," *Current History*, Vol. 10, No. 2 (May 1919), pp. 280–281.

21. George F. Kennan, *Russia and the West Under Lenin and Stalin* (Boston: Little, Brown, and Company, 1961), p. 117.

22. *Foreign Relations of the United States, 1920*, Vol. 3, pp. 466–468, cited in perhaps

the best study of early Soviet diplomacy, Teddy Uldricks's *Diplomacy and Ideology: The Origins of Soviet Foreign Relations: 1917–1930* (London: Sage, 1978), p. 51.

23. Kennan, op. cit., p. 137.
24. Ibid., p. 138.
25. Bailey, *America Faces Russia,* p. 257.
26. Stoessinger, op. cit., p. 143.
27. Ibid., p. 143.
28. *Literary Digest,* Vol. 116 (December 2, 1933), p. 13.
29. Louis Fisher, *Russia's Road from Peace to War* (New York: Harper & Row, 1969), p. 261.
30. Indeed, some have suggested that the brutal purges in 1937 can be seen as a means of ridding the Soviet Union of potential opposition to a *modus vivendi* with Hitler. See Kennan, op. cit., pp. 315–316. Thomas Maddux suggests that Stalin "backed away" from active cooperation with the West in early 1936. See Maddux, "Watching Stalin Maneuver Between Hilter and the West: American Diplomats and Soviet Diplomacy, 1934–1939," *Diplomatic History,* Vol. 1, No. 2 (Spring 1977).
31. Kennan, op. cit., p. 317.
32. *The Times* (London), September 28, 1938, and John Wheeler-Bennett, *Munich: Prologue to Tragedy* (London: Macmillan, 1948), pp. 157–158.
33. The American role was minor but noteworthy for the sense of guilt that it caused. Roosevelt stated to Hitler, just before Munich, that Germany did not have to concern itself about American protest. "The Government of the United States has no political involvements in Europe," Roosevelt declared, "and will assume no obligations in the conduct of the present negotiations." Robert A. Divine, *Roosevelt and World War II* (Baltimore: Johns Hopkins University Press, 1969), p. 22.
34. Adam B. Ulam, *Expansion and Coexistence, History of Soviet Foreign Policy, 1917–1967* (New York: Praeger, 1968), p. 263 *passim.*
35. The British did not want to be responsible for defending the Baltic states but were requesting the Soviets to aid Holland and Belgium.
36. Winston S. Churchill, *The Grand Alliance,* Vol. III of *The Second World War* (Boston: Houghton Mifflin, 1950), p. 369.
37. George F. Kennan, *Memoirs, 1925–1950* (Boston: Little, Brown, 1967), pp. 133–134.
38. Divine, op. cit., p. 81–82.
39. Ibid., p. 84
40. Kennan, *Russia and the West Under Lenin and Stalin,* pp. 350–351.
41. As the U.S. Chiefs of Staff reported in 1941, "It should be recognized as an almost invariable rule that wars cannot be finally won without the use of land armies." M. Watson, War Department, Chief of Staff; *Pre-War Plans and Preparations (United States Army in World War II).* Washington, D.C.: U.S. Government Printing Office, 1950, pp. 400–410; cited in John Bagguley, "The World War and the Cold War," in David Horowitz, ed., *Containment and Revolution* (Boston: Beacon, 1967), p. 91.
42. Churchill, op. cit., pp. 645–651.
43. James MacGregor Burns, *Roosevelt: The Soldier of Freedom* (New York: Harcourt Brace Jovanovich, 1970), p. 231.
44. Churchill, op. cit., pp. 457–458.
45. Paul Carell, *Hitler Moves East: 1941–1943* (New York: Ballantine, 1963), p. 196 *passim.*
46. Ibid., p. 202.
47. Churchill, op. cit., pp. 469–470.
48. Churchill, *The Hinge of Fate,* Vol. IV of *The Second World War* (Boston: Houghton Mifflin, 1950), p. 201.

49. Burns, op. cit., pp. 111–112.
50. John L. Gaddis, *The United States and the Origins of the Cold War, 1941–1947* (New York: Columbia University Press, 1972) , p. 7.
51. Robert E. Sherwood, *Roosevelt and Hopkins* (New York: Harper & Brothers, 1948), p. 577.
52. Churchill, *The Hinge of Fate*, p. 342.
53. H. C. Butcher, *The Years with Eisenhower* (New York: Simon & Schuster, 1946), p. 12.
54. Ibid., p. 29; and Stephen Ambrose, *Rise to Globalism: Amerian Foreign Policy Since 1938* (Baltimore: Penguin Books, 1970), p. 53.
55. Burns, op. cit., p. 236.
56. Churchill, *The Hinge of Fate*, p. 475.
57. Cited in Andre Fontaine, *History of the Cold War* (New York: Vintage Books, 1968), p. 160.
58. Bagguley, "The World War and the Cold War," in David Horowitz, ed., *Containment and Revolution* (Boston: Beacon Press, 1967), p. 91; and Churchill, *The Hinge of Fate*, Vol. IV of *The Second World War* (New York: Bantam Books, 1962), Appendix A, Book 2, Memo: Prime Minister to Ismay, January, 1943, p. 806, and March 3 and 4, 1943, p. 816.
59. Churchill, *The Hinge of Fate*, Bantam ed., pp. 663–679, and Memos: Prime Minister to Ismay, March 4, 1943, p. 816.
60. Richard M. Leighton and Robert W. Corkley, *Global Logistics and Strategy: 1943–1945, The United States Army in World War II* (Washingon, D.C.: Office of the Chief of Military History, 1968), p. 846.
61. Gordan A. Harrison, *The European Theater of Operations: Cross-Channel Attack (The United States Army in World War II)* (Washington, D.C.: Office of the Chief of Military History, 1951), p. 141.
62. Fontaine, op. cit., p. 160.
63. Ibid., pp. 160–161.
64. Indeed, the Joint Chiefs of Staff had predicted as much. Burns, op. cit., pp. 312–316.
65. Bagguley, op. cit., p. 95.
66. Basil Liddell Hart, *History of the Second World War, Vol. II* (New York: Capricorn, 1972), p. 488; Vojtech Mastny, "Stalin and the Prospects of a Separate Peace in World War II," *The American Historical Review*, Vol. 77, No. 5 (December 1972), pp. 1365–1388; and Lynn Etheridge Davis, *The Cold War Begins: Soviet American Conflict over Eastern Europe* (Princeton, N.J.: Princeton University Press, 1974), pp. 51–52.
67. Herbert Feis, *Churchill, Roosevelt and Stalin* (Princeton, N.J.: Princeton University Press, 1957), p. 584. The Germans, and especially Himmler, were apparently very interested in piquing the Western Allies' interest in a separate deal. Such a move would, at the least, cause disruption in the Allied cause, and might become serious. As Himmler explained to the Swedish diplomat Count Bernadotte, a deal with the Western Allies would save as great a part of Germany as possible from a Russian invasion. "I am willing to capitulate on the Western Front in order to enable the Western Allies to advance to the East." Gar Alperovitz, *Cold War Essays* (Cambridge, Mass.: Schenkman, 1970), p. 26.
68. Allen Dulles, *Secret Surrender* (New York: Harper & Row, 1966), pp. 146–151.
69. Joseph Stalin, *Correspondence Between the Chairman of the Council of Ministers of the U.S.S.R. with Churchill, Atlee, Roosevelt and Truman, 1941–1945*, Vol. II (New York: Dutton, 1958).
70. Gaddis, op. cit., p. 93.
71. Michael A. Pezke, article in the *Journal of the American Aviation Historical Society*,

cited in *The New York Times*, November 8, 1973.

72. Sherwood, op. cit., p. 899.
73. Ibid., pp. 899–900.
74. Churchill, *The Grand Alliance*, p. 391.
75. John A. Lukacs, *The Great Powers and Eastern Europe* (New York: American Book, 1953), p. 506.
76. Divine, op. cit., pp. 91–92.
77. Divine, *Foreign Policy and U.S. Presidential Elections 1940–1948* (New York: Franklin Watts, 1974), pp. 130–137.
78. Burns, op. cit., p. 572.
79. Gaddis, op. cit., p. 173.
80. W. Averell Harriman, *America and Russia in a Changing World: A Half Century of Personal Observation* (Garden City, N.Y.: Doubleday, 1971), pp. 35–36.
81. Milovan Djilas, *Conversations with Stalin* (New York: Harcourt, Brace & World, 1962), p. 114, and Ronald Steel, "Did Anybody Start the Cold War?" *New York Review*, Vol. 26 (September 2, 1971), p. 26.
82. See Arthur Schlesinger, "The Origins of the Cold War," *Foreign Affairs*, Vol. 46 (October 1967), pp. 22–52.
83. Ambrose, op. cit., pp. 58–59. Jews were still persecuted, unable to practice professions, attend schools, or own property; Arabs continued to be beaten and exploited; the French generals who had cooperated with the Nazis and fought the Americans lived in splendor amid the squalor that surrounded them.
84. *Times* (London), April 17, 1945.
85. Churchill, *Triumph and Tragedy*, Vol. VI of *The Second World War* (New York: Bantam, 1962), p. 258.
86. Ibid., 247, *passim*.
87. Ibid., p. 610.
88. Perry McCoy Smith, *The Air Force Plans for Peace: 1943–1945* (Baltimore: Johns Hopkins University Press, 1970). American plans at sea were to put U.S. ships "everywhere" so, in the words of one planner, the U.S. fleet would outnumber the fleets of the world. Thomas G. Paterson, *On Every Front* (New York: Norton, 1979), p. 81, and unpublished monograph by James E. King.
89. Kennan, *Memoirs*, p. 57. For Harriman's views see Daniel Yergin, *Shattered Peace: The Origins of the Cold War and the National Security State* (Boston: Houghton Mifflin, 1977), pp. 81, 84, and 93.
90. Kennan, op. cit. p. 70.
91. Edward R. Stettinius, *Roosevelt and the Russians* (Garden City, N.Y.: Doubleday, 1949), p. 347.
92. Harry S. Truman, *Memoirs*, Vol. II, *Year of Decision* (Garden City, N.Y.: Doubleday, 1955), p. 71.
93. Ibid., p. 82. For a milder rendition of this conversation, see Robert J. Donovan, *Conflict and Crisis* (New York: Norton, 1977), p. 42, fn. 33, and p. 445.
94. Churchill, *Triumph and Tragedy*, Bantam ed., pp. 421–422. This quotation is partly a paraphrase of Stalin's words by Churchill and partly a direct quote of Stalin's message to Churchill.
95. William D. Leahy, *I Was There* (New York: Whittsley House, 1950), pp. 384–385.
96. Gabriel Kolko, *The Politics of War* (New York: Vintage Books, 1968), pp. 439–444; and Schlesinger, op. cit., p. 43.
97. Alperovitz, *Cold War Essays*, p. 98.
98. Sherwood, op. cit. p. 894.
99. And, in the view of some observers, it may have been a bureaucratic mistake: Gaddis, op. cit. p. 219.

100. Truman, op. cit., p. 87.
101. Jonathan Daniels, *The Man of Independence* (Philadelphia: J. B. Lippincott, 1950), p. 266. Also see Martin J. Sherwin, *A World Destroyed: The Atomic Bomb and the Grand Alliance* (New York: Alfred A. Knopf, 1975). pp. 188, 191 for a dispute about exactly when the bomb and Poland became bound together as issues.
102. Gar Alperovitz, *Atomic Diplomacy* (New York: Random House, 1965), p. 64. For a critique of Alperovitz's "delayed showdown" thesis, see Martin J. Sherwin "The Atomic Bomb, Scientists, and American Diplomacy During the Second World War" (unpublished doctoral dissertation, University of California, Los Angeles, 1971) pp. 252–269. On the other hand, see Yergin, op. cit., p. 101 and p. 115, who apparently accepts part of Alperovitz's controversial thesis about a showdown with the Soviets until after there was a successful test of the atom bomb. His rather elliptical essay on this point can be found in his notes of p. 433, fn. 19, where he suggests Alperovitz "overinterprets" the data.
103. Gaddis, op. cit., p. 234.
104. Truman, op. cit., p. 314.
105. Churchill, *Triumph and Tragedy* (Houghton Mifflin ed.), p. 639.
106. William A. Williams, *Tragedy of American Diplomacy*, rev. ed. (New York: Delta, 1962), p. 249.
107. Ibid.
108. Churchill, *Triumph and Tragedy* (Houghton Mifflin ed.), pp. 545ff.
109. Walter Millis, ed., *The Forrestal Diaries* (New York: Viking, 1951), p. 78.
110. Truman, op. cit., p. 412.
111. Gaddis, op. cit., p. 264.
112. Cited in Alperovitz, *Cold War Essays*, p. 70.
113. Harry S. Truman, *Public Papers of the President—1945* (Washington, D.C.: U.S. Government Printing Office, 1961), p. 212.
114. Cited in Alperovitz, *Cold War Essays*, p. 54.
115. Herbert Feis, *The Atomic Bomb and the End of World War II* (Princeton, N.J.: Princeton University Press, 1966), pp. 111–116.
116. *The United States Strategic Bombing Survey*, "Japan's Struggle to End the War," War Department, July 1, 1946, p. 13, and Alperovitz, *Cold War Essays*, pp. 62–63. The thesis that the bomb might not have been a military necessity is sharply challenged but not refuted by Professor Edward Shapiro, "The Military Options to Hiroshima: A Critical Examination of Gar Alperovitz," *Naval War College Review*, Vol. 30, No. 4 (Spring 1978), pp. 101–113. The thesis that the Japanese would not have surrendered until at least the first atomic bomb is argued by John Toland, *The Rising Sun: The Decline and Fall of the Japanese Empire, 1936–1945* (New York: Random House, 1970), pp. 809–866. See also the comments of former U.S. ambassador Edwin O. Reischauer in *Washington Post*, August 3, 1983, p. D1.
117. Discussions of these options may be found in Feis, op. cit., and Alperovitz, *Cold War Essays*. Also see the remarks of Isidor Rabi, a Nobel laureate, conversant with both the physics and politics of the decision not to warn the Japanese ahead of time, in Donovan, op. cit., p. 61 and p. 95 for Truman's thinking on this matter.
118. Feis, op. cit., p. 194. The decision to use the bomb may have been reinforced by a certain momentum that was somewhat independent of diplomatic or strategic subtleties. Among the elements that could have been at work in this regard, one might note:

    1. The expenditure of $2 billion, in secret, would have to be presumably justified some day.
    2. Thousands had already been slaughtered in Europe and Japan in air raids

against civilian targets. The raid against Japan did not seem all that extraordinary and was perhaps facilitated by popular racist beliefs about Japan.

3. As Ambrose points out, "The bomb was there . . . to use it seemed inevitable." To Truman, it appeared little else than an ace in the flush hand of military capability. It was only after their use, and some reflections, that atomic weapons created the respect they now command for themselves. See also Donovan, op. cit., chaps. 5, 7, and 10.

Still another argument drawing on the implicit momentum of the development process by emphasizing Truman's inexperience is advanced by Kenneth M. Glazier, Jr., "The Decision to Use Atomic Weapons Against Hiroshima and Nagasaki," *Public Policy*, Vol. 18 (Summer 1970), pp. 463–516. See also the important essay by Barton Bernstein, "Roosevelt, Truman and the Atomic Bomb," *Political Science Quarterly*, No. 90 (Spring 1975), pp. 23–29, for some of the uncertainties policymakers harbored regarding the efficacy of the bomb. On balance, however, their hopes for the weapon seem beyond question. See Yergin, op. cit., p. 120.

119. Kolko, op. cit., p. 599.
120. Gaddis, op. cit., p. 119.
121. Gaddis, op. cit., p. 241.
122. Charles Bohlen, Minutes of Second Meeting, February 5, 1944, *Foreign Relations of the United States, Diplomatic Papers: The Conferences of Malta and Yalta, 1945* (Washington, D.C.: U.S. Government Printing Office, 1955), pp. 620–621.
123. Lloyd C. Gardner, *Architects of Illusion: Men and Ideas in American Foreign Policy, 1941–1949* (Chicago: Quadrangle, 1970), p. 98.
124. Atomic scientist Leo Szilard wrote of his conversations with Byrnes at this time, that his "sense of proportion" was appalling. Szilard recalls:

> I shared Byrnes' concern about Russia's throwing around her weight in the post-war period, but I was completely flabbergasted by the assumption that rattling the bomb might make Russia more manageable.
>
> I began to doubt that there was any way for me to communicate with Byrnes in this matter, and my doubt became certainty when he turned to me and said, "Well, you come from Hungary—you would not want to stay in Hungary indefinitely, but what Byrnes said offended my sense of proportion. I was concerned at this point that by demonstrating the bomb and using it in the war against Japan, we might start an atomic arms race between America and Russia which was not disposed at this point to worry about what would happen to Hungary.

Leo Szilard, "Reminiscences" in Donald Fleming and Bernard Bailyn, eds., *Perspectives In American History II* (Cambridge, Mass.: Harvard University Press, 1968), pp. 94–151.
125. Feis, *From Trust to Terror: The Onset of the Cold War 1945–1950* (New York: W. W. Norton, 1970), p. 54.
126. Gaddis, p. 291.
127. The Stuttgart Speech, Typscript, National Archives, Washington, D.C., Regional File of the Department of State 740–00119 (Germany), p. 8. For an important dissent on the meaning of the Stuttgart address and review of the literature see John Gimbel, "On the Implementation of the Potsdam Agreement: An Essay on U.S. Post War German Policy," *Political Science Quarterly*, Vol. 87 (June 1972), pp. 242–269.

Chapter 2
The Onset of the
Cold War

By late 1945 it was apparent that Soviet and American policies were no longer joined by even the most tenuous of the strands that had held the wartime alliance together. During the last months of 1945 and through-out 1946 a new and inexperienced American president sought to master American policy even as that policy collided with Soviet interests on a global scale, first in Germany and then simultaneously in the Middle East, Asia, and the United Nations. It was, as former Secretary of State Dean Acheson put it, a time of "learning."[1] And out of it emerged the political culture, reflexes, and some of the most fundamental policy parameters for the next quarter century.

A WORLD VIEW TAKES SHAPE

As positions hardened in Germany, the Soviets and the West issued what Walter LaFeber has called "appropriate declarations of the Cold War."[2] In a speech on February 9, 1946, Stalin took note of the relatively weak position of the Soviet Union and its need, in spite of the hardships of the war, to redouble its efforts to achieve economic recovery. In Stalin's view, the power of the West did not allow the Soviet Union the luxury of returning to a peacetime footing; instead, high industrial production targets and an emphasis on the production of modern weapons systems were to be the order of the day for the next fifteen years.[3] Stalin asserted that communism and capitalism were incompatible and that true peace was impossible until the former supplanted the latter. Most people in the United States received the speech as a warlike call to confrontation be-tween communism and the West.[4]

Less than a month later, Winston Churchill replied with his famous "iron curtain" speech at Fulton, Missouri, in which he asserted that the Soviets did not want war but rather "they desire . . . the fruits of war and the indefinite expansion of their power and doctrines."[5] The proper re-sponse, in Churchill's view, was a show of strength: "There is nothing they admire so much as strength, and there is nothing for which they have less respect than for military weakness."[6] It was the "duty," there-fore, of the United States and Great Britain to join in a "fraternal association of the English-speaking peoples" to counter Soviet expansionism. Churchill's position seems to have been quite compatible with a fairly widespread but basically private mood of American policymakers, a mood that had been articulated in an eight-thousand-word telegram from the chargé d'affaires of the Moscow Embassy, George F. Kennan, two weeks after Stalin's speech and a week before Churchill's.

The Soviet Threat Defined

The "long telegram" of February 22, 1946, was a response to an exasperated Department of State request for some explanation of Soviet behavior. Kennan states that he had been trying for the preceding eighteen months to get Washington to move toward a firmer policy line. "Now, suddenly, my opinion was being asked. . . . Nothing but the whole truth would do. They had asked for it. Now, by God, they would have it."[7] What they got was an extremely frightening picture of a Soviet Union that would expand inexorably unless opposed:

> Soviet power [is] . . . [i]mpervious to logic of reason, and it is highly sensitive to logic of force. For this reason it can easily withdraw—and usually does—when strong resistance is encountered at any point. Thus, if the adversary has sufficient force and makes clear his readiness to use it, he rarely has to do so."[8]

Although Kennan's recommendations concerning what American policy should be in the face of this threat were rather vague,[9] his description of the horrors and implied horrors of failing to confront communist power had tremendous impact and was a crucial element in subsequent American foreign policy. The message was read from the president on down and circulated widely in the Department of State and the military. The conclusion seems to have been drawn that the United States was confronted with a multidimensional threat aimed at nothing less than Western civilization. The only apparent remedy to Soviet power was struggle and confrontation because all they understood was force. Negotiations were viewed as being of limited utility if not impossible. Therefore the manipulation of the threat of war had to become the most important facet of diplomacy when dealing with the Soviets.

The inference that force was a primary instrument for dealing with the Russians was drawn, although Kennan claims, in retrospect, to have been uncomfortable with it.[10] A few other officials within the government openly displayed their opposition to the emerging anti-Soviet consensus of the Truman administration. Most prominent was Secretary of Commerce and former Vice President (under Roosevelt) Henry Wallace.

Wallace represented a diminishing number of liberal Democrats who continued to advocate a policy of lowered voices and continued negotiation with the Russians.[11] Truman's reaction to these concerns was to ignore them, and when Wallace took a similar position publicly in September 1946, he was fired.[12] The message was clear; the policy of getting tough with the Russians was now official orthodoxy, and those who challenged it did so at their peril. The hard line articulated in Churchill's public warning and Kennan's private epistle was matched by the events of 1946.

"Another War Is in the Making"

In January 1946 a purportedly pro-Soviet government came to power in Iran and began to negotiate with the Soviet-supported Azerbaijanian "autonomous region" in northern Iran, then occupied by Soviet forces. Truman sent a stiff note to Stalin demanding that all Soviet troops be withdrawn consistent with schedules agreed to during World War II discussions and warning that the American fleet and troops were being prepared to move to Iran within six weeks.[13] By early April 1946, Stalin had backed away from the confrontation, and under U.S. pressure the internal policy of Iran began to shift. In Turkey the Russians sought throughout 1945 and much of 1946 to fulfill their historic desire to exercise control over the Dardanelles, the link between the Black Sea and the Eastern Mediterranean. Soviet pressure on the Turkish government was met by a display of American arms as Truman dispatched to the area in August the aircraft carrier *Franklin D. Roosevelt* along with a reinforced naval unit including a contingent of Marines. Furthermore, in the following month the secretary of defense announced that the Navy would maintain a permanent presence in the Eastern Mediterranean.

In the meantime the political situation in China began to deteriorate rapidly. In December 1945 General George C. Marshall had been dispatched to China to work out a reconciliation between the Communists under Mao Zedong and Chiang Kai-shek's Kuomintang. By February 1946 he had succeeded in bringing about a ceasefire, but he could not convince Chiang to enter into a coalition government with Mao. Fighting renewed in April 1946. And by autumn Mao, with the aid of large stores of captured Japanese weapons turned over to him by the Russians as their occupation forces withdrew from Manchuria, had assumed an offensive that would bring victory in less than two years.

It was apparent, by late 1946 and early 1947, that Chiang's military ineptitude was exceeded only by the corruption of his civil administration and his consequent loss of popular support. Significant American intervention might have saved Chiang although the Maoist forces fought virtually unaided, excepting the Russian gift of captured Japanese weapons. Mao was, of course, a Communist, but Soviet involvement in the Chinese civil war was unenthusiastic. Throughout the war, the Russians continued to recognize Chiang as the head of China. More important, there was profound disagreement between Mao and Stalin over the course to political power in China that dated back to the 1920s. Indeed, there is evidence that Stalin feared a postwar China united under the strong leadership of Mao. But Washington's primary concern in 1946 was the Soviet-American confrontation in Europe and the implementation of stiffening U.S. posture vis-à-vis the Russians. Chiang was provided inspiration and limited material aid. He was not given the commitment of American troops probably necessary to save what Marshall reported to be a militarily inept and politically corrupt regime. Nonetheless, as the situation worsened in Europe, the Russians became identified as agents of China's internal agony.

Yet another element in this mix of developments was the total breakdown of efforts to establish some form of international control over atomic energy. The original U.S. position, the so-called Acheson-Lilienthal plan, called for the gradual passing of control of atomic weapons to an international body under the UN. During the proposed transition, the United States would maintain its favored military position while other parties to the agreement would agree to be inspected by international agencies. To make the plan more acceptable to Congress and the American people, Truman decided to entrust Bernard Baruch, a well-known, admired, but vain confidant of public officials, the task of formally making the proposal to the UN. Baruch insisted, however, that the possibility of Soviet veto power, left vague in the control arrangements in the original proposal, be explicitly eliminated in the draft submitted to the UN.

The Soviets rejected Baruch's formulation, calling instead for a reversal of the process being proposed. The first step, they argued, should be the destruction of all atomic weapons and then the evolution by stages of international control within which they would maintain their veto power. Thus, at the very outset of the cold war, the problem of parity and perceived gaps in capability impinged on efforts to control arms. The Soviets, perceiving themselves behind in nuclear weapons technology and thus vulnerable, were not prepared to commit themselves to any scheme of arms control that implied freezing the Soviet Union into a position of permanent inferiority. They would seek a level of equality either through the destruction of existing atomic stockpiles and then discuss the possibilities of control or by building their own atomic weapons. The United States, on the other hand, viewed Soviet fears of the American atomic monopoly as evidence of neurotic stubbornness and as a smokescreen to camouflage their attempts to gain the nuclear secret (an atomic spy ring had been broken in Canada in 1946).[14]

The shift in tenor and tactics begun in late 1945 was complete by the end of 1946. In late 1945, former Secretary of War Henry L. Stimson had cautioned Truman against too blatant a use of American possession of atomic weapons in postwar diplomacy for the fear that Russian "distrust of our purposes and motives will increase."[15] A year later he was proposing full production of the weapons.[16] Moreover, in January 1946, Mr. Truman had written to Secretary of State Byrnes:

> There isn't a doubt in my mind that Russia intends an invasion of Turkey and the seizure of the Black Sea Straits to the Mediterranean. Unless Russia is faced with an iron fist and strong language, another war is in the making. Only one language do they understand—"How many divisions have you?"
>
> I do not think we should play compromise any longer. I'm tired of babying the Soviets.[17]

Kennan's long telegram followed in February, Churchill's speech in March, the Iranian confrontation in the same month, the resumption of the Chinese civil war in April, the deterioration of the German situation in April and May, Baruch's proposal in June, and in August the United States reacted to Soviet probes in Turkey with the threat of war. Finally, in September, Secretary of State Byrnes in his Stuttgart speech had made it clear that the United States was prepared to stay in Germany indefinitely—a unified Germany preferably, but a divided one if necessary.

Arranged in this way, the major international political events of 1946 would seem to form a pattern, almost a design. We should not conclude, however, that there was some sort of scheme being worked out by Washington or Moscow. Events retrospectively abstracted from the milieu in which they were embedded invariably appear to have interrelationships that policymakers usually perceived only dimly at the time if at all. On the other hand it would be naive to conclude that there was no relationship among the events. The stiffening and toughening of American policy in 1946 was based on an assessment of Soviet ideology, pronouncements, and activities. The linking by President Truman of an "iron fist" and "strong language" and the talk of "another war" implies that by 1946 he and others in his administration were drawing parallels between the world of 1946 and the world of 1938 and 1939, when war had come about because the British did not draw the conceptual linkage between force and order now drawn by President Truman. Truman (an avid and voracious reader of history and prone to drawing historical analogies), his advisers, and their British allies had only just brought to a close the horrible consequences of the failure to show an iron fist and strong language to Hitler. That mistake was not going to be repeated by the Truman administration.

The American Public
and the Onset of Cold War

If there was an element of discontinuity in the initial attempt to define United States–Soviet relations it was due in no small measure to the domestic situation confronting the Truman administration. Apart from the inevitable difficulties surrounding his assumption of the presidency, Truman was faced with an American public whose concerns ran to anything but foreign policy in 1946. The war was over, and most Americans were interested in returning their personal lives to a state of normalcy. What they found in 1946, however, was hardly normal.[18] In April the nation's coal miners went on strike for forty days, and in May the railroads were struck. Meanwhile unemployment was growing in those industries where wartime contracts were being cancelled. With the removal of wartime price controls the cost of living exploded upward, and by the end of 1946, prices were 33 percent higher than they had been five years earlier when Japanese bombs fell on Pearl Harbor. Prices were going up but there was also little to buy. Black markets, under-the-table deals, even bartering reached a scale beyond that undertaken during the war and its attendant rationing.

Socially, "the ill-tempered, the mean, the vicious in human beings pushed to the fore."[19] There were two race riots in the North and six lynchings in the South. Jewish atomic scientists such as Robert Oppenheimer, who had been the architect of the American atomic bomb but became concerned over its implications for mankind, were harassed. At the same time the pent-up desire for luxuries drove people to buy television sets, and the public mood seemed to allow "[a]ny night . . . to burst into New Year's Eve."[20]

The presidency became, as it almost invariably does, the focus of these frustrations and jarring discontinuities. Much of the power of the president stems from his position at the center of the American people's image of their government. But this fact is not only a source of presidential power, it can also become a source of weakness. The man in the White House for the preceding fourteen years strode like a giant through the Depression and then World War II. Truman was inevitably the center of invidious comparisons and the enormous expectations following the war; he was also the target of the frustrations that set in. For his own part, Truman seemed unable to gain control of the domestic situation, and although his foreign policy had begun to take shape by the end of 1946, to most Americans foreign affairs were but gathering storm clouds. People worried about the Russians, but the price of meat was understandably more important. All of it, the economic disruption, the social malaise, and the uneasiness concerning foreign affairs, culminated in the 1946 elections. The Republicans, who had not controlled the Congress or the White House since Herbert Hoover, asked the American people, "Had enough?" and the American electorate responded by sending fifty-six new Republicans to the House, putting thirteen new Republican senators in the Senate, thereby giving the GOP control of both houses of Congress.

The perceptions of and reactions to this domestic situation on the part of the Truman administration are in some respects even more important than the perceptions and reactions to external events during this period. To many of the men around Truman, this unfolding spectacle of public disorientation and self-indulgence seemed to confirm all of their preconceptions concerning the isolationism of the American public. Indeed, Undersecretary of State Acheson was of the view that "focusing the will of 140,000,000 people on problems beyond our shores . . . [when] people are focusing on 140,000,000 other things" was perhaps the most important problem confronting American foreign policy.[21]

There was some basis for the fears of Acheson and others. Public opinion polls taken during this period indicate that throughout 1946, less than 25 percent of the American people felt that foreign problems were the most vital ones confronting the country.[22] On the other hand, one suspects that such a finding need not be surprising given the state of the economy and the understandable expectations of a nation only recently dragged through one of the most intense periods of involvement in foreign affairs in Amerian history. Furthermore, it is not entirely clear that poll findings were indicative of the isolationism feared by those in the Truman administration, who were anxious to exhibit an iron fist and to talk tough with the Russians. It should be recalled that less than one year earlier, the American people and their representatives in Congress had been convinced of the necessity of accepting and participating in one of the greatest efforts at institutionalized multilateralism and internationalism undertaken up to that time, the founding of the UN. Unlike 1919 and 1920, the response was overwhelmingly positive. Beyond this, Winston Churchill's "iron curtain" speech calling for Anglo-American stewardship of world order had not received what could be characterized as universal support. The Department of State, sensing public support for the UN, ordered Acheson to *avoid* appearing on the platform with Churchill (when he delivered an address in New York ten days after the

Fulton, Missouri, speech) for fear that the undersecretary's presence might imply official acceptance of the former prime minister's position. It may have been the private view of the Truman administration that a shift in policy toward the Soviet Union was needed. But the signals sent to the American people were as yet garbled.[23]

It may well be, therefore, that a portrayal of American public opinion as infected with a deep isolationism is not entirely accurate. There were, in fact, cross curents in American opinion that reflected the ambiguities of American policy. On the one hand, there was a commitment to the UN; but on the other hand, there was popular and congressional reluctance to extend financial assistance to Great Britain and Europe to help them overcome the economic chaos and deprivation of the immediate postwar period. Similarly, the UN had been put across as the curator of the postwar peace; but now Truman was going before Congress and asking for a continuation of the draft and universal manpower training along with a $15 billion defense budget. In point of fact, public opinion at this juncture might be more accurately characterized as confused and disoriented—aware of the world and its problems, but aware of its own immediate problems as well. Furthermore, the Truman administration, although circulating copies of Kennan's long telegram internally, was, at least prior to the summer of 1946, still taking a somewhat conciliatory *public* stance toward the Russians. Indeed, the increasingly bitter negotiations at Yalta, Potsdam, and subsequent meetings of foreign ministers were kept secret—thereby feeding public suspicion and lending credibility to Republican charges of appeasement, sellouts, and secret agreements. In short, the level of public awareness and sensitivity was disoriented and reluctant to accept greater burdens. But as subsequent events were to demonstrate, they were also permissive and accepting of executive leadership when it was provided. "The people react to what the President does," Kenneth Waltz has observed.[24] To many Americans in 1946, the president appeared to be doing very little or, at a minimum, very contradictory things.

To Truman and his closest advisers, there seemed little public awareness of the awesome threat they perceived and with which they had been dealing since early in 1945. The situation was only slightly better in Congress. It was true that Senator Arthur Vandenberg had come around during and immediately after the war to an internationalism that tended to support the stance developing within the Truman administration. But the extent to which the senator's newly gained world view extended to others in the Republican party was questionable. Indeed, what the Truman administration saw, as it confronted the 80th Congress, was a Republican majority that had lambasted the Democrats the previous November for their appeasement of communism but now would cut the administration's budget by $4.5 billion—including significant reductions in the defense budget.

From within the administration, and particularly the Department of State, it seemed that the direction of history was hanging in the balance. The post–World War II international system was perceived as on the verge of being overwhelmed by the onslaught of Soviet expansion. It was felt that this expansion could be checked by the United States; and the events in Iran and Turkey in the preceding months seemed to validate this. "The danger of these Soviet moves," despaired one inside chronicler, "was not generally realized by the American people;"[25] and without such a realization, the full power of the United States could not be mobilized to curb the impending disaster. Thus, when the British informed Washington in February 1947 that they were no longer able economically to deal with the volatile Greek domestic situation, which had once again flared into open civil war, the administration viewed the situation as both a crisis and an opportunity.

WORLD VIEW BECOMES POLICY: THE TRUMAN DOCTRINE AND THE MARSHALL PLAN

The combination of one of the worst winters in history and the economic consequences of World War II had, by February 1947, reduced Great Britain to a state of bankruptcy. Unable to afford even the import of cigarette tobacco the British informed the United States that they could not continue economic and military assistance to either Greece or Turkey beyond March 31, 1947. The situation in Greece was deemed far more important by the Truman administration in view of the ongoing insurgency, which was purportedly communist led. A communist victory was feared if the British economic relief programs were to break down. All of this was communicated to the Department of State on February 21; and on March 12, 1947, President Truman requested $400 million in economic assistance for Greece and Turkey in a spectacular special message to Congress that is now referred to as the Truman Doctrine.

Joseph M. Jones, one of the drafters of Truman's statement, has observed that the British "had within the hour handed the job of world leadership, with all its burdens and all its glory, to the United States."[26] Yet, "[r]apidly, in an orderly manner, and with virtually no dissent, the executive branch of the government decided to act."[27] The lack of dissent indicates how well established the predisposition was toward U.S. intervention in the face of perceived Soviet expansion. Indeed, by 1947 those who stood in opposition to such a policy had been eliminated from the government or sufficiently intimidated by the experience of Henry Wallace, that they were not prepared to speak up. Thus U.S. involvement in Greece and Turkey was never really in question in the Truman administration. If there was a crisis in the spring of 1947, it concerned whether Congress and the American people could be convinced to enlist in the crusade that had been taking shape within the Truman administration for over a year.

A meeting with congressional leaders was held on February 27 and assumed dramatic proportions. The newly appointed secretary of state, George C. Marshall, argued for the Greek-Turkish aid program on abstract and broadly humanitarian grounds. Accounts of the meeting all agree that the congressional leadership largely reflected Republican skepticism about the need for U.S. economic assistance and the implication of increasing budgets. The congressmen stood mute after the distinguished secretary's restrained arguments were presented. Then, Undersecretary of State Dean Acheson spoke out and reframed the proposed United States response. Acheson later described the atmosphere of the meeting in terms that convey an image of history breaking open: "I knew we were met at Armageddon," he wrote.[28] His response was appropriately apocalyptic:

> These congressmen had no conception of what challenged them; it was my task to bring it home. . . . Never have I spoken under such a pressing sense that the issue was up to me alone. No time was left for measured appraisal. In the past eighteen months, I said, Soviet pressure on the Straits, on Iran, and on Northern Greece had brought the Balkans to the point where a highly possible Soviet breakthrough might open three continents to Soviet penetration. Like apples in a barrel infected by one rotten one, the corruption of Greece would infect Iran and all to the east. It would also carry infection to Africa through Asia Minor and Egypt, and to Europe through Italy and France, already threatened by the strongest domestic Communist parties in Western Europe. The Soviet Union was playing one of the greatest gambles in history at minimal cost. It did not need to win all the possibilities. Even one or two offered immense gains. We and we alone were in a position to break up the play. These were the stakes that British withdrawal from the Eastern Mediterranean offered to an eager and ruthless opponent.[29]

The members of Congress were stunned by Acheson's presentation, and there seemed to be general agreement that they would support the president if he would go before Congress and the American people and state matters in the same forceful manner as Acheson's presentation.[30] The Department of State, charged with drafting the President's speech, was determined to convince the American people of the existence of a mortal danger and the need for a decisive American response.[31] Thus, from the very outset, the Truman Doctrine had a dual purpose. First, it was a public statement of the foreign policy assumptions and positions that formed the basis of deep consensus within the Truman administration. Second, Truman's statement was aimed at the American public. For in it, he attempted to convince the American people to view world security as jeopardized and then mobilize Americans in support of a world role for the United States.[32] Thus Truman sought and in large measure succeeded in setting forth the idiom of the debate and the cental questions of American foreign policy for twenty-five years. Truman's speech was to be, in Hans Morgenthau's words, the "intellectual capital" of the cold war.[33]

The Truman Doctrine

President Truman's presentation to the Congress centered on what he termed the "broader implications" of U.S. assistance to Greece and Turkey. The world, Truman asserted, was divided between two antithetical ways of life: one based on freedom, the other on coercion.[34]

The president emphasized that it had long been "one of the primary objectives of the foreign policy of the United States (to create) conditions in which we and other nations will be able to work out a way of life free from coercion."[35] He continued:

> We shall not realize our objectives, however, unless we are willing to help free peoples to maintain their free institutions and their national integrity against aggressive movements that seek to impose upon them totalitarian regimes. This is no more than a frank recognition that totalitarian regimes imposed upon free peoples by direct or indirect aggression, undermine the foundations of international peace and hence the security of the United States.[36]

Truman thus displayed the assumptions for post–World War II American foreign policy. The security of the United States, the most basic of foreign policy values, was found only in "international peace," that is, in a system of international order. Unless that international order was secure the United States could not be counted secure; thus it followed that

> it must be the policy of the United States to support free peoples who are resisting attempted subjugation by armed minorities or by outside pressures.
>
> I believe that we must assist free peoples to work out their own destinies in their own way.[37]

The specific concern of Truman on this day was a request for $400 million in economic and military assistance for Greece and Turkey, but he made it clear that the broader framework articulated in the speech stretched beyond those troubled countries:

> It would be an unspeakable tragedy if these countries which have struggled so long against overwhelming odds, should lose that victory for which they sacrificed so much. Collapse of free institutions and loss of independence would be disastrous not only for them but for the world. Discouragement and possibly failure would quickly be the lot of neighboring peoples striving to maintain their freedom and independence.[38]

Acheson had privately spoken of "rotten apples . . . spreading corruption and infection," the president was now speaking of "confusion and disorder," the "collapse of free institutions," and "discouragement," and future American leaders would warn of falling dominoes—but the underlying premise was the same. Peace and world order were now indivisible. Hence the loss of one country carried with it ominous implications for the entire structure of world order. (This, after all, was the lesson of Munich.) In essence, therefore, the security of the world and the security of the United States were entwined, perhaps synonymous. It was now imperative that the United States build and then maintain a world order congenial to its own values or way of life. In the analysis of Truman and his advisers, if aggression were allowed to proceed, then the fabric of global security would unravel, and American security would inevitably be jeopardized.

Truman's statement implied, however, that U.S. policy involved a great deal more than a simple internationalism. The threat to international security was defined in terms of the regimes and domestic systems of other members of the international system. The internal affairs of other states were now an important component of world order. Whether a country's political, economic, and social system was "totalitarian," "democratic," "communist," or "capitalist"—whether, in short, its way of life conformed to the American vision of what was best or the Soviet vision—was now central to the question of world order. The internal politics of states were fused with the quality of world order; and intervention in the former was now regarded as legitimate so as to preserve an American vision of the latter.

Although the existence and objectives of the UN were duly noted, they were dismissed with the observation that "the situation is an urgent one requiring immediate action and the UN and its related organizations are not in a position to extend help of the kind that is required."[39] Roosevelt's conception of the nations of the world working through a multilateral structure for the building and preservation of world order (a conception drawn in turn from Wilson) was therefore set aside. A singularly American vision of world order, built and maintained through American instrumentalities, was put in its place. The UN itself had been an American idea, and from the outset the central role of the Security Council with its provision of great-power vetoes ensured a pivotal role for American interests. But now, with the Truman Doctrine, multilateralism became an instrument of American unilateralism.

Important to the Congress was the scope of the Truman Doctrine. Did this new Truman Doctrine mean, the Congress now asked, that we are "adopting a policy where we say the United States of America will be interested all over the world in any country that is seeking democratic freedom?"[40] The administration sought to ease concern that the Truman Doctrine was the opening of a global ideological crusade while at the same time maintaining for itself maximum latitude. Acheson, in soliciting aid to Turkey and Greece before the Senate Foreign Relations Committee, engaged in colloquy with the committee chairman, Senator Vandenberg:

> *The Chairman:* . . . In other words, I think what you are saying is that wherever we find free peoples having difficulty in the maintenance of free institutions, and difficulty in defending against aggressive movements that seek to impose upon them totalitarian regimes, we do not necessarily react in the same way each time, but we propose to react.
> *Secretary Acheson:* That, I think, is correct.[41]

The Truman administration's reluctance to extend further aid or Amerian combat support to Chiang Kai-shek and Acheson's staunch refusal to concede under intense questioning in his appearance before the House Foreign Affairs Committee that the Chinese and Greek cases were comparable seems to confirm that there were, indeed, limitations to the scope of the Truman Doctrine. But, Acheson's ready acceptance of Vandenberg's expansive paraphrasing of the president's speech reveals an activist and globalist impulse to American policy that was to transcend the temporary hedging of the American bet in China and play itself out over the next decades in Korea, Lebanon, Berlin, the Bay of Pigs, the Dominican Republic, and Vietnam.

The president seemed unequivocal about the instruments to be employed to buttress this doctrine: "I believe that our help should be primarily through economic and financial aid which is essential to economic stability and orderly political processes."[42] And, at first glance, Truman's request for $400 million was not unlike the loans and credits extended to Belgium, France, the Netherlands, and Norway during 1945 and 1946. Furthermore, the amount requested for Greece and Turkey was small when compared to a $3.4 billion loan extended to Britain the previous year. Thus, the use of economic assistance had well-defined and substantial precedent and was linked to a broad conception of world economic order. Economic recovery had been tied by the Roosevelt and now the Truman administrations to the creation of an international economic order predicated upon the reduction and eventual elimination of tariffs and other obstacles to free trade. A fundamental element in free and expanding international trading systems was stable international monetary affairs, the absence of which during the 1930s had, in this view, brought on the general economic collapse of the Depression and thereby contributed directly to World War II. To prevent a recurrence of this situation and establish the basis for stable world economic order, a set of loosely related institutions had been set up during and after the war: the International Monetary Fund (IMF), the International Bank for Reconstruction and Development (World Bank), and the General Agreement of Tariffs and Trade (GATT).[43] But by 1946 the entire constellation of institutions and processes seemed insufficient to provide needed postwar aid and recovery.

Simple altruism was not the motive force of the Truman economic policy. The brief termination of lend-lease aid to Russia in May of 1945 and the so-called loss of a Soviet request for a billion dollar loan later in 1945 indicated that the Truman administration was prepared to use economic instrumentalities in pursuit of political objectives. A primary thrust of American economic policy prior to the Truman Doctrine can be seen as economic recovery, reconstruction, and ultimately the development of a strong and monetarily stable free-trading international economic system as an end in itself. Yet even then, the central role of the dollar and the solitary strength of the American economy undoubtedly ensured American well-being in and even domination of such a system.[44] Furthermore, given American hegemony in the world economy, one could certainly anticipate the intrusion of American political objectives into the nascent world economic order of 1945 and 1946. Nevertheless, Richard Cooper is probably justified in his contention that the framers of this economic order sought somehow to separate trade and other international economic questions from those political and security issues that comprise what is sometimes referred to as "high diplomacy."[45]

The Truman Doctrine suggested, however, that the perceived imperatives of high policy might transcend the desire or logic of treating international economics and other political questions as separate domains. Truman had asserted that "the seeds of totalitarian regimes are nurtured by misery and want. They spread and grow in the evil soil of poverty and strife."[46] Thus President Truman seemed to view the two tracks of economic and politico-military policy as interrelated. Indeed, his appeal for economic assistance assumed that the relationship of "totalitarian regimes" and the "evil soil of poverty" was reversible, that the instrumentalities and processes of "low foreign policy" could be employed to bring about international order in the realm of high diplomacy. In summary, there was the germ of a grand design implied by the Truman Doctrine: the transformation of a heretofore piecemeal use of economic assistance for recovery into a comprehensive assault on the conditions that gave rise to totalitarian regimes.

The Marshall Plan and the Soviet Union:
The Truman Doctrine's Meaning Emerges

Even as Truman spoke and Acheson sought to soothe congressional fears of a far-reaching American involvement, external events and developments within the administration were merging to bring about the "transformation of American foreign policy."[47] During March and April 1947 a special interdepartmental group had tentatively concluded that future United States economic and military assistance would have to proceed within a carefully planned comprehensive framework emphasizing a strong European regional economy including a reconstructed Germany.[48] But the problem of European recovery raised a troublesome issue: What was to be the relationship of the Soviet Union and Eastern Europe to this integrated European economy? How could a continent-wide recovery and integration take place in an atmosphere of deteriorating Soviet-American relations? The idea of giving priority to democracy-oriented governments while simultaneously minimizing aid and comfort to "communist-dominated countries" could only contribute to the fears and distrust in the Kremlin. Coupling this to an economically strong Germany could hardly be viewed by the Russians as mere altruism. And finally, to assume and propose that the Soviets and their satellites willingly enter into such a Western-oriented politico-economic structure would seem, at a minimum, illusory, naive, or unserious. At worst, the Soviets might take this posture as support for their assumption that the United States was advancing such proposals so as to penetrate and fragment economically the Soviet Union's Eastern European hegemony.[49]

An indication of the Soviet reaction to this or similar proposals was the tough position taken by Molotov at the Moscow foreign ministers conference held during March and April 1947. The conference was about the future shape of Germany, its postwar economy, and its relationship with the remainder of Europe. The United States and Great Britain proposed at the outset a federal structure for the German government with limitations on the powers of the central government. Even so, German economic recovery was viewed as a piece with the general economic recovery of Europe. The Russians reacted with suspicion, and attacked the proposals for a weak central German government as protecting the position of former Nazis and other anticommunist elements. In contrast, the Soviets argued for a stronger central government administering an economic recovery directed not at European integration but rather meeting as yet unfulfilled reparations commitments under the Potsdam agreements of 1945.[50]

Underlying economic claims and counterclaims, however, were bedrock differences over the future political and economic shape of Europe. The United States and Britain sought an economically strong Germany within a context of European economic recovery and integration. The French eventually came to accept much of this view, although at the outset they were reluctant to move too rapidly toward supporting a resurgent German economy. The Soviets' general desire, on the other hand, was to keep Germany in an economically weak and dependent status and hence less likely to reemerge as a threat to their security. Predictably, therefore, the conference deadlocked and Secretary of State Marshall returned to the United States with apparent confirmation that the Truman Doctrine accurately portrayed obdurate Soviet behavior. Needless to say, the view of the world from the Kremlin was increasingly a mirror image of that held on the Potomac.

In the meantime, some of the remaining ambiguities of the Truman Doctrine were being removed, as Washington's worst fears— deteriorating economic conditions leading to social and political chaos—seemed ready to bloom with the spring thaw of 1947. The disastrous winter of 1946–1947 had severely reduced coal production in Europe and thus further diminished industrial productivity. European livestock herds were decimated, and projections of reduced crops in the following year were becoming commonplace. In France the spring saw an extreme government crisis as a lack of supplies led to rationing followed by inflation. French government controls on prices and wages precipitated a dissolution of the coalition of Communists and socialists that made up the cabinet; widespread strikes followed. In Italy a similar series of developments seemed imminent. In this environment Acheson indicated the position that had been evolving within the administration.[51]

First, the United States was seen as having to absorb large quantities of imports so as to stimulate productivity abroad. Second, further emergency U.S. financing would be necessary. Furthermore, he stated: "We must take whatever action is possible immediately, *even without full Four Power agreement, to effect a larger measure of European, including German,* recovery."[52] In calling for European recovery and including German recovery and participation, Soviet objections notwithstanding, the opportunity for avoiding a further deterioration of Soviet-American relations was reduced. Acheson's emphasis on using American assistance to promote and defend democratic institutions when they were subjected to totalitarian pressure indicated an acceptance, even encouragement, of a bifurcated Europe, and by implication a divided Germany as well. International economic instrumentalities and processes were, therefore, absorbed into the national security equation of the Truman Doctrine. International political and economic order, American national security, totalitarian (Soviet) threats to American national security were all integrated by Acheson into a statement of American "duty."[53]

The fully elaborated European Recovery Program was proclaimed by Secretary of State Marshall at the Harvard University commencement in early June 1947. The secretary's speech restated the nexus of political and economic order at the heart of the administration's policy: "It is logical that the United States should do whatever it is able to do to assist in the return of normal economic health in the world, without which there can be no political stability and no assured peace."[54] From this it followed that American policy "should be the revival of a working economy in the world so as to permit the emergence of political and social conditions in which free institutions can exist."[55] The substance of Marshall's speech was a proposal for European economic integration rather than a piecemeal aid program. It required that the Europeans assume the initiative in establishing the structure within which they would receive American aid. At the same time, the Europeans could hardly refuse the American offer—and preconditions. Thus the United States might realize its postwar objective of an integrated economic system encompassing most of the market economies of the world. Still, there was an unspoken dilemma: How were the Soviets to fit into this scheme?

Soviet participation in the Marshall Plan seemed inconsistent with the explicit linkage of economic instrumentalities and American national security drawn by Acheson. Furthermore, members of the Department of State feared that allowing Soviet participation in the planning and administration of the program would lead to Soviet disruption of European integration and political exploitation of the continuing economic stagnation. In addition, there was some concern that Soviet and Eastern European participation could undercut congressional support for the billions of dollars that would have to be requested. Nevertheless, there were disadvantages in not at least inviting the Russians: The onus for precipitating the inevitable political and economic division of Europe would fall on the United States and the Western Europeans if the Russians were snubbed. The resolution of the dilemma lay in a course of action proposed by Kennan: The Soviets would be invited to participate,[56] but only on the condition that they would contribute raw materials and abide by any arrangements for mutual planning and economic integration that emerged.[57]

In other words, the Soviets were to be asked to open up their economic planning and control and the economies of Eastern Europe to the scrutiny and implied control of capitalistic Western Europeans and ultimately the United States. Furthermore, they were to contribute raw materials to the reconstruction of these same Western states, including Germany. The prospect was breathtaking. For the Soviets were being asked, in effect, to accept absorption into the American vision of world economic and political order. "If they were unwilling to do this," Kennan said, "we would simply let them exclude themselves. But we would not ourselves draw a line of division through Europe."[58] Of course, one cannot help but wonder if there was any real possibility that the Soviets could do anything else but exclude themselves and thereby place themselves in the position of being blamed for the division of Europe.

Rather unexpectedly and to the dismay of much of Washington, the Soviets, under Molotov's leadership, arrived at the initial planning sessions in Paris in late June 1947 with scores of economic experts, thus indicating interest in the program. Perhaps they felt that the position set forth by the Americans was an initial bargaining point that might be changed; or perhaps the plan genuinely interested them in view of possible assistance for their own beleaguered economy.[59] In any event, they came and participated in initial discussions and urged a plan that, though continental in scope, would nevertheless preserve the integrity of sovereign prerogatives concerning domestic economic planning. When it became apparent that the American preconditions were not negotiable and that Soviet participation would have to be on American terms, there was really little else for Molotov to do except walk out. As Molotov left, he issued an angry warning that acceptance of the American plan would mean the imposition on Europe of a supranational planning body with the power to intervene in domestic economic and, by extension, political affairs; the resurgence of Germany; and the eventual domination of the European economy by American capital and corporations. Molotov returned home. And immediately afterward the Soviets proposed their own rather uninspiring plan for the economic integration of Eastern Europe and established the Cominform—a uniting of the ruling parties of Eastern Europe and the Communist parties of France and Italy.

The Soviets had been maneuvered precisely as Kennan had projected; thus post–Marshall Plan diplomacy may be viewed as a brilliant tactical victory for American diplomacy. But in the long run it proved to be a decisive turn toward the depths of the cold war. The Soviets now seemed convinced that American policy was committed to European hegemony and ultimately the political and economic penetration of Eastern Europe.[60] With the formation of Cominform, the Communist parties of France and Italy moved from the collaborationist posture they had adopted immediately after the war to one of resistance to the Marshall Plan. All of this was viewed in the West as evidence of an ideological offensive.[61] The American reaction was a redoubling of efforts to bring about European economic integration, including a decision to go ahead with German redevelopment and European partnership. In early December, the French entered into discussions with the British and the Americans concerning the integration of the French zone of occupation into the previously merged British and American zones. Further steps were therefore taken towards the creation of an independent West German state. In Herbert Feis's words, "The rift over Germany became an irreparable rupture,"[62] On December 19, 1947, a Marshall Plan request for $17 billion was submitted to Congress for approval, and at the end of the month informal talks were begun on the formation of some kind of Western European defense arrangement.

THE SUMMING UP:
CONTAINMENT IS DEFINED

In the summer of 1947, George Kennan, writing under the pseudonym "X," published a public restatement of his earlier theses concerning Soviet behavior and added a somewhat more distilled set of policy prescriptions.[63] There is perhaps no better summary statement of official thinking at this time than Kennan's article; for it encompasses most of the prevailing American assumptions concerning Soviet behavior and the appropriate American response to the situation.

As with the 1946 telegram, Kennan emphasized his perception of the internal weaknesses of the Soviet political system. From this vantage point he sees a Soviet foreign policy that emphasizes flexibility of means: Soviet policy is "a fluid stream which moves constantly, wherever it is permitted to move, toward a given goal. Its main concern is to make sure that it has filled every nook and cranny available to it in the basin of world power."[64]

The flexibility of Soviet policy suggested dangers, but the internal weaknesses of their system also provided opportunities. In the first place, Soviet pressure would be ongoing and not easily discouraged; rather, "if it finds unassailable barriers in its path, it accepts these philosophically and accommodates itself to them."[65] Kennan felt, however, that

> the United States has it in its power to increase enormously the strains under which Soviet policy must operate, to force upon the Kremlin a far greater degree of moderation and circumspection than it has had to observe in recent years, and in this way to promote tendencies which must eventually find their outlet in either the break-up or the gradual mellowing of Soviet power.[66]

This was so because "no mystical, Messianic movement—and particularly not that of the Kremlin—can face frustration indefinitely without eventually adjusting itself in one way or another to the logic of that state of affairs."[67] The manner whereby these "frustrations" and "strains" were to be induced and "moderation" and "circumspection" brought about is the prescriptive core of Kennan's argument:

> In these circumstances it is clear that the main element of any United States policy toward the Soviet Union must be that of a long-term vigilant containment of Russian expansive tendencies.... The Soviet pressure against the free institutions of the Western world is something that can be contained by the adroit and vigilant application of counter-force at a series of constantly shifting geographical and political points, corresponding to the shifts and maneuvers of Soviet policy.[68]

Kennan's statement provided a coherent summation of the policy and assumptions that had been developing incrementally over the preceding two years. It was, in some respects, a more subtle and moderate assessment of Soviet behavior and prescription for American behavior than the public statements of other members of the Truman administration. One suspects, for example, that Kennan's admonition "that such a policy has nothing to do with outward histrionics; with threats or blustering or superfluous gestures of outward 'toughness' "[69] was directed at no less a figure than the president himself; for Kennan and others (notably Secretary of State Marshall) were known to have reacted negatively to the ideologically belligerent tone of the Truman Doctrine.

Nevertheless, because the article was a reflection of a consensus about the roots of Soviet behavior and a suitable response, Kennan's statement was also characterized by much of the expansive optimism and vague rhetoric of officials in the Truman administration. Thus he, like Acheson, offered his "gratitude to a Providence which, by providing the American people with this implacable challenge, has made their entire security as a nation dependent on their pulling themselves together and accepting the responsibilities of moral and political leadership that history plainly intended them to bear."[70]

More important, in retrospect, his language about a "firm containment designed to confront the Russians with unalterable counter-force at every point where they show signs of encroaching upon the interests of a peaceful and stable world" was more than a faint echo of Truman's and Acheson's rhetoric. The interrelated motifs of containment, confrontation, and "unalterable counter-force at every point" were sufficiently open-ended as to allow more militant prosecutors of American policy to recast Kennan's vision of political and economic containment of Soviet power in Europe to one of global military containment.[71]

SUMMARY . . . AND MORE QUESTIONS

Thus Kennan's public "X" article reaffirmed publicly the doctrine that had been developing within the Truman administration since the end of the war: early Soviet-American disagreements over Germany contributed to a growing predisposition toward toughness within the administration—a predisposition supported by Kennan's extended analysis of Soviet international behavior in the long telegram. Events in Iran, Turkey, and to a lesser extent, China seemed to support Kennan's analysis. Thus, by early 1947 President Truman was prepared to move America into a posture of confrontation with the Soviet Union. American public opinion, however, did not seem to allow such a departure. A popular as well as congressional isolationist mood seemed in evidence. Acheson and others concluded that only a dramatic statement, even overstatement, of the Soviet threat was necessary to expand the limits of public permissibility. The Greek-Turkish crisis of early 1947 provided such an opportunity, and the president dramatically set forth a concept of American national security that required that America—alone if necessary—build and then maintain global order. Indeed, American national security was deemed synonymous with that global order.

Questions concerning the means and scope of American policy remained. The Marshall Plan proposal seemed to clarify the issue in that it expanded the initial Truman Doctrine's foreign assistance proposal to a comprehensive program of European economic redevelopment. However, the structure of the program consciously precluded Soviet participation on any but American terms. The Soviets' worst fears—fears that American policy, now embracing German recovery, was directed at the economic and political penetration of their Eastern European empire —were therefore confirmed. Thus a program subsequently heralded by Winston Churchill as the "most unsordid act in history"[72] stands as an ambiguous marker at an important fork along the road to the cold war.

The economic recovery and integration of Western Europe was undoubtedly a worthy, perhaps noble, end in itself. But we should realize that in the view of the world held by the Truman administration it was also an instrument of the containment of Soviet power. For their part, however, the Soviets viewed both the Marshall Plan and Kennan's concept as something more than a defensive Western posture. These policies were perhaps seen by men such as Truman, Acheson, and Marshall as limited, well-intentioned, and ultimately peaceful responses to Soviet expansion. But by the time Kennan published his exposition of American policy, the Soviets were no longer able or willing to view the deteriorating relationship in this light. The Soviet-American relationship moved, therefore, from the crumbling edge of a tenuous wartime alliance into a crevice of distrust, fear, and, ultimately, terror.

NOTES

1.   Dean Acheson, *Present at the Creation* (New York: W. W. Norton, 1969), p. 196.
2.   Walter LaFeber, *America, Russia and the Cold War 1945–1971* (New York: John Wiley, 1972), p. 30.
3.   Marshall Shulman, *Stalin's Foreign Policy Reappraised* (New York: Atheneum, 1963), pp. 13–21.
4.   For examples of American reaction see John L. Gaddis's discussion of the speech and its aftermath in *The United States and the Origins of the Cold War, 1941–1947* (New York: Columbia University Press, 1972), pp. 299–302.
5.   Winston Churchill, "The Sinews of Peace," March 5, 1946, *Vital Speeches of the Day,* Vol. 12 (March 15, 1946), p. 332.
6.   Ibid.
7.   George F. Kennan, *Memoirs, 1925–1950* (Boston: Little, Brown, 1967), p. 293.
8.   Kennan, "Excerpts from Telegraphic Message from Moscow of February 22, 1946," in *Memoirs, 1925–1950,* pp. 557–558. Kennan has admitted that he now reads the long telegram with "horrified amusement" in that "it reads like one of those primers put out by alarmed congressional committees or by the Daughters of the American Revolution, designed to arouse the citizenry to the dangers of the Communist conspiracy" (Ibid., p. 294).
9.   Kennan's recommendations in this regard are not unlike the proposals of Seantor J. William Fulbright two decades later, that America should become "an intelligent example to the world" [Fullbright, *The Arrogance of Power* (New York: Vintage, 1967), p. 257]. Kennan suggested, for example, that the United States should "apprehend, and recognize [the Soviet Union] for what it is," "see that our public is educated to the realities," take "courageous and incisive measure[s] to solve internal problems of our own society," "formulate and put forward for other nations a much more positive and constructive picture of the sort of world we would like to see," and

"have courage and self-confidence to cling to our own methods and conceptions of human society" (Kennan, op. cit., pp. 558–559).

10. See, for example, Kennan's admonition in the "long telegram" that the United States approach the problem of dealing with the Soviets "calmly" and "with good heart" and avoiding "prestige-engaging showdowns" (Kennan, op. cit., p. 558). For recent scholarly debate about Kennan's view of military strength and its utility at this time see John Lewis Gaddis, "Containment: A Reassessment," *Foreign Affairs*, Vol. 55, No. 4 (July 1977), pp. 873–887, and Edward Mark, "The Question of Containment: A Reply to John Lewis Gaddis," *Foreign Affairs*, Vol. 56, No. 2 (January 1978), pp. 430–440 and Gaddis' response in Ibid., pp. 440–441. There is a final minisalvo between these two in the *Newsletter* of the Society for Historians of American Foreign Relations, Vol. 9, No. 3, (September 1978), pp. 28–31.

11. Harry S. Truman, *Memoirs I: Year of Decisions* (Garden City, N.Y.: Doubleday, 1955), p. 555; and D.F. Fleming, *The Cold War and Its Origins*, Vol. II (London: Callen & Unwin, 1961), pp. 420–421.

12. Truman, *Year of Decisions*, p. 556. Interestingly enough, Wallace had personally cleared his speech with Truman before delivering it. Truman, either through oversight or incomprehension, did not glean its departure from the tougher line he wished to establish with the Soviets. Truman did not fire Wallace, however, until Byrnes, his secretary of state, in Paris at a foreign ministers' meeting threatened to resign "immediately." Richard Walton, *Henry Wallace, Harry Truman and the Cold War* (New York: Viking, 1976), and Robert J. Donovan, *Conflict and Crisis: The Presidency of Harry S. Truman, 1945–1948* (New York: Norton, 1977), pp. 224–228.

13. Herbert Feis, *From Trust to Terror: The Onset of the Cold War, 1945–1950* (New York: W. W. Norton, 1970), p. 84.

14. See Shulman, op. cit., pp. 21–24, and Thomas W. Wolfe, *Soviet Power and Europe, 1945–1970* (Baltimore: Johns Hopkins University Press, 1970), p. 37. David Holloway, "Entering the Nuclear Arms Race: The Soviet Decision to Build the Atomic Bomb, 1939–1945," *Working Papers, The Wilson Center* (Washington, D.C., July 25, 1979), p. 47. Most of the supposed secrets delivered to Soviet agents during the war were already known to Soviet physicists, ibid., fn. 76, p. 58.

15. Quoted in LaFeber, op. cit., p. 21.

16. Gaddis, op. cit., p. 335.

17. Harry S. Truman, *Year of Decisions*, p. 552, and Gaddis, op. cit., p. 289.

18. Eric F. Goldman, *The Crucial Decade—And After: America, 1945–1960* (New York: Vintage, 1960), pp. 25–41.

19. Ibid., p. 42.

20. Ibid., p. 41.

21. *Department of State Bulletin*, Vol. 14, No. 363 (June 16, 1946), p. 1045.

22. See Gabriel Almond, *The American People and Foreign Policy* (New York: Praeger, 1960), p. 73.

23. For a review of the Acheson incident, see Gaddis, op. cit., p. 309.

24. Kenneth N. Waltz, "Electoral Punishment and Foreign Policy Crises," in James N. Rosenan, ed., *Domestic Sources of Foreign Policy* (New York: Free Press, 1967), p. 293.

25. Joseph M. Jones, *The Fifteen Weeks* (New York: Harcourt, Brace & World, 1965), p. 47. For some idea of the word as viewed from within the Department of State at this time see pp. 39–47.

26. Ibid., p. 7.

27. Ibid., p. 11.

28. Reprinted from *Present at the Creation* by Dean Acheson. By permission of W. W. Norton, and Hamish Hamilton, Ltd. Copyright © 1969 by Dean Acheson.

29. Ibid.
30. There is some disagreement concerning exactly what Vandenberg said. Acheson recalls Vandenberg saying: "Mr. President, if you will say that to the Congress and the country, I will support you and I believe that most of its members will do the same" (p. 219). Goldman, on the other hand, has Vandenberg saying: "Mr. President, if that's what you want, there's only one way to get it. That is to make a personal appearance before Congress and scare the hell out of the country" (Goldman, op. cit., p. 59).
31. Jones reports that the interdepartmental committee responsible for an initial draft of the speech indicated that there were three primary objectives of the speech: "1. To make possible the formulation of intelligent opinions by the American people on the problems created by the present situation in Greece through the furnishing of full and frank information by the government. 2. To portray the world conflict between free and totalitarian or imposed forms of government. 3. To bring about an understanding by the American people of the world strategic situation" (Jones, op. cit., p. 152).
32. For an extended discussion of the Truman Doctrine as essentially domestic propaganda, see Richard M. Freeland, *The Truman Doctrine and the Origins of McCarthyism: Foreign Policy, Domestic Policies, and Internal Security, 1946–1948* (New York: Schocken, 1974).
33. Hans J. Morgenthau, *A New Foreign Policy for the United States* (New York: Praeger, 1969), p. 1.
34. Harry S. Truman, "The Truman Doctrine: Special Message to the Congress on Greece and Turkey, March 12, 1947," *Public Papers of the Presidents of the United States. Harry S. Truman, 1947* (Washington, D.C.: U.S. Government Printing Office), p. 178.
35. Ibid.
36. Ibid.
37. Ibid., pp. 178–179.
38. Ibid., p. 179.
39. Ibid., p. 177.
40. U.S. Congress, Senate Foreign Relations Committee, *Hearings on S. 938 Assistance to Greece and Turkey,* 80th Cong., 1st Sess., March 24, 1947, p. 19.
41. Ibid., pp. 30–31.
42. Truman, "The Truman Doctrine: Special Message to the Congress . . . ," p. 179.
43. For a straightforward introduction to the often baffling world of international economic policy the reader is referred to Joan Spero, *The Politics of International Economics,* 2nd ed. (New York: St. Martin's, 1981).
44. See Harry Magdoff, *The Age of Imperialism: The Economics of U.S. Foreign Policy* (New York: Monthly Review, 1968), esp. pp. 54–113, for a Marxist exposition of this thesis. William Diebold's *The United States and the Industrial World: American Foreign Economic Policy in the 1970's* (New York: Praeger, 1972) provides the conventional and more benign view of American policy. David P. Calleo and Benjamin Rowland's *America and the World Political Economy: Atlantic Dreams and National Realities* (Bloomington, Ind.: Indiana University Press, 1973) is somewhat less conventional in its assessment.
45. Richard Cooper, "Trade Policy is Foreign Policy," *Foreign Policy,* No. 9 (Winter 1972–73), pp. 18–21.
46. Truman, "The Truman Doctrine," p. 180.
47. See Charles Bohlen, *The Transformation of American Foreign Policy* (New York: W. W. Norton, 1969).
48. For a detailed account of the formation, activities, and recommendations of the Special Committee, see Jones, op. cit., pp. 199–209.
49. Ibid., p. 205.

50. For a more detailed consideration of the Conference, see Feis, op. cit., pp. 208–220.
51. Once again, a good detailed account of these developments is in Jones, op. cit., pp. 206–213.
52. Dean Acheson, "The Requirements of Reconstruction," *Department of State Bulletin,* Vol. 16 (May 18, 1947), p. 994 (emphasis added).
53. Ibid.
54. George C. Marshall, "European Initiative Essential to Economic Recovery," *Department of State Bulletin,* Vol. 16 (June 15, 1947), p. 1160.
55. Ibid.
56. Ibid.
57. Accounts of Kennan's position are numerous but essentially alike. See Kennan, *Memoirs, 1925–1950,* p. 342; and Feis, op. cit., pp. 242–243. See also Jones, op. cit., p. 253.
58. Kennan, *Memoirs, 1925–1950,* p. 342.
59. Adam Ulam, *The Rivals* (New York: Praeger, 1973), pp. 128–129.
60. Shulman, op. cit., pp. 14–15, and Ulam, op. cit., p. 130.
61. See Ulam, op. cit., p. 133.
62. Feis, op. cit., p. 281.
63. "X" (Geroge F. Kennan), "The Sources of Soviet Conduct," *Foreign Affairs,* Vol. 25 (July 1947), pp. 566–582.
64. Ibid., p. 575.
65. Ibid.
66. Ibid., p. 582.
67. Ibid.
68. Ibid., p. 575–576.
69. Ibid., p. 575.
70. Ibid., p. 582.
71. See Kennan, *Memoirs; 125–1950,* pp. 364–365; and Ronald Steel, "Man Without a Country," in his *Imperialists and Other Heroes: A Chronicle of the American Empire* (New York: Vintage, 1973), pp. 53–55.
72. Cited in Jones, op. cit., p. 256.

Chapter 3
From the
Marshall Plan
to Global
Containment

The distrust generated by the initial clashes of antithetical Soviet and American visions of world order hardened into confrontation and cold war during the thirty months between the winter of 1947–1948 and June 1950. Throughout most of the period, as in the immediate postwar years, the cockpit was Europe and specifically Germany as the Truman administration sought to make the Marshall Plan—European recovery including a reconstituted Germany—the central component in the policy of containment. Stalin reacted with a brutal consolidation of his East European empire, including the termination of limited Czechoslovakian democracy, and increasingly anxious protests concerning the West's efforts to create a new German state free of the Four Power administration agreed to at the Potsdam meeting of 1945. In a last desperate effort to forestall this disaster for Soviet foreign and security policy, Stalin blockaded Western surface access to Berlin in 1948 and demanded a reversal of the Western thrust toward a West German state.

With the blockade, East-West relations turned, perhaps irrevocably, into the darkest days of cold war. The West responded by redoubling its efforts to bring about the creation of the Federal Republic of Germany. Even more important, the previously somewhat amorphous economic structure of containment in Europe crystallized into a military alliance, the North Atlantic Treaty Organization (NATO) in mid-1949. Almost simultaneously, in late 1949, Mao Zedong's communist revolution achieved victory on the Chinese mainland and the Soviets exploded their first atomic device. These events contributed to a top-level reassessment of American policy in late 1949 and early 1950. The outcome was a call for a decisive shift away from European-focused containment and dependence on the political and economic instruments embodied in European reconstruction and a weak NATO to a remobilization of American political and military power equal to the tasks of global containment. Indeed, American domestic priorities were to yield to the demands of a confrontation of indefinite length.

In retrospect these events seem to have about them a decisive, almost inevitable inherent direction. In fact, there was much uncertainty and internal debate within the United States. There were similar uncertainties and perhaps an even greater sense of vulnerability in the Soviet Union, and these fears contributed directly to the evolution of Western policy. Most of this chapter will be concerned with an overview and analysis of the playing-out of these uncertainties into the hard-edged confrontation of cold war.

THE COLD WAR

If the view of the world from Washington was grim in the winter of 1947–1948, it was no less so from Moscow. Under American leadership, the capitalist countries seemed to be consolidating their position. Stalin may have surmised that American political and economic hegemony of the West would be the first step in forming a strong base for bringing pressure to bear on the Soviet dominance of Eastern Europe. The initial pressure on the Soviets may have been limited to economic enticements, but then again the Americans would in time perhaps become sufficiently bold to instigate and support unrest in Eastern Europe. In sum, Soviet security seemed to require the maintenance of a strong Soviet political, economic, and military presence in the Eastern European countries occupied after the war.[1]

The Red Army, though reduced in size,[2] was adequate to whatever immediate external military threat may have existed. Internally, however, Stalin felt compelled to strengthen his hand. He purged Eastern European regimes of anticommunist elements as well as nationalist Communist parties that were unwilling to subordinate themselves to the Soviet vision of the future. Stalin's policy collided most spectacularly with that of Tito in Yugoslavia. Tito's nationalism undercut Stalin's drive for consolidation of Eastern Europe. Consequently, tensions heightened, replete with veiled threats, and eventually, in mid-1948, Tito broke with Stalin.[3]

In the meantime, replication of this insolence and insubordination had to be anticipated. A quick crushing of the Yugoslavs might have served Stalin's ends, but there seems to have been some doubt on Stalin's part that he could end the matter quickly. The possibility of resource-consuming guerrilla conflict with Yugoslav Communists led by the same Tito who had two and a half years earlier successfully prosecuted a largely partisan war against the Germans could not have been appealing to Stalin. Stalin is said to have boasted that he could "shake my little finger and there will be no more Tito"—but he did not behave as if he believed it. The image of the Russian bear grappling perhaps ineffectually with the Yugoslav midget would not inspire awe on the part of other Eastern Europeans. The Yugoslav situation deteriorated slowly while more decisive moves were made elsewhere. In Hungary, Bulgaria, and the other communist countries "potential Titos were tracked down, demoted, tried, and often executed. In none of the other satellites was there in fact that combination of factors which had enabled Yugoslavia to launch her defiance, but the Soviets were not taking chances."[4]

The Czechoslovakian Coup

Nowhere was this militancy more manifest and with greater consequence for the future of East-West relations than in Czechoslovakia. Prior to 1948, Czech opposition parties coexisted in a coalition government with the Communists maintaining a slight popular plurality entitling them to nine cabinet positions including that of prime minister. By February of 1948, however, the Communists were instructed to eliminate independent parties, thereby consolidating Communist control in a country whose borders touched western and eastern Germany, Poland, Hungary, and the Soviet Union. Czechoslovakia was perhaps the most industrialized of the Central European states, and unlike eastern Germany and Poland, its industrial base had come through the war more or less intact. In short, Czechoslovakia was the geographic and industrial heart of the Soviet Central European glacis.

But the avowed American intention to integrate Western Europe, including Germany, into the Marshall Plan (which was received favorably among noncommunist Czechs), the fears of the possible magnetic effect of Western European recovery and even future political and economic penetration, intimations of a Western European alliance, and now the intra-empire Titoist threat were apparently seen by Stalin as dangerously cumulative. In such an environment he felt that he could not tolerate a Czech government whose president, Eduard Beneš, had proclaimed in May 1946, "Culturally we are Europeans. We will never range ourselves with East alone, or with the West alone, but always with East and West simultaneously."[5] Accordingly, on February 25, 1948, with the Russian army arrayed on the border and local Communists poised in and around Prague, the Czech Communist party took control of the government. Stalin, with the establishment of the Cominform, the purging of East European regimes, and the Czech coup, seemed to have consolidated his position.

The West Reacts

In the West, however, Stalin's actions were seen as anything but defensive. The elimination of a few Eastern European Communists with nationalist visions was one thing—but the Czechs being bullied into submission created "coursing emotion" and "gave an emotional tone to the Western reaction."[6] General Lucius Clay, the military commander of American occupation forces in Germany, informed the Pentagon that he perceived a subtle but ominous change in the Soviet attitude—a change that might presage the onset of war. Clay was to concede later that he never had any confirming evidence that war was on the horizon.[7]

Nevertheless, the immediate reaction was an intensification of tentative discussion among the Western Europeans and Americans concerning some form of defensive alliance. With the Czechoslovak coup, matters quickly came to a head; and by the third week in March, Britain, France, the Netherlands, Belgium and Luxembourg signed in Brussels a fifty-year mutual assistance pact "clearly directed at the Soviet Union."[8] On March 17, 1948, President Truman informed Congress that the growing menace of the Soviet Union was threatening the reconstruction of Europe. He called upon Congress to provide full support for Western Europe and especially those countries that were, as Truman spoke, linking themselves through the Brussels accord.

Still, Truman and his top advisers moved cautiously. For even though there was agreement within the upper levels of the administration on the general direction of American policy, there was disagreement concerning the instrumentalities to be employed. Second, there was also broad and deep concern about support from a Republican-dominated Congress for the imminent departure in policy toward a peacetime military alliance. Finally, we should not overlook Truman's domestic political circumstances: The fall of 1948 was to be a national time of reckoning. And in view of the Republican majorities in both houses of Congress, which had resulted from the 1946 election, and the generally held opinion that the Republicans were already ahead in the race for the White House, it is understandable that Truman was uncertain of his base for a bold foreign policy.

President Truman's ultimately successful but prodigious electoral effort vied for his attention and energy throughout much of 1948. In the meantime, he had to build support in a hostile Congress, and especially in the Senate, for the Marshall Plan and presidential discretion in working out the as yet ambiguous relationship with Western Europe. The memory of Wilson's humiliation over the League of Nations at the hands of Congress inspired Truman to instruct Undersecretary of State Robert Lovett during April and May 1948 to work with Senator Vandenberg to produce a declaration of senatorial support for an American–Western European alliance. Simultaneously, the State Department entered into preliminary talks with the British, Canadians, and other representatives of the Brussels Pact concerning the structure and obligations of signatories of such an arrangement.[9] On May 19 Vandenberg, well briefed by high State Department officials, introduced his resolution; three weeks later, on June 11, 1948, the Senate passed the Vandenberg Resolution by a margin of 64–4. President Truman could now claim bipartisan support for whatever course he chose.

DEBATE CONCERNING THE INSTRUMENTS OF CONTAINMENT

The successful steering of the Vandenberg Resolution through the Senate seemed to confirm the existence of some operational latitude for President Truman. But the president faced seemingly irreconcilable, conflicting demands. His sense of fiscal needs and his domestic political strategy compelled him to advance his domestic programs aggressively yet within a framework of fiscal responsibility. On the other side, however, was the ominous drift of events in Europe, which seemed to confirm the need for some kind of unified Western response, presumably underwritten by the United States. Indeed, the president had encouraged this in his March speech supporting the Brussels Pact and his subsequent effort to get a Senate resolution of support for his European policy. But now he was being warned that a significant increase or the mere consideration of new defense spending could so inflate the economy that extensive controls on the economy would be inevitable—an unpleasant prospect in an election year.[10]

Complicating matters further was that, as of early 1948, no clear-cut strategic policy had yet emerged. The air force and congressional airpower advocates were urging reliance on an atomic-armed, long-range air force as the basis for the American defense posture. However, there was a good deal of skepticism concerning the viability of this posture.[11] The production of American atomic warheads was lagging due to shortages and problems of uranium delivery, and there were doubts concerning bomb potency during this early period. There was also limited confidence in the delivery systems available to the United States.[12]

It is probable, therefore, that in the event President Truman had been predisposed to rely heavily on military instrumentalities, the means were not available. In fact, Truman's approach to postwar defense requests indicates that the president was not so predisposed. His rhetoric was tough, even belligerent, but in the aftermath of the Czech coup it was Marshall's European Recovery Program that received the president's support as the best means for filling out the American relationship with the Europeans. He would support some increase in the defense budget, but not the $9 billion being requested. In contrast to the Marshall Plan, which received complete and intensive support when it went before Congress, Truman cut the Defense Department's supplemental request by two-thirds.

An identifiable structure of policy and programmatic assumptions seemed to be crystallizing. The most fundamental assumption set forth by Marshall, and apparently accepted by Truman, was that there was not going to be a war with the Soviet Union in the forseeable future. The recent behavior of Stalin suggested that the Soviets would seek an oppressive politico-economic control of Eastern Europe, undergirded by Soviet conventional military strength. But it was also assumed that the Soviets did not then have and were unlikely to possess atomic weapons within the next five years. American strategic superiority was not in question. Prudence and the need for bureaucratic compromise might dictate that the new Department of Defense be allowed to develop and maintain the ability to deal with a theoretical Soviet strategic threat. However, Marshall and the president did not perceive the threat as imminent. Indeed, the Soviet threat was deemed manageable within the resources provided by a $15 billion-a-year defense budget, less than fifty bomber groups (which would be about fifty more bomber groups than the Russians would possess), an army of fewer than six hundred thousand men, and a navy equipped very much as it had been at the end of the war. Far more important to the American posture envisioned by Truman and Marshall at this time was the economic reconstruction of Europe.

THE MARSHALL PLAN AS A
POLITICO-ECONOMIC CONCEPT

The idea of European recovery as the foundation of American policy had many appealing qualities. Not the least of these was the possibility that through European recovery the United States might simultaneously frustrate the Soviets, unify all of Europe, and reduce or even eliminate the future need for massive U.S. economic assistance appropriations.[13] There were collateral benefits. A productive and economically integrated Western European economy might prove irresistible to Eastern Europeans and ultimately the Soviets themselves. Further, containment, and perhaps the eventual taming of communist excesses, could be implemented while avoiding the domestic dislocations brought on by the development and maintenance of a large military establishment. Thus, the response to Truman's call for international commitment and involvement could be both dynamic and economically finite.

In the longer run, a growing capitalist Western Europe promised benefits for the postwar American economy. European recovery through the Marshall Plan held out the promise of an Atlantic community. This American-European relationship might become the basis of an even larger global economic system. In such a liberal, free-trading, and essentially capitalistic world, the United States, its economy unscathed by World War II, could not help but benefit, indeed, predominate.

In 1948 American efforts focused on the short-run dimensions of this Atlantic vision. The immediate problem had been set forth in the Truman Doctrine and was reiterated by Secretary of State Marshall.[14] Europe's desperate economic straits were being exploited by "those small groups who aspire to dominate by the method of police states."[15] The prevailing and largely bipartisan understanding of this crisis[16] was that European cooperation and even unification were the only means for using U.S. aid effectively and thus retrieving the political situation.[17]

In line with these sentiments were the crucial decisions in 1947 to formally merge the economics of the American and British zones of western Germany into "Bizonia," and the relaxation of the rigid occupation directives of 1945. Thus, the denazification programs instituted immediately after the war would be eased; similarly, the dismantling of German industrial capacity, and decartelization—the elimination of monopolistic organizations—was slowed. Those measures once viewed essential for preventing the resurgence of German political and military power were now viewed as contradictory to German and, more importantly, European recovery. In January 1948 German officials were urged to consider the formation of more centralized government structures that might assume some political functions.[18] And on January 22, 1948, the British called for a meeting for the following month in London to discuss the future of Germany. Invitations were extended to the Americans, the French, and the Benelux countries. Pointedly, the Russians were not invited.

West German Statehood Is Ratified

Decisions were reached in three broad areas at London. First, the earlier implicit moves toward full German participation in the European Recovery Program were ratified. Moreover, it was agreed that not only would Bizonia participate, but also the French zone. Finally, the London Conference urged the Western zones to move quickly toward the establishment of West German political institutions and processes which would allow the West Germans to assume control of their own political and, in large measure, economic affairs.[19] The means whereby this West German federal constitution was to be drawn up, ratified, and its relationship to the three occupation administrations defined were to remain points of contention until early 1949. Communists as well as some conservatives in the French parliament were especially reluctant to accept the degree of German autonomy implied by the conference recommendations and urged that greater control be reserved to the occupation powers.[20] Despite French ambivalence concerning reconstructed German economic power, the London conference summarized and institutionalized the developments of the preceding two years. The Western powers had now officially recognized "that German reconstruction is essential to the well-being of Europe."[21] Of equal importance, the commitment to the formation of a West German state and the exclusion of Soviet interests in that decision marks yet another intensification in the reciprocating dynamics of East-West distrust.

THE DEATH OF DIPLOMACY

The thrust and specifics of the Marshall Plan proved discomforting to the French; to the Russians they must have been appalling. As events unfolded in late 1947 and early 1948, Stalin's worst fears were materializing: There were internal problems in Eastern Europe. Now the Western powers were moving resolutely toward the reestablishment of the European political economy. Perhaps more distressing to Stalin, the seed of a new German state had finally sprouted with the completion of the London Conference. Prior to mid-1947, U.S. policy had been rhetorically tough, but there had been limited action to go with American posturing. Now, however, the United States had initiated a comprehensive and apparently long-run program of economic assistance designed to set in motion Western European economic integration and the creation of a new West German state that would eventually control the important Ruhr Valley industrial complex.[22] Moreover, the Soviets were isolated from and unable to influence these events directly. The Soviet Union's isolation was in part a product of its own actions beginning with Molotov's walk-out at the Paris conference in June 1947.[23] But the United States was not entirely displeased with Soviet behavior, and in the development of the Marshall Plan had sought to structure the proposal, its promulgation, and its operation so as to make it unacceptable to the Soviets.[24]

The London Conference of early 1948 was the culmination of Western unilateralism[25] in that it expressly excluded Soviet participation. The communique of the London Conference stated that "The present recommendations . . . in no way preclude and on the contrary should facilitate eventual 4-power agreement on the German problem. . . ."[26] The establishment of guidelines for the creation of the West German state, trizonal economic integration, and especially the recommendations on the Ruhr, all without Soviet participation, however, could not help but communicate a message to the contrary. And if there was any uncertainty concerning the intentions of the West, it was made clear that any future Four Power agreements would have to be consonant with the measures the West was initiating.[27]

In sum, both sides shared responsibility for the breakdown of diplomacy. Insofar as both sides were using the Control Council and foreign ministers' meetings for little more than public posturing, they both debased the medium of diplomatic exchange. The early postwar period had been marked by tough negotiations and sometimes bitter diplomatic exchanges; nevertheless, there had been more than the semblance of diplomatic interaction as the two sides felt their respective ways through the ambiguities of the new postwar world. Now things were taking an uglier turn, for East-West relations "had begun to assume the proportions of a struggle between two competing theologies. It had passed out of the realm of ambiguity into a period of moral clichés based on absolute definitions of good and evil that were to blight relations between the super powers for over a decade."[28]

The increasing diminution of diplomacy left each side with the crudest and most dangerous of means for communicating with the other: threat, counterthreat, confrontation, and the escalation of confrontation. The actions and intentions of the adversary were to be evaluated in the worst light. The modalities of interaction were now to be played out within a syndrome of tests and demonstrations of will, a reciprocating and mutually reinforcing diplomacy of threat.

The Berlin Blockade

The norm of future East-West interaction emerged from Stalin's efforts to check what he now perceived to be a concerted Western effort to undermine Soviety security. First he turned to the remaining point of institutionalized diplomatic contact in what may have been at best a half-hearted attempt to communicate his concerns about what was, to him, a deteriorating German situation. In February 1948 he filed a formal protest in the Control Council before the London talks began and again in March when the conference ended. When, during the March meeting, the Russians were unable to get information on or a discussion of the London meeting, they broke off the talks. Stalin now turned to more direct means in an attempt to communicate his position and influence Western behavior so that the German question could be reopened.

In April 1948 Stalin halted Western military supplies to West Berlin, located deep within the Russian zone. The Western reaction was to press on with the plans laid out at the London Conference. Specifically, the West approved in early June the initial step in the formation of the West German state. The Russians responded in turn with further interference with traffic into Berlin. Finally, in mid-June, at preceisely the moment Tito's heresy broke into a total rupture with Stalin culminating in Tito's formal expulsion from the Cominform (after a Russian-inspired coup directed at Tito had failed), the Western powers initiated a currency reform in all their sectors except Berlin. This seemingly innocuous move was regarded by the Soviets as a precursor to economic chaos in their zone because they envisioned the old devalued German currency being dumped in the eastern zone. The initial Soviet reaction was to initiate a currency change of their own, but when the new Western reform was extended to West Berlin, they responded on June 24, 1948, with a full blockade of Berlin. The West countered with their own economic blockade of the entire eastern zone.

All surface movement in and out of Berlin was at a complete standstill, and both sides quickly defined the situation as a mutual testing of will. General Clay, in messages described as "pulsating," implored the president to resist and break the blockade with force; others advised conceding Berlin to the Russians. Truman never seriously contemplated the latter; Forrestal noted in his diary:

> When the specific question was discussed as to what our future policy in Germany was to be—namely, were we to stay in Berlin or not?—the President interrupted to say that there was no discussion on that point. We were going to stay, period.[29]

On the other hand, Truman did not adopt the bold course of action proposed by Clay. Instead, he ordered an airlift of supplies into West Berlin. Two weeks later he ordered two groups of atomic-capable B-29's to England, although it is not clear that nuclear weapons were in fact deployed outside the United States. Nevertheless, by the end of July more than sixty B-29's were in Europe, and there was no effort to conceal the fact.[30]

In August 1948 Stalin granted an interview with the ambassadors of the Western Allies. The Allied ambassadors were interested in reasserting Western access routes to West Berlin, whereas Stalin sought to shift negotiations to the broader question of recent events in West Germany, most notably the outcome of the London Conference. He wanted nothing less than the cessation of efforts to form a West German government and the full restoration of Four Power control of Germany, in which case the Western powers were welcome back in Berlin. It seems, therefore, that Stalin was attempting to use the blockade as leverage to get at the far more salient issue of Germany's political future. The West, on the other hand, was now committed to a diametrically opposed course; for the West Germans were to begin drafting a constitution within weeks. The West's response to the Stalin proposal, therefore, was to try to shift discussion back to the narrower questions of access rights. Talks deadlocked, and the situation in Germany reached a perilous state as Truman asked his advisers in early September to "brief me on bases, bombs, Moscow, Leningrad, etc. I have a terrible feeling . . . that we are close to war. I hope not . . . Berlin is a mess."[31]

Border incidents or conflict in and around Berlin were available if either side had wanted to fight. The airlift itself provided ample opportunity. From June–July 1948 until Febrary 1949, food and fuel deliveries increased to more than seven thousand tons daily. To accomplish this, the Western Allies were landing a plane in West Berlin every two minutes. There was, therefore, no lack of targets for the Soviets if they had sought an igniting incident. Harassment continued, but no provocative incident occurred.

The unwillingness or inability of the Soviets to provoke open conflict may be attributed to the ambiguous threat posed by the American B-29's. More likely is the fact that Stalin was simply not interested in pushing the West out of Berlin. Rather, he hoped by blockading Berlin to force the West to negotiate about the political and economic future of all Germany. Simple diplomacy had proved inadequate during the preceding months, for the Western Allies had gone ahead unilaterally with their plans for the integration of a West German state into the European Recovery Program. Stalin undertook, therefore, the slow strangulation of West Berlin as a means for dramatizing his own demands.

If this was Stalin's intent, he misread feelings in Washington, London, Paris, and Ottawa. Officials in these capitals responded to Stalin's actions by accelerating the very trends the Soviet dictator sought to deflect.[32] From July through early September 1948, European military and diplomatic representatives met with counterparts from the United States and Canada and began developing a concrete proposal for joining the North Atlantic countries in a defense pact. In December 1948 the language of a draft treaty was prepared. In January 1949 Truman made passing reference to the new defense treaty in his State of the Union message, and by February 1949 negotiations on the final language of the treaty were underway. Paralleling these events, a West German parliamentary council was elected in August 1948 and began drafting a West German constitution in September 1948. Simultaneously, the Americans, British, and French began developing terms for the international authority of the Ruhr as well as drafting a new occupation statute, which would define Allied authority once the new West German state was in place. These arrangements included German management and in some instances German ownership of the Ruhr industries. Moreover, rules of exclusion for former Nazis, although included in the statutes, were now little more than symbolic inasmuch as some of the men recommended for trusteeship positions had been involved with the management of German industry during the war.[33] Agreement on the West German constitution moved more slowly, but by the spring of 1949 a constitution or basic law was approved by the military governors in the three Western zones. The new constitution was accepted on the same day, May 12, 1949, that the Soviets lifted their blockade.

The lifting of the blockade, even as the basic law was accepted in principle is an especially strong indication of how desperate the Soviet diplomatic position had become by mid-1949. It must have been clear to Stalin by early 1949 that the blockade would fail and that its effect had been totally unproductive. Rather than split the Western Allies and hasten the resumption of negotiations on Germany's future, the blockade brought the Allies together and probably facilitated intra-Allied bargaining on such contentious questions as the Ruhr authority and occupation rights.[34] In addition, the Western powers, when confronted with the blockade, had moved quickly to extend the Brussels Pact into a North Atlantic defense arrangement that now included the United States. All of this activity pointed to a divided Germany with the West German state increasingly a part of an economically integrated Western Europe operating under an as yet undefined American military commitment.

Faced with these cumulating reverses, Stalin sought a way back from the confrontation of the blockade while at the same time trying to hold off the formation of West Germany. The blockade had originally been used as a stick with which Stalin sought to prod the West into acceptance of his position. Now he would try unsuccessfully to use the removal of the blockade as a carrot.

The Blockade
Is Lifted—The West Ascendant

In January and February 1949 the Russians made public overtures through press conferences followed by secret contacts at the United Nations proposing that, if the formation of West Germany could be delayed until after a foreign ministers meeting, the Soviets would consider lifting the blockade. Acheson, who had taken over as secretary of state in the second Truman administration, agreed only to "simultaneously lifting the blockade and counterblockade, and fixing a date for a meeting of the Council of Foreign Ministers."[35] Acheson was aware of the thrust of Stalin's diplomacy:

> We . . . saw the danger in allowing Stalin to edge his way into the incomplete and delicate negotiations among us regarding our relations among ourselves and with the Germans in our zones, which could lead to disunity among us and no progress in lifting the blockade. The greatest danger of disunity lay in any postponement of our tripartite preparations together and with the Germans.[36]

The Soviets continued the secret contacts throughout April 1949, seeking some form of commitment to postpone preparations for the formation of the West German government, but the West would not yield. On May 4 the Russians finally agreed to go ahead with the lifting of the blockade on May 12, 1949, because it was clear now that private negotiations could take them no further. Perhaps Stalin concluded that public negotiations would bring pressure to bear on the West to make concessions. At a minimum, Stalin could end the blockade and perhaps save face.[37]

In the meantime, Secretary of State Acheson was working almost feverishly to ensure the complete isolation of the Soviets. In April 1949, while negotiations on the lifting of the blockade were underway, the NATO pact was completed and the German constitution drafted. In addition, the Western Allies hammered out agreements on virtually all outstanding issues concerning Germany: the Ruhr, their respective occupation rights, agreements on Berlin and its relationship to the new West German state, future reparations, unresolved boundary questions, and a memorandum of main principles of policy toward Germany.[38] Moreover, just prior to the foreign ministers' meeting, a common understanding concerning tactics and procedures at the conference was reached. The Western powers' consensus hinged on the idea that they would turn down any Soviet proposal concerning Germany's political and economic future if that proposal was based on any other than Western policy and procedure.[39] In summary, the only things the Soviets wanted to discuss were to be nonnegotiable; or, as at Paris in 1947, negotiable only on Western terms.

The West expected very little from the conference, and in putting forward (in Acheson's words) "our requirements for a 'good opportunity'" which were admittedly "severe,"[40] the prophecy became a reality. "Our requirements" were deemed "not impossible"[41] by Acheson, but the Russians found them so, and the Paris meeting quickly settled into mutual recrimination. By all accounts, President Truman was not unhappy with the results of the conference. He publicly applauded Acheson for the skill with which he had carried off the tasks of ending the blockade while simultaneously maintaining the thrust of American policy in Europe. For the Russians, however, the dismal end of the conference marked the collapse of their effort to counter the Marshall Plan, the formation of West Germany, and NATO. It was, as Professor Marshall Shulman has noted, the "low point of Soviet diplomacy."[42] Washington's attention was now free to focus on the problem of institutionalizing and providing resources for the alliance that had been struck in the heat of the Berlin crisis—and the deteriorating situation in Asia.

FORMATION OF THE NORTH ATLANTIC TREATY ORGANIZATION

The passage of the Vandenberg Resolution and the imposition of the blockade gave impetus to a period of intense contacts between U.S. representatives and members of the Brussels Pact. By December 1948 there was general agreement on one point: the geographic scope of the pact should include Scandinavian, North Atlantic, and Mediterranean powers so as to provide protection for the flanks of the main powers.[43] A second and more difficult point concerned the substance of the pact.

Conflicting Concepts of Alliance Emerge—and Are Compromised

Robert E. Osgood, in his study of the early years of the NATO alliance,[44] has suggested that two conflicting concepts of the NATO alliance emerged in late 1948 and persisted even after the signing in April and ratification of the treaty in July 1949. First there was the view, held for the most part by American and European military planners, that NATO should be a large and fully integrated "trans-Atlantic military coalition."[45] In line with this view, the defense ministers of the Brussels Pact countries had agreed that the alliance should proceed with a common defense policy under some sort of integrated command buttressed by a permanent group concerned with logistical and supply problems.[46] The American Joint Chiefs of Staff were already on record as supporting such a concept, including an American supreme commander if fighting actually occurred.[47] Furthermore, this concept of the alliance carried with it the implication of a local and forward defense of Western Europe. This was necessary because it was assumed that the most basic threat to

European security was the large standing army of the Soviet Union. Moreover, from a continental perspective, there was the concern that unless the alliance formally committed to the forward defense of the continent, the Americans, the British, or both might revert to the kind of peripheral strategy they had adopted in World War II. The continental powers and especially France did not look forward to another prolonged liberation struggle. The logic of this position, therefore, was to commit the alliance partners and especially the Americans and the British to an automatic response to external aggression.[48]

There was opposition to this view in the Department of State, the White House, and the Congress. Instead of viewing the alliance as an American military trip wire, the treaty was interpreted as "intending to provide political and psychological reinforcement in the continuing political warfare of the Cold War."[49] This view held that it was the political, economic, and social weakness of Western Europe itself that opened up subversive opportunities for Soviet communism. The purported propensity for the Soviets to use force, as displayed in Czechoslovakia and Berlin, was viewed as "defensive reactions on the Soviet side to the initial success of the Marshall Plan initiative and to the preparations . . . to set up a separate German government in West Germany." Critics of a well-reinforced military "plate glass" shield to Europe saw the communist-inspired strikes in France and Italy in the autumn of 1947 as "Moscow's attempt to play, before it was too late, the various political cards it still possessed on the European continent."[50]

Many advocates of a more political concept of NATO believed that communist political and economic pressure in the shadow of Soviet conventional military strength might force the Western Europeans into a neutral stance between East and West (in the jargon of a later time, they might be "Finlandized"), thereby threatening the Marshall Plan. But in this view the response was the intensification and success of the Marshall Plan itself, not a comprehensive and expensive U.S. military commitment to Europe's defense. At most, NATO was to be a "modest military shield" behind which the primary task of economic construction would go forward and European self-confidence reestablished.[51] From the perspective of many in the U.S. Congress, such a political and economic commitment should not entail an automatic commitment of U.S. military involvement.

The procedural question of automatic commitment was to be the most contentious issue in the drafting of the final language of the treaty. The Senate, with Acheson serving as both advocate and mediator, and the Western ambassadors struggled over this point during February and March 1949 and produced a compromise. The United States was not automatically committed to war if the treaty[52] came into force, thereby satisfying American minimalists, particularly those in the Senate. On the other hand, by signing the treaty the United States was committed to its provisions, which implied certain obligations on the part of the United States, including mutual aid, but what those obligations were and how they were to be fulfilled were not yet clear. But then precision was not required in the spring of 1949, for in the heat of the Berlin crisis, a show of unity and agreement in broadest principle was all that was deemed necessary; operational specifics could be resolved later.

In his memoirs, Acheson noted that the April 4, 1949, NATO treaty signing ceremony was "dignified and colorful." He adds: "The Marine Band added a note of unexpected realism as we waited for the ceremony to begin by playing songs from the currently popular musical play *Porgy and Bess,* 'I've Got Plenty of Nothin' and 'It Ain't Necessarily So.'"[53]

Support for NATO and More
Compromise on Strategic Concepts and Means

The debate on the $1.3 billion Mutual Defense Assistance Program (MDAP), which was conceived by the Truman administration as the first installment on the NATO agreement, in no way clarified the strategic thinking underlying U.S. policy.

The NATO treaty was described by Acheson to the Senate as limited in its commitment of assistance. Indeed, the administration presented the request for the MDAP only after the treaty was approved in July 1949, thereby separating the more explosive question of material support from the principle of the alliance. When asked by Republican Senator Bourke Hickenlooper of Iowa whether the treaty would lead to the United States sending large numbers of troops to Europe "as a more or less permanent contribution to the development of these countries' capacity to resist," Acheson replied, "The answer to that question, Senator, is a clear and absolute 'no.'"[54]

Acheson was to eat these words eighteen months later. In the meantime, the administration's gambit was to minimize the apparent costs of the commitments under the NATO agreement; but this was, in the final analysis, a tactical extension of their own belief in the primacy of the Marshall Plan and that the material cost and implications of NATO could be minimized. The best evidence of this lies in the less than $15 billion defense budget President Truman had recommended to Congress in January 1949, the midpoint of the Berlin crisis. Furthermore, the logic of the fiscal year 1950 budget was carried forward with even greater vigor in the planning for fiscal year 1951. Louis Johnson replaced Forrestal in the Defense Department in 1949,[55] and held the fiscal year 1951 budget to a $13.5 billion ceiling. The secretary of defense chose as the target of his reductions the Army and especially the Navy's desire for a piece of the strategic bombing mission. His efforts during mid-1949 to cut the size of the Navy's air arm led to an explosion within the military as the Navy fought back by forcing a congressional investigation of the Air Force's new strategic B-36 bomber. These hearings during August and October 1949, although beginning with allegations concerning the procurement of the B-36, ultimately moved to the broader strategic questions of which service branch could best carry out a strategy of maximum atomic retaliation on the Soviet Union.[56] Congressional sentiment tended to run with the air power advocates and the thrust of Truman's policy remained intact.

The MDAP was received less enthusiastically, however, for it implied that the alliance was based on a doctrine of large-scale land war in Europe and was, therefore, inconsistent with the strategic doctrine that supposedly underlay the budget request. Moreover, the armed services, especially the Army, did not show much enthusiasm for the proposal, for the military assistance program had been and continued to be a competitor for funds. The MDAP stalled in Congress and was passed only after being reduced to $1 billion and only after the president announced in late September that the Soviets had exploded their own atomic bomb. The effect of Truman's announcement was described in *Atomics* magazine as "a minor panic; many radio commentators have the country practically at war with Russia."[57] However, its passage in this manner, resulting in large measure from the perceived urgency of the moment, obscured and left unanswered the many questions raised in the preceding months.[58] Nevertheless, alliance planning went forward in the months after MDAP's passage and the explosion of the Soviets' atomic bomb. The specifics of initial NATO planning were not published, but Osgood has speculated that they involved the assignment of strategic bombardment and protection of sea lines of supply and communication to the United States and foresaw Europe providing the basis of conventional land forces.[59]

Summary

By 1950 the political and economic reconstruction of Europe encompassing that of West Germany was well underway. Furthermore, an alliance structure had been established with Western Europe and a modicum of defense integration achieved that anticipated the reconstruction of European conventional capability by means of U.S. assistance. In the meantime, U.S. strategic superiority, coupled with the accelerating success of the Marshall Plan, was deemed adequate to the task of containing Soviet power in Europe.

In the long run, however, if American strategic superiority could be eliminated, even as its monopoly on atomic power was now broken, then the prospect of some form of mutual atomic deterrance arose in which a conventional balance of forces would assume more and perhaps decisive importance.[60] Of course, an erosion of American atomic superiority was not going to occur overnight, given the paucity of Soviet intercontinental delivery aircraft. Furthermore, it is doubtful that Stalin contemplated strategic warfare five years after the appalling losses of World War II. Indeed, Stalin's primary concern at this time was his vulnerability to the West's nuclear advantage.[61] No one in the administration, in short, saw war with the Soviets as imminent.

Nevertheless, the explosion of the Soviet atomic bomb contributed to the cross-currents and implicit contradictions that underlay the compromises and apparent success of American European policy in late 1949. In addition, the Chinese civil war built to a climax in late 1949, and with the collapse of the Nationalist Chinese a chain of events was set in motion that eventually consumed the Truman administration.

CRISIS AND COLLAPSE IN ASIA

The momentous events in China did not take the Truman administration unawares. In view of American involvement in China during and immediately after World War II, it cannot be said the administration lacked information or concern about events in China. It is true, however, that the evolution of events in China was a lower-priority item for the Truman administration. China, indeed Asia, was felt to be on the periphery of the "basin of world power" of which Kennan had written. If countries or continents were to be reconstructed by and in the likeness of America, better that they be at the epicenter of world politics. On the periphery America would, in Acheson's words, "wait until the dust settles," and then concern itself with the emergent balance of forces. But this was not enough for those in America who thought they had heard a call for world ideological confrontation and crusade in the Truman Doctrine.

The Civil War in China—and in Congress

Marshall had spent a good deal of 1946 in China trying to bring about some kind of reconciliation between the Communists and Chiang Kai-shek. By the end of the year, however, negotiations had collapsed and Marshall had been recalled to Washington to assume direction of the Department of State. In January 1947 Marshall's report on the Chinese situation was made public. In it, Marshall pronounced a plague on both the Communist and Nationalist Chinese houses for their mutual distrust and extremism. By the end of January, the United States terminated all efforts at mediating the struggle; and in February and March 1947, full-scale fighting was renewed.

American policy was characterized by ambivalence, incrementalism, and what must have appeared to both the Communist Chinese and the conservatives in Congress as disingenuousness. In June 1947 more than $6 million in ammunition was provided the Nationalists, while Marshall claimed that the sale did not signify U.S. support for Chiang's regime. In July 1947 Marshall noted U.S. concern over the economic conditions in China and asserted that U.S. assistance would be forthcoming only as conditions developed that seemed to promise that such assistance would be beneficial. To evaluate conditions, Lieutenant General Albert Wedemeyer was sent to China on a fact-finding mission and to inform Chiang that future assistance would be under American supervision and predicated upon internal reform. Wedemeyer's report was unfavorable to the Nationalists and suggested that the Nationalists could succeed only by undertaking far-reaching political and economic reforms to correct what Wedemeyer saw as widespread corruption and inefficiency. Nevertheless, the Truman administration found itself unable or unwilling to cut Chiang's regime completely adrift. Thus, in November 1947 Marshall announced a new $300 million economic assistance program for China to begin the following year, although he conceded that the United States was finding it difficult to develop a course of action in which American funds could be expended with expectations of "getting about a 70-percent return in effectiveness of use."[62]

Increasingly, therefore, the Truman administration found itself in Asia in the position of a gambler faced with a run of bad cards and a crowd of jeering kibitzers—in this case, a growing band of conservative Republicans who were charging that the Truman administration was doing too little. The gambler knows that the probabilities are that the next cards will be as bad as his previous hands. Indeed, he begins to suspect that the game might be rigged. However, although his losses have begun to mount, they are not yet unacceptable and there is the hope that one more play might recoup those losses; thus, yet another bet is made.

The Truman administration seemed to have convinced itself that the best strategy in 1947 and early 1948 was to stay in the Chinese game by means of economic assistance. No one seems to have been terribly optimistic—but then maybe something would turn up. The alternatives seemed unpleasant: China would fall to the Communists and the administration would be open to a merciless attack—in an election year—from the Republicans that even as Roosevelt had sold out Eastern Europe at

Yalta, Truman and the Democrats had now lost China. Moreover, cutting the Nationalists loose might threaten the bipartisan support so carefully nurtured for the administration's policy in Europe.[63] The important thing in the short run, therefore, was not to lose nerve—press on, commit the minimum resources necessary to keep in the game in Asia and simultaneously hold domestic critics at arm's length until after the election in November. Once the election was over, the entire situation could be reassessed.

In the meantime, this incremental holding strategy could never satisfy the Republicans who were calling for an all-out commitment similar to that in Europe. More important in the long run, the provision of *any* aid to Chiang, no matter how symbolic, could only reinforce Mao's suspicion and distrust, thereby complicating any future effort at reconciliation. By Christmas of 1947 Mao was publicly calling the Nationalists "reactionary forces" and "running dogs of American imperialism." Simultaneously Chiang's regime and the Republicans were blaming President Truman for increasing communist control in Manchuria. Throughout the first half of 1948, political pulling and pushing over the size and conditions to be attached to American aid to Chiang persisted in the Congress. The game was not unlike the one to be played out twenty years later in Southeast Asia by another Democratic president—for both gamblers, the good hand was never dealt.

But nothing changed in China, as the military reverses accumulated. On September 24, Jinan (Tsinan) fell; on October 20, the Manchurian capital of Changchun; and on November 1, 1948, Shenyang (Mukden), the key to all of Manchuria, fell. In October 1948 a report of the House Foreign Affairs Subcommittee on World Communism had called for an American guarantee "of territorial and political integrity"[64] of China. But while the House committee was demanding a firm position, Secretary Marshall and the State Department remained ambivalent. Earlier in August, Secretary Marshall had advised the American embassy in China that the United States would not support a coalition government that included Communists. On the other hand, the United States would not try to mediate the civil war again. Beyond the provision of some economic and military assistance, Mr. Marshall advised the embassy that it was "not likely that the situation will make it possible for us at this juncture to formulate any rigid plans for our future policy in China."[65]

A Decision to "Let the Great Tree Fall"

President Truman's reelection in 1948 allowed the administration to resist a commitment of full support for Chiang. Thus, when two weeks after the election Chiang requested an increase in aid to save his regime,

President Truman was noncommittal. Moreover, when Chiang's wife arrived in Washington in December with a request for $3 billion in aid, she was ignored by the administration. Just prior to her arrival the administration had received the report of Major General David Barr, Director of the U.S. Military Advisory Group to the Government of China. General Barr's feeling was that:

> The military situation has deteriorated to the point where only the active participation of United States troops could effect a remedy. . . . No battle has been lost since my arrival due to lack of ammunition or equipment. Their military debacles in my opinion can all be attributed to the world's worst leadership and many other morale destroying factors that lead to a complete loss of will to fight. . . . The Generalissimo has lost much of his political and popular support.[66]

Secretary Marshall agreed that the only way to save Chiang's regime was to commit American troops, but he would not recommend such a course.

The inference was clear: The administration would now attempt to put even more distance between itself and the Nationalist Chinese although not moving to a position of real neutrality. To do so would have further provoked those conservative Republicans who were urging higher levels of assistance and U.S. commitment. Thus, during January and February 1949, when the Nationalist government was being forced to move from Nanjing (Nanking) to Guangzhou (Canton) in the face of advancing Communist forces, the White House instructed the State Department "that in order not to discourage Chinese resistance to communist aggression, military aid should not be suspended, but no effort should be made to expedite it."[67] Congressional pressure continued, but Acheson persistently reiterated that there would be no change in American policy.

Throughout May, June, and much of July 1949, major cities in southern China continued to fall to the Communists, but the administration stood fast in its refusal to intervene. Earlier, in February 1949, Acheson had been asked by members of Congress to predict the course of events in China and had responded that "when a great tree falls in the forest one cannot see the extent of the damage until the dust settles."[68] Acheson insists that his "waiting until the dust settles" was not a description of American policy, but it was taken as such.[69] Certainly Acheson's willingness to watch mutely the chain of Nationalist disasters in China stood in marked contrast to his feverish activity during this same period concerning American European policy. He was clearly not prepared to let the great European tree fall.

With the NATO treaty ratified in mid-July 1949 and the MDAP

submitted to Congress, Acheson prepared to go to the public with what had been American policy for months. On July 27 he announced that American policy in Asia would be subjected to a full review. Ten days later the Department of State released a White Paper of more than a thousand pages that sought to absolve the United States of all responsibility for the impending collapse of the Nationalist Chinese. The White Paper emphasized that the only manner in which the Nationalists could be saved would be through American intervention but noted that such an intervention would have been "resented by the mass of the Chinese people, would have diametrically reversed our historic policy, and would have been condemned by the American people."[70]

The report was met with a firestorm of criticism from all sides but especially from the right, where senators Bridges, Knowland, and Wherry—all Republicans—and Democratic Senator McCarran labeled it "a 1,054-page whitewash of a wishful, do-nothing policy which has succeeded only in placing Asia in danger of Soviet conquest."[71] But the rage of Nationalist China's supporters in the Congress could not prevent what Acheson was prepared to accept when he took office. On September 21, 1949, the Nationalist Chinese tree crashed to the ground as the People's Republic of China was proclaimed. On October 1, Mao Zedong's new government was inaugurated in Beijing (Peking) with Zhou Enlai as premier and foreign minister. By the end of the year Chiang Kai-shek had ensconced himself on Taiwan and was calling for American aid.

AMERICAN POLICY REAPPRAISED

The combined reverberations of the Nationalist Chinese collapse and the Soviets' atomic explosion gave impetus to a reassessment of American policy. The result in early 1950 was Policy Paper Number 68 of the National Security Council, "United States Objectives and Programs for National Security," or NSC-68, which became an overarching conceptual framework incorporating past American policy up to 1950 and establishing important parameters for future policy.[72] Before it was completed, however, one of the questions of late 1949 was resolved, for on January 31, 1950, the president decided to go forward with the development of the hydrogen bomb.

The Hydrogen Bomb Decision

One of the most immediate effects of the Soviet atomic bomb explosion was a debate within the American foreign and defense policymaking community over how the United States might maintain its pre-1949 nuclear superiority. The debate was intensified by the fact that moving up to the next level of nuclear weaponry, the hydrogen bomb, would involve a truly awesome increase in explosive capacity—a thousandfold increase over the atomic weapons used at Hiroshima and Nagasaki. The military advantages seemed more decisive than had been the case with atomic weapons, hence the military attractiveness of technological escalation. But this very fact of a quantum leap in destructiveness made the weapon especially repugnant to many in the scientific community. Within the government all of the members of the General Advisory Committee to the Atomic Energy Commission (AEC), as well as a majority of the commission itself, opposed going forward. The Defense Department favored development on a crash basis, but AEC Chairman David Lilienthal refused to move until all the foreign-policy implications of the hydrogen bomb had been considered. This meant, of course, that the Department of State was brought into the debate, but within the department there was also disagreement.

George Kennan, who was leaving as director of the Policy Planning Staff, had prepared a memorandum on the question of the hydrogen bomb and more broadly, U.S. nuclear policy as it related to international control.[73] In this memorandum Kennan underscored what he regarded as extreme ambiguity and confusion in American policy on nuclear weapons and their use. He urged, therefore, that there be a complete review of the entire question of the "first use" of these weapons by the United States, and emphasized that he was opposed to any doctrine of "first use." He did not challenge the necessity of maintaining such weapons until some form of disarmament arrangements could be worked out. In the meantime, however, Kennan urged that "we remain prepared to go very far, to show considerable confidence in others, and to accept certain risks for ourselves, in order to achieve international agreement on their removal from international arsenals."[74] In opposition to this position were Paul Nitze, the new director of the State Department's Policy Planning Staff, and Dean Acheson. Both were joined in "measuring the risks on a different scale,"[75] and seemed persuaded that immediate research and development should begin, given the likelihood that Soviet research was undoubtedly proceeding.[76] President Truman concurred with Acheson's view that further delay would not be wise, and announced on January 31, 1950, that the United States would proceed with the development of the hydrogen bomb.

Thus, on the hydrogen bomb decision the worst-case assumption concerning Soviet capabilities and behavior was made and assumed primary importance in the American decision. George Kennan and others on the Policy Planning Staff were prone to considering first what the Soviets' intentions were and using this as the basis or, at a minimum, a fundamental part of American policy. Now, however, Kennan sensed a "growing tendency in Washington . . . to base our own plans and calculations solely on the *capabilities* of a potential adversary, assuming him to be desirous of doing anything he could to bring injury to us, and to exclude from consideration, as something unsusceptible to exact determination, the whole question of that adversary's real *intentions*."[77] Kennan's concerns were regarded by Acheson and Nitze as "obscure argument" based on a kind of intuitive approach to policy making. Such an approach, Acheson conceded, had great utility and applicability in foreign operations; however, in his view, "its value . . . was limited in Washington."[78] In Acheson's opinion, "what [the president] needed was communicable wisdom, not mere conclusions, however soundly based in experience or intuition. . . ."[79] Acheson saw himself providing such "communicable wisdom" in the hydrogen bomb decision, and he sought to do the same in the drafting and promotion of NSC-68.

NSC-68

The drafting of NSC-68 was undertaken by a group of Department of State and Department of Defense planners working under the immediate direction of Paul Nitze and the Policy Planning Staff. Not unlike the authors of the Truman Doctrine, the authors of NSC-68 saw the world as essentially bipolar, only now there were no vague references to antithetical ways of life. The polarization of world politics and power was not a temporary one, but rather a "fundamentally altered" distribution of world power such that two nations, the United States and the Soviet Union, confronted one another with profoundly antithetical objectives and ideals in an international system in which "conflict has become endemic."[80] The Soviets' objectives were threefold and involved: (1) consolidation of their hold on the Soviet Union as the ideological and political center of world communism; (2) consolidation of control over existing and extension of control to new satellites; and (3) the "complete abolition or forcible destruction" of power centers that opposed the Soviet aspiration for world hegemony.

"The fundamental design of those who control the Soviet Union and the international communist movement," the report argued, is "the complete subversion or forcible destruction . . . of the non-Soviet world and their replacement by an apparatus and structure subservient to and controlled from the Kremlin." Soviet objectives were "wholly irreconcilable" with the objectives of a free society. Moreover, "the assault on free institutions is worldwide now, and in the context of the present polarization of power a defeat of free institutions anywhere is a defeat everywhere. . . ." "In a shrinking world which now faces the threat of atomic warfare, it is not an adequate objective merely to seek to check the Kremlin design, for the absence of order among nations is becoming less and less tolerable. This fact imposes on us, in our own interest, the responsibility of world leadership,"[81] which would require "a much more rapid and concerted build-up of the actual strength of both the United States and the other nations of the free world. . . . [T]his will be costly and will involve significant domestic financial and economic adjustments."[82]

NSC-68 provided a generally bleak assessment of the respective capabilities of the United States and the Soviet Union in this total struggle between "free society" and the "implacable purpose of the slave state." First, the nuclear superiority of the United States was deemed to be of limited duration with a stalemate of nuclear power anticipated in 1954, although the United States might extend its advantage if hydrogen weapons were perfected rapidly. But the Joint Chiefs of Staff were cited as concluding that the Soviets would be able by 1950 to overrun most of Western Europe, drive into the Middle East, consolidate control of Asia, and initiate air and sea attacks in the Atlantic basin including attacks on "selected targets with atomic weapons, now including targets in Alaska, Canada, and the United States."[83]

Faced with this grim prospect, what should the West, and especially the United States, do? First, Western European recovery and the NATO alliance should be fully implemented, for only in this way could the purported Soviet conventional military advantage be countered. But the prospect was long-run unrelieved tension and danger, and under these circumstances the framers of NSC-68 recommended "a rapid build-up of political, economic, and military strength in the free world" with the United States as the center of the effort. Furthermore, the reconstructed military capability of the United States and the West should be such that it surpassed that of the Soviet Union, and the West should be prepared to employ the capability in a clear-cut, unequivocal, and even "offensive" manner when challenged by communist power.[84]

The authors of NSC-68 were fully cognizant of the domestic implications of this proposal:

> Budgetary considerations will need to be subordinated to the stark fact that our very independence as a nation may be at stake.
>
> A comprehensive and decisive program to win the peace and frustrate the Kremlin design should be so designed that it can be sustained for as long as necessary to achieve our national objectives. It would probably involve . . .
>
> A substantial increase in expenditures for military purposes. . . .
>
> A substantial increase in military assistance programs. . . .

Reduction of Federal expenditures for purposes other than defense and foreign assistance, if necessary by the deferment of certain desirable programs.

Increased taxes.[85]

More specifically, the paper argued that the national economy was sufficiently dynamic that "in an emergency the United States could devote upward of 50 percent of its gross national product . . ." to national security if necessary. That is, rather than the $13–15 billion defense budgets of the postwar years, military budgets proportionate to those of World War II were acceptable—and perhaps essential in view of the threat confronting the United States and the free world.[86]

Summary

The picture painted by Nitze's group was, to say the least, a dark one. Past American policy was not criticized, but the inference was that the policies developed within the Marshall Plan framework were no longer adequate. For the fall of China and the acquisition of nuclear weapons by the Soviets suggested "a permanent and fundamental alteration in the shape of international relations."[87] "The issues that face us are momentous, involving the fulfillment or destruction not only of this Republic but of civilization itself."[88] Under these circumstances, if the ideals and objectives of "American life" were to be protected and furthered, an equally permanent and fundamental change in American policy must occur. Significantly, NSC-68 concluded that in such a transformation of American policy, negotiations and especially negotiations concerned with nuclear weapons, mutual arms reduction, or the control of atomic energy were not likely to be beneficial.

> Negotiation is not a possible separate course of action but rather a means of gaining support for a program of building strength, or recording, where necessary and desirable, progress in the cold war, and of facilitating further progress while helping to minimize the risk of war. Ultimately, our objective [is] to negotiate a settlement with the Soviet Union . . . on which the world can place reliance as an enforceable instrument of peace. But it is important to emphasize that such a settlement can only record the progress which the free world will have made in creating a political and economic system in the world so successful that the frustration of the Kremlin's design for world domination will be complete.[89]

In sum, negotiations were conceived not as viable good faith instruments of Soviet-American interaction, but rather as benchmarks of or ratifications of "progress in the cold war." In any event:

> The present world situation . . . is one which militates against successful negotiations with the Kremlin—for the terms of agreements on important pending issues would reflect present realities and would therefore be unacceptable, if not disastrous, to the United States and the rest of the free world. After a decision and a start on building up the strength of the free world has been made, it might then be desirable for the United States to take an initiative in seeking negotiations in the hope that it might facilitate the process of accommodation by the Kremlin to the new situation. Failing that, the unwillingness of the Kremlin to accept equitable terms or its bad faith in observing them would assist in consolidating popular opinion in the free world in support of the measures necessary to sustain the build-up.[90]

In view of this jaundiced and narrowly instrumental conception of negotiations, it is not surprising that the thrust of the proposal was that the United States and the West must seek and maintain military superiority over the Soviet Union so as to confront and override the inevitability of Soviet aggression at each turn. Indeed, NSC-68 refused to rule out the first use of nuclear weapons by the United States.[91] Finally, such superiority would have to be maintained even at the expense of other elements on the national public policy agenda.

THE POLICY REAPPRAISAL APPRAISED

Thinking at the top of the Department of State had turned very nearly 180 degrees in less than two years. Whereas Marshall concerned himself, to an extent, with how the Russians might perceive and react to an American action, Acheson seemed to care primarily about Russian capabilities. Attempts to evaluate Soviet intentions were deemed "interesting," but not really applicable to the task confronting the new secretary of state. The task as Acheson saw it was a redirecting of American policy away from the "soft" political and economic containment of the Marshall Plan. World politics was now cast in harsh relief—the grim remorseless struggle of nuclear-armed and ideologically driven combatants: "our analysis of the threat combined the ideology of communist doctrine and the power of the Russian state into an aggressive expansionist drive, which found its chief opponent and, therefore, target in the antithetic ideas and power of our own country."[92]

In Secretary Acheson's view, and the view of the other men who drafted NSC-68, however, the power of America was not yet realized. That power was not realized because too many in the United States persisted in two outmoded beliefs: The first had been held by Marshall when he was secretary of state—that the primary threat to world peace was the social and economic chaos of Western Europe, a threat that could be eliminated through American economic and moral assistance culminating in the economic unification of Europe. "This I did not believe," Acheson asserts.

> The threat to Western Europe seemed to me singularly like that which Islam had posed centuries before, with its combination of ideological zeal and fighting power. Then it had taken the same combination to meet it: Germanic power in the east and Frankish in Spain, both energized by a great outthrust of military power and social organization in Europe. This time it would need the added power and energy of America, for the drama was now played on a world stage.[93]

The crisis was not mere economic recovery; the barbarian was once again quite literally at the gates of Europe. And once again it would require "a great outburst of military power and social organization"—a reconstructed Europe but, most importantly, NATO (including "Germanic power")—in order that civilization might hold. Mobilizing Europe was necessary, but not sufficient, for the barbarian was at the gates everywhere and in this global confrontation American "energy and power" was also necessary. Acheson and his colleagues were convinced that this energy and power, if mobilized, would also be sufficient.

But the mobilization of American power on the scale deemed necessary ran up against the second of the great misconceptions thought to be widely held in Washington—that domestic ruin would follow on the heels of the reallocation of resources proposed by Secretary Acheson. The problem was complicated by the fact that no less a figure than the president and his White House staff seemed sympathetic to this view, for the president was in early 1950 sticking to his $13 billion ceiling for the Defense Department's fiscal 1951 budget and, as Paul Hammond notes, "Talk of even a $10 billion budget ceiling for fiscal 1952 was serious enough to have prompted preliminary soundings on it."[94]

On the other hand, the administration was obviously not of one mind. NSC-68 had been, after all, presidentially commissioned and signed, and Truman was certainly not unaware of his new secretary of state's predispositions concerning the Soviets and the threat they posed. Moreover, the rationale for his hydrogen bomb decision indicated Truman's receptivity to the views that were set forth in the document even though his economic instincts may have forced him to recoil. Acheson did not suffer from any indecisiveness. Hence, he relates, "The purpose of NSC-68 was to so bludgeon the mass mind of 'top government' that not only could the President make a decision but that the decision could be carried out."[95] Indeed, much of the emphasis on and overstatement of the Soviet threat can and has been explained as a rhetorical tactic adopted by Nitze and Acheson as a means for stating the case for an increased American defense effort as persuasively as possible.[96]

> The task of a public officer seeking to explain and gain support for a major policy is not that of the writer of a doctoral thesis. Qualification must give way to simplicity of statement, nicety and nuance to bluntness, almost brutality, in carrying home a point. It is better to carry the hearer or reader into the quadrant of one's thought than merely to make a noise or to mislead him utterly.[97]

The perspective and policies to which the listeners were to be persuaded were not without their detractors. Within the Department of State, George Kennan and Charles Bohlen, the two foremost Soviet experts in the U.S. government, were skeptical of both the analysis of Soviet policy set forth in the NSC-68 and the way in which the analysis was to be employed. Kennan persisted in a more subtle and complex view of Soviet behavior and viewed Nitze's statement of Soviet intent as simplistic. Both Bohlen and Kennan regarded Soviet behavior as being too complex to encompass in such a planning document. Indeed, they expressed reservations concerning the entire exercise because it forced extremely complex and delicate considerations of policy into the sterile abstractions of a planning document. From such a statement, higher officials lacking perspective and a sense of nuance, would be prone to draw even more simple-minded conclusions.[98] Acheson's perceived need for serving as militant missionary among the benighted of the Truman administration underscores and extends Kennan's point. For, having bludgeoned the top minds of government, can one realistically expect that same government to respond to the ambiguity and change of world politics with sophistication and conceptual elegance?

Let us reemphasize, however, that there were fundamental substantive differences between the positions represented by Kennan and Acheson. To Kennan the real threat confronting the West was political and economic. He saw no real military threat either to Western Europe or Western ideals. Ironically, as we have traced in this chapter, the policies developed and pursued by Marshall, although he may have regarded them as limited and no real threat to Soviet security, were taken as such by Stalin. An economically strong Western Europe, including a new German state, when combined with his own difficulties in Eastern Europe and at home, were unacceptable pressures from Stalin's increasingly isolated standpoint. Moreover, the means adopted by the West for implementing their policies excluded Soviet participation, hence Stalin through the Berlin crisis tried to force his way into the

West's decisions on Germany. The Berlin crisis became in turn the opportunity for the emergence of the position represented by Acheson: The threat to Western Europe was essentially military and Stalin's moves were not—as Kennan argued—desperate, but limited actions by an isolated Soviet dictator playing his last cards. The fall of China and the explosion of the atomic bomb by the Soviets seemed to confirm that Stalin represented a deeper and darker threat, a dislocation of history, to which NATO, the Mutual Defense Assistance Program, the hydrogen bomb, and a massive increase in U.S. military preparedness were the answers.

In summary, the president, the bureaucracy, Congress, and the country were suspended in mid-1950 between a past that was captured in Kennan's admonition that American policy must be "that of a long-term vigilant containment" of Soviet power which avoided "outward histrionics: without threats or blustering or superfluous gestures of outward 'toughness'" and Acheson's Wagnerian vision of "the road to freedom and to peace," which was "a hard one." In Acheson's view:

> The times in which we live must be painted in the dark sombre values of Rembrandt. The background is dark, the shadows deep. Outlines are obscure. The central point, however, glows with light; and, though it often brings out the glint of steel, it touches colors of unimaginable beauty. For us, that central point is the growing unity of free men the world over. This is our shaft of light, our hope, and our promise.[99]

The main difference in these perspectives lay in their proposals for action. Kennan, like Acheson, saw a prolonged confrontation, but it was to be one of political and economic containment, like the Marshall Plan, a largely symbolic alliance, and even taking risks to bring about arms control and broader negotiations. Acheson feared world domination by Soviet ideology and military power, the containment of which would require a full-fledged military alliance with Europe abroad and a subordination of domestic priorities to national security needs, which were in fact indistinguishable from global security needs. Moreover, meaningful negotiations were deemed unlikely except when carried out in the presence of Western political, economic, but above all, military strength—in short, "the glint of steel."

President Truman apparently stood somewhere between those perspectives and prescriptions. Perhaps by mid-1950 he was somewhere closer to Acheson's view of the threat, but unwilling to pursue vigorously Acheson's response.[100] The policy proposed in NSC-68 remained, therefore, tentative. But on June 24, 1950, the North Korean army crossed the 38th parallel into South Korea, and most of the remaining uncertainties vanished. Acheson's road would be taken.

NOTES

1. Adam Ulam, *The Rivals: America and Russia: Since World War II* (New York: Viking Press, 1971) and Marshall D. Shulman, *Stalin's Foreign Policy Reappraised* (New York: Atheneum Publishers, 1965), pp. 14–15, 258.
2. The actual size of the Soviet military at this time is a question of some dispute. For a review of the issue and the numerous estimates see Thomas W. Wolfe, *Soviet Power and Europe, 1945–1970* (Baltimore: Johns Hopkins University Press, 1970) pp. 9–11.
3. Ulam, op. cit., pp. 139–140.
4. Ibid., pp. 140–141. Ulam notes that Stalin's boast concerning Tito's destruction is probably not a literal quotation, but Professor Ulam observes, "that is how he felt" (p. 140).
5. Quoted by Herbert Feis, *From Trust to Terror: The Onset of the Cold War, 1945–1950* (New York: W. W. Norton & Company, 1970), p. 292.
6. Ibid., p. 294.
7. See Clay's autobiography, *Decision in Germany* (Garden City, N.Y.: Doubleday, 1950), p. 354, and Feis, op. cit., p. 296.
8. Ibid.
9. Truman's careful preparation was not always successful. The *sine qua non* of a meaningful alliance was seen by the Army as a sufficient standing army. The first time that universal conscription was suggested to Congress, it was voted down. There were reports, as the *Chicago Tribune* put it, that "in March, apparently in desperation, the Army handed President Truman a false intelligence report which 'pictured the Soviet Army as on the move,' when 'actually the Soviets were redistributing their troops to spring training stations'" (*Chicago Tribune,* June 19, 1948). Thus, when Truman called a joint emergency session of Congress to consider issues of defense, he had "evidence" that aided the passage of conscription as well as the Vandenberg Resolution.
10. For the most thorough analysis of the Truman administration's fiscal policy and its relationship to defense spending see Warner R. Schilling, "The Politics of National Defense: Fiscal 1950," in Warner R. Schilling, Paul Y. Hammond, and Glenn H. Snyder, *Strategy, Politics, and Defense Budgets* (New York: Columbia University Press, 1962). Most accounts of Truman's planning and budgeting eventually draw upon this excellent set of essays; the following analysis is no exception.
11. For a full account see George H. Quester, *Nuclear Diplomacy: The First Twenty-Five Years* (New York: Dunellen, 1970), p. 6 *passim.*
12. Ibid., pp. 5–6, 34–36 and Report of the President's Air Policy Commission, *Survival in the Air Age* (Washington, D.C.: U.S. Government Printing Office, 1948) and David MacIsaac, "The Air Force and Strategic Thought 1945–1951," *Working Paper* No. 8, Wilson Center, International Security Studies Program, June 21, 1979, Washington, D.C., p. 27.
13. See the testimony of Undersecretary of State Robert Lovett before U.S. Congress, Senate Committee on Foreign Relations, *Interim Aid for Europe,* 80th Congress, 1st Session, 1947. The following exchange is especially revealing (p. 99):

    > *The Chairman* [Vandenberg]: The thing I was trying to highlight at the moment was simply the general concept that we are approaching . . . this subject this time in a totally different fashion than ever before.
    >
    > *Secretary Lovett:* Absolutely, completely different.

The Chairman: And that it does involve an attempt to set down an effective *quid pro quo* and to produce an ultimate emancipation of the obligation of the United States for any further relief.

Secretary Lovett: That is its purpose.

14. Testimony of Secretary George C. Marshall before U.S. Congress, Senate Committee on Foreign Relations, *U.S. Assistance to European Economic Recovery,* 80th Congress, 2nd Session, 1948, p. 4.
15. Ibid.
16. Ibid., pp. 589, 591.
17. Ibid., p. 591. John Foster Dulles, a prominent Republican attorney and close adviser to the Department of State, reflected administration assumptions and thinking when he testified in support of the Marshall Plan:

> The importance of unity is clearly brought out by the fact that Western European unity is the feature of the Marshall idea which has particularly aroused Soviet leaders to attack. They are supremely confident that if Western Europe can be kept divided, the governments can, one by one, be discredited and economic conditions made so hopeless that the people will, in despair, accept a Soviet-dictated peace. On the other hand, they know that a unity of upward of 250,000,000 people in Western Europe, industrious and educated as they are, could not easily be reduced even by Soviet power.
> Unity is thus a vital aspect of the present struggle. So long as it is not achieved, Soviet expectations will justifiably be high and their efforts will be prolonged. Once unity is achieved, their struggle will be lost and efforts to prolong it will be abandoned (p. 588).

But, Dulles emphasized—again reflecting a growing sentiment within the administration—German recovery was essential to European recovery.

18. John Gimbel, *The American Occupation of Germany: Politics and the Military, 1945–1949* (Stanford, Calif.: Stanford University Press, 1968) pp. 195–196. Gimbel notes that relations within the Bizonal Economic Council had deteriorated through the latter half of 1947 as internal German political disagreements between the Social Democratic party and the Christian Democrats–Christian Socialists concerning the control of the council and struggles growing out of food shortages brought decision making to a standstill (pp. 186–194).
19. "London Conference Recommendations on Germany: Text of Communique," *Department of State Bulletin,* Vol. 18 (June 20, 1948), p. 808. This discussion is drawn, for the most part, from Gimbel, op. cit., and from Feis, op. cit., pp. 318–323.
20. "London Conference Recommendations on Germany: Explanation of the Conference," *Department of State Bulletin,* Vol. 18 (June 20, 1948). p. 812. The "explanation" under its section on "security" noted French concern explicitly: "The French Government in particular has been acutely aware of the possible dangers inherent in the reconstruction of a German state and the substantial revival of German economy."
21. Ibid., p. 811.
22. Testimony of John Foster Dulles in Hearings before U.S. Congress, Senate Committee on Foreign Relations, *U.S. Assistance to European Economic Recovery,* 80th Congress, 2nd Session, 1948, p. 589.
23. Actually, the confrontation at the November–December 1947 foreign ministers' conference was forecast by Marshall Sokolovsky's vitriolic attacks on the West during a meeting of the Control Council on November 21. See Feis, op. cit., pp. 276–277.

24. See the preceding chapter, and Feis, op. cit., pp. 267–274.
25. Testimony of Secretary of State George C. Marshall before U.S. Congress, Senate Committee on Foreign Relations, *U.S. Assistance to European Economic Recovery,* 80th Congress, 2nd Session, 1948, p. 12.
26. "London Conference Recommendations on Germany: Text of Communique," p. 808.
27. Ibid.; Feis, op. cit., pp. 320–321.
28. John G. Stoessinger, *Nations in Darkness* (New York: Vintage, Random House, 1971), p. 148.
29. Walter Millis, ed., *The Forrestal Diaries* (New York: Viking, 1951), entry dated June 28, 1948, p. 454; quoted by Feis, op. cit., p. 342.
30. Quester, op. cit., 48–49.
31. Quoted by Feis, op. cit., p. 352.
32. This historical review is reconstructed from ibid., pp. 366–383.
33. Ibid., pp. 370–371.
34. Ibid., p. 373.
35. Reprinted from *Present at the Creation* by Dean Acheson. By permission of W. W. Norton, Inc., and Hamish Hamilton, Ltd. Copyright © 1969 by Dean Acheson, p. 272.
36. Ibid., p. 272.
37. Shulman, p. 73.
38. See Acheson, op. cit., 286–292.
39. Ibid., p. 292.
40. Ibid.
41. See ibid.
42. Shulman, op. cit., p. 77.
43. Feis, op. cit., p. 377. Feis's conclusion is drawn from his conversations with many of the participants in these talks carried out during late 1948.
44. Robert E. Osgood, *NATO: The Entangling Alliance* (Chicago: University of Chicago Press, 1962).
45. Ibid., p. 33.
46. Feis, op. cit., p. 377.
47. Walter Millis, *Arms and the State* (New York: Twentieth Century Fund, 1958), p. 237.
48. Osgood, op. cit., pp. 29–31, 36–39.
49. Ibid., p. 30.
50. George F. Kennan, *Memoirs, 1925–1950* (Boston: Little, Brown, 1967) p. 401.
51. Osgood, op. cit., p. 35.
52. U.S. Congress, House Committee on Foreign Affairs, "North Atlantic Treaty Between the United States of America and Other Governments," *Collective Defense Treaties,* 91st Congress, 1st Session, 1969, p. 77.
53. Acheson, op. cit., p. 284.
54. U.S. Congress, Senate Committee on Foreign Relations, *Hearings on the North Atlantic Treaty,* 81st Congress, 1st Session, 1949, p. 47.
55. According to psychohistorian Arnold Rogow, James Forrestal, the first secretary of defense, "regarded the final outcome of the 1948 defense debate as both a personal defeat and conclusive evidence that the nation lacked the leadership and stamina necessary for victory in the Cold War. The personal defeat, he felt, had been administered less by Congress than by Truman, and [Secretary of the Air Force] Symington." On March 28, 1948, Forrestal resigned. On April 2, 1948, he was formally admitted to Bethesda Naval Hospital in Washington. On Sunday, May 22, despondent that what he regarded as a coalition of high administration dupes of Jews and

Communists had chosen him "as their Number One target for liquidation as a consequence of his efforts to alert Americans to the Communist menace," Forrestal leapt
to his death from his sixteenth-floor suite at the hospital. Arnold A. Rogow, *James
Forrestal: A Study of Personality, Politics and Policy* (New York: Macmillan, 1963),
pp. 6–7 and 299.

56. See Paul Y. Hammond, "NSC-68: Prologue to Rearmament," in Schilling et al., op.
cit., pp. 280–282.

57. Cited by Robert Sherrill, "The War Machine," *Playboy*, Vol. 17 (No. 5, 1970), p. 220.

58. Osgood, op. cit., p. 45.

59. Ibid., pp. 46–47.

60. For a discussion of the scenarios thus presented, see Quester, op. cit., p. 32.

61. Wolfe, op. cit., p. 32.

62. Committee on Foreign Affairs, U.S. Congress, *Hearings on Emergency Foreign Aid*,
80th Congress, 1st Session, 1947, p. 14.

63. See Acheson, op. cit., pp. 303–304.

64. Quoted in *China and U.S. Far East Policy 1945–1967* (Washington, D.C.: Congressional Quarterly Service, 1967) p. 45.

65. Quoted in ibid.

66. U.S. Department of State, *United States Relations with China with Special Reference to the Period 1944–1949* (Washington, D.C.: U.S. Government Printing Office,
1949), pp. 358–359.

67. Acheson, op. cit., p. 306.

68. Ibid.

69. Mr. Acheson contends that the analogy was used to emphasize his inability to peer
into the future. He continues: "Of course, any stick is good enough to beat a dog, but
this was an example of my unhappy ability—if I may mix a metaphor—to coin a
stick" (p. 306).

70. Letter of transmittal, *United States Relations with China*, p. xvi.

71. *China and U.S. Far East Policy*, p. 47.

72. NSC-68, described by Dean Acheson as one of the most important documents of
American history, has now been declassified after more than twenty years of secrecy:
NSC-68, A Report to the National Security Council: *United States Objectives and
Programs for National Security* (Washington, D.C.: Photocopied, April 14, 1950).
Hereafter cited as "NSC-68." Previously analyses of it had to be drawn from second-
ary sources. Of these, there is wide consensus that the account of Paul Y. Hammond,
"NSC-68: Prologue to Rearmament," in Schilling et al., op. cit., pp. 305–308, is the
best review. Acheson's autobiography is also useful, especially pp. 344–349 and
373–381.

73. A full review of the memorandum, described by Kennan as "in its implications one
of the most important, if not the most important, of all the documents I ever wrote in
government," may be found in his *Memoirs, 1925–1950*, pp. 471–476.

74. Ibid., p. 474.

75. Acheson, op. cit., p. 347 and Robert J. Donovan, "The Devastating Times: The
Hydrogen Bomb, China, and Korea," *Working Paper* No. 6, Wilson Center, International Security Studies Program, Washington, D.C., April 19, 1979, p. 23.

76. Acheson, op. cit., p. 349.

77. Kennan, op. cit., p. 475 (emphasis in original).

78. Acheson, op. cit., p. 347.

79. Ibid., and Samuel Wells, Jr., "Sounding the Tocsin: NSC-68 and the Soviet Threat,"
Working Paper No. 7, Wilson Center, International Security Studies Program,
Washington, D.C., September 26, 1979, p. 11.

80. "NSC-68," p. 4.

81. Ibid., pp. 6–9.
82. Ibid., pp. 63–64.
83. Ibid., pp. 17–18.
84. Ibid., pp. 54–55.
85. Ibid., pp. 56–57.
86. Ibid., p. 58.
87. Ibid., p. 3
88. Ibid., p. 4.
89. Ibid., p. 48.
90. Ibid., p. 64.
91. Ibid., pp. 39–40.
92. Acheson, op. cit., p. 375.
93. Ibid., p. 376
94. Hammond, op. cit., p. 331.
95. Acheson, op. cit., 374.
96. Hammond, op. cit., pp. 309–318.
97. Acheson, op. cit., p. 375.
98. Hammond, op. cit.
99. Acheson, op. cit., p. 380.
100. Hammond, op. cit., pp. 340–341. As RAND Analyst Paul Hammond notes, there was some effort to incorporate NSC-68 guidelines into Defense Department budgeting in early 1950.

Chapter 4
Korea and the Militarization of Containment

More than anything else, two events, the Soviet Union's first successful atomic test in the fall of 1949 and the Korean War beginning in the late spring of 1950, confirmed the increasingly military definition of America's global role. Indeed, the Soviet test was seen privately as something of a blessing. Acheson relates: "once again the Russians had come to the aid of an imperiled nonpartisan foreign policy, binding wounds and rallying the divided Congress."[1] Similarly, the crisis of communist military action in Asia pushed forward the rearmament advocated in NSC-68. One of Acheson's aides remembered the trepidation which the administration felt when contemplating the "sale" of NSC-68 to the American people: "We were sweating over it, and then . . . thank God, Korea came along."[2]

THE ORIGINS
OF THE FIRST LIMITED WAR

The focus of containment in Asia was vague in NSC-68. As Acheson explained American interests on January 12, 1950, to the National Press Club, "this defensive perimeter runs along the Aleutians to Japan and then goes to the Ryukus [sic] . . . [then] . . . runs from the Ryukus to the Philippine Islands."[3] In defining American interests in this manner, Acheson's analysis seemed like an ambiguous call for local self-help from countries on the mainland. If military attacks were to come, "the initial reliance must be on the people attacked to resist it and then upon the commitments of the entire civilized world under the Charter of the United Nations."[4] The primary threat in these areas was not military aggression, but rather "subversion and penetration that cannot be stopped by military means."[5]

Conspicuous by its absence in this outline of American security interests in Asia was Taiwan. The week before Acheson's speech to the National Press Club, the president had made it clear that the United States had no intention of providing more than economic assistance to

Chiang Kai-shek's government.[6] Indeed, the eventual fall of Taiwan was assumed by the Department of State, which was so certain of Chiang's doom and the fall of Taiwan that ". . . [it] had already prepared and distributed an information paper to be used as a guide for information officers on what they were to say after the Chinese Communists had overrun the islands."[7]

Korea seemed an even more remote concern than Taiwan. Under the postwar occupation agreements the United States had been responsible for the administration of South Korea until reunification under UN auspices could take place. When the Soviets refused to submit the question of Korean reunification to the United Nations, separate administrations were established. As early as 1947, President Truman asked the Joint Chiefs to evaluate the military significance of Korea. In September 1947 they reported "that, from the standpoint of military security, the United States has little strategic interests in maintaining the present troops and bases in Korea."[8]

Nevertheless, both Soviet and American assistance continued to their respective clients during 1948 and 1949. But by 1950 Syngman Rhee, the president of the South Korean regime, was becoming something of an embarrassment to the Americans. He severely restricted civil liberties, balked at holding elections, and did so only after withdrawal of American aid was threatened. Between September 1948 and April 1949 over eighty thousand people were arrested in South Korea. There were sporadic demonstrations in the capital and by October 1949, 7 percent of the national assembly had been jailed by Rhee. By spring of 1950 economic conditions had worsened dramatically. Although Rhee arrested more than two dozen of his opponents prior to the May 30, 1950, elections, he lost heavily, and more than half of the new assembly favored a move toward reunification with the North.[9]

To many in the Truman administration, Rhee was taking on all the attributes of a lesser Chiang Kai-shek. The most explicit public statement of growing ambivalence toward the South Koreans came from Democratic Senator Tom Connally of Texas, the chairman of the Senate Committee on Foreign Relations. Just after the elections, in an interview Senator Connally asserted that South Korea might have to be abandoned.[10] Secretary of State Acheson refused to comment on the Connally interview, thereby heightening the uncertainty, or at a minimum, seeming indifference, of American policy in early May of 1950.

There is little or no evidence that Beijing was in any way involved in the North Korean attack on the South that came in late June. The North Koreans were armed with Soviet weapons and had been trained by Soviet advisers, leading most observers to regard the North Koreans as a Soviet satellite.[11] A victory by the North Korean Communists might benefit the Chinese in that it would undercut the image of American power in Asia. Still, for Beijing, the main military problems remained the conquest of Taiwan and Tibet, the pacification of southern and central China, and the reduction of military expenditures so as to relieve inflationary pressures.[12]

Soviet interest in Korea was long-standing and focused in part on its proximity to Japan and the geopolitical centrality of the peninsula in East Asian politics. It was possible that a communist victory in Korea might lead the Japanese to reconsider their relationship with the Americans. Even if the Americans responded by intensifying their commitment to Japan, the Russians may have reckoned that this would require a drawing down of the American presence in Europe. Then, too, an increased American presence in Asia would contribute to increased Chinese dependence on the Soviets.[13] Thus, for the Soviets, the benefits to be gained from encouraging or allowing a North Korean attack on the South seemed significant, the costs quite acceptable.

The evidence that the Soviets *directed* the attack is inconclusive at best. Next to speculation in the West that Stalin instigated the Korean adventure (he may well have known about it), there is Khrushchev's testimony: "I must stress that war wasn't Stalin's idea, but Kim Il-Sung's. Kim was the initiator."[14] Khrushchev's accusation can be supported. There had been, since 1948, a declining number of Russian advisers in North Korea who might have exercised an effective veto on Kim's action. In 1948 there were one hundred fifty Russians per North Korean army division, but by spring 1950 a State Department historian estimates that there were only from three to eight Russians to advise each North Korean division,[15] perhaps a total of fewer than forty[16] at the moment of attack. Soviet intentions, as interpreted in Washington, were, in the words of Assistant Secretary for Far Eastern Affairs Dean Rusk, "fuzzy."[17] And as Harvard Kremlinologist Adam Ulam speculates:

> The American reaction to the North Korean invasion on June 25 must have been one of the greatest surprises of Stalin's life. Having acquiesced in the loss of China, these unpredictable people now balked at the loss of a territory they themselves had characterized as unimportant. . . . Had there been any inkling . . . the Soviet delegate would not have boycotted the Security Council since January . . . and Moscow would have been ready with diplomatic notes and propaganda campaigns. . . . Between June 27 and July 3, the news from Korea was tucked in the back pages of the Soviet press.[18]

If Korea's place in the U.S. defense perimeter had been left ambiguous in January by Secretary of State Acheson, and very nearly disavowed by his silence in May,[19] then why was it a security interest in June? In part, Korea was seen as an overt communist military attack; that is, the form of communist aggression had changed decisively.[20] But also, the North Korean attack was deemed a Soviet probe by proxy, aimed at Japan. And Japan was most definitely a well-marked American interest. If Korea was perceived by mainland Asians as a bridge for Japanese aggression, the Japanese had historically conceived of Korea as a dagger pointed at their heart. The combination of a weak South Korean regime and a strong Soviet-backed North Korean government, in the analysis of President Truman and his advisers, provided the means for extending communist control of the peninsula at minimal cost.

But to President Truman and his advisers that danger was more than specific to any country. The menace was now aggression and its attendant dangers to global order:

> Communism was acting in Korea just as Hitler, Mussolini, and the Japanese had acted ten, fifteen, and twenty years earlier. I felt certain that if South Korea was allowed to fall Communist leaders would be emboldened to override nations closer to our own shores. If the communists were permitted to force their war into the Republic of Korea without opposition from the free world, no small nation would have the courage to resist threats and aggression by stronger communist neighbors. If this was allowed to go unchallenged it would mean a third world war, just as similar incidents had brought on the second world war.[21]

Thus President Truman's decision to seek a UN mandate for military assistance to the South Koreans, the immediate interpositioning of the Seventh Fleet between Taiwan and the mainland, and increases in assistance to the Philippines and the French in Indochina which grew out of the Korean crisis, were acts to demonstrate American will. In so acting, "the safety and prospects for [the] peace of the free world would be increased."[22] The rationale and the rhetoric should be familiar, for they are virtually synonymous with that of March 1947 . . . or August 1964. Even if the substantive essence of the Truman Doctrine might remain European, its applicable limits now became global.

NSC-68 summarized this notion about the integrity of world order and also predicted military probes and feints by the Soviets that had to be answered. Otherwise, as Acheson explained, "To back away from this challenge [in Korea] would be highly destructive of the power and prestige of the United States. By prestige I mean the shadow cast by power, which is of great deterrent importance."[23] Thus, the United States would escalate its commitment, for if the aggressor was not stopped on the frontiers of containment, then the integrity of the entire concept would be compromised. If the commitment were debased, it would indicate a lack of will to defend the heart of the system—Europe. Korea was not, therefore, essential in the same sense as Germany or Britain. Nonetheless, President Truman and his advisers were convinced that "the Korean situation [was] vital as a *symbol of the strength and determination of the West.*"[24]

To President Truman and his advisers, intervention in Korea held great dangers. First, there was the danger of world war. Once the decision had been made to use force, the possibility increased that the violence might get out of hand and escalate into a Soviet-American confrontation. Consequently, an overriding consideration was keeping the Soviets out of the conflict. At the very outset, therefore, the Soviets were not accused of starting the war. They were simply asked to disavow any responsibility for the attack. Some observers have suggested that this approach by the United States, when combined with President Truman's reluctance to equate explicitly the Soviet Union with communism in his June 27 statement, indicates that the United States was not convinced that the Soviets had started the war.[25] In any event, the Soviets replied that the South Koreans had started the fight and that they (the Soviets) advocated a policy of noninterference by outside powers in Korea. Secretary Acheson and the State Department's Russian experts took this response, the lack of any further follow-up by the Soviets, and the cumulating string of North Korean victories as conclusive evidence that the Soviets would not intervene in the short run.[26]

There was also concern about Chinese intervention, although here the immediate threat was perceived to be an attack on Taiwan. Ostensibly this was the basis for moving the Seventh Fleet into the Taiwan Strait. President Truman recognized, however, that Communist Chinese intervention might be provoked by Chiang Kai-shek's actions. Consequently, he called upon Chiang to cease all actions against the mainland and declined, on Secretary Acheson's advice, the offer by Chiang and General Douglas MacArthur of some thirty thousand Nationalist Chinese troops.

The delicacy of the Nationalist Chinese position in the crisis was compounded by the militancy of the China lobby in the United States, and also by the presence in Asia of General MacArthur, who had long disagreed with the European focus of American policy. Ironically, this European orientation of U.S. policymakers allowed General MacArthur to build for himself, in Asia after the war, a position of considerable personal power and a network of personal contacts and confidences among East Asian anticommunists including a strong attachment to Chiang and his cause. A European-oriented White House, State Department, and Defense Department were prepared to leave the administration of American policy—which was primarily occupation policy—to the Supreme Commander of the Allied Powers in Tokyo. From his

Pacific command in Tokyo, General MacArthur possessed power and authority comparable to that of a head of state, powers never before possessed by an American military man. Indeed, his staff compared him to Napoleon and Alexander.[27] As President Truman put it later, "there was never anybody around to keep him in line. . . . He just wouldn't let anybody near him who wouldn't kiss his ass . . . there were many times when he was . . . out of his head."[28]

From his position of virtual control of American military and political policy in Asia, General MacArthur was uniquely situated to assist Chiang and Rhee in their struggle for survival. In late 1949 Rhee had sought out General MacArthur's help in obtaining an increase in American arms. Almost simultaneously the South Korean defense minister stated after a conference with General MacArthur "that he would gladly march on Pyongyang," the North Korean capital. Also in early 1950, Rhee visited General MacArthur in Tokyo, outlined his increasingly desperate position, and reportedly called for an Asian anticommunist crusade under General MacArthur's leadership.[29]

The MacArthur problem would eventually dominate war and domestic policy, but in the meantime a buildup of military forces was culminating on both sides of the 38th parallel. From March 1949 until June 1950, Rhee expanded his military forces from 114,000 to more than 150,000 men. Rhee's American arms were light weapons, perhaps reflecting U.S. anxiety concerning his intentions.[30] In contrast, the North Koreans began a rapid buildup of their forces to a level of 135,000 men after January 1950, with large shipments of Soviet equipment, including armor, arriving as late as April and May. Despite the North Korean advantages in armor, American intelligence, fully aware of the mini-arms race then underway, reported that Rhee was fully capable of defending the South.[31]

Tensions between the two Korean governments grew steadily. Philip Jessup, a State Department official, declared in April 1950 that "the boundary at the 38th parallel . . . is a real front line. There is constant fighting. . . . There are very real battles, involving one or two thousand men."[32] As one authority on Korea, Robert Simmons, summed up the situation: "Koreans were accustomed to the fighting and the possibility of war; each side believed that an early unification was worth a war."[33] As tensions and arms increased along the 38th parallel, John Foster Dulles (then acting as Republican special consultant to the State Department) visited Asia. In a speech before the South Korean national assembly on June 18, 1950, Dulles struck a rather different note than indicated by Secretary of State Acheson in his January "defense perimeter" speech. Dulles denounced the North Koreans and then added, concerning South Korea, "you are not alone. You will never be alone as long as you continue to play worthily your part in the great design of human freedom."[34] Dulles did not promise any specific form of aid. But these statements before a national assembly controlled by Rhee's opponents must have encouraged Rhee—and frightened the North Koreans. After leaving Korea, Dulles traveled to Tokyo, and after meeting with General MacArthur made vague references to positive action by the United States in the future.

Thus the circumstances surrounding the outbreak of fighting in Korea remain, after three decades, confusing. The American perception of the importance of the peninsula was deeply divided between MacArthur's desire for action and Washington's ambivalence, which was resolved only when the fighting began. The calculus of interests regarding the motives of the Soviet Union, China, and the two Koreas is no less controversial. But the hazy facts now surrounding the origins of the Korean War did not inhibit the crystallization of a policy consensus that allowed President Truman to insert swiftly an American military presence in Korea when the apparent North Korean attack came on June 25, 1950.[35] Stewart Alsop remembered that even George Kennan (now, in 1950, seen as an iconoclast in his views about how to manage Soviet power) did a "jig of delight" on hearing that the United States would now confront "Stalin's carefully calculated challenge in Korea."[36]

THE "FOG OF WAR"

On the morning of June 24, 1950 (June 25, Korean time), about ninety thousand men of the Korean People's Army of North Korea (KPA), supported by more than one hundred Russian-built T-34 tanks, crossed the 38th parallel, the border between North and South Korea.[37] Within hours the North Koreans were claiming that their forces had pushed ten to fifteen miles into the Republic of Korea. Confusion as to what was happening was extensive. At least one official in General MacArthur's headquarters in Tokyo believed that the South Koreans had attacked the North Koreans. Some observers characterized events as a complete surprise followed by the fairly rapid collapse of South Korean resistance. Other, more skeptical analysts have suggested that the Republic of Korea (ROK) Army recovered quickly from a North Korean surprise attack, launched a counterattack, and had established a more or less stable defensive line by June 26.[38]

In any case, news in Washington throughout June 27 and 28 was still confused. General MacArthur and Syngman Rhee predicted imminent collapse. But other journalistic sources suggested that any report from the battlefield had to be viewed cautiously.[39] Hanson Baldwin, military correspondent of *The New York Times*, reported on June 29: "The normal fog of war—greatly accentuated in the Korean campaign by the paucity of communications—has left Washington with insufficient information to determine with precision our future course."[40]

The response in Washington to these perplexing reports was, nonetheless, decisive. Secretary of State Acheson had received the news from Korea, and before contacting the president—who was in Independence, Missouri, on family business—requested that the UN Security Council be called into session. The council met on the afternoon of June 25. Absent was the Russian delegate, who was boycotting the council over the issue of its exclusion of the People's Republic of China as the legitimate representative of China to the United Nations. An American-drafted resolution was quickly passed, which labeled the North Koreans aggressors and demanded their withdrawal from the South.[41]

By June 26 President Truman had returned to Washington. There he received an alarming message from General MacArthur: "South Korean units unable to resist determined Northern offensive. . . . [O]ur estimate is that a complete collapse is imminent."[42] Mr. Truman has recorded his reaction to this message:

> There was now no doubt! The Republic of Korea needed help at once if it was not to be overrun. . . . I told my advisers that what was developing in Korea seemed to me like a repetition on a large scale of what had happened in Berlin. The Reds were probing for weaknesses in our armor; we had to meet their thrust without getting embroiled in a world-wide war.[43]

President Truman was prepared, in short, to assume the worst, draw what were becoming the conventional analogies of his administration, and move.

The president ordered American air and naval forces into action in support of what were assumed, in Washington, to be retreating South Korean units. The President then requested that the UN Security Council meet again the next day, June 27, and recommend that the member states provide assistance to South Korea. The council was thus put in the position of meeting to consider whether it should approve sanctions against the North Koreans that the United States had already initiated. Inasmuch as the council had already declared the North Koreans aggressors on June 25, the decision was a foregone conclusion. The Security Council passed a resolution that recommended that "members of the United Nations furnish such assistance to the Republic of Korea as may be necessary to repel the armed attack and to restore international peace and security in the area."[44] The command of UN forces was under General Douglas MacArthur. It was clear, therefore, that the UN effort in Korea would be United States conceived, administered, and implemented.

THE LIMITED WAR AT HOME:
DOMESTIC POLITICS AND REARMAMENT

The Korean War cannot be understood as merely a military operation, a case study in the problems of limited war[45] or primarily a problem of civil-military relations.[46] It was also seen by the Truman administration as a crucial part of the complex and interrelated domestic and foreign milieu of 1950.

Domestic Politics

The concept of a limited war was never completely understood by the American people. This was due in some measure to the combination of President Truman's actions and his hyperbolic rhetoric. As the war progressed, the public grew uneasy with the notion that the United States was circumscribing its military activities both geographically and in terms of the means employed. Discontent was perhaps increased by the fact that many of the men called upon to carry the brunt of this limited war had only five years earlier brought to a successful close a massive total war effort. Moreover, World War II had been conducted so as to crush the same forces of aggression that were said now to be loose again.

Exacerbating the domestic situation immeasurably was a second factor: an executive-legislative struggle with conservative Republicans pitched against President Truman and Secretary of State Acheson. The battle was engaged by men with mixed motives, who had not held the presidency and had held a congressional majority only once in twenty years. Conservatives such as senators Knowland, Bridges, Jenner, Wherry, Taft, and McCarthy are frequently identified as isolationists in that they attacked the Truman administration's deepening involvement in Europe. Curiously, however, these same men assailed Truman, Marshall, and Acheson for not doing enough in Asia to stop the spread of communism. The inconsistency is striking and confusing unless one admits the possibility that the majority of congressional Republicans as well as a significant portion of congressional Democrats were simply ideological conservatives opposed to every facet of Truman's public policy as crypto–New Dealism. The backdrop of conservative suspicion was what they saw as Roosevelt's "treasonous maneuvering" over Eastern Europe. The only remedy suggested by Republicans to amend Roosevelt's perfidy was liberation, not containment. Containment was seen as involving coexistence with, and thus the continuation of communism—not its destruction. And to many conservatives the final proof that containment would not work could now be found in Asia: first in Mao Zedong's success in China and now in the attack on South Korea.

Under these circumstances, Truman administration policy in Asia became a target of criticism from the right. Republicans reproached Truman not for any love they may have had for Asia (although this was undoubtedly the case for a few of Truman's critics such as Congressman Walter Judd, wo had a long personal attachment as a missionary doctor in China prior to Mao's victory), but simply because containment in Asia was beset by difficulties in contrast with the apparent success of containment in Europe.

The expediency of the conservative position is apparent: Republicans could support Truman's decision to intervene in Korea while simultaneously criticizing the administration's policy for having brought on the attack in the first place. They charged that all of this could have been avoided if the Truman administration had been willing to commit U.S. troops and greater aid to save China and support Asian anticommunists such as Syngman Rhee. Ironically these were the same conservatives who supported Truman's reduction of U.S. conventional military strength and advocated a greater reliance upon air power.

The Senator from Wisconsin: "A Pig in a Minefield"[47]

Perhaps the best example of the political opportunism underlying much of the attack from the right is to be found in the rise of Senator Joseph McCarthy to national prominence. Beginning in February 1950 and continuing until December 1954, Senator McCarthy maintained that the U.S. government was and had been for a decade infiltrated with Communists, former Communists, communist sympathizers, and unknowing instruments of communism. Their presence throughout the government, but especially in the Department of State, was the explanation for all the failures of American foreign policy during the preceding decade. Their influence explained the willingness of the Roosevelt administration to accept the Soviets in Central Europe and, above all, communist influence among the Department of State's Asian experts explained the loss of China.[48]

On February 9, 1950, Senator McCarthy unveiled his blunderbuss: "While I cannot take the time to name all the men in the State Department who had been named as members of the Communist Party and members of a spy ring, I have here in my hand a list of two hundred and five that were known to the Secretary of State as being members of the

Communist Party and who, nevertheless, are still working and shaping policy in the State Department."[49] On other occasions Senator McCarthy referred to 207, 57, 10, 116, 121, 106, and 81 Communists in "foggy bottom," and sometimes he merely spoke of a "lot" of subversives. In July a Senate committee and then a full vote of Congress attested that there was nothing to Senator McCarthy's charges. But Republicans, as journalist David Halberstam writes, "welcomed him; the more they assaulted the Democrats the better for the Republicans." "Joe," said John Bricker, one of the more traditional conservatives and a candidate for vice president in 1944, "You're a real SOB. But sometimes it is useful to have SOB's around to do the dirty work."[50]

The assault on Democratic and State Department integrity and patriotism was a clever strategy. It explained how it was that Americans were now fighting a curious war in Asia without confronting the complexities and ambiguities of world politics and American policies: There were traitors in high places. Moreover, it appealed to America's alienated and preyed on an endemic fear deeply rooted in American society: the fear that America might not be equal to the task of global involvement.[51] Senator McCarthy's answer was reassuring: America's difficulties were not the product of inexperience and naivete, but rather treason.

Senator McCarthy was a much-sought speaker. He coveted the publicity that rapidly came to him. His simplistic views articulated the fears and confusion of many Americans. In time, it would be demonstrated that he "was in many ways the most gifted demagogue that ever lived on these shores. No bolder seditionist ever moved among us—nor any politician with a surer, swifter access to the dark places of the American mind."[52] But even in early 1954, as he neared censure in the U.S. Senate, 50 percent of the American people held a favorable opinion of him; only 29 percent reacted negatively. "It was a melancholy time," Richard Rovere has observed, "and the Chief Justice of the United States was probably right when he said at the time that if the 'Bill of Rights were put to a vote, it would lose.' "[53]

McCarthy's meteoric rise made him the rallying point for the rather large number of Americans who found American foreign policy under Harry Truman confusing and burdensome. It was this characteristic that made Senator McCarthy attractive to the Republican leadership in the Senate, including "Mr. Republican," Senator Robert A. Taft.

Senator Taft's association with McCarthy is striking in view of Taft's reputation for conservative probity and sensitivity to civil liberties, all of which was in contrast with McCarthy's insensitivity and demagogic excesses. However, Senator Taft wanted the Republican presidential nomination in 1952, and he was going to do nothing that would cost him the support of conservative Senate Republicans. When it became clear that the center of Republican opinion, searching for any means to strike at Truman, had begun to move with or was at least willing to tolerate McCarthy, Taft abandoned his early uneasiness with McCarthy and began to support him. Senator Taft began castigating "the procommunist group in the State Department who surrendered to every demand of Russia at Yalta and Potsdam, and promoted at every opportunity the communist cause in China."[54] Taft's biographer, William W. White, has said of the senator at this time, "it seemed to some of his friends and admirers that he began, if unconsciously, to adopt the notion that almost *any* way to defeat or discredit the Truman plans was acceptable. There was . . . a blood in the nostrils approach."[55]

On June 2, 1950, Senator Margaret Chase Smith, Republican of Maine, issued what she termed a "Declaration of Conscience" in which she attacked the Republican leadership. She noted, "The nation sorely needs a Republican victory. But I do not want to see the Republican Party ride to political victory on the Four Horsemen of Calumny—fear, ignorance, bigotry, and smear."[56] It is a mark of the effects of Truman's stunning victory in 1948 on Robert Taft and the Republican party, Taft's personal ambition, and the fear and the polarization brought about by McCarthy, that Senator Taft could not or would not associate himself with Senator Smith's declaration.[57]

Rearmament

Against this backdrop of increasing vitriolic conservative opposition, President Truman sought to use the emergency of Korea and, subsequently, Chinese intervention in the war, to flesh out the framework of NSC-68. As Paul Nitze, chairman of the committee that drafted NSC-68, recalled:

> The dilemma involved in choosing between an unbalanced budget, higher taxes, and more stringent economic controls on the one hand, and an adequate military posture on the other was not resolved at the policy decision level until some three months prior to the outbreak of the North Korean aggression. Those decisions were translated into specific action *only after* the aggression into South Korea had given *concrete and bloody confirmation to the conclusions already produced by analysis.*[58]

By the end of 1951, total requests for defense spending had reached $74 billion. NSC-68 had argued that American defense spending expand from $13.5 billion to $50 billion. The added difference of some $24 billion represented the cost of Korea *per se* and a sudden inflationary surge to the economy under the impact of war. The sheer magnitude of this defense spending is awesome given the defense budgets and philosophy that had existed for the past several years. Even more important, however, was the programmatic content of the requests, for what was being funded carried implications far beyond Korea.

The fiscal year 1952 budget request reflected the administration's decision to go over to a basically conscript army. The president asked that draft authority be extended to 1955 and a permanent military obligation of eight years total and two years active duty be imposed on all males between the ages of eighteen and twenty-six. Expansion of the American overseas military base system was proposed to Congress. More than seventy new bases and support facilities were to be constructed in the United States, North Africa, and the Middle East. The Air Force was to be placed within striking range of the Soviet Union, expanded, and its strike capability augmented by the decision to deploy a new bomber, the B-47. The construction of atomic weapons forged ahead to the point that the secretary of the air force could claim in November 1951 that the United States had entered the age of atomic plenty. At the same time, the last technical problems standing in the way of a thermonuclear device or hydrogen bomb were surmounted in the spring of 1951. The Navy was in no sense left out of this quantum jump in American global capability. With virtually no opposition, the Congress approved $2.4 billion in fleet construction and modernization. Included in this program was the first super-carrier, the fifty-seven-thousand-ton *Forrestal,* and the first nuclear submarine, the *Nautilus.* If, as envisaged in NSC-68, a "year of maximum peril" was closing on the United States in 1953 or 1954, the Truman administration would be ready.

In 1951 the foundations were also established for a permanent U.S. defense presence in Asia. Most important was the Japanese Peace Treaty, signed in September 1951. The treaty simultaneously excluded any Russian involvement in the future of Japan and ensured future American basing. The Japanese treaty was supplemented by a similar arrangement with the Philippines and a third mutual security treaty with Australia and New Zealand. An increase in aid to the French in Indochina was also extended. Finally, the administration moved toward permanent support of Chiang Kai-shek's regime on Taiwan as U.S. military assistance increased.

In short, the fiscal year 1952 budget that went before and was approved by Congress in 1951 provided the basis for the expanded military capability envisaged by NSC-68. But there was more to Truman's budget than a request for increased spending; he also proposed increasing the number of American troops stationed in Europe. In so doing, Truman sparked a great debate on both sides of the Atlantic: with Senator Taft, on the one hand, attacking the premises of the president's policy, and with the Europeans, on the other hand, concerned with the future of NATO.

The Great Debate

Truman's announcement on December 19, 1950, that now U.S. troops would be needed in Europe prompted Senator Taft to argue for a "re-examination" of the entire course of postwar foreign policy. Taft charged that Truman, "without authority . . . involved us in the Korean War. Without authority he is now attempting a similar policy in Europe. This matter must be debated."[59] Taft did not wish to return to the old isolationism of one hemisphere hegemony but the senator was bothered by the financial and constitutional costs involved in securing and maintaining a global role. Thus, he implored the Truman administration to "not assume obligations by treaty or otherwise which require any extensive use of American land forces."[60] The defense of Japan and an unequivocal commitment to Chiang Kai-shek were exceptions, Taft argued, but the American obligation to Europe was fulfilled with the mere existence of NATO—nothing else was mandated.[61] Otherwise the country's economy would be seriously distorted through a disastrously inflated economy, deficit spending, and hence a mortgaged future. To control a spiraling arms budget would require, according to Senator Taft, wage and price controls—controls that would eventually extend to other dimensions of American life. In short, the very antithesis of the free-market capitalist domestic system that comprised the ideological bedrock for conservatives such as himself.[62]

The only recourse, to Senator Taft and his followers, was a defense policy predicated upon air and naval superiority. Taft also called for an aggressive effort to sell the American system abroad by means of propaganda and, where necessary, clandestine infiltration and support of "those millions who yearn for liberty in satellite countries. . . ."[63] Sympathetic elements of Soviet-bloc nations would be cultivated, for Taft hoped that they "may be organized to seize power wherever they have support of their fellow citizens."[64] Senator Taft recognized the irony implicit in this policy: It would rely on the very methods of those he would fight.[65] But it was essential, he believed, to pursue a course of subversion and propaganda if a limited military posture was to succeed.

Three days after Senator Taft spoke, a resolution was introduced into the Senate by the conservatives that would require congressional action before any troops could be moved to Europe. During February and March of 1951, the administration sent a parade of witnesses before the Senate Foreign Relations Committee to counter Senator Taft's position, including his proposition that the president did not, in fact, already have the authority to move the troops to Europe. Similarly, military leaders including General Dwight Eisenhower testified in favor of European deployment. Administration officials led by Acheson and Marshall emphasized that the United States was thinking in terms of four to six divisions. By April 1951 conservative opposition began to diminish[66], and the Senate acted on President Truman's request, passing a retroactive endorsement of the president's decision and approving the appointment of General Eisenhower as NATO commander.

CONVENTIONAL FORCES FOR NATO: PLANS AND STALEMATE

Parallelling the great debate in the United States was another within NATO. The outbreak of fighting in Korea provided the Truman administration with some leverage on the stalemated situation within the NATO alliance. Prior to the Soviet acquisition of atomic weapons, American planning for the defense of Europe was based solely on the deterrent capacity of American atomic superiority. The Soviets' test explosion in 1949 brought American deterrence into question. The American nuclear umbrella to others, now, at least potentially, was a risk. First, the umbrella could be swept away if the Soviets ever attained the ability to launch a disarming blow. Second, sharing the American umbrella implied that an ally was not only a target but also, perhaps, a negotiable asset. After all, the French, Germans, and British would muse, why would America want to risk Chicago for Dusseldorf or Lyons? Could not European targets become chips in a great power poker game unless the Europeans became equipped to play the game too and obtained nuclear weapons for themselves?

The questions were still hypothetical. Most Europeans continued to believe, and correctly, that American military predominance would not be effectively undercut for some time to come. The problem was viewed with greater urgency in the United States and especially by Secretary of State Acheson. The conclusion of NSC-68—that rearmament should begin immediately in both the United States and NATO—was in anticipation of a nuclear stalemate predicted to materialize in the mid-1950s. By then, it was estimated, the balance of conventional forces would assume overriding importance.

Consequently the American position at the foreign ministers' meeting of the North Atlantic Council in May 1950 was that planning for increased European conventional forces was essential. For their part, the Europeans were reluctant to move rapidly toward reinvigorating their military establishments. They feared that an emphasis on rearmament would divert scarce resources away from the continuing economic re-construction of Europe including a proposal for integrating the coal and steel industries of Europe as "the setting-up of common foundations for economic development as a first step in the federation of Europe."[67]

From the very outset the concept upon which NATO conventional force planning was based was weakened by what proved to be an ir-resolvable tension between the needs of imperial powers, such as the French, Dutch, Belgian and Portuguese, to retain control of crumbling empires and the requirements of a collective ground force. In the end, the NATO allies settled for a vague statement of principle and an equally vague concession from the Americans and the British that they would increase their levels of participation in the defense of the continent. Obviously, there was another source of manpower—Germany. But the idea of German rearmament was still very nearly unmentionable given French sensitivity to a new *Wehrmacht*.[68] Hence on the eve of the Ko-rean War the NATO allies were forced to admit that there were grave differences between their rhetoric and the resources they were willing to commit to any collective effort.

The outbreak of the Korean War caused some movement on these problems. American assistance was now predicated upon an increased effort on the part of the Europeans.[69] Truman skillfully forced the issue by linking his announcement of the increased American contribution to NATO with an insistence that the question of a German contribution be confronted at the September 1950 NATO conference where a forward strategy for the defense of Europe was adopted. A conventional defense of Western Europe as far east as possible clearly required troop levels above those that the Europeans were prepared to raise. Thus the NATO council also accepted, as a matter of great urgency, the consideration of how the Germans might best be integrated into the common effort and formally approved the idea of an integrated military force under a cen-tralized command structure. Still, the precise nature of German partici-pation in all of this was not resolved. Nor could the issue be forced by the Americans in view of European uneasiness with the entire notion of German rearmament. However, it was clear that the Germans would be integrated in some way into the European army concept that now seemed to be emerging.

Yet, as one authority, Robert Osgood, has noted, there was great uncertainty as to just what kind of aggression would be deterred by the NATO structure, whether skeletal or fully muscled. Acheson does not seem to have believed that the Russians could be matched along every military dimension, but he and the Joint Chiefs clearly sought to avoid Europe's being overrun. However, this seemed to require a NATO force of almost one hundred divisions. As Robert Osgood observes, "Yet in

1951 it was already obvious that only the fear of imminent invasion . . . could conceivably inspire the Europeans to make sufficient contribution of men, money, and equipment to support a strategic objective which the United States herself expected to support primarily with airpower."[70]

By 1951, however, the Korean emergency lost its catalytic force as negotiations for a cease fire began. Moreover, throughout Europe, rearmament cut into the social welfare efforts of European governments and brought on the defeat of the Labor government in Britain and the reassumption of power by Winston Churchill in 1951. Churchill immediately emphasized his belief that nuclear deterrence was still quite valid. Although he agreed that NATO's conventional forces were a problem, he stated that the British would have to stretch out their general armament plan; similar problems and sentiments emerged throughout Western Europe. When the Truman administration announced that its fiscal year 1953 budget would show some cuts in defense spending, it was a clear signal to Europeans that military imperatives could be compromised in the face of domestic political and economic realities.[71]

UP AND DOWN THE KOREAN PENINSULA

In the meantime, the military events that had given rise to the great debate and the parallel intra-alliance negotiations were approaching a turning point. General MacArthur had consolidated the UN position at the tip of the South Korean peninsula around Pusan and was preparing to take the offensive—an offensive that would crush the North Korean army, pull the Chinese into the war, and bring the general and the president into conflict *mano a mano*.

MacArthur Takes the Offensive

By September 1950 four American divisions had been committed to Korea—twice what General MacArthur had first requested—and they had been driven with their backs to the sea in the Pusan perimeter. Nevertheless, UN troop strength began to mount until it surpassed that of the North Koreans. Total UN air superiority complicated the North Koreans' position, for their lines of supply now stretched the length of the peninsula and were therefore very vulnerable to air interdiction. Even as the North Koreans pushed deep into the South, General MacArthur had begun planning for an amphibious landing far in their rear at the port city of Inchon on the west coast of the Korean peninsula just west of Seoul below the 38th parallel. Simultaneously, UN forces would break out of the Pusan perimeter, push up the peninsula, and link up with General MacArthur's forces at the 38th parallel. The landing at Inchon would be extremely dangerous: One military planner said, "We drew up a list of every conceivable natural and geographic handicap and Inchon had 'em all."[72] But General MacArthur did not heed nearly unanimous advice. Instead, in his own words, he heard "the voice of his father telling him years before 'Doug, councils of war breed timidity. . . .'" And General MacArthur was nothing if he was not bold.[73]

The Joint Chiefs came to Korea to counsel against the adventure and refused General MacArthur what he considered an adequate number of Marines for the assault. Rear Admiral James Doyle, his amphibious commander, said, "I have not been asked . . . my opinion about this landing. If I were asked however, the best I can say is that Inchon is not possible."[74] Inchon had incredible tides. Water would rise and then fall some thirty feet each day. As the tide came wooshing out, vast banks of mud reaching some three miles from shore were exposed. Some landing assault and troop vehicles drew twenty-nine feet of water; there were only two days each year when high tide would be up enough to allow the vessels to port at the harbor of Inchon. Even then the LSTs would have only two or three hours to debark their Marines—not on the beach, for there was none, but on a concrete seawall—before they would be pounded into the murky slime of Inchon. Not only were the logistics difficult, the purported advantage of surprise, the key to the operation, had been lost for some time. In Japan the plans for the assault had become a topic of barroom conversation, where it was termed "operation common knowledge." Indeed, the landing preceded a Korean mine-laying effort by a hairsbreadth. Yet it was undeniable that if the two phases of the operation, the assault from the sea and the drive from the south, could be carried out, the North Korean army would be trapped between the pincers of General MacArthur's UN force. If it worked, the original objectives of the UN action would be attained.

On September 15, 1950, the Inchon landing was effected with remarkably low casualties. Within two days, the port was secured and the push toward Seoul began as UN troops began to rush up from their enclave in the South. By September 23 North Korean resistance was collapsing. And by September 26 virtually the entire North Korean army had been cut off and destroyed, with only thirty thousand North Koreans able to retreat across the 38th parallel. On September 27, 1950, Seoul was retaken after terrible destruction, described by one historian as "apocalyptic"—the result of massive U.S. firepower turned on the city.[75] By the end of September UN forces were back on the 38th parallel.

After Inchon, the military momentum grew infectiously. General

MacArthur apparently assumed from the outset that his mandate extended to the military reunification of Korea.[76] But after the collapse of the North Korean army resistance his ambitious designs for Korea became the Western norm. Louis Halle remembers:

> The political leaders in Washington, in London, and elsewhere were themselves in a state of *hubris* brought on by success after long failure. They were themselves swept along by the momentum of victory, and they allowed themselves to be swept along the more readily because anything else was politically impossible for them.[77]

With victory, Washington now believed that American power could control events beyond the 38th parallel. President Truman was preparing to go beyond containment into the uncharted terrain of liberation.

There were, of course, domestic political considerations that undoubtedly influenced Truman's decision. The Republican leadership had already announced that it would regard failure of the administration to go north of the 38th parallel as evidence of appeasement. In addition, there were midterm elections coming up in November. Total victory in Korea on the eve of the elections would, perhaps, undercut the McCarthyites. Domestic realities, therefore, limited Truman's ability or willingness to respond to Chinese hints of a desire for a political settlement or take seriously similar Soviet proposals in early October 1950. The forward dynamic of policy was gathering and on September 30, 1950, UN Ambassador Warren Austin submitted a U.S.-drafted resolution calling on UN forces to take measures "to ensure conditions of stability throughout Korea."[78] The UN General Assembly approved overwhelmingly the motion which sanctified the destruction of North Korean military forces and unifying the country under a UN command led by General MacArthur. There is some evidence that George Kennan and others at the Department of State did have reservations about the American advance toward China.[79] These men, however, were precisely those toward whom McCarthy was then directing his withering fire. It was a time, as one inside observer could remember, when "a noble boldness, rather than a craven timidity, became the order of the day—and everyone wanted to be identified with it."[80]

Sinologist and former intelligence official Harold Hinton described how the Chinese must have felt about events in Korea:

> [O]ne need only imagine American reaction if a large Soviet army, under an especially anti-American commander, were to move up the Lower California peninsula toward the California frontier. The analogy is improved if

one further imagines that Southern California is the main heavy industrial region in the United States, as Manchuria was (and is) in the CPR.[81]

The Chinese were not coy or hesitant in airing their view of the imminent collapse of North Korea. In late September the chief of staff of the Chinese People's Liberation Army informed the Indian ambassador to China that the People's Republic would not "sit back with folded hands and let the Americans come to the border." Again, on September 30, Zhou Enlai gave a public warning: "The Chinese people . . . will not supinely tolerate seeing their neighbors being savagely invaded by the imperialists." Chinese warnings were accompanied by a redeployment of their best troops into the Yalu frontier area. American intelligence was aware of the troops, although their exact disposition and intentions remained unclear.[82] Finally, on October 1, when ROK units entered North Korea, the Indian ambassador was called. In a midnight meeting he was informed by Zhou that although the Chinese were not concerned about the South Koreans, the movement of U.S. troops north of the 38th parallel would be regarded by the Chinese as a reason for Chinese entry into the war. Professor Allen S. Whiting, a former State Department official, notes, "In the next few days Washington received additional reports of [Zhou's] warning through allied and neutral channels and through American embassies in Moscow, Stockholm, London and New Delhi."[83] Evidently, President Truman brushed aside Zhou Enlai's warnings by discounting the credibility of the Indian ambassador who served as the channel of communication.[84] And Secretary of State Acheson, astonishingly, asserted that Zhou was not an authoritative spokesman.[85]

Mao Zedong, General MacArthur, and Harry Truman: Three's a Crowd

The political *hubris* that attended General MacArthur's punch toward the north on October 7 seemed to sweep away doubts about Chinese ability or interest in Korea. The peninsula would be unified by the victorious UN juggernaut. On October 9, President Truman informed General MacArthur:

> Hereafter in the event of the open or covert employment anywhere in Korea of major Chinese Communist units, without prior announcement, you should continue the action as long as, in your judgment, action by forces now under your control offers a reasonable chance of success.[86]

Moreover, Truman also seemed ready at least to consider actions against China itself. In place of the earlier absolute prohibition on operations against China, the commander-in-chief closed his October 9 dispatch to

General MacArthur with the cryptic statement: "In any case you will obtain authorization from Washington prior to taking any military action against objectives in Chinese Territory."[87]

Since the North Koreans had been beaten, China made repeated attempts to explain that they were concerned about their own security more than they fretted over the future of a fraternal communist state. The Chinese even hinted that they might be able to live with the conquest of North Korea, providing that North Korea were occupied by South Koreans and the Americans stayed below the 38th parallel. Even after U.S. troops crossed the 38th parallel, the Chinese indicated that they could live with a rump North Korean state that would buffer China's Manchurian boundary.[88] Mao Zedong, it has been reported, was up seventy-two hours before making his decision, which took effect October 16, when Chinese General Lin Biao's Fourth Field Army began crossing the Yalu at night and in secret.

On October 19 the North Korean capital of Pyongyang fell to American forces and General MacArthur prepared to press on for his much-heralded quick victory. North Korean Premier Kim fled to the Yalu, leaving behind vast supplies of military equipment. Soon the North Korean defeat turned into a rout. U.S. soldiers parachuted in front of the retreating Koreans and Kim's forces began to surrender *en masse*. By the end of October more than 135,000 North Koreans had been captured.

General MacArthur's plan called for the Eighth Army to move up the west coast of Korea to the Yalu River and the Tenth Corps to move toward the Yalu somewhat farther east. But the spine of mountains running down the middle of the peninsula separated the two elements of General MacArthur's force by more than fifty guerrilla-filled miles. The Chinese would exploit this tactical blunder within weeks. But in mid-October General MacArthur and his commanding general were eyeing an early and easy victory. Lt. General Walton H. Walker, the commander of the Eighth Army, for instance, thought the entire advance was not unlike a quail shoot in his native Texas.[89] On October 24, 1950, General MacArthur ordered his commanders to move all units, Korean and non-Korean, forward to the Yalu, thus violating Joint Chiefs directives of late September. When reminded of this by Washington, General MacArthur cited a personal message of Marshall's giving MacArthur tactical and strategic discretion. The matter was dropped. Was it reasonable, Washington pondered, to countermand the man who had masterminded the amazing Inchon landing? By October 26, elements of a South Korean division on the American Eighth Army's eastern flank reached the Yalu; that night they were surrounded by Chinese Communist troops, ambushed, and sent fleeing south, encountering Chinese ambushes throughout the withdrawal.

By November 1 U.S. forces were heavily engaged by Chinese troops. Yet, on November 7, curiously, almost as swiftly as the Chinese had attacked, they broke off contact. During this two-week period MacArthur's analysis of what was taking place along the front swung from optimism to deep pessimism. He urgently requested and received permission to bomb the Yalu River bridges, and then, once his request was satisfied, he manifested a kind of befuddled optimism. General MacArthur was still not prepared to view those initial, sharp contacts with the Chinese as conclusive proof of Chinese intervention.

On November 15 he proposed to the Joint Chiefs that he press forward with his advance. But November 15 was the date the Communist Chinese had been invited to the United Nations to discuss the Taiwan situation and perhaps Korea as well. Nevertheless, Washington approved MacArthur's advance. In the meantime, the Chinese announced that their arrival at the United Nations would be delayed until November 24. Inexplicably, MacArthur delayed his attack until then, and on that date he pressed forward again announcing that the "boys would be home by Christmas." Needless to say, the Chinese diplomats refused to proceed with negotiations as the UN offensive churned ahead.

General MacArthur's final blow had only a day's momentum when the Eighth Army was hit by a strong Chinese attack. By November 26 it was clear that a full-scale counterattack was underway by six Chinese armies. In two days, the entire right flank of the UN forces was collapsing. During the next eight days the UN forces fought heroically for their lives as they retreated south. Pyongyang was evacuated in early December, and by Christmas the boys were back on the 38th parallel.[90]

As the military defeat began to unfold, the tenuous politico-military consensus that had marked the onset of the campaign disintegrated. While victorious armies had marched north, all parties sought identification with General MacArthur's successes. Now, however, politicians and generals alike sought to disassociate themselves from each other and of course the deepening disaster on the Korean peninsula. This self-serving and confused scramble revealed the deep disagreements between Washington and UN military headquarters in Tokyo, brought into the open Europe's unease and exacerbated the profound domestic frustration with the war and President Truman's foreign policy.

THE MACARTHUR PROBLEM

If there were any worries within the highest levels of the Truman administration about expanding the war, they centered on General MacArthur and not his mission. These misgivings were reflected in the hedged, frequently contradictory language of the directives sent to the general. Both the White House and the Pentagon were sensitive to General MacArthur's domestic following and his personal vanity. Indeed, during World War II, the general's independence came to be thought of as the "MacArthur problem."[91] Consequently, it was deemed necessary to qualify heavily most of his orders to ensure control of his military activities.

With the outbreak of the Korean War, the MacArthur problem resurfaced. One example occurred on July 31, 1950, when General MacArthur paid a visit to Chiang Kai-shek on Taiwan, ostensibly to inform him of the progress of the fighting in Korea and explain the decision not to use his troops. However, General MacArthur pointedly refused to invite a State Department representative to the talks, claiming that only military matters were to be discussed. Nevertheless, both MacArthur and Chiang issued statements after the conference was over in which they praised one another's great leadership and called for closer Sino-American cooperation. Washington was upset, given the implications of these statements, that is, that the United States should support Chiang's desire to return to the mainland.

MacArthur's position was that the United States remove its prohibition against Taiwan's attacks on the mainland. To clarify Washington's position, Averell Harriman was immediately sent to Tokyo to discuss matters with General MacArthur. MacArthur told Harriman: "We should fight the communists every place—fight them like hell!"[92] After Harriman left, MacArthur issued a public statement defending his talks with Chiang and charged that his purpose was being "maliciously misrepresented to the public by those who invariably in the past have propagandized a policy of defeatism and appeasement in the Pacific."[93]

Again on August 17, 1950, MacArthur lashed out at the Truman administration. In a letter to the Veterans of Foreign Wars to be read at their annual meeting on August 28 and also printed in *U.S. News & World Report*, General MacArthur stated that it was merely his intent to evaluate the strategic position of the United States in Asia. However, the letter, which was never cleared in Washington, went on to emphasize the vital position of Taiwan in America's strategic posture. General MacArthur asserted: "Nothing could be more fallacious than the threadbare argument by those who advocate appeasement and defeatism in the Pacific that if we defend [Taiwan] we alienate Continental Asia."[94] President Truman and his advisers reacted, in Truman's words, with "surprise and shock," and Truman apparently considered relieving MacArthur of his command.[95] In the end, however, Truman merely ordered MacArthur on August 26 to withdraw the statement, although the action came too late to prevent its public appearance in *U.S. News & World*

Report. By late August the plans for the Inchon landing were well advanced, as was the decision to invade North Korea. To have fired MacArthur at the end of August 1950 would have destroyed the building momentum. Moreover, Truman's decision to invade the North brought him into line with MacArthur's aggressive spirit. And given the sense of forward movement after months of retreat, forcing the issue of MacArthur's independence could be politically disastrous. An ultimate confrontation was, therefore, avoided. By October, however, Truman felt compelled once again to discuss the relationship of his political objectives to the general's military activities. On October 9 two U.S. Air Force aircraft had attacked a Soviet airfield near Vladivostok, some sixty-two miles inside the Soviet Union. This was hardly a routine cold war border incident, and this was precisely the kind of event that could provoke the larger conflict Truman hoped to avoid. It was certainly the sort of thing that might heighten Truman's distrust of MacArthur and trigger any latent desire of the president to communicate face to face with the general.[96]

On October 10, 1950, three days after American troops had crossed the 38th parallel, President Truman announced that he would be flying to Wake Island in the Pacific to discuss the military effort with General MacArthur. However, the hasty manner in which the conference was arranged and its brevity once undertaken—the talks lasted only five hours—have puzzled observers. Truman has stated that he went to Wake simply because he had never met MacArthur personally and felt that the general should have a better appreciation of the "situation at home."[97] It would seem, however, that such matters and the establishment of personal contacts would have been more appropriate prior to the launching of the northern invasion. What now seems likely is that some emergency had arisen, perhaps caused by MacArthur or members of his command—such as the Vladivostok incident—that precipitated a meeting Truman may indeed have wanted for some time.

Although the meeting was brief and, on the surface, somewhat *pro forma,* it nevertheless betrayed some of the tension between the men. When, for example, the president stepped from the plane, General MacArthur greeted him cordially. But the general was dressed in a casual manner and did not salute the president, his commander-in-chief. Truman, on the other hand, planted an eavesdropping secretary behind a partially opened door adjacent to private conversations between the president and the general, who, supplied with legal pad and pen, automatically took down everything she overheard. Later when relations between Truman and MacArthur collapsed over the crisis brought on by the Chinese intervention, MacArthur's assurances that the Chinese would face the "greatest slaughter" if they intervened, were released.

Truman seemed, said the *New York Times* reporter who covered the conference, "like an insurance salesman who has signed up an important prospect." MacArthur, in contrast, was said to seem "dubious." His mood was not improved, notes a biographer, when Truman left the general's entourage without transportation from the spot from where the president's plane took off. He tried to hail a passing jeep but was unsuccessful. Finally, he thumbed a ride in a pickup truck.[98]

In less than a month, of course, Truman would have reason to question the success of his Pacific journey on grounds far more consequential than the general's lack of attention to protocol. At Wake Island, General MacArthur had been confident that Chinese intervention would not occur, and that if it did take place he expected no more than fifty to sixty thousand Chinese troops.[99] But almost as MacArthur spoke the Chinese began moving tens of thousands of troops into North Korea. Between mid-October and the first of November 1950, the Chinese had deployed between 180,000 and 228,000 members of the Fourth Field Army across the Yalu. The disaster of late November followed in due course.

MacArthur's Last Stand

Even as UN forces began their retreat back to the 38th parallel, General MacArthur released self-serving public explanations of his military strategy and the defeat he now confronted. His difficulties, General MacArthur explained, could be traced to the limitations imposed upon him by Washington. This most serious burden, MacArthur complained, was his inability to do anything about the Manchurian sanctuary beyond the Yalu. This was, he said, "[a]n enormous handicap, without precedent in military history."[100] The implication was clear; he could have avoided the present disaster if he had been free of Washington's constraints.

What MacArthur presented as an unnecessary tactical inhibition was, of course, the very heart of Truman's attempt to keep the war limited, and MacArthur knew this. In short, MacArthur was attempting to use the crisis presented by the Chinese intervention to force the issue that had divided him and his congressional supporters from the administration. Truman recognized from the very outset of the fighting what MacArthur was attempting to do. Truman's reasons for not firing the general at this juncture are, one suspects, not entirely candid. Truman's explanation was that "I did not wish to have it appear as if he were being relieved because the offensive failed. I have never believed in going back on people when luck is against them, and I did not intend to do it now."[101] Truman's humanity and compassion notwithstanding, much public and certainly conservative congressional opinion still supported the general.

Thus Truman's only real response to MacArthur's challenge was a presidential directive, issued on December 5 to all "officials overseas, including military commanders, and diplomatic representatives," that all public statements on foreign and defense policy be cleared in Washington. The president's domestic situation was sufficiently delicate that he had to camouflage a direct order to MacArthur to stop engaging in behavior for which Truman was confident MacArthur would have justifiably court-martialed a second lieutenant.[102] In the meantime, confusion, bordering at times on despair, settled over Washington. On November 30, President Truman caused great consternation as he stated in a press conference that the United States was and always has been actively considering the use of the atomic bomb in Korea. The British were almost panicked, and Prime Minister Clement Attlee urgently requested an immediate conference with Truman, which took place between December 4 and 8. Truman's loose talk about using nuclear weapons had given rise to a British desire to participate in some manner in any future decision on the use of nuclear weapons. Most important, however, was what the British perceived to be a dangerous incipient reversal of American security priorities. Unlike congressional conservatives and MacArthur who were pressuring Truman to do more in Asia, Attlee wanted the Americans to do much less, thereby returning containment to its original dimensions. The best way to accomplish this, in the opinion of the British, would be to begin negotiations with the Chinese Communists concerning an end of the war as well as recognition of the Beijing regime. Little was resolved, however, for alliance concerns were overtaken by the more demanding crisis represented by General MacArthur.

During December General MacArthur's reports underscoring the threats to his small command deepened the gloom and near despondency in Washington. MacArthur restated his public position that the fight should be taken to China itself, emphasizing the "great potential" of guerrilla war in China and attacks from Taiwan. The White House and the Pentagon were besieged by a series of hysterical cables from MacArthur, requesting "permission to take whatever measures necessary to save his command. His plans . . . including the use of 20–30 atomic bombs against China, the laying down of a radioactive belt across North Korea to seal it off from China and the use of half a million Chinese Nationalist troops."[103] The Joint Chiefs rejected flatly MacArthur's proposed retaliatory measures on China. On January 13, 1951, the administration opened a counteroffensive as President Truman sent a personal letter to MacArthur urging him to hold his position or, at a minimum, only withdraw to islands off the coast of Korea. For emphasis, Truman sent generals J. Lawton Collins and Hoyt Vandenberg of the Joint Chiefs of Staff to Korea; they confirmed what the Truman administration had come to suspect: General MacArthur was consciously overestimating the threat to his command in an effort to gain approval for an attack on the Chinese mainland. Truman responded by sacking General Emmett O'Donnell of the Far East Air Force Bomber Command, a well-known advocate of bombing China. It was a clear signal to MacArthur to keep his own advocacy of attacks on China to himself and support the counteroffensive soon to be launched by General Matthew Ridgeway. Ridgeway's willingness to stand and fight *in* Korea marked him as more responsive to Washington's concept of how the war should be fought. Moreover, as military historian David Rees noted, "Henceforward, MacArthur [located in Tokyo], who had now ceased to exercise close supervision over the Eighth Army, was increasingly bypassed by Truman and the JCS in dealing with Ridgeway."[104]

In mid-February the general went public again. MacArthur branded Ridgeway and Washington's strategy "wholly unrealistic and illusory."[105] On March 7 in a press statement, General MacArthur called the prevailing limited approach to the war as "Die for [a] Tie"[106] and pointed to Washington as being responsible for the "savage slaughter that the current strategy would bring about."

By March 12 Ridgeway reached the 38th parallel and Seoul was retaken. President Truman now prepared a diplomatic initiative that anticipated the beginnings of cease-fire negotiations and a settlement of the entire Korean question. Moreover, this was to be followed, in turn, by consideration of other problems in Asia. Presumably this referred to the entire China question, including recognition and UN representation.[107] When the news of this overture to China was sent to General MacArthur, he was requested not to initiate any major advance north of the parallel while negotiations were in the offing. MacArthur sullenly agreed.

But suddenly, without any forewarning, General MacArthur thundered his own public ultimatum to the Chinese before the president had taken his planned initiative. The general arrogantly threatened the Chinese with an expansion of the war and marked his terms for negotiations:

> [T]here should be no insuperable difficulty in arriving at decisions on the Korean problem if the issues are resolved on their own merits, without being burdened by extraneous matters not directly related to Korea, such as [Taiwan], or China's seat in the United Nations.[108]

The legendary warrior then, magnanimously, offered his services as a negotiating partner to end the war—on Western terms.[109]

President Truman's pending offer would have signaled that he was tacitly offering the Chinese the opportunity to discuss their broader concerns in Asia if they would begin negotiations on a cease fire. General MacArthur's ultimatum explicitly precluded Truman's offer and indicated to the Chinese instead that they could expect a general war if they would not come to the negotiating table. He must have known that his ultimatum would so complicate matters for the administration that it would be unable to proceed with its diplomatic effort. Finally, it has been suggested that he was also aware that his action would jeopardize his career; for in making this public statement he was clearly in violation of Truman's December 6, 1950, directive that all public statements by theater commanders be cleared by Washington.

The man in the White House was infuriated.[110] Still, Truman did not relieve MacArthur. Instead the president reminded MacArthur of his December order concerning public statements and awaited the general's response. His response came in a letter to Congressman Joseph Martin, the House Minority Leader, who had said earlier that he had "good reason" to believe that MacArthur and the Pentagon had favored using "800,000" Chinese Nationalist troops in Taiwan to fight with the United States in Korea. "If we are not in Korea to win," Martin concluded, "then Truman's administration should be indicted for the murder of thousands of American boys." Martin sent a copy of the speech to MacArthur and asked for the general's comments. On March 20, MacArthur congratulated the Republican leader for having "lost none of your old time punch" and ended by writing:

> It seems strangely difficult for some to realize that here in Asia is where the communist conspirators have elected to make their play for global conquest, and that we have joined the issue thus raised on the battlefield; that here we fight Europe's war with arms while the diplomats there still fight it with words; that if we lose this war to communism in Asia the fall of Europe is inevitable; win it and Europe most probably would avoid war and yet preserve freedom. As you have pointed out, we must win. There is no substitute for victory.[111]

The breaking point had now been reached. Truman initiated a week-long round of discussions with his top advisers concerning his next step. All agreed the president had but one course of action open to him: the removal of MacArthur and his replacement by Ridgeway. The announcement was made on April 11, and the nation was immediately caught up in one of the great spectacles of U.S. history as the general came home.

Truman was vilified throughout the country. He and Acheson were burned in effigy, and his public approval ratings dropped to less than 30 percent according to the Gallup poll. In Congress, calls for impeachment of Truman, Acheson, and Marshall were commonplace. Senator Richard Nixon characterized Truman's action as "appeasement of communism" and demanded that Truman be censured if the general were not reinstated. Others were less discreet. Senator McCarthy declared that the president was a "son-of-a-bitch,"[112] and Senator William Jenner of Indiana spoke for many when he charged on the floor of the Senate:

> This country today is in the hands of a secret inner coterie which is di-
> rected by agents of the Soviet Union. We must cut this whole cancer-
> ous conspiracy out of our government at once. [Applause from the public
> gallery.] Our only course is to impeach President Truman and find out
> who is the secret invisible government which has so cleverly led our
> country down the road to destruction.[113]

The general and his wife arrived in San Francisco on April 17, 1951, and paraded fourteen miles in two hours to their hotel. The next day the general told a crowd that "he was not running for President. . . . The only politics I have is contained in a single phrase well known to you—God Save America."[114] On April 19 he appeared in the House of Representatives for his farewell address. He described the global communist menace and reviewed his proposals for ending the war in Korea. Next MacArthur hammered away at his conception of war—a conception shared by millions of Americans—and its relationship to events in Asia:

> [O]nce war is forced upon us, there is no other alternative than to apply
> every available means to bring it to a swift end. . . . War's very object is
> victory, not prolonged indecision.

He concluded, choked with tears:

> I am closing my 52 years of military service. When I joined the Army even
> before the turn of the century, it was the fulfillment of all my boyish hopes
> and dreams. The world has turned over many times since I took the oath on
> the Plains at West Point, and the hopes and dreams have long since van-
> ished. But I still remember the refrain of one of the most popular barracks
> ballads of that day which proclaimed most proudly that, "Old Soldiers
> never die; they just fade away." And like the old soldier of that ballad, I
> now close my military career and just fade away—an old soldier who has
> tried to do his duty as God gave him the light to see that duty.
>   Good-by.[115]

The scene on the floor of the House of Representatives was pan-
demonium. Senators, members of Congress, and spectators leaped to

their feet, many with tears streaming down their faces. Afterwards, Harvard-educated Congressman Dewey Short proclaimed, "We saw a great hunk of God in the flesh, and we heard the voice of God."[116] Former President Herbert Hoover saw only a "reincarnation of St. Paul into a great General of the Army.'[117] A distinguished senator was overheard to remark after the speech, "I have never feared more for the institutions of the country. I honestly felt . . . that if [the General's] speech had gone on much longer there might have been a march on the White House."[118] If the senator had been outside he would have been concerned that the march had in fact begun; for as David Rees has noted:

> In the afternoon MacArthur drove down Pennsylvania Avenue to be given the freedom of the City of Washington. It was a public holiday and, as hundreds of thousands watched, bombers and jet fighters flew overhead and artillery boomed out over the capital.[119]

The next step for the legendary American general, who had led American troops into one of the greatest military disasters since the first battle of Bull Run and openly flouted his oath of office with his insubordination of his commander-in-chief, was New York. The city gave him a six-hour-and-five-minute parade, longer and larger than any in its history, including that given for Lindbergh in 1927, and twice as large as Eisenhower's victorious return in 1945. The New York Police Department estimated that there were more than seven million people along the parade route. Signs along the way read, "God Save Us from Acheson," and the city hired sky-writing fliers who spelled in two-mile-long heavenly script, "Welcome Home" and "Well Done."[120]

The MacArthur Hearings:
Denouement of Domestic Confrontation

Clearly the general was not just fading away. There followed a series of speeches throughout the country. MacArthur extolled the simple virtues of a pastoral America he hadn't seen for over fifteen years. Yet the years of his absence, especially the five years since the war, were among the most crucial in America's history.[121] Containment, Truman, Marshall, and Acheson had argued, was a commitment to world involvement and expensive military strength. But power had to be employed in a limited and controlled manner lest events elude them and war ensue. By the time of Korea, Americans had begun to accommodate themselves to this new situation. But Korea ripped at the emerging consensus, and MacArthur represented, for many Americans, a needed point of reference and seeming stability. It was reassuring for the general to state: "though without authority or responsibility, I am the possessor of the proudest of titles. I am an American."[122] In city after city MacArthur appeared with one arm around Mrs. MacArthur, another around his son. The general seemed the unabashed symbol of home and patriotism and what he delighted in calling the simple eternal truths of the American way.[123]

But for tens of millions of other Americans the Depression, World War II, and the onset of the cold war had proved that there were no more simple eternal truths. Truman recognized this and counterattacked effectively by using the forum presented in the Joint Senate Foreign Relations and Armed Services Committee hearings on MacArthur's dismissal and the conduct of the war. MacArthur led off the hearings and stated once again his objection to any concept of a limited war under the close control of political leadership.[124]

The Truman administration responded as it had in meeting Taft's challenge. A solid phalanx of administration officials—Marshall, all of the Joint Chiefs, and Acheson—carefully detailed MacArthur's insubordination and attacked his notion of all political control shifting to a theater commander once war began as beyond the pale of the American civil-military tradition and the Constitution. Moreover, MacArthur's broader strategic vision was deemed dangerously in error in that his proposals would not result in an end to the war, but a wider war that would divert American resources from the truly fundamental confrontation with the Soviet Union. Finally, the administration witnesses instructed the Congress that a commitment to a full-scale Asian conflict was opposed by our European allies. Therefore, pursuing the course advocated by the general might drive a wedge between us and the Europeans. The specter of a weakened or collapsed NATO was outlined, and the fulfillment of Soviet objectives in Europe was detailed.

The result of Truman's effort was to deflect MacArthur's simplistic appeal to patriotism, which masked a notion of civil-military relations subversive of the American Constitution. The Joint Chiefs supported Truman's conception of American priorities and would not allow wedges to be driven between them and the civilian leadership of the administration. Most important, however, was the united front maintained on the issue of civilian supremacy and agreement on MacArthur's violation of this precept. Because the administration was generally successful in framing the debate in these terms, it was successful in shifting the focus of confrontation. Questions of grand strategy could and did provoke disagreement. But the principle of civilian supremacy was broadly accepted. Once the issue was set in these terms, the emotion of the general's return began to settle, and public opinion shifted away from MacArthur.

Moreover, as the hearings ended, negotiations finally got underway in Korea. The Chinese advance south stalled under the combined weight of appalling casualties inflicted by American firepower and overextended lines of supply, vulnerable to UN air superiority. The burst of optimism that greeted the opening of talks and military success would turn to growing cynicism in the fall and winter of 1951 as the talks deadlocked and stalemated fighting resumed. But in the summer of 1951 the news of negotiations in a domestic context of a booming, if inflated, economy produced an atmosphere little conducive to MacArthur's case.

THE OLD COLD WARRIOR FADES AWAY: THE END OF THE TRUMAN ADMINISTRATION

In the longer view, however, President Truman's success in exploiting the MacArthur hearings was but a holding action for he was never able to translate his victory into increased support for himself. He may have been able to convince a majority of the American people that Douglas MacArthur and the conservative Republicans did not possess a prudent and constitutionally acceptable way out of the cold war and Korea, but he could not convince the same group that Harry Truman knew where the exit lay.

Further diminishing Truman's domestic support was a series of revelations beginning in 1950 and running throughout 1951 of deficient and even corrupt administration within many agencies of the government.[125] The succession of scandals and Truman's announcement in March of 1952 that he would not seek reelection reduced the Truman administration to virtual caretaker status unable to conclude the war through negotiations or force. Senator McCarthy unleashed a renewed attack on the members of the Truman administration, starting with Marshall, whom he characterized as being a member of "a conspiracy so immense, an infamy so black, as to dwarf any in the history of man."[126] The vilification of Acheson grew, and one commentator noted that "many people burst into profanity at the mere mention of Truman's name."[127]

In July 1952 the parties nominated their candidates and went to the American people. Adlai Stevenson and the Democrats told the nation for the next three months that they "never had it so good" and raised the specter of another depression if the Republicans were elected. The Republicans behind Eisenhower, who had defeated Taft for the nomination, systematically attacked the Democrats concerning Korea, communism, and corruption. The Democrats, it was charged, had given the American people a corrupt administration at home, compounded by subversion by Communists and communist sympathizers. The endless war in Korea was proof that containment as a foreign policy was, in the words of the Republican platform (drafted largely by John Foster Dulles, who was assumed to be the next secretary of state if Eisenhower was elected), "negative, futile and immoral."

As the campaign seemed to be gaining momentum for the Republicans, it was revealed that Richard Nixon, the Republicans' vice presidential nominee, had been the beneficiary of an $18,000 special fund established for him by some wealthy California businessmen. General Eisenhower was furious and demanded that Nixon explain matters to the American people if he was going to remain on the ticket. Senator Nixon then went before the nation through a televised address on September 23, 1952, and delivered his now famous "Checkers" speech, in which he denied that he had ever used any of the money for his personal use; it had all been used to clean out the Communists and crooks in Washington. He emphasized that he, like many Americans, had found it difficult to meet payments on his car and his mortgage, and that he and his wife were struggling financially. He did admit to one gift, however:

> Do you know what it was? It was a little cocker spaniel dog in a crate . . . sent all the way from Texas. Black and white spotted. And our little girl— Trisha, the six year old—named it Checkers. And you know the kids love the dog, and I just want to say this right now, that regardless of what they say about it, we're going to keep it.[128]

The public response was overwhelmingly positive, for Nixon succeeded in aligning himself and the Republican party with the little man struggling with inflation, the war, the corruption, and the desire for a better life.[129] It may have been corny, tear-jerking stuff, but in the domestic malaise of 1952, it was devastating electoral politics.

A month later General Eisenhower, whose attacks on Truman had become more and more pointed and slashing, announced that the first thing he would do, if elected, was make a trip to Korea for a personal assessment of the situation. This promise and a stunningly effective nationally televised speech by General MacArthur on October 27 brought the campaign to an end. A week later, twenty years of Democratic party rule came to an end in the landslide election of Dwight Eisenhower.

CONCLUSION

The Korean experience was critical in a number of ways. As Professor Robert Tucker has noted:

> In the decade following the initiation of containment, Korea stands out as the decisive event in the evolution of American policy. The Korean experience largely determined the form and course that the great transformation

in American foreign policy eventually took. . . . In Europe, the Korean conflict led to the reestablishment of American forces, the establishment of an integrated command structure, the decision to rearm Germany, and the agreement on a common defense strategy. In Asia, the Korean War led to American intervention in the Chinese civil conflict and prompted the conclusion of a series of bilateral and multilateral alliances that continue today roughly to define the extent of the American commitment in that area.[130]

In the end, this effort was widely adjudged by American academic and policy makers to be a success. Robert Osgood, for instance, observes that "one can hardly overestimate the importance of the United States achievment in containing the Communist attack on South Korea without precipitating total war. By this achievement the nation went a long way toward demonstrating that it could successfully resist direct military aggression locally by limited war in the secondary strategic areas. . . ."[131] Yet if the war was limited, it was only in some rather specific aspects. It was limited geographically, and nuclear weapons were not used on the peninsula. Beyond this, however, Korea was one of the most destructive wars ever fought. An estimated four million Koreans were killed out of a population of about thirty million.

General O'Donnell, head of the U.S. Bomber Command in the Far East, testified: "I would say that the entire, almost the entire Korean peninsula, is just a terrible mess. Everything is destroyed. There is nothing standing worthy of the name." Just before the Chinese came in, he elaborated, "We were grounded. There were no more targets in Korea." General MacArthur testified on May 3, 1951, "The war in Korea already almost destroyed that nation. . . . I have never seen such devastation. I have seen, I guess, as much blood and disaster as any living man, and it just curdled my stomach, the last time I was there. After I looked at that wreckage and those thousands of women and children and everything, I vomited."[132] The authoritative military publication, *The Armed Forces Yearbook*, said in its 1951 edition:

> The war was fought without regard for the South Koreans, and their unfortunate country was regarded as an arena rather than a country to be liberated. As a consequence, fighting was quite ruthless, and it is no exaggeration to state that South Korea no longer exists . . . its towns have been destroyed . . . its people reduced to a sullen mass dependent on charity. . . . Few attempts were made to explain to the American soldier why they were fighting. . . . The South Korean . . . was regarded as a "gook" like his cousins North.[133]

The war also introduced the notion of relating force to political objectives prior to achieving a thorough military victory. Negotiating while fighting was obviously not congruent with the "unconditional" military posture employed by U.S. forces just six years earlier. As Professor Thomas Schelling elaborates, "the war in Korea [was] a 'negotiation' over the political status of the country. But, as in most bargaining processes, there was also implicit bargaining about the rules of behavior, about what one would do, or stop doing, according to how the other side behaved."[134] Or as Dean Rusk has observed, "in the Korean war there came a point when the other side was ready to negotiate. . . . [I]n the Korean war . . . we . . . tried to use the amount of force that [was] required to achieve the essential objectives without letting it escalate."[135] Thus, "diplomacy of violence"[136] received its conceptual baptism in Korea. The Truman administration's response in Korea consummated a trend toward primary reliance upon military instrumentalities and the use of the threat of war as the basis of containment. The economic tools of the Marshall Plan and global economic cooperation were now subordinated to military assistance and the use of force.

The war reversed an emerging policy of differentiating between the new Communist Chinese regime and the Soviet Union. After American troops were committed to Korea, and the Seventh Fleet blocked Mao from storming the Nationalist redoubt on Taiwan, and especially after Chinese and American forces began to bloody each other, normal relations became almost impossible to contemplate. Indeed, the domestic distortions and convulsions of the Korean experience—epitomized by the antics of Senator McCarthy—would scar the American consciousness. Communism, not just Soviet power, but a sinister conspiracy, became the whipping boy of ruthless men and the fear of Americans great and small.

The war also had the effect of being something of a self-fulfilling prophecy. Earlier, Dean Acheson in his January 12, 1950, "defense perimeter" remarks to the National Press Club, had tried to distinguish between historic Chinese and Russian aspirations by asserting that eventually Chinese nationalism would turn against Soviet imperialism. After the Korean conflict had begun, Assistant Secretary of State Dean Rusk would say of China in 1951: "It is not the government of China. It does not pass the first test. It is not Chinese."[137]

But early relations between Mao's new China and the Soviet Union were not those of partners. The initial formal state instrument between Communist China and Soviet Russia was negotiated by Mao in Moscow in February 1950. It took Mao three months to secure the treaty, and he was gone so long "that rumors arose about Mao being detained against his will."[138] Stalin, according to Adam Ulam, "was . . . incredibly stingy," negotiating an "embarrassingly small loan," a "pittance." Even the European satellites had "received . . . credits greater than now extended to the most populous country in the world."[139]

After the Korean War had begun, however, China became increasingly dependent on the Soviet Union. The Chinese were forced to borrow at least $2 billion in order to finance the Korean War, and the Soviets charged interest. The Soviets became a deterrent force on which the Chinese were forced to rely, and it was the Soviet Union that now was the voice of the Chinese position in international councils. Occasionally, the Soviets did not always inform the Chinese as to how they were proceeding in the Chinese interest, but the Chinese, in a period of profound isolation, had little choice but to use Moscow as their intermediary.[140]

The Korean War served ultimately to debase the United Nations by employing expedient stratagems to avoid the processes elaborated in the charter. Using the Soviet absence from the Security Council to vote UN sanctions against a Soviet client, although of questionable legality, would not likely be precedent if the Soviets remained alert in the future. But using the General Assembly to obtain a warrant to move into North Korea would come to haunt the United States when the character of the General Assembly was to dramatically change in the early 1960s. The Uniting for Peace Resolution, proposed by Acheson, "provid[ed] for an emergency session of the General Assembly upon twenty-four hours' notice if the Security Council should be prevented from acting."[141] Under the charter the assembly can only "recommend," not authorize action. But the Uniting for Peace Resolution blurred the distinction between recommendation and authorization.* By the mid-1960s, when the number of members of the UN Assembly had expanded enormously and proved unresponsive to U.S. pressure, the United States tried to move important decisions back to the Security Council. Bit by bit, however, the General Assembly slipped from U.S. control and influence.

The decision to go into Korea was predicated on the perception that American will was being tested. Although the arena was peripheral, the United States, it was believed, must respond in order to establish a reputation for action that would deter probes at the center. The perception may have been in error given the murky origins of the Korean civil war. Yet having committed American reputation or honor on the periphery, the principle of containment was instantly extended to that periphery and, in theory at least, virtually everything within it.

In February of 1950, Secretary of State Acheson observed:

> The only way to deal with the Soviet Union, we have found from hard experience, is to create situations of strength. Wherever the Soviet detects

---

*Thus when the assembly recommended that "all appropriate steps be taken to ensure conditions of stability throughout the whole of Korea," it was taken as a legal justification by the United States for crossing the 38th parallel.

weakness or disunity—and it is quick to detect them—it exploits them to the full. . . . [W]hen we have eliminated all of the areas of weakness that we can—we will be able to evolve working agreements with the Russians.[142]

During the Korean War, the Truman administration set about creating situations of strength on a global scale. Thus the Japanese Peace Treaty, encompassing military basing rights as well as similar arrangements in Australia, New Zealand, the Philippines, the Middle East, and North Africa, began the process of institutionalizing global containment. Likewise, support of the French in Indochina, the Dutch in Indonesia, or extension of aid to Chiang Kai-shek could be rationalized as essential to this process of establishing a global network of situations of strength.

However, as Coral Bell has emphasized in her analysis of the 1950s, negotiating from strength is elusive at best and probably a contradiction in terms, especially if strength is conceived of as superiority—as seems to have been the case in NSC-68.

> The idea of negotiation from strength has had . . . the true mirage-like quality of some of the most effective political myths: shimmering promisingly, always a little farther off, across a stony waste of effort, keeping its distance at each apparent advance.[143]

If the United States found superiority and strength to be the only prudent posture from which to negotiate, why should the Soviet Union settle for less? Why should it be prudent for the Soviets to negotiate from relative weakness?

The Korean War caused profound distortions at home. Arms expenditures reached 67 percent of the budget by 1952. There were dramatic price rises and shortages, and wage and price controls were imposed as wholesale prices began to rise at the rate of 25 percent a year. In September 1950 Congress passed the McCarran Act, banning aliens who had belonged to "totalitarian organizations." In June 1951, in the case of *Dennis v. United States*, the Supreme Court held that, given the state of tension in the world, advocating or teaching revolutionary philosophy constituted a crime. The State Department began to lose some of its best people—especially in Asian affairs—as experienced diplomats were asked if they had ever dealt with Communists. After all, communism was killing American sons in Korea; why should those who truck with it at home, or on the job abroad, be given the benefit of the doubt?

Finally, the United States became tied to a client regime with a reputation for terror that gnawed the conscience of jurists and journalists who witnessed the political conditions of South Korea. The American effort to liberate both North and South Korea had contributed to the maintenance of highly militarized, authoritarian regimes: North Korea, according to Amnesty International, is the most closed society in the world, and in South Korea, documentation about the abuse of human rights is abundant.[144] Thomas Schelling is, no doubt, correct when he points out: "We lost thirty thousand dead in Korea to save face for the United States and the United Nations, not to save South Korea for the South Koreans." Schelling's conclusion is, however, at the least, debatable: "It was," he writes, "undoubtedly worth it."[145]

NOTES

1. Reprinted from *Present at the Creation* by Dean Acheson. By permission of W. W. Norton and Hamish Hamilton, Ltd. Copyright © 1969 by Dean Acheson.

2. Edward W. Barrett in a debriefing seminar for Acheson and his close associates, Princeton University, October 10–11, 1953. Box 65, Acheson Papers, cited by Thomas G. Paterson, *On Every Front* (New York: W. W. Norton, 1979), p. 171.

3. Dean Acheson, "Crisis in Asia—An Examination of U.S. Policy," *Department of State Bulletin*, Vol. 22 (January 23, 1950), p. 116. Acheson was paraphrasing MacArthur's observation of the preceding year: "Our defensive dispositions against Asiatic aggression . . . starts from the Philippines and continues through the Ryuku Archipelago, which includes its main bastion, Okinawa. Then it bends back through Japan and the Aleutian chain to Alaska." *The New York Times*, 2 March 1949, quoted in Acheson, *Present at the Creation*, p. 357.

4. Acheson, "Crisis in Asia," p. 116.

5. Ibid.

6. "Statement: United States Policy Towards Formosa," *Department of State Bulletin*, Vol. 22 (January 16, 1950), p. 79.

7. John Spanier, *The Truman-MacArthur Controversy and the Korean War* (New York: W. W. Norton, 1965), p. 56. For an exegesis of recently declassified documents confirming that the U.S. fully expected Taiwan to fall, see Robert R. Simmons, "Contradictions in 'Fraternal Relationships': Moscow, Peking, P'yongyang and the Korean War," *Conference on Security Arrangements in Northeast Asia from 1945 to Present*, Harvard University, June 19–23, 1978, pp. 7–8.

8. Quoted in Merle Miller, *Plain Speaking: An Oral Biography of Harry Truman* (New York: Berkeley, Medallion, 1974), pp. 286–287. See also the testimony of General L. Bolte, Director of Plans and Operations in testimony for the Korean Assistance Act, June 16, 1950, *United States Policy in the Far East*, Vol. VIII, Historical Series of the Committee on Foreign Relations, United States Senate, 1976, p. 46. A good review of Acheson's view of the significance of Korea is in David S. McLellan, *Dean Acheson: The State Department Years* (New York: Dodd, Mead, 1977), pp. 209–211.

9. Robert R. Simmons, "The Korean Civil War," in Frank Baldwin, ed., *Without Parallel* (New York: Pantheon, 1974), p. 149.

10. World Policy and Bipartisanship: An Interview with Senator Tom Connally," *U.S. News & World Report*, Vol. 28 (May 5, 1950), p. 30.

11. Allen S. Whiting, *China Crosses the Yalu: The Decision to Enter the Korean War* (Stanford, Calif.: Stanford University Press, 1960), pp. 42–43.

12. Ibid., p. 45.

13. Harrison E. Salisbury, "Image and Reality in Indochina," *Foreign Affairs*, Vol. 49 (No. 3, April 1971), p. 388. Mr. Salisbury has speculated that the real target of the North Korean offense, "instigated" by Stalin, was Communist China. He writes: "I think it reasonable to assume that Stalin felt he could take Washington's word—that we did not feel obligated to rise to the defense of South Korea. . . . [I]f he could overrun all of Korea he would be able to dominate Peking from positions in Mongolia, Manchuria and Korea. He would possess the power to deal with Mao as he once said he would deal with Tito. . . ."

14. Strobe Talbott, tr. and ed., *Khrushchev Remembers* (Boston: Little, Brown and Company, 1970), p. 378. See also, Robert M. Slusser, "Soviet Far Eastern Policy, 1945–1950; Stalin's Goals in Korea," in *The Origins of the Cold War in Asia* edited by Yonosuke Nagai and Akira Iriye (Tokyo and New York: University of Tokyo Press, 1977), pp. 141–142, 146.

15. U.S. Department of State, *North Korea: A Case Study in the Technique of Takeover* (Washington, D.C.: U.S. Department of State, 1961), p. 114.

16. According to a purported defector, Lt. Col. Kyril Kalinov, "How Russia Built the North Korean People's Army," *Reporter Magazine* (September 26, 1950), pp. 4–8. Also see Robert R. Simmons, *The Strained Alliance: Peking, P'yongyang, Moscow and the Politics of the Korean War* (New York: Free Press, 1975), p. 120 *passim*.

17. Glenn D. Paige, *The Korean Decision, June 24–30, 1950* (New York: Free Press, 1968), p. 97. (Paige is citing an interview he had with Rusk in 1955.)

18. Adam B. Ulam, *The Rivals: America and Russia Since World War II* (New York: Random House, Vintage, 1971), p. 171.

19. Moreover, the year before, Truman was extraordinarily cautious when arguing for a $150 million military aid bill. "It is a question of defense by the Southern Korean government . . . against Koreans from the North. I do not think our forces should be mixed up in that. The Russians would love to see that. . . . They would sit back and laugh their heads off if we got our forces engaged at all . . . and the one thing that causes me some surprise is that the Russians have not realized how much damage they could do if they really did begin to let military events start in Southern Korea. I will feel relieved when we get these [American troops] out of there" (*United States Policy in the Far East, Part II, Korean Assistance Act*, Vol. VIII, U.S. House, Committee on International Relations, Historical Series, 1976, pp. 33, 46).

20. Statement by President Truman, "U.S. Air and Sea Forces Ordered into Supporting Action," *Department of State Bulletin*, Vol. 23 (July 3, 1950), p. 5.

21. Harry S. Truman, *Memoirs: Years of Trial and Hope* (Garden City, N.Y.: Doubleday, 1956), p. 333.

22. Ibid., p. 340.

23. Acheson, *Present at the Creation*, p. 405.

24. Truman, op. cit., p. 339 (emphasis added).

25. Joyce and Gabriel Kolko, *The Limits of Power: The World and United States Foreign Policy* (New York: Harper & Row, 1972), pp. 579–582. In any event, even if they did not initiate the conflict, there is good reason to believe that: (1) they probably knew about it in advance and did not attempt to prevent the conflict and (2) they probably could have had the North Koreans withdrawn early and with honor if they were willing to exercise sufficient influence. In this sense the Soviets' relation to the North Koreans may have been similar to Russian-Syrian and Egyptian relations in 1973. The Soviets may not have provoked the Arab attack *per se*, but the Arab attack was preceded by large arms delivery and Soviet advisers were at Arab command headquarters and with Arab field units. (3) No matter what the initial Soviet reason for acquiescence in the North Korean adventure, there is some evidence that the

Soviets made it clear that they would not become involved in what they called a "Korean *civil* war" (emphasis added) but that the Chinese had more direct interests. The Chinese, in turn, tried to implicate the Soviets without success. See Simmons, "Contradictions in 'Fraternal Friendships,'" pp. 11–13.

26. Ulam, *Expansion and Coexistence* (New York: Praeger, 1968) pp. 523–525, and Acheson, *Present at the Creation*, pp. 408–412.

27. David Rees, *Korea: The Limited War* (Baltimore: Penguin Books, 1964), pp. 67–69.

28. Quoted in Miller, op. cit., p. 313.

29. Kolko and Kolko, op. cit. p. 572.

30. Ibid., and *The New York Times*, February 17, 1950.

31. Kolko and Kolko, op. cit., pp. 573–574.

32. Philip Jessup, in *Department of State Bulletin*, Vol. 22, No. 564 (April 24, 1950), p. 627.

33. Simmons, op. cit., p. 152.

34. John Foster Dulles, "The Korean Experiment in Representative Government," *Department of State Bulletin*, Vol. 23 (July 23, 1950), esp. p. 13.

35. Some observers, notably journalist I.F. Stone and historian Gabriel Kolko, have drawn from these events in Seoul and Tokyo an interesting hypothesis combining the circumstances in the months before the war with the confusion and curiously contradictory reports emanating from the battlefield during the week of June 25. Specifically, the U.S. command in Tokyo is viewed as being quite aware of the North Korean buildup and seeking to provoke a fight or perhaps maneuver the North Koreans into attacking. Thus, Dulles, as a representative of Republican conservatism, along with General MacArthur, publicly supported an increasingly belligerent Rhee. Such support, it is argued, could only have increased tensions and fears in the North, perhaps raising the fear that American military assistance was about to increase dramatically. If there was a new rapid buildup in the South, then the North Koreans would lose their recently acquired arms advantage. Once the attack occurred, whether started by South Korean incursions (as Stone suggests) or as the result of a preemptive strike (Kolko), General MacArthur and Syngman Rhee, the revisionists suggest, allowed the situation to deteriorate so as to ensure a significant U.S. intervention. Washington was, in this analysis, rather ignorant of this maneuvering. President Truman and his advisers were more or less dependent upon General MacArthur for information as to what was going on in Asia. Having been misled by General MacArthur, they were pulled into the involvement and consequent redirection of American policy in Asia desired by General MacArthur, Syngman Rhee, and Chiang Kai-shek. See I.F. Stone, *The Hidden History of the Korean War*, Second Modern Reader Edition (New York: Monthly Review, 1952), esp. pp. 1–107.

36. Cited by George F. Will, "Right Out of the '30s," *Washington Post*, January 17, 1980, p. A27.

37. Numerous accounts of the Korean War are available. Among the more concise yet comprehensive are David Rees, op. cit., and John Spanier, op. cit. Also important and provocative is the revisionist I. F. Stone, op. cit. Shorter but useful accounts and analyses are provided by Bernard Brodie, *War and Politics* (New York: Macmillan, 1973), pp. 57–112, and Martin Licterman, "Korea: Problems in Limited Wars," in Gordon B. Turner and Richard D. Challener (eds.), *National Security in the Nuclear Age* (New York: Praeger, 1960), pp. 31–58. The major documentary source on the war is U.S. Congress, Senate Committee on Armed Services and Committee on Foreign Relations, *Military Situation in the Far East*, 82nd Congress, 1st Session, 1951. Finally the civilian-military implications are dealt with in Spanier, op. cit., and also in Walter Millis, *Arms and the State* (New York: Twentieth Century Fund, 1958), pp. 259–332.

38. Rees, op. cit., pp. 3–7, 21–26 and Kolko and Kolko, op. cit. pp. 579–582. Recently debate concerning the origins of the war resurfaced in the pages of *China Quarterly*. Karwnakar Gupta argues that South Korean forces attacked first at the North Korean border city of Haeju on June 25, 1950, and the the North Korean onslaught was a response. See Gupta's "How Did the Korean War Begin," *China Quarterly* (October–December 1972), pp. 699–716. This article prompted a refutation and a rejoinder by Gupta. See Chang-sik Lee, W. E. Skilend, and Robert Simmons, "Comment," *China Quarterly* (April–June 1973), pp. 354–368.

39. *The Times* (London), June 29, 1950, quoted in Kolko and Kolko, op. cit., p. 583.

40. Hanson Baldwin, "Ground Aid in Korea," *The New York Times*, June 29, 1950, p. 4.

41. *Department of State Bulletin*, Vol. 23 (July 3, 1950), pp. 4–5.

42. Quoted in Truman, op. cit., p. 337.

43. Ibid., p. 337.

44. "Text of Security Council Resolution," *Department of State Bulletin* (July 3, 1950), p. 7.

45. See Brodie, op. cit., or Licterman, op. cit.

46. See Spanier, op. cit.

47. David Halberstam, *The Best and the Brightest* (New York: Random House, 1972), p. 119.

48. Perhaps the best short analysis of McCarthy is Richard H. Rovere's *Senator Joe McCarthy* (New York: Harper & Row, 1959).

49. Halberstam, op. cit., p. 118.

50. Ibid., p. 119.

51. Hans J. Morgenthau, *The Purpose of American Politics* (New York: Random House, Vintage Books, 1960), p. 146.

52. Rovere, op. cit., p. 3.

53. Ibid., p. 23. McCarthy's influence had a half-life of over a generation. Even after his name had become an oath, in 1968 when *Eugene* McCarthy challenged Lyndon Johnson in the snows of a New Hampshire primary as an anti-Vietnam War peace candidate, many of his supporting votes were cast in the belief that he was *Joe* McCarthy.

54. Richard P. Stebbins, *The United States in World Affairs, 1950* (New York: Harper & Row, 1951), p. 57.

55. William S. White, *The Taft Story* (New York, Harper & Row, 1954), pp. 84–85.

56. Margaret Chase Smith, "Declaration of Conscience," *Congressional Record*, Vol. 96, Part 6 (June 1, 1950), p. 7894.

57. Indeed, only six other Republicans did: Tobey of New Hampshire, Aiken of Vermont, Morse of Oregon, Ives of New York, Thye of Minnesota, and Hendrickson of New Jersey.

58. Paul H. Nitze, "The United States in the Face of the Communist Challenge," in C. Grove Haines, ed., *The Threat of Soviet Imperialism* (Baltimore: Johns Hopkins University Press, 1954), p. 374 (emphasis added).

59. Senator Robert A. Taft, *Congressional Record*, January 5, 1951, 82nd Congress, 1st Session, p. 59.

60. Ibid.

61. Ibid., p. 58.

62. Ibid., p. 60.

63. Ibid., p. 61.

64. Ibid.

65. Ibid.

66. See Acheson, *Present at the Creation*, pp. 494–495 on this point. However, Acheson quoted Taft saying "[I] would not object to a few more divisions simply to show the

Europeans that we are interested and will participate in the more difficult job of land warfare while we carry out also our larger obligations" (p. 495).

67. Announcement of the French government, May 9, 1950, quoted in Acheson, *Present at the Creation,* p. 384. The Schumann Plan envisaged that the integration of German heavy industrial capacity would make more difficult the development of independent military power. The French and any other Europeans who chose to join would sacrifice some of their sovereignty, but in return they would gain an unprecedented margin of control over German productive capability.

 A split immediately developed between the British and the French. The British perceived problems with the Schumann Plan apart from their ancient ambivalence concerning the continent and the more recent notion that the British possessed a special relationship with the Americans that would be diminished as the result of close political and economic ties with the continent. Specifically, the Labor government in power in the spring of 1950 feared that entering into any such supranational arrangement would diminish their capacity to exercise socialist principles of domestic economic planning. All this was sufficient to keep the British out of the new European economic integration for almost two decades.

68. Ibid., p. 399.

69. See Robert E. Osgood, *NATO, The Entangling Alliance* (Chicago: University of Chicago Press, 1962) for further elaboration.

70. Ibid., pp. 80–81.

71. Ibid., *passim.*

72. Malcolm W. Cagle and Frank Manson, *The Sea War in Korea* (Annapolis, Md.: U.S. Naval Institute, 1957), p. 81.

73. Robert Leckie, *The Wars of America,* Vol. II: *San Juan Hill to Tonkin* (New York: Bantam, 1969), pp. 357–358.

74. Capt. Walter Karig, Comdr. Malcolm Cagle, and Lt. Cmdr. Frank A. Manson, *The War in Korea Battle Report,* Vol. VI (New York: Holt, Rinehart & Winston, 1952), p. 5.

75. This description is drawn from Rees, op. cit., pp. 77–97; see esp. pp. 90–92 for an account of the fighting in and around Seoul.

76. Millis, op. cit., p. 274.

77. Louis J. Halle, *The Cold War as History* (New York: Harper & Row, 1967), p. 220.

78. *Department of State Bulletin,* Vol. 23 (October 9, 1950), p. 580.

79. Halle, op. cit., p. 220.

80. Ibid.

81. Harold C. Hinton, *Communist China in World Politics* (Boston: Houghton Mifflin, 1966), p. 213.

82. Rees, op. cit., p. 109.

83. Whiting, op. cit., pp. 108–109.

84. Truman, op. cit., p. 362.

85. Acheson, *Present at the Creation,* p. 452.

86. Truman, op. cit., p. 362.

87. Ibid.

88. This offer was conditional on a withdrawal of diplomatic recognition, protection, and aid to the Nationalists on Taiwan. *Manchester Guardian,* November 18, 1950, cited by Harold Hinton, op. cit., p. 213.

89. Rees, op. cit., p. 128.

90. The best short account of the military action from October 19 through the Chinese intervention is Rees, op. cit., pp. 123–177. The classic study of the Chinese offensive is S. L. A. Marshall, *The River and the Gauntlet* (New York: William Morrow, 1953). There has been some speculation that MacArthur's battle plan had been betrayed by

the now notorious British spy "Kim" Philby and his associates. Philby was a Soviet mole in the British Embassy in Washington and a liaison between the British and the Central Intelligence Agency. The British had a commonwealth brigade under MacArthur's command; much information regarding common concerns was channeled through the British Embassy. See William Manchester, *American Caesar: Douglas MacArthur, 1880–1964* (New York: Dell, 1979), pp. 711–713.

91. Millis, op. cit., p. 267, although Truman was fairly successful in his relationship with the general while MacArthur was Supreme Commander for the Allies Pacific.

92. Quoted by Harriman in Truman, op. cit., p. 353.

93. Quoted by Spanier, op. cit., p. 73.

94. Douglas MacArthur, "Formosa Must Be Defended," *U.S. News & World Report,* Vol. 29 (No. 9, September 1, 1950), p. 34.

95. Truman, op. cit., pp. 355–356.

96. Stone, op. cit., pp. 145–150.

97. Truman, op. cit., pp. 362–363.

98. Manchester, op. cit., pp. 706–709.

99. Richard H. Rovere and Arthur M. Schlesinger, Jr., *The General and the President* (New York: Farrar, Straus & Young, 1951), p. 258.

100. "MacArthur's Own Story," *U.S. News & World Report,* Vol. 29 (December 8, 1950), p. 17.

101. Ibid., p. 384.

102. Ibid.

103. Douglas MacArthur, "Reply to the Joint Chiefs of Staff, December 30, 1950," in U.S. Congress, Senate Committee on Armed Services and Committee on Foreign Relations, *Hearings on the Military Situation in the Far East,* 82nd Congress, 1st Session, 1951, p. 2180; and Gaddis Smith, "After 25 Years—The Parallel," *The New York Times Magazine,* June 22, 1975, p. 20.

104. Rees, op. cit., p. 183.

105. Quoted in ibid., p. 206.

106. Ibid., p. 207.

107. Truman, op. cit., pp. 439–440.

108. Ibid., p. 441.

109. Ibid.

110. Ibid., p. 442.

111. Manchester, op. cit., p. 736, and Rees, op. cit., p. 213.

112. John Spanier, op. cit., p. 212.

113. Rees, op. cit., p. 222.

114. Quoted in ibid., p. 224.

115. Quoted in ibid., p. 226.

116. Spanier, op. cit., p. 220.

117. Ibid.

118. Quoted in William S. White, *Citadel: The Story of the U.S. Senate* (New York: Harper & Row, 1957), p. 244.

119. Rees, op. cit., p. 227.

120. Spanier, op. cit., p. 217.

121. See Eric Goldman, *The Crucial Decade and After: America 1945–1960* (New York: Vintage, 1960).

122. Ibid., p. 208.

123. Ibid., pp. 208–209.

124. MacArthur, *Hearings,* p. 45.

125. For a review of the details, see Cabell Phillips, *The Truman Presidency: The History of a Triumphant Succession* (Baltimore: Penguin Books, 1969), pp. 402–414.

126. Senator Joseph McCarthy, *Congressional Record,* June 14, 1951, Vol. 97, Part 5, p. 6556.
127. Quoted by Rees, op. cit., p. 386.
128. Richard M. Nixon, "My Side of the Story," *Vital Speeches of the Day,* October 15, 1952, pp. 11–15.
129. Goldman, op. cit., p. 232.
130. Robert W. Tucker, *Nation or Empire? The Debate over American Foreign Policy* (Baltimore: Johns Hopkins University Press, 1968), p. 28.
131. Robert E. Osgood, *Limited War: A Challenge to American Strategy* (Chicago: University of Chicago Press, 1957), p. 178.
132. U.S. Congress, Senate Committee on Armed Services and Committee on Foreign Relations, *Hearings on the Military Situation in the Far East,* 82nd Congress, 1st Session, 1951, pp. 3075, 3082.
133. Cited in Stone, op. cit., p. 313.
134. Thomas G. Schelling, *Arms and Influence* (New Haven, Conn.: Yale University Press, 1966), p. 136.
135. Dean Rusk, "The Revisionist Historians," *Firing Line* (Transcript), PBS broadcast, January 27, 1974 (Columbia, S.C.: Southern Educational Communications Associations, 1974), pp. 7–8.
136. See James A. Nathan and James K. Oliver, "The Diplomacy of Violence," *Society,* Vol. 11 (September/October 1974), pp. 32–40.
137. Marvin Kalb and Elie Abel, *Roots of Involvement: The U.S. in Asia, 1784–1971* (New York: W. W. Norton), p. 65.
138. Adam Ulam, *Expansion and Co-Existence,* p. 493.
139. Ibid., p. 495; see also Salisbury, op. cit.
140. Allen S. Whiting, "'Contradictions' in the Moscow-Peking Axis," *Journal of Politics,* Vol. 20, No. 1 (February 1958), p. 120. Apparently, for instance, when Soviet Ambassador Malik made his speech of June 23, 1951, calling for negotiations to bring the war to a close, the Chinese were surprised, not having been informed prior to Jacob Malik's proposal (Simmons, op. cit., p. 165).
141. Acheson, *Present at the Creation,* p. 450.
142. Dean Acheson, *Department of State Bulletin,* Vol. 22, No. 559 (March 20, 1959), pp. 427, 429.
143. Coral Bell, *Negotiations from Strength* (New York: Knopf, 1963), p. 5.
144. Amnesty International, *Report on Torture* (London: Duckworth, 1973), pp. 143–145; see also Gregory Henderson, "The 'Other Boot' in Seoul," *New York Times,* January 16, 1980.
145. Schelling, op. cit., p. 124.

Chapter 5
Conserving
Containment

The two dominant figures in the formulation of American foreign policy during the Eisenhower years were the president and his secretary of state. The two men had come to power as the result of deep national and partisan disaffection. Most of the animus was directed toward the Democratic architects of a foreign policy that had been served by both Dulles and Eisenhower with considerable distinction during and after World War II. The fact that they had helped build and served that policy explains much of the continuity underlying the campaign rhetoric announcing the new administration.

Eisenhower's wartime and immediate postwar role is well known to most Americans. As commander of Allied forces in Europe during World War II he had directed the closing of Churchill's ring—thus destroying the Nazis. But there had been much more: postwar commander of U.S. forces in the European theater; governor of the American zone of occupation; army chief of staff; president of Columbia University; and finally, supreme commander of NATO. As military chief of NATO, he had gone before the Senate as an advocate of President Truman's plan to increase the American presence in Europe. This associated him with the European-centered policies of the Truman administration, created deep suspicion of him within the right wing of the Republican party and guaranteed the struggle with Robert Taft for the presidential nomination in 1952.

Even with his resounding victory over Taft, there were some counter-indications about the continuity of foreign policy. For example, there was the long meeting with Taft in September out of which came Taft's assertion that he and Eisenhower were in "full agreement" on virtually every aspect of domestic and foreign policy. This concession to the right was, perhaps, politically essential given the make-up of the Republican party. For the first two years of the Eisenhower administration the Republicans controlled the House and Senate, and the leadership of the congressional Republicans was in the hands of the right. Eisenhower repeatedly displayed ambivalence toward this ideological bloc within his own party. The result was a tendency to yield before what he feared would be disruptive attacks from the right.[1] Nevertheless, Eisenhower was personally committed to the global structure of containment and the commitments that were implied by this doctrine. Indeed, he was vastly to enlarge the scope of these commitments.

The designation of John Foster Dulles as secretary of state had a certain air of inevitability about it.[2] All the same, the convoluted career of Dulles, especially during the Truman administration, indicates that he, like Eisenhower, seemed to be swimming against strong currents within the Republican party. Dulles, despite the almost frothing partisanship he displayed in drafting the foreign policy statement in the 1952 Republican platform, undeniably represented the internationalist Republican party of Thomas Dewey. His intensely moralistic conception of the postwar Soviet-American confrontation set him apart from the more pragmatic tone of the Democratic secretaries of state he served as a special consultant. Nevertheless, he had assisted in the development and defense of the Marshall Plan and the negotiation of the Japanese Peace Treaty. To the extent that he was successful in his bipartisan role, he was suspect among the Republican partisans Taft, Knowland, Jenner, and McCarthy. Furthermore, as a high-level adviser to the State Department he had watched Acheson and Truman attempt to shield the department and its foreign policy from the onslaught of what Acheson termed "the primitives."[3] Consequently, achieving the stewardship of American foreign policy required careful timing in joining the Eisenhower bandwagon, a delicate feat of ideological nimbleness, and a fine sensitivity to the policy preferences and political power of the right.

Eisenhower's past military involvement with the Roosevelt and Truman administrations was as suspect to the right as Dulles's diplomatic service to the political and diplomatic architects of containment. Eisenhower's immense personal popularity provided him with a fund of political capital that Dulles never could possess, but Eisenhower was no less sensitive than Dulles to what had happened to the Truman administration. The Republican party was under the thrall of Joseph McCarthy, the man who had viciously attacked Eisenhower's mentor and commander-in-arms, General George Marshall, a man of enormous prestige.[4] Thus from the very outset, Eisenhower and Dulles were lined up in a mutual effort to contain the Republican right.

CONTAINING THE REPUBLICAN RIGHT

During the first two years of his administration, President Eisenhower refused to rebut Senator McCarthy's brutalizing of the foreign service and State Department. Instead the president adopted a strategy of waiting for McCarthy's excesses to double back on the senator and destroy him.[5] In the meantime, John Foster Dulles would proclaim the rhetoric of rolling back communist power and liberating so-called captive peoples, while appeasing Senator McCarthy by allowing him and his cohorts virtual freedom to investigate and vilify the foreign service.

Dulles approved the appointment of a McCarthy confidant, Scott McCleod, as chief of personnel security—a man who had a plaque on his desk with his personal motto: "an ounce of loyalty is worth a pound of brains." When Charles Bohlen, the distinguished diplomat and friend of President Eisenhower, was appointed by the new president to be American ambassador to the Soviet Union, he underwent cruel lecturing by Senator McCarthy because of Bohlen's association with the Roosevelt and Truman administrations. President Eisenhower remained aloof, however, and it fell to Secretary Dulles to steer Bohlen's nomination through the Senate over the objections of McLeod and McCarthy. Dulles did so but with trepidation lest he (Dulles) be personally associated with the nomination. So great was Dulles's fear that at one point he asked Bohlen that the two of them not be photographed together. Finally, when the nomination ordeal was over and Bohlen indicated that he would be traveling to the Soviet Union in advance of his family, Dulles, ever fearful, cautioned against the plan because "such a circumstance could open him to veiled charges of homosexuality no matter how baseless such charges might be."[6]

Similarly, Dulles allowed John Carter Vincent and John Paton Davies to be fired although he personally concluded that both men were not security risks as charged by McCleod. Both men were among those foreign service officers who had warned that Chiang Kai-shek was corrupt and must inevitably fall before Mao Zedong's revolutionaries. From the standpoint of Senator McCarthy and his followers, however, they were responsible for what had happened, and would have to go. Dulles acquiesced, although in both instances he officially refused to reinstate the men not because they were security risks, but because they had not demonstrated "sound judgment"—a standard that was never defined by Dulles.[7] Years later Bohlen reflected on these early months of the Eisenhower administration:

> Dulles was a man who lived in mortal terror that events would conspire to turn the McCarthy attack on him, that ". . . so strong were his preoccupations with his job and staying in it, that this affected his attitudes and actions" in nearly every realm. Dulles was a man with "one obsession: to remain Secretary of State."[8]

President Eisenhower probably did not feel these pressures as intensely. However, he, too, was not prepared to take on McCarthy publicly.[9] This reluctance on President Eisenhower's part according to many, including his vice president, was due to Eisenhower's naïveté and inexperience in political warfare.[10] But this analysis is now undergoing a revision. As Gary Wills points out, Eisenhower

> rose in the peacetime professional army, where ambition is thwarted of its natural object (excellence in war) and falls back on jealousy and intrigue. Eisenhower climbed that slippery ladder of bayonets with a sure step and rare instinct for survival.[11]

He was a soldier, but unlike a Patton, he did not romanticize war. He was above all a realist who was conserving and deliberate in the use of his resources, not a man to come out swinging against a McCarthy. In 1953 he assumed the presidency of a country that was torn by suspicion and hysteria. He would in later life assert that his greatest domestic accomplishment as president was the calming of this mood.[12] Insofar as Eisenhower is justified in his claim, he "got the job done, without trumpets."[13]

This temperate attitude and approach was institutionalized in his staff system.[14] Especially in the areas of foreign and defense policy, President Eisenhower replicated the elaborate staff system to which he had become accustomed and employed so successfully in the army. The National Security Council (NSC) expanded dramatically, as committees and subcommittees proliferated. The NSC was managed by Robert Cutler, who dampened dissent and diffused accountability by firmly insisting on the confidentiality of both the substance of recommendations and the process of arriving at decisions in the NSC. Congress, Cutler believed, was not a proper party to this process. Undoubtedly this slowed the decision process; decision papers moved at a more measured pace. But it was Eisenhower's view that the frantic effort to build the wall of containment in the preceding administration had led to the overextension of American power, and the accompanying charged domestic atmosphere contributed to the destruction of Truman's authority and threatened containment itself.

Perhaps Gary Wills is correct: "Eisenhower had the true professional's instinct for making things look easy. He appeared to be performing less work than he actually did. And he wanted it that way. An air of ease inspires confidence."[15] Furthermore, Eisenhower's style "allowed him to evade responsibilities, in the sense that if any head had to roll, it would not be his."[16]

The relationship of Dulles and Eisenhower, though strained at first, came to embody this approach. Dulles appeared to dominate American foreign policy.[17] Dulles always seemed out front, belligerently proselytizing his moralistic message of a new "political offensive" within "a policy of boldness."[18] The front page of the morning papers seemed at times permanently highlighted with pictures of the secretary of state grimly boarding or deplaning either in Washington or some other world capital. President Eisenhower, in contrast, was affable, relaxed, always smiling. His speeches on foreign policy frequently emphasized the positive, the opportunities for relaxing East-West tensions. Eisenhower articulated a deep and seemingly genuine desire to end the confrontation of Soviet and American power that, by now, was the key to world politics. And if Dulles's photographs seemed to come from the travel section, Eisenhower's came from the sports pages, for the president seemed to be perpetually teeing-off at Burning Tree or Augusta.

There were undoubtedly important differences between the two men and, perhaps, disagreements as to relations with the Soviet Union. But there seemed to be agreement concerning the immediate national security problems before the Eisenhower administration: Korea, and, beyond that, retrenchment and consolidation of America's defense posture. Both men knew that their own party would be harassing them as they dealt with these problems. In retrospect, however, Eisenhower's style and especially his relationship with Dulles were admirably suited to dealing with his priorities of Korea and conserving containment within the politically dangerous domestic environment confronting his administration.

Regarding Korea, Eisenhower had reached some very definite conclusions. He had carried out his campaign pledge of visiting Korea during the first week of December 1952. He came away with the conviction that further offensive military action would be enormously costly and ultimately fruitless given the strong defensive positions established by the Chinese and North Koreans during the year of stalemated negotiations.[19] To go for anything less than total victory,[20] however, risked bringing the wrath of the Republican party right down upon the administration. Unless the fact that Eisenhower was now pursuing the same war aims as Truman could be in some way masked, the Eisenhower administration might suffer the same political fate. Yet Eisenhower possessed in his secretary of state exactly what he needed. By allowing Dulles to take the public initiative with his tough and belligerent rhetoric and, in some instances, adopting the same stance publicly and privately himself, President Eisenhower put forth an image that many in Congress and America wanted to see. Though morally repugnant and ultimately destructive of the State Department Dulles's and Eisenhower's willingness to sacrifice the careers of many in the foreign service also contributed to the functional equivalent of a smoke screen. In the meantime, Eisenhower moved to end the war in Korea in a manner for which President Truman might well have been impeached.

A Korean Truce: Continuing
Containment along the 38th Parallel

On returning to the United States from Korea, Eisenhower noted that America was dealing with an enemy that could not be impressed by words "however eloquent, but only deeds—executed under circumstances of our own choosing."[21] The deeds came very quickly, a pattern of escalating military pressure that would be replicated in another Asian war almost two decades later. In his State of the Union Address in February 1953, Eisenhower announced that the Seventh Fleet would be removed from the Taiwan Strait—a clear threat to the mainland Chinese, for Eisenhower was indicating a willingness to allow the Nationalists to step up their guerrilla activities against the mainland and perhaps go even further. There seems to have been little belief that Chiang Kai-shek could launch a full-scale attack; but to the Communists, Eisenhower's action could be read as a toughening of America's posture. It could also be read in the same light by those in Congress who sought total victory, in spite of the fact that Eisenhower had no intentions of seeking such an outcome.

Eisenhower was prepared to use threats and words as well as deeds, and the threat that followed was blunt and awesome, though quietly communicated.[22] "In February, at his orders," Peter Lyons reports, "word had been discreetly passed that if the truce negotiations did not begin to show results, a few atomic weapons might, to use the jargon of the military, be 'wasted.'"[23]

Eisenhower and others in his administration believed that these threats were responsible for subsequent movement in the peace talks in March. This is arguable; for an event of monumental importance for the communist world occurred at the end of March—Stalin died. Suddenly the symbol of Soviet and communist power and intransigence was gone. An extended period of transition followed in the communist world during which long-standing policies underwent important change. Among these changes was some increase in the policy latitude available to Beijing. Within weeks of Stalin's death, the Chinese decided to move to end the Korean War. In April 1953, an exchange of sick and wounded took place, but negotiations bogged down on the repatriation issue. The problem was how to handle those prisoners in the hands of the South Koreans who might choose to stay in the South after an armistice.

Eisenhower again privately threatened the use of nuclear weapons and simultaneously bombed the only remaining strategic targets in North Korea. On May 10 and 11, hydroelectric dams on the Yalu River were attacked, followed on May 13, 1953, by attacks on five irrigation dams in North Korea. The May 13 attacks were directed at civilian populations. Such raids had been undertaken by the Nazis in Holland in 1944 and 1945 and "as all military leaders everywhere well knew, [had] been stigmatized as a war crime by the Nuremberg Tribunal."[24] A dozen or more dams remained, but the message was clear—the United States was prepared to do virtually anything, including the starvation and/or incineration of North Korea (and China?), to end the war.[25] On June 8, 1953, the Communists signed an agreement that seemed to meet most of the objectives of the Americans.

In the meantime, however, Syngman Rhee was digging in his heels. The specter of a settlement that left him little better off than in 1950 loomed before him. Indeed, Rhee would now confront a strong Chinese presence in addition to a war-devastated South Korea. In April and May 1953, Rhee denounced the negotiations, called instead for yet another march to the Yalu, said he would withdraw his troops from the UN force if the Chinese remained in the North, boycotted the talks at Panmunjom, and when it was announced that the repatriation obstacle had been surmounted, organized street demonstrations against the impending settlement. Finally, on June 18, 1953, Rhee started releasing more than twenty-five thousand prisoners in the hope that North Koreans would be sufficiently embarrassed by the reality of thousands of their former soldiers choosing to stay in the South that the Chinese would break off the talks and resume fighting. Rhee's action received support from some military men in Korea, notably General Mark Clark. In Congress, Senator McCarthy commented that "freedom-loving people throughout the world should applaud" Rhee's actions.[26]

Eisenhower did not applaud. In fact an air of crisis settled on the White House as the president feared that the Chinese would ("and, I must confess, with some right") simply refuse to participate in any further talks given the Americans' apparent inability to control their ally. But the Chinese, having made a firm decision to end the war, waited for the Americans to bring Rhee in line. By July 12, 1953, the Americans had succeeded, but only after promising Rhee a mutual security treaty, hundreds of millions of dollars in military assistance and economic aid, a voice in any postwar conferences concerning Korea, and thinly veiled threats to remove Rhee from power.[27]

On July 13 and 14 the Chinese struck at South Korean units, pushing them back several miles and inflicting thousands of casualties. The American Eighth Army stood by while Rhee's forces took a terrific pounding. As Eisenhower notes: "One possibly useful result was to remind President Rhee of the vulnerability of his forces if deprived of United Nations support."[28] On July 19 the chief UN negotiator informed the Chinese that the UN command would honor any armistice reached no matter what the ROK did.[29] Final arrangements were quickly worked out for the repatriation of remaining prisoners, and the truce was signed on July 27.

A year earlier the secretary of state had written into the Republican platform strong words concerning "hampering orders" on the part of the Truman administration leading to "stalemate and ignominious bartering with our enemies . . . [with] no hope of victory" in Korea.[30] The Eisenhower administration had countermanded some of the hampering orders and allowed the bombing of irrigation dams and threatened the use of nuclear weapons, thereby providing the appearance of having decisively forced the end of the war. But in the end there had been no victory. Moreover, some of the most "ignominious bartering" of the war was of necessity carried out between America and its South Korean allies. Finally, when the war ended the Eisenhower administration found itself agreeing, through the truce and promise of massive aid to South Korea, to accept a militarily stalemated line not unlike the one that had existed in June 1950.[31] In summary, the use of escalating force and the threat of nuclear weapons combined with even more important changes in the communist world had the net effect of formalizing the preexisting balance of political and military power on the Korean peninsula.

Reassessment and Continuity

Under the urging of Senator Taft and his own economic advisers, President Eisenhower reduced the outgoing Truman administration budget by more than $6 billion. At the same time, Eisenhower announced what he termed a radical departure in his first defense budget, which would be sent to Congress in January 1954. The so-called radical nature of this approach referred to Eisenhower's rejection of the year of crisis concept that had appeared in NSC-68 and other planning documents of the Truman administration. In its place Eisenhower would substitute the notion of the long haul: "providing a strong military position which can be maintained over the extended period of uneasy peace."[32] The implication was that the older planning concepts were unsound because they introduced into military budgets and planning a feast or famine cycle rather than sustained effort.[33]

In fact, Eisenhower's rhetoric was a misrepresentation of Truman's policies.[34] President Truman's rearmament proposals were presented to a Congress that was, prior to June 1950, reluctant to proceed as the president desired. The notion, presented in NSC-68, of a year of maximum peril, 1954, served as a device to emphasize and dramatize the target date for completion of the buildup. The years between 1952 and 1954 were portrayed as the crucial period for American rearmament to gain a position of strength.[35] The Eisenhower administration felt that it could stretch out the build-up in military capability called for in NSC-68, achieving its target levels in 1957 rather than the end of 1955. Eisenhower gave to his defense planning, however, the image of a new departure. It was after all essential—as in Korea—that the appearance of change be maintained. At a minimum, Eisenhower's own party had to be convinced that a transformation was taking place.

In summary, the Eisenhower administration's assumptions and expectations concerning a period of extended Soviet-American confrontation were very similar to those held by the Truman administration. However, the Eisenhower administration held that the rearmament effort, already well under way as a result of the Korean War, could be completed and sustained at a lower rate of expenditure than planned by Truman. This contention was the fundamental principle of Eisenhower's planning: national security was a function of a balanced budget and economic principles must be incorporated into all military planning. The new Joint Chiefs of Staff had been selected by Eisenhower (and with the approval of Taft) so as to ensure that they would be totally responsive to the new administration's defense priorities and concepts. Nonetheless, the broad foreign policy concepts on which the defense posture rested were increasingly similar to those held by Truman's administration.

As in the case of defense policy, Eisenhower had set in motion a parallel reassessment of foreign policy. Task forces were established to study and make recommendations concerning three alternative politico-military strategies:

1. *Containment*: a continuation of the basic structure of policy during the Truman years.
2. *Global deterrence:* American commitments would be actually extended and communist transgressions met with severe punishment.
3. *Liberation:* political, psychological, economic, and even paramilitary warfare designed to penetrate the communist empire, "roll it back," and liberate the captive peoples.

The last two options clearly bore the stamp of John Foster Dulles, who had previously called for heavy reliance upon the threat of nuclear weapons as the best means for checking the threat of communist military aggression. Global deterrence was a defensive or deterrent military posture; but if aggression occurred, the response of the West would not be confined to a limited conventional response à la Korea. If American interests were global and indistinguishable, and the threat to those interests was monolithic, undifferentiated Soviet Communist aggression, then the United States and the free world now felt free to direct a response directly against the Soviets (or any other communist aggressor such as China). Moreover, Dulles claimed that having thus resolved the problem of military defense, the free world "can undertake what has been too long delayed—a political offensive:"[36]—liberation.

Eisenhower, however, was skeptical about the notion of liberation. He did not understand how Dulles could ever effectively implement his political offensive. In fact, as the planning exercise was underway, the first opportunity for liberation occurred in June 1953. East Berlin workers, ostensibly reacting to the imposition of higher production quotas, rioted. The United States did nothing beyond an offer of free food and the establishment of soup kitchens in West Berlin. The uprising was crushed. The detonation in August 1953 of the Soviets' first hydrogen bomb made explicit what Eisenhower knew all along: given the Soviets' growing military capacity and the importance of Eastern Europe to their security designs, liberation was at best an incredibly dangerous policy. The option was "firmly rejected."[37] In contrast, the deterrence option, with its emphasis on air and sea power, was clearly looked upon favorably by Eisenhower. The appointment of Arthur William Radford ("whose maxim as a carrier Admiral in the war against Japan had been 'kill the bastards scientifically'"[38]) as chairman of the Joint Chiefs and the economic constraints issued him with his initial planning directives led almost inevitably to support for a less manpower-intensive defense posture.

The outcome of the policy review set in motion by President Eisenhower was the rejection of Secretary Dulles's proposed policy of boldness and political offensive, and a confirmation of the posture advocated by Eisenhower from the very outset: the continuation of containment but with a shift in the instruments away from conventional force and toward the technology of air and sea power. This was Senator Taft's conception of what American military policy ought to be, not that of Dulles.

The New Look and Massive Retaliation

In October 1953 the task of integrating foreign policy assumptions and defense planning into the first Eisenhower budget was begun. The president approved an NSC paper that allowed the services to "plan on using nuclear weapons, tactical as well as strategic, whenever their use would be desirable from a military standpoint."[39] Apart from small brush fire conflicts, all wars were now assumed to be, at a minimum, tactical nuclear wars. Moreover, massive retaliatory capability rather than ground troops was now regarded as the major deterrent to Soviet aggression, although what specifically the form of aggression might be was never made explicit. It was agreed that some American ground forces should be available to deter local aggression, but there was vagueness concerning the assumption that local indigenous forces would be employed. These decisions, especially cuts in the size of the Army, opened the way for a reduction in the military budget through 1957, when the administration intended to complete the implementation of the new look.[40]

On January 12, 1954, Dulles, in a speech before the Council on Foreign Relations, explained the outcome of the new administration's policy deliberations and planning. The speech included criticism of the purported defensive, reactive, and expensive character of Truman's containment.[41] The Eisenhower administration was advancing a new conception of American policy—"a maximum deterrent at a bearable cost,"[42] in which

> local defenses must be reinforced by the further deterrent of massive retaliatory power. . . . The way to deter aggression is for the free community to be willing and able to respond vigorously at places and with means of its own choosing.[43]

Dulles succeeded through the massive retaliation speech in projecting an American policy with a tough and rigid image that obscured the administration's decision to continue American policy within the frame-work of containment developed by the Truman administration.[44] If anything, the options were now fewer in number; in the event of local aggression the United States would rely on local forces, perhaps backed by American air and sea support. If that was not sufficient or if the aggression was major, there remained only nuclear war.

CONTAINMENT IN A CHANGING WORLD

The rapid contraction of British power in the Middle East and the French in Southeast Asia accelerated the struggle for national independence in the non-Western world. To Eisenhower and Dulles, these momentous changes were understood in terms of the quasi-theological dogma of confrontation between communism and the free world. The Middle East, Latin America, and Vietnam were, therefore, "vacuums" into which Soviet and Chinese communism would move unless anticipated by a free world—that is, American—presence. The remnants of the Chinese civil war in and around the Taiwan Strait were formalized as the eastern frontier of the cold war and the testing ground for the notion of deterrence.

There was also a continuation of economic motives in U.S. policy in these years. The Truman Doctrine and the development of the Marshall

Plan underscored the interdependence of economic, political, and military considerations in American policy in Europe. Eisenhower and his secretary of state generally framed their policies in the lofty rhetoric of ideological confrontation. But, as was the case in the Truman administration, the freedom that American power was to protect usually encompassed a notion of a particular way of life. Moreover, that way of life—its political forms and, inseparably, its economic essence—was deemed appropriate to the rest of the world.

Thus, concerning Vietnam and Indochina, Eisenhower stated:

> The loss of all Vietnam, together with Laos in the west and Cambodia in the southwest, would have meant the surrender to Communist enslavement of millions. On the material side, it would have spelled the loss of valuable deposits of tin and prodigious supplies of rubber and rice. It would have meant that Thailand, enjoying buffer territory between itself and Red China, would be esposed on its entire eastern border to infiltration or attack.
>
> And if Indochina fell, not only Thailand but Burma and Malaya would be threatened, with added risks to East Pakistan and South Asia as well as to all Indonesia.[45]

All the elements of the world view developed after World War II are here: the enslavement of millions, raw materials, and the strategic concern for buffer territory and proliferating threats to others. One element might assume dominance in a particular case. Yet whether it was an economic or strategic question or a matter of the internal political regime of other nations, it always stood inseparably in the context of the ideological whole.

During the Eisenhower administration, a primary objective was to protect world economic and ideological order in the emerging third world of the 1950s. The containment doctrine developed for Central Europe in the late 1940s was extended. However, this effort reflected a profound misunderstanding of the forces at work in the Middle East, Southeast Asia, East Asia and Latin America. To Eisenhower and his advisers, the revolutionary changes that seemed to be activated all over the globe by the collapse of European colonial empires were not viewed as the result of complex and fragile traditional societies being thrust into the crucible of rapid decolonization and modernization. Instead, the often violent unrest was regarded as merely the newest form of world communist aggression, requiring an American response not unlike that undertaken in Europe.

The effort to restructure emerging societies in the American image had three consequences: First, the frequently brusque shouldering aside of America's European allies as they proved unable to deal with what was perceived as communist penetration of the non-Western world introduced near irreconcilable strains in the NATO alliance. Second, this assumption of the postcolonial Western presence in the non-Western world also meant that the Americans would now be confronted with forces they could not understand until the United States was itself tragically and irretrievably enmeshed in a colonial war in Asia. Finally, the preoccupation with formalizing containment outside of Europe contributed to the inability of Eisenhower and Dulles to explore developments in Soviet-American relations that might have allowed movement into a postcontainment phase of world politics. Unhappily, the formal abrasiveness of the "new look" prevailed. American foreign policy was fixed against the revolutionary tide of the postwar international system.

Vietnam

By the early 1950s, after seven years of bloody counterrevolutionary warfare in Indochina, it was inescapably apparent that French colonial control could not be reestablished. American assistance was substantial but could not offset the material and psychological costs of the war the French had been waging against the Viet Minh, a Communist-led coalition of Vietnamese revolutionaries under the direction of Ho Chi Minh. The Viet Minh, with the active support of the American Office of Strategic Studies (the forerunner of the CIA), had fought the Japanese effort to impose their political and economic order on Indochina during World War II. When the French attempted to reimpose colonial rule after the war, the Viet Minh continued to fight for national independence. By 1954, the price the French were paying to deny self-government to the Viet Minh had become inordinate. The French suffered 92,000 dead and 114,000 wounded.[46] But many in the French government feared that to grant Vietnamese independence would cost even more. For it might encourage revolutionary activity in other colonial areas such as Morocco, Tunisia, or most important, Algeria.

The dilemma was a painful juxtaposition of national pride and waning imperial glory against a hemorrhage of blood and treasure. In early 1954 the French, with garrison of fifteen thousand surrounded at Dien Bien Phu, accepted a Russian proposal for a five-power foreign ministers conference—to include the Soviet Union, United States, Britain, France, and Communist China—that would discuss both the Korean and Indochinese situations. Dulles and the president were concerned that an important and vital front in the cold war was about to be compromised. Both worried that the outcome of negotiated withdrawal of France would lead to "shift[s] in the power relations throughout Asia and the Pacific

[that] could be disastrous. . . ."[47] Neither man viewed what was going on in Vietnam as the continuation of a struggle for independence. To Eisenhower, "Ho Chi Minh was, of course, a hard-core Communist, while the Viet Minh, the forces under his command, were supported by the Chinese Communists in the north."[48] The Eisenhower administration came to see the imminent collapse of French power as the breaching of the dike holding back the tide of Chinese Communist-promoted aggression throughout southeast Asia. As the president explained in April 1954:

> First of all, you have the specific value of a locality in its production of materials that the world needs.
> Then you have the possibility that many human beings pass under a dictatorship that is inimical to the free world.
> Finally, you have . . . what you would call the "falling domino" principle. You have a row of dominoes set up, you knock over the first one, and what will happen to the last one is the certainty that it will go over very quickly.[49]

With the Geneva Conference beginning at the end of April 1954, an air of crisis developed in Washington. The immediate reaction, especially on the part of the head of the Joint Chiefs of Staff, Admiral Radford, was for military intervention by means of an air strike, with nuclear weapons if necessary, on the Viet Minh positions around Dien Bien Phu. Dulles was no less prone to intervention, although he announced publicly that any U.S. action should be within the context of "united action." This ambiguous notion reflected Eisenhower's view that any U.S. intervention would have to meet certain preconditions. First, American intervention would have to have the support of Congress, and second, any intervention would have to be undertaken in concert with the Southeast Asians and the British.[50]

Eisenhower wanted a victory as intensely as anyone in Washington. But Eisenhower, perhaps more than most, was aware of the domestic limits in the situation. Korea had ended less than a year earlier, and the military situation in Vietnam seemed to require a commitment of American manpower similar to Truman's effort at military containment in Asia. Aside from the fact that the manpower necessary for such an engagement would not be available under the new look, Eisenhower sensed that there was no national stomach for another fight and probably knew that Congress, the Republican right wing notwithstanding, would not support another engagement in Asia. In fact, the congressional leadership, when consulted, further strengthened the president's hand against immediate military intervention by echoing his precondition of British approval and support for military involvement.

To meet Eisenhower's and Congress's preconditions would require a considerable diplomatic effort which precluded a quick intervention. Therefore, Dulles set about the tasks of getting British and Southeast Asian support against Ho Chi Minh and minimizing the possible damage growing out of the Geneva Conference. Eisenhower and Dulles wanted no involvement in any negotiated settlement of the Indochinese situation that resulted in a *de facto* communist victory. The way to avoid this, according to Eisenhower, would be the creation of "a new, *ad hoc* grouping or coalition" comprised of the United States, Britain, France, Cambodia, Laos, Australia, New Zealand, Thailand, and the Philippines. This coalition would provide material and moral support, and "it must be willing to join the fight if necessary."[51] In short, the coalition would provide the French with the wherewithal to avoid having to negotiate any agreement at Geneva. Eisenhower and Dulles simply did not want the French to give up.

The Indochina phase of the Geneva Conference began the day after the commander of Dien Bien Phu, on May 7, after fifty-seven days of siege, surrendered all his remaining men to the Vietnamese leader, General Giap. Dulles and Eisenhower persisted in their view that the United States had to prevent any settlement that undercut the containment of communism in Southeast Asia. Thus, they refused to participate formally in the talks or state an unambiguous position concernig the outcome. American policy was one of no participation in any agreement and limiting to the maximum extent possible any communist gains made through the negotiations. The sum of the American position was to impede any progress toward a settlement at Geneva; and if this failed, to refuse any ratification of the agreement.

This obstructionist position ran counter to all other participants, especially the British, who under Foreign Minister Anthony Eden's skilled direction attempted to move the conference toward a settlement. In the meantime, Washington persisted in private contacts with the French concerning American intervention including, then French Premier Georges Bidault would later claim, the possibility of using nuclear weapons. These overtures only served to inhibit French willingness to come to an agreement with the Viet Minh and further exacerbated American relations with the British, who were attempting to move matters to a settlement. By late May 1954, the conference had stalemated, the French government fell, and the talks were suspended pending French elections.

By the end of June 1954 the French had elected as premier Pierre

Mendès-France, who assumed direct responsibility for the negotiations and promised to have a settlement within thirty days. The Geneva Conference now moved quickly to a conclusion. The substance of the agreement was to provide for a resolution of the military conflict by means of a temporary partition of the country at the 17th parallel. The final declaration of the conference explicitly stated that, "the military demarcation line is provisional and should not in any way be interpreted as constituting a political or territorial boundary."[52] The political future of the country was to be resolved in 1956 in national elections.

In summary, two countries were not formed and there were no political preconditions established for the elections. Subsequent South Vietnamese and U.S. justifications for refusing to undertake or carry out the election provisions of the Geneva Accords rested on the assertion that "conditions in North Vietnam during that period were such as to make impossible any free and meaningful expression of popular will."[53] In fact, the participants in the talks agreed that the establishment of democratic institutions or the free and meaningful expression of popular will was not something to be guaranteed by the Geneva Accords. Rather, democratic institutions and processes would be a product of elections. The elections were not dependent upon any specified political conditions in the provisional regroupment zones. And the zones were clearly not viewed as political units or nascent nation-states.[54]

On the understanding and misunderstanding of these agreements rest the respective claims concerning American intervention in Vietnam. If one construes the Geneva Accords to have established two Vietnamese states, then American involvement appears legally unexceptional. If, on the other hand, the language of the final declaration is interpreted as above, then subsequent development of the Vietnam War is clearly a civil war and not a case of aggression as insisted by the Eisenhower, Kennedy, Johnson, Nixon, and Ford administrations.

Dulles and Eisenhower moved immediately to undo the results of the Geneva agreement on Indochina. "The important thing," Dulles said, shortly after the conference broke up, "is not to mourn the past but to seize the future opportunity to prevent the loss in Northern Vietnam from leading to the extension of Communism throughout Southeast Asia and the Southwest Pacific."[55] Within six weeks Dulles convened a meeting in Manila of representatives of the United States, Britain, France, Australia, New Zealand, Pakistan, Thailand, and the Philippines for the purpose of establishing a Southeast Asia Treaty Organization (SEATO) to prevent the extension of communism. Dulles sought but could not get, either from the participants in the conference or from the Congress, the kind of precommitments to the defense of the area embodied in the NATO agreement. Instead, SEATO would "meet the common danger in accordance with its constitutional processes. . . ." Beyond this were equally vague agreements to consult in the event of subversion, guerrilla warfare, or similar kinds of activity.[56]

Dulles also sought to include the French Associated States of Laos and Cambodia, and the state of Vietnam, in SEATO. This was resisted vigorously by the French. The French pointed out that such an act would violate the Geneva Accords proscription against Vietnam or the other associated states from entering into alliances. However, Dulles persisted and got everyone to agree to at least a protocol to the SEATO agreement that extended the protection of the treaty to Laos, Cambodia, and the "free territory under the jurisdiction of the state of Vietnam."[57] What had been left by the signatories as a nonpolitical provisional separation of the parties in Vietnam pending elections, Dulles and Eisenhower set out to make politically permanent. The United States had failed to stop the Geneva Conference, but the SEATO agreement and the reference in the protocol to the treaty to the "free territory" in Vietnam was a clear indication of Eisenhower and Dulles's intent to transform the 17th parallel into a permanent political boundary with American support going to a separate state of South Vietnam. Indeed, the SEATO protocol extended protection to South Vietnam even before it existed.

During and immediately after the Geneva Conference a confused struggle for power developed in the southern part of Vietnam. Ho Chi Minh was in firm control in Hanoi, but in Saigon the locus of power was in doubt, at least until the United States entered the picture. The government of the Vietnamese chief of state, Emperor Bao Dai, had served as a front for French colonial control since 1948. With the impending collapse of French power Bao Dai had left Vietnam seeking refuge in France, and in 1954 Ngo Dinh Diem became prime minister. Diem, a Catholic, had spent much of the preceding four years in the United States and gained the support of the American Friends of Vietnam, an analogue of the China lobby. He was also supported by a collection of American politicians including such senators as Mike Mansfield, Hubert Humphrey, and John F. Kennedy; a spectrum of academics; and Catholic religious leaders, most notably Francis, Cardinal Spellman.

In November of 1954 full U.S. support for Diem was announced and, with the removal of those Vietnamese military leaders opposed to Diem, the way was cleared for the consolidation of Diem's power in Saigon. To ensure Diem's control, more than $325 million in economic and military assistance was pumped into the South. Included in this aid were, by some accounts, more than $12 million which Diem employed in early 1955 to bribe the leadership of the remaining domestic political opposition.[58] In October 1955, Diem organized a referendum in which the South Vietnamese had to choose between Diem and Bao Dai. Diem won more than 98 percent of the vote, and on October 26, 1955, the prime minister proclaimed the founding of the Republic of Vietnam and himself the first president.

Meanwhile, Diem had refused to begin negotiations with the Viet Minh concerning elections. In July 1955 Diem asserted that he had not signed the Geneva agreements and that he could not, therefore, be bound by them. In this, Diem was merely reflecting the position of Dulles, who had claimed, in June 1955, that the preconditions for free elections did not exist in the North. Hence, there was no obligation on Diem's part to proceed. Instead, Diem continued his consolidation of control and, with the establishment of the Republic of Vietnam, provided the United States with a political entity in name as well as fact.

Iran

As in Southeast Asia, American intervention in the Middle East was related to the collapse of colonial control on the part of an American ally, in this case Great Britain. In 1951 the Iranians had nationalized the Anglo-Iranian Oil Company. The major oil companies had subsequently boycotted Iranian oil, bringing on a near-impossible economic situation in the country. The Truman administration had tried to straddle the issue. Fearing Soviet involvement if the Iranian economic structure collapsed, Truman had maintained a low-level economic assistance program even as he refused to prevent the oil companies from trying to bring Iran and the nationalist government of Premier Mohammed Mossadegh to their knees.

Eisenhower and Dulles decided very early in their administration that Mossadegh would have to go. Significantly, however, it was not Eisenhower's intention merely to retrieve British interests and influence in the area. Rather, the president sought to replace the British in Iran even as he replaced the French in Indochina and would try to replace the British throughout the Middle East during 1956 and 1957. There was the conviction that British power was forever broken, thereby leaving a politico-strategic vacuum in the area. But underlying these balance of power abstractions were the realities of oil.

Eisenhower's election had been heavily financed by the American oil industry; and of the men Eisenhower counted as his closest friends numerous oil men, investment bankers, and other titans of the corporate world constituted a clear majority. He was, therefore, intuitively responsive to their interests and concerns, and his entire conception of the national economy and America's role in the global economy was pervaded with their views concerning free enterprise, access to raw materials, and world markets.[59] It is unlikely, therefore, that the dangerous implications of a nationalist success in Iran for American oil interests throughout the Middle East escaped him. And finally, the situation in Iran, if carefully orchestrated, provided an opportunity for replacing British power and its economic presence.

In March 1953, Eisenhower, Dulles, and Undersecretary of State Walter Bedell Smith had agreed with Eden to seek "alternatives to Mossadegh."[60] This understanding was reached after the United States had tried and failed in the first weeks of the Eisenhower administration to bring Mossadegh in line with a threatened cut-off in U.S. economic assistance. Mossadegh had responded that he would turn to the Soviet Union if need be, although he would prefer to work with the Americans. The Americans urged the Iranian premier to settle with the British, then the United States would consider further aid. Mossadegh refused, and in early August 1953, Kermit Roosevelt, Theodore Roosevelt's grandson and the Central Intelligence Agency's primary operative in the Middle East, was despatched to Iran for the purpose of bringing down Mossadegh's government and turning U.S. support to the Shah.

The situation in Iran was seething by this time and amenable to Roosevelt's efforts. On August 19, Roosevelt, using a Tehran basement as a command post, engineered a coup.

> One authority has it that Kim Roosevelt's Iranian agents emptied the athletic clubs and steam rooms of Teheran, producing a pride of weight-lifters, gymnasts, wrestlers, and assorted musclemen who paraded through the bazaars braying pro-Shah slogans and gathering great crowds along their way. Another authority speaks of "a lumpenproletarian mob, armed with knives and clubs" moving on the center of the city. There is no essential discord. All agree the uprising brought riots, terror, violence, bloodshed, death.[61]

Within three days, Mossadegh had been arrested and the Shah returned from Rome where he had been consulting with Allen Dulles, the head of the CIA. Earlier, on August 21, Eisenhower received a note, probably from Roosevelt, which read in part: "The Shah is a new man. For the first time, he believes in himself because he feels that he is king of his people's choice and not by arbitrary decision of a foreign power."[62] Iran was immediately extended $45 million in economic assistance, and a month later Kermit Roosevelt was awarded the National Security Medal by Eisenhower.[63]

Next the United States undertook the negotiation of a new oil arrangement which reduced substantially the British position while increasing the American share. The five major American oil companies— New Jersey Standard, Mobil, Texaco, Gulf, and Standard Oil of California—received 40 percent of a new international consortium developed to exploit Iranian oil. British Petroleum received 40 percent, Royal Dutch Shell 14 percent, and the French 6 percent. American antitrust laws were adjusted to permit the formation of the American portion of the cartel, and Iranian oil production was carefully controlled by the consortium to avoid a reduction of world oil prices.[64]

Guatemala

The situation in Guatemala a year later was somewhat different than the Iranian case in that the regime of Jacobo Arbenz Guzmán accepted and depended upon domestic Communists for support.[65] The existence of leftist and Marxist politics in Guatemala is not surprising, in view of the country's postwar history. Prior to 1944 a series of dictators had served as a governmental front for a vast concentration of private American political and economic power, the United Fruit Company. Since the late nineteenth century it had bought hundreds of square miles of banana-producing and nonproducing acreage, employed forced labor, and controlled the only railroad in the country. In 1944, however, the last dictator, General Jorge Ubico, who admired and compared himself favorably to Hitler, was overthrown and replaced by a military junta which included Arbenz.

Arbenz was subsequently elected president in 1951, and Marxist activity increased as Communists were taken into the government. Moreover, during 1952 and 1953 heavy-handed suppression of anticommunist labor and political leaders became commonplace, although this activity cannot be dissociated from the ongoing antigovernment and anticommunist activities of United Fruit, which included the end of tourism promotion by American companies and, more important, the reduction of both international and bilateral economic assistance from the United States. In March 1953 matters came to a head as Arbenz expropriated more than two hundred thirty thousand acres of uncultivated land for which United Fruit was compensated $600,000 in long-term interest-bearing bonds—the low valuation previously placed on the land by United Fruit to escape Guatemalan taxes. The president of United Fruit reportedly remarked at this time: "From here on out it's not a matter of the people of Guatemala against the United Fruit Company; the question is going to be communism against the right of property, the life and security of the Western Hemisphere."[66]

Washington saw matters in a similar light. U.S. Ambassador to Guatemala John E. Peurifoy described his first impression of Arbenz in 1953:

> It seemed to me that the man thought like a Communist and talked like a Communist, and if not actually one, would do until one came along. I so

reported to Secretary Dulles, who informed the President; and I expressed to them the view that unless the Communist influences in Guatemala were counteracted, Guatemala would within six months fall completely under Communist control.[67]

This was hardly news to Eisenhower and Dulles. They had, in fact, sent Peurifoy to Guatemala to coordinate the activities of the CIA and other U.S. ambassadors in Central America—activities explicitly directed at the overthrow of the Arbenz regime.[68] Dulles had prepared the way in March 1953 by getting the Tenth Inter-American Conference to pass a resolution declaring that intervention against a state whose political institutions were dominated or controlled by "the international Communist movement" would not constitute an abrogation of hemisphere principles of political and territorial integrity.[69]

The coup itself did not come until June 1954, for the liberation army had to be prepared. The CIA employed Carlos Castillo Armas, a graduate of the U.S. Army Command and General Staff School, to lead a band of mercenaries from their base camp in Honduras with air support flown by American CIA pilots out of Managua International Airport in Nicaragua. Eisenhower closed a personal review of the coup d'état plans on June 16, 1954, with the observation, "I want all of you to be damn good and sure you succeed. I'm prepared to take any steps that are necessary to see that it succeeds. When you commit the flag, you commit it to win."[70]

On June 18, 1954, Castillo Armas, driven in an old station wagon, led his would be army across the border as the CIA's rebel air force of four P-47 Thunderbolts bombed the Guatemalan capital. Little progress was made, however, as no popular uprising occurred and half the CIA's planes were knocked out of action. On June 20 Eisenhower approved the sale of two P-51 fighter bombers to Nicaragua; the planes promptly entered the liberation struggle. On the ground Castillo Armas was making little headway, but Arbenz, facing possible rebellion in his own army, capitulated and turned over control of the government to an army colonel named Díaz, who proved reluctant to go much beyond the abolition of the Communist party.

Peurifoy, who had displayed singular anticommunist skills in similar operations in Greece while he was an ambassador there, had had enough. Strapping a .45 pistol to his hip and taking along his marine embassy guard, the ambassador strode down the street to meet with the new Guatemalan leader. As the conference proceeded, American pilots bombed the radio station and army headquarters. Díaz then agreed that another governmental change would be in order. Within a week Castillo Armas arrived in Peurifoy's private plane and assumed power.

The first act of Castillo Armas in the aftermath of the coup was disenfranchisement of about 70 percent of the population. Next, an election was held in which Castillo Armas received 99.9 percent of the votes cast. There was no opposition. Eisenhower noted in his memoirs:

> Castillo Armas was . . . confirmed . . . by a thundering majority, as President. He proved to be far more than a mere rebel; he was a farseeing and able statesman . . . he enjoyed the devotion of his people.[71]

This "farseeing and able statesman" proceeded to suspend congress and all constitutional rights, end agrarian reform thereby returning all land to United Fruit, and end all rights and privileges of labor organizations. Finally, Castillo Armas established a committee for defense that could secretly name anyone, without appeal, a Communist who was in turn subject to arrest and death; 72,000 people were so named within four months.[72] For this display of leadership the Castillo Armas regime received $90 million in American aid over the next two years. In contrast, from 1944 through 1953 the leftist regimes received—apart from road-building subsidies—less than $1 million in economic assistance.[73]

Intervention and Containment

In April 1953 the President had proclaimed that among the "few clear precepts, which govern its conduct in world affairs, the United States counted: . . . Any nation's right to form a government and an economic system of its own choosing is *inalienable*. . . . Any nation's attempt to dictate to other nations their form of government is *indefensible*."[74] In view of the preliminary planning then underway for both the Iranian and Guatemalan coups, how are we to explain the gross inconsistency of this statement with contrary policies already in motion?

One answer might be simply to discuss the Iranian and Guatemalan coups as sordid but nonetheless deviant cases designed to protect the particular interests of political benefactors, past business associates present investments, or future employment opportunities. Eisenhower's connection with American oil interests has been noted. As a lawyer, John Foster Dulles had drawn up the contracts between United Fruit and the Guatemalan government by which whole provinces were turned over to the company; the assistant secretary of state for inter-American affairs at the time of the coup held a significant block of United Fruit stock; Allen Dulles, the head of the CIA, had been president turned over to the company; the assistant secretary of state for inter-

American affairs at the time of the coup held a signficant block of United Fruit stock; Allen Dulles, the head of the CIA, had been president of the company; and Walter Bedell Smith, the undersecretary of state, would join the board of directors of United Fruit upon leaving the State Department.

Although this line of analysis is straightforward and on its face powerful, the Guatemalan and Iranian coups must be placed in a broader context of policy development during the early Eisenhower administration. Viewed in relation to parallel events in Vietnam there is apparent a systematic set of attitudes and pattern of policy with respect to change in the non-Western world. In all these instances, anti-Western nationalism or revolutionary leftist political activity was viewed by Washington as externally derived, the product of international communist penetration. Men such as Eisenhower and Dulles found it impossible to accept that revolutionary change in the non-Western world could result solely or even primarily from indigenous conditions. And if they did accept the possibility, such change was nevertheless a threat to their conception of acceptable political and economic order. Moreover, even if they had regarded such revolutionary change as legitimate—and there is no evidence whatsoever that they did—perceived domestic politial constraints were such that they could not admit it.

In summary, then, the Eisenhower administration had begun during its first years in office to develop and elaborate a conception of containment in those non-Western areas regarded as peripheral by Kennan, Acheson, and the other framers of the containment policy. The modalities of containment in the non-Western world were as yet crude— these coups were frenetic affairs conducted by romantic types straight out of contemporary fiction. Indeed, Eisenhower recorded in his personal diary concerning the Iranian coup, "our agent there, a member of the CIA, worked intelligently, courageously and tirelessly. I listened to his detailed report, and it seemed more like a dime novel than an historical fact."[75] The image of a Kermit Roosevelt directing a nation's destiny from a basement or an American ambassador personally conducting a coup d'état with a gun appended to his hip is almost comical until we reflect on the consequences of their actions for the people of the countries in question. Nevertheless, their activities were consistent with Eisenhower's view that containment must be carried out at lower cost than in the Truman years if it was to be domestically acceptable. From this standpoint the immediate ends achieved, the salaries, bribe funds, limited equipment required by a Roosevelt or Peurifoy, and subsequently a few hundred million dollars in military and economic assistance compared favorably to the tens of thousands of casualities and billions of dollars consumed by containment in Korea.

CONTAINMENT
THROUGH BRINKMANSHIP

The crisis of the Taiwan Strait during 1954 and 1955 is another example of the Eisenhower view of global containment. Because the crisis involved the Chinese civil war, the situation was perhaps as dangerous domestically as it was internationally. On no other issue was the Republican right more vocal; indeed, it had emerged as an important political force because of the China issue. Consequently, the contours of the crisis were shaped by Eisenhower's concern for this domestic right flank. Through the crisis, the Eisenhower administration confirmed its willingness to threaten nuclear war. By the end of the crisis, Dulles would formalize nuclear threats as the preeminent component of an American-constructed peace.

The Onset of the Crisis

The tensions of 1954 were the ongoing essence of the relationship between Chiang's regime in Taipei and Mao's in Beijing. During 1953 and early 1954, the Eisenhower administration announced that it was removing the Seventh Fleet from the Taiwan Strait, and, in response to strong lobbying, increasing American economic and military assistance to Chiang. The Chinese Communists, anticipating increased military pressure from Taiwan, felt compelled to signal their disfavor. By midyear 1954, the Communists and Chiang were exchanging threats of invasion. Air and naval incidents gradually intensified and increased in number. In August 1954, Syngman Rhee, speaking in the U.S. House of Representatives, called for the United States to join him and Chiang Kai-shek in a full-scale invasion of the mainland. In September 1954 the Communists began shelling the Nationalist island of Quemoy two miles off the mainland and the confrontation was joined.

Perhaps the most difficult aspect of this early phase of the escalating confrontation was in Washington, where Senate hawks demanded a decisive response to the Communists' use of force. The Joint Chiefs recommended that the offshore islands be defended and Chiang allowed to bomb communist gun emplacements on the mainland and further inland if necessary. If this precipitated a communist invasion, then the United States should join the battle. Eisenhower emphasized, however, that such a step could not be kept limited. He foresaw only two likely outcomes: a Korea-type engagement or world war. Both were unacceptable. Nevertheless, he had to respond to the domestic pressures and his own inclination that Dulles was correct in his assessment: "The Chinese communists, Dulles said, were probing; unless we stopped them, we faced disaster in the Far East."[76] The initial American response was a proposal to submit the issue to the United Nations, but Chiang refused, fearing that the United Nations might resolve the broader question of the civil war against him. The only apparent remaining course, therefore, was the defense treaty with Chiang that was negotiated and eventually signed on December 2, 1954.

The Communists may have begun their escalation as an essentially "preemptive or spoiling attack."[77] By the end of the year, however, they were confronted with a U.S. guarantee of mutual assistance to Chiang. Moreover, the public agreement was ambiguous concerning the American commitment to the defense of the offshore islands and the use of force by Chiang. It is probable that this ambiguity was inevitable and consciously contrived. Eisenhower and Dulles sought simultaneously to balance the pressures of the congressional hawks who would have been infuriated by any withdrawal of U.S. support; Chiang's desire to extend U.S. commitment and involvement; and the administration's private wish to avoid precisely such involvement and commitment.[78] Eisenhower had, therefore, succeeded in the manipulation of an extremely ambiguous diplomatic and domestic political situation. Mao continued probing. In this instance, however, the actions included the bombing of the strategically insignificant Tachen Island and an amphibious assault on the island of Ichiang near Tachen, routing in the process a garrison of Nationalist irregulars. The Eisenhower administration now had to deal with an escalation of the crisis. The mutual security treaty may have contained the home front, but clearly it had not stabilized the situation in East Asia.

The Crisis Goes to the Brink

Eisenhower resolved that the most appropriate response would be an embellishment of the treaty—a precommitment on the part of Congress to give the president discretion in the implementation of the treaty and in meeting the renewed crisis. The resulting "Formosa [i.e., Taiwan] Resolution" found the Congress affirming Eisenhower's "inherent powers" to deal with the situation as he saw fit.[79]

The specifics were left vague and ominous, a condition heightened by Secretary Dulles in a press conference on January 24, 1955:

> Well are you going to nail your flag to this little bit of rock . . . which in fact could be pretty easily pulverized by artillery fire from the Mainland, and make that into a Dien Bien Phu? You certainly wouldn't want to do that. Nor would you want to give a notice to the communists that they can come in and pick it up without a fight.[80]

Ambiguity and its manipulation were, however, the essence of the American position. By confronting the Communists with uncertainty, Dulles and Eisenhower hoped to induce caution into their behavior. Still, there was more to the Eisenhower-Dulles policy. It also sought a confirmation of the status quo in the Taiwan Strait—a cease fire—something the Communists seemed reluctant to grant while the United States continued increasing the pressure.

After a trip through Southeast and East Asia, Dulles returned to Washington in March 1955, and informed President Eisenhower that the odds were even that the crisis could not be resolved without war and that war would require the use of nuclear weapons. Vice President Nixon publicly noted that "tactical atomic explosives [are] now conventional"[81] and Eisenhower seemed to agree: "I see no reason why they shouldn't be used just exactly as you would use a bullet."[82] The president's statement was qualified with disclaimers as to the difficulties of using these weapons on a battlefield; however, this orchestration of ambiguity and threat brought the crisis to a peak. The Joint Chiefs, through a public statement by Admiral Robert Carney, chief of naval operations, recommended a preemptive strike, but American allies such as Britain and Canada stated flatly that they would not join in any fight to protect the offshore islands.

Eisenhower now found himself caught between his administration's rhetoric and domestic hawks urging escalation and America's allies who were quickly placing distance between themselves and the United States. Eisenhower reacted as he had in September of the previous year. The position of the Joint Chiefs was undercut by leaking a statement denying dire predictions of imminent aggression from the mainland (and subsequently not reappointing Carney to the Joint Chiefs). Moreover, in April 1955 Eisenhower moved diplomatically by urging Chiang to withdraw his troops from Quemoy and Matsu in exchange for an increase in the American military presence on Taiwan. Chiang demurred but there was no further escalation and the crisis petered out in late April 1955. The Communists, like the United States, were under pressure from third parties, in this case third world countries urging a reduction in tension. Desiring greater influence with these countries and perhaps concerned about American threats, the Communists relaxed the pressure on the offshore islands.[83]

An Appraisal

Dulles would, in subsequent months, take this as evidence that the threat of massive retaliation was a viable foundation for American policy. Creating an atmosphere of risk and ambiguity was by definition dangerous, the secretary of state would argue, but it could be managed to deter your opponent:

> You have to take chances for peace just as you must take chances in war. Some say that we were brought to the verge of war. Of course we were brought to the verge of war. The ability to get to the verge without getting into the war is the necessary art. If you cannot master it, you inevitably get into war. If you try to run away from it, if you are scared to go the brink, you are lost. We've had to look it square in the face—on the question of enlarging the Korean War, on the question of getting into the Indochina War, on the question of Formosa. We walked to the brink and we looked it in the face. We took strong action.[84]

Dulles's brinkmanship in the Taiwan crisis seems to have been directed as much toward American and world opinion as toward China.[85] Dulles, it is true, tried to force a cease fire with his nuclear brinkmanship, but he also attempted to demonstrate the administration's willingness to work at the outer limits of the diplomacy of violence. A reputation for recklessness was a weapon with many surfaces. Its psychological purpose was not meant to be limited to just Quemoy and Matsu.

The payoff in East Asia was limited. Eisenhower gained through the treaty with Chiang nothing more than a formal restatement of the relationship and balance of forces that had existed prior to the crisis, an institutionalization of the status quo as it were. More important, perhaps, Eisenhower and Dulles were able to put on display in early 1955 the operational crux of the new look—deterrence by means of threatening massive nuclear retaliation. The dramatic display of will, the bold walking to the brink, assumed added importance. For in the early spring of 1955, the pressures on the United States to meet the Soviets at the summit were becoming irresistible. Eisenhower and Dulles agreed with the general assessment of Truman and Acheson that if there were to be negotiations then they should be conducted from positions of strength.

NEGOTIATING FROM
STRENGTH AND CONTAINING DETENTE

In mid-1955, the Eisenhower administration seemed to be making considerable headway in its effort to consolidate global containment. Paradoxically, the presumed source of America's and the free world's danger was undergoing significant changes. Stalin's death released great anxiety and confusion within the Soviet ruling elite. Fears of a coup prompted the dispersal of security troops throughout Moscow, and the members of the Presidium sought to avoid disintegration of the government by agreeing to form a fragile collective dictatorship with Georgi M. Malenkov as prime minister. By July 1953, an uneasy equilibrium of ambition and power seemed to have developed.[86] In the meantime, Malenkov and the Presidium started to de-Stalinize Soviet life and Soviet foreign policy. Ten days after Stalin's death Malenkov proclaimed that there were no disagreements or disputes between the Soviet Union and other states, but especially the United States, that could not be resolved by peaceful means.

The View from Washington

Washington's reaction to the death of Stalin was, at the outset, as confusing as the events in Moscow. By the end of March 1953, Eisenhower had decided that a speech acknowledging and reviewing the changed circumstances was in order. In private conversations with Emmet John Hughes, a presidential adviser and speech writer, Eisenhower asserted, "Look, I am tired—and I think everyone is tired—of just plain indictments of the Soviet regime. I think it would be wrong—in fact, asinine—for me to get up before the world now to make another one of those indictments."[87] In contrast to Eisenhower's instinct to respond positively, Secretary Dulles was prepared to stand Eisenhower's argument on its head. Yes, there was indeed an oportunity available to the United States in Stalin's demise—an opportunity to take advantage of what we saw as the fatal weakness of the Soviet or any totalitarian society—the problem of leadership transition. Dulles argued that any apparent concessions on the Soviets' part resulted "because of outside pressures, and I don't know anything better we can do than to keep up these pressures right now."[88] For months after news of Stalin's death Dulles seemed preoccupied and enthusiastic about the possibility that the new leadership would devour itself as its members struggled for power.[89]

Accordingly, Dulles fought a vigorous rearguard action against the speech. When it was clear that the president intended to give it anyway, Dulles worked to make its tone as tough and uncompromising as possible or to qualify it so as to render it meaningless. When the speech was finally delivered on April 16, 1953, it emerged as a mix of new hope and cold war gamesmanship.

President Eisenhower, while proclaiming that "[t]his is one of [the] times in the affairs of nations when the gravest choices must be made, if there is to be a turning toward a just and lasting peace,"[90] required of the Soviets nothing less than a renunciation and reversal of their entire foreign policy since the end of the war. He demanded that the Soviets halt revolutionary activity in Asia and Korea, all of which assumed a control of events on the part of the Soviets that they did not possess. Preconditions of on-sight inspection of any disarmament proposal ran directly counter to the known position of the Soviet Union. He tied West Germany's future to that of NATO[91] and thereby could not help but raise Soviet fears. Finally, his prerequisites concerning Germany and Eastern Europe, "free choice of their own forms of government," clearly reflected the thinking of John Foster Dulles and involved nothing less than the removal of the foundations of Soviet postwar security policy. On balance, therefore, Eisenhower saw a "chance for peace" only if the Soviets would concede—as "genuine evidence of peaceful purpose"— every point at issue in the cold war.

Significantly, the Soviets published the Eisenhower speech in its entirety and publicly responded to it on April 25, 1953, using the front page of *Pravda* to do so.[92] But nothing else followed; perhaps it was too much to expect a breakthrough. Both governments were caught up in their respective periods of governmental transition, with the Soviets perhaps facing the more difficult task.[93] In any event, Eisenhower seems not to have expected an immediate response and suggests that the speech was as much for the record as it was a serious effort to indicate negotiations.[94] The Soviets in their response indicated a willingness to proceed to "serious businesslike discussions," but as Peter Lyon notes, "in the White House nobody picked up the telephone."[95]

An Opportunity Missed?

Some students of American and Soviet foreign policy have suggested that this period was one of those rare moments when serious Soviet-American negotiations on the future of Europe could have been undertaken.[96] Even prior to Stalin's death the Soviet Union on March 10, 1952, had proposed Four Power talks on a German peace treaty, and agreed to the rearmament of a reunified Germany if it accepted strict neutrality and nonalignment with any block or coalition.[97] A neutralized Germany, though rearmed, was clearly more appealing to the Russians than a rearmed West Germany integrated into an avowedly anti-Soviet military alliance. Stalin's proposal for a neutral, rearmed Germany made in his last days may have been mere propaganda, but Adam Ulam emphasizes that

> the fear of a German Army backed by the United States and on the borders of the Soviet empire was a real fear felt by the Soviet policy-makers, unlike the fear, partly the product of genuine apprehension but also a bogey for propaganda purposes, of the evil machinations of American Capitalists. And to conjure away his real fears Stalin was ready to pay highly.[98]

Of near equal importance in evaluating this period of Soviet-American relations was the nature of the strategic balance between the two countries. Perhaps at no other time than between 1952 and late 1953 did the United States possess greater strategic superiority over the Soviet Union. The Soviets possessed a very limited supply of atomic weapons and no intercontinental bombers with which to deliver them. Moreover, even the Soviet explosion of a thermonuclear device, in August 1953, did not transform this situation, for it would be still another year or more before the Russians would acquire credible intercontinental delivery capability.[99] Thus, if there ever was a situation in which the United States could negotiate from strength it was during the last year of the Truman administration and the first year to two years of the Eisenhower administration.

Churchill clearly thought the time was auspicious, for on May 11, 1953, he made a major speech to the House of Commons in which he called for a summit conference to seize the moment. "The great Khan is dead," he exclaimed as he suggested that although some settlement of outstanding issues as a prelude to such a meeting might be desirable, nevertheless, "It would be a mistake to assume that nothing could be settled with Soviet Russia unless or until everything is settled."[100] Churchill thought he saw "a profound movement of Russian feeling" and hoped that the West would move to encourage the positive development of this situation. During both 1953 and 1954 Soviet budgetary allocation for defense declined.[101] In Washington, however, detente would have to contend with Dulles and a curiously reluctant Eisenhower. The whole thing, Dulles grumbled, was a "phony peace campaign."[102]

By early 1954, however, the opportunity, if it had ever existed, began to slip away. The understandable American preoccupation with ending the Korean War, and Churchill's severe illness in mid-1953, worked to slow whatever thrust toward negotiations may have existed in the West. By the end of the year Eisenhower and Dulles agreed to participate in a foreign ministers' conference on Germany to be held in Berlin in early 1954, but by the time the conference was under way a subtle but important shift had begun within the Soviet Union. During the Berlin conference the Russians removed their offer of a unified but neutralized Germany and advocated a settlement that would maintain the two Germanies.[103]

It is not clear in any event that the American delegation, headed by Secretary of State Dulles, was in any frame of mind to negotiate. One cannot discount the intangible impact of the ghost of Yalta on Dulles, the man who in the Republican platform had called for the repudiation of secret understandings assumed to have been made in 1945 with the

Russians.[104] An incident observed by Ambassador Bohlen, who attended the Berlin conference,[105] indicates the spirit of Dulles's approach:

> At this meeting, Dulles had a Russian-speaking lip-reader watching the Soviet delegation. The idea was to find out what the Russians were talking about and possibly to pick up some secrets. I do not believe the lip-reader learned anything of importance.[106]

The Twilight of Opportunity

The stiffening Soviet posture at Berlin may have been a reflection of an evolving debate within the Presidium. Malenkov's priorities had their opponents among the military, and there were those within the Presidium, notably Nikita Khrushchev, the leader of the Soviet Communist party, who were prepared to use these disagreements to their own personal ends.

The debate in the Kremlin leadership centered on Malenkov's downgrading of the traditional Soviet emphasis on heavy industry and his denigration of nuclear weapons as realistic war-fighting implements. In contrast, Khrushchev, though accepting the necessity for reform of the agricultural system and a better balancing of heavy industry and consumer-oriented production, nevertheless opposed Malenkov's overall priorities. Khrushchev sided with those in the collective leadership who remained skeptical of Malenkov's contention that the use of nuclear weapons had become unthinkable. As the debate gained momentum in the Soviet Union, it was fed by Dulles's statement concerning "massive retaliation" in January 1954, the rumblings of nuclear intervention in Vietnam during April and May, and then similar overtones to the Quemoy-Matsu crisis as it developed during late 1954.

Moreover, developments within NATO confirmed the central role of nuclear weapons in American strategy. In view of the new look, it was clear that the United States would not be providing increased manpower. Furthermore, the political and economic evolution of the other NATO members made it equally clear that they were not going to support higher manpower levels. The only recourse, therefore, was the implementation in Europe of "a strategy based upon a tactical nuclear response to conventional aggression in order to support this objective [the defense of Western Europe] at a level of economic and manpower contributions that the allies were willing to pay"[107]—and the rearmament of Germany. The Germans unilaterally pledged not to manufacture nuclear, chemical, or biological weapons or missiles, warships, or long-range bombers, thereby making German rearmament more palatable to the French. In return, the German Federal Republic gained full sovereign status. Finally, the United States and Great Britain agreed to maintain their own military presence on the continent.[108]

In the Soviet Union, the new look, the evolving strategy of brinkmanship, a nuclear strategy for NATO, and the prospect of German rearmament could not help but reinforce those within the Presidium who argued against Malenkov. Throughout 1954 the debate intensified, and by the end of the year the alternative views were being aired openly in the Soviet press.[109] Ambassador Bohlen in Moscow reported throughout the year that Khrushchev's prominence was increasing,[110] and added that he believed the question of German rearmament might well be the decisive test of the collective leadership given the extreme sensitivity of the Soviets to the reemergence of West German military potential.[111] Bohlen advised that unless Eisenhower and Dulles approached the issue circumspectly, the Soviets would respond in kind.

This is, in fact, what happened. With the announcement in December 1954 of West German rearmament, the Soviets moved to formalize in 1955 their military presence in Eastern Europe with the formation of the Warsaw Pact—in many respects a more tightly integrated image of NATO.[112] The debate within the Presidium came to an end, with Khrushchev supplanting Malenkov as the primary spokesman for the collective leadership. With the shift of control in early 1955, the odds in favor of serious negotiations about Germany, arms control, or any other issues may have decreased decisively. Whereas Malenkov seemed willing to accept for the foreseeable future the implications of Soviet strategic inferiority and work toward a minimum deterrence posture, Khrushchev was not. In time, Khruschev would come to display ambivalence concerning the costs of achieving anything near parity with the United States. But in 1955 one of his first acts was to increase the defense budget by 12 percent.

Simultaneously, Khrushchev sought to minimize the image of Soviet weakness. Khrushchev knew that the prospects were good that the Soviet Union would make considerable progress in developing long-range rocket capability in the immediate future.[113] Therefore, within the next few years the Soviets would be able to pursue seriously an intercontinental ballistic missile capability that might cut into the gap between the Soviet Union and the United States.[114] In the meantime, Soviet strategic capability was inferior. But Khrushchev was prepared to exploit the limited Soviet strategic capability then available to create an image of strength.

By early 1955 the Soviets had developed a marginal intercontinental bomber capability in the form of a handful of heavy bombers. In July 1955 these were dramatically put on display during Aviation Day in what seemed to be great numbers, and sufficiently impressed Western observers that they calculated that the Soviets had secretly built up a large bomber fleet. In fact, the Soviets were not building large numbers of bombers, for they were sinking their resources into missile technology. The CIA has since concluded that the image of large numbers of strategic bombers at the Aviation Day display was accomplished by over-flying the same squadron of rather short-ranged Bison bombers repeatedly in a large circle at the May Day parade to impress Western military observers.[115]

The fact that the West could be so easily deceived into overestimating Soviet capability was not lost on Khrushchev. His willingness to gamble on and exploit Western gullibility and suspicion is revealing of the problem now before American diplomacy. By not vigorously exploiting the opportunities presented after Stalin's death, Eisenhower and Dulles may have undercut forces working for detente. In the place of Malenkov, they got Khrushchev, a man who was prepared to use anything including, in a figurative sense, mirrors, to gain for the Soviet Union a position of strength from which he might negotiate. This is not to say that Khrushchev was never serious in his off-and-on pursuit of detente over the next decade. He was clearly a far tougher adversary, however, than Malenkov might have been simply because he, like Dulles and Eisenhower, did not believe in negotiating from a position of apparent weakness. Consequently, after February 1955 the United States and the Soviet Union were once again led by men whose behavior would, as in the late 1940s, reinforce their respective suspicions about one another.[116]

The "Spirit of Geneva"

Following the 1954 elections, in which the Democrats recaptured the House and Senate, the new Democratic leadership in Congress was urging Eisenhower toward the summit. Since Eisenhower was now dependent upon the Democrats for support of his programs, he found it difficult to resist their urgings for a Soviet-American meeting. Furthermore, Khrushchev began to maneuver in early 1955 to cut away some of the preconditions thrown up by Dulles and Eisenhower. There were two simultaneous and dramatic Soviet actions. In April 1955, the Soviets requested that the foreign ministers of the four major powers meet in Vienna to work out a treaty to end the occupation of Austria, thereby neatly removing one of Dulles's preconditions to negotiations. Dulles held, however, that the neutralization treaty was one more piece of evidence that the hard line worked, for he took the treaty as evidence of the liberation of Austria.[117]

The second major Soviet overture concerned disarmament and involved the Soviets' accepting positions of the disarmament position previously adopted by the United States. The Soviets dramatically reversed their previous policy: dropping their demand for the abolition of nuclear weapons at the outset and accepting Western European (but not U.S.) proposals on manpower level reduction formulas. Finally, they accepted the notion of international control, including some form of inspection and access to internal military budgetary processes and defense installations.[118] There were "jokers" in the Soviet proposal: a ban on nuclear testing at the outset (unacceptable to the West); the use of nuclear weapons would have to be approved by the UN Security Council (thereby subject to Soviet veto); force levels would be conditional upon the end of all overseas bases (thus the end of U.S. bases in NATO, SEATO, North Africa, and Japan); and uncertainties concerning inspection.[119] Nevertheless, they caught the United States absolutely unprepared.

There followed a good deal of embarrassed obfuscating on the part of President Eisenhower as his administration scrambled to prepare a fall-back position. The outcome was the administration's "open skies" inspection proposal. It called for the exchange of detailed information about the respective defense establishments and open aerial inspection of each other's territory; however, such information about the American defense establishment was relatively available and information about the Soviets' was not. Thus, the Soviet Union had little to gain by accepting the American proposal. Indeed, open aerial inspection might reveal the magnitude of Soviet weakness and make impossible the kind of deception engaged in during the Aviation Day fly-by.[120] The plan was unacceptable to the Russians, and Eisenhower and Dulles apparently anticipated that it would be. Eisenhower recalled: "We knew the Soviets wouldn't accept, we were sure of that."[121]

Thus both the United States and the Soviet Union approached a summit conference that had been gestating for years with limited expectations and skepticism: the Soviets in the hope that they could gain time to close the strategic gap with the United States[122] and the United States because they could not gracefully avoid going and because of their difficult propaganda position. Dulles was, as might be expected, extremely concerned that the United States not be taken in at the conference.[123] But by mid-May 1955 a summit conference became inevitable. Dulles urged that Eisenhower avoid any substantive negotiating, arguing the conference be considered the beginning of a process of negotiations, the technical details to be left to the experts (Dulles). Dulles even suggested at one point that Vice President Nixon should go instead of the president. Furthermore, it was Dulles's view that the president suppress his instinct for relaxed and open socializing, avoid being photographed with the Soviets, and where it was inevitable maintain "an austere countenance."[124] "[T]he wolf was to put on a new set of sheep's clothing," said Dulles, and then confusing the menagerie a bit, "while it is better to have a sheep's clothing on than a bear's clothing on, because sheep don't have claws, I think the policy remains the same."[125]

Under the circumstances, the conference—at least as a public relations exercise—would have to be counted something of a success. Eisenhower's open skies proposal, dropped extemporaneously and unannounced into a formal discussion on disarmament, had the desired effect: maximum press coverage, minimum Soviet response apart from momentary confusion, and a vague commitment to study the proposal. There was no movement on other agenda items, as virtually all substantive items were deferred to a foreign ministers' conference to follow in the fall. Moreover, informal discussions outside the conference meetings did not go especially well, as Eisenhower held to a minimum his social contacts with the Russians.[126] Nonetheless, in those formal and the few informal contacts that did occur, one American observer notes that the president, to the chagrin of Dulles, succeeded in "project[ing] an earnest and pacific intent, a serious yearning for conciliation, a readiness to grant the other side a rectitude no less than his own."[127] The Soviets responded with what Eden termed a "new found . . . enthusiasm for free and easy methods."[128] Virtually all observers agree that at a minimum it was a refreshing change in style for all concerned and that there was indeed a new spirit of discourse among the heads of state. On the issues, however, there was no movement either at the Geneva Conference or later at the foreign ministers' conference in October 1955.

The notion of a *spirit* of Geneva is therefore appropriate, for it conveys the idea of something ethereal and lacking in substance. There may have been opportunities for serious negotiations at the Geneva Conference. However, given the attitude with which the United States and the Soviet Union approached the conference, they were extremely narrow. In fact, Dulles was expressly opposed to substantive negotiations. It would have required a remarkable act of will on Eisenhower's part to move East-West relations beyond the exchange of good feelings and reassurances. Of course, not all the obstacles were imposed by the United States. There is good reason to believe that the Soviets sought to foster and exploit the spirit of detente not as an end in itself but rather as a defensive gambit. A *spirit* of relaxing cold war tensions is probably all that was possible after Khrushchev's faction won out and the Eisenhower-Dulles team had gone through the fires of coup d'état and crisis during 1954 and early 1955.

The period of opportunity passed when the Soviets achieved thermonuclear status and began moving toward building their own positions of strength in 1954. Earlier, during the period of leadership transition in both countries, the United States seemed to possess the strength, even superiority, that it had deemed the necessary prerequisite for negotiations since the end of the war.[129] Kennan, in his long telegram, had argued that it was incumbent upon the United States to be able to respond to what he thought would be the inevitable domestic changes in the Soviet Union. In the early 1950s the United States possessed the military superiority to have risked a testing of the Soviets' responsiveness. But the signal that the United States was willing to move into a postcontainment era was at best ambiguous and perhaps unwillingly sent. Once Khrushchev began consolidating his power, it was no longer clear that anyone was listening. By then, Khrushchev sought to anticipate and contain the pressures in Soviet foreign and domestic policy foreseen by Kennan.

NOTES

1. Perhaps this interpretation of President Eisenhower's early administration is most thoroughly and eloquently developed by Emmet John Hughes, *The Ordeal of Power* (New York: Dell, 1964), especially chaps. 3 and 4.

2. Dulles came from a family long associated with the formulation and administration of American foreign policy. His grandfather had served briefly as secretary of state during 1892 and 1893. In 1907 he accompanied his grandfather, then an adviser to the Chinese government, to the Second Hague Peace Conference of 1907. In 1917 he performed diplomatic service in Latin America for his uncle, Robert Lansing, President Wilson's secretary of state, and served with distinction as a legal adviser to the American delegation to the Versailles Peace Conference following World War I. For a complete review of Dulles's early life see Townsend Hoopes, *The Devil and John Foster Dulles* (Boston: Little, Brown, 1973), pp. 9–61.

3. Hans J. Morgenthau, "John Foster Dulles: 1953–1959," in Norman A. Graebner, ed., *An Uncertain Tradition: American Secretaries of State in the Twentieth Century* (New York: McGraw-Hill, 1961), p. 293.

4. Eisenhower's concern for his domestic flank, and specifically Joseph McCarthy, was apparent during the campaign. While speaking in Wisconsin, Eisenhower had carefully deleted an intended tribute to General Marshall. Some accounts have it that Eisenhower did this only under the most intense pressure from Republican politicians who trembled before the junior senator from Wisconsin. Nevertheless, Eisenhower would not risk McCarthy's ire, even though the man for whom the tribute was intended had fostered Eisenhower's military career throughout the war. See the account of this incident in Peter Lyon, *Eisenhower: Portrait of the Hero* (Boston: Little, Brown, 1974), p. 522.

5. Hughes, op. cit., pp. 81–83.

6. Hoopes, op. cit., p. 160, paraphrasing an oral history interview with Bohlen, See also Bohlen's account of these events in Charles E. Bohlen, *Witness to History, 1929–1969* (New York: W. W. Norton, 1973), pp. 309–336.

7. Joseph C. Harsch, "John Foster Dulles: A Very Complicated Man," *Harpers Magazine*, Vol. 213, No. 1276 (September 1956), p. 30. It is reported that when Dulles held his final interview with Vincent, he offered his name as a reference if Vincent wanted to use it in the future. Dulles confided to the departing official that the chief problem had been simply that "Mr. Vincent's critics in the Senate talked louder than his supporters." On the purge of the "China Hands," see Gary May, *China Scapegoat: The Diplomatic Ordeal of John Carter Vincent* (Washington, D.C.: New Republic, 1978).

8. Hoopes, op. cit., p. 160, quoting and paraphrasing an oral history interview with Bohlen.

9. Lyon, op. cit., p. 524.

10. See Richard M. Nixon, *Six Crises* (Garden City, N.Y.: Doubleday, 1962), p. 97.

11. Gary Wills, *Nixon Agonistes: The Crisis of the Self-Made Man* (Boston: Houghton Mifflin, 1970), p. 119. Wills's essay on Eisenhower is a brilliant and perceptive piece. For a similar analysis focused on Eisenhower's administrative style, see Fred Greenstein, *The Hidden Hand Presidency* (Washington, D.C.: New Republic, 1979).

12. Ibid., and Lyon quoting CBS Reports, Eisenhower on the Presidency, Part I, October 12, 1961, on p. 851.

13. Wills, op. cit., p. 133.

14. See James A. Nathan and James K. Oliver, *Foreign Policy Making and the American Political System* (Boston: Little, Brown, 1983, chap. 2.

15. Wills, op. cit., p. 131.

16. Ibid., p. 132.

17. See Morgenthau, op. cit.

18. See John, Foster Dulles, "A Policy of Boldness," *Life*, Vol. 32, No. 20 (May 10, 1952), pp. 146–160.

19. Eisenhower, *Mandate For Change* (Garden City, N.Y.: Doubleday, 1963), p. 95.

20. General Mark Clark, *From the Danube to the Yalu* (London: Harrap, 1954), p. 221, quoted in David Rees, *Korea: The Limited War* (Baltimore: Penguin Books, 1964), p. 402.

21. Lyon, op. cit., p. 472.

22. Eisenhower, op. cit., p. 181.

23. Lyon, op. cit., p. 534. See also the newly released documents on Eisenhower's inclination to use nuclear weapons; Bernard Gwertzman, "U.S. Papers Tell of '53 Policy to Use A-Bomb in Korea," *The New York Times*, June 8, 1984, p. A8.

24. Ibid., p. 536.

25. See ibid., and Joyce Kolko and Gabriel Kolko, *The Limits of Power: The World and United States Foreign Policy, 1945–1954* (New York: Harper & Row, 1972), p. 681. Kolko adds that in view of these attacks the communist charges of bacteriological warfare assumed added credibility (ibid., fn. 10, p. 794).

26. Quoted in Lyon, op. cit., p. 541.

27. Eisenhower, op. cit., p. 185, *The New York Times*, August 4, 1975 and "Eisenhower Considered A-Bomb in Korea," *Washington Post*, June 9, 1984, p. A8.

28. Ibid., p. 189.

29. At the same time, however, the South Koreans were informed that the United Nations would not use force to stop them from breaking an armistice. What really emerged in the unspoken agreement between the two sides on July 19 was that if Rhee's army was foolish enough to attack the Communists, the war need not be expanded if the Chinese merely pulverized the South Korean forces without involving the United Nations' Command's western divisions.

30. Republican Platform in *National Party Platforms, 1840–1968*, compiled by Kirk H.

Porter and Donald Bruce Johnson (Urbana, Ill.: University of Illinois Press, 1970), pp. 497–498.

31. There had been some adjustment of the border between North and South Korea as the result of the fighting. The ROK had gained some 2,350 square miles on the eastern end of the main line of resistance but lost 850 square miles to the west. Military historian David Rees is of the view that the newer line was more defensible than the old boundary (Rees, op. cit., p. 431).

32. "Message of the President: National Security," *The Budget of the United States Government for the Fiscal Year Ending June 30, 1955* (Washington, D.C.: U.S. Government Printing Office, 1954), p. M-38.

33. Ibid., p. M-39.

34. This analysis is drawn from Glenn H. Snyder, "The New Look of 1953," in Warner Schilling, Paul G. Hammond, and Glenn H. Snyder, *Strategy, Politics, and Defense Budgets* (New York: Columbia University Press, 1962), pp. 401–406.

35. Although Eisenhower and the Republicans had implied this in the campaign.

36. Dulles, op. cit., p. 152.

37. Hoopes, op. cit., p. 195, and Snyder, op. cit., pp. 408–409.

38. Quoted by Hoopes, op. cit., p. 194.

39. Snyder, op. cit., p. 436. The top secret internal study NSC-162/2 seriously considered nuclear weapons in a wide range of circumstances. At one point Eisenhower even suggested to Dulles that preventive war might have to be considered. John Lewis Gaddis, *Strategies of Containment* (New York: Oxford University Press, 1982), pp. 149–150.

40. A complete account of the struggle of the army against these cuts can be found in ibid., pp. 443–455. See also Hanson W. Baldwin, "'New Look' of the U.S. Armed Forces Is Emerging at the Pentagon," *The New York Times*, December 13, 1953, p. 5E, the *Budget for FY 1955*, op. cit., p. M-45, and Snyder, op. cit., pp. 457–460. See also the testimony of Secretary of Defense Charles E. Wilson and Admiral Arthur William Radford before U.S. Congress, Senate Committee on Appropriations, *Department of Defense Appropriations, 1955*, 83rd Congress, 2nd Session, 1954, pp. 2–15 and 79–91.

41. John Foster Dulles, "The Evolution of Foreign Policy," speech made to Council on Foreign Relations, January 12, 1954, *Department of State Bulletin*, Vol. 30, No. 761 (January 25, 1954), p. 107.

42. Ibid., p. 108.

43. Ibid.

44. Robert R. Bowie interview, Oral History Research Office, Columbia University, quoted in Lyon, op. cit., footnote on p. 520.

45. Eisenhower, op. cit., p. 333.

46. Joseph Buttinger, *Vietnam: A Dragon Embattled*, Vol. II: *Vietnam at War* (New York: Praeger, 1967), pp. 797–798, and Lauran Paine, *Viet Nam* (London: Robert Hale, 1965).

47. Eisenhower, op. cit., p. 346.

48. Ibid., p. 333.

49. News Conference, April 7, 1954, *Public Papers of the Presidents, Dwight D. Eisenhower, 1954* (Washington, D.C.: U.S. Government Printing Office, 1960), pp. 382–383.

50. Eisenhower, op. cit., pp. 340–341.

51. Ibid., p. 347.

52. "United States Declaration on Indochina," July 21, 1954, in Richard A. Falk (ed.), *The Vietnam War and International Law* (Princeton, N.J.: Princeton University Press, sponsored by the American Society of International Law, 1968), p. 558.

Though refusing to sign the agreement, the United States did make a "unilateral declaration in which Under Secretary of State Walter B. Smith stated that the United States will refrain from the threat or the use of force to disturb" the agreements. Smith made no reference to a North or South Vietnam, and although he refused to sign any documents the American declaration could certainly be taken as American acceptance of the politically provisional nature of the agreement. The U.S. offer of atom bombs is recounted in John Prados, *The Sky Would Fall: Operation Vulture, The Secret U.S. Bombing Mission to Vietnam, 1954* (New York: Dial, 1983), p. 152.

53. "The Legality of United States Participation in the Defense of Viet Nam, March 4, 1966," in ibid., p. 596.

54. See the excellent discussion of this point in George M. T. Kahin and John W. Lewis, *The United States in Vietnam*, rev. ed. (New York: Dell, 1969), pp. 48–57.

55. Marvin Kalb and Elie Abel, *Roots of Involvement: The U.S. in Asia, 1784–1971* (New York: W. W. Norton, 1971), p. 89.

56. Southeast Asia Collective Defense Treaty, Article IV, in Falk, op. cit., p. 562.

57. Protocol to the Southeast Asia Collective Defense Treaty, in Falk, op. cit., p. 564.

58. Kahin and Lewis, op. cit., p. 70.

59. Lyon, op. cit., pp. 497–499 and 513–514.

60. Eden, op. cit., p. 236.

61. Lyon, op. cit., p. 551.

62. Quoted in ibid., p. 552, and drawn from *Mandate for Change*, p, 165. Eisenhower claims that he did not know who had written the memorandum, ibid., p. 164.

63. Ibid., and see also Richard Barnet, *Intervention and Revolution*, rev. ed. (New York: Mentor, 1972), pp. 264–268.

64. See Leonard Mosely, *Power Play: Oil in the Middle East* (New York: Random House, 1973), pp. 219–222, and Lyon, op. cit., pp. 553–554.

65. Throughout the Iranian crisis, Eisenhower and Dulles had tried to tie Mossadegh's activities to the influence of the Iranian Communist party, the Tudeh. The effort was transparent. Mossadegh's National Front coalition had repeatedly refused to include the Communists. In fact, in 1951 the premier turned the army on a Tudeh demonstration against the oil companies, killing 100 and injuring another 500 Communists. Once again, during the American-inspired coup attempts of mid-August, 1953, Mossadegh unleashed the army against Tudeh demonstrators. Manfred Halprin, "The Middle East and North Africa," in *Communism and Revolution: Uses of Political Violence* (Princeton, N.J.: Princeton University Press, 1964), pp. 316–319, and Barnet, op. cit.

66. Quoted by Lyon, op. cit., p. 590.

67. Testimony before U.S. Congress, House Select Committee on Communist Aggression, Hearings Before the Subcommittee on Latin America, 83rd Congress, 2nd Session, 1954, pp. 24–26.

68. See the testimony of Ambassador Whiting Willauer before the Senate Internal Security Subcommittee, 87th Congress, 1st Session, 1961, as quoted by Lyon, op. cit., pp. 590ff.

69. See "Declaration of Solidarity for the Preservation of the Political Integrity of the American States Against the Intervention of International Communism," in U.S. Department of State, *Tenth Inter-American Conference* (Washington, D.C.: U.S. Government Printing Office, 1955), pp. 156–157, and Philip B. Taylor, Jr., "The Guatemalan Affair: A Critique of United States Foreign Policy," *American Political Science Review*, Vol. L, No. 3 (September 1956), pp. 790–792.

70. Quoted in Lyon, op. cit., p. 611.

71. Eisenhower, op. cit., p. 426.

72. Lyon, op. cit., p. 614, and Barnet, op. cit., pp. 275–276.

73. Barnet, op. cit., p. 275.
74. Dwight D. Eisenhower, "The Chance for Peace," an address delivered before the American Society for Newspaper Editors, April 16, 1953, in *Public Papers of the Presidents, Dwight D. Eisenhower, 1953* (Washington, D.C.: U.S. Government Printing Office, 1960), p. 180, and Barnet, op. cit.
75. Dwight David Eisenhower's Personal Diary, entry of October 8, 1953, quoted by Lyon, op. cit., p. 552.
76. Eisenhower, *Mandate for Change*, p. 464.
76. Eisenhower, *Mandate for Change*, p. 464.
77. Harold C. Hinton, *China's Turbulent Quest* (Bloomington, Ind.: Indiana University Press, 1972), p. 67.
78. See Hoopes's discussion of these factors, op. cit., pp. 268–272. The latter position was confirmed in an exchange of private understandings between Dulles and the Nationalist foreign minister that the use of force from territory controlled by the Nationalists would have to be approved by the United States.
79. "The Formosa Resolution," 69 Stat. 5, January 29, 1955.
80. Dulles press conference of January 24, 1955, quoted in Hoopes, op. cit., p. 273.
81. *The New York Times*, March 18, 1954.
82. Eisenhower press conference, March 16, 1955. *Public Papers of the Presidents, Dwight D. Eisenhower, 1955* (Washington, D.C.: U.S. Government Printing Office, 1959), p. 332.
83. See Hinton, op. cit., pp. 68–69, and Hoopes, op. cit., pp. 282–283.
84. James Shepley, "How Dulles Averted War," *Life*, Vol. 40, No. 3 (January 19, 1956), p. 78. In contrast to Dulles's explication of the necessary art of war prevention in the straits crisis is the note Eisenhower penned to himself when the crisis seemed most intense: "hostilities are not so imminent as is indicated by the forebodings of a number of my associates" *(Mandate for Change*, pp. 478–479) and his leak to the press in April that "the best political and military intelligence reaching the White House is that the Chinese Reds have not yet undertaken the kind of military and aviation buildup that would make an attack likely in the near future." (Attributed to Eisenhower by Hoopes, op. cit., p. 281.) Furthermore, after January the Communists had not again increased their level of threat. In fact, the probability is that they could not escalate further short of launching air strikes against Quemoy or Matsu. And, as Eisenhower noted, Chinese Communist ability to engage in aerial warfare was limited at best.
85. Hoopes, op. cit., p. 277.
86. Adam Ulam, *Expansion and Coexistence: Soviet Foreign Policy 1917–1973*, rev. ed. (New York: Praeger, 1974), pp. 539–540, and Bohlen, op. cit., pp. 354–355.
87. Hughes, op. cit., p. 90.
88. Ibid., p. 96.
89. Bohlen, op. cit., p. 356.
90. Eisenhower, "The Chance for Peace," p. 183.
91. Ibid.
92. Lyon, op. cit., pp. 533–534.
93. Ulam, op. cit. pp. 540–541.
94. Eisenhower, *Mandate for Change*, p. 148.
95. Lyon, op. cit., p. 534.
96. See especially Coral Bell, *Negotiation from Strength: A Study in the Politics of Power* (New York: Knopf, 1963), pp. 100–136, for perhaps the best treatment of this subject and also Ulam, op. cit., pp. 534–571. The following discussion is drawn

primarily from these analyses and that of Bohlen, who was the American ambassador to the Soviet Union during this crucial period.

97. See Ulam's analysis, op. cit., pp. 535–536, and the text of the Soviet proposal in *Documents on International Affairs, 1952* (London: Royal Institute for International Affairs, 1955), p. 88.

98. Ulam, op. cit., p. 537.

99. Arnold L. Horelick and Myron Rush, *Strategic Power and Soviet Foreign Policy* (Chicago: University of Chicago Press, 1966), p. 17.

100. Winston Churchill, House of Commons debate, 5th Series, Vol. 515, cols. 896–897, quoted in Bell, op. cit., p. 106.

101. Raymond L. Garthoff, *Soviet Strategy in the Nuclear Age* (New York: Praeger, 1958), p. 23, and Horelick and Rush, op. cit., pp. 18–20.

102. Private memorandum, late April 1953, Dulles Papers. Quoted by Hoopes, op. cit., p. 173. See also Bohlen, op. cit., p. 371.

103. Ulam, op. cit., pp. 551–552.

104. Hoopes, op. cit., pp. 176–177. There was no such agreement.

105. Although he notes that he had no substantial role to play, it is noteworthy, of course, that he had been at Yalta as an adviser and interpreter, and this fact was used against him in his struggle for nomination as ambassador.

106. Bohlen, op. cit., p. 362.

107. This strategy was formally ratified in December 1954. It promptly generated turmoil within NATO over control of the nuclear trigger, an issue that would plague the alliance for the next two decades. See Robert Osgood, *NATO: The Entangling Alliance* (Chicago: University of Chicago Press, 1962), p. 116.

108. Ibid., pp. 95–98.

109. Horelick and Rush provide a useful review of this aspect of the debate, pp. 23–26; also Mackintosh, op. cit., pp. 90–97.

110. Bohlen, p. 366; Horelick and Rush note that Malenkov was upon occasion now retreating publicly from his earlier position, p. 21.

111. Bohlen, op. cit.

112. See Malcolm Mackintosh, *The Evolution of the Warsaw Pact*, Adelphi Paper No. 58, June 1969 (London: International Institute for Strategic Studies). For Bohlen's reporting during this period see Bohlen, op. cit., pp. 366–367.

113. Horelick and Rush, op. cit., pp. 27–31.

114. Ulam, op. cit., pp. 560–562.

115. Allen Dulles, *The Craft of Intelligence* (New York Harper & Row, 1963), p. 149.

116. Bohlen, op. cit., p. 371.

117. Dulles maintained that it was "just one of these breaks that comes if you steadily, steadily [keep] the pressure on." Cited by Vojtech Mastny, "Kremlin Politics and the Austrian Settlement," *Problems of Communism* (July/August, 1983), p. 37.

118. One of the best detailed reviews of these proposals is in John W. Spanier and Joseph L. Nogee, *The Politics of Disarmament: A Study in Soviet-American Gamesmanship* (New York: Praeger, 1962), pp. 86–92.

119. Ibid., pp. 88–89.

120. Ibid., for a review of "open skies," esp. p. 92.

121. Lyon, op. cit., p. 653 fn.

122. A strong statement of this view can be found in Malcolm Mackintosh, "Three Detentes: 1955–1964," in Eleanor Lansing Dulles and Robert Dickson Crane (eds.), *Detente: Cold War Stategies in Transition* (New York: Praeger, 1965), pp. 103–120.

123. On Dulles's attitude see Hoopes, op. cit., pp. 290–295.

124. Briefing memorandum for Eisenhower, June 18, 1955, Dulles Papers, quoted in Hoopes, op. cit., p. 295.
125. Dulles Press Conference, May 15, 1955, quoted in Lyon, op. cit., p. 653.
126. Eden was especially concerned about this. See Eden, op. cit., pp. 341–342.
127. Hoopes, op. cit., p. 297.
128. Eden, op. cit., p. 341.
129. Ibid., p. 215. See also Mastny, op. cit, passim, who argues that NATO "messmerized" the Soviets and gave the U.S. an opening for negotiations but let it pass.

Chapter 6
Crisis and
Salvaging the
Status Quo

If the vision and spirit was perhaps emerging at Geneva, the body of one of the participants soon failed. Upon returning from Geneva, Eisenhower, now sixty-five years of age, took a long vacation in Colorado that included strenuous and extended rounds of golf, sometimes twenty-seven or thirty-six holes a day. Suddenly, after days of trout fishing, golf, and a few hours work, the president suffered a heart attack. On September 23, 1955, the president lay near death in Fitzsimmons General Hospital in Denver. And for almost a year, the effects of the heart attack and an intervening attack of ileitis were to be apparent. In the meantime, perhaps the greatest crisis of his administration was set in motion in the Middle East.

THE SUEZ CRISIS

The Suez crisis had its origins in Dulles's and Eisenhower's obsession with international communism and their inability to grasp fully non-Western nationalism. In early 1955 the British, sensing that their hold on their base at Suez was increasingly tenuous, sought to shore up their Middle East military presence and isolate the nationalist views of Egyptian President Gamal Abdel Nasser. American interests paralleled those of the British. Dulles wanted to replicate the SEATO arrangement in the Middle East to prevent communist penetration of the area. At length, in February and April 1955, an alliance—"The Baghdad Pact"—was completed that linked the so-called northern tier of states in the region, Turkey, Iraq, Iran, and Pakistan, with Britain. The United States declined formal association in deference to the Israelis. Nasser was deeply disturbed by this instrusion of what he took to be neocolonialist meddling directed at him personally and launched a vigorous propaganda campaign against the alliance. Nasser calculated that British influence might best be offset by going to the Soviets for military assistance. After long negotiation, a Soviet-Egyptian arms deal was consummated in September 1955—almost the very day Eisenhower had his heart attack. The Russians now had leapfrogged the Baghdad Pact defensive alliance.

Nasser attempted to maintain his image of neutrality by approaching the World Bank and the United States to gain financing for the construction of a high dam across the Nile River at Aswan. The Soviets had also offered to provide aid, but Nasser preferred to work with the West. The dam was to be the centerpiece of Nasser's plans to modernize Egypt; and, at least at the outset, the fact that he turned to the West for financing impressed the usually skeptical Dulles with Nasser's protestations of neutrality. On December 19, 1955, a tentative American decision to loan the Egyptians the money was made and negotiations were opened. Yet Nasser, suspicious of losing control of the Aswan project to his creditors, bargained slowly, a delay that was reciprocated on the American side.

Nasser now grew anxious about his loan and hedged his bet. He turned East. Nasser extended recognition to the Chinese Communists as a possible alternative source of arms. Dulles, grumbling that Nasser was playing both sides,[1] informed the Egyptians on July 19, 1956, that the United States would withdraw its support from the Aswan project.[2] Dulles reportedly handled the matter with insensitivity to Egyptian pride, accusing them of blackmail and making gratuitous comments on the state of the Egyptian economy.[3] A week later, a deeply hurt and furious Nasser, in an impassioned speech, announced that he was nationalizing the Suez Canal and would operate it himself.

A crisis was now all but inevitable. Both the British and the French protested that Nasser's foot was on their necks. For Anthony Eden, his health and domestic political base deteriorating,[4] the canal seizure seemed more than adequate justification for the use of force to eliminate a menace he compared to Mussolini. But Eden's bellicosity ran counter to Eisenhower's political needs of the moment, for the last thing Eisenhower needed going into a presidential campaign was a war in the Middle East in which two NATO allies were acting in clear violation of international law. Eden, however, had lost control of his own emotions and was determined to push the issue through to a definitive conclusion.

There followed throughout August, September, and most of October 1956 frantic diplomatic activity. The Americans sought to prevent Anglo-French intervention, and Eden, in a near frenzy of persistence, pushed the crisis forward.[5] Dulles's role was that of ambivalent middleman between a president who absolutely refused to countenance Anglo-French military intervention (but seemed to acquiesce in other forms) and the British and French, who sought to pull the United States into the intervention in some form or, if they could not gain American support, ensure noninterference. Dulles's ambivalence stemmed from his sympathy for the Anglo-French position, for he shared their antipathy toward Nasser's action and ideology. Moreover, he tended to view Nasser's Arab nationalism as being, if not communistic, then vulnerable to communist penetration. At the same time, Dulles was secretary of state and, therefore, an advocate of Eisenhower's interest, which was quite simply—no war.

The only way out of the box was to try to buy time through delay and the development of a negotiated settlement that would be nevertheless beneficial to the British and the French. Dulles proposed the establishment of a Suez Canal Users Association (SCUA) in which the users of the canal would not take over the canal but would simply join together, provide their own canal pilots, and pay tolls to SCUA. Some portion of these funds would be passed on to the Egyptians. The plan was "as any casual observer could confirm . . . possessed [of] a transparently grotesque, unreal quality,"[6] for Dulles's proposal simply ignored the political and economic claims of Egyptian sovereignty. Nasser rejected the proposal out of hand and suggested with bitter irony that in its place there be established "an association of the users of the Port of London and all ships bound for London would pay to it."[7] Eden was not sure what Dulles's SCUA proposal meant.[8] However, the British ambassador communicated to Eden that Dulles had given assurances that "the United States would *do* everything required to assert the authority of the Suez Canal Users Association."[9]

Dulles's view seems to have been designed to allow the Europeans to put whatever interpretation they desired on his ambiguous assurances as he tried to buy time and save the situation. Eden, thinking that the Americans had finally committed themselves to the elimination of Nasser, by force if necessary, adopted the proposal for a users association and took it to Parliament. During a heated two-day debate in Parliament on the crisis, Eden defended the scheme by alluding to the apparent willingness of Dulles to use force in support of the association.

Dulles, realizing that Eden's statement placed him (Dulles) in opposition to the president, publicly reversed the ambiguous position he had taken in his private diplomacy with the British. Eden and his foreign minister, Harold Macmillan, now looking quite foolish, were plunged into a black fury. More important, Dulles's actions strained the alliance to the point of collapse, for "it cut the last remaining strands of trust and engendered an enduring bitterness."[10] The British and French now felt free to go their own way.

In late September 1956, the French, who had been supplying the Israelis with arms in anticipation of a major Israeli attack in the Sinai, decided to use the Israeli attack as a pretext for their own involvement. By mid-October the Franco-Israeli plans had neared completion and the British were brought into the conspiracy. Between October 16 and 24,

1956, the three countries agreed on a plan that would have the Israelis attack Egypt's Sinai positions and push toward the canal. The British and French would then issue an ultimatum for the fighting to stop. The Israelis would "fail" to respond, and the British and French would then "intervene" to "protect," that is, seize the canal. On October 16 the British and French cut off the flow of normal communications with Washington, and the president was forced to employ high-altitude U-2 aerial surveillance flights over the Middle East to gain generally inconclusive information as to what was going on.

On October 23 the confusion of Anglo-French silence, a brewing crisis, and a presidential election was compounded by the eruption of an uprising in Hungary against Soviet power. For a week Dulles and Eisenhower watched what Dulles hoped would be the fulfillment of his wish for liberation, but there was litttle else that could be done for events were surging to a climax in the Middle East. The Israelis launched the attack against Egypt on October 29. The British and French vetoed a U.S. and Soviet cease-fire resolution in the Security Council, and joined the assault on October 31. The fighting continued for another five days as the Israelis routed the Egyptians and the insertion of British and French troops was carried out. While the assault on Egypt was underway, the Russians crushed the Hungarian revolt; and, on the night of November 2, Dulles, in extreme pain, entered the hospital for abdominal surgery that revealed the presence of cancer which would kill him in a little over two years.

At the height of the crisis, Eisenhower employed diplomatic and economic instruments against both the Israelis and the Anglo-French effort. French and British sensibilities were important, for Eisenhower was concerned about the impact of the crisis on the alliance. However, the delicacy of the situation did not prevent extreme anger and toughness on Eisenhower's part when he learned that the British and French were using force on a mere pretext without consulting their major NATO benefactor. Eden and Eisenhower had exchanged lengthy communications in the days prior to the Israeli attack, but Eden, of course, never mentioned the Anglo-French plans. When Eisenhower pieced together the Anglo-French collusion on October 30, Lyon reports, his "amiability" turned to "flint," and "the air in the oval office became briefly a blue haze. . . . The President was very angry, but it was a carefully frigerated wrath. From that moment Eden's ambitions were destined to go smash."[11] It is reported that on the next morning, October 31, Eisenhower placed a personal call to Eden and in "less official and tougher army life, tongue lashing language told the Prime Minister of his 'deep concern' over the drastic action implied by the ultimatum and its probable consequences. The Prime Minister burst into tears."[12] Three weeks later, his health broken, Eden would be ordered by his doctors to take a three-week rest.

Eisenhower, in addition to verbal abuse, hit the British at their most vulnerable point—their economy. As October turned to November it became apparent that the pound sterling was under immense pressure and the United States was not only doing nothing to help but may, in fact, have encouraged the drain of reserves. Specifically, in the week of November 5 the Bank of England was forced to draw down its gold and dollar reserves by some 15 percent to meet the demands for gold and dollars from holders of sterling—more than $250 million. Much of the large-block selling was taking place in New York, and there was speculation that it was being initiated by the Treasury Department at Eisenhower's direction. Foreign Secretary Macmillan now warned Prime Minister Eden of British economic collapse. Macmillan knew that there was no help in Washington[13] and that there would be a financial transfusion only if there was an immediate cease fire. It came on November 6.

As the crisis waned in late November and early December, American diplomacy turned to the task of patching up the damage, especially in NATO. The damage within the alliance was a complex mix of personal bitterness and the inevitable sensitivity of those who had once possessed great imperial power now being confronted with the reality of their impotence. Nevertheless, during February and March 1957, talks were held with the French and British in which much of the personal rancor was dispelled. It was clear, however, that the French, and especially the British, were rethinking the nature and magnitude of their NATO commitment. The French had withdrawn most of their conventional combat units from NATO to deal with a new colonial struggle in Algeria, and the British, for economic reasons, were moving toward similar reductions in their conventional forces.

The other area in which the pre-Suez crisis status quo was threatened was the Middle East itself. As the result of Eden's foolishness, Dulles's bungling, and Eisenhower's pressure during the preceding months, British power and credibility had collapsed in the area. Eisenhower concluded that an American presence was urgently required even as the lingering problem of Israeli withdrawal was being dealt with. Thus the president went before Congress and urged the adoption of a special program of economic and military assistance in the Middle East. He asked for a congressional prior commitment "to use armed forces to assist any nation or group of such nations requesting assistance against armed aggression from any nation controlled by international Communism." The presidential discretion to use force was essential, Eisenhower argued, because the Middle Eastern vacuum had to be "filled by the United States before it is filled by Russia."[14] However, a Democrat-controlled Congress refused to move quickly on what was now referred to as the Eisenhower Doctrine.

Extensive hearings provided a forum for criticizing Dulles's behavior during the Suez crisis and the resultant disarray in the alliance. Dulles's alarmism about an imminent penetration of the area by international communism no longer startled a Congress that had been asked to prepare for the coming of the wolf almost daily for four years. In fact, Dulles was forced to concede that there were no nations in the Middle East controlled by communism. Moreover, Congress, under intense pressure from American Jewish groups, refused to legitimize any effort to force the Israelis out of the Sinai. The onus fell, therefore, on Eisenhower, who publicly avowed his intention of cutting off U.S. assistance to Israel as well as eliminating tax loopholes for private American contributors to Israel's welfare. On March 1, 1957, the Israelis gave way and withdrew. Only after the Israelis moved out of Sinai did Congress pass the Middle East Resolution.

It had been a desperate fall and winter. Yet as the Washington spring of 1957 blossomed the Eisenhower administration seemed to have come through the crisis in fairly good shape. The NATO alliance had gone through a traumatic and wrenching experience, and Dulles had earned the everlasting enmity of many Europeans, but the 1957 springtime NATO conferences provided some reason to believe that relations were on the mend. Even more impressive was the way Eisenhower had moved to expand the American presence in the Middle East. Indeed, Dulles could point out before the Senate Foreign Relations Committee that with the Eisenhower Doctrine, the United States had now succeeded in closing a ring of American power, alliances, and commitments around the communist world: NATO in Europe; the Eisenhower Doctrine and Baghdad Pact in the Middle East; SEATO; the Korean and Taiwan mutual security agreements; the treaties Dulles had negotiated in the late Truman years—ANZUS and the Japanese arrangements; and finally, of course, the revised Rio Pact with its heightened defenses against communist subversion.[15] In sum, Eisenhower and Dulles seemed to have succeeded by early 1957 in institutionalizing containment on a global scale.

But beneath the image of a carefully nurtured and now stable system of containment there were signs that all was not well. The most distressing feature of this policy was the inability to grasp the magnitude and nature of revolutionary change in the non-Western world. Militant anti-Western and anti-American nationalism was consistently equated with international communism and therefore subject to unilateral American policing under such abstract rationales as the Eisenhower Doctrine.

Thus, when a relatively minor domestic upheaval occurred in Jordan in April 1957 and similar unrest, at the same time, in Syria (coupled with a Syrian-Soviet arms deal), Dulles sniffed communism and Eisenhower moved the Sixth Fleet into position to intervene.

In neither Jordan nor Syria, however, did overt intervention occur. In the more serious case of Syria conservative Arab states withdrew their support of U.S. plans, pointing out to Washington that intervention against leftist Syria would merely make states such as Saudi Arabia and Jordan the next targets of Nasser-inspired Arab nationalism. There was no power vacuum and no external communist threat—both Syria and Egypt had jailed the members of their indigenous Communist parties— and the conservative Arab leaders indicated that Washington might best let the Arabs work out their own respective regional *modus vivendi*. Dulles was apparently upset and puzzled by this attitude. But without Arab support, American intervention would look painfully like the Anglo-French disaster of the previous year. Prudence and the need for continued American credibility seemed to dictate, therefore, a temporary tactical adjustment of the American position away from intervention and toward restraint.[16]

THE NEW LOOK CHALLENGED

In August 1957 the Soviet Union announced that it had successfully tested a long-range intercontinental ballistic rocket. In October the Soviets orbited the first artificial earth satellite, Sputnik I; in November 1957 and May 1958, the second and third Soviet satellites went into orbit. In the meantime Khrushchev made sure, through a seemingly endless stream of interviews and public statements, that the strategic implications of this feat would not be lost on the West.[17]

The point was a simple one: Soviet space accomplishments were evidence that the Soviet Union now possessed strategic weapons delivery technology equal to and perhaps even surpassing that of the West. This was untrue, but from 1955 to 1961 Khrushchev exploited the American tendency to overestimate Soviet weapons capability. Khrushchev's ability to deceive the United States was aided by the inability of the United States to penetrate with certainty Soviet secrecy.[18] Soviet rocket development seemed instantly to have compromised the entire structure of the new look. By all appearances the Soviets could now equal the American threat of massive retaliation. If this were the case, was the nuclear threat that constituted the underpinning of Eisenhower and Dulles's foreign policy any longer credible? Was it not necessary to reexamine the entire question of force in the nuclear age? Sputnik provided, therefore, the immediate fillip to a reexamination of American defense posture.

The Attack on Massive Retaliation

As early as 1956, the sophisticated army chief of staff, Maxwell Taylor, had been lobbying diligently for an army role and capability to deal with the changed strategic environment.[19] Taylor was concerned that the army was being dangerously shortchanged by the reliance on an airborne deterrent. Strategic weapons might prevent a massive general war but they could not be used believably, especially with the advent of potential Soviet retaliation, as an instrument of policy for controlling local pressures.[20] Coups d'état in the Middle East, insurgencies in Asia, Soviet pressure on Berlin could not be credibly countered by brandishing atomic weapons. Containment by nuclear weapons at the points where communism pressed would be like a housewife using a shotgun on a hornet that was about to enter her kitchen. It might work; but even if it did, the effects on the environment—the hornet's and the housewife's—might be disproportionate. Then again, it might not work. In which case the sting might not only be painful, but would also show the kitchen vulnerable to all kinds of similar pests.

Among the leaders of concerned scholars in this area was Harvard instructor Henry Kissinger, who became director of a study group formed in 1954 of "exceptionally qualified individuals" whose mandate was to "explore all factors involved in making and implementing foreign policy in the nuclear age."[21] In 1956 Kissinger maintained that the use of nuclear weapons was inevitable if war were to break out between the Soviet Union and the United States. The question, therefore, was how to limit the scope of the war.[22] In *Nuclear Weapons and Foreign Policy*, Kissinger argued for a spectrum of military capability available to American policymakers: "a twentieth century equivalent of 'showing the flag,' an ability and readiness to make our power felt quickly and decisively, not only to deter Soviet aggression but also to impress the uncommitted without capacity for decisive action." In short, a willingness to meet any level of force with at least an equivalent response,[23] including a strategy of limited war, using tactical nuclear weapons which promised "the best chance to bring about strategic changes favorable to our side" from Indochina and Korea, to Eastern Europe and Berlin.[24] Kissinger wrote:

> The key problem of present-day strategy is to devise a spectrum of capabilities with which to resist Soviet challenges. These capabilities should enable us to confront the opponent with contingencies from which he can extricate himself only by all-out war, while deterring him from this

step by a superior retaliatory capacity. Since the most difficult decision for a statesman is whether to risk the national substance by unleashing an all-out war, the psychological advantage will always be on he side of the power which can shift to its opponent the decision to initiate all-out war. All Soviet moves in the post-war period have had this character. They have faced us with problems which by themselves did not seem worth an all-out war, but with which we could not deal by an alternative capability. We refused to defeat the Chinese in Korea because we were unwilling to risk an all-out conflict. We saw no military solution to the Indochinese crisis without accepting risks which we were reluctant to confront. We recoiled before the suggestion of intervening in Hungary lest it unleash a thermonuclear holocaust. A strategy of limited war might reverse or at least arrest this trend. Limited war is thus not an alternative to massive retaliation, but its complement. It is the capability for massive retaliation which provides the sanction against expanding the war.[25]

By the end of 1958, most strategists in the scholarly community had written off massive retaliation as a viable strategic concept. They agreed that the United States needed the capacity and will to fight limited wars.[26] The only contention left centered on the point at which nuclear weapons should be introduced into a "local war." By early 1960, Kissinger abjured the early use of tactical weapons and argued, instead, for a wide-ranging conventional capability so that the nuclear option "becomes the *last* and not the *only* recourse."[27]

The Notables Bless "Flexible Response"

The Gaither report, prepared in 1958 by the head of the Ford Foundation, H. Rowan Gaither, and assisted by great industrialists, eminent educators, scientists, and former high-level officials, pronounced America's defense capability to be in a desperate condition.[28] The report argued that the Soviet Union's economic strength was growing at a pace twice as fast as the American economy and that Soviet expenditures for arms were presently at least equal to American expenditures. By 1959, the report forecast, the Soviet Union would have one hundred ICBMs and be in a position to attack preemptively the vulnerable U.S. strategic bomber force, docked on crowded airfields.[29] The committee recommendations implied "that the government was dangerously underestimating the gravity of the Soviet threat."[30] The Gaither Committee called for a massive defense build-up including a multibillion-dollar fallout shelter program, shelters housing U.S. strategic aircraft dispersed on civilian and military fields, and a large but unspecified sum to be spent on arms research and development. The report was laden with contingencies that pushed the total recommendation for increased spending on missile forces, strategic air command dispersion, and ground forces to over $60 billion, an increase of some $25 billion over what the Eisenhower administration had expected to spend.[31]

Eisenhower and Dulles Hold the Line

The Gaither report and the defense intellectuals were proposing an immediate shift in the American defense posture requiring billions of dollars beyond the conservative ceilings acceptable to Eisenhower. Many of those who were pushing for a reenergized defense posture were Democrats associated with the cold war from the earliest days of the Truman administration. No doubt this ingredient, plus the deep suspicion Eisenhower harbored of an unbalanced budget and what he later termed the military-industrial complex, allowed him to resist the burgeoning pressure for an increased American military capability. Eisenhower did, however, initiate a long-term process of transforming the American strategic posture by authorizing the development of a new sea-based nuclear deterrent based on nuclear submarines and the new, solid-fueled Minuteman missile. At the November 1957 NATO conference the United States urged an increase in the number of tactical nuclear weapons and intermediate-range ballistic missiles in Europe. Many in Western Europe were now inclined to pursue some kind of negotiated settlement with the Russians, but Eisenhower and Dulles would not yield significantly. It was increasingly clear that "[i]nitiative had passed to the adversary. Washington was governed by old, tired, unimaginative men. It seemed a time of twilight."[32]

POLICY IMMOBILITY

All about the Eisenhower administration change was accelerating, dramatically transforming the terrain of world politics. Most important was the momentous schism within the communist world as Khrushchev's concern for Soviet strategic inferiority and preoccupation with Europe brought him into conflict with his ideologically intense and more bellicose Chinese brethren.

The last year of the Eisenhower-Dulles partnership was marked by a predictable sameness. The observer of the events in the Middle East and Asia in 1958 experienced a sensation of *déjà vu*. In May pro-Nasser Lebanese nationalists rebelled against a conservative government that announced that it would remain in power beyond its constitutional term. The Lebanese and Jordanian governments were in a state of panic, fearing imminent intervention from Iraq, Syria, or both. They urged immediate Anglo-American intervention. Eisenhower decided to go in: "the question was whether it would be better to incur the deep resentment of nearly all of the Arab world (and some of the rest of the Free World) and in doing so to risk general war with the Soviet Union or to do something worse—which was to do nothing."[33] On July 15 the United States landed the first of 14,300 troops in Lebanon and the British put more than 3,000 troops in Jordan. But the crisis was more intense in Washington than in Lebanon.

> Combat marines came ashore across the bathing beaches in front of Beirut's expensive hotels. One private looked at the cluster of bikini-clad young women who were taking the sun, idly watching the operation or wholly indifferent. He put down his rifle, thoughtfully scanned the scene, and proclaimed in tones of wonder and appreciation: "So this is Eye-Rack."[34]

A compromise arrangement was worked out. The Lebanese government stepped down and was replaced by another acceptable to all parties. Indeed, Nasser had suggested precisely such a solution a month earlier. Coming from Nasser it was unaceptable; only terms arrived at by the State Department could be regarded as legitimate. In the meantime, hatred of the United States was increased and the Arab left was driven closer to the Russians.

During the summer and fall of 1958 the Taiwan Strait crisis was rerun as the Communists resumed the shelling of Quemoy, and Chiang Kai-shek dispatched a frenzied call for help to Washington. As in the earlier crisis, Dulles marched to the brink, claiming that the American commitment to the defense of the offshore islands was unequivocal and total. And once again, Eisenhower let matters ride at the outset as Dulles and the Joint Chiefs of Staff began talking privately of "no more than small air bursts without fallout. That is of course an unpleasant prospect, but one I think we must face up to."[35] Khrushchev added his ambiguous threats; naval and air incidents increased, and the world became extremely nervous. At the same time Khrushchev refused to provide Mao Zedong with a guarantee of support up to and including the use of nuclear weapons. Thus, Mao's capacity to escalate the crisis was truncated, as was in fact the entire Sino-Soviet relationship. In the United States, congressional and allied support for Dulles's tough posture began to break, Eisenhower apparently intervened, and Dulles reversed himself publicly and drew back from the brink. There was, the president stated, no commitment to defend the offshore islands or, for that matter, to help Chiang return to the mainland. The fundamental structure and assumptions of U.S. foreign policy remained unchanged, however.[36]

In Europe, Khrushchev had grown anxious to resolve what was for him the dangerously ambiguous question of Germany. Khrushchev's concern by late 1958 was that the West Germans, as they were integrated into NATO, would gain access to nuclear weapons. To counter this, Khrushchev had backed the proposal made in late 1957 by the Polish foreign minister, Adam Rapacki, that Central Europe be transformed into a nuclear-free area. In January 1958, Rapacki had issued through Soviet Premier Bulganin a call for a summit to discuss this and other issues.

The Rapacki proposal posed a number of difficulties for NATO planners. The elimination of nuclear weapons without a parallel reduction of manpower by the Warsaw Pact threw NATO defenses into what was deemed to be an impossible disadvantage. Nevertheless, the Soviet call for a summit conference was viewed favorably by many in Europe, especially the British. Khrushchev took dead aim at this soft spot by declaring on November 27, 1958, that he would turn over all remaining Soviet occupation functions in Berlin to the East Germans within six months unless there was a summit conference to create a normal situation in Germany. The image of a renewed Berlin blockade ran through Europe. Only now the confrontation would be even more dangerous. Demands for a conference rose throughout Western Europe.

Dulles and Eisenhower, once more on the defensive, sought to hold the alliance in line. Dulles was now only six months away from death. All who saw him were struck by his declining physical appearance.[37] Yet in December 1958 and February 1959 Dulles made two trips to Europe in an effort to hold things together. Those who met with him were awed by his courage but they, and one suspects Dulles as well, knew that he would no longer captain containment. The initiative was now in the hands of the more pliant and pragmatic Macmillan. The British prime minister, in an eleven-day visit to Moscow in February and March 1959,[38] found Khrushchev willing to defer the crisis deadline as long as diplomatic movement was in evidence. Later in March, Macmillan arrived in Washington to get American consent to the arrangements. His substantive talks were all with Eisenhower who, although distracted by Dulles's desperate situation at Walter Reed Hospital, ratified Macmillan's diplomacy. A new and final phase of the Eisenhower presidency had begun.

THE OPENING TOWARD DETENTE

With John Foster Dulles dead, Eisenhower assumed personal control of American foreign policy and sought, through sheer force of his personality, to redirect American policy in the time left to his administration. The result, according to one student of the Eisenhower years, was "a turn so swift and sharp that the pattern of six years was utterly broken and the world was left in startled wonder."[39] Eisenhower's attempt to exploit personal diplomacy was paralleled by his Soviet counterpart. Khrushchev, although prone to mercurial theatricality and even boorishness, was also attempting to impose his own personal stamp on a Soviet foreign and defense bureaucracy that was, in many respects, the mirror image of that in the United States. Thus, Khrushchev's domestic needs, his interest in expanding economic contact with the West, the bitter fight with the Chinese, and perhaps his own personal instincts as well, moved him toward a positive response to Eisenhower's new departure.

The Confluence of Personal Diplomacies

In December 1959 Eisenhower "began to reexamine the image of America across the world" and discovered that he "did not like much of what he saw."[40] Eisenhower's global perusal had mixed motivations. The 1958 election had not been successful for the Republicans, the economy was in the third and deepest recession of his administration, and Eisenhower's personal prestige among independent voters and the press had been eroded by his ambivalence toward the black civil rights movements in the South. Sometimes reporters laughed at his circumlocutions at press conferences. References to the "program of the President" drew laughter from members of Congress and staffers.[41] And there were jokes on television about the Eisenhower doll: you would wind it up and it wouldn't do anything. Then, too, there was the contrast of the Russians and the Chinese, both actively on the offensive in the third world pursuing nonaligned nations with aid offered at nominal interest and with no visible strings attached. Khrushchev became the first Soviet leader to make diplomatic travels abroad, leaving in his wake major loans for projects with high visibility.[42] Similarly, China had broken her diplomatic isolation and had begun a small, but increasingly effective effort to convince neutralist nations of Chinese good intentions.

Given the seeming loss of *élan* in America and a declining prestige abroad, Eisenhower prepared to undertake a series of global tours of good will. Eisenhower's itinerary took him to Europe, Asia, and, less successfully, to Latin America. It was motivated by a desire to assert an image of American leadership for the benefit of the increasingly disoriented American people and the Republican party.[43] Perhaps Eisenhower believed that he could combat expanding communist influence by the force of his enormous personal prestige in four separate visits to all corners of the globe, and arrange, if possible, the beginnings of detente with the Soviets.

It was clear to Eisenhower that the ultimate extension of personal diplomacy would have to be talks with the Soviets themselves. Khrushchev was prepared to stake much prestige and a good deal of his reputation on his ability to deal with Eisenhower. By January 1960, for example, Khrushchev would use his relationship with Eisenhower to convince the Soviet military to accept a cutback of about one-third of Soviet forces.[44] But Khrushchev had significant domestic opposition to a detente with the United States.[45] Molotov, ideologically not unlike a Soviet Dulles, writing from exile as ambassador to Mongolia, sent an article to *Kommunist* that recounted the older themes of the inevitable incompatibility of communism and capitalism and the need for vigilance.[46] The Chinese proclaimed that they were "able to see no substantial change in the imperialist war policy, the policy of the United States Government and of Eisenhower himself."[47] The Western press began to report the Soviet Union's internal disagreements, and Khrushchev indicated that there was considerable truth in them. He complained bitterly about the "libelous tales" that "other socialist countries [China and Albania] are demanding that the Soviet Union abandon its policy of detente." Khrushchev objected that it was "the silliest inventions . . . that officers and generals who lost their jobs owing to a cutback in the armed forces are opposed to [peaceful coexistence.]."[48]

The Spirit of Camp David

Clearly, therefore, Khrushchev was taking a chance in his pursuit of detente through personal diplomacy. But his hugely successful trip through the United States in September 1959 seemed to justify the risks. Indeed, the talks at the presidential retreat at Camp David, Maryland, may have led Khrushchev, and perhaps the president as well, to believe that a duopolistically managed detente was after all possible.[49] For a time, it seemed that the crucial territorial issues of the cold war might be arranged by a series of summit conferences. First there was the remarkable meeting of Khrushchev and Eisenhower at Camp David, then a series of consultations among the allies of both camps, followed by a meeting of the Big Four scheduled to take place in Paris in the spring of 1960. The planned capstone of all this activity was to be Eisenhower's visit to Moscow, scheduled to take place in the summer of 1960. It was, in short, a curious harbinger of the manner in which detente would unfold some fourteen years later. In 1960, however, almost as soon as detente assumed an identifiable shape, it shattered. The most dramatic fracture was to occur with the downing of an American aerial surveillance aircraft, the U-2. For after the plane and its pilot, Francis Gary Powers, appeared in a field near the Soviet city of Sverdlovsk, the cold war reemerged as detente's nascent form suddenly evaporated—almost without a trace.

Nikita Khrushchev's 1959 visit had startled Americans.* On his arrival Khrushchev behaved as if he were running for office. He lunched with Hollywood stars Bob Hope, Marilyn Monroe, and Frank Sinatra, and had his picture taken laughing and joking with corn farmers in Iowa. Then, at the end of his journey, Khrushchev visited the Eisenhower farm at Gettysburg and played with the Eisenhower grandchildren. Both the press and the public had the impression that these two benign men, both grandfathers, had become partners for peace.

About to leave, Khrushchev delivered an amazing farewell to the American people over national television. The speech was almost completely devoid of what the Soviet premier termed the "old boring arguments of the Cold War period." "Goodevening, American friends," he began. After complimenting America's "beautiful cities and kindhearted people," the nominal leder of the world communist movement referred to scripture and Christ to explain to the American people Soviet socialism. Then, in English, Khrushchev concluded his farewell speech, "Goodbye, good luck, friends."[50] Historian and former State Department official Louis Halle commented: "All this is not a dream. The record of the visit is there."[51]

It was a remarkable break with the past. Senator Stuart Symington, then a potential presidential candidate, in contrasting the domestic change that accompanied the Soviet premier's visit, averred that if Harry Truman had invited Stalin to dinner at the White House, he would have been impeached.[52] To Halle, the Khrushchev trip signified no less than the end of the cold war. "All that remained," Halle wrote, "was to put it into practice."[53]

THE OLD REFLEXES REEMERGE

Yet almost as soon as Khrushchev departed, the spirit of Camp David appeared steadily less substantial. To be sure, there was some initial appearance of forward movement at the disarmament meeting in Geneva. On February 16, 1960, the Soviets proposed that Western inspection teams be allowed to visit "the site of virtually any earth tremor in the Soviet Union in order to see if this was due to natural causes or an atom-

*Most of the argument from here to page 221 is adapted from James A. Nathan, "A Fragile Detente: The U-2 Incident Re-examined," *Military Affairs*, October 1975, pp. 97–104, with permission. Copyright 1975 by the American Military Institute. No additional copies may be made without the express permission of the author and of the editor of *Military Affairs*.

ic test." To the British prime minister, Harold Macmillan, this offer seemed to be a "complete reversal of the previous Soviet position." But Macmillan sensed an inexplicable lack of interest by the United States.[54] By March the reaction of many American officials to the prospect of negotiation seemed increasingly unenthusiastic. Secretary of State Christian Herter confessed to the Senate Foreign Relations Committee on March 22, 1960, that "I am frank to admit I'm not too optimistic that the summit will produce very great results."[55] Herter told the Senate the most that could be reasonably expected from a summit meeting would be the beginning of the shaping of the guidelines that would set the framework for protracted negotiations, at lower levels, on substantive matters. Herter emphasized, however, that even in the context of a very tentative first step, the May summit was a "gamble."[56] Clearly, the atmosphere of good will at Camp David had begun to dissipate.

In part, the hardening of the American position was a response to pressure from America's allies. The French were apparently most responsible for the delay between Khrushchev's visit in September 1959 and the Paris Summit in May 1960. Both Eisenhower and Khrushchev had expected to meet again soon, first in Paris and then in Moscow sometime in early summer. But French President Charles de Gaulle wanted time to consolidate his domestic position and, moreover, he wished to negotiate only after there had been a successful test of France's new atomic bomb. De Gaulle did not want to be excluded from great conferences and, following the reasoning of British labor leader Aneurin Bevan, who had argued earlier that the British bomb allowed England not to stand "naked at the conference chamber,"[57] De Gaulle, too, desired a nuclear fig leaf.[58] De Gaulle's principal purpose, however, in seeking the delay was to undercut the beginnings of a great power condominium—a situation in which France, in or out of an atomic loin cloth, would not be relevant. De Gaulle calculated that he could successfully delay the summit so that it would have to be placed in the shadow of a presidential election in order that it would be less likely that a lame duck president could be able to undertake any startling innovation with the Russians.

In the meantime, Khrushchev let the timing of his November 1958 six-month deadline on Berlin become ambiguous.[59] He told the East Germans that "the conditions are not yet ripe for a new scheme of things." The date for a final settlement had become open-ended with the September 1959 meeting at Camp David. But instead of seizing upon this element of apparent retreat, the State Department, concerned about how to ameliorate fissures in the alliance and worried about long-range Soviet intentions, chose to respond as if a final treaty might still be signed by Khrushchev. A final treaty meant that Germany would be permanently divided, and that Soviet claims in Eastern Europe would gather some additional legitimacy. But to acknowledge the Soviet position in Eastern Europe threatened Western unity because it could weaken the German Federal Republic under Konrad Adenauer. Adenauer's Germany held an enormous number of displaced Germans who had fled before the Russians entered Central Europe in the last days of World War II and who had escaped the comparatively harsh conditions of East Germany via Berlin. Each year some three hundred thousand East Germans had escaped to the miraculously prosperous West Germany of the late 1950s. By late 1959 some three million East Germans had come to West Germany by the Berlin route alone. The West's nonrecognition of the Soviet position in East Germany and Poland, but tactical inaction about pushing the Russians out, stabilized internal West German affairs by pacifying, somewhat, Germans separated from their traditional lands, and yet managed to dangle in front of displaced Germans the image of a Russian conqueror who held these territories, making it seem that the only remedy could be found in the context of a Western alliance. But whenever talk in the West turned to "disengagement" or some other form of settling World War II, Adenauer conjured up the startling Soviet-German rapprochement of the 1920s. And nobody in Western Europe or the United States desired that kind of reversal.[60] Adenauer did not even want the issue of Berlin brought up, and counseled that the only permissible and fruitful issue that might be discussed at Paris would be disarmament.[61]

To meet these fears, real and imagined, Undersecretary of State C. Douglas Dillon spoke before the AFL-CIO conference on world affairs and warned Khrushchev that by threatening a separate peace with the German Democratic Republic he was "skating on very thin ice":

> Germany . . . represents a critical test of Soviet good faith. . . . [T]he problem of Germany and Berlin can only be solved through German reunification. This the Soviets have so far rejected. . . . But we cannot abandon our goals. . . . It would be highly optimistic to pretend that the prospects of . . . agreement are bright. . . . [But i]s the Soviet Union willing to remove its forces from East Germany and the East European countries on which they are imposed? Is it willing to grant self-determination to the East Germans and to permit the people of the Soviet-dominated states in East Europe to choose their destiny? Is it willing to abandon the fiction of a separate north Korea and permit the entire Korean peoples to reunite? We . . . know that to the Soviet Union "peaceful coexistence" . . . includes the use of military force whenever it suits their purpose.[62]

The tone of Dillon's speech seemed to indicate that Berlin would be placed in the context of all the outstanding issues between the Soviets and the United States since World War II—even the nature of world order itself was on the table. Similar statements made by Secretary of State Herter and Vice President Nixon made it obvious that the United States intended in no way to move away from its Berlin stand of the past. The Soviets, through a variety of channels, expressed dismay at this toughening of the American position in the wake of Camp David and on the eve of the Paris summit.[63]

THE CURIOUS DEATH
OF DETENTE: THE U-2 INCIDENT

Fourteen days before the scheduled conference in Paris, on the morning of May 1, over Sverdlovsk, a large industrial area in the Urals, twelve hundred miles deep in the Soviet Union, there appeared a black plane with a peculiarly large tail and enormous wings. The pilot, Francis Gary Powers, carried two military identification cards, a U.S. and an international driving license, a Selective Service card, a Social Security card, a PX ration card, a medical certificate, two flying licenses, American, French, Turkish, Italian, German and Soviet currencies, two gold watches, gold coins, and seven gold rings, as Khrushchev put it sarcastically, "for the ladies."[64] Indeed, Powers was a multilingual billboard for American espionage. Along with his pistol with a silencer, morphine, and flares, he also carried a "large silk American flag poster" in fourteen languages reading "I am an American and do not speak your language. I need food, shelter and assistance. I will not harm you. I bear no malice toward your people. If you help me, you will be rewarded.[65] Somewhat incongruously, he also had a needle dipped in curare. The U-2 also contained a destructor unit with 2½ pounds of plastic explosive activated by a delayed timing switch. If the pilot were to use his ejection seat, the destructor button would be set off automatically.[66]

It is not clear how the plane descended to earth. The Soviets claim that they shot it down. So much of the plane was intact that the lettering U-2 could plainly be seen on the huge fragment of the plane's fuselage and tail displayed in Gorky Park in Moscow. Eisenhower was told by the Joint Chiefs and the CIA that the plane "would virtually disintegrate" in the event of a "mishap," so "fragile" was the plane's construction.[67] When Khrushchev announced that "the uninjured pilot of a reconnaissance plane, along with much of his equipment was intact, was in Soviet hands," Eisenhower was flabbergasted. It was, he wrote, "unbelievable."[68]

Powers was paid a salary of almost $30,000 a year to steer an aircraft from Pakistan to Norway by way of the Soviet Union.[69] His high pay was presumably a reflection as much of the risks of his profession as his skill. Moreover, *Aviation Week,* the prestigious aerospace trade journal, noted that Powers's "embarrassing survival was not in the best tradition of the USAF which trained him or the CIA who employed him."[70] When Powers parachuted to earth he should have had, by the code of his profession, only two possible distinguishing characteristics. He could have been "deniable" and he could have been dead—or, and perhaps preferably, he could have been both. Powers contends that his instructions were that if he were caught he could "tell them everything" he knew, because they could probably get it out of him anyway. The nonuse of the curare needle with which Powers was supplied was also supported in the CIA public statement upon his release.[71] In any case, he should not have been caught, and if caught he should not have talked and talked and talked.

The Paris Summit Is Aborted

On May 5 Khrushchev announced to the Supreme Soviet that an aircraft had penetrated Soviet airspace but neglected to mention that Powers or much of his plane and equipment were intact and in Soviet hands. Khrushchev asked, "Who sent this aircraft across the Soviet frontier? Was it the . . . President? Or was this token aggressive act carried out by Pentagon militants?"[72] Lincoln White, the Department of State spokesman, responded to Khrushchev emphatically, "There was absolutely no—n-o—, no deliberate attempt to violate Soviet airspace. There has never been."[73] But on May 7, Powers was shockingly produced, alive. Khrushchev claimed, however, that he was prepared to grant that the president had no knowledge of a plane being dispatched to the Soviet Union and failing to return.[74] It was Eisenhower's worst fear. Eisenhower had been trying to stop the flights since 1958.[75]

The American response was hardly a disavowal.[76] On May 11, just four days before the conference was scheduled to open and six days after Khrushchev had asked the president to tell him it was not true that it was he who was responsible, Eisenhower spoke to the American people saying the U-2 flight and flights like it were a "vital necessity" because the Russians "make a fetish of secrecy and concealment." And echoing a statement by Secretary of State Herter on May 9, he indicated that the flights would be continued.[77] Walter Lippmann commented, "*To avow* [emphasis his] that we intend to violate Soviet sovereignty . . . makes it impossible for the Soviet government to play down this particular incident because now it is challenged openly in the face of the world. It is compelled to react because no nation can remain passive when it is the avowed policy of another to intrude upon its territory."[78] Nonetheless,

Khrushchev still insisted that he would come to Paris. When asked in an informal conference in Moscow on May 11 if "this plane incident [will] influence Soviet public opinion when Mr. Eisenhower visits Moscow," Khrushchev replied, "I can only say the Soviet people . . . are very polite, so there will be no excesses, but questions will be asked. . . . The people will say, 'Are you nuts?' " But, he assured the president again, "our people are courteous, they let off steam in words and leave the government to act. They will not indulge insulting behavior."[79]

But on May 16, Khrushchev, pale and with shaking hands, appeared in front of world television at a Paris news conference side by side with his splendidly decorated defense minister, Marshall Rodin Malinovsky, and proceeded to roast President Eisenhower, who Khrushchev claimed was like "a thief caught red-handed in his theft. . . . The President," Khrushchev demanded heatedly, "must apologize for his wrong and punish his responsible confederates, if a meeting would proceed." It was not certain, by now, if Khrushchev could have proceeded even if he had wished. According to Bohlen, who was at Paris, "Khrushchev had come to Paris determined to get an apology."[80] And if he could not elicit Eisenhower's regrets, then Khrushchev, speculated Bohlen, "was not authorized to participate in the conference."[81] Khrushchev recalled in his memoirs that "I went out of my way not to accuse President Eisenhower in my own statements. As long as [he] was dissociated from the U-2 affair, we could continue our policy of strengthening Soviet-U.S. relations." But Eisenhower publicly acknowledged that "he had known about the U-2 flight in advance and he had approved it. . . . It was no longer possible for us to spare the President. He had, so to speak, offered us his back end, and we obliged him by kicking it as hard as we could."[82]

At Paris when Khrushchev personally demanded of Eisenhower a formal apology and assurances of no more American reconaissance flights over Russia, he said his interpreter overheard Eisenhower ask Secretary of State Herter, "Well, why not? Why don't we go ahead and make a statement of apology?" Herter said no—and he said it in such a way, with such a grimace on his face, that he left no room for argument on the issue. Khrushchev said that this incident demonstrated that "if Eisenhower had followed his own good instincts and used his considerable intelligence, he would have done the right thing and given in to our demand . . . but unfortunately Eisenhower wasn't the only one who determined foreign policy for the United States."[83]

Eisenhower did start to edge away from his position of May 11, that espionage was "a distasteful but vital necessity."[84] But it was too late. Khrushchev had already asked in a press conference that Eisenhower's visit be "postponed" until "conditions for the visit . . . mature."[85] After a thirty-six hour delay, perhaps waiting for Eisenhower to change his position, Khrushchev departed, saying that he hoped he would be able to deal with the new administration more successfully than he had with Eisenhower.[86] Suddenly, the promise of peace was dashed and Eisenhower would write: "the Paris summit, had it been held, would have proved to be a failure and thus would have brought the free world only further disillusionment."[87] And it was with obvious pride that Secretary of State Herter told the Senate Foreign Relations Committee: "One of the most impressive things I have ever seen was the meeting of NATO that took place after the aborted, so-called summit conference. I have never seen such unanimity, such firmness, such determination, as exhibited at that meeting."[88]

The Strange Odyssey of Francis Gary Powers

Adlai Stevenson summarized the Paris Conference: "We handed Khrushchev that crowbar and sledge-hammer to wreck the meeting."[89] Khrushchev recalls that he was "haunted by the fact that just prior to this meeting the United States had dared to send its U-2 reconnaissance plane against us. It was as though the Americans had deliberately tried to place a time bomb under the meeting, set to go off just as we were about to sit down with them at the negotiation table."[90]

The anomalies surrounding the U-2 flight are numerous. First, there are unanswered questions concerning the altitude of the plane, whether it was in fact shot down, and why it landed in such pristine condition.[91] Second, there is the problem of the curious timing of the flight, shortly before a summit conference, a schedule all the more strange because previous U-2 flights had been cancelled before and during no more important diplomatic events than the Paris Conference.[92] Third, Powers told all to a crowded courtroom full of reporters, but twenty-one months later was retrieved by the CIA in exchange for Rudolph Abel, widely reported to be the most important Soviet agent ever captured in the United States.[93] Finally, few questions were asked by Congress on the day Powers gave public testimony to the Senate about his performance, testimony preceded by a still secret briefing provided by CIA chief John McCone. Moreover, Powers was rewarded on returning home with the highest honor the CIA can bestow—the Intelligence Star—and given a comfortable job that lasted some years as a test pilot for the Lockheed Aircraft Corporation, which built the U-2.[94] As Macmillan noted on May 8, 1960, "It seemed a very queer story."[95] The complex truth of the U-2 incident and the Paris conference may never be known. Macmillan felt that the situation might have been "retrieved" if it had not been for Eisenhower's "unlucky admission."[96] It is reasonable to suppose that Eisenhower felt he had little choice but to confess that he had responsibility for the flights; after all, he was the top civilian and military administrator. Nevertheless, suspicion remains that the conference was one that Americans had apparently initiated and then took advantage of every device to see that it was unsuccessful. Investigative reporters Wise and Ross concluded: "By lying, when it could have remained silent, by admitting it had lied, by disclaiming Presidential responsibility, then admitting Presidential responsibility, and finally by implying the flights would continue, the United States all but made it impossible for the summit meeting to take place."[97] As De Gaulle summarized, "Khrushchev *does* want detente—*does* want disarmament . . . but . . . except perhaps for Eisenhower, the Americans want neither."[98] Nor has the passage of time diminished the curious nature of the U-2 incident. Thus as he was leaving the Senate in 1975, Senator J. William Fulbright observed:

> [W]hen Khrushchev came here in '60, he had it in mind to seek what we would now call detente, so as to devote more Soviet resources to Soviet development. I often wondered why, in the midst of these efforts by President Eisenhower and Khrushchev to come to some understanding, the U-2 incident was allowed to take place. No one will ever know whether it was accidental or intentional.[99]

Francis Gary Powers seemed like a human monkey wrench tossed into the emerging East-West relationship and then, later, unaccountably retrieved and refurbished. When the U-2 went down, there was indeed some private speculation, in Eisenhower's words, that the president had been the "victim of overzealous subordinates." Eisenhower denied this. "After all," he pointed out, since he had approved the flights in principle he "did not want it to appear that [he] could not, in important matters . . . speak authoritatively" for the United States.[100]

Denouement

The effect of the U-2 was dramatically and immediately apparent. On May 14, *the day before* the conference ended, but when all the heads of government were in Paris, the American secretary of defense, Thomas Gates, announced a worldwide military alert as a "sound precautionary measure."[101] In Washington, the Joint Chiefs interpreted Gates's message to mean that a "type 3" nuclear alert was called for.[102] Walter Lippmann despaired:

> On Sunday night Mr. Macmillan and General De Gaulle were still struggling to find some way out of the affair of the spy plane. Yet this was the time chosen by the Secretary of Defense to stage a worldwide readiness exercise

which, though not the last stage before actual war, is one of the preliminary stages to it.

... The timing of the so-called exercise makes no sense whatever. For if the alert was concerned with a possible surprise attack, when in the name of common sense could there be less danger of a surprise attack on the Western World than when Mr. K. in person was in Paris?[103]

On Tuesday, May 18, an irate Khrushchev, with Malinovsky at his side, berated Eisenhower: he was ready, he boomed, "to divest the Western powers of the right to have occupation troops in West Berlin. And when we see fit we shall take up our fountain pens from our pockets—the drafts are all ready—sit down, sign and make the announcement."[104] Khrushchev's parting shot at Paris apparently terrified Western leaders. He used incredibly insulting language, being particularly abusive toward the German "bastards" of the Adenauer regime. To Macmillan and the British press it was reminiscent of Hitler at his worst.[105]

The position of the United States and the West hardened to what appeared to be a renewed Soviet offensive led by a man whose posture as an effective diplomatist paled beside the memory of his insults at Paris delivered with an unblinking and obviously approving representative of Soviet military power at his side. Indeed, enthusiasts for all-out preparedness such as columnist Joe Alsop used the incident to demand that the "facts be faced ... appropriations are needed to speed ... reconnaissance satellites ... and the B52H bomber."[106] To some, the results of the Paris meeting seemed no surprise. Defense Secretary Gates testified at the official summit postmortem, "In January I repeat[edly] stated we didn't expect to have any significant substantive conclusions. We believe there was a tactic on the part of the Soviet Union. We didn't know how long it would last ...[107] [so] as late as April we went back with a major revision in our military programs to the appropriations committees."[108]

THE MORE THINGS CHANGED ...

With the collapse of the Paris summit conference, the Eisenhower administration's capacity to pursue detente or, for that matter, his personal diplomacy vis-à-vis America's allies was circumscribed. Anti-American demonstrations in Tokyo forced cancellation of his trip to Japan. His ability to deal with the Russians on any basis other than by means of the traditional cold war modalities had ended. The opening of lines of communication by means of personal diplomacy required above all else the credibility of the instrument of personal diplomacy. But Eisenhower's personal credibility with Khrushchev had been shattered by the U-2 incident. Indeed, continued positive interaction with Eisenhower was a liability for Khrushchev: the U-2 and the aborted summit conference made Khrushchev's personal diplomatic efforts suspect to Soviet hardliners and to the Chinese, who were now prepared to bring their feud with Moscow into the open.

Moreover, the Twenty-second Amendment, with its prohibition on presidential succession after two terms, now decisively entered into the picture. The Eisenhower administration would, of necessity, pass from the scene within a matter of months. In the meantime, Khrushchev could simultaneously refuse to deal with Eisenhower and attack him, thereby underscoring the president's impotence. Khrushchev's ebullient and sometimes belligerent personality had, therefore, a clear field during the election and transition period. And he exploited the situation to its fullest by berating Eisenhower but also trying to replace detente on the agenda of the incoming administration. For its part, "the Eisenhower administration ran steadily down like a tired clock, its energies spent, its coherence blurred."[109] Under the circumstances, it fell back reflexively upon the cold war stance of the Dulles years.

To preserve containment, Eisenhower and Dulles constructed a ring of commitments around the perimeter of a communist world that, by the end of the 1950s, was fractious and preoccupied with its internal problems but perceived the United States as being monolithic and expansive. The circle of treaties, guarantees, and bases were predicated on clear American strategic superiority. The United States seemed to possess, especially at the outset of the Eisenhower and Dulles years, the requisite strength to negotiate the issues of the cold war, but the second phase of containment foreseen by Kennan never took place:

> The failure consisted in the fact that our government, finding it difficult to understand a political threat as such and to deal with it in other than military terms, and grievously misled, in particular, by its own faulty interpretations of the significance of the Korean War, failed to take advantage of the opportunities for useful political discussion when, in later years, such opportunities began to open up, and exerted itself, in its military preoccupations, to seal and to perpetuate the very division of Europe which it should have been concerned to remove. It was not "containment" that failed; it was the intended follow-up that never occurred.[110]

But in relying on the maintenance of a policy implemented through the threat of war, Eisenhower, perhaps unwittingly, institutionalized the very thing against which he would warn the nation in his farewell address:

We have been compelled to create a permanent armaments industry of vast proportions. . . .

This conjunction of an immense military establishment and a large arms industry is new in the American experience. The total influence— economic, political, even spiritual—is felt in every city, every statehouse, every office of the federal government. We recognize the imperative need for this development. Yet we must not fail to comprehend its grave implications. Our toil, resources, and livelihood are all involved; so is the very structure of our society.

In the councils of government we must guard against the acquisition of unwarranted influence, whether sought or unsought, by the military-industrial complex. The potential for the disastrous use of misplaced power exists and will persist.[111]

An irony of the Eisenhower-Dulles era, therefore, is that although there was no war during their stewardship, their most significant legacy to America was an institutionalized cold war. And not the least of its manifestations and consequences was the massive and potent union of U.S. government and private politico-economic power necessary to wage that cold war and man the defenses of containment—a joining of public and private power that would, as Eisenhower, Dulles, and Taft feared, come to dominate the institutions and spirit of America during the next decade.

There was an additional, external legacy in Eisenhower and Dulles's policy of institutionalized and globalized containment. By failing to distinguish international communism and nationalist or anticolonial revolution, by seeing the latter as indistinguishable from the former, Eisenhower and Dulles set American policy against the nationalist revolutions of the non-Western world. There was much of real and imagined economic necessity in this: the presumed need for raw materials, export markets, and the implied integrated world economy built on low tariffs and the free flow of U.S. private investment.[112] But this was very quickly subordinated to the incompatible imperatives of what was thought to be a more immediate threat: the penetration of the global political economy by international communism *through* these anti-Western nationalist revolutions. Thus, Ho, Nasser, Mossadegh, Arbenz, and the mobs that attacked Richard Nixon in Venezuela in 1958 were not viewed as primarily products of a collapsing colonial and traditional milieu, they were instead the political and even military instruments of communism.

The threat of massive or tactical nuclear retaliation based on U.S. strategic superiority could check communist expansion in Europe or the Taiwan Strait, but in the third world something else was required if Korea was not to be replicated. The answer was intervention in a counterrevolutionary mode. The form of intervention was often crude, as in

Lebanon, Iran, or Guatemala. Such intervention, although it did not always work, was nevertheless relatively cheap. But by the end of the Eisenhower-Dulles era, a somewhat more sophisticated range of instrumentalities was being employed, including the use between 1952 and 1959 of $37.3 billion in foreign aid, of which almost $21 billion was military assistance in support of essentially counterrevolutionary regimes on the periphery of the communist world and incorporated into Dulles's alliance system. Moreover, the economic aid was usually structured, as in South Vietnam after 1956, to benefit those most likely to resist revolutionary activity.[113]

Nevertheless, the thrust of the Dulles-Eisenhower effort was the politico-military containment and suppression of non-Western political, social, and economic revolution. Economic instruments were simply not, in the emerging view of the 1950s, sufficient in themselves to this great task. As in Europe and Japan, American power supplemented by economic and military aid would establish the political preconditions for world economic order, integration, and stability. In this respect, what Eisenhower and Dulles tried to do in the non-Western world was merely an extension of what Truman, Marshall, and Acheson saw themselves doing in Europe after World War II. The legacy for the 1960s was that insofar as Eisenhower and Dulles succeeded, they set their faces and the face of American power against history. They were, at least superficially, successful in the short run of their eight years. But in the meantime, revolutionary forces were growing, and the 1960s would demonstrate that American political and military power was ultimately and tragically limited in its ability to contain them.

TRANSITION

During the seven months following the collapse of the Paris summit conference, Khrushchev held the diplomatic initiative. As the attention of the American people turned to the presidential campaign between Richard Nixon and John Kennedy, the Soviet leader unleashed a frequently vicious diplomatic offensive directed at the hapless Eisenhower administration. At the same time Khrushchev indicated a willingness to renew the quest of detente with a new administration, especially if it was Democratic.

For the balance of 1960, however, the Eisenhower administration fought a diplomatic holding action in a world that seemed perpetually in turmoil. The worst of it exploded in the newly independent Congo (now Zaire), where rape, riot, murder, mayhem, and eventually civil war accompanied the departure of Belgian colonial rule. The flood of anarchy in the Congo, it was feared, might spread to any one of the recently independent nations of Africa. Seventeen nations gained independence in 1960 alone, and the precedence of chaos and savagery in the Congo appeared to incite great power conflicts.

When the Congolese army mutinied, Prime Minister Patrice Lumumba appealed to the United Nations to restore order. He also appealed to the Soviet Union, which Macmillan believed was "sinister evidence of his sympathies."[114] Acting under a Security Council resolution, in which the Soviets concurred, the United States airlifted Tunisian and Moroccan troops into the Congo and provided these troops with relief food, airplanes, and helicopters and sent a U.S. aircraft carrier to the mouth of the Congo River. In September, UN Secretary-General Dag Hammarskjold reported that Soviet fliers and military personnel might begin operations to support Lumumba. To Eisenhower, the Soviet presence was "an invasion" that the United Nations, shored up by American support, was obligated to resist.[115] More UN peace-keeping troops arrived and attempted to keep order between the central government of the Congo and the secessionist factions. In this confused situation the pro-Western Colonel Joseph Mobutu gained power and demanded that the Russian advisers leave, in Macmillan's words, "Lock, stock and barrel . . . it is too good to be true!"[116]

The situation in the Congo sputtered on but at the high point of the crisis, Macmillan, known for his unflappability, brooded, "ever since the breakdown of the summit in Paris I have felt uneasy about the summer of 1960. It has a terrible similarity to 1914. Now Congo may play the role of Serbia. Except for the terror of the nuclear power on both sides, we might easily slide into the 1914 situation."[117] The Russians, losing politically in the Congo, attempted to recoup by refusing to recognize the Mobutu government and claimed with many African and other nonaligned nations that Lumumba was the legitimate head of state. Simultaneously, the Soviet pressed for the removal of Secretary Hammarskjold and a reorganization of the United Nations.

Khrushchev next took his attack on the United Nations and the lame duck Eisenhower administration to the United Nations itself when he announced that he would return to the United States to head the Soviet delegation to the General Assembly on September 20, 1960. The visit would also place him precisely in the middle of the American presidential election campaign. While at the United Nations Khrushchev conspicuously conferred with leaders of the third world, notably Fidel Castro, the new leader of the increasingly anti-American Cuban regime. During debate in the General Assembly Khrushchev pressed his attack on the West and Hammarskjold's purportedly pro-Western UN leadership. This performance reached its peak during a speech by Macmillan as Khrushchev's rather startling and discourteous interruptions were climaxed by the Soviet leader removing his shoe and alternately banging on his desk and waving it at the imperturbable British leader.[118] It was a shocking and frightening spectacle in which the Kremlin appeared to be headed by a man so reminiscent of earlier totalitarians that the world of negotiation seemed barely applicable.

In marked contrast with this behavior, however, was Khrushchev's attitude toward the American election and the new president-elect. During the campaign, Khrushchev made references to the unacceptability of Richard Nixon as the next president—an oblique endorsement of Kennedy that nonetheless contributed to much discomfort in the young senator's camp.[119] And following Kennedy's victory, Khrushchev's persistent overtures to the president-elect during the interregnal period between November 1960 and the inauguration in January 1961 sounded the refrain of harmony and new opportunities for detente.

However, during the postelection period, the Soviets were confronted with and seemed to have been somewhat perplexed, even chagrined, by Kennedy's cool but correct silence.[120] Khrushchev undoubtedly hoped for some reinforcement for his effort to renew detente—but there was at best an ambiguous response. Perhaps little else could be expected from the president-elect. Kennedy had earlier emphasized that the responsibility for policy making remained with President Eisenhower until January 20, and that he (Kennedy) had no intention of usurping it. Reaction to the Russian overtures was determined in part, therefore, by Kennedy's conception of a president-elect's status. An additional inhibiting factor was the enormity of the administrative changeover itself. Although the Eisenhower administration willingly extended itself in order to facilitate the orientation of Kennedy's appointees, those appointees, particularly in the top decision-making positions, still were faced with the formidable job of grasping the magnitude of their particular positions. Thus, even if Kennedy had been inclined to respond to the Russian approaches at this time, a considered response would have been difficult to construct.

More fundamental, however, was that the incoming Kennedy administration was no less an advocate of negotiating from strength than its predecessors. On October 8, 1960, during the second of the famous televised debates between Kennedy and Nixon, Kennedy had agreed completely with Nixon concerning the preconditions of negotiation with the Soviets:

> Before we go into the summit, before we ever meet again, I think it's important that the United States build its strength—that it build its military strength, as well as its own economic strength.

If we negotiate from a position where the power balance or wave is moving away from us, it's extremely difficult to reach a successful decision on Berlin, as well as the other questions.[121]

This statement was more than mere campaign puffery designed to demonstrate that the Massachusetts Democratic senator was as tough as his experienced Republican opponent. One would be hard-pressed to find a more straightforward statement of this most fundamental conception of world politics and Soviet-American relations during the cold war. John Kennedy, along with the "best and the brightest" he brought to the presidency, would continue the vigorous pursuit of military superiority before any serious effort would be made to negotiate the outstanding issues of the cold war. Thus Kennedy's conception of America's world role, and the hostile nature of the international system within which that role would have to be played out, was consistent with the principles that had guided American foreign and national security policy during the preceding fifteen years.

NOTES

1. Townsend Hoopes, *The Devil and John Foster Dulles* (Boston: Little, Brown, 1973), p. 337.
2. Eisenhower's role in this decision seems to have been minimal. In early June he suffered a recurrence of the ileitis. His intestinal problem required major surgery and during the crucial five-week period that the Suez Crisis was set in motion, Dulles had near total control of policy.
3. Hoopes, op. cit., pp. 341–342.
4. Anthony Nutting, *No End of a Lesson: The Story of Suez* (New York: Clarkson Potter, 1967), pp. 32–33.
5. Among the accounts of the crisis perhaps the standard analysis has been that of Herman Finer, *Dulles' Own Suez: The Theory and Practice of His Diplomacy* (Chicago: Quadrangle, 1964). However, Finer's book was, of necessity, written without benefit of access to Dulles's papers. For an account that does have benefit of this primary source, see Hoopes, op. cit., pp. 318–414. The following analysis draws most heavily on the latter.
6. Hoopes, op. cit., p. 359.
7. Kenneth Love, quoting Nasser in *Suez: The Twice Fought War* (New York: McGraw-Hill, 1960), p. 429.
8. Finer, op. cit., p. 218.
9. Ibid., pp. 217–218 (emphasis in the original).
10. Hoopes, op. cit., p. 361.
11. Peter Lyon, *Eisenhower: Portrait of the Hero* (Boston: Little, Brown, 1974), p. 715.
12. Finer, op. cit., p. 386.
13. His request that a portion of British capitalization in the International Monetary

Fund be rebased in order to support the pound had been referred to the I.M.F. in Washington and rejected.

14. Dwight D. Eisenhower, *Waging Peace* (Garden City, N.Y.: Doubleday, 1965), p. 178.
15. Notes for testimony before the Senate Foreign Relations Committee, February 1957, in the Dulles Papers, quoted bv Hoopes, op. cit., p. 408.
16. Earlier, U.S. interventionism had been in evidence in Syria where a coup had been planned. The operation was aborted by the Israeli attack. See Wilker Crane Eveland, *Ropes of Sand: America's Failure in the Middle East* (New York: W. W. Norton, 1980) and Donald Neff, *Warriors at Suez: Eisenhower Takes America into the Middle East* (New York: Linden, 1981), pp. 383ff.
17. For a review of Khrushchev's claims see Arnold L. Horelick and Myron Rush. *Strategic Power and Soviet Foreign Policy* (Chicago: University of Chicago Press, 1966), pp. 42–50.
18. Ibid., p. 110.
19. His efforts are recounted in Maxwell D. Taylor, *The Uncertain Trumpet* (New York: Harper & Row, 1960).
20. Ibid., p. 185.
21. Gordon Dean, former head of the Atomic Energy Commission, writing in the foreword of Henry Kissinger's *Nuclear Weapons and Foreign Policy* (New York: W. W. Norton, 1957), p. vii.
22. Henry Kissinger, "Force and Diplomacy in the Nuclear Age," *Foreign Affairs,* Vol. 34 (April 1956), pp. 349–366.
23. Kissinger, *Nuclear Weapons and Foreign Policy*, p. 264.
24. Ibid., p. 147.
25. Ibid., pp. 144–145.
26. Morton Halperin, *Limited War in the Nuclear Age* (New York: John Wiley, 1963), p. 62.
27. Henry Kissinger, "Limited War: Conventional or Nuclear? A Reappraisal," in Donald G. Brennan (ed.), *Arms Control, Disarmament and National Security* (New York: Braziller, 1961), p. 146. Italics in the original.
28. This report was declassified in February 1973. It is entitled "Deterrence and Survival in the Nuclear Age," Security Resources Panel of the Science Advisory Committee, NSC Cover Sheet 5724, November 7, 1957, Office of Presidential Libraries, Reference Copy No. 43.
29. Ibid., p. 6.
30. Morton L. Halperin, "The Gaither Committee and the Policy Process," *World Politics,* Vol. 13 (April 1961), pp. 360–384.
31. See the Gaither Report, op. cit., table "C." For Eisenhower reaction see *Waging Peace*, pp. 220–221.
32. Hoopes, op. cit., p. 430.
33. Eisenhower, op. cit., p. 274.
34. Meaning Iraq; Hoopes, op. cit., p. 436.
35. Harold Macmillan, *Riding the Storm* (London: Macmillan, 1971), pp. 547–548. The Joint Chiefs' inclination to use atomic weapons became almost a fixation according to Morton Halperin, a Defense Department official in the Johnson administration.
36. Hoopes, op. cit., pp. 442–457.
37. Macmillan, op. cit., p. 587.
38. Ibid., pp. 592–632.
39. Hoopes, op. cit., p. 492.
40. See Hoopes, pp. 492–494. See also Emmett John Hughes, *The Ordeal of Power* (New York: Dell, 1964), pp. 247–248 and Merriman Smith, *A President's Odyssey* (New York: Harper & Row, 1961), p. 250.

41. Richard Neustadt, *Presidential Power* (New York: Signet, 1964), p. 83.
42. Marshall Goldman, *Soviet Foreign Aid* (New York: Praeger, 1967), p. 116.
43. Hoopes, op. cit., p. 493.
44. Michael Tatu, *Power in the Kremlin: From Khrushchev to Kosygin*, translated by Helen Katel (New York: Viking, 1969), p. 50.
45. Ibid., pp. 49–52.
46. Ibid., p. 51
47. Ibid., p. 48.
48. Ibid., p. 44.
49. Hoopes, op. cit., p. 496.
50. Text reprinted in *The New York Times*, September 28, 1959; see also Khrushchev's Press Conference, *The New York Times*, September 28, 1959.
51. Louis Halle, *The Cold War as History* (New York: Harper & Row, 1967), p. 366.
52. *The New York Times*, September 28, 1959.
53. Louis Halle, op. cit., p. 367.
54. Harold Macmillan, *Pointing the Way* (London: Macmillan, 1972), p. 179. Macmillan wrote that he was "concerned at the slow American reaction to these undoubted advances."
55. *The New York Times*, March 23, 1960.
56. Ibid.
57. *The Times* (London), October 4, 1957, quoted in Robert E. Osgood, *NATO, The Entangling Alliance* (Chicago: University of Chicago Press, 1962), p. 242.
58. Coral Bell, *Negotiation from Strength* (New York: Knopf, 1963), p. 203, and *Le Monde*, October 22, 1959.
59. Adam Ulam, *Expansion and Coexistence: Soviet Foreign Policy 1917–1967* (New York: Praeger, 1968), pp. 626–627.
60. See James Richardson, *German and the Atlantic Alliance: The Interaction of Strategy and Politics* (Cambridge, Mass.: Harvard University Press, 1966), pp. 33–34.
61. Bell, op. cit., p. 204 and *The New York Times*, November 22, 1959.
62. C. Douglas Dillon, "American Foreign Policy Today," *Department of State Bulletin*, Vol. 42, Speech of April 20, 1960, pp. 724–725, 727.
63. See Charles E. Bohlen, *Witness to History, 1929–1969* (New York: W. W. Norton, 1973), p. 451; David Wise and Thomas B. Ross, *The U-2 Affair* (New York: Random House, 1962), p. 141; and *Current Digest of the Soviet Press*, Vol. 12 (May 25, 1960), p. 7.
64. See Khrushchev's remarks as reported in *The New York Times*, May 8, 1960, and Wise and Ross, op. cit., pp. 125–126.
65. Francis G. Powers and Curt Gentry, *Operation Overflight* (New York: Holt, Rinehart and Winston, 1970), p. 45.
66. L. Fletcher Prouty, *The Secret Team* (Englewood Cliffs, N.J.: Prentice-Hall, 1974), p. 374. Prouty maintains that procedure for these flights invariably included a "skin search," where pilots were stripped naked and then given a flying costume without pockets. "The zipper might be made in Denmark, the shoes in India, and the underclothes in Hong Kong," Prouty told James Nathan in a telephone interview, June 3, 1974.

   Powers contends in *Operation Overflight* that curare is a "horrible" death (like self-strangulation) [p. 143]. (This is correct.) But, Powers says, he refused to take the profferred cyanide capsule (which toxicologists indicate to be the suicide "drug of choice") because he was afraid it would break in his pocket [p. 53]. (Checking with the chief toxicologist and former army chemical warfare researcher at the Du Pont Company's Haskell Laboratory we find that cyanide capsules are not gelatin coated but "hard as walnuts" and have to be cracked with the back teeth. There is no chance they will break in one's pocket.) Nevertheless, Powers tossed away the silver dollar covering of a poorly constructed [p. 144] and poorly sheathed curare plunger and put it in his pocket where it remained undetected for several days [p. 88] until he revealed its presence to the KGB even though he claims that he still feared torture [pp. 102–107]. In any case, he took this needle, he says, not as a suicide device, but as a weapon. However, his ostentatiously silenced "extra long barreled" [p. 146] semi-automatic pistol with the initials U.S.A. on the handle [p. 77] was, he contends, only for hunting game.

One speculation arising from these contradictions might be that the curare needle and the gun were but mere dramatizations of Powers's role as a spy. Powers explained that he did not "reach for the destruct switches . . . but I thought I had better see if I can get out of here before using this. I knew that there was a seventy second time switch delay." Powers was worried the seventy seconds was not enough time and maintains, to this day, that he simply bailed out. David Wise and Thomas R. Ross, *The Invisible Government* (New York: Bantam, 1964), p. 132, citing Hearings, Francis G. Powers, U-2 pilot, Senate Committee on the Armed Services, March 6, 1962.

67. Eisenhower, op. cit., p. 546. Indeed, in September 1956 a U-2 "simply disintegrated" in mid-air when passed by two curious Canadian jets and caught in the wake of the interceptors. Powers and Gentry, op. cit., pp. 49–50. Eisenhower told a group of Congressional leaders at a breakfast meeting that a picture of the plane showed bullet holes, but no Soviet plane could reach the U-2's altitude. "The present theory," Eisenhower said, was the "plane's engines flamed out." "Memorandum of conversation, breakfast with the President," The White House, May 26, 1960. Eisenhower Library. The authors would like to thank Thomas G. Paterson for bringing this memorandum to their attention.

68. Eisenhower, op. cit., pp. 549–550. Some former intelligence men have speculated that the plane simply ran out of fuel. Prouty, op. cit., p. 424. Although Powers radioed on May 1 an "engine flame out," he later became insistent that he was, in fact, shot down. See Eisenhower, op. cit., pp. 543 and 558, and Powers and Gentry, op. cit., p. 82. Powers claims that his radio could not reach over 400 miles and he did not radio back. There is some reason to believe that Powers may well not have radioed back as Eisenhower recalls in *Waging Peace*, for Undersecretary of State C. Douglas Dillon testified, "But we did not have any specific information that it was down in the Soviet Union . . . until Mr. Khrushchev made the statement of Thursday morning [May 5]." *Events Incident to the Summit Conference,* Hearings before the Senate Committee on Foreign Relations, 86th Congress, 2nd Session, May 27, June 1 and 2, 1960, p. 48; hereafter cited as *Events.*

69. Powers's 1956 contract for employment was a complex arrangement between Lockheed, NASA, and the CIA. See Wise and Ross, *The Invisible Government,* p. 240.

70. *Aviation Week,* Vol. 72, No. 20 (May 16, 1960), p. 21; see also *Newsweek,* May 23, 1960, p. 29.

71. Cited by Powers and Gentry op. cit., p. 315. It is instructive to compare Powers's cooperative attitude with that of Navy Commander Lloyd Bucher of the *Pueblo,* captured off North Korea in 1968. Bucher resisted, but, unlike Powers, was tortured and collaborated only marginally with his captors. The navy, however, court-martialled, reprimanded, and consigned him to the ignominy of commanding a mine-sweeper. One of the presiding admirals investigating the *Pueblo* incident explained, "I know that when I put on a blue uniform, I'm expected to stand in harm's way." (Admiral Bergner, quoted in Trevor Armbrister, *A Matter of Accountability* [New York: Coward McCann, 1970], p. 385.) Bucher's "failure to put up any

resistance . . . was incredible . . . shocking . . . and unforgivable." (According to one senior admiral of the court, ibid., p. 387.)

72. *The New York Times*, May 6, 1960.

73. *Events*, p. 49.

74. *The New York Times*, May 8, 1960. Speech of May 7, 1960.

75. Memorandums of recorded conversations. A. J. Goodpaster recording, September 3, 1958, March 4, 1959, February 8, 1960, April 11, 1969. John D. Eisenhower recording, N.S.C. Meeting, February 12, 1959. The authors thank Professor Larry Haapanen, Baker University, for bringing these materials to their attention.

76. Wise and Ross, *The U-2 Affair*, p. 100, Jack Shick, *The Berlin Crisis, 1958–1962* (Philadelphia: University of Pennsylvania Press, 1971), p. 114, and *The New York Times*, May 8, 1960.

77. *The New York Times*, May 12, 1960; one unexplored possibility was simply to claim that Powers was unauthorized to intrude on Russian air space and that he had simply disobeyed orders. The U.S. government could have then stuck by its denial enough so as not to have been embarrassed, "apologized," and asked the "insubordinate" or "demented" pilot to be returned for punishment. This kind of line is fairly frequent. One of the best-known examples occurred at the height of the Cuban missile crisis when a U-2 "strayed" into Soviet air space.

78. Cited by Wise and Ross, *The U-2 Affair*, p. 132 (emphasis added). Similarly, Emmett Hughes, Eisenhower's biographer, speech writer, and friend, wrote later, scathingly, that the president had claimed espionage was "a sovereign right." (Hughes, op. cit., p. 361.)

79. *The New York Times*, May 13, 1960, reprinted in *Events*, pp. 204 and 208. And there were other favorable signs. For after some hesitation, a Soviet military delegation accepted an invitation to visit the United States the same day that Khrushchev averred that the Soviet people would think him mad that he was keeping open his invitation for the president to visit Russia.

80. Apologies for spying, even insincere apologies, are not an uncommon practice in international affairs. A ceremonial declaration of regrets was insisted upon when Japan in 1937 "mistakenly" bombed for three hours the American ship *Panay*. A similar formal apology was elicited from the Israelis when they "mistakenly" sank the U.S. "Elint" [electronic intelligence] vessel *Liberty*, in the 1967 Middle East War. On December 23, 1968, Major General Gilbert Woodward signed a document prepared by North Korea which stated that the United States "solemnly apologizes for the grave acts of espionage committed by the U.S. Ship *Pueblo* . . . and gives firm assurance that no U.S. ships will intrude again . . . into the territorial waters . . . of North Korea." Woodward proclaimed as he signed: "My signature will not and cannot alter the facts. I will sign . . . only to free the crew" (Armbrister, op. cit., p. 340).

81. Charles Bohlen, op. cit., p. 470.

82. Nikita Khrushchev, *Khrushchev Remembers: The Last Testament*, translated and edited by Strobe Talbott (Boston: Little, Brown, 1974), pp. 447–448. For Khrushchev's insistence that Powers was shot down, see p. 445. It was always in the Soviet interest to maintain, as Khrushchev does in his memoirs, that the Russians possessed "surface to air missiles" that were literally "rolling off the production line." Khrushchev maintains that Powers "ejected from his plane when hit and parachuted to earth." Given the characteristics of the plane and the altitude (twenty-one thousand meters) at which he hints the U-2 was operating (although he does not come out and directly claim that it was hit at that altitude), it is unrealistic that Powers or his plane could have made it to earth in such pristine condition. As translator Talbott explains, Khrushchev's recollections are marked with "deliberate deceptions" as well as "revelations" (p. xxii). If Powers were not "shot down" and

the Soviets did not possess an antiaircraft capability of reaching a U-2 and Khrushchev revealed this, he would have, in the words of Edward Crankshaw, "subjected [himself] and his heirs to charges of disloyalty and the laws governing state secrets" (p. xviii).

83. Ibid., pp. 454–455.
84. *The New York Times,* May 12, 1960.
85. *Events,* p. 244; *The New York Times,* May 17, 1960.
86. *Events,* pp. 238–248.
87. Eisenhower, op. cit., p. 558.
88. *Events,* p. 47.
89. *The New York Times,* May 30, 1960.
90. Khrushchev, op. cit., pp. 450–451.
91. It was said that the plane flew well over 80,000 feet, yet the CIA is also reported to have concluded that it was downed by remarkably accurate SA-2 missiles. Powers, in his "recollections," claims that he was "shot down at his assigned altitude" (implying that it was well over 75,000 feet), and he rejected Khrushchev's claim that the plane was shot down at 20,000 meters or 65,616 feet. However, SA-2 missiles of 1960 vintage had a ceiling of only 60,000 feet. But there is a curious and unexplained loss of 10,000 to 15,000 feet under the plane's normal height [*Military Review,* Vol. 41, No. 5 (May 1961), p. 105; Ross and Wise, op. cit., pp. 130–31]. *Aviation Week* claimed that some U-2s could fly over 100,000 feet and that the version Powers was flying could do at least 90,000 feet [*Aviation Week,* Vol. 72, No. 20 (May 16, 1960), p. 26)]. *Aviation Week* puzzled over the details of the incident for four weeks. Why were the pilot, plane, and gear, the editors wondered, in such "exceptionally clean" condition? After thirty days, the journal concluded that Powers must have made a "belly landing," and that no other explanation fit the facts. [See ibid., pp. 33–34 and *Aviation Week,* Vol. 72, No. 22 (June 6, 1960), p. 28.] Although Powers insisted that he was "shot down" above 68,000 feet, the administration clearly did not believe at the time that he was struck by a Soviet rocket at high altitude. Secretary Herter told the Foreign Relations Committee, "We are very skeptical and there are certain evidences that it was not shot down from [its maximum] altitude." Senator George Aiken then asked, "Does it seem unlikely to you that the U-2 was brought down with a one shot rocket?" Secretary Herter responded, "It seems very unlikely." (*Events,* p. 37 and p. 41.) Secretary Herter went on, "I am not skilled enough in the techniques of shooting down planes. But I should think it is very doubtful if he was hit by a rocket whether either he or the plane would have come down intact" (*Events,* p. 61). Eisenhower was equally skeptical. He said, "In the Soviet allegations there are many discrepancies. For example, there is some reason to believe that the plane in question was not shot down in high altitude" (ibid., p. 199). Russian radar would have had to have been superior to the then-existing state of the art in American electronics for the Russians to have successfully tracked the U-2. When the U-2 was being tested against the "probability of being detected" in the United States, American radar, "even when warned of strange airplanes flying over national territory," could not see or if picked up could not track the plane at the U-2's operating altitude. Moreover, neither American nor Soviet interceptors could then reach an altitude beyond 50,000 feet (Eisenhower, op. cit., pp. 545–546).
92. The official explanation for the flight is controversial. Notwithstanding the claim that there was good weather forecast for the day of the flight, there were many clear days over the Urals in the spring. Moreover, it was claimed that Russian radar would be reduced in the area because of a holiday. Yet on this same festive day it was claimed that there was to be an important test launch of a new missile, surveillance of which required Powers's flight. And would Soviet radar operators go on holiday no matter

what the occasion? Finally, there is evidence that there had been no missile activity in the Sverdlovsk area for the preceding two years, and there is some doubt if there had ever been any there at all. (Sanche de Gramont, *The Secret War Since World War II* (New York: G. P. Putnam's Sons, 1962), p. 256; Fletcher Prouty, op. cit., p. 422; Jack Anderson, "United States Heard Russians Chasing U-2," *Washington Post*, May 11, 1960. Gramont gives no source, Anderson cites only "official reports." Apparently this was the official explanation given to the press. See *Newsweek*, May 16, 1960, and *Time*, May 16, 1960. See Horelick and Rush, op. cit., pp. 74–75).

Powers, in his book, claims that this was the first trans-Russian flight. All others had been relatively short incursions. The Powers flight was to cover 3,800 miles in all, 2,900 inside Soviet airspace, giving the Soviets a long time, indeed, to notice it. The men who ordered the U-2 flights and controlled the flight schedules fully realized that the Soviets knew of them and that a U-2 had been lost over Russia a year earlier. (Powers and Gentry, op. cit., p. 74). Powers claims that this particular flight was personally approved by Eisenhower, and, in fact, the flight was delayed thirty minutes before communication from the White House was secured. (Ibid., p. 78). The flights had been going on since August 1955, but the Russians could not profit from revealing their existence until a live pilot unavoidably descended on them. Indeed, when Air Force General Nathan Twining was invited to visit the Soviet Union in 1956, Khrushchev revealed (on May 9, 1960), that a U-2 had penetrated Soviet airspace as far as Kiev but the Russians did not protest (Tatu, op. cit., p. 54). And just three weeks prior to the May summit conference on April 9, 1960, another U-2 transversed the Soviet Union, and Khrushchev "for his own reasons . . . said nothing of it" (Chalmers Roberts, *Washington Post*, May 27, 1960, and Eisenhower, op. cit., p. 547). According to one account at the time, Eisenhower had cancelled the U-2 flights before and during delicate negotiations. For example, he ordered the flights stopped in September 1956 while engaged in talks with the Egyptians and the Russians at the height of the Suez crisis. Overflights were also halted during Khrushchev's trip to the United States in September 1959. So the diplomatic implications of the flights were not unknown to the administration.

Eisenhower complained that he was the "only principal" who feared the repercussions of a U-2 failure over Soviet territory:

> Secretary Dulles, for instance, would say laughingly, "If the Soviets ever capture one of these planes, I'm sure they will never admit it. To do so would make it necessary for them to admit also that for years we had been carrying on flights over their territory while the Soviets had been helpless to do anything about the matter" (Eisenhower, op. cit., p. 546).

Moreover, in the months leading up to the flight, Eisenhower had expressed his skepticism concerning the wisdom of the flights. According to a "memorandum of conference with the President" of 7 April 1959, General Andrew Goodpaster, Secretary to the NSC, reported Eisenhower's concern "over the terrible propaganda impact that would be occasioned if a reconnaissance plane were to fail." Nonetheless, Eisenhower approved one last U-2 flight—Powers's flight of May 1. The Goodpaster memorandum and others outlining Eisenhower's anxiety over the U-2 were uncovered in the Eisenhower Library by Larry Haapanen of Baker University. We would like to thank Haapanen for making this material available to us. See also Milton Eisenhower, *The President Is Calling* (New York: Doubleday, 1974), p. 335.

93. It seemed extraordinary that a young technician of the cold war should be traded for a seasoned master spy—especially when the technician had failed so spectacularly in his mission. There was considerable public speculation about Powers's courage,

character, and ability. Indeed, there were stories in the press that former Assistant U.S. Attorney General W. F. Tompkins, the prosecutor of Abel, had complained, "It's like trading Mickey Mantle for the average ball player" (Powers and Gentry, op. cit., p. 296). Rudolph Abel's lawyer concurred. He described Powers as a kind of calm, likable mercenary hillbilly but not in the same class as Col. Abel. "Suppose you wished to recruit an American to sail a shaky espionage glider over the heart of hostile Russia at 75,000 feet. . . . Powers was a man, who, for adequate pay, would do it; and as he passed over Minsk, would calmly reach for a salami sandwich [James B. Donovan, *Strangers On A Bridge: The Case of Colonel Abel* (New York: Atheneum, 1964), p. 421].

94. The CIA issued an unusual statement even before he took the stand. The dispatch said that Powers had fulfilled his contract, lived up to "his obligations as an American," and would get $52,500 back pay. [Statement concerning Francis Gary Powers, Central Intelligence Agency, March 6, 1962, released by Carl Vinson (Dem., Georgia), Chairman of the House Armed Services Committee, partially quoted in Powers and Gentry, op. cit., pp. 300–301 and Ross and Wise, *The U-2 Affair*, p. 257.] Senator Richard Russell set the tone of the hearing, "I understand from Senator [Harry] Byrd that you are a Virginia boy." Ninety minutes of gentle questions later, the official inquest into the incident was over and Powers was on his way, leaving in the words of a *Time* magazine reporter, a "persistent feeling that some of his story remains untold" (*Time*, March 16, 1962, p. 19).

The report of the CIA released upon Powers's return was obviously less than frank. For instance, in an attempt to explain that even if the destructor unit had been detonated, the U-2 would have been identifiable and the pilot would have survived, the CIA said, "The purpose of the destruct mechanism was to render inoperable the precision camera and other equipment, not to destroy them or the plane." But as Wise and Ross note, "Army ordinance . . . describes cyclonite . . . as one of the most powerful explosives in the world. Three pounds . . . could blow up four trucks" (Wise and Ross, The *U-2 Affair*, p. 18, fn. 2).

Although there was not inconsiderable speculation in the press about why Powers had used neither his needle nor his destruct button, the terms of the discussion were captured by one headline, which read "Hero or Bum?" Powers adds, interestingly, that Attorney General Robert Kennedy opposed the Powers-Abel trade and wanted him tried for treason (Powers and Gentry, op. cit., p. 302). The Lockheed Aircraft Corporation announced on November 3, 1962, that Powers had "taken a routine test pilot job . . . checking out the U-2's that are modified, maintained and overhauled"—a plane that was obsolete and was being phased out. Powers worked for Lockheed until the company hit a stretch of financial trouble in 1970 and was layed off. He later worked as a helicopter pilot for the Los Angeles Police Department and was killed in a helicopter crash August 1, 1977. (Wise and Ross, *The Invisible Government*, p. 197.

95. Macmillan, op. cit., p. 197.
96. Ibid., p. 201.
97. Wise and Ross, *The U-2 Affair*, p. 261.
98. Macmillan, op. cit., p. 193; April 5, 1960. Macmillan is citing a conversation with De Gaulle (emphasis Macmillan's, paraphrasing De Gaulle in an official dispatch).
99. J. William Fulbright: "Reflections on a Troubled World," interview conducted by Warren Howe and Sarah Trott, *Saturday Review*, January 11, 1975, p. 14.
100. Eisenhower, op. cit., p. 553. Eisenhower told a group from Congress that "he didn't want the CIA on the spot. . . ." The Speaker of the House, Sam Rayburn, summed up Congressional opinion: "whether mistakes had been made or not, we're all in this together." "Breakfast Meeting Memorandum," op. cit. The Congressional inquiry

has recently been made available. U.S. Senate, *Executive Sessions of the Senate Foreign Relations Committee,* 86th Congress, 2nd Session, November 1982.

No less than pilot Powers confessed to suspicions that the U-2 was betrayed. To Powers, it now seems curious that official approval for his flight was given over an open telephone line because radio communications between Germany and Turkey broke down. Thus, Powers concludes, "there is a possibility that the Russians knew I would be taking off even before I did." Powers also feels that defectors, including Lee Harvey Oswald, might have given the Soviets the technical capacity to track the U-2. This seems a bit fanciful at best, and Powers's demonstration of the connection is only by the assertion that Oswald had access to height-finding equipment while in the Marines and that six months after he defected, the U-2 was shot down. Powers and Gentry, op. cit., pp. 356–358.

101. *Aviation Week,* Vol. 72, No. 23 (June 6, 1960), p. 26.
102. Wise and Ross, *The U-2 Affair,* p. 146.
103. Walter Lippmann, "First of All," *Washington Post,* May 19, 1960.
104. "Press Conference of N. S. Khrushchev in Paris on May 18," *Current Digest of the Soviet Press,* Vol. 12, No. 20 (June 15, 1960), p. 9.
105. Macmillan, *Pointing the Way,* p. 212.
106. *Chicago Sun Times,* May 22, 1960.
107. But on May 10, 1960, Khrushchev had pointed out that in the last eighteen months he had "unilaterally cut the armed forces in the Soviet Union by one-third . . . to 24 million men." *The New York Times,* May 10, 1960. Between 1955 and 1960 the armed services had been cut by 2 million, and an additional 1.2 million cut had been announced for 1960–1961. CIA Report, May 1960, reprinted in *Events,* p. 288.
108. *Events,* p. 134.
109. Hoopes, op. cit., p. 504.
110. George F. Kennan, *Memoirs: 1925–1950* (Boston: Little, Brown, 1967), p. 365.
111. Eisenhower, op. cit., p. 616.
112. See Joyce and Gabriel Kolko, *The Limits of Power, 1945–1954* (New York: Harper & Row, 1972), esp. the "Introduction" and "Conclusion."
113. U.S. Congress, Senate Committee on Foreign Relations, *Some Important Issues in Foreign Aid,* 89th Congress, 2nd Session, 1966, pp. 6–7 and table 1.
114. Macmillan, op. cit., p. 261.
115. A supplemental appropriation of $100 million was sought from Congress. Eisenhower, op. cit., p. 575.
116. Dispatch of January 16, 1960, in Macmillan, op. cit., p. 269.
117. Ibid., pp. 264–265.
118. *The New York Times,* September 30, 1960.
119. Arthur M. Schlesinger, Jr., *A Thousand Days: John F. Kennedy in the White House* (Boston: Houghton Mifflin, 1965), p. 50.
120. *The New York Times,* December 29, 1960. See also Schlesinger, op. cit., pp. 126–127.
121. "Transcript of the Second Nixon-Kennedy Debate on Nation-Wide Television," *The New York Times,* October 8, 1960, p. 11.

Chapter 7
Containment on
the New Frontier

John F. Kennedy and his administration had a flair and style that set them apart from the generation that had shaped American policy during the late 1940s and then institutionalized the cold war during the mid-1950s. As he eloquently proclaimed in his inaugural address, "The torch has been passed to a new generation of Americans." Nevertheless, it was a generation "tempered by war, disciplined by a hard and bitter peace, proud of our ancient heritage." Not the least of the elements retained from that heritage were the old objectives and reflexes of the "hard and bitter peace."

When the Democratic nominee, John Kennedy, rose to give his acceptance speech, his central theme was the interrelationship between world affairs and the American mission. It seemed an almost cosmic challenge, "a new frontier" where we would be asked "more sacrifice instead of more security." "Can a nation organized and governed such as ours endure?" asked Kennedy. "Have we the nerve and the will? . . . Can we carry through in . . . a race . . . for mastery of the sky and the oceans and the tides the far side of space and the inside of men's minds?"[1] The American people, declared Kennedy, stood "at a turning point in history," and must choose "between the public interest and private comfort, between national greatness and national decline . . . all mankind awaits upon our decision."[2]

The Kennedy victory in the 1960 election was razor thin; but the sense of power and vitality that the young president brought to the tasks thus won was almost contagious. On Inauguration Day Kennedy stood before the American people and called them to their destiny: "Let every nation know, whether it wishes us well or ill, that we shall pay any price, bear any burden, meet any hardship, support any friend, oppose any foe to assure the survival and success of liberty. We will do all this and more." Thus the first message of the new administration was an eloquent reaffirmation of the Truman Doctrine. It was containment with vigor. The problem, as Kennedy saw it, was not the objectives of the Eisenhower administration but its reluctance to develop and exploit a full range of American instrumentalities to implement containment. "Eisenhower," Kennedy complained, "had escaped" the burden of making good on the far-flung commitments rendered during his administra-

236

tion. Kennedy, however, had premonitions that "all the pigeons are coming home on the next President."[3]

THE THREATENED NEW FRONTIER

The view from the new frontier was frightening. The domestic preoccupations of the Communists during the mid-1950s had provided the Eisenhower administration a respite. But during that time deep forces had been at work throughout the international system. By the end of the decade the members of the Kennedy administration thought they could discern the shape of these forces. Indeed, they felt that the Eisenhower administration had seen them as well, especially those in the third world, but had chosen to ignore them or confront them with the inapplicable rigidities of the new look and massive retaliation. The years since 1957 were viewed as an unrelieved succession of cumulating disasters. Soviet missile strength seemed to grow, and the pressure on Berlin became very nearly unbearable. Simultaneously the Soviets and the Chinese expanded their activities in the Middle East, South and Southeast Asia, as well as Africa. Castro's victory in the Cuban civil war marked the penetration of the western hemisphere.

In the face of this burgeoning assault on fifteen years of American order, America seemed no longer able to respond either spiritually or materially. Thus, the Kennedy administration moved immediately to reinvigorate American will through the bedazzling rhetoric and energy of the New Frontier. It was, however, but an eloquent reaffirmation of the absolutism of John Foster Dulles and the sense of mission of Dean Acheson. As for the instruments of containment on the new frontier, they would have to be commensurate with the scope of the purported challenge. Since the challenges were apparent at every level of potential conflict, then it seemed imperative that the United States be able to respond at all levels and arenas of potential conflict. "We are moving," Kennedy told Americans, "into a period of uncertain risk and great commitment . . . thus we must be able to respond with discrimination and speed, to any problem at any spot on the globe at any moment's notice."[4]

This search for a wide-spectrum response to the far-ranging demands of containment prompted the development of interrelated instrumentalities and doctrine ranging from general nuclear war to the problems of public health in the third world. Military forces were conceived and designed for a flexible response: to fight total thermonuclear war, limited nuclear war, conventional wars in Europe or Asia, or unconventional warfare anywhere in the world. At the same time, the Kennedy administration sought to expand American military and economic assistance programs in an effort to anticipate and defeat communist efforts in the third world. The problem of building nations that reflected American political and economic values was but a natural extension of the effort to maintain an international strategic environment conducive to historic American purposes and principles. Indeed, American involvement in nation-building, whether by means of military or politico-economic intervention, constituted a demonstration of the will and commitment deemed crucial to the maintenance of the strategic balance.

The Kennedy administration's concern with the problem of nation-building resulted in part from the circumstances existing in the third world when Kennedy assumed office. The situation in the Congo, insurgencies in Laos and Vietnam, and Castro's success in Cuba meant that in virtually every corner of the third world the Kennedy administration felt compelled to deal with revolutionary developments. This concern was given even more urgency by the prevailing view of the nature of the Soviet and Chinese relationship to these events. The American perception of these events was complicated by the Sino-Soviet schism. But disputes within the communist world notwithstanding, the conclusion was drawn that the third world was to be a major if not the primary testing ground of communist and American will. Consequently, nation-building within the third world revolutionary context became much more than an end in itself. It was to become a major element in the overarching global struggle.

The Sino-Soviet Dispute, Revolutionary War, and American Policy

By the early 1960s American officials knew that communism was no monolith. The Sino-Soviet dispute was apparent to all but the most insensitive observer even by the late 1950s. In the wake of Khrushchev's refusal to back the Chinese during the last Taiwan crisis in 1958, what had been latent Sino-Soviet tension broke into open conflict. Khrushchev withdrew all technical advisers. Unfinished cement factories were abandoned as Russian engineers returned to the Soviet Union, taking their architectural drawings with them. China was militarily deprived of the Soviet nuclear shield and at supposedly fraternal international conclaves was denounced as "irresponsible" by the Soviets. The Chinese were bitter in the extreme. They had expected that the appearance of a Soviet retaliatory capability as manifested by the launching of Sputniks and working model ICBMs and large thermonuclear explosions could be used to contain American pressure on China. When their hopes did not materialize, the Chinese rhetorically reverted to a kind of exorcism of danger. The Americans with their atomic bombs, they declared, as much to Russia as to the United States, were paper tigers. War with the capitalists, they pointed out, was inevitable, and although other societies might perish, "victorious peoples would create very swiftly a civilization thousands of times higher than the capitalist system and a truly beautiful future for themselves."[5] To believe otherwise was proof of declining ideological purity, revolutionary will, and capacity for leadership of the communist world.

Official Washington, as well as alert readers of *The New York Times*, were aware, therefore, that the one-time "Sino-Soviet monolith" was cracking.[6] But the Kennedy administration, ever sensitive to the memory of Truman's difficulties in trying to differentiate between Moscow and Beijing, though perhaps accepting that the two powers were now analytically distinct, nevertheless dealt with them as functional equivalents. In the young president's first State of the Union message, only ten days after his inauguration, Kennedy told the nation that "each day we draw near the hour of maximum danger" in foreign affairs. The "great obstacle," proclaimed Kennedy, was the Soviet Union and Communist China. "We must never be lulled into believing that either power has yielded its ambitions for world domination. . . . On the contrary, our task is to convince them that aggression and subversion will not be profitable routes to pursue these ends."[7] Secretary of State Dean Rusk made the same point some six months later when he told the National Press Club: "The central issue . . . is the announced determination to impose a world of coercion upon those not already subject to it . . . it is posed between the Sino-Soviet empire and the rest, whether allied or neutral; and it is posed on every continent."[8]

Sino-Soviet Enthusiasm for Emerging Nations

The consequence of this image of the Sino-Soviet relationship held by the new administration and the Sino-Soviet perception of revolutionary war is critical to the history of this period. The military doctrine of the Soviet Union traditionally had shown little attention to the third world.[9] But in 1955, as part of the new effort at world activism assumed by the Khrushchev regime, Moscow made new overtures to the developing nations. Yet rather than working to promote revolution, Soviet strategy, after the Bandung Conference of 1955, strove toward detaching former colonial areas from the imperialist bloc by working with the national bourgeoisie. Indeed, the nonaligned nations might jail local Communists and still count on Soviet moral and material development assistance.[10]

By the end of 1960, however, the ebullient and chimerical Khrushchev began to propound a theory of "wars of national liberation" which neatly mirrored the analysis of American defense intellectuals who were arguing for a capacity to wage limited war. The Soviets announced that they were prepared to sponsor and promote insurgencies. Although they had refrained from military activity previous to 1960 in the third world, support would now be forthcoming: first, in the form of doctrinal approval; and, second, with economic assistance. This policy was articulated on January 6, 1961, two weeks before Kennedy's inauguration, in which Khrushchev reviewed the full range and dangers of modern war and declared:

> The armed struggle by the Vietnamese people or the war of the Algerian people, which is already in its seventh year, serve as the latest examples of national liberation wars. These wars began as an uprising by the colonial peoples against their oppressors and changed into guerrilla warfare. Liberation wars will continue to exist as long as imperialism exists, as long as colonialism exists. These are revolutionary wars. Such wars are not only admissible but inevitable, since the colonialists do not grant independence voluntarily. Therefore, the peoples can attain their freedom and independence only by struggle, including armed struggle. . . .
> What is the attitude of the Marxists toward such uprisings? A most positive one.[11]

But Khrushchev's analysis of the need to support wars of national liberation was tempered by his awareness of the need for caution in the face of the potential price.[12] Thus, Khrushchev's redefinition of Soviet strategy was part of his rejection of the traditional historical inevitability of communism's triumph in any circumstance—even war. But Khrushchev's call to support wars of national liberation helped him counter Chinese charges that Russia had grown too soft to challenge capitalism. Nevertheless, he remained essentially cautious; he circumspectly chastened the Chinese:

> We must be realistic in our thinking and understand the contemporary situation. Of course, this does not in any way mean that if we are so strong, we should test the stability of the capitalist system by force. This would be wrong. The peoples would not understand and would never support those who took it into their heads to act in such a way. We have always been against predatory wars. Marxists have recognized and still do recognize only wars of liberation, wars that are just, and have condemned and still do condemn wars that are predatory and imperialistic.[13]

China, it was widely purported, held markedly more activist and militant doctrines.[14] But it is debatable that Mao Zedong's notion of "people's war" was a grand design for world conquest. However, Mao's writings on guerrilla warfare, penned from the perspective of his defensive war against the Japanese and civil war against Chiang Kai-shek, were not taken as a description of a defensive effort carried out by indigenous nationalist revolutionaries. Rather, Dean Rusk and others in the policy-making community believed that the resurrection of Mao's writings on people's war was an advocacy of a formula for aggressive Chinese Communist expansion. In fact, however, from 1949 there was a seventeen-year hiatus in which Chinese officials made almost no statements that could be interpreted as actively encouraging wars of national liberation, and Lin Biao's 1965 statement concerning revolutionary war (called a Chinese *Mein Kampf* by Secretary of State Rusk) had ambiguous support at best. As Arthur Huck, an Australian scholar working at London's International Institute for Strategic Studies, wrote: "Far from being a blue print for the direct expansion of Chinese influence [Lin Biao's] 'Long Live the Victory of People's War'[15] argues that revolution cannot be exported and that the people's forces must be almost entirely self-reliant."[16]

The American Misperception

But American policymakers chose to believe that China's militant rhetoric of the late 1950s and early 1960s, although directed at Moscow and primarily the product of the Sino-Soviet ideological and political dispute, indicated an intensely aggressive nature, especially with respect to South and Southeast Asia. The threat of insurgent communist war as articulated by Khrushchev was therefore interpreted to be as much a Chinese menace to world order as were the purported designs of Stalin and his successors.

The trumpet of worldwide testing, then, had been sounded over the issue of the expansion of power from *either* the Soviets or the Chinese. The issue was, as it had been since the days of Woodrow Wilson, whether aggression was tolerable in an orderly world environment where American ideals and institutions would prosper. In this way, it made no difference what its source or instruments, disorder had to be contained. It was this conviction that could lead Dean Rusk to explain to the Senate Foreign Relations Committee that the differences among the great communist rivals did not erase their fundamental similarities.

> *Secretary Rusk:* It was said here the other day that Hilter was a unique phenomenon. Well, there were some unique aspects. An airedale and a great dane are different but they are both dogs.
> Now, we have this phenomenon of aggression.
> *Senator Aiken:* They bite you in different places.
> *Secretary Rusk:* That is right. We have the phenomenon of aggression.

Hitler could see that the Japanese militarists in Manchuria were not stopped. He saw that Mussolini was not stopped in Ethiopia. This encouraged him.

Now, what happens here in Southeast Asia, if Peiping [Beijing] discovers that Hanoi can move without risk or can move with success? What further decisions are they going to make? What difference will that make in Moscow about what would happen to our commitments elsewhere, whether they should make choices as between peaceful coexistence and a more militant policy of world revolution?[17]

Secretary Rusk's response to an assumed communist challenge was one in which Sino-Soviet differences did not really matter.[18] Intellectually, therefore, Americans had by 1960 changed very little from the view expressed by Truman that global order was seamless web, which if threatened by aggression anywhere was liable to collapse into Armageddon. As President Truman stated the notion of American policy matters in a radio talk April 11, 1951:

If history has taught us anything, it is that aggression anywhere in the world is a threat to peace everywhere in the world. When that aggression is supported by the cruel and selfish rulers of a powerful nation who are bent on conquest, it becomes a clear and present danger to the security and independence of every free nation.[19]

The instruments of aggression were different, for now as Robert McNamara observed:

The faces of *World Communism* operate in the twilight zone. Their military tactics are those of the sniper, the ambush and the raid, their political tactics are terror and assassination. We must help the people of threatened nations to resist these tactics.[20]

Moreover, a new and in some ways more perplexing arena of conflict had been opened up in the emergence of revolutionary political and economic dynamics in the third world. But if there was the slightest doubt as to the necessity of a multifaceted response, they were dispelled by events in Cuba and the failure of Kennedy's first crude attempt at counterrevolution in the style of the 1950s.

The Bay of Pigs

In Cuba, a handful of men under the leadership of Fidel Castro had arrived by boat in 1956 to begin a successful three-year struggle to topple a dictator who was an American client. After seizing power on New

Year's Day in 1959, Castro had begun to restructure Cuban institutions while professing a socialist-revolutionary ideology profoundly disturbing to Americans. Almost at a stroke, one of the most advanced nations in Latin America had been converted to socialism. If only a few dozen men or so could manage such a feat in a traditional zone of American preeminence, then what, American policymakers despaired, would be the fate of countries in areas that were in dispute among the superpowers? The Kennedy administration saw the third world symbolically interlaced in a structure of political and economic order in want of an American guarantee to maintain order.

It is not surprising, therefore, that Kennedy did not stop the preparations set in motion by the CIA with Eisenhower's approval for an invasion of the island by Cuban exiles to overthrow Castro's regime. Arthur Schlesinger, Jr., and Theodore Sorensen have tried to portray Kennedy as being misled about the operation by the Eisenhower holdovers in the CIA and Defense Department.[21] And it may well be that Kennedy was unclear concerning the details of the intervention. But Kennedy did approve the intervention. That is to say, he accepted the underlying premise of Eisenhower's policy—the Castro regime should be destroyed.

The operation itself was an absolute disaster. Somewhat fewer than fifteen hundred Cuban exiles hit the beaches at the Bay of Pigs, and some five hundred men were promptly and efficiently cut to pieces by Castro's well-disciplined forces. The remaining one thousand men were ignominiously captured. Contrary to what the CIA had confidently predicted, there was no uprising of the Cuban people to greet the invaders and provide the necessary assistance.[22] The full dimensions of the disaster were apparent and Kennedy accepted complete responsibility for the failure. Kennedy's candor and remarkable rapport with the press and the willingness of the American people to rally around the presidency at moments of crisis eased the administration's handling of the failure at home. Covertly, however, the Kennedy administration established an extensive clandestine operation against the Castro regime using the Cuban exile community in south Florida as a source of manpower under CIA direction. This harassment and several attempts to assassinate Castro would continue until Kennedy's assassination more than two years later.

The Bay of Pigs fiasco is important for what it tells us of the Kennedy administration's attitude toward revolution and intervention. In a speech only hours after it was clear that the invasion had failed, Kennedy warned of the dangers posed by the "menace of external communist intervention and domination in Cuba."[23] Kennedy reemphasized the intention of his administration to reorient American force structure to be able to counter the revolutionary challenge to American power. "We dare not fail," he asserted, "to see the insidious nature of this new and deeper struggle. We dare not fail to grasp the new concepts, the new tools, the new sense of urgency we will need to combat it—whether in Cuba or South Vietnam."[24] This was essential if "the United States was to win in a struggle in many ways more difficult than war, where disappointment will often accompany us."[25] Kennedy concluded with reaffirmation of the grim vision of the inaugural address:

> I am convinced . . . that history will record the fact that the bitter struggle reached its climax in the late 1950s and the early 1960s. Let me then make it clear as the President of the United States that I am determined upon our system's survival and success, regardless of the cost and regardless of the peril![26]

Activism and American involvement were absolutely essential and, as in Europe after World War II, the United States was prepared to act with or without the assistance of others.

> Let the record show that our restraint is not inexhaustible. Should it ever appear that the inter-American doctrine of noninterference merely conceals or excuses a policy of nonaction—if the nations of this hemisphere should fail to meet their commitments against outside communist penetration—then I want it clearly understood that this govenment will not hesitate in meeting its primary obligations which are to the security of our nation![27]

The possibility of American intervention remained; indeed, Kennedy had proclaimed that the national security of the United States required that the "right" of intervention be retained by the United States. In the meantime, "any free nation under outside attack of any kind can be assured that all of our resources stand ready to respond to any request for assistance."[28]

NATION-BUILDING
AND COUNTERREVOLUTION

The preoccupation of the Kennedy administration with the role of communism in the third world led to a search for economic, cultural, and social instrumentalities that could parallel military counterinsurgent tactics and lead to a stabilizing of revolutionary situations in the underdeveloped world. Communism would not be allowed a foothold or would be stifled while it was little more than an idea. Revolution was perhaps inevitable, but the Kennedy administration sought a way to redirect revolution away from a communist conclusion.

Nation-Building

Khrushchev's January speech about "sacred wars of national liberation" prompted Kennedy to reconvene in February 1961 one of his transition task forces under the leadership of Adolph Berle and Thomas Mann with a mandate "to develop politics and programs which channel the revolution . . . in Latin America . . . and prevent it being taken over by the Sino-Soviet bloc."[29] Earlier the task force had reported to the new president that the social revolutionaries were targets for "capture by Communist power politics."[30] According to the report, the Communists intended "to convert the Latin American social revolutionaries into a Marxist attack on the United States itself." This threat, the report warned, "is more dangerous than . . . the Nazi Fascist threat."[31] The report held that the primary threat was of armed revolutionaries and the essential remedy was a combination of military action and development aid.

The report, stimulated by the relationship Castro had established with Moscow, was the foundation of Kennedy's March proposal for "a vast new ten-year plan for the Americas." The Alliance for Progress was envisioned as a $20 billion development assistance program whereby the nations of Latin America would establish a new legitimacy through reforms of archaic tax and land systems and through expanded assistance to the public sector: education, housing, and health. But there was more to the proposal than an economic assistance program having as its objective simply the economic development of Latin America or the third world. The entire national security establishment was coordinated by a special interdepartmental task force chaired by the attorney general, Robert Kennedy, who in turn reported to his brother after each meeting. The resources detailed to the Special Counterinsurgency Group constituted a massive undertaking "blazing new and uncharted paths in the tradition of such recent triumphs as the Marshall Plan."[32]

There evolved with the Alliance for Progress and the revitalized aid program an infusion of governmental funds to universities and think tanks designed to foster a body of scholarship that was to support the policy objectives of the Kennedy administration in the third world. Political development or political modernization was to emerge in the early 1960s as a distinct subfield of social science, bridging such diverse disciplines as psychology, sociology, political science, and economics. The purpose of this study was to describe, predict, and ultimately assist in the management of the process of development.

Nation-building was a heady undertaking. Yet few government officials or academics hesitated before the exhilarating prospect of social architecture.

> As a house can be built from timber, bricks, and mortar, in different patterns . . . according to the choice, will and power of its builders, so a nation can be built according to different plans, from various materials, rapidly or gradually, by different sequences of steps, and in partial independence from its environment.[33]

The prescriptive elements and the tools of the study of nation-building are a bit chaotic to summarize easily; but, essentially, they shared a belief that the poor nations of the world would achieve a modest prosperity without succumbing to what Walt Rostow called "the scavengers of modernization," communism.[34] As a society modernized, became more Western, urbanized, and literate in its attitudes, there was an assumption that liberal governmental and capitalist economic forms would take hold. In short, in winning the battle of modernization in the developing societies the developing countries would expunge communism and, perforce, attune themselves to a process of building a stable, orderly community where American ideals would be vindicated and would flourish. As one academic put it to a War College audience in 1963:

> Here is one place where "winning over communism" has clear and specific meaning. When we look ahead over the next ten years our aim should be to have laid the foundation for good relations with those countries *after* they have passed through the first rude stages of transition from colony to nation, from asleep to awake, from medieval to twentieth century. Our investment today in these countries is in many ways a great gamble, with very real costs of which the financial is only one.
> The only meaningful payoff to this great investment is in the establishment of societies in the new countries that will be friendly to us, democratic in political complexion, and preferably capitalist rather than socialist in their economic structure.[35]

The search for the secret of how to make developing societies compatible with the historic American purpose was the essential endeavor of the theorists and practitioners of modernization. To many of the academic devotees of nation-building, a developed society was cohesive. Tribalism, multiethnicity, or autonomous regions were not believed to be congruent with development. The growth of a city-dwelling population was deemed especially important. Urbanization was seen as related to integration and the beginning of differentiation where urban dwellers begin to have specialized services, market facilities, access to societal agents of socialization, and political learning. Further, urban environments bring security from the unpredictable, overpopulated, and perhaps insecure countryside. Moreover, urbanization provides the setting for the building of strong central institutions. After all, what could be more useful than a recognizable capital with some ambit of control and the possibility of diffusing its control outward from a central policy. To development theorist Samuel Huntington, "modernization is, in large part, measured by the growth of the city."[36] Professor Huntington praises the great serendipity that

> [i]n an absent-minded way the United States in Vietnam may well have stumbled upon the answers to "wars of national liberation." The effective response lies neither in the quest for conventional military victory nor in the esoteric doctrines and gimmicks of counterinsurgency warfare. It is instead forced-draft urbanization and modernization which rapidly brings the country in question out of the phase in which a rural revolutionary movement can hope to generate sufficient strength to come to power.[37]

Paralleling integration—purportedly the by-product of urbanization—was the need for strong institutions: "A society with weak institutions lacks the ability to curb the excesses of personal and parochial desires."[38] Almost by definition, weak institutions lack authority and cannot do their job. They are "immoral in the same sense in which a corrupt judge, a cowardly soldier or an ignorant teacher is immoral."[39] But also by definition, there are few strong institutions in developing societies—with one exception: in developing societies, one almost universally strong institution is the military. The purpose, therefore, of American military and economic assistance was to strengthen the most logical central institution that has been widely conceived of as providing the *sine qua non* of development—security and order.

> All nation-building efforts will encounter resistances requiring a combination of persuasion and coercion. In the earliest stages, coercion must be a primary instrument and nation-builders must give prime attention to improving organizational capability (e.g., army, police, foreign assistance) in this area. The degree of coercion will vary with he degree of heterogeneity (e.g., class, religion, ideology, economic development) a would-be national territory manifests.[40]

The support of military regimes seemed an almost inexorable conclusion of the nation-builders because

> contemporary coups in Asia and Africa may be regarded as providing necessary and tolerable periods of transition. The coup is a necessary link in

the process of modernization. For the new nations, it seems far better to accept a military government that preserves law and order than to face radical subversives or guerrilla warfare.[41]

Thus, in order to rival the appeals of communism in the third world, the prescription of many American development theorists and practitioners was to search for strong leadership in command of well-functioning institutions who could form alternatives to communism.[42] This, then, was the struggle that development theorists saw between revolution and collectivist doctrines on the one hand and "liberal development" on the other.[43] It was the same Manichean struggle of the Truman doctrine given new terms: WHAM—Winning Hearts and Minds.

Counterrevolution

The ultimately counterrevolutionary thrust of nation-building was apparent in the Alliance for Progress, the ten-year, $20 billion economic assistance program established to counter the influence of Castro throughout Latin America. Schlesinger has written that Kennedy was quite sensitive to the need to remain responsive to revolutionary demands if reform and development were to take place.[44] But then the court historian of Camelot, Arthur Schlesinger, Jr., also recounts that Kennedy employed revealing criteria to test whether a regime could be supported:

> There are three possibilities in a descending order of preference: a decent democratic regime, a continuation of the Trujillo regime [a right-wing dictatorship], or a Castro regime. We ought to aim at the first, but we really can't renounce the second until we are sure that we can avoid the third.[45]

Decent democratic regimes were clearly desirable, but it is clear from this arraying of preferences that Kennedy would settle for a good deal less if there was a chance he might get a replication of Castro.

Kennedy sought through the alliance to bring about a 5.5 percent annual economic growth rate in Latin America, but the conditions under which the program was implemented included the provision that American aid had to be spent on American goods and services, which were more expensive than could be obtained elsewhere. The real infusion of resources was, therefore, correspondingly reduced. The alliance was, however, successful in encouraging private American corporations to expand their holdings in Latin America during the period.[46] Finally, and most indicative of the purpose of the alliance, was that even as the economic assistance programs were receiving special attention, the Department of Defense was emphasizing the training of Latin American units in counterinsurgency and counterguerrilla activity at Fort Bragg, North Carolina, home of the Green Berets, and in the Jungle Warfare School in the American-controlled Panama Canal Zone. In addition, hundreds of Latin American policemen were given special instruction in pacification and civic action at an Agency for International Development school also based in the Canal Zone.

Kennedy, in effect, simultaneously supported economic and (presumably) democratic political development, but would not risk Latin America's extant social structure and pattern of privilege if the cost might include revolution from the left. The former was, of course, the declaratory policy of the alliance. However, if development took an unfavorable turn to the left, then the Kennedy administration wanted to be able to draw upon those indigenous forces that would be able to stem or channel the revolutionary tide. Furthermore, if U.S. intervention was necessary, there would be available material to construct a pro-American regime.

The Dominican case is illustrative. Following Trujillo's ouster by assassination, Juan Bosch, a leftist but noncommunist writer who had been in exile for twenty years, was elected president. Bosch appeared weak, however. He was described by Schlesinger as a "literary figure, better as short story writer than as statesman."[47] Consequently, Kennedy maintained support of the Dominican military, which subsequently overthrew Bosch in 1963 just before Kennedy's death. Theodore Draper summarizes Kennedy's policy and problems succinctly: "When the latter decided to stage the coup, this double bookkeeping proved to be the undoing both of Bosch's regime and Kennedy's Dominican policy."[48]

Beset by such anomalies and contradictions, the alliance did not prosper. The hoped-for 5.5 percent growth projections could not be achieved until the fifth year of the program, and then it required a good deal of prodding and juggling of indicators. It was apparent that the countries of the alliance would not respond to the simplistic notion that growth would come about primarily as the result of the infusion of American capital. Social and political transformation were essential to the development effort. But transformation implied a disruption of class structures and patterns of privilege. How could those who had the most to lose be expected to lead a campaign that would enervate their power? In nations where survival looked almost like comfort, and in countries where personalist rule prevailed and a civic culture was but a transplanted social science fantasy, the whole notion of a ruling elite being a party to its own enfeeblement was absurd. Moreover, forceful removal of these elites would have placed Kennedy in the quadrant of the collectivists and revolutionary elements he opposed. Thus, Kennedy was forced to fall back on the contradictory notion that

[t]he men of wealth and power in poor nations "must lead the fight for those basic reforms which alone can preserve the fabric of their own societies. Those who make peaceful revolution impossible will make violent revolution inevitable. These social reforms are at the heart of the Alliance for Progress."[49]

It might be said that Kennedy's developmental programs saw three possibilities in descending order of preference: development in all its dimensions was desirable; stability was the minimum that was acceptable; and leftist revolution was simply unacceptable. The Kennedy administration would aim for development, but under no circumstances would the second be surrendered in the face of the third possibility. Kennedy's warning to the elites of Latin America and the third world that they might well be crushed by violent revolution if they stood in the way of reform reflects an important ambivalence in Kennedy and his administration. He was, on the one hand, sensitive and perhaps emotionally responsive to the revolutionary ferment of the third world. On the other, however, he saw America locked in mortal struggle with world communism, and from this higher strategic vantage point, revolutionary ferment was conceived as more of a threat than an opportunity. Accordingly, revolution was to be anticipated by means of development.

But the effect of such an approach was the subordination of development as an end in itself. Development assistance became an instrument in the larger strategic struggle and was justified to Congress primarily as an instrument in the cold war. Indeed, a report prepared for the Senate Foreign Relations Committee in 1966 concluded that among the numerous rationales advanced by all administrations since 1950, the most common were first, the enhancement of American national security; second, containment of communist aggression; and then, third, "to assist economic development in the less-developed countries." Moreover, American foreign assistance has been concentrated—more than 75 percent in most years—in a handful of forward or confrontation countries on the periphery of the Soviet Union and China.[50] Contrary to the charge that American aid has been distributed indiscriminately in pursuit of unrealistic altruistic ends, it has in fact served as an instrument of American national security policy.

Thinking of nation-building in this way meant that the American attitude toward development in the third world was and would be marked by a perhaps irreconcilable ambivalence. On the one hand, decent democratic development could be, was, and continues to be thought of by many Americans as an end in itself—the ultimate long-run preemption of communism in the third world. At the same time, however, Kennedy and his successors saw an immediate problem of revolutionary unrest that had to be stabilized through support of strong institutions if the perceived Sino-Soviet threat was to be contained.

One cannot be sure that the elimination of this ambivalence would have ensured the success of American aid as an instrument of nation-building and development. Indeed, it is now increasingly apparent that the development of so-called decent regimes in the third world is an immensely more complex task than envisioned by the proponents of nation-building. In any event, development was at best one, and probably not the primary, objective of nation-building. As an objective it has always competed with another generally overriding objective—containment of communism's advance in the third world. Thought of in this way, nation-building is understood as a major addition to the spectrum of political, economic, unconventional and conventional military, and strategic capability—otherwise known as flexible response—that the Kennedy administration sought to develop and employ during the decade of the 1960s.

FLEXIBLE RESPONSE

At the other end of this spectrum of capability was the realm of conventional and strategic military power. And as with nation-building, Kennedy called for a reappraisal and augmentation of American potential. In his first State of the Union message the new president noted:

> *We must strengthen our military tools.* . . . In the past, lack of consistent, coherent military strategy . . . [has] made it difficult to assess accurately how adequate—or inadequate—our defenses really are. I have, therefore, instructed the Secretary of Defense to reappraise our entire defense strategy.[51]

The signal that a massive infusion of funds would be available to the various defense agencies set off an internal wrangle over the allotment of funds among the various services. The Air Force asked for 3,000 new solid-fuel Minuteman missiles to replace the huge, liquid-fueled Titan. The Air Force had more than 50 Titan missiles. They were comparatively vulnerable, and were enormously expensive. A squadron of nine Titan IIs cost hundreds of millions of dollars.[52] Some requests for new missiles apparently went as high as 10,000 missiles. McNamara "compromised" and submitted a request for appropriation to build 950 new Minutemen.[53]

The Air Force insistence on massive superiority illuminates a remarkable coincidence of manipulation of information for bureaucratic reasons and the Kennedy administration's sense that the way to deal with the Russians was to outdistance them at every level of armaments. Indeed, the notion of a missile gap originated with inspired leaks from the Air Force. *The New York Times,* on January 17, 1959, based an article on interviews with "numerous persons having intimate knowledge of the defense effort" and estimated that by 1962 Soviet ICBMs would outnumber American missiles by 1,000 to 130 and would increase in 1964 to 2,000 to 130.

In his farewell speech President Eisenhower had told Congress that the missile gap showed every sign of being a fiction.[54] Eisenhower's evidence was fairly conclusive. The U-2 flight of May 1, 1960, was the last of a series that had revealed, according to Eisenhower, "information of the greatest importance to the nation's security. In fact, their success has been nothing short of remarkable."[55] What the U-2 flights (and other intelligence means) had demonstrated was that there were only a handful of Soviet missiles, perhaps 30 to 35. More important, there was no massive build-up underway.

By the end of 1960 Khrushchev knew that the United States probably was aware that there was no missile gap, and he made several attempts to signal the incoming administration of the possibility of limiting deployment on both sides. In the December 1960 "Pugwash" Conference on disarmament, W. W. Kuznetsov worriedly approached the American representatives, Walt Rostow and Jerome Wisner, about the campaign rhetoric concerning the missile gap. Kuznetsov suggested that if the new administration went in for massive rearmament, it could not expect the Russians to sit still. Rostow told the Soviet official "that any Kennedy rearmament would be designed to improve the stability of the deterrent, and the Soviet Union should recognize this as in the interests of peace."[56]

Schlesinger despairs that Kuznetsov, "innocent of the higher calculus of deterrence recently developed in the United States, brusquely dismissed [Rostow's] explanation."[57] Apparently the higher calculus was one of overwhelming American superiority. For as the prestigious International Institute for Strategic Studies (IISS) has noted, the acceleration of United States ICBM and submarine-launched ballistic missile (SLBM) production during the first two years of the Kennedy administration created a missile gap—but a gap clearly advantageous to the United States. The IISS comparisons of American and Soviet strategic missile deployment at the end of the Eisenhower years and during the Kennedy administration are shown in Table 7-1.

As the Kennedy administration assumed office in early 1961, it found already in place a two- or three-to-one American advantage in strategic weapons. Moreover, the Eisenhower administration had provided the basis for maintaining such an advantage for the immediate future. It will be recalled that the response of Eisenhower to the ferment of the late 1950s following the launch of Sputnik and the reappraisal of massive retaliation was a modest increase in American strategic weapons programs, especially the Polaris and Minuteman systems. By 1960–1961 these strategic systems had been moved from the research, development, and testing phase to actual procurement. Therefore, at least at the strategic level, Eisenhower had provided Kennedy with more than ample resources to deal with whatever threat might have existed.

Indeed, it was argued by McNamara that the Eisenhower-approved strategic bomber, the B-70, was unnecessary and perhaps of obsolete strategic capability. Professor Schlesinger suggests that McNamara accepted the arguments for massive ICBM superiority because the new defense secretary

> was already engaged in a bitter fight with the Air Force over his effort to disengage from the B-70, a costly, high-altitude manned bomber rendered obsolescent by the improvement in the Soviet ground-to-air missiles. After cutting down the original Air Force missile demands considerably, he perhaps felt that he could not do more without risking public conflict with the Joint Chiefs and the vociferous B-70 lobby in Congress. As a result, the President went along with the policy of multiplying Polaris and Minuteman missiles.[58]

But even if one grants this bureaucratic political necessity, one should not lose sight of the fact that Kennedy and McNamara sought to maintain overwhelming strategic superiority over the Soviets. Thus, in spite of some administration doubts and perhaps abetted by some administration log-rolling, the first ten months of the Kennedy administration witnessed a $6 billion increase in the military budget, from $43,685,000 to $49,878,000. The capacity to produce Minuteman missiles was increased 100 percent, and the number of Polaris subs to be produced by 1964 was increased by 50 percent. Moreover, about one-quarter of the Strategic Air Command bomber force was put on 50 percent alert, thus increasing by 50 percent the number of long-range bombers on alert status. This build-up was undertaken although, as Schlesinger has pointed out, Kennedy and the White House staff "wondered whether the new budget was not providing more missiles than national security required" and thereby threatened the Soviets' retaliatory capability. But the "President," reports Schlesinger, "was not prepared to overrule" the recommendation of Secretary of Defense McNamara.[59]

TABLE 7-1. Growth of ICBM/SLBM Strength, 1960–1964 (Mid Years)

		1960	1961	1962	1963	1964
USA	ICBM	18	63	294	424	834
	SLBM	32	96	144	224	416
USSR	ICBM	35	50	75	100	200
	SLBM	—	some	some	100	120

Source: The Military Balance 1970–1971 (London: International Institute for Strategic Studies, 1971), p. 106. Reprinted by permission.

Considering the level of strategic superiority when Kennedy took office, these increases were awesome. Congressman Melvin Laird entered into the *Congressional Record* some estimates of the considerable baseline from which the Kennedy team advanced:

> . . . two Polaris submarines with a combined total of 32 missiles, each missile capable of much more destruction than was rained upon Hiroshima.
> . . . about 16 Atlas ICBM's.
> . . . over 600 long-range B-52 jet bombers, each carrying more destructive explosive power than that used by all the combatants in World War II.
> . . . nearly 1400 B-47 medium-range jet bombers based abroad and at home with a 4500-mile range and distances beyond with air-to-air refueling.
> . . . B-58 Hustlers, the first U.S. supersonic medium-range jet bombers.
> . . . Fourteen aircraft carriers able to launch more aircraft than the entire Soviet heavy bomber force.
> . . . eighteen wings of tactical aircraft, each wing with a substantial nuclear attack capability deployed globally.
> . . . Sixty Thor IRBM's (intermediate-range ballistic missiles) deployed in England, capable of raining nuclear destruction on Russia, and thirty Jupiter IRBM's being installed at bases in Italy, from which Russia can be hit.

or "well over 2000 nuclear carrying vehicles capable of reaching Russia."[60]

Kennedy was also willing to move toward expansion of American military capability at the subnuclear level. "Flexible response," as Henry Kissinger had indicated in the late 1950s, required superiority not only at the strategic level but at all levels of potential conflict. Thus at the same time as American strategic forces were being augmented, Kennedy and McNamara moved to build up the conventional capability that Eisenhower had cut back. During the first eighteen months of the Kennedy administration, McNamara strove to increase the size of the Army, the Navy, and the Air Force. By mid-1962, after a year of intense and escalating crises (to be described below), McNamara would have available sixteen combat-ready divisions (up from eleven), along with twenty-one tactical air wings (up from eighteen), three marine divisions and their air wings, or the equivalent of a ten-division strategic reserve. William Kaufmann notes:

> With it, he could handle a Korean size engagement and still have several divisions left over for another emergency. Alternatively, he could triple the size of the American forces in Europe, and do so in fairly short order, since he had prepositioned in Europe the equipment for two divisions and was continuing to expand the airlift and sealift to move the strategic reserve. . . . His conventional options were expanding steadily.[61]

The interfaces between strategic nuclear and conventional war on the one hand and conventional war and nation-building on the other were not ignored. The basis for a graduated response between conventional war and strategic nuclear war was already present in the Eisenhower administration's tactical nuclear capability. Apart from improving existing systems, therefore, all that remained to be done was the development of a doctrine of controlled use or graduated escalation from conventional war up to and through limited or tactical nuclear war to, finally, general war. But throughout this spectrum of force McNamara sought options:

> Our new policy gives us the flexibility to choose among several operational plans, but does not require that we make any advance commitment with respect to doctrine or targets. We shall be committed only to a system that gives us the ability to use our forces in a controlled and deliberate way.[62]

Finally, McNamara developed an American potential for dealing with what he termed the "gray areas" of the third world. Nation-building was conceived as an anticipation of unconventional military conflict. But if conflict or what Khrushchev had called wars of national liberation broke out, the United States was to be prepared to respond in kind. Specifically, McNamara called for a more than $1.5 billion increase in military assistance, and soon noted proudly that the ability to fight guerrilla wars had been augmented by a 150 percent increase in antiguerrilla forces in all services but especially the Army's Special Forces or Green Berets.[63]

In time McNamara would come to question elements of this doctrine, especially the notion of the controlled and limited use of nuclear weapons. By the late 1960s McNamara would be publicly warning that neither the United States nor the Soviet Union possessed or could attain the capacity for a nuclear first strike against the other without inviting the certainty of unacceptable nuclear destruction in retaliation.[64] He would also shift to an advocacy of deterrence grounded in "assured destruction capability" as the basis of American strategic planning and forces. But in 1961 and 1962, nuclear weapons were viewed as but one of several instrumentalities to be employed—a "complement" to nonnuclear antiguerrilla forces which, taken together, "aimed at achieving the best balance of military capabilities—over the entire range of potential conflict, in the various areas of the globe where the Free World has vital interests, and over the years, as far ahead as we can reasonably plan."[65]

In summary, the Kennedy administration feverishly prepared for confrontation with communist aggression at whatever level of conflict or wherever it appeared. In the meantime, however, Khrushchev continued to pursue the more moderate diplomacy that had marked his overtures to Kennedy during the interregnal period.

AMERICAN AIMS IN THE
FIRST ROUND: THE BERLIN CRISIS

Immediately following Kennedy's inauguration, Khrushchev moved dramatically to demonstrate his desire to improve communications between the United States and the Soviet Union. On January 21, 1961, Khrushchev met for two hours with U.S. Ambassador Llewellyn E. Thompson and informed him that he earnestly desired an improvement in communications between the United States and the Soviets. To demonstrate this, Khrushchev announced to Thompson that he would release the two survivors of the RB-47 shot down in July 1960. Khrushchev noted that he had deliberately waited until now so as to benefit Kennedy rather than the Republicans.[66] Finally, Khrushchev made it clear to Thompson that he was very interested in a meeting with Kennedy as soon as possible.[67] This Russian overture, announced by Kennedy in his first news conference on January 25, was taken by the new administration as an indication that the Russians wanted a reduction in tensions, but Khrushchev's "Wars of National Liberation" speech of January 6 was not overlooked. Khrushchev's gesture was, therefore, accepted, but with a note of caution.[68]

Kennedy's cautious receipt of Khrushchev's overture indicated a basic need of the new administration at this stage in the transition—time. Kennedy had been in office less than a week. He was confronted with a crush of demands, including the preparation of numerous messages for the new Congress and the completion of his legislative program. Furthermore, Kennedy had not yet had an opportunity to confer with his Soviet experts as to a future course of action. An immediate and dramatic response to Khrushchev at this point was, therefore, not forthcoming, although Kennedy did announce during his January 25 news conference that during his administration, the U-2 flights would not be resumed. The door was not, however, closed on a meeting between Kennedy and Khrushchev, but at this point Kennedy did want more time before moving to the summit level of negotiations. This point was communicated to Khrushchev by Ambassador Thompson in his meeting with the Russian premier on January 21, and apparently Khrushchev did not challenge Kennedy's request. Rather, he restricted himself to an expression of his wish that lines of communication might be reopened.[69]

Russian reaction to Kennedy's February announcement of a stepped-up strategic armaments program was noticeably restrained. *Pravda*, for example, confined itself to a bland denunciation of the defense passages in the address and urged that the new administration follow a course of peaceful coexistence.[70] Beyond this there was little official reaction on the part of the Kremlin. The Russians seemed content to exercise a degree of restraint until Kennedy's position would be more clearly spelled out.

In the meantime, events were transpiring which endangered the still-developing contacts between the Soviet Union and the United States. The civil strife in Laos was an explosive situation given the presence of Russian aid and a commitment of American prestige. Kennedy moved to demonstrate to Khrushchev that he was willing to commit U.S. troops in order to ensure in Laos what he called in his first press conference a "peaceful country—an independent country not dominated by either side."[71] The Communist-backed Pathet Lao forces launched an offensive against Vientiane in early March, and Kennedy on March 23 gravely warned that there could be no peace unless the external support of the Pathet Lao was halted.[72] Kennedy followed up his warning by moving American troops into neighboring Thailand across the Mekong River from Vientiane. Apparently the show of force had its desired effect; for by April Khrushchev had agreed to discuss proposals for the neutralization of the country.

An earlier event in February, which also implied difficulties for Soviet-American relations, was the very peculiar murder of Patrice Lumumba in the Congo.[73] The Russian reaction to the event indicated, however, that they would confine their attacks to charges against Secretary-General Dag Hammarskjold and the United Nations, while avoiding direct attacks against the United States. Indeed, on the day of the incident, February 13, Khrushchev, in a reply to a congratulatory telegram from Kennedy (on the occasion of the launching of a Soviet Venus probe), indicated that he was interested in exploring joint Soviet-United States space efforts.

The event that evoked the greatest concern for Soviet-American relations, however, was the abortive Bay of Pigs invasion. If the Russian actions with respect to Laos and the Lumumba murder provided some hope that Soviet-American relations might be improving, the sharp diplomatic exchange between Kennedy and Khrushchev over Cuba seemingly returned those relations to their preinauguration status.[74] Within three weeks following the U.S. Caribbean failure, however, events were to take a dramtic turn as Khrushchev renewed his request for a summit meeting and Kennedy replied positively and agreed to meet with Khrushchev in Vienna on June 3 and 4, 1961.

Kennedy's decision to go to Vienna can be attributed to the deterioration of the position of the United States resulting from the Bay of Pigs disaster. Kennedy feared that Khrushchev might miscalculate the strength and position of the United States and thereby dangerously overestimate his position, thus the opportunity for talks was seized by Kennedy as a means for making the U.S. position clear. Khrushchev's motivations were, however, somewhat problematic. One might surmise that Khrushchev was as anxious as Kennedy to take the measure of his counterpart and may also have felt that the American president's position had been sufficiently weakened by the Cuban affair as to make him prone to bullying—a tactic that Khrushchev had shown some propensity to use in the past.[75] There is also evidence that Khrushchev's specific intent was to attempt to force the German question to a solution.[76] Khrushchev reportedly informed the American ambassador, Llewellyn Thompson, that he had waited long enough on the Berlin question, and noted that the matter of his own prestige was involved. Thompson reported in turn that Khrushchev was faced with a Communist party congress in the fall and needed some action on the Berlin question to protect himself.[77]

Kennedy's desire that he enter into negotiations from a position of apparent strength manifested itself in a disconcertingly tough speech to Congress on May 25, less than two weeks before the Vienna summit. The title of his message was "On Urgent National Needs." He explained his appearance by declaring: "These are extraordinary times . . . and . . . I am here to promote the doctrine of freedom." The Soviets, he declared, "possess a powerful intercontinental striking force, large forces for executing war, a well trained underground in nearly every country . . . the capacity for quick decision, a . . . society without dissent . . . and long experience in the techniques of violence and subversion."[78] The challenge was formidable. But the young president proceeded to describe a wide range of strategies to meet it. Along with his request for increased conventional and unconventional war capability, Kennedy also announced a new national fall-out shelter program. Every federal, state, and local building, and even private homes, were to be subsidized by an immediate tripling of the then-pending budget request. A great civil defense effort had been advocated by civilian strategists, notably Harvard's Henry Kissinger and Herman Kahn, then at RAND.

This school of strategists believed that a massive fall-out shelter program and new methods for quick evacuation of cities and dealing with the results of thermonuclear destruction by improved communication capabilities would prepare for the worst and could well save millions of lives; and, more important, would demonstrate the United States' willingness to take the worst the Soviets had to offer, if the stakes were high enough. In short, fall-out shelters were a concrete, burlap, and sandbag symbol of national will to uphold commitments at any level of violence necessary. Critics, however, pointed out that shelters could also be interpreted by the Soviets as a preparation for an American first strike. Given the number of missiles and planes that the Soviets could send to the United States after they had been hit by a disarming blow, fall-out shelters would minimize damage to an extent where an American victory could be contemplated without the thought of a mountain of American corpses. To that extent, critics held, the program was provocative. Political scientist J. David Singer wrote worriedly in the *Bulletin of Atomic Scientists*:

> [T]he Kremlin strategists might well want to ask how useful a shelter program would be to the nation whose doctrine is a purely retaliatory one. More specifically, how many lives would be saved by such a program if we were the victims of a surprise attack?
>
> If the [surprise] attack were against our cities, it is evident that very few people would be able to get to their shelters in time, and those that did would not find them particularly protective. . . . [Therefore] the Soviets must begin to wonder whether the shelters are for protection against [a] surprise attack, or whether they may not reflect a first-strike strategy.[79]

Kennedy and McNamara were later to yield to these arguments. But in the meantime, so near to the summit, the announcement of vastly enlarged civil defense programs had a clear and immediate diplomatic purpose. "Our greatest asset," Kennedy concluded "in this struggle [for freedom] is the American people['s] willingness to pay any price. . . . It is heartening to know, as I journey abroad, that our country . . . is ready to do its duty."[80]

The Vienna Conference

The Vienna Conference, described as "useful" in the joint communique issued at the conclusion of the meetings on June 4, produced substantive agreement on only one point, Laos. Agreement was reached on the second day of the talks that the conclusion on a cease fire should be a "priority matter."[81] The remainder of the conference produced frank, well defined, but courteous disagreement.

The first day of the conference was devoted to a thorough airing of the world views of both leaders. By becoming involved in such an ideological debate, Kennedy was forced to talk on Khrushchev's grounds, hence Khrushchev apparently held the initiative throughout this initial day of talks. Such ideological debate was, as Schlesinger has pointed out, inevitably fruitless.[82] Kennedy sought, therefore, in the second day of the talks, to turn the discussion to more concrete matters. On disarmament a complete stalemate was reached. The discussion then turned to Berlin and the German question, and in so doing the first great confrontation on the new frontier was initiated.

Khrushchev repeated the oft-stated position of the Soviet Union that a peace treaty had to be signed so as to eradicate the threat of the West German militarists starting a third world war. He wanted agreement with the West, but if none was forthcoming he would sign a separate treaty with East Germany. A free city of West Berlin would be established, with control of all access in the hands of the German Democratic Republic. Kennedy replied that, unlike Laos, Berlin was considered by the United States to be a point of vital interest. The position of the United States vis-à-vis Berlin and Germany was the result of legal contractual rights as decided by World War II. If the United States withdrew from Berlin, it would ultimately mean the abandonment of the rest of Europe. In summary, Kennedy made it clear to Khrushchev that he would not accept an ultimatum from the Soviet Union. He would not "acquiesce in the isolation of his country."[83]

Khrushchev now became considerably more harsh. He repeated that he only wanted to assure that the "most dangerous spot in the world" would not cause war. He in effect closed the question as he noted that nothing could possibly prevent him from signing a peace treaty with East Germany by the end of the year;[84] and from that time on, any infringement on the sovereignty of the German Democratic Republic would be considered as an act of aggression.[85]

The Berlin Crisis: Emergence from Transition

Khrushchev had given to Kennedy at Vienna two *aide-mémoires* which restated in more formal diplomatic language the position advanced by Khrushchev during his conversations with Kennedy.[86] The memoranda did not include Khrushchev's pledge that he would sign a peace treaty by the end of the year, but his television and radio talk to the Russian

people on June 15, 1961, did state the pledge clearly.[87] Kennedy's statement a week earlier was:

> I made it clear to Mr. Khrushchev that the security of Western Europe and
> therefore our own security are deeply involved in our presence and our
> access rights to West Berlin, that those rights are based on law and not on
> sufferance, and that we are determined to maintain those rights at any
> risk.[88]

When joined with Khrushchev's pronouncement, this announced to the
world that another Berlin crisis was full blown.

Throughout the summer the crisis was gradually escalated. On June
21 Khrushchev noted that the United States was increasing its appropriations for military expenditures. The Soviet leader indicated that such a
move might necessitate a similar increase on the part of the Soviet
Union. Khrushchev went further and threatened to resume nuclear testing if the United States did so.[89]

On the following day, Secretary of State Rusk reaffirmed the inten-
tion of the United States to stay in Berlin, and refused to consider the
Russian peace treaty as valid.[90] The president, in his news conference of
June 28, solemnly restated the position of the United States to honor its
commitments and warned the Russians not to "underestimate the will
and unity of democratic societies where vital interests are concerned."[91]
Khrushchev reciprocated these sentiments and stepped up the pressure.
On July 8 he announced that, in response to increased U.S. defense
expenditures, the Soviet Union would be forced to increase its own
defense preparations by suspending all proposed reductions in the size
of the Soviet armed forces until the German question was resolved and
increasing defense spending of 3,144,000,000 rubles.[92]

The initial reaction of the United States to this new Soviet move
came in the form of a note given to the Soviet Union on July 17. This note
was, in fact, a reply to the Soviet *aide-mémoires* of June 4, and was
comprised of a legalistic point-by-point refutation of that document.[93]
The White House seems to have been disappointed by the document,
particularly with the "maddening" slowness with which it had been
produced by the State Department.[94] Kennedy was reportedly dismayed
that the document was only a "compilation of stale, tedious, and negative
phrases, none of them very new."[95] Kennedy felt that a new and more
dynamic statement of the United States was needed; a clear delineation
of the over-all response of the United States to the German question had
to be presented to the American people and the world.

Kennedy's new response was delivered in a televised report to the

American people on July 25, 1961. At the outset the president repeated the intention and right of the United States to be in Berlin. Again he restated that the U.S. position was considered as being vital to the national interest:

> We cannot and will not permit the Communists to drive us out of Berlin, either gradually or by force. For the fulfillment of our pledge to that city is essential to the morale and security of Western Germany, to the unity of Western Europe, and to the faith of the entire Free World.[96]

Kennedy next set forth his specific proposals, which were to constitute his response to Khrushchev's escalation of the crisis. The president called for an additional $3,247,000,000 in defense appropriations. He asked for an increase in the size of the Army from 875,000 men to approximately 1 million, an increase in the Navy and Air Force of respectively 29,000 and 63,000 men. The draft was to be doubled and then tripled within the near future, and Kennedy announced that he was requesting authority to call upon reserve units. The numbers required were unstated but soon more than 150,000 men, veterans of Korea and World War II, and National Guardsmen, were called from their jobs to active service. Also, the planned deactivation of ships and aircraft such as the B-47 was to be delayed. Fifty percent of "our missile power . . . and of our B-52 and B-47 bombers" were on "ground alert which would send them on their way with 15 minutes warning." Moreover, Kennedy announced that $1.8 billion of the funds he had requested would be spent for the procurement of nonnuclear war materials.[97] Defense programs were to be enlarged yet another $205 million. The year's appropriation of $3.5 billion for civilian defense was to be applied toward procuring adequate food, water, first aid kits, household warning kits to detect dangerous levels of home radiation, and a national air raid warning system ranging from sirens to telecommunications.

The Berlin crisis did not, of course, end with Kennedy's speech. In the tension-filled weeks following Kennedy's talk, the exodus of refugees from East Berlin increased thereby prompting Khrushchev to seal off East Berlin on the night of August 12 and, in the days that followed, to construct the Berlin wall. Possibly this cessation of the flow of refugees to the West was seen by Khrushchev as his only obtainable goal (other than using the circumstances as a pretext for renewing atmospheric testing); for after inconclusive negotiations had been initiated, Khrushchev announced, in a six-hour report to the 22nd Congress of the Communist Party, that he would no longer insist on a peace treaty.[98]

Just before Khrushchev rose to make his speech, the probability of a Soviet-American showdown seemed unusually high. The calling up of

150,000 American reservists, the increase in the American arms budget, the inauguration of a nationwide fallout shelter system that indicated Americans would be prepared to accept the worst from the Soviets and still, in the words of the Pentagon's second in command, "not be defeated," all indicated an assurance that America's full might could well be called into play in Berlin. Reports of the wall—the sordid details of land mines, barbed wire, and watchtowers—reached the morning papers in Washington on an especially inauspicious Friday, October 13, 1961. General Lucius Clay, the U.S. military governor general of Berlin, who was largely responsible for the Berlin airlift, returned to the city. As he arrived, White House spokesmen announced that a battle group of fifteen hundred men was heading down the Autobahn to reinforce the American garrison in Berlin.

While the 22nd Congress was being held in Moscow, the East German authorities began to slow Western traffic, including American armored columns, headed for Berlin. On October 26 Soviet tanks moved in the East Berlin sector so as to be separated by a strip less than seventy-five yards from the position of American tanks. There were reports that American bulldozers had joined the American tank columns and infantry positions. In his memoirs, Khrushchev claims that Marshal Ivan Konev reported to him that the Americans were preparing to cross the frontier and destroy the wall.[99] But on October 27 Khrushchev spoke to the 22nd Congress: "What counts most," he declared, "is not the particular date" of the settlement of the German problem, "but a businesslike and honest settlement of the question."[100] Soviet tanks withdrew as Khrushchev finished speaking.

The apparent successful manipulation of threats and signals again seemed to indicate Soviet susceptibility to the diplomacy of threat. After the Cuban missile crisis, this lesson seemed to displace almost all other approaches for dealing with America's most powerful adversary. Soviet power was depreciated. For a while, Americans believed that an American-constructed international system would endure without challenge for the foreseeable future. Yet the Berlin crisis and the successful installation of the Berlin wall had further significance. Khrushchev was probably correct in pointing out that Western acquiescence to the implied permanent division of Germany that the wall portended also prepared the ground for future German leaders to live with the results of World War II. Khrushchev claimed that he "forced Kennedy and the Western Allies to swallow a bitter pill."[101] In the long run, the medicine did not seem pernicious. In the short run, both the patient and the good Soviet doctor almost died as the cold war moved to a climax in the waters off Cuba.

CONCLUSION

Nation-building and a flexible response provided the Kennedy administration with a policy construct predisposed toward activism. Flexible response, of course, was in part rooted in the concepts of the past; however, the thrust of the Kennedy administration was to free itself of the "reactive elements" that to them characterized the massive retaliation of the Eisenhower years. That is to say, Kennedy, through Robert McNamara and his collection of defense intellectuals, sought to develop a spectrum of usable force in addition to an expanded and embellished strategic retaliatory capacity at the upper end of the scale of possible violence. Indeed, with the incorporation into the Kennedy Department of Defense of many of the men who had criticized the massive retaliation doctrines of the 1950s, American nuclear forces began to reflect a limited nuclear war potential as well as an expansion of conventional capability, Nowhere is the propensity toward an activist interventionist posture more apparent than in the area of unconventional warfare. In fact, the doctrines of insurgency and counterinsurgency stand as a kind of conceptual and practical bridge between the diplomacy of violence embodied in the doctrines of flexible response and the ostensibly peaceful activism of nation-building.

Nation-building as a concept and policy was clearly activist and interventionist. Whether the intervention was to be by means of a Peace Corps volunteer or a massive aid grant, the objective was the same. Forces of economic, social, and cultural development were to be set in motion and then monitored so as to allow the country to take off toward self-sustaining economic growth. At the same time, however, this economic growth "should aim at the strategic goals of a stronger national independence, an increased concentration on domestic affairs, greater democracy and a *long-run association with the West*."[102] President Kennedy concerned himself with the development of a world marked by "diversity and independence," but "above all, 'this emerging world is incompatible with the communist world order.'"[103] The direction of history, Kennedy asserted, "represent[ed] the very essence of our view of the future of the world."[104]

But like the Truman administration, the Kennedy administration could not leave the historical process alone. America was now thought to be benefactor and monitor of the development process. This was the corollary of the mission set forth in the Truman Doctrine: to build and maintain a global order among great powers such that American values of political economy might flourish. Moreover, the burden was now doubly great, for had not Khrushchev proclaimed support of national wars of liberation a primary thrust of Soviet policy? Previously, external aggression was clear warrant for American intervention. Now the presence of armed insurgents was *ipso facto* grounds for intervention. The Kennedy administration accepted wholeheartedly, therefore, the somewhat enigmatic charge of the Truman Doctrine that we must help others "work out their own destiny in their own way."

Yet this was a slippery slope; for intervention pulled the United States into a process inevitably marked by enormous social, cultural, and economic discontinuity. Traditional structures were, of necessity, cracked open, often violently. But the mechanistic concepts and policies of nation-building were marked by a naïve belief that somehow violence could be avoided. Indeed, if violence persisted, it was not unreasonable to assume that it was related in some way to Khrushchev's January 2, 1961, pledge, in which case reliance upon military force either indigenous or external was perfectly appropriate to the development process. The paradox was that in turning to the military and others of a conservative bent in the developing world, the United States was aligning itself with those least predisposed to a world of diversity and social justice. Moreover, it is notable that despite his protestation of willingness to allow pluralistic forces to work, Kennedy adopted and maintained intense personal interest in the Green Berets, that elite group of men responsible for insurgency and counterinsurgency—the gray nether world that joined nation-building to flexible response.

The doctrinal basis of the Kennedy administration foreign and defense policy was, therefore, a return to the activism of the late Truman administration. By adopting many of the modalities implied by NSC-68, the Kennedy administration worked to build and maintain an international system not unlike that envisioned in the 1950s as well as the 1940s. Indeed, what is commonly regarded as the finest hour of the Kennedy administration, the Cuban missile crisis, was a classic example of the brinkmanship of the 1950s.

NOTES

1. Theodore H. White, *The Making of the President: 1960* (New York: New American Library, Signet Edition, 1967), pp. 204–205.
2. Theodore C. Sorensen, *Kennedy* (New York: Bantam, 1966), p. 189.
3. Ibid., p. 256.
4. John F. Kennedy, "Annual Message to the Congress on the State of the Union, January 30, 1961," *Public Papers of the President, 1961* (Washington, D.C.: U.S. Government Printing Office, 1962), pp. 23–24.

5. "Long Live Leninism!" *Red Flag*, April 16, 1960, translated in *Peking Review*, No. 17 (1960).
6. Bernard S. Morris, *International Communism and American Policy* (New York: Atheneum, 1968), pp. 133–148.
7. Kennedy, op. cit., p. 23.
8. Cited by John Kenneth Galbraith, "The Moderate Solution," in John R. Boettiger, ed., *Vietnam and American Foreign Policy* (Lexington, Mass.: D.C. Heath, 1968), p. 130.
9. For a good review, see Herbert Dinerstein's classic *War and the Soviet Union*, rev. ed. (New York: Praeger, 1962). There had been some writing on partisan warfare and some attention by Trotsky and Lenin to the revolutionary potential in the third world, but the dominant part of Soviet intellectual energy had been to diagnose the nature of capitalist ambitions and capacities and prepare a deep defense. Soviet diplomatic and revolutionary activity in Asia were especially muted as Stalin's campaign began in the late 1920s to build "socialism in one country" after disastrous attempts to bestir communist revolution in the colonial world.
10. John A. Armstrong, "Soviet Policy in the Middle East," in Kurt London, ed., *The Soviet Union: A Half-Century of Communism* (Baltimore: Johns Hopkins University Press, 1968), pp. 423–454, esp. pp. 440–450.
11. Reprinted in "Selected Readings: Counter Insurgency" (U.S. Army War College, Carlisle Barracks, Pa., 1962), and in *Selected Readings in Guerrilla and Counter Guerrilla Operations* (U.S. Infantry School, Fort Benning, Ga., July 1967), pp. 54–62. Also see his speech reprinted in *World Marxist Review,* January 1961, and Robert McNamara's exegesis of it in his speech given to the Fellows of the American Bar Association, February 17, 1962, reprinted in *Selected Reading in Guerrilla and Counter Guerrilla Operations,* pp. 9–17.
12. Khrushchev in January 6, 1961, "Za Novye Pobedy Mirovogo Kommunisticheskogo Dvizheniia Kommunist" (January 1961), p. 20; cited by Michel P. Gehlen, *The Politics of Coexistence: Soviet Methods and Motives* (Bloomington, Ind.: Indiana University Press, 1967), p. 105.
13. Cited in Gehlen, op. cit., pp. 105–106.
14. Especially important in perpetuating this understanding was the influential translation of Mao Zedong, *On Guerrilla Warfare* by Samuel Griffith (New York: Praeger, 1961), especially p. 4, where Griffith equates a statement made in November 1949 by Liu Shaoqi to the effect that other Asian revolutions "would follow the Chinese pattern," to Khrushchev's remarks in December 1960 and January 1961 on national liberation wars. Griffith's translation was considered "classic," and the Praeger distribution was the first major dissemination of Mao's thought in English by an American publishing firm.
15. *Peking Review,* No. 36 (September 3, 1965) for the full text.
16. Arthur Huck, *The Security of China: Chinese Approaches to Problems of War and Strategy* (New York: Columbia University Press, 1970), p. 50.
17. Dean Rusk, in U.S. Congress, Hearings before the Senate Committee on Foreign Relations, *Supplemental Foreign Assistance, Fiscal Year 1966, Vietnam,* U.S. 89th Congress, 2nd Session, p. 596.
18. But this view was not confined to policy makers. It was also a perception widely shared by academics. As Professor Frank Trager of New York University wrote, "To support this view of the communist challenge in Southeast Asia, one does not have to argue for a supposed total identity of Sino-Soviet objectives, strategies and tactics in the area: that is, for world monolithicism . . . [v]ariations help make it possible for Moscow and Peking to advance their overriding communist objectives. Separately or together, they acquire more strings to their respective bows for the greater success of

the communist symphony . . . there should be no doubt that basic purpose of the exercise in both Moscow and Peking is to overwhelm, that is to communize Southeast Asia." Frank N. Trager, in William Henderson, ed., *Southeast Asia: Problems of United States Policy* (Cambridge, Mass.: The M.I.T. Press, 1963), pp. 163–164.

19. *Public Papers of the President of the United States: Harry S. Truman—1951* (Washington, D.C.: U.S. Government Printing Office, 1965), p. 224.

20. Secretary Robert McNamara, February 17, 1962, speech to the American Bar Association in Chicago, p. 11 (emphasis ours), cited in *Selected Readings in Guerrilla and Counter Guerrilla Operations.*

21. Arthur Schlesinger, Jr., *A Thousand Days* (Boston: Houghton Mifflin, 1965), pp. 296–297; and Sorensen, op. cit., pp. 332–333.

22. Richard J. Walton, *Cold War and the Counterrevolution: The Foreign Policy of John F. Kennedy* (New York: Viking, 1972), pp. 44–45. In a press conference five days before the invasion on April 17, Kennedy skillfully dissembled when asked about American support for any such invasion, rumors of which had been in the press for weeks. Castro had obviously learned from the Guatemalan experience. The Cubans made more far-reaching land reforms, dismantled the pre-revolutionary military, and organized the peasantry to fight off invasion. See Richard H. Immerman, *The CIA in Guatemala: The Foreign Policy of Intervention* (Austin, Tex.: University of Texas Press, 1982), p. 196.

23. "Speech to American Society of Newspaper Editors," in *Public Papers of the President of the United States: John F. Kennedy—1961* (Washington, D.C.: U.S. Government Printing Office, 1962), p. 305.

24. Ibid., p. 306.

25. Ibid.

26. Ibid.

27. Ibid., p. 304.

28. Ibid., p. 305.

29. Schlesinger, op. cit., p. 202.

30. Ibid., p. 195.

31. Ibid.

32. Douglas A. Blaufarb, *The Counter-Insurgency Era: U.S. Doctrine and Performance, 1950 to Present* (New York: Free Press, 1977), p. 88.

33. Karl W. Deutsch and William J. Foltz, *Nation-Building* (New York: Atherton, 1966), p. 3.

34. "Guerrilla Warfare in the Underdeveloped Areas," address made at graduation ceremonies at the U.S. Army Special Warfare School, Ft. Bragg, N.C., June 28, 1961, *Department of State Bulletin*, Vol. 45, No. 1154 (August 7, 1961), p. 234.

35. Lincoln S. Bloomfield, "Vital Interests and Objectives of the United States," paper delivered to the Naval War College on August 26, 1963, reprinted in Wesley Posvar et al., eds., *American Defense Policy* (Baltimore: Johns Hopkins University Press, 1965), pp. 18–19 (emphasis in the original).

36. Samuel Huntington, *Political Order in Changing Societies* (New Haven, Conn.: Yale University Press, 1968), p. 72.

37. Samuel P. Huntington, "The Bases of Accommodation," *Foreign Affairs*, Vol. 46 (July 1968), p. 652.

38. Huntington, *Political Order in Changing Societies*, p. 24.

39. Ibid., p. 28.

40. Joseph La Palombara, "Political Science and the Engineering of National Development," in Monte Polner and Larry Stern, eds., *Political Development in Changing Societies: An Analysis of Modernization* (Lexington, Mass.: D.C. Heath, 1971), p. 52.

41. David W. Chang, "The Military and Nation Building in Korea, Burma and Pakistan," *Asian Survey*, Vol. 9, No. 11 (November 1969), p. 830.

42. See especially Charles Wolf, Jr., *The United States Policy and the Third World: Problems and Analysis* (Boston: Little, Brown, 1967), for an elaborate panegyric to the military contribution to development.

43. See Gabriel Almond and J. S. Coleman, eds., *The Politics of the Developing Areas* (Princeton, N.J.: Princeton University Press, 1960), or Edward C. Banfield, *American Foreign Aid Doctrines* (Washington, D.C.: American Enterprise Institute, 1963).

44. Schlesinger, op. cit., p. 201. Professor Schlesinger writes:

> But the revolutionary point remained primary. For Kennedy fully understood—this was, indeed, the mainspring of all his thinking about Latin America—that, with all its pretensions to realism, the militant anti-revolutionary line represented the policy most likely to strengthen the communists and lose the hemisphere. He believed that, to maintain contact with a continent seized by the course of revolutionary change, a policy of social idealism was the only true realism for the United States.

45. Ibid., p. 769.

46. See, for example, *U.S. Department of Commerce, Statistical Abstract of the United States, 1971* (Washington, D.C.: U.S. Government Printing Office, 1972), p. 755.

47. Schlesinger, op. cit., p. 773.

48. Theodore Draper, "The Dominican Crisis: A Case Study in American Policy," *Commentary*, Vol. 40, No. 6 (December 1965), p. 34.

49. Schlesinger, op. cit., quoting Kennedy, p. 789.

50. Legislative Reference Service, Library of Congress, *Some Important Issues in Foreign Aid*, A Report Prepared for the Senate Committee on Foreign Relations (Washington, D.C.: U.S. Government Printing Office, 1966), pp. 10–13 and Agency for International Development, *U.S. Overseas Loans and Grants and Assistance from International Organizations: Obligations and Loan Authorizations, July 1, 1945–June 30, 1972* (Washington, D.C.: U.S. Government Printing Office, 1973), *passim*.

51. Annual Message to the Congress on the State of the Union, January 30, 1961, in *Public Papers of the Presidents, John F. Kennedy, 1961* (Washington, D.C.: U.S. Government Printing Office, 1962), p. 24 (emphasis added).

52. Louis Fitzsimmons, *The Kennedy Doctrine* (New York: Random House, 1972), p. 233, citing an oral history interview with Doctor Herbert York.

53. Ibid., pp. 233–234.

54. *The New York Times*, January 12, 1961.

55. Television and Radio Address of May 25, 1960, *Department of State Bulletin*, Vol. 42, No. 1093 (June 6, 1960), p. 900.

56. Schlesinger, op. cit., p. 301.

57. Ibid.; I. F. Stone, in *New York Review of Books*, April 23, 1970, p. 21.

58. Schlesinger, op. cit., p. 500.

59. Ibid., pp. 499–500.

60. Melvin Laird, *Congressional Record*, January 25, 1961, House p. 1228; also cited by I. F. Stone, *New York Review of Books*, April 23, 1970, p. 22. In addition, Stone notes that Republicans pointed out that under the final Eisenhower budgets, there would be "600" Minuteman missiles by the end of 1964; 129 Atlas and 126 Titan ICBM's by the end of 1962; 4 more Polarises in service by the end of 1961, with 64 more missiles; and . . . 15 Jupiter IRBMs."

61. William W. Kaufmann, *The McNamara Strategy* (New York: Harper & Row, 1964), pp. 79–80.

62. Robert S. McNamara's Address in Atlanta, Ga., November 11, 1961, quoted in ibid., p. 75.
63. Ibid., pp. 69–72.
64. See, for example, McNamara's speech before the annual convention of United Press International editors and publishers at San Francisco, Calif., on September 18, 1967, printed in *Department of State Bulletin*, Vol. 57, No. 1476 (October 9, 1967), pp. 443–451.
65. Quoted in Kaufmann, op. cit., p. 76.
66. Schlesinger, op. cit., pp. 301–302. See also Seymour Topping, "Kremlin Initiation Step," *The New York Times*, January 22, 1961, pp. 1–3.
67. Sorensen, op. cit., p. 541.
68. See "Secretary Rusk's News Conference of February 6," *Department of State Bulletin*, Vol. 44, No. 1131 (February 27, 1961), p. 302.
69. There does exist some disagreement on the question of whether Khrushchev forcefully pushed for an immediate meeting with Kennedy. Sorensen, as we have noted, merely states that Khrushchev expressed a desire for such a meeting. Others, notably Dana Schmidt, "Kennedy to Seek Delay in Parley and Atom Test Ban," *The New York Times*, January 25, 1961, p. 1, and William Jorden, "U.S.-Soviet Approaches Studied," *The New York Times*, January 25, 1961, p. 2, report that Khrushchev was not forceful in his expression of a desire for talks. Apparently the wish was expressed but not pushed.
70. "Only Sane Course Is Peaceful Coexistence," *Current Digest of the Soviet Press*, Vol. 13 (March 1, 1961), pp. 29–31.
71. "The President's News Conference of January 25, 1961," *Public Papers of the President, 1961*, p. 16.
72. "The President's News Conference of March 23, 1961," *Public Papers of the President, 1961*, pp. 213–214.
73. The authors of a Senate investigation some fifteen years later wrote: "The chain of events revealed by the documents and testimony is strong enough to permit a reasonable inference that [a] plot to assassinate Lumumba was authorized by President Eisenhower." But even though "[t]he Congo station [of the CIA] had advanced knowledge of the Central Government's plans to transport Lumumba into the hands of his bitterest enemies, where he was likely to be killed, . . . there is no evidentiary basis for concluding that the CIA conspired in *this* plan. . . ." U.S. Congress, Select Committee on Governmental Operations with Respect to Intelligence Activities, *Alleged Assassination Plots Involving Foreign Leaders*, Report No. 94–463, November 20, 1975, pp. 48 and 51.
74. "Message from N. S. Khrushchev, Chairman of the U.S.S.R. Council of Ministers, to U.S. President John F. Kennedy," *Current Digest of the Soviet Press*, Vol. 13 (May 17, 1961), pp. 4–5; and "Message to Chairman Khrushchev Concerning the Meaning of Events in Cuba, April 18, 1961," *Public Papers of the President, 1961*, pp. 286–287. Also in "United States and Soviet Union Exchange Messages in Regard to Events in Cuba," *Department of State Bulletin*, Vol. 44, No. 1141 (May 8, 1961), pp. 661–667.
75. Schlesinger, op. cit., p. 344. Schlesinger is the only person who has spoken of the exact contents of Khrushchev's letter; see also Louis J. Halle, "The Job to Be Done at the Summit," *The New York Times Magazine*, May 28, 1961, p. 48.
76. "For New Victories of the World Communist Movement," *Current Digest of the Soviet Press*, Vol. 13 (February 22, 1961), p. 10.
77. Schlesinger, op. cit., p. 347.
78. "Special Message to the Congress on Urgent National Needs, May 25, 1961," *Public Papers of the President, 1961*, pp. 396–397.

79. Ibid., pp. 402–403; and J. David Singer, "Deterrence and Shelters," *Bulletin of the Atomic Scientists*, Vol. 17, No. 8 (October 1961), p. 313.

80. "Special Message, May 25, 1961," p. 406.

81. Schlesinger, op. cit., pp. 367–368; and Sorensen, op. cit., pp. 548–549.

82. Schlesinger, op. cit., p. 367.

83. Ibid., p. 371.

84. Sorensen, op. cit., p. 585. There is some disagreement between Sorensen and Schlesinger on chronology here. Schlesinger does not mention Khrushchev's pledge of an end-of-the-year treaty until after lunch of the second day. Sorensen records the pledge as being made during the morning talks.

85. Schlesinger, op. cit., pp. 370–374; and Sorensen, op. cit., pp. 584–586.

86. "On the Memorandum Handed by N. S. Khrushchev to U.S. President Kennedy," *Current Digest of the Soviet Press*, Vol. 13 (July 5, 1961), pp. 4–7.

87. "Radio and Television Address by N. S. Khrushchev on June 15, 1961," *Current Digest of the Soviet Press*, Vol. 13 (July 12, 1961), pp. 3–8. The East German leader Walter Ulbricht added emphasis to Khrushchev's statement by noting that he intended to maintain absolute control of access when the treaty was signed. "Ulbricht Warns on Berlin Access," *The New York Times*, June 16, 1961, pp. 1–2.

88. "Radio and Television Report to the American People on Returning from Europe, June 6, 1961," *Public Papers of the President, 1961*, p. 444.

89. "Speech by Comrade N. S. Khrushchev at Meeting of the Representatives of Moscow Public Park to Mark 20th Anniversary of Beginning of Great Patriotic War, June 21, 1961," *Current Digest of the Soviet Press*, Vol. 13 (July 19, 1961), p. 20.

90. "Secretary Rusk's News Conference of June 22," *Department of State Bulletin*, Vol. 45, No. 1150 (July 10, 1961), p. 51.

91. "The President's News Conference of June 28, 1961," *Public Papers of the President, 1961*, p. 477.

92. "Speech by Comrade N. S. Khrushchev at Reception for Graduates of Military Academies of U.S.S.R. Armed Forces, July 18, 1961," *Current Digest of the Soviet Press*, Vol. 13 (August 2, 1961), p. 5.

93. "Note from the United States to the Soviet Union, Replying to the Soviet Aide-Memoire Handed to President Kennedy at Vienna, July 17, 1961," *Department of State Bulletin*, Vol. 45 (August 7, 1961), p. 224.

94. Schlesinger, op. cit., p. 406.

95. Sorensen, op. cit., p. 587. Schlesinger describes the reply as "a tired and turgid rehash of documents left over from the Berlin crisis of 1958–1959," p. 384.

96. "Radio and Television Report to the American People on the Berlin Crisis, July 25, 1961," *Public Papers of the President, 1961*, p. 534.

97. Ibid., pp. 535–536.

98. "Report of the Central Committee of the Communist Party of the Soviet Union to the 22nd Congress—II," *Current Digest of the Soviet Press*, Vol. 13 (November 3, 1961), p. 5.

99. Nikita Khrushchev, *Khrushchev Remembers: The Last Testament*, Strobe Talbott, ed., (Boston: Little, Brown, 1974), pp. 506–507.

100. "Concluding Remarks by Comrade N. S. Khrushchev at the 22nd Party Congress, October 27, 1961," *Current Digest of the Soviet Press*, Vol. 13, No. 46 (December 13, 1961), p. 24.

101. Khrushchev, *Khrushchev Remembers*, p. 509.

102. Schlesinger, op. cit., p. 588 (emphasis added).

103. Schlesinger noting Kennedy, op. cit., p. 617.

104. "Address in Berkeley at the University of California, March 23, 1962," *Public Papers of the President, 1962*, p. 265.

Chapter 8
The Apotheosis
of Containment

Historians know there is a rhythm to their craft. Events are examined, and orthodoxies are established. Then comes a chipping away of previously held convictions. New understandings emerge and stand—for a while; and then comes another tide of reevaluation. Similarly, the Kennedy administration's shimmering hour—the Cuban crisis—is now subject to review in terms of the assumptions, policy processes, and relationships of the cold war. Our contention is that the crisis became something of a misleading model for the foreign policy process and diverted attention from profound changes under way in the world political economy.[1]

Concerning the former model there are seven central tenets, each of which was confirmed by the lessons of the Cuban crisis:

1. Crisis is typical of international relations. The international environment is a constant collision of wills that is, at once, both a surrogate of war and takes place at the doorstep of war. Crises are objective elements of the international system—but they also have a profoundly psychological element of will and resolve.
2. Crises are assumed to be manageable. Those skills of personality, training, and organizational expertise that had developed in the national security machinery during the previous twenty-five years could be orchestrated by a vast bureaucracy in controlled and responsive movements.
3. Although crises are a characteristic of the international system, the domestic system is one of order and consensus and is insulated from the necessities of international politics. Public opinion, in this view, can be controlled to lend support for a particular foreign policy.
4. Diplomacy is a mixture of force and bargaining. An essential element of crisis management is the ability to reconcile the inherent forward dynamic of violence, threats of violence, and the instruments of violence with negotiation.
5. Americans can control the process of crisis negotiation to win.
6. The Soviets seldom negotiate serious matters except under extreme duress.
7. Military questions are too critical to be left in the hands of military men and organizations that are not in step with the needs of crisis

management. Crisis management can and must be a civilian enterprise.

After the Cuban missile crisis, there were the beginnings of detente with the Soviet Union. The test ban treaty, the hot line, and a more civil exchange between the two powers are widely believed to stem from the favorable resolution of the missile crisis. Yet the model and its inherent assumptions on the meaning of Cuba can be challenged. Cuba does indeed stand as a watershed in the cold war and the history of the international system. But it is properly understood as a part and product of the cold war; indeed, the Cuban crisis was in many ways the climax of the cold war.

Even as the crisis occurred, evidence was emerging that the structure of the world's political economy was changing irrevocably and in a manner that would constrain the future exercise of American political and military power. More than a decade of American foreign military spending could no longer be dismissed as temporary or nonrecurring. The surfeit of American dollars in foreign hands—formerly the necessary liquidity for a rebuilding Western economy—was by the early 1960s regarded by Europeans as a threat to their new prosperity. But the Americans, now reinvigorated by the successful management of the Cuban crisis, saw such concerns as secondary. Granted that communism had been faced down at the brink of nuclear Armageddon, there was now a new crisis in the rice paddies of Southeast Asia.

MASTERY OR LUCK?

By far the most intense experience in East-West relations began on October 14, 1962, when the Russians were discovered to have placed forty-two medium-range missiles in Cuba. For the next week an ad hoc committee of top officials met in secret to consider the American response. This executive committee, or ExCom as they called themselves, arrived at two options: (1) an air strike on the missile sites or (2) a blockade of the island coupled with a demand that the missiles be removed. In a dramatic, nationally televised speech on October 22, President Kennedy announced that the United States was imposing a blockade around Cuba which would be removed only if the missiles were taken out by the Soviets. If they were not, and Soviet ships carrying new missiles encountered the Navy's warships, a Soviet-American military conflict seemed likely.

During the next four days, some ships carrying Russian goods were stopped and searched and some Soviet vessels carrying missiles turned back, but the crisis held. On October 26, Khrushchev sent an emotional private message to Kennedy indicating a willingness to remove the missiles if the United States would guarantee that it would not invade Cuba. The next day, however, a more formal and much tougher message was delivered to Kennedy which demanded that the United States remove its missiles in Turkey (missiles which Kennedy had earlier ordered removed because they were deemed obsolete) in exchange for the removal of the Soviet missiles from Cuba. Kennedy, not wanting to bargain, took the advice of his brother Robert, who had been a major participant in the ExCom deliberations, to accept the offer made in the private message and ignore the second, more belligerently phrased message. President Kennedy agreed and in private talks between Robert Kennedy and Soviet Ambassador Anatoly Dobrynin on October 27, the Soviets agreed to remove the missiles in return for the U.S. non-invasion pledge and ambiguous assurances that the missiles in Turkey would be removed if the NATO countries agreed. The next day, October 28, the Soviets announced that the missiles would be removed and the world exhaled.

In Khrushchev's apt description, it was a time when "a smell of burning hung heavy" in the air.[2] Kennedy's apparently controlled and masterful way of forcing Khrushchev to withdraw the missiles in the thirteen-day crisis has become a paradigmatic example of the way force can be harnessed to a policy by an elaborate manipulation of threats and gambits, negotiation and intimidation. Academic and government analysts have viewed Kennedy's response as a highly calibrated dissection of alternatives instead of seeing his actions as largely an intuitive response to a threat to his administration's electoral future, pride, and strategic posture. As Hans J. Morgenthau, the eminent scholar and a critic of the Kennedy administration, concluded: "The Cuban Crisis of 1962 . . . was the distillation of a collective intellectual effort of a high order, the like of which must be rare in history."[3] Much of this analysis—so drenched in the cool light of hindsight—bears a suspicious resemblance to the logical and psychological fallacy of reasoning *post hoc ergo propter hoc*.[4] Nevertheless, the dominant lesson Americans have drawn from the Cuban experience has been a joyous sense of the United States regaining mastery over history.

For many years Americans had felt threatened by the Soviet challenge to world order—especially since that challenge had been reinforced by growing Russian strategic capability. But after Cuba, the fears of precipitate expansion of a Soviet-American dispute into a final paroxysm of nuclear dust were dissipated. After Cuba, escalation became the *idée fixe* of academics and policymakers—a vision of a ladder of force with rungs separated by equivalent spaces of destruction, each with its own "value," running out toward darkness. Escalation became the dominant metaphor of American officialdom. Each rung could be ascended or descended with the proper increment of will and control. Events and military machines could be mastered for diplomatic ends. As Robert McNamara exalted after the exciting and frightening Cuban climax: "There is no longer any such thing as strategy, only crisis management."[5] Dennis Healy, the British Labor party "shadow" defense minister, called the Kennedy administration's performance a "model in any textbook on diplomacy."[6] Journalist Henry Pachter described Kennedy's execution of crisis management as "a feat whose technical elegance compelled the professionals' admiration."[7] Similarly, Albert and Roberta Wohlstetter made Cuba into a general historical principle about the use of force in times of great stress: "where the alternative is to be ruled by events with such enormous consequences, the head of a great state is likely to examine his acts of choice in crisis and during it to subdivide these possible acts in ways that make it feasible to continue exercising choice."[8]

The decisions as to what steps should be taken to deal with the implantation of the missiles were hammered out in the ExCom meetings. Although court chroniclers of the Kennedy administration have pored over each detail, the impression now is not one of all choices having been carefully weighed and considered. Rather, in retrospect, there appears to have been a gripping feeling of uncertainty and pressure. Robert Kennedy, for instance, at the height of the crisis, looked across at his brother and almost fainted at the horror of what they were contemplating: "Inexplicably, I thought of when he was ill and almost died; when he lost his child, when we learned that our oldest brother had been killed; or personal times of strain and hurt. The voices droned on, but I didn't seem to hear anything."[9]

There were reports that one assistant secretary was so disconcerted and fatigued that he drove into a tree at 4 A.M. Robert Kennedy recalled, "The strain and the hours without sleep were beginning to take their toll. . . . That kind of pressure does strange things to a human being, even to brilliant, self-confident, mature, experienced men." Robert Kennedy suspected that Dean Rusk, the secretary of state, "had a virtually complete breakdown mentally and physically."[10] And President Kennedy, although deliberately pacing himself, wondered how many of his principal advisers might suffer mental collapse from the long hours and pressure. Tense, fearful, and exhausted men planned and held together the American policy response to the Russian missiles.

Strain and fatigue commonly produce actions that are "caricatures of day-to-day behavior."[11] Although the stress of crisis decisionmaking concentrates and focuses the collective mind, it does not necessarily allow for the kind of elegant dissection of events that is now read into the Cuban affair. Events can take charge of decision makers; on October 25,

1962, Robert Kennedy reported that he felt, as Soviet ships drew near the edge of the American quarantine, that "[W]e were on the edge of a precipice with no way off. . . . President Kennedy had initiated the course of events, but he no longer had control over them."[12] John F. Kennedy's calm public face, discipline, and cool control gave a sense of intellectual engagement in the crisis that yielded no hint of the mute wasteland he was contemplating. But his private anxiety is well recorded, and a case can be made that dispassionate analysis was interlaced with cold war reflexes and constrained by bureaucratic politics.

It was very close. The military and the "hawks"—a term coined by journalistic descriptions of the ExCom deliberations—were pushing for actions ranging from a "surgical strike" to an all-out invasion of Cuba. Such options would have demanded the stark choice of an even greater Soviet humiliation or a Soviet response in kind. Ironically, a surgical strike was not really practical, for there was no guarantee that more than 90 percent of the missiles could be extirpated. Even after an American air attack, some of the missiles could have survived and been launched. And "surgical" always was a misnomer to describe an estimated twenty-five thousand Cuban fatalities, not to speak of the five hundred sorties that American planes would have had to run in order to destroy the Soviet missiles and bombers. Nevertheless, if six out of fourteen members of the ExCom group had had their way, the blockade of Cuba would have been an attack, which Robert Kennedy called a "Pearl Harbor in reverse." It is no wonder that President Kennedy estimated the world's chance of avoiding war at between one out of three and even.[13]

The illusion of control derived from the crisis was perniciously misleading. Although many Americans shared the belief of historian Arthur Schlesinger that the Cuban crisis displayed to the "whole world . . . the ripening of an American leadership unsurpassed in the responsible management of power . . . [a] combination of toughness . . . nerve and wisdom, so brilliantly controlled, so matchlessly calibrated that [it] dazzled the world,"[14] President Kennedy's control was in fact far from complete.

McNamara had sensed the Navy's lack of responsiveness to civilian commands and had gone to the "Flag Plot," or Naval Operations Center, where he could talk to ship commanders directly by voice-scrambled radio. McNamara pointed to a map symbol indicating that a ship was in a spot where he had not wanted it. "What's that ship doing there?" he asked. Chief of Naval Operations Admiral William R. Anderson confessed, "I don't know, but I have faith in my officers."[15] McNamara's unease with the apparent lack of responsiveness of the Navy to civilian command prompted him to inquire what would happen if a Soviet captain refused to divulge his cargo to a boarding American officer. Anderson picked up a Manual of Naval Regulations and rose to defend the Navy against any implied slight about Navy procedure. "It's all in there," Anderson asserted. McNamara retorted, "I don't give a damn what John Paul Jones would have done. I want to know what you are going to do, now!" The last word—again—however, was the Navy's: Admiral Anderson patronizingly soothed the fuming defense secretary, "Now, Mr. Secretary, if you and your deputy will go to your offices, the Navy will run the blockade."[16] As McNamara and his entourage turned to leave, Anderson called to him, "Don't worry, Mr. Secretary, we know what we are doing here."[17]

Just when the first Soviet-American encounter at sea seemed imminent, William Knox, the president of Westinghouse International, who happened to be in Moscow, was surprised by an abrupt summons from Premier Khrushchev. The voluble Soviet leader, perhaps half-convinced that Wall Street really manipulated American policy, gave a frightening summary of the strategic situation in the Caribbean. He warned that if the U.S. Navy began stopping Soviet ships, Soviet subs would start sinking American ships. That, Khrushchev explained, would lead to World War III.[18]

Only a little latter, the Navy began to force Soviet subs to the surface in order to defend its blockade—well before Kennedy had authorized contact with surface vessels. Kennedy was appalled when he learned that military imperatives are distinct from diplomatic necessities and can, all too often, conflict. When he found out that the Navy was intent on surfacing Soviet submarines, he was horrified: "Isn't there some way we can avoid having our first exchange with a Russian submarine—almost anything but that?" McNamara replied flintily, "No, there's too much danger to our ships. There is no alternative." Robert Kennedy wrote that "all six Russian submarines then in the area or moving toward Cuba from the Atlantic were followed and harassed and, at one time or another, forced to surface in the presence of U.S. military ships."[19] One can only wonder what would have happened if one of the Russian subs had refused to surface and had instead turned on its pursuers.

Events were only barely under control when, at the height of the crisis, on October 26, an American U-2 plane fixed on the wrong star and headed back from the North Pole to Alaska via Siberia. To compound matters the Alaskan Air Command sent fighter-bombers to escort the plane home, and the U.S. fighters and the spy plane met over Soviet territory before proceeding back.[20] To survive a Dr. Strangelove series of incidents like these, even given the assumptions of the day, can hardly be characterized as more than luck. It would not seem to be the mastery that Schlesinger and other court scribes delight in recalling and extolling.

THE DOMESTIC FACTOR

Why was there a crisis in the first place? The answer was found, in part, in one of the unacknowledged necessities in the conduct of American international affairs—domestic political considerations.[21] The Kennedy administration's sense of its own precarious electoral position, the coming of the November mid-term elections, and the place Cuba had occupied in public debate, all augured for an immediate and forceful response, no matter what the strategic reality was of having Russian missiles near American borders. The imperatives of American domestic politics during an election year had been building for some time. On August 27, 1962, for example, Republican Senator Homer E. Capehart of Indiana declared, "It is high time that the American people demand that President Kennedy quit 'examining the situation' and start protecting the interests of the United States."[22] Former Vice President Nixon, on the gubernatorial campaign stump in California, proposed that Cuban communism be "quarantined" by a naval blockade.[23] Republicans in both houses had warned the administration that Cuba would be "the dominant issue of the 1962 campaign."[24] The chairman of the Republican national committee jabbed at Kennedy's most sensitive spot— his concern for foreign policy resolve: "If we are asked to state the issue in one word, that word would be Cuba—symbol of tragic irresolution of the administration."[25]

The pressure mounted. As the political campaign began, one observer spotted a sign at a Kennedy rally in Chicago that read, "Less Profile—More Courage."[26] The widely respected and conservative London *Economist* reported that America had become "obsessed" by the "problem" of Cuba;[27] and I. F. Stone despaired in his *Weekly* that Cuba was a bogey that shook Americans, in the autumn of 1962, even more than the thought of war.[28] The domestic pressure on the American president was so intense that one member of Camelot, former Ambassador John Kenneth Galbraith, wrote: "Once they [the missiles] were there, the political needs of the Kennedy administration urged it to take almost any risk to get them out."[29] This skeptical view was shared by none other than former President Eisenhower, who suspected "that Kennedy might be playing politics with Cuba on the eve of Congressional elections."[30]

Nor, as Ronald Steel pointed out, were the principals—the ExCom—insulated from domestic considerations in their deliberations.[31] One Republican member of the crisis planners sent Theodore Sorensen—Kennedy's alter ego—a note that read: "Ted—have you considered the very real possibility that if we allow Cuba to complete installation and operational readiness of missile bases, the next House of Representatives is likely to have a Republican majority?"[32] Similarly,

McGeorge Bundy, chief adviser to two presidents, wondered, when the missiles were first reported, whether action could be deferred until after the election.[33] If the missile installations were completed earlier, there would be, arguably, both a strategic and an electoral problem facing the administration.

What was the worrisome substance of change in the strategic balance represented by the placement of forty-two missiles? To Robert McNamara, the secretary of defense, it seemed that "a missile is a missile. It makes no great difference whether you are killed by a missile from the Soviet Union or from Cuba."[34] About two weeks later, on television, Deputy Secretary of Defense Roswell Gilpatric confirmed the debatable meaning of the missiles: "I don't believe that we were under any greater threat from the Soviet Union's power, taken in totality, after this than before."[35] Indeed, Theodore Sorensen wrote in a memorandum to the president on October 17, 1962—five days before the blockade was ordered—that the presence of missiles in Cuba did not "significantly alter the balance of power." Sorensen explained, "They do not significantly increase the potential megatonnage capable of being unleashed on American soil, even after a surprise American nuclear strike." Sorensen confessed, in conclusion, that "Soviet motives were not understood."[36]

JUST A DIRTY TRICK?

To Khrushchev, the missiles offered the appearance of what former State Department analyst Roger Hilsman called a "quick fix" to the Soviet problem of strategic inferiority. Khrushchev was under enormous pressure from the Russian military, who rejected his promise of "goulash communism" and were pushing for a vast increase in the Soviet arms budget.[37] The Cuban missile ploy was probably Khrushchev's response to the prospect of Russian strategic inferiority, which was reported by the Kennedy administration as it admitted that the Democratic preelection charge of a missile gap had not been based on fact. The American announcement that the gap had been closed was accompanied by a Defense Department plan, dated October 19, 1961, for production of more than one thousand missiles by 1964.

One purpose of the Soviet moves in Cuba was, therefore, to gain the *appearance* of parity with the Americans. The employment of twenty-four MRBMs and eighteen IRBMs *seemed* to be a dramatic movement in that direction. But such an increase posed no real threat to American retaliatory strength, or to increasing American superiority. As Henry Kissinger noted at the time: "The bases were of only marginal use in a defensive war. In an offensive war their effectiveness was reduced by the enormous difficulty—if not impossibility—of coordination of a first strike from the Soviet Union and Cuba."[38]

The Kennedy administration knew that the Soviets were not striving for more than an appearance of strategic equality. As Kennedy later reflected, they were not "intending to fire them, because if they were going to get into a nuclear struggle, they have their own missiles in the Soviet Union. But it would have politically changed the balance of power. It would have appeared to, and appearances contribute to reality."[39] In the 1970s, by contrast, appearances were less important while the Americans were arranging a complex international order that verged on duopoly. Indeed, beginning in 1970, Soviet missile-firing submarines and tenders began to visit Cuban ports.[40] What protest there was by the Nixon administration seemed so muted as to be almost inaudible.[41]

Why was Kennedy so concerned about appearances? Perhaps he felt that the American people demanded an energetic response, given their purported frustration over Cuba. The administration's evaluation of the public mood supported the notion that firmness was a requisite of policy. Although repeated Gallup polls before the crisis showed 90 percent of Americans opposing actual armed intervention in Cuba,[42] Kennedy's own sense was, as his brother pointed out, that if he did not act, he would be impeached.[43]

Another explanation for Kennedy's concern that he would not appear credible to Khrushchev dates from the time, less than two years earlier, when he decided not to use air support for the Bay of Pigs invasion. According to James Reston's impression upon seeing Kennedy ten minutes after the two leaders had met in Vienna, "Khrushchev had studied the events of the Bay of Pigs; he would have understood if Kennedy had left Castro alone or destroyed him; but when Kennedy was rash enough to strike at Cuba but not bold enough to finish the job, Khrushchev decided he was dealing with an inexperienced young leader who could be intimidated and blackmailed."[44] Similarly, George F. Kennan, then the U.S. ambassador to Yugoslavia, met the president after the Vienna summit session and reported that he found Kennedy "strangely tongue-tied" during these talks. Later, he recalled for a Harvard oral history interviewer:

> I felt that he had not acquitted himself well on this occasion and that he had permitted Khrushchev to say many things which should have been challenged right there on the spot.
> I think this was definitely a mistake. I think it definitely misled Khrushchev; I think Khrushchev failed to realize on the occasion what a

man he was up against and also that he'd gotten away with many of these talking points; that he had placed President Kennedy in a state of confusion where he had nothing to say in return.[45]

Kennedy expressed concern to Reston and others that Khrushchev considered him a callow, inexperienced youth and that he soon expected a test. "It will be a cold winter," he was heard to mutter as he left the Vienna meeting. Khrushchev may indeed have been surprised at the forceful reaction of Kennedy, particularly after the young president had accepted the Berlin wall in August 1961 with no military response and had temporized in Laos in 1961 and 1962.

Perhaps, as Hilsman has argued, the Soviets assumed that the fine American distinctions between "offensive and defensive" missiles were really a *de facto* acknowledgment of the Soviet effort in Cuba. One could conjecture that this was what led Khrushchev to promise, and to believe that Kennedy understood, that no initiatives would be taken before the elections. In any case, Kennedy's concern about his appearance and the national appearance of strength kept him from searching very far for Soviet motivation. His interpretation was that it was a personal injury to him and his credibility, as well as to American power. He explained this sentiment to *New York Post* reporter James Wechsler:

> What worried him was that Khrushchev might interpret his reluctance to wage nuclear war as a symptom of an American loss of nerve. Some day, he said, the time might come when he would have to run the supreme risk to convince Khrushchev that conciliation did not mean humiliation. "If Khrushchev wants to rub my nose in the dirt," he told Wechsler, "it's all over." But how to convince Khrushchev short of a showdown? "That son of a bitch won't pay any attention to words," the President said bitterly on another occasion. "He has to see you move."[46]

TRUE GRIT AND CRISIS DIPLOMACY

The missile crisis illuminates what came to be considered a requisite personality trait of the cold war: being tough. Gritty American determination had become the respected and expected stance of American leaders under stress in confrontations with the Soviets from the earliest days of the cold war. When Truman, for example, dispatched an aircraft carrier, four cruisers, a destroyer flotilla, and the battleship *Missouri* to counter Soviet pressure on the Turkish Straits, he told Acheson, "We might as well find out whether the Russians [are] bent on world conquest now as in five or ten years."[47] Clark Clifford gave more formal expression to this sentiment when he advised Harry Truman, in a memo, in late

1946: "The language of military power is the only language which disciples of power politics understand. The United States must use that language in order that Soviet leaders will realize that our government is determined to uphold the interest of its citizens and the rights of small nations. Compromise and concessions are considered, by the Soviets, to be evidence of weakness and they are encouraged by our 'retreats' to make new and greater demands."[48]

The American concern with its appearance of strength was a mark of the Kennedy administration. One White House aide recalled that, especially after the failure of the Bay of Pigs, "Nobody in the White House wanted to be soft. . . . Everybody wanted to show they were just as daring and bold as everybody else."[49]

In the Cuban crisis, the cold war ethic of being tough exacerbated the discrepancies between the necessities of force and the necessities of diplomacy and negotiation. As a result, diplomacy was almost entirely eclipsed. In fact, it was hardly tried. According to Adam Yarmolinsky, an inside observer of the executive committee of the National Security Council, "90 percent of its time" was spent studying alternative uses of troops, bombers and warships. Although the possibility of seeking withdrawal of the missiles by straightforward diplomatic negotiation received some attention within the State Department, it seems hardly to have been aired in the ExCom. "Yarmolinsky confesses that it is curious that no negotiations were considered. Nor were economic pressures ever suggested by the foreign affairs bureaucracy. Only a series of military plans emerged, and they varied from a blockade to a preemptive strike.[50]

Kennedy knew the Russians had deployed missiles on October 16. But instead of facing Soviet Foreign Secretary Gromyko with the evidence while the Russian was giving the president false assurances that missiles were not being installed, the president blandly listened without comment. Whether or not the Russians believed that Kennedy must have known, the effect of the charade was an absence of serious negotiations. Instead of using private channels to warn the Russians that he knew and intended to act, Kennedy chose to give notice to the Russians in a nationwide TV address. After that, a Soviet withdrawal had to be in public, and it almost had to be a humiliation. When the Soviets attempted nonetheless to bargain for a graceful retreat, their path was blocked. Kennedy refused Khrushchev's offer of a summit meeting "until Khrushchev first accepted, as a result *of our deeds* as well as our statements, the U.S. determination in the matter."[51] A summit meeting, Kennedy concluded, had to be rejected; for he was intent on offering the Russians "nothing that would tie our hands." We would only negotiate with that which would "strengthen our stand."[52] If there were to be any deals, Kennedy wanted them to seem a part of American munificence.

He did not want a compromise to be tied to the central issue of what he conceived to be a test of American will and resolve. "[W]e must stand absolutely firm now. Concessions must come at the end of negotiation, not at the beginning," Robert Kennedy cautioned.[53]

In other words, the Soviets had to submit to American strength before any real concessions could take place. When Khrushchev offered to exchange the Cuban missiles for the Jupiter missiles stationed in Turkey, Kennedy demurred, even though he had ordered the missiles out months earlier; in fact, he had thought they were out when Khrushchev brought them to his attention. (The Jupiters were all but worthless. A marksman with a high-powered rifle could knock them out. They took a day to ready for firing, and the Turks did not want them.)[54] Kennedy, however, did not want to appear to yield to Soviet pressure even when he might give little and receive a great deal. An agreement would have confounded the issue of will. As Kennedy's Boswell put it, the president wanted to "concentrate on a single issue—the enormity of the introduction of the missiles and the absolute necessity of their removal."[55]

In the final act of the crisis, Kennedy accepted one of two letters sent almost simultaneously by Khrushchev. One contained the demand for removal of the Turkish missiles; the other did not. Kennedy accepted the latter. Khrushchev's second letter began with a long, heartfelt, personal communication and made no mention of a *quid pro quo*. Kennedy's response was a public letter to Khrushchev, temperate in tone, in which he accepted the more favorable terms he preferred and further detailed American conditions. It is said that Kennedy published his response "in the interests of both speed and psychology."[56] But this procedure of publishing the private terms of an interchange with another head of state was a considerable departure from diplomacy. It was not negotiation; it was, in this context, a public demand. Public statements during a crisis lack flexibility. Compromise is almost foreclosed by such a device, because any bargaining after the terms have been stated seems to be a retreat that would diminish a statesman's reputation. Because reputation was the stake in Cuba as much as anything else, Kennedy's response was hardly more than a polite ultimatum. In private, Kennedy was even more forceful. Robert Kennedy told Soviet Ambassador Dobrynin: "We had to have a commitment by tomorrow that those bases would be removed. . . . If they did not remove those bases, we would remove them. . . . Time was running out. We had only a few more hours—we needed an answer immediately from the Soviet Union. . . . We must have it the next day."[57]

As a result of the crisis, force and toughness became enshrined as instruments of policy. George Kennan observed, as he left forty years of diplomatic service: "There is no presumption more terrifying than that of those who would blow up the world on the basis of their personal judgment of a transient situation. I do not propose to let the future of mankind be settled, or ended, by a group of men operating on the basis of limited perspectives and short-run calculations."[58] In spite of occasional epistles from the older diplomatist, the new managers who proliferated after Cuba routed those who most favored negotiations. In an article in the *Saturday Evening Post,* one of the last moderates of the Kennedy administration, Adlai Stevenson, was attacked for advocating "a Munich." The source of the story, it was widely rumored, was President Kennedy himself.[59]

The policy of toughness became dogma to such an extent that nonmilitary solutions to political problems were excluded. A moderate in this circumstance was restricted to suggesting limited violence. Former Undersecretary of State George Ball explained his later "devil advocacy" in Vietnam, in which he suggested that there be a troop ceiling of seventy thousand men and bombing be restricted to the South: "What I was proposing was something which I thought had a fair chance of being persuasive . . . if I had said let's pull out overnight or do something of this kind, I obviously wouldn't have been persuasive at all. They'd have said 'the man's mad.'"[60]

This peculiar search for the middle ground of a policy defined in terms of force was abetted by the sudden sense on the part of Kennedy's national security managers that the military was filled with Dr. Strangeloves. There was some warrant for this fear. Time and time again, during the crisis, the military seemed obsessed by the opportunity to demonstrate its potential. When asked what the Soviet reaction would be to a surgical raid on their missiles and men, General Curtis LeMay snapped, "There will be no reaction." When the crisis ended on Sunday, October 25, one of the Joint Chiefs suggested that they go ahead with a massive bombing the following Monday in any case. "[T]he military are mad," concluded President Kennedy.[61] Robert Kennedy recalled acidly that "many times . . . I heard the military take positions which, if wrong, had the advantage that no one would be around at the end to know."[62]

In part, it was a result of the Cuban crisis that the civilians of the American defense and foreign policy bureaucracy grew to despise the military. Hilsman reports that later in the Kennedy administration, an official prepared a mock account of a high-level meeting on Vietnam in which Averell Harriman "stated that he had disagreed for twenty years with General [Brute] Krulak [commandant of the Marines] and disagreed today, reluctantly, more than ever; he was sorry to say that he felt General Krulak was a fool and had always thought so." It is reported that President Kennedy roared with laughter upon reading this fictitious account.[63] Hilsman also delighted in telling a story about General Lyman Lemnitzer, chairman of the Joint Chiefs of Staff, who once briefed President Kennedy on Vietnam: "This is the Mekong Valley. Pointer tip hit the map. Hilsman, watching, noticed something, the pointer tip was not on the Mekong Valley, it was on the Yangtze Valley."[64] Hilsman's recollection of the general's error became a common office story.

Ironically, while the military was increasingly thought to be rather loutish and ill-prepared, civilians were starting to rely more and more on military instrumentalities in the application of which, with few exceptions, they were not trained, and whose command structure they depised as being second-rate at best. Civilian crisis managers felt, after Cuba, that they should have control and that the military could not be trusted and had to be made more responsive to the political and civilian considerations of policy. To many observers, as well as to these managers, the failures of the Cuban missile crisis were not failures of civilian judgment but of organizational responsiveness. The intelligence establishment, for instance, had not discovered the missiles until the last minute. McNamara never really secured control over the navy. U-2 flights were sent near the Soviet Union to excite Soviet radar at the height of the crisis. Until Kennedy ordered their dispersal, American fighters and bombers were wing to wing on the ground, almost inviting a preemptive Soviet blow. Moreover, American tactical nuclear weapons and nuclear-tipped IRBMs in Turkey and Italy were discovered to be unlocked and lightly guarded.[65] All this led observers and policy makers to believe that crisis management demanded the president's organizational dominance and control, because the military and intelligence organizations were inept and their judgment was not reliable or at times even sane.

CUBA AND THE AMERICAN CENTURY

After Cuba, confidence in the ability of U.S. armed superiority to command solutions to crises in a way that would favor American interests expanded in such a way that Americans again began to speak of the American century. For a period before the crisis there had been a national reexamination. There were fears of national decline in the face of startling Soviet economic growth. Advances in Russian rocketry had led Americans to believe that not only were they in a mortal competition with the Soviets, but that the outcome was uncertain. Now, however, most of these doubts seemed to have dissipated.

The Cuban missile crisis revived the sense of the American mission. Henry R. Luce once rhapsodized in a widely circulated *Life* editorial that Americans must "accept wholeheartedly our duty and opportunity as the most powerful and vital nation in the world and in consequence to exert upon the world the full impact of our influence for such purposes as we see fit, and by such means as we see fit."[66] After the crisis, Arthur Schlesinger could lyrically resurrect this tradition: "But the ultimate impact of the missile crisis was wider than Cuba, wider than even the western hemisphere. . . . Before the missile crisis people might have feared that we would use our power extravagantly or not use it at all. But the thirteen days gave the world—even the Soviet Union—a sense of American determination and responsibility in the use of power which, if sustained, might indeed become a turning point in the history of the relations between east and west."[67]

Similarly, Zbigniew Brzezinski, then a member of the planning council of the Department of State, proclaimed that American paramountcy was the lesson of Cuba. Brzezinski explained, "The U.S. is today the only effective global military power in the world."[68] In contrast to the United States, Brzezinski declared, the Soviets were not a global power. Although Khrushchev may at one time have believed otherwise, the Cuban crisis demonstrated the limits of Soviet capabilities. "The Soviet leaders were forced, because of the energetic response by the United States, to the conclusion that their apocalyptic power [nuclear deterrent power] was insufficient to make the Soviet Union a global power. Faced with a showdown, the Soviet Union didn't dare to respond even in an area of its regional predominance—in Berlin. . . . It had no military capacity to fight in Cuba, or in Vietnam, or to protect its interests in the Congo." No doubt the historic American sense of divine purpose and the almost Jungian need to be the guarantor of global order received a strong fillip from the Cuban crisis. Brzezinski concluded: "What should be the role of the United States in this period? To use our power responsibly and constructively so that when the American paramountcy ends, the world will have been launched on a constructive pattern of development towards international stability. . . . The ultimate objective ought to be the shaping of a world of cooperative communities."[69]

The overwhelming belief of policymakers in American superiority seriously eroded deterrence. The Soviet Union reached the same conclusion as the United States—that a preponderance of military power, ranging across the spectrum of force from PT craft to advanced nuclear delivery systems, was the *sine qua non* of the successful exercise of political will. Before the fall of 1962, Khrushchev's strategic policy, in the words of a RAND Kremlinologist, "amounted to settling for a second-best strategic posture."[70] The missile crisis, however, manifestly demonstrated Soviet strategic weakness and exposed every Soviet debility that Khrushchev's verbal proclamation of superiority had previously covered.

CUBA AND DETERRENCE

After Cuba, the Soviet military, responding to the humiliating American stimulus, demanded a higher priority to strategic arms and a cutback on the agricultural and consumer sectors of the Soviet economy. Although Khrushchev and Kennedy were by then moving toward a detente—best symbolized by the signing of the test-ban accords of mid-1963—many in the Kremlin saw this as but a breathing spell in which the Chinese might be isolated and Soviet arms could catch up. Naval preparations, especially the building of Polaris-type submarines, were intensified.[71] Soviet amphibious landing capability—something in which the Soviets had shown little interest before—was revitalized and expanded. As Thomas W. Wolfe noted: "From the time of the first test-launching . . . of 1957 to mid-1961 only a handful of ICBM's had been deployed. . . . After Cuba, the pace of deployment picked up, bringing the total number of operational ICBM launchers to around 200 by the time of Khrushchev's ouster."[72] Although the West still outnumbered the Russians by four to one in numbers of launchers at the time, the Russians worked furiously and by September 1968 they commanded a larger force than the United States.[73] Worldwide "blue water" Soviet submarine patrols were initiated; and a decision was made under Brezhnev and Kosygin to extend the Soviet navy to "remote areas of the world's oceans previously considered a zone of supremacy of the fleets of the imperialist powers."[74]

After the missile crisis, the cold war establishmentarian John McCloy, representing President Kennedy, was host to Soviet Deputy Foreign Minister V. V. Kuznetzov. McCloy secured an affirmation from Kuznetzov that the Soviets would indeed observe their part of the agreement to remove the missiles and bombers from Cuba. But the Soviet leader warned, "Never will we be caught like this again."[75]

The Soviets were to yield again to U.S. strength in Vietnam and the Middle East. But each time, the usable strategic leverage of the United States grew weaker. Thus the structure of the international system and international stability was shaken in three ways.

First, the United States became confident that its power would prevail because global politics had become "unifocal."[76] But American military primacy began to erode as soon as it was proclaimed, when the Soviets fought to gain at least a rough strategic parity.

Second, nations, once cowed, are likely to be less timid in the next confrontation. As Kennedy admitted some time later, referring to the Cuban missile crisis, "You can't have too many of those."[77] Just as Kennedy feared that he had appeared callow and faint-hearted in successive Berlin crises and thus had to be tough over Cuba, the Soviets were likely to calculate that they must appear as the more rigid party in future confrontations or risk a reputation of capitulationism. For weeks after the missile crisis, the Chinese broadcast their charges of Russian stupidity and weakness to the four corners of the globe. The Chinese labeled Khrushchev an "adventurist" as well as a "capitulationist," and therefore not fit for world communist leadership. The Russian answer was to accuse the Chinese of being even "softer" than they for tolerating the Western enclaves of Macao and Hong Kong.[78] The charge of who was the most capitulationist, the Chinese or the Russians, grew almost silly; but these puerile exchanges had their own dangers in terms of deterrence.

Third, once a threat is not carried out—even after an appearance of a willingness to carry it out has been demonstrated—the ante is upped just a bit more. Morgenthau described a two-step process in nuclear gamesmanship, "diminishing credibility of the threat and ever bolder challenges to make good on it. . . . [T]he psychological capital of deterrence has been nearly expended and the policy of deterrence will be close to bankruptcy. When they reach that point, the nations concerned can choose one of three alternatives: resort to nuclear war, retreat, or resort to conventional war."[79]

Morgenthau's observation captured the dilemma of American policymakers after Cuba. The problem was that nuclear superiority had been useful, but each succeeding threat (because no nuclear threat has ever been carried out) would necessarily be weaker than the last. Yet how could security managers translate military power into political objectives without such threats? Daniel Ellsberg recalled the quandary of U.S. security managers:

> McNamara's tireless and shrewd efforts in the early sixties, largely hidden from the public to this day, [were to] gradually control the forces within the military bureaucracy that pressed for the threat and use of nuclear weapons. [He had] a creditable motive for proposing alternatives to nuclear threats. . . . [I]n this hidden debate, there was strong incentive—indeed it seemed necessary—for the civilian leaders to demonstrate that success was possible in Indochina without the need either to compromise Cold War objectives or to threaten or use nuclear weapons.
>
> Such concerns remained semi-covert: for it was seen as dangerous to lend substance to the active suspicions of military staffs and their Congressional allies that there were high Administration officials who didn't love the Bomb.[80]

But after a Cuban crisis, the option of low-level violence became more and more attractive. Conventional and limited deployments of force became increasingly necessary as conventional force was considered less forbidding than the nuclear abyss. After all, the symbolic or psychological capital of deterrence rested on the notion of resolve. And one way to demonstrate political will was through the resurrection of conventional force as an instrument of demonstrating commitment—a commitment whose alternative form was a threat of nuclear holocaust. The latter was bound to deteriorate with the advent of a viable Soviet retaliatory capability and the knowledge that the Soviets had collapsed once under a nuclear threat and might not be willing to be quite so passive again. Many national security managers found they could navigate between the Scylla of nuclear war and the Charybdis of surrender with the serendipitous discovery of the lifeboat of the 1960s—limited war. It would not prove to be a sturdy craft.

Of course, the assumptions of the planners of limited war—as they emerged victorious from the Cuban crisis—were as old as the cold war. They dated from the Truman Doctrine's Manichean presentation of a bipolar global confrontation where a gain to one party necessarily would be a loss to the other. A world order of diverse centers of power, with elements of superpower cooperation, where gains and losses would be less easily demonstrable, was not so demanding of military remedy. A multipolar world would be less congenial to the belief that the only options available to policymakers were either military force or retreat. Maneuver and negotiation, in such a world, would again become part of diplomacy. But such a development was to come about only after the tragic failure of the military remedy had been demonstrated in Vietnam.

THE BY-PRODUCTS OF SUCCESS

There were other effects related to the exuberant reaction to the Cuban crisis. As the United States began to feel that power and force were successful solvents to the more sticky problems of the cold war, the role of international law declined precipitously.[81] Hypocrisy, in the words of H. L. Mencken, "runs, like a hair in a hotdog, through the otherwise beautiful fabric of American life."[82] Moral pontifications appeared increasingly hypocritical after Cuba. The participants in the crisis knew the blockade was an act of war that had little basis in international law. After the crisis was over, even lawyers began to see law as but another instrumentality of American policy. The conclusion reached by American academics was that "International law is . . . a tool, not a guide to action. . . . It does not have a valid life of its own; it is a mere instrument available to political leaders for their own ends, be they good or evil, peaceful or aggressive. . . . [The Cuban missile crisis] merely reconfirms the irrelevance of international law in major political disputes."[83]

Dean Acheson summarized the code of the cold war as it was confirmed by the Cuban experience: "The power, prestige and position of the United States had been challenged. . . . Law simply does not deal with such questions of ultimate power. . . . The survival of states is not a matter of law."[84] George Ball, former undersecretary of state, wrote: "No one can seriously contend that we now live under a universal system or, in any realistic sense, under the 'rule of law.' We maintain the peace by preserving a precarious balance of power between ourselves and the Soviet Union—a process we used to call 'containment' before the word went out of style. It is the preservation of that balance which, regardless of how we express it, is the central guiding principle of American foreign policy."[85] The United Nations was used in the Cuban crisis, not as Kennedy had told the General Assembly the year before, as "the only true alternative to war,"[86] but as a platform where Adlai Stevenson, the eloquent American representative, could deal "a final blow to the Soviet case before world opinion."[87]

Epitomized by Cuba, crisis after crisis pointed out the stark irony: Americans, who had so long stroked the talisman of international law, now seemed to do so only when their interests were not jeopardized. Otherwise, law became merely a rhetorical flourish of U.S. policy. International law was still a part of the admonition that armed aggression and breaches of the peace cease and desist. But behind these legalistic and moralistic injunctions, the armed cop became more and more apparent. As Charles de Gaulle had observed earlier, the conclusion that American idealism was but a reflection of the American will to power became almost inescapable after the Cuban crisis.[88] Few obeisances about the need for law in international society disguised the sense that America had abandoned its ancient, liberal inheritance in the zesty pursuit of world order.

Another effect of the crisis was to differentiate the great powers— the United States and the Soviet Union—from other states, which were literally frozen out of a major role in structuring global politics. After all, the major chips of big-power poker were simply not accessible to other governments—even those with modest and nominally independent nuclear forces. For no other nations had the capability of making even plausible calculations of either preemptive or second-strike blows against a great power, much less basing national strategies on such possibilities. As a result, Europeans were offered the appearance of some control in their nuclear lot with the ill-fated multilateral force. But the nuclear trigger was still in the hands of the United States, and so was the final squeeze. Not only were the weapons of great-power diplomacy increasingly inaccessible to other states, but the other tools of statecraft also receded from the grasp of those with modest resources. The spy, for instance, was largely replaced by satellite reconnaissance. Intellectual musings on great-power conflicts became differentiated from other strategic thinking. Gradually, the Soviets and the Americans created a shared private idiom of force; and a curious dialogue began between the congressional budget messages of the secretary of defense and the periodic revisions of *Military Strategy* by Marshal Sokolovsky.[89]

Allies became mere appurtenances of power whose purpose, in the duopolistic structure of international society, was increasingly symbolic. Thus, for example, the Organization of American States was asked to validate the U.S. blockade at the same time the American quarantine was announced. Similarly, Dean Acheson flew to Paris and other European capitals to confer with American allies about the coming confrontation over Cuba.

> "Your President does me great honor," de Gaulle said, "to send me so distinguished an emissary. I assume the occasion to be of appropriate importance." Acheson delivered President Kennedy's letter, with the text of the speech to be delivered at P-hour, 7 P.M. Washington time. He offered to summarize it. De Gaulle raised his hand in a delaying gesture that the long-departed Kings of France might have envied. "May we be clear before you start," he said. "Are you consulting or informing me?" Acheson confessed that he was there to inform, not to consult. "I am in favor of independent decisions," de Gaulle acknowledged.[90]

For the Europeans, Gaullists and leftists alike, it appeared that there was a high likelihood of nuclear annihilation without representation.[91] In spite of European gestures of support, the alliance received a shock from which it did not recover. The British, in the midst of a vicious internal debate about whether or not to abandon nuclear weapons, decided they were necessary to buy even minimum consideration from their American allies. The French did not debate; they accelerated their nuclear programs while withdrawing from a military role in the alliance in 1964. Henceforth, NATO would be, in Henry Kissinger's words, a "troubled partnership."[92]

On the Soviet side, it was equally apparent that Russian interests would not be sacrificed to fellow socialist states. Castro was plainly sold out. The weak promise tendered by the Kennedy administration not to invade the island was probably cold comfort as Castro saw his military benefactors beat a hasty retreat from American power. Embarrassingly, Castro began to echo the capitulationist theme of Chinese broadcasts. Privately Castro said that if he could, he would have beaten Khrushchev to within an inch of his life for what he did. Soviet Foreign Minister Mikoyan was dispatched to Cuba and stayed there for weeks, not even returning to the bedside of his dying wife, but Castro's fury was unabated. Whatever the motive for Khrushchev's moves in Cuba, the Chinese were also enraged.[93] Any attempts the Soviets had made to dissuade the Chinese from assuming a nuclear role prior to October 1962 lost their validity when it became obvious that the Russians would not risk their own destruction for an associate.

By 1963 a new era of East-West relations was unfolding. The Americans still cultivated the asymmetrical assumptions of the cold war, but the Soviet Union was at least admitted as a junior partner in a duopolistic international system that was now increasingly characterized as one marked by detente.

Indications of this new spirit appeared in the administration's desire for improved economic relations with the Soviet Union. This effort extended into the early years of the Johnson administration as Lyndon Johnson spoke enthusiastically of improved East-West economic relations as a bridge-building exercise and Zbigniew Brzezinski wrote early in 1965 in his book *Alternative to Partition*, sponsored by the prestigious Council on Foreign Relations, "The Cold War in Europe has lost its old meaning. There was a vitality and a passion to it as long as either side had reason to believe that it could prevail and as long as either side felt genuinely threatened by the other. Neither condition truly exists today."[94] The relaxation was favorable to Kennedy, who wanted to explore diplomacy with the Soviets without the ideological rancor that had poisoned previous relations and who had a vision of Soviet responsibility that would be enlarged upon by succeeding administrations. The Soviets too sought a detente. Another series of confrontations, given their acknowledged strategic inferiority, could hardly be successful. Moreover, the Chinese began to present formidable ideological and political difficulties for the Soviets. The Soviets' new interest in improved relations with the Americans brought intense fears from China of American-Soviet collusion. At the same time, the Soviets began to fear a Sino-American agreement that would be detrimental to their interest. As chief ideologue of the Soviet Union, Michael Suslov explained, in early 1964:

> With a stubbornness worthy of a better cause the Chinese leaders attempt to prevent the improvement of Soviet-American relations, representing this as "plotting with the imperialists." At the same time the Chinese government makes feverish attempts to improve relations with Britain, France, Japan, West Germany, and Italy. It is quite clear that they would not refuse to improve relations with the United States but as yet do not see favorable circumstances for such an endeavor.[95]

THE ECONOMICS OF CONTAINMENT

The events of October 1962 and the euphoria and renewed sense of American power that followed this great climax of the cold war also had as a by-product the obscuring of economic elements of the new era of world politics that seemed to be opening up. By 1961 and 1962 the international position of the American dollar had begun to weaken markedly. A favorable balance of payments situation in the years after World War II had turned to a small but nagging deficit of around $1.4 billion a year by 1956. Between 1958 and 1960 this average annual deficit had jumped to more than $3.5 billion and during the early 1960s persisted at just over $2.5 billion annually.[96]

Making this situation especially perplexing was the fact that this deteriorating U.S. balance of payments position could not be readily explained in a conventional manner. Normally a persistent deficit in a nation's balance of payments situation can be attributed to domestic circumstances, usually inflation, leading to its goods and services being too expensive to maintain a competitive position in world markets. Under these circumstances (and assuming relatively low barriers to trade) a nation imports more than it exports, leading to a net outflow of wealth and a deficit in its balance of payments. Another source of such a deficit might be an export of currency to finance foreign investment, but in this case the return of profits, fees, and royalties should in the long-run equal or even exceed outflow, leading ultimately to a net gain for balance of payments.

Recent analysis of the American international economic position during the cold war years suggests that the growing balance of payments problem cannot be explained in these traditional terms. Indeed, for the fifteen years following World War II, U.S. private sector transactions showed an annual average surplus. Between 1960 and 1964 these private transactions slipped slightly into deficit (less than $400 million a year on the average), then recovered to a surplus of more than $1.2 billion in 1965 and 1966, before sliding into deficit again between 1967 and 1970. However, even in the troubled decade of 1960 to 1970, the more than $2 billion annual average deficit cannot be explained easily by conventional economic factors. Throughout the late 1950s and well into 1963 and 1964 the American domestic economy was actually in recession, the recovery from which during late 1963, 1964, and 1965 was marked by sustained economic growth without significant inflation. Thus, it would not seem that American goods were priced out of the world market, leading to an excess of imports. Moreover, American export strength has never rested with low-price goods, but rather with relatively high-priced but technologically sophisticated goods and agricultural commodities.

International conditions facilitating the movement of private capital developed after 1958 and led to an outflow of American private investment in the late 1950s and early 1960s, especially to Europe. But it is not clear that these seemingly negative short-run transactions were detrimental to the American balance of payments situation in the long run. Thus, Raymond Vernon, a foremost student of American multinational corporations and their investment behavior has noted[97] that one outcome of this investment activity in the late 1950s and early 1960s has been development of substantial American claims on the assets of other countries. Moreover, by the end of the 1960s much of what the United States was exporting to the world was in the form of services:[98] "The rewards to the U.S. economy from these activities are to be found not in the merchandise balance, but in sales of business services, in interest and dividends, and in the build-up of the earnings left abroad in subsidiaries and branches. When these are taken into account, the U.S. performance appears a good deal less bleak."[99] Thus it would seem that the balance of payments problems of the 1950s and early 1960s cannot be easily explained by focusing on private foreign economic transactions. Instead, we must turn our attention to the foreign expenditures of the U.S. government, and in so doing we are drawn to the economic dimension of the diplomacy of violence.

America's International Economic Position in the 1960s

The underlying causes of the balance of payments crisis that confronted the Kennedy administration in the early 1960s seem best understood in terms of the long-run and accumulating costs of containment increasingly dependent on the instrumentalities of military threat and capability. Containment relied originally on the Marshall Plan and then in time came to rest on NATO, military intervention in Korea, and subsequently large economic and military assistance to Europe and the third world— in short, foreign expenditures by the U.S. government that in most instances did not have a financial return as private foreign investment might have yielded. The upshot was, logically and in practice, a net deficit in American balance of payments. It is, of course, accurate to respond that these expenditures purchased something of great value for the United States—national security. However, this is a form of transaction that cannot be factored into a balance of payments statement.

These large public expenditures contributed decisively to a negative balance and accumulating quantities of American dollars in the hands of foreigners. Moreover, during the 1950s and 1960s, as this quantity of dollars grew steadily, the amount of gold backing them remained relatively unchanged. As long as those governments and traders holding dollars maintained their confidence in the capacity and willingness of the U.S. government to back these dollars, they might be content to hold and use the currency. By 1960, however, foreign confidence in the recession-ridden American economy's ability to sustain growth (while the Eisenhower administration continued to expand military assistance and other forms of foreign expenditure) dwindled. By October 1960, the American deficit had become sufficiently large that many of those holding dollars were willing to gamble that the United States would have to devalue the dollar. Accordingly, dollars were exchanged for gold on the London free gold market, forcing up the price of gold from $35 to $41 an ounce. This speculative surge was fueled in some measure by expressions of official concern about the balance of payments situation.

The roots of this situation go back to the Marshall Plan. During the late 1940s, the reconstruction of Western Europe—the bedrock of containment—required a large infusion of American foreign assistance to the West Europeans so that they might finance the purchase of American goods and services necessary to European recovery. Similarly, between 1949 and the early 1950s, the United States provided large amounts of assistance to fund the establishment of NATO through the MDAP and, subsequently, spent billions extending containment to Asia. This combination of economic and military assistance meant that the United States was running slight deficits in its balance of payments by 1956, although net private transactions were in the black by more than $3 billion annually. Nevertheless, these government expenditures were not regarded in the early years of the cold war as normal transactions, and they were not, therefore, viewed with alarm. By and large, they were seen as temporary and, over the long-run, nonrecurring.[100] In any event, they were thought essential to the national security and acceptable as long as the annual deficit remained, as it did, around $1.5 billion a year.

Between 1958 and 1960, however, the deficits increased dramatically—up to an average of $3.7 billion per year. A combination of factors contributed to some deterioration (although not a net deficit) in private transactions. For the most part, these events marked the culmination of trends set in motion by the Marshall Plan. Thus, between 1958 and 1960 the industrialized economies of Western Europe had recovered sufficiently to be able to enter into export competition with the United States. At the same time and with the encouragement of the United States, Europeans moved forward with the creation in 1958 of the European Economic Community (EEC) or the Common Market. A key element of the Common Market included some tariff protection to encourage even more rapid development of a truly European economy. At the same time all European currencies became convertible with one another so as to facilitate the movement of capital for investment purposes. Finally, this combination of economic growth and internationalization of capital *behind* the Common Market tariff wall served as incentives for American investment to move behind these tariff barriers. Trade through these tariffs proved difficult, but on the other hand the internationalization of capital within Europe and growing European economies led to American businessmen "discovering" Europe, and there occurred a tripling of their investment there in the late 1950s and early 1960s.[101]

In the short run, therefore, there was a reduction in the positive private transactions balance. Far more important, however, was the fact that American foreign and military expenditures could no longer be regarded as temporary. Indeed, if anything, increased Soviet activism implied an indefinite and perhaps growing level of such expenditures. As this fact began to sink in during the late 1950s, concern with the constantly growing deficit began to increase in official American circles and, inevitably, abroad. This concern was high in Western Europe and especially in France, where this seemingly unending stream of U.S. government spending came to be viewed as a potential threat to new-found prosperity.

The European position was paradoxical in that in the past they had encouraged U.S. foreign assistance to stimulate their own growth. Similarly, during the late 1940s and early 1950s and even at the start of the 1960s, the Europeans benefited from the American military presence. At the same time, however, the European economy was now being forced to absorb large quantities of public as well as private investment dollars—dollars that seemed to have less and less gold to back them. The problems posed for the Europeans were twofold. First, of course, was the growing doubt that the Americans would be able to exchange gold for their dollars, and as the number of dollars increased, the doubts could only increase. Nevertheless, if governments and international traders were willing to continue using the dollars as if they had backing (i.e., as the international money rather than the gold to which the dollar was theoretically pegged in value under the postwar Bretton Woods system of monetary agreements), there need not be an international monetary crisis. However, for this forebearance, the Europeans had to pay an increasing price in terms of their own domestic economies.

Insofar as the Europeans remained faithful to the postwar International Monetary Fund rules. Thus, for example, the German, French, or British governments were obligated to exchange their currencies for dol-devaluations or revaluations upward were not permitted under International Monetary Fund rules. Thus, for example, the German or French or British governments were obligated to exchange their currencies for dollars at a fixed rate whenever the holders of dollars (e.g., a French, British, or German merchant engaged in export-import trade) wanted to convert them into francs, pounds, or marks. As long as the holders of dollars were willing to use them, there was little consequence for European domestic economies. But as confidence in the dollar began to slip, the demand for other, seemingly stronger currencies or gold would increase. The governments responsible for the currencies in demand were obligated to supply the marks, francs, pounds, or whatever.

The net effect of this process was an increasing supply of the Europeans' currencies in their own economies as they sought to sop up the steady stream of dollars and maintain the fixed exchange rate system. To the extent that their own economies grew faster than this supply of money, inflation might be controllable. But it was apparent to European national bankers and economic planners that the expanding presence of dollars constituted a virtually uncontrollable inflationary pressure both in the short and especially in the long term. As long as the fixed exchange rate system remained in place, the European domestic money supply would have to increase, not necessarily because of real growth in the production of their own goods and services (although this was taking place as well), but in response to diminishing confidence in the bloated quantity of dollars sloshing about in the European and world economy.

Thus, by the end of the 1950s, American economic policy had finally succeeded in fostering the rebirth of the European economy but, paradoxically, the decline of European confidence in the dollar. At the same time, the American foreign and defense policymaking community was not prepared to forego what it regarded as an essential instrument of containment—U.S. foreign and military assistance—at the very moment the cold war seemed to be reaching a point of tolerable adjustment.

Sound and Fury . . . and More of the Same

The American response did not attempt to remove the source of the balance of payments problem—American economic assistance and military spending abroad. Instead, during the last two years of the Eisenhower administration, conditions were attached to these programs that were designed to increase American exports and otherwise reverse or restrain the flow of dollars abroad. First, in the case of economic assistance, recipient countries were required to use their American economic assistance dollars to purchase American goods and services. Second, military expenditure regulations were restructured so as to emphasize a "Buy America" approach. By the 1960s, these latter provisions required that government agencies purchase American goods, although this meant frequently paying as much as 50 percent more for goods and services than would have been the case if purchased from foreign suppliers. By the late 1960s, more than 90 percent of U.S. economic assistance funds were being spent in the United States. In many instances, however, this meant that the cost of aid projects increased by as much as 30 percent to recipient countries.[102]

In summary, the cost of the Buy America measures led to the cost of government overseas programs increasing for the American taxpayer. At the same time, American economic assistance recipients, forced to spend their receipts on more expensive American goods and services, were actually receiving less for their aid dollars. Moreover, aid recipients were frequently subsidizing noncompetitive American exporters. In terms of balance of payments, however, these measures combined with loan repayments from previous years, allowed the United States actually to make money on much of its economic program in the 1960s. Nevertheless, military assistance spending remained high, and the net flow of U.S. government-generated dollars was, therefore, only slowed but not stopped.

The Kennedy administration maintained the "tied aid" concept and undertook a number of scattered measures including minor adjustments in the tax laws and interest rates in an effort to repatriate more U.S. private dollars. When these actions did little to change the rate of private investment by the mid-1960s, President Johnson introduced a program of voluntary constraints that were subsequently made mandatory. Moreover, presidents Kennedy and Johnson initiated vigorous arms sales programs abroad in an effort to improve the American export picture.

In the area of export expansion, Kennedy sought and received new trade legislation from Congress, the Trade Expansion Act of 1962. The negotiating authority under the Trade Expansion Act (TEA) was to be used by the administration to bring about significant mutual reduction in tariffs between the United States and Europe so as to allow for the expansion of U.S. exports. There were, however, other motives involved. Specifically, the TEA gave the president the authority to negotiate tariff reductions of 50 percent across the board and to eliminate tariffs altogether on those product groups where U.S. and EEC exports equaled 80 percent or more of world exports.[103] In the latter case, however, this "dominant supplier" provision was meaningful only if the British were in the Common Market, for otherwise there were very few EEC-U.S. traded product groups that could meet the 80 percent requirement.

Thus the TEA of 1962 was oriented toward export expansion, but the United States was also trying to use the TEA's dominant supplier provision as an inducement to the EEC countries to admit the British into the EEC. It was the Kennedy administration's hope that British entry would offset the economically and politically troublesome French and transform the EEC into an outward-looking Europe more open to U.S. exports. De Gaulle saw through the American effort, however, and fearing that Britain would serve as an American Trojan horse in Europe, vetoed British entry into the EEC in 1962.[104] Kennedy's "grand design" for export expansion, British entry in the Common Market, and the diminution of De Gaulle's political and economic influence in Europe was never consummated. Some tariff reductions were brought about over the extended "Kennedy round" of negotiations, but, generally the EEC turned increasingly inward and fostered expansion of its internal trade.[105] American exports did increase, but only rapidly enough to very nearly balance American imports—and certainly not enough to offset the continued export of American dollars associated with U.S. military spending.

Indecision and Marginal Measures

By the mid-1960s, therefore, the various American efforts to check or reverse the U.S. balance of payments deficits could claim only the most marginal success. Indeed, after 1965 and 1966, the deficit began to creep back up toward $2 billion plus, in spite of a booming U.S. economy in which U.S. exports were increasing. American military spending continued to expand at a rate far in excess of the surplus generated by private trade and investment income. And, of course, a major source of this growing hemorrhage of dollars was the escalating conflict in Southeast Asia. Moreover, once the war became thoroughly Americanized after 1966, the costs of military spending cut even deeper. Not only did the export of dollars directly attributable to military spending increase to more than $3.2 billion annually, but the domestic inflation set in motion by the war undercut the American competitive position abroad as the prices of American exports increased.

Choosing 1967 as a typical year for the international economic position of the United States during the 1960s, economist Robert Stevens summarizes the conditions underlying the American balance of payments situation:

> When we compare the gross and net impacts on the figures of these three major types of outflow, we find that in 1967 Pentagon-inspired arms exports offset only 29 percent of gross foreign military spending, whereas 86 percent of U.S. foreign aid was offset by purchases made in the United States and 133 percent of private investment outflows were offset by return flows of foreign investment income. Thus, viewed in this context, the government's net foreign military spending has had a much more deleterious

effect on the balance of payments than foreign aid or private foreign investment.[106]

This situation could always be rationalized domestically, however, for the outflow of dollars was presumably buying security and, until very late in the 1960s, the American economy felt no negative effects of this spending.

The situation abroad, especially in Europe, was of course quite different, for Europeans were more or less compelled to absorb the exported American dollars. Insofar as the dollar was the basis of the industrialized world's economy, serving as the key currency (and the United States as a kind of banker for the system), the United States could, unlike other countries, escape until very late the need to settle its deficits. As the banker, the United States possessed seemingly unlimited credit symbolized by an unending series of deficits, which the rest of the world and primarily Europe were asked to assume by holding rather than converting American dollars. In time, however, the feared inflation of European economies began, and pressure for international action increased.

During the 1960s a series of short-run measures were developed to deal with speculative pressures as currency swaps, short-term credit arrangements, and an international gold pool were established. In addition, the United States created a new form of credit with issuance of medium-term securities (Roosa bonds) designed to repatriate some of the excess dollar assets in European and other central banks. For a while, these arrangements stemmed somewhat the short-term flow of dollars and diminishing American gold into Europe. Nonetheless, these measures did not get at the fundamental weakness of the dollar's position—a currency that was serving as the key international currency even as it was being used to finance global containment. This patched-up system stumbled through most of the 1960s, then staggered under the added burden of even more military spending in the late 1960s and, along with the foreign policy it was to finance, collapsed in the swamp of Vietnam.

By the end of the 1960s it was increasingly clear, therefore, that the American dollar could no longer be viewed as an instrument simultaneously serving American foreign policy and the international economic system. The actors comprising this system now had economic and political interests of their own. It mattered not that American balance of payments deficits had in large measure financed the development of those interests. For they were no longer congruent with an American foreign policy that seemed to require that industrialized countries of the world passively and indefinitely absorb American dollars as their own economies inflated.

CONCLUSION

Thus, by the mid 1960s, the beginning of the end of the cold war had precipitated a change in the global structure of power even as it deflected attention from another growing crisis. American paramountcy had been self-proclaimed, the seeds of detente were sown by a shared vision of nuclear oblivion, and the ingredients for a great power condominium were becoming clear. Tragically and ironically, however, the lessons of the Cuban missile crisis—that success in international crisis was largely a matter of national guts; that the opponent would yield to superior force; that presidential control of force can be suitable, selective, swift, effective, and responsive to civilian authority; and that crisis management and execution is too dangerous and events move too rapidly for anything but the tightest secrecy—all these inferences contributed to the Johnson decision to use American air power against Hanoi in 1965. Even the language of the Gulf of Tonkin Resolution was almost identical to that which Kennedy's legal advisers had drawn up for the OAS in October 1962.[107]

The Cuban crisis changed the international environment but riveted American expectations to the necessities of the diplomacy of violence. Although the Cuban crisis created substantial changes in distinguishing superpowers from other states, the realization both of the parity of the superpowers and the indications that they could join in a relationship that had some elements of condominium and other elements of the classic balance of power was suppressed until the end of the Vietnam War.

Finally, the shimmering image of the "American century" blinded American policymakers to the magnitude of an emerging crisis in the industrialized world's political economy. The construction of containment and the surmounting of the apparent strategic crisis of 1961 and 1962 were all immesnsely costly, requiring a steady flow of American capital into the reconstruction of the industrialized world's political economy. Just as the Soviet-American political-military confrontation at the center of the cold war climaxed in Berlin and in the waters off Cuba, the political economic dynamics that the Marshall Plan and the flow of American government dollars had sought to set in motion finally took hold in Europe. The eventual result would be the establishment of an international political economy of interdependence that no single government could control. But reflection, modesty, and humility were not characteristic traits of the activists who had just managed one of the great turning points of history. Thus, the importance of the opportunities and risks attendant to these new transnational economic forces seems to have been misunderstood or, if comprehended, deemed manageable as the missile crisis had been managed.

In retrospect, therefore, the great cold war strategic crisis of 1961 and 1962 and the economic crisis of the early and mid-1960s seems to mark the beginning of a major transformation of the international system and American foreign policy. The realization of this profound fact was obscured in some measure by the management of the crises themselves. In any event, the full implications of this transformation could not be dealt with until the American agony in Vietnam drew to a close.

NOTES

1. Revisionist critiques of the Cuban crisis are becoming more frequent. But most are rather polemical and thin. For a sample of some of the better ones, see Richard J. Walton, "The Cuban Missile Crisis" in *Cold War and Counter Revolution* (Baltimore: Penguin Books, 1972), pp. 103–43; Leslie Dewart, "The Cuban Crisis Revisited," *Studies on the Left*, Vol. 5 (Spring 1965), pp. 15–40; John Kenneth Galbraith, "Storm over Havana: Who Were the Real Heroes?" (review of *Thirteen Days* by Robert F. Kennedy), *Book World*, January 19, 1969, p. 16; Ronald Steel, "Endgame," (review of *The Missile Crisis* by Elie Abel), *New York Review of Books*, March 13, 1969, reprinted in Ronald Steel, *Imperialists and Other Heroes* (New York: Vintage, 1971), p. 115; Louise FitzSimmons, *The Kennedy Doctrine* (New York: Random House, 1972), pp. 126–173, and R. Ned Lebow, "The Cuban Missile Crisis: Reading the Lessons Correctly," *Political Science Quarterly*, Vol. 98 (Fall 1983), pp. 431–458. For a criticism of the interpretation developed here see Irving Janis, *Group-think*, 2d ed. (Boston: Houghton Mifflin, 1982), p. 291.
2. Roger Hilsman, *To Move a Nation* (New York: Dell, 1967), pp. 48, 157; also cited in Steel, op. cit., p. 115.
3. Hans J. Morgenthau, *Truth and Power, Essays of a Decade, 1960–1970* (New York: Praeger, 1970), p. 158.
4. A current review of this enormous literature is contained in Charles F. Hermann, ed., *International Crises: Insights from Behavioral Research* (New York: Free Press, 1972).
5. Cited by Coral Bell, *The Conventions of Crisis: A Study in Diplomatic Management* (London: Oxford University Press, 1971), p. 2.
6. Alexander George et al., *The Limits of Coercive Diplomacy* (Boston: Little, Brown, 1971), p. 132.
7. Henry Pachter, "J. F. K. as an Equestrian Statue: On Myths and Myth Makers," *Salmagundi* (Spring 1966), cited in George, op. cit.
8. Albert and Roberta Wohlstetter, "Controlling the Risks in Cuba," *Adelphi Paper No. 17* (London: Institute for Strategic Studies, April 1965), p. 19.
9. Robert F. Kennedy, *Thirteen Days: A Memoir of the Cuban Missile Crisis* (with afterword by Richard Neustadt and Graham T. Allison) (New York: W. W. Norton, 1971), p. 48.
10. Ibid., p. 22; Theodore C. Sorensen, *Kennedy* (New York: Bantam, 1969), p. 705. Hermann, op. cit., p. 33 and Arthur M. Schlesinger, Jr., *Robert Kennedy and His Times* (New York: Ballantine, 1979), pp. 546–547.
11. See Thomas W. Milburn, "The Management of Crisis," in Herman, op. cit., esp. pp. 263–266. But see Janis, op. cit.

12. Kennedy, op. cit., pp. 48–49.
13. Sorensen, op. cit., p. 705.
14. Arthur M. Schlesinger, Jr., *A Thousand Days* (Boston: Houghton Mifflin, 1965), pp. 840–841.
15. Jack Raymond, *Power at the Pentagon* (New York: Harper & Row, 1964), pp. 285–286.
16. Elie Abel, *The Missile Crisis* (Philadelphia: Lippincott, 1969). Abel interviewed the witnesses to this episode, some of whom did not agree as to Anderson's exact words. Anderson, Abel reports, could not recall ever having said this.
17. William A. Hamilton, III, "The Decline and Fall of the Joint Chiefs of Staff," *The Naval War College Review*, Vol. 24 (April 1972), p. 47.
18. Abel, op. cit., p. 151–152; Hilsman, op. cit., p. 214; W. E. Knox, "Close-up of Khrushchev During a Crisis," *The New York Times Magazine*, November 18, 1962, p. 128.
19. Kennedy, op. cit., p. 55.
20. Irving Janis, *Victims of Group Think* (Boston: Houghton Mifflin, 1972), p. 163; Henry Pachter, *Collision Course* (New York: Praeger, 1963), p. 58.
21. Leslie Gelb and Morton Halperin, "The Ten Commandments of the Foreign Affairs Bureaucracy," *Harpers*, Vol. 244 (June 1972), pp. 28–37; Leslie Gelb, "The Essential Domino: American Politics and Vietnam," *Foreign Affairs*, Vol. 50 (April 1972), pp. 459–476.
22. Homer E. Capehart: "U.S. Should Act, Stop 'Examining Cuba,' " *U.S. News & World Report*, September 10, 1962, p. 45.
23. *The New York Times*, September 19, 1962.
24. "Cuban Crisis," *Data Digest* (New York: Keynote Publications, 1963), p. 35, cited by Thomas Halper, *Foreign Policy Crisis: Appearance and Reality in Decision Making* (Columbus, Ohio: Merrill, 1971), p. 132.
25. "Notes of the Month: Cuba: A U.S. Election Issue," *World Today*, Vol. 18, (November 1962), p. 543; Halper, op. cit., p. 132.
26. Quincy Wright, "The Cuban Quarantine of 1962," in John G. Stoessinger and Alan Westin (eds.), *Power and Order* (New York: Harcourt, Brace and World, 1964), p. 186.
27. *Economist*, October 6, 1962, p. 15.
28. "Afraid of Everything but War," *I. F. Stone's Weekly*, September 17, 1962, p. 1.
29. Quoted in Steel, op. cit., p. 119.
30. Abel, op. cit., p. 78.
31. Steel, op. cit., p. 121.
32. Sorensen, op. cit., p. 688.
33. George et al., op. cit., p. 89.
34. Hilsman, op. cit., p. 195.
35. *The New York Times*, November 12, 1962.
36. *Wilmington Morning News*, January 25, 1974.
37. Walter W. Layson, "The Political and Strategic Aspects of the 1962 Cuban Missile Crisis," unpub. Ph.D. Diss. (University of Virginia, 1969), pp. 18–87; Thomas W. Wolfe, *Soviet Power and Europe, 1945–1970* (Baltimore: Johns Hopkins University Press, 1970), pp. 73–99, 100–194.
38. Henry Kissinger, "Reflections on Cuba," *The Reporter*, Vol. 27 (November 22, 1962), p. 22.
39. Interview, December 17, 1962, *Public Papers of the Presidents, John F. Kennedy* (Washington, D.C.: U.S. Government Printing Office, 1963), p. 898.
40. *The New York Times*, December 6, 1970. According to the authoritative *Aviation*

Week, the Russians also began to schedule regular stops of long-range aircraft at about the same time. December 21, 1970, pp. 16–17.

41. For a description and forceful but private insistence that the building of the Soviet submarine base at Cienfuegos, Cuba, be halted, see Henry Kissinger, *The White House Years* (Boston: Little, Brown, 1979), pp. 636–651. Nevertheless, sporadic press reports indicate that missile-firing Soviet submarines were putting into Cuba long afterwards; see Barry Blechman and Stephanie Levinson, "U.S. Policy and Soviet Subs," *New York Times,* October 22, 1974; *Washington Post,* October 12, 1979, p. A15. Pincus reports that in 1972 a nuclear armed "Golf II" submarine anchored off Cuba and was serviced by a Soviet tender. Another visit was made in May of 1974, by another "Golf II"—a submarine which usually carries three missiles. Neither time were the visits protested.

42. "How U.S. Voters Feel about Cuba," *Newsweek,* October 13, 1962, p.138; Halper, op cit., p. 133.

43. Kennedy, op. cit., p. 45, and "Afterword," p. 114.

44. Reston, "What Was Killed Was Not Only the President but the Promise," *The New York Times Magazine,* November 15, 1964, p. 126.

45. *The New York Times,* September 1, 1970; *New York Daily News,* August 31, 1970.

46. Schlesinger, *Thousand Days;* op. cit., p. 391.

47. Walter Millis (ed.), *The Forrestal Diaries* (New York: Viking, 1951), p. 192.

48. Arthur Krock, *Memoirs* (London: Cassel and Co., 1968), pp. 228–229.

49. Hugh Sidey, *John F. Kennedy, President* (New York: Atheneum, 1964), p. 127.

50. Adam Yarmolinsky, *The Military Establishment* (New York: Harper & Row, 1971), p. 127.

51. Kennedy, op. cit., pp. 44–45 (emphasis added).

52. Sorensen, op. cit., p. 699.

53. Schlesinger, op. cit., p. 811.

54. Hilsman, op. cit., p. 202. Donald F. Hafner, a State Department officer, in an article, "Bureaucratic Politics and those 'Frigging Missiles': JFK, Cuba and U.S. Missiles in Turkey," *Orbis,* Vol. 21 (Summer 1977), p. 313, claims that Kennedy was not surprised that the missiles were in place and that the assertion that Kennedy refused to negotiate is a "myth." More recently, however, Arthur Schlesinger, in *Robert Kennedy and His Times,* supports the idea that Kennedy was surprised (p. 559) and engaged in "no *quid pro quos*" but thought that in 4 or 5 months "matters would be resolved" (p. 563).

55. Schlesinger, *A Thousand Days,* op. cit., p. 810.

56. Sorensen, op. cit., p. 714.

57. Kennedy, op. cit., p. 87.

58. Schlesinger, op. cit., p. 397; also cited by I.F. Stone, *In a Time of Torment* (New York: Random House, 1968), p. 23.

59. Walton, op. cit., p. 119. The article was by Stewart Alsop and Charles Bartlett, "In Time of Crisis," *Saturday Evening Post,* December 8, 1962.

60. Gelb and Halperin, op. cit., p. 36.

61. Schlesinger, op. cit., p. 831; Neustadt and Allison, in "Afterword," in Kennedy, op. cit., p. 126.

62. Ibid., p. 26.

63. Hilsman, op. cit., pp. 512–513; John McDermott, "Crisis Manager," *New York Review of Books,* Vol. 9 (September 14, 1967), pp. 4–10. The fictitious paper, written by James Thompson, also took on the whole Vietnam decision-making team.

64. David Halberstam, *The Best and the Brightest* (New York: Random House, 1971), p. 255.

65. *Washington Post,* May 26, 1974.
66. Luce, *The American Century* (New York: Farrar and Rinehart, 1941), p. 23; and *Life,* February 17, 1941, p. 63. Actually, Luce had been on record with this message from the age of twenty. See W.A. Swanberg, *Luce and His Empire* (New York: Dell, 1972).
67. Schlesinger, op. cit., pp. 840–841.
68. "Background" remarks to a conference for editors and broadcasters, May 22, 1967, cited in Hans J. Morgenthau, *A New Foreign Policy for the United States* (New York: Praeger, 1969), p. 19. For Brzezinski's edited remarks, see "The Implications of Change for United States Foreign Policy," *Department of State Bulletin,* Vol. 57 (July 3, 1967), pp. 19–23.
69. Ibid.
70. Wolfe, op. cit., p. 134.
71. David Woodward, *The Russians at Sea: A History of the Russian Navy* (New York: Praeger, 1964), pp. 229–230.
72. Wolfe, op. cit., pp. 182–183.
73. Statement by Secretary of Defense Clark M. Clifford, *The Fiscal Year 1970–1974 Defense Program and Defense Budget,* Department of Defense, January 15, 1969, p. 35.
74. Fleet Admiral V. Kasatonov, "On Battle Watch," *Krasnaia Zvezda,* July 30, 1967; cited in Wolfe, op. cit., p. 446.
75. John Newhouse, *Cold Dawn: The Story of SALT* (New York: Holt, Rinehart and Winston, 1973), p. 68.
76. George Liska, *Imperial America: The International Politics of Primacy* (Baltimore: Johns Hopkins University Press, 1967), pp. 36ff.
77. K. J. Holsti, *International Politics,* 2nd ed. (Englewood Cliffs, N.J.: Prentice-Hall, 1972), p. 325.
78. Michel Tatu, *Power in the Kremlin: From Khrushchev to Kosygin* (New York: Viking, 1968), pp. 319–320.
79. Hans J. Morgenthau, *A New Foreign Policy for the United States,* pp. 212–213.
80. Daniel Ellsberg, *Papers on the War* (New York: Simon and Schuster, 1972), pp. 292–293.
81. Dean Rusk reflected earlier obligatory American statements about international legal order and American foreign policy when he declared:

> Our foreign policy has been reflected in our willingness to submit atomic weapons to international law, in feeding and clothing those striken by war, in supporting free elections and government by consent, in building factories and dams, power plants and railways, schools and hospitals, in improving seed and stock and fertilizer, in stimulating markets and improving the skills and techniques of others in a hundred different ways. Let these things stand in contrast to a foreign policy directed towards the extension of tyranny and using the big lie, sabotage, suspicion, riot and assassination as its tools. The great strength of the United States is devoted to the peaceful pursuits of our people and to the decent opinions of mankind. But it is not healthy for any regime or group of regimes to incur, by their lawless and aggressive conduct, the implacable opposition of the American people. The lawbreaker, unfortunately in the nature of things, always has the initiative, but the peace-making peoples of the world can and will make themselves strong enough to insist upon peace. [Cited in Halberstam, op. cit., p. 327.]

82. H. L. Mencken, "Editorial," *American Mercury,* Vol. 9 (November 1926), p. 287. Cited in Halper, op. cit., p. 157.

83. William P. Gerberding, "International Law and the Cuban Crisis," in Lawrence Scheinman and David Wilkinson, eds., *International Law and Political Crisis: An Analytic Casebook* (Boston: Little, Brown, 1968), pp. 209–210

84. Richard J. Barnet and Marcus Raskin, *After Twenty Years* (New York: Random House, 1965), p. 229n.

85. George Ball, "Slogans and Realities," *Foreign Affairs,* Vol. 47 (July 1969), p. 624.

86. John F. Kennedy, "Let Us Call a Truce to Terror,"address to the General Assembly of the United Nations, September 23, 1961, *Department of State Bulletin,* October 16, 1961, p. 619.

87. Schlesinger, op. cit., p. 824.

88. For General De Gaulle's analysis, see his *Mémoires de Guerre,* Vol. 2, *L'Unité* (Paris: Librairie Plon, 1956), pp. 97–98.

89. Marshal Z. D. Sokolovsky, *Military Strategy: Soviet Doctrine and Concepts* (Introduction by Raymond Garthoff) (New York: Praeger, 1963). (Subsequent editions were translated by RAND for internal use by government officials.)

90. Abel, op. cit., p. 112.

91. Amitai Etzioni, *Winning Without War* (Garden City, N.Y.: Doubleday, 1965), p. 46.

92. Henry Kissinger, *The Troubled Partnership: A Reappraisal of the Atlantic Alliance* (Garden City, N.Y.: Doubleday, 1966).

93. Adam Ulam, *Expansion and Coexistence* (New York: Praeger,1968), p. 675. Ulam (pp. 668–670) suggested that Khrushchev aimed at precluding both Chinese and German acquisition of nuclear weapons.

94. Zbigniew Brzezinski, *Alternative to Partition: For a Broader Conception of America's Role in Europe* (New York: McGraw-Hill, for the Council on Foreign Relations, 1965), p. vii.

95. Cited by Ulam, op. cit., p. 691.

96. These figures and much of the following review of the deteriorating American international economic situation are based on the refreshingly clear analysis of Robert Warren Stevens in *A Primer on the Dollar in the World Economy: United States Balance of Payments and International Monetary Reform* (New York: Random House, 1972), esp. pp. 108–174. See also Lawrence Krause, *Sequel to Bretton Woods: A Proposal to Reform the World Monetary System* (Washington, D.C.: Brookings, 1971).

97. Raymond Vernon, "A Skeptic Looks at the Balance of Payments," *Foreign Policy,* No. 5 (Winter 1971–1972), pp. 52–65.

98. See Lawrence Krause, "Why Exports Are Becoming Irrelevant," *Foreign Policy,* No. 3 (Summer 1971), pp. 62–70.

99. Vernon, op. cit., p. 60.

100. On this point see Stevens, op. cit., pp. 119–121.

101. Ibid., and David P. Calleo and Benjamin M. Rowland, *America and the World Political Economy: Atlantic Dreams and National Realities.* (Bloomington, Ind.: Indiana University Press, 1973), pp. 118–192.

102. Stevens, op. cit., p. 130.

103. For a detailed analysis of the TEA of 1962, see Ernest H. Prieg, *Traders and Diplomats* (Washington, D.C.: Brookings, 1970).

104. See Nora Beloff, *The General Says No: Britain's Exclusion from Europe* (Baltimore: Penguin Books, 1963), *passim.*

105. See Calleo and Rowland, op. cit., pp. 123ff.

106. Stevens, op. cit., p. 138.

107. Remarks by William P. Bundy, October 16, 1973, University of Delaware, Newark.

Chapter 9
Containment
"Turns the Corner"
. . . into the Swamp

By the 1980s the running sore of the Vietnam War had become a scar. Vietnam, no longer a subject of sometimes violent public debate and confrontation, had become the object of cinematic art, the novel, the memoir, and the historian. But those foreign policy analysts of this period who still surveyed the smoke and ruin of Vietnam and the concomitant domestic turmoil and near disintegration, like the ancient Mediterranean oracles who opened the bellies of oxen and burned their entrails to understand the past and predict the future,[1] asked: How did it happen and what did it mean?

CONTAINMENT ON THE MEKONG

To write of American combat involvement in the Indochina war in the past tense strikes the authors as somewhat odd. Both were politicized during the truncated Kennedy years and then lived through what seemed to be an interminable succession of presidential statements and news conferences in which corners were turned and light seen at the end of the tunnel. One fought to maintain some sense of the human implications of the dehumanized jargon of the decade: "gooks" and "slopes," "search and destroy," "free fire zones," "pacification," and that omnipresent obscenity of the late 1960s, the daily "body count." And yet in retrospect, what appeared to be an endless torrent of indistinguishable days, weeks, months, and years can be seen to have fallen into more or less definable periods or phases containing specific and crucial decision points. In this way the war seems to have had an identifiable structure and, more important for our purposes, was an intellectual and historical culmination of the fundamental elements of American foreign policy mapped out in previous chapters.

The Period of Limited
but Escalating Commitment

John Kennedy's investment in the problem of Vietnam was unusual. He was one of the founding members of the American Friends of Vietnam. The Friends were established in the fall of 1955 in order, as then-Senator Kennedy explained at one of their meetings, to offer an alternative to "revolution—a political and social revolution far superior to anything the Communists can offer."[2] Senator Kennedy's explanation to the assembly of Friends summarized the rationale for American involvement in Indochina as it was to stand for the next sixteen years:

> Vietnam represents the cornerstone of the Free World in Southeast Asia, the keystone to the arch, the finger in the dike. Burma, Thailand, India, Japan, the Philippines, obviously Laos and Cambodia are among those whose security would be threatened if the red tide of communism overflowed into Vietnam. . . . Her economy is essential to the economy of all of Southeast Asia; and her political liberty is an inspiration to those seeking to obtain or maintain their liberty in all parts of Asia—and indeed the world. . . .[3]

When President Kennedy came to the Vietnam question, therefore, his beliefs were already well defined and, in general, they conformed to the prevailing concept of America's interests in the non-Western world and Southeast Asia. President Kennedy was aware, however, that the Diem regime had not conformed to the image one expects in a supposed proving ground for democracy. Between 1955 and 1961 Diem's control of the South had become more and more repressive. In late 1956, a Western observer described South Vietnam as a "quasi-police state characterized by arbitrary arrests and imprisonment, strict censorship of the press and the absence of an effective political opposition."[4] By 1959 Diem had abolished most local government at the village level and carried out a program of land reform that did little or nothing to break the hold of large and absentee land owners. Finally, in 1959, ordinances were passed that gave Diem's military courts very nearly complete latitude and the people no right to appeal the courts' decisions.[5]

Diem was soon confronted with a thriving indigenous insurgency. Organized opposition to Diem emerged in 1957 and 1958 but did not have the support of the Communists in the North. Indeed, Radio Hanoi repeatedly attacked this new South Vietnam Liberation Front comprised of Viet Cong, southern Viet Minh from the struggle against the French, and the newly disaffected. The Communists in the North apparently feared, throughout 1958 and 1959, that this new political force in the South, though articulating an avowedly communist program of action, nevertheless constituted a threat to any subsequent reunification effort. Furthermore, the primary concern of the North at this time seems to have been its own internal economic reconstruction and development, not fomenting revolution in the South. By 1960, however, the South's opposition to Diem was threatening to move totally beyond the control of Hanoi. Thus, in September 1960, the Northern leaders moved to endorse the activities of the Southern insurgents. Nevertheless, the "socialist revolution in the North was to be regarded as the 'most decisive task for the development of the whole Vietnamese revolution for the cause of national reunification,' but the Southerners were now encouraged to take direct and militant action."[6] By the end of 1960 and into early 1961, the insurgency had escalated. Political assassinations, terrorism, and large battalion-sized battles were not infrequent. Contrary to what the American government would claim subsequently, observers at the time noted: "the insurrection is Southern rooted; it arose at Southern initiative in response to Southern demands."[7]

Upon assuming office, Kennedy sent, in succession, Vice President Lyndon Johnson, Chairman of the Joint Chiefs of Staff Maxwell Taylor, White House adviser Walt Rostow, and the secretaries of state and defense to Southeast Asia to evaluate the situation and recommend a course of action. All reported to Kennedy in essential agreement with Rusk and McNamara:

> The loss of South Vietnam would make pointless any further discussion about the importance of Southeast Asia to the free world; we would have to face the near certainty that the remainder of Southeast Asia and Indonesia would move to a complete accommodation with Communism, if not formal incorporation with the Communist bloc.
> The loss of South Vietnam to Communism would not only destroy SEATO but would undermine the credibility of American commitments elsewhere.[8]

Like Korea a decade earlier, the loss of a country on the periphery would not only undercut regional security and "involve the transfer of a nation of 20 million people from the free world to the communist bloc,"[9] it would also undermine the entire structure of global containment. Moreover, warned McNamara and Rusk, there was yet another Korean ghost abroad in Southeast Asia: the "loss of South Vietnam would stimulate bitter domestic controversies in the United States and would be seized upon by extreme elements to divide the country and harass the Administration."[10] In sum, Kennedy's year-long review of the situation confirmed Eisenhower and Dulles's domino theory of aggression in Southeast Asia. Furthermore, Kennedy's advisers emphasized that at the end of the row of international dominoes was what Leslie Gelb, one of the authors of the *Pentagon Papers,* would term the "essential domino," American public opinion.[11] It seemed to Kennedy—a man who had been elected by less than one percentage point, stained by the disaster at the Bay of Pigs, again tarnished by the construction of the Berlin wall following the difficult Vienna Conference, and confronted with an even more rapidly deteriorating situation in Laos than in Vietnam—that there was really no choice; he would have to stay.

The next year and a half provided some apparent basis for optimism. A strategic hamlet program which removed South Vietnamese peasants from insecure areas was initated and as American troop strength went from 500 Green Berets and other advisers in May of 1961 to more than ten thousand. Secretary of Defense McNamara reported that "Every quantitative measurement we have shows that we're winning this war."[12] Taylor had called in the previous year for both a troop increase as well as the bombing of the North. Kennedy had given him some of the personnel but had refused to initiate the bombing, and it seemed by early 1963 that Kennedy's limited response was working well. Indeed, by 1963 McNamara had initiated planning for U.S. troop withdrawals and, on paper at least, was able to show a one-thousand-man reduction in force in December 1963. In the meantime, however, apparent success turned decidedly sour.

The Collapse of the Diem Regime

The sense of movement associated with the American build-up in 1962 had provided a deceptive image of progress. The strategic hamlets proved a disaster, as Diem used the program to disrupt traditional Vietnamese society in an effort to extend his authority. A program designed to increase security became, ironically, a contribution to the potential pool of insurgents. Within the South Vietnamese army the situation was actually worsening. Government weapons losses increased as did Viet Cong terrorism. In May 1962 the resentment among the nation's Buddhist majority toward the Catholic minority symbolized by Diem and his brother, Ngo Dinh Nhu, broke into the open. During a demonstration in Hue, on May 8, government troops fired into a crowd of demonstrating Buddhists. Demonstrations escalated and during the fall of 1962 and the summer of 1963 took a grisly turn as seven Buddhist monks committed suicide by public self-immolation, an act of protest sarcastically characterized by Nhu's wife as a "barbecue show."[13] Finally, in August, Nhu ordered government troops to raid major Buddhist pagodas throughout the country and arrest the Buddhist leadership; schools were closed, and the public suicides continued.

By September 1963 things were clearly out of control. Kennedy sent McNamara to South Vietnam with instructions to Diem that reforms must be forthcoming or U.S. assistance would be reduced. In the meantime, the U.S. embassy learned of a conspiracy within the army to overthrow Diem. Orders went out from Washington that the coup should be encouraged and supported if the plan showed likelihood of success. By November, after one false start, the planning for the coup was completed with assistance from the CIA and the American embassy, notably Ambassador Henry Cabot Lodge, and was carried out on November 1, 1963. Diem and his brother were assassinated, and an unstable Military Revolutionary Council took over.[14]

Kennedy was now increasingly ambivalent:

> In the final analysis, it is their war. They are the ones who have to win it or lose it. We can help them, we can give them equipment, we can send our men out there as advisers, but they have to win it—the people of Vietnam—against the Communists. . . . [A]ll we can do is help, and we are making it very clear.

"But," cautioned Kennedy, "I don't agree with those who say we should withdraw. That would be a great mistake."[15] As evidence of this conviction, American personnel reached fifteen thousand in November. At the same time, however, Kennedy intimates have reported that the president, fearing that the war was becoming an American war, was moving toward a decision in 1963 to end American involvement in 1965. The immediate restraining factor was, of course, the presidential election of 1964, the last time Kennedy would have to face the electorate. In the spring of 1963, Kennedy informed Senator Mike Mansfield, who, though an early supporter of Diem, now called for a complete American withdrawal, that he (Kennedy) now agreed, "But I can't do it until 1965— after I'm reelected."[16] Kenneth O'Donnell, a confidant of the president, recalled:

> After Mansfield left the office, the President told me that he had made up his mind that after his reelection he would take the risk of unpopularity and make a complete withdrawal of American forces from Vietnam. "In 1965, I'll be damned everywhere as a Communist appeaser. But I don't care. If I tried to pull out completely now, we would have another Joe McCarthy red scare on our hands, but I can do it after I'm reelected. So we had better make damned sure that I *am* reelected."[17]

The country would never learn whether Kennedy's decision was a firm one, for he was himself assassinated three weeks after Diem. Lyndon Johnson came into office with the knowledge that the situation in the South was rapidly disintegrating. As McNamara would report in December 1963:

> Vietcong progress has been great during the period since the coup, with my best guess being that the situation has in fact been deteriorating in the countryside . . . to a far greater extent than we realized because of our undue dependence on distorted Vietnamese reporting. . . . We should watch the situation very carefully, running scared, hoping for the best, but preparing for more forceful moves if the situation does not show early signs of improvement.[18]

McNamara's closing recommendation would prove to be a prophetic description of American policy for the next four years. The situation would never show more than illusory signs of improvement, especially during 1964, when seven South Vietnamese governments moved in and out of Saigon, and Lyndon Johnson became increasingly fearful of a resurgent Republican right wing in the November 1964 elections.

Transforming the War into an American War

Throughout early 1964 the United States steadily escalated the scale of American involvement in a covert war against North Vietnam in the hope that collapse of the South Vietnamese government could be staved off. The authors of the *Pentagon Papers* characterize Johnson's decision making at this time as being one of pursuing "noncommitting" actions, however, the covert war involved clandestine raids and attacks inside North Vietnam, air strikes in Laos, and destroyer patrols in the Gulf of Tonkin. Most important in the view of the authors of the *Pentagon Papers*, this covert war "carried with it an implicit symbolic and psychological intensification of the U.S. commitment. . . . A firebreak had been crossed."[19]

Significantly, almost no one in the Johnson administration believed that these covert actions would be sufficient to prevent the loss of the South. In May of 1964, after the Joint Chiefs of Staff had developed their proposals,[20] William P. Bundy prepared a scenario for the escalation of American involvement culminating in an all-out bombing campaign against the North. Included in the proposal was a draft congressional resolution that would give to the president the authority "to use all measures, including the commitment of armed forces" to ensure the survival of South Vietnam.[21] Thus by midyear 1964, Johnson had secretly developed a plan for the escalation of American involvement in Southeast Asia even as he was executing a clandestine low-level war against the North and in Laos.

In spite of a steadily deterioriating situation in South Vietnam, Johnson shelved the proposed escalation temporarily. The president had already moved into the 1964 campaign against Senator Barry Goldwater and was portraying himself to the American people as a man who would not pursue a rash escalation of the war because it would undercut his pursuit of the Great Society at home. Goldwater, in contrast, was calling for an escalation of force in Southeast Asia including the bombing of the North, with nuclear weapons if necessary. Johnson reorted that such a step would dangerously widen the war, perhaps bringing the Chinese or Russians into the conflict; it might also require the commitment of American ground troops to the war, a step that Johnson had scorned during the campaign: "We are not going to send American boys nine or ten thousand miles away from home to do what Asian boys ought to be doing for themselves."

Privately, however, Johnson was approving the very steps that he was publicly attacking Goldwater for recommending. As in the previous decisions to initiate covert actions against the North, the bombing was rationalized as a limited means to prevent collapse of the political situation in the South. The president could not begin the bombing immediately in view of the position he was taking in the presidential campaign. In the meantime, however, he was able to get the Southeast Asia Resolution passed in August as the result of extremely confusing and uncertain August naval engagements in the Gulf of Tonkin. The purported North Vietnamese attacks came in the wake of a provocative covert naval action against the North approved earlier in the year by the president. Moreover, Assistant Secretary of Defense John McNaughton suggested after the Tonkin "attacks," President Johnson's air strikes in retaliation, and the hurried congressional passage of the open-ended Tonkin Gulf Resolution, that yet another incident might be staged later as a part of a "provocation strategy" to provide a pretext for the initiation of additional bombing of the North.[22]

The impression of deceit surrounding the Tonkin Gulf Resolution has, of course, been intensified by revelations subsequent to the events of August 1964. It is now apparent that there was considerable confusion and uncertainty surrounding the purported attacks on the *Maddox* and *C. Turner Joy*.[23] The *casus belli* for sending fighter bombers to bomb and strafe North Vietnam was said to be a second North Vietnamese attack on American warships in forty-eight hours. The administration maintained the ships were on "routine" patrol on the high seas and the "attacks" were "piracy." But the vessels, as Anthony Austin points out in his account, "were not engaged in 'routine' sea patrol . . . but in a special espionage mission that took the ships well within North Vietnamese waters. . . . The *Maddox* [was] running in and out of territorial waters" before the first real attack by North Vietnam, and twenty-four hours after the *Maddox* was found by the *C. Turner Joy* on the night of August 3 and 4, the *Maddox* again attempted to "excite" North Vietnamese radar. There was, in Austin's words, "considerable evidence that one objective of the patrol was to provoke the North Vietnamese and bloody them if they responded."[24]

A White House official in a "position to know" confided to the *New York Times* columnist Tom Wicker "that the President had been carrying around the text of the resolution 'in his pocket' long before the Tonkin episode gave him the right opportunity to lay it before Congress."[25] When opportunity knocked, the secretary of defense hurriedly sent American fighter bombers over North Vietnam, bombing oil storage and port facilities. Secretary McNamara could report to the president that the "retaliatory" air strikes were a huge success. "Smoke was observed rising to 14,000 feet," he declared. Johnson was elated. One reporter heard him gloat, "I didn't just screw Ho Chi Minh; I cut his pecker off."[26] The Tonkin resolution was then brought out of Johnson's pocket to be used as the basis for legitimizing the planned expansion of the war—all that had been needed was an event to set things in motion. Publication of the *Pentagon Papers* makes the claims put forward in support of the resolution patently transparent. The *Papers* themselves and the documents published with them make it clear that from February to August 1964 the United States was consciously pursuing a policy of escalating the conflict in Southeast Asia by overt and covert means. With the election safely behind him, President Johnson moved to the crucial decisions on the escalation and transformation of the war. Detailed plans for initiating a bombing campaign against the North were tentatively approved in early December. For the time being, however, the president gave final approval only to increased, but secret, bombing of the infiltration routes in Laos.

By the end of 1964 American aircraft had been shot down over South Vietnam, domestic political chaos had increased in Saigon, and the South Vietnamese army seemed on the verge of collapse. Furthermore, much of the intelligence community was now warning the president that the increased U.S. military action envisioned in the bombing proposal could not save the situation on the ground in South Vietnam. Early 1965 was, therefore, a critical decision point, perhaps the most crucial period in the evolution of American policy in Southeast Asia. The administration was confronted with the undeniable fact that previous efforts had not halted the decline in the South. When the Viet Cong struck an American installation at Pleiku in February, Johnson ordered the initiation of Operation Rolling Thunder, the sustained bombing of strategic targets in the North which would continue for the next three years. This was probably not the only option available to the United States at this time, for Hanoi had initiated peace feelers during December and January. At a time when circumstances in the South were so obviously bad the appearance of negotiating from weakness was a concern in Washington, therefore, talks were to be avoided until more military pressure could be brought to bear on the North.

The bombing of the North, including areas surrounding Hanoi, came as Soviet Premier Aleksei Kosygin arrived in North Vietnam. The Soviet Premier was widely reported as a moderate, and many Western intelligence analysts saw his visit as a means of dampening the war and reasserting Russian influence in the area against Chinese ambitions. But while Kosygin was in Hanoi the bombs fell. The Soviet Premier bitterly told Kissinger and Nixon some eight years later, "I shall never forget it."[27] David Halberstam relates a story that indicated it was not the attack on Pleiku that prompted American reprisal but rather that it was an opportune moment to head off negotiation and increase the pace of the war:

> A few days after the bombing campaign had begun, a White House reporter came across Bundy in the White House barbershop. Bundy was sitting there being lathered, and since he could not easily escape, the reporter thought it was a good time to ask Bundy something that had been bothering him since the incident. "Mac," he said, "what was the difference between Pleiku and the other incidents?"
>
> Bundy paused and then answered, "Pleikus are like streetcars" (i.e., there's one along every ten minutes).[28]

Nevertheless, the bombing could not prevent the next decision facing Johnson. The South Vietnamese army was collapsing, and bombing the North was not going to reverse this trend any more than covert raids and incremental increases of U.S. advisers had stopped the growth of the Viet Cong during the preceding two to three years. The authors of the *Pentagon Papers* underscore the dilemma:

> Once set in motion, however, the bombing effort seemed to stiffen rather than soften Hanoi's backbone, as well as the willingness of Hanoi's allies, particularly that Soviet Union, to work toward compromise. . . .
>
> The U.S. was presented essentially two options: (1) to withdraw unilaterally from Vietnam leaving the South Vietnamese to fend for themselves, or (2) to commit ground forces in pursuit of its objectives.[29]

On April 1, 1965, President Johnson ordered that American troops would be used in offensive action in South Vietnam. In a National Security Action Memorandum issued on April 6, 1965, the president approved: an eighteen-thousand- to twenty-thousand-man increase in U.S. forces, the deployment of two marine battalions in northern South Vietnam; and a change of mission for all marine battalions in South Vietnam "to permit their more active use." The memorandum also cautioned, "The President desires that with respect to the actions . . . premature publicity be avoided by all possible precautions."[30]

"I Want to Leave
the Footprints of America There"[31]

On April 7, 1965, in a speech at Johns Hopkins University, the president sought to explain why the war must be fought. The reasons given were familiar ones:

> We are . . . there because there are great stakes in the balance. Let no one think for a moment that retreat from Vietnam would bring an end to conflict. The battle would be renewed in one country and then another. The central lesson of our time is that the appetite of aggression is never satisfied. To withdraw from one battlefield means only to prepare for the next. We must say in Southeast Asia—as we did in Europe—in the words of the Bible: "Hitherto shalt thou come, but no further."[32]

Vietnam was in fact no different from Europe before World War II, Johnson implied. Furthermore, Hanoi was analogous to Nazi Germany, for "the first reality is that North Vietnam has attacked the independent nation of South Vietnam. Its object is total conquest." This was no civil war; indeed: "Over this war—and all Asia—is another reality: the deepening shadow of Communist China. The contest in Vietnam is part of a wider pattern of aggressive purposes."[33] The rationale for action put before the American people was, therefore, the same that had been advanced for almost two decades. There was a hint of the decision already secretly taken and of what was to come: "We know that air attacks alone will not accomplish all of these purposes."[34] By the end of the year there would be 184,314 American troops in South Vietnam.

In June and July 1965, those opposed to further escalation of the war marshalled their arguments, which had been passed over at the time the April decisions to commit American ground troops had been made. Central Intelligence Agency Director John McCone had argued for an increased air effort to avoid ground combat in this jungle quagmire.[35] By mid-1965 the "doves" insisted that even with an increase in the air war, McCone's prophecy would be fulfilled. But on July 28, 1965, President Johnson announced that "We did not choose to be the guardians at the gate, but there is no one else. . . . [W]e learned from Hitler at Munich that success only feeds the appetite of aggression. . . . I have asked the commanding general, General [William] Westmoreland, what more he needs to meet this mounting aggression. He has told me. We will meet his needs. . . . Additional forces will be needed later, and they will be sent as requested."[36]

This was clearly not a decision made in the absence of any debate or indication of what might come. There was full awareness on the part of the administration that they were now embarked on a new course. The Pentagon analysts who prepared the three thousand page analysis of the Vietnam War provide the best summation of these private mid-1965 decisions.

> The major participants in the decision knew the choices and understood the consequences. . . . [The mid-July decision to approve forty-four maneuver battalions] was perceived as a threshold—entrance into an Asian land war. The conflict was seen to be long, with further U.S. deployments to follow. The choice at that time was not whether or not to negotiate, it was not whether to hold on for a while or let go—the choice was viewed as winning or losing South Vietnam. . . . This was sanctioned implicitly as the only way to achieve the U.S. objective of a noncommunist South Vietnam.
>
> The acceptance of the search and destroy strategy . . . left the United States commitment to Vietnam open-ended. The implications in terms of manpower and money are inescapable.
>
> Final acceptance of the desirability of inflicting defeat on the enemy rather than merely denying him victory opened the door to an indeterminate amount of additional force.[37]

American policymaking now assumed a kind of tragic predictability. On July 2, 1965, the Joint Chiefs were requested to estimate "the forces required to win in South Vietnam."[38] But it was soon apparent that no one knew, and Washington deferred to Westmoreland's estimate of what he said he needed. By August 1966 Westmoreland requested 542,588 men by the end of 1967. The war would be over, he said, by the end of 1967; 1968 was, of course, an election year.[39]

As American escalation of the ground war continued throughout 1966, the air war followed a similar pattern as previously untouched pretroleum, oil, and lubricant supplies were hit and destroyed. Nevertheless, the North continued to match each American escalation; and by the fall of 1966 a special report of the Institute for Defense Analysis commissioned by the Department of Defense concluded that

> [a]s of July 1966 the U.S. bombing of North Vietnam . . . had had no measurable direct effect on Hanoi's ability to mount and support military operations in the South at the current level. . . .

The available evidence clearly indicates that Hanoi has been infiltrating military forces and supplies into South Vietnam at an accelerated rate during the current year. Intelligence estimates have concluded that North Vietnam is capable of substantially increasing its support.

Finally, the report concluded with the observation:

There is currently no adequate basis for predicting the levels of U.S. military effort that would be required to achieve the stated objectives—indeed, there is no firm basis for determining if there is *any* feasible level of effort that would achieve these objectives.[40]

In October McNamara went to Vietnam for another evaluation of the war, and upon returning to Washington reported to Johnson that he was in substantial agreement with the institute's conclusions. This report by McNamara in October was accompanied by his recommendation that the United States set a limit to its troop levels and shift the pattern of American bombing away from the Hanoi-Haiphong area to infiltration routes in preparation for a negotiated settlement of the conflict. This recommendation sparked an intense debate within the administration, with the Joint Chiefs standing in opposition to McNamara. The Johnson administration was now split as to the future course of the war. The president compromised by allowing McNamara to cut the military's requested troop level to 469,000 by the end of 1968, but approving yet another step-up in the air war despite CIA findings that 80 percent of the casualties in North Vietnam during 1965 and 1966 were civilians. In February 1967, Johnson approved an increase in B-52 sorties from sixty to eight hundred monthly.[41]

Midway into 1967 the debate within the administration was at its peak and was intensified by General Westmoreland's request for 200,000 troops, or an ultimate troop strength of more than 670,000 troops by mid-July 1968. Moreover, pressure from within the military began to rise for unlimited bombing, an invasion of Cambodia, Laos, or even North Vietnam, as well as attacks on the port of Haiphong.[42] Johnson continued to resist the pressure for an expansion of the war on land. At the same time the preconditions he attached to any peace overtures offered the North Vietnamese were such as to preclude real negotiations. These prior conditions were little changed from those Johnson offered in 1965 and 1966 when the president ordered bombing pauses while offering that if the North Vietnamese and the Viet Cong would concede that they were the aggressors in the war and stop their infiltration of the South, then the United States would end its bombing and begin negotiations. The entire position was rooted in the contention that the war was not a civil war, a position that was unacceptable and hence nonnegotiable to the North. The fighting continued.

By late 1967 disaffection with the war had begun to swell in the United States. Draft resistance increased during 1966 and 1967, and during these same years the War on Poverty turned into a skirmish because of the budgetary demands of the war; widespread rioting became almost commonplace in black ghettoes. Radical politics seemed to be the norm on many college campuses. And within Congress, the bipartisan consensus of foreign policy disintegrated as congressional doves led by Senator J. William Fulbright and other liberal members of the Foreign Relations Committee openly challenged the administration's policies in Southeast Asia. Indeed, by the end of 1967 there was virtually no communication between the Foreign Relations Committee and the administration. Public opinion remained uneasily behind the president. But as the nation approached the 1968 elections, polls found growing opposition to American policy in Indochina, especially the bombing of the North and the refusal of the Johnson administration to facilitate negotiations.

In the face of this disintegrating domestic base, Johnson reiterated the now worn justifications for the war, increased secret domestic surveillance on American antiwar dissidents, and brought General Westmoreland before the Congress to extol progress and eminent success in the war. It would all be over in two years, the general said, if, of course, he got the necessary forces. But Johnson would not go this far; instead, there would be more bombing and greater use of indiscriminate firepower as ever-larger areas of South Vietnam were declared "free fire zones." Anyone found in these areas was assumed to be the "enemy" and therefore subject, in the jargon of the day, to being "blown away," or "wasted." By one estimate, one-third to one-half of the people of Southeast Asia had become refugees.[43] Vast areas of land had been defoliated by American herbicides and weed killers. Between 1961 and 1971 the United States dropped more than one hundred million pounds of herbicide on South Vietnam (six pounds of herbicide for every man, woman, and child in South Vietnam). Dioxin, one of the ingredients of the defoliant Agent Orange, is now known to cause genetic mutation, liver damage, and cancer, according to a National Academy of Science study completed in February 1975. About one-seventh of the territory of South Vietnam was sprayed in order to destroy crops and jungle canopy which supposedly sheltered the Viet Cong. The 1925 Geneva treaty on chemical and biological warfare prohibits the deployment of gases and toxins. Just the same, some 36 percent of the mangrove swampland—the breeding ground of the staples of fish and rice of the Vietnamese diet—had been destroyed by 1974. The seventeen scientists commissioned to study the effect of these toxins estimated that it could take over 100 years for the swamps to recover.[44] Moreover, by the late 1970s and early 1980s this campaign would produce a grim irony as the United States government faced suits from American veterans of the war who had been exposed to the defoliants and were experiencing abnormally high rates of cancer. The damages claimed in the suits could run into the billions of dollars.

Between 1965 and 1971 the enormous quantity of ordnance expended in Indochina as a whole represented some 142 pounds of explosives per acre of land and 584 pounds per person. "The average rate of detonation was 118 pounds per second," which equaled, in terms of explosive power, the equivalent of 450 Hiroshima-type atomic bombs.[45] Craters filled with water, causing mosquito populations to intensify and malaria to spread. Unexploded shells killed and maimed those who dared remain to work the land. The timber industry was wiped out. Workers attempting to cut wood with power saws risked being hit from shrapnel buried in the wood. The rubber industry was ruined, and the landscape of the once rich Mekong Delta became, according to observers, "gray porridge . . . torn as if an by an angry giant." Senator Gaylord Nelson noted that "There is nothing in the history of warfare to compare with [it]. A 'scorched earth' policy has been a tactic . . . throughout history, but never has a land been so massively altered and mutilated."[46]

By the end of 1967 more bombs had been dropped on Vietnam than in the entirety of Europe during World War II. McNamara now began to testify openly that the air war had failed to stop the infiltration of men and supplies into the South and the destruction inflicted on the North could not be said to have broken Hanoi's will to go on. It was a remarkable departure for the secretary of defense to contradict publicly and powerfully the Joint Chiefs. But McNamara had changed. Previously, students at Harvard had nearly overturned his car when he made one of his last public addresses in defense of what was once known as McNamara's War. Then he shouted, "I'm tougher than you. I was tougher in World War II and I'm tougher now!" But his doubts grew. He commissioned the Pentagon Papers. When the papers were handed to him, he confessed to a friend, "You know they could hang people for what's in there."[47] McNamara's son began turning up at peace demonstrations and McNamara's behavior, once so controlled, determined, and calculating, became "erratic."[48] In the end, he was given to public weeping. He was the third secretary of defense in less than twenty-five years to break in office.

On January 31, 1968, the start of the Buddhist Tet holiday, the Communists launched large-scale attacks throughout South Vietnam. Communist forces penetrated to the heart of every major city in the South, including Saigon. Hue was captured, and it was only after weeks of fighting and the literal destruction of most of the ancient and culturally important city that it was retaken. Parts of Saigon and other cities could be saved only by calling destructive and indiscriminate air strikes down on them. The Communists took enormous casualties, and the Pentagon claimed a major battlefield victory, but in fact Tet marked the end of the open-ended American war in South Vietnam. If, after almost three years of steady escalation and expansion of the effort, the Communists could launch an attack of the magnitude of the Tet offensive, then it was clear that a change in policy was necessary.

The crucial decision was made by Clark Clifford, who had replaced McNamara as secretary of defense in February 1968. Faced with a new Westmoreland request for 206,000 additional troops, Clifford recommended that it be denied. Moreover, the new secretary of defense asked on March 5, 1968, that the chairman of the Joint Chiefs of Staff evaluate a proposal from the Department of State that the bombing in the North be curtailed or halted, implying that he (Clifford) favored such a move. The domestic domino began wobbling as an avowed peace candidate, Senator Eugene McCarthy, claimed a moral victory in the New Hampshire primary with 40 percent of the Democratic vote. Then the American casualty figures were released. They numbered 139,801—exceeding the overall Korean War losses. At the same moment, an emergency meeting of European and American bankers was held in Washington to stem a rush on gold as the price soared. And on March 13 Senator Robert Kennedy announced that he would seek the Democratic party nomination for president in 1968. The day Senator Kennedy announced he would, Johnson rejected Westmoreland's troop request. Within a week, the president recalled the general to become Army chief of staff.[49]

The Tet offensive simply could not be ignored, for it ran completely against the years of deceptively optimistic official reporting.[50] The president was forced to reconsider the entire course of the war. On March 25 Johnson convened a Senior Informal Advisory Group, which consisted of former members of the foreign and defense policy community and was informally headed by Dean Acheson. Almost without exception these were men who had been hawks for years; many of them, such as Acheson and Omar Bradley, traced their service back to the immediate postwar period.[51] After a two-day review of the situation, this group, informally known as the "wise men," dramatically recommended that the president reverse course and deescalate the war. The president, according to the authors of the *Pentagon Papers*, was stunned by the position now taken by this group, which in previous years had recommended escalation. On March 31, 1968, the president announced that he was cutting back on the bombing. Moreover, he announced that in order to facilitate the search for peace he would not seek the presidential nomination in 1968. The domestic domino had fallen.

In his 1965 Johns Hopkins speech Johnson had stated a desire to bring a $1 billion economic assistance program to Vietnam. "The vast Mekong River," he said, "can provide food and water and power on a scale to dwarf even our own TVA." He also noted that "we often say how impressive power is. But I do not find it impressive at all. The guns and bombs, the rockets and the warships, are all symbols of human failure . . . they are witness to human folly."[52]

UNDERSTANDING THE QUAGMIRE AND THE STALEMATE MACHINE

A combination of a misperception of the nature of the revolutionary conflict in Vietnam, the relationship of that conflict to America's broader world role, and presidential politics set a framework within which we might understand America's (and Vietnam's) Vietnamese tragedy. At the confluence of these streams lies the swamp into which American foreign policy was knowingly carried during the 1960s. John Kennedy was murdered even as he seemed to recognize the peril confronting his administration. Lyndon Johnson's administration died in the swamps as he tried to extricate himself from that quagmire first through violence and then through negotiations.

The International Costs of "Losing"

Those who have tried to grasp and explain America's deadly fascination with and involvement in Vietnam have frequently employed the image of a man floundering helplessly in a quagmire into which he had inadvertently slipped.[53] Other students of American policy have argued that American presidents in no way stumbled into the Vietnamese swamp. Rather they entered knowingly into the bog. There may have been times, such as early and mid-1965, that the intense desire for victory made the wish seem a real possibility. But for the most part American policymakers were aware that the actions they were taking at a particular moment would at best allow them to hold their position on what seemed eternally shifting and treacherous grounds, and at worst would probably require subsequent additional commitment.[54]

If in their frantic effort to press on or extricate themselves from the swamp, Kennedy, Johnson, and the "best and the brightest" who made up their administrations maimed and killed other creatures who lived in the swamp, the Americans should not be blamed, guilt should not be apportioned, for American intentions were good. It was necessary, or so it seemed, to Truman, Eisenhower, Kennedy, and Johnson, that we be in Vietnam, not because Vietnam itself was so vital to American security, but because if we were not willing to go in and stay there, "our word" and reputation would suffer. "We are there," said Johnson, "because we have a promise to keep. . . . We are also there to strengthen the world order. Around the globe from Berlin to Thailand are people whose well-being rests . . . on the belief that they can count on us."[55]

Assistant Secretary of Defense John McNaughton put matters in perspective in a memo he wrote laying out American war objectives as the Johnson administration approached the fateful escalation decisions in late 1964 and early 1965. American aims should be:

> 70 pct.—To avoid a humilitating U.S. defeat (to our reputation as a guarantor).
> 20 pct.—To keep SVN (and then adjacent) territory from Chinese hands.
> 10 pct.—To permit the people of SVN to enjoy a better, freer way of life. Also—To emerge from crisis without unacceptable taint from methods used.
> [American aims should] not [be]—To "help a friend," although it would be hard to stay in if asked out.

McNaughton went further: even if the Viet Cong were not defeated, American involvement "would demonstrate that the U.S. was a 'good doctor' willing to keep promises, be tough, take risks, get bloodied and hurt the enemy badly."[56]

The McNaughton ranking of American priorities does suggest a plausible set of benchmarks against which the employment of American means were evaluated, otherwise one would have to argue that the Kennedy and Johnson administrations were filled with willful sadistic monsters. If the well-being of one's ally is evaluated on the order of magnitude of 10 percent out of a 100, whereas the avoidance of a "humiliating defeat" stands at or near 70 percent, then clearly the figurative and quite literal destruction of one's ally is a small price to pay if "humiliation" is avoided. If, as a doctor, you believe that your worth to society will be evaluated primarily in terms of your cool willingness to enter a potentially bloody operating room, then it does not matter much that the patient be disabled, disfigured, or die a horrible and lingering death.

Johnson's desire that the United States leave behind in Vietnam that which he regarded as truly "impressive"—schools, dams, a better life—

is more understandable in this light. There is no reason to doubt that the president set forth in all honesty and with deep conviction this image of what Indochina could be. What is more important, however, was his belief that first "we must deal with the world as it is, if it is ever to be as we wish." The building of the world that we wish must be deferred as we deal with and contain the perceived threats and disorder of the contemporary system. In this vision, if the road be painful, so be it: "this nation [must] hazard its ease, its interest, and its power." Ultimately, however, we must do so not primarily, as Johnson implied, "for the sake of a people so far away," but rather because the American vision of the political and economic order of the world demands it. The difficulty and danger for those people "so far away" is, however, that the pursuit of that vision, as in Vietnam, frequently requires that *they* hazard *their* ease, *their* interest, and *their* power so that the American vision might be realized.

In one sense only, therefore, the quagmire metaphor is useful. Kennedy and Johnson, but especially Johnson, did behave as if they were men in a swamp. That part of the swamp in which they found themselves, Vietnam, was but a part of a much larger morass—a quagmire created and sustained, it was believed, by the flow of Chinese and Soviet communism. If that source of aggression threatened to turn the entire international system into a swamp, then it was essential that the United States try to dam up Asian and Soviet communism. If that meant in turn that the United States must stay in the swamp indefinitely, then it was, nevertheless, essential.

The persistence of Kennedy, Johnson, and subsequently Richard Nixon, once in the swamp, is understandable in terms of their fears of the international consequences of losing Vietnam. Given the perceived all-encompassing nature of the threat, to lose once is to lose everything. It does not follow, as Dulles used to insist, that one must win finally and definitely. But one must certainly not lose. All American presidents faced with the problem of Vietnam desired the final defeat of the Viet Cong and North Vietnamese. Yet the larger international imperatives demanded at a minimum that the American client not be defeated. Thus, when Johnson found that, to avoid such a defeat, the commitment of American troops was necessary, he proceeded with the escalation of the war. And once in, of course, it was not only the American client who was at stake; rather it was the United States itself. Indeed, the client was only a symbol of the higher stakes of battle. As Kissinger readily confessed in January 1969, Vietnam may not have been important intrinsically, but "the commitment of five hundred thousand Americans . . . settled the issue of the importance of Vietnam." Kissinger continued:

For what it involved now is confidence in American promises. However fashionable it is to ridicule the terms "credibility" or "prestige," they are not empty phrases; other nations can gear their actions to ours only if they can count on our steadiness. . . . In many parts of the world—the Middle East, Europe, Latin America, even Japan—stability depends on confidence in American promises.[57]

In 1965, 1966, and early 1967, Johnson believed that the United States could have final victory. Certainly events in the Dominican Republic in 1965, even as he was escalating the Vietnam War, might have suggested as much to him. In that case when an American-backed regime was "deserted by everyone"[58] and subsequently attacked by leftists and conservatives, Johnson landed the Marines and imposed order. The original pretense was the protection of Americans in Santo Domingo, but subsequently the United States published a hastily drawn and largely inaccurate list of Communists and "Castroite leaders who were purportedly active in the revolution." A stable conservative government was installed.

The thrust of this policy was repeated throughout Latin America as Lyndon Johnson's new assistant secretary of state for inter-American affairs, Thomas Mann, redirected much of what was left of the Alliance for Progress to military governments, such as that established in Brazil in 1964 following a coup that overthrew a liberal-leftist regime. The apparent success of these efforts may have reinforced Johnson's propensities to escalate the scale of military involvement in Vietnam. Arthur Schlesinger speculates that Johnson also "found it viscerally inconceivable that what Walt Rostow kept telling him was 'the greatest power in the world' could not dispose of a collection of nightriders in black pajamas."[59] Further, insofar as the Dominican intervention was carried out without much negative public outcry in the United States, it is conceivable that Johnson concluded that his domestic base was supportive.

Presidential Politics and the Cost of Losing

In contrast to Johnson's bold escalation of the fighting and American participation in it after 1965, there was the covert war, secret preparation for the escalation, and the outright public deception of 1964. These facts suggest that there was more than the fear of the international consequences of a loss or overconfidence concerning U.S. power at work. Presidents have indeed been afraid of losing in Vietnam because of the international implications of such a loss, but they have also been preoccupied with its domestic consequences. Moreover, this concern and preoccupation with losing to Communists or looking "soft" when confronted with a communist challenge has extended to more than Vietnam.

We have noted the import of this factor on the Truman and Eisenhower administrations previously. John Kennedy's emotional and bellicose reaction to the Bay of Pigs disaster was due in some part to his fear that he would suffer during the next election or because he perceived the American people chastising him not for the blatant illegality of the act but for his failure. Similarly, the Cuban missile crisis over a year later seems to have been fed by this same anticipation of a popular backlash to a posture more conducive to a negotiated resolution of the conflict.

These fears were clearly at work throughout the Vietnam escalation. For Kennedy and Johnson the war could not be lost if they and their administrations were to survive. Kennedy may have decided by late 1963 that he would have to reverse course, but he did not see his way clear to do so until after the 1964 election. The choice for Lyndon Johnson was even more complex. Johnson could no more "lose" the war before the 1964 election than the murdered Kennedy but Johnson could not lose the war after the election either, because he hoped to face the electorate again in 1968. At the same time, Johnson sought to maintain an image of a calm moderate so as to set himself apart from Goldwater's bellicose proposals. To save the situation on the ground in Vietnam was difficult, for Johnson and his advisers knew that matters were disintegrating rapidly. Thus the covert war, actually conceived in the Kennedy administration, was employed to hold the situation until November 1964. In the meantime, Johnson was planning secretly to do what Goldwater was proclaiming publicly that the United States should be doing.

Underlying this balancing act by Johnson was a perception of the American people with which Kennedy could have agreed:

> I knew our people well enough to realize that if we walked away from Vietnam and let Southeast Asia fall, there would follow a divisive and destructive debate in our country. . . . A divisive debate about "who lost Vietnam" would be, in my judgment, even more destructive to our national life than the argument over China had been.[60]

In Johnson's view this debate would in turn undercut the capacity of the United States to play its global role.[61] Thus the two streams converged precisely where the president of the United States stood. For Lyndon Johnson as well as his predecessors and his successor, the only way to survive in the midst of the cross-currents was to avoid a loss in Vietnam. Or, as Daniel Ellsberg has argued, the end of policy became the production and maintenance of a stalemate.[62]

The problem after the 1964 election was no less complex, for by then the situation in Vietnam had become desperate as governments came and went and the South Vietnamese army fought indifferently. If the situation was to be held for another four years, it was clear that the Americans would have to do it. Now, however, Johnson sought a middle way along the escalatory path he had chosen. On one side were the doves who demanded withdrawal. The latter could be placated, at least in the short run, with breathless bombing pauses and peace initiatives. The hawks could be bought off by dribbling out the troop escalations that everybody knew were coming and inching up the bombing campaign while warning of the dangers of Chinese or Soviet intervention if the escalation went too fast or too violently. Finally, to maintain the support of that large number of confused and disoriented people in the middle, Johnson carefully avoided for as long as possible taking those steps that would significantly disrupt the lives of the average American. Thus he resisted tax increases and a call-up of the reserves until 1967 and maintained draft deferments for college-age males as long as possible.[63]

At the same time, however, the incremental escalation necessitated by this approach simplified the problem of matching the escalation on the part of the North Vietnamese. There can be little doubt that Hanoi was quite aware of the nature of Johnson's domestic circumstance and sought to exploit it:

> American public opinion was the essential domino. Our leaders knew it. Hanoi's leaders knew it. Each geared its strategy—both the rhetoric and the conduct of the war—to this fact.
>
> Hanoi adopted what seems to have been a . . . strategy to cause U.S. withdrawal from Vietnam by playing on American domestic politics. The . . . aim was to try to convince Americans that unless U.S. forces withdrew, the killing of Americans would never end.[64]

The *Pentagon Papers* seemed to confirm that Johnson and his advisers were quite aware of Hanoi's appeal to the American public. Moreover, Johnson also knew that the course he had chosen would be arduous and long: "Johnson . . . knew that the intelligence analysts offered little promise of victory ever, while no one (except, most of the time, Walt Rostow) promised it quickly."[65] But the president also knew (or thought he knew) what the American people would do if he caved in. Thus he was compelled to hang on and hope that something would turn up. These judgments fated him to play out the scenario presented to him by Undersecretary of State George Ball, perhaps the leading dove in the Johnson administration, who argued for no further escalation and lost in mid-1965:

The South Vietnamese are losing the war to the Viet Cong. No one can assure you that we can beat the Viet Cong or even force them to the conference table on our terms, no matter how many hundred thousand white, foreign (U.S.) troops we deploy. . . . The decision you face now, therefore, is crucial. Once large numbers of U.S. troops are committed to direct combat . . . [and] once we suffer large casualties, we will have started a well-nigh irreversible process. Our involvement will be so great that we cannot—without national humiliation—stop short of achieving our complete objectives. Of the two possibilities I think humiliation would be more likely than the achievement of our objectives—even after we have paid terrible costs.[66]

Negotiating in Quicksand

After the Tet offensive and the collapse of his political career, Johnson was more or less personally free of presidential politics. These pressures remained for his party and his vice president, Hubert Humphrey, who would become the Democratic party candidate. Nevertheless, after March 1968 the American public, which had been hawkish earlier, no longer had any stomach for the war. In short, the opportunities for a negotiated settlement in Vietnam seemed better than at any time since the 1950s. The North Vietnamese, in responding to Johnson's limited bombing halt of March 1968, agreed to discuss only the full cessation of the bombing at the outset; if there was to be only a limited bomb suspension, they would engage in only limited talks. The central questions of the war, unification and the illegitimacy of the Saigon regime, remained nonnegotiable issues. The North Vietnamese probably concluded that time was on their side, for as the elections drew closer, the Americans might become more forthcoming.

In the meantime, however, Johnson refused to take the minimum steps necessary to move the talks to the level of true negotiations. Throughout April, May, and most of June 1968, the United States insisted that the bombing could completely stop only if the North Vietnamese demonstrated some restraint on the battlefield. The North Vietnamese refused any concession to the American demand, for to do so would be an indirect admission that they were aggressors in South Vietnam. Since the North Vietnamese refused to concede that South Vietnam existed and insisted that the United States was in fact the aggressor against Vietnam, there could be no *formal* and *public* concession of this most fundamental of points.

During June, July, and August 1968, however, the Viet Cong and North Vietnamese drastically reduced their offensive action, and the North Vietnamese reportedly withdrew more than eighty thousand of their troops as a gesture to the Americans. Johnson refused to respond, however, apparently believing that further concessions could be gained by the continued application of force. Furthermore, he was now under pressure from Saigon to make no concession that in any way recognized the Viet Cong; they should not be given any recognition at formal negotiations. To do so, argued President Nguyen Van Thieu of South Vietnam, would be to concede the point of the entire war.

In late July and early August the administration took the position that the informal signals from the North were no longer adequate. There would have to be a formal statement or assurance of what the North Vietnamese would do in the way of a response if the United States stopped the bombing. In effect, the United States had not modified its original hard position. The United States would maintain its military presence and pressure, thereby protecting the Thieu regime, but the North would have to withdraw—then true negotiations could begin. From the perspective of the North this U.S. demand was tantamount to saying that the North must surrender what the United States had not been able to win on the battlefield, then negotiations could begin.[67] The North refused and promptly reescalated the violence in the South, with rocket attacks against major cities and the partial overrunning of Tay Ninh City in the northern part of South Vietnam. By early autumn 1968 American casualties rose dramatically after the marked decline during the lull of the preceding months.

By mid-October, with the election deadline closing fast but Hubert Humphrey lagging seriously, Johnson finally made a major concession which went to the heart of the twenty-year war. In an effort to move the informal talks to the level of full negotiations, he offered to allow the National Liberation Front (the South Vietnamese Communists) full representation at the conference, thereby extending tacit recognition of the Communists. In return, the North Vietnamese would accept a representative of Saigon. Johnson got around the question of bombing by not requiring a formal concession from Hanoi. Johnson merely stated that he would halt the bombing and not resume it unless the demilitarized zone was violated or the Communists attacked Southern cities. The president announced the proposal publicly on October 31, 1968, less than a week before the elections, and the North Vietnamese and the NLF accepted immediately.[68]

Now, however, the South Vietnamese exercised what amounted to a veto. They simply refused to sit down with the United States, the North Vietnamese, and the NLF. For two months they argued over any arrangements that implied recognition of the NLF, with the shape of the conference table becoming the symbolic issue over which the procedural wrangling continued. In the meantime, a surge of Humphrey support in the wake of the announcement that formal negotiations might be getting under way petered out just before election day as the delays by the Saigon regime created confusion. Only after president-elect Richard Nixon urged the Saigon regime to begin negotiations did the South Vietnamese reluctantly go along. Formal negotiations began on January 24, 1969, four days after Nixon had become president.[69]

Conclusion

The Nixon administration entered office intimating it had a secret plan to end the war. The plan consisted of a largely secret effort in 1971 and 1972 to negotiate a cease fire, the return of American prisoners of war, and the conditions of postwar political processes in the South. In the meantime, however, the fighting continued for four more years. There was secret bombing[70] and subsequent invasions of Cambodia and Laos by American and South Vietnamese troops, massive bombing of Hanoi and the mining of Haiphong harbor, and the Nixon administration initiated and carried out a program of Vietnamization in which American troops were withdrawn incrementally as the South Vietnamese army received the latest American equipment and training neglected for the most part during the Americanized portion of the war.

In at least one narrow respect, the Johnson administration's policy of stalemate was successful. The Johnson administration never formally recognized communist claims in South Vietnam, and the Viet Cong flag was not run up over Saigon during its years in office. With respect to the broader and more important aspects of that policy, however, the outcomes are more problematic. First, Johnson's pursuit of stalemate cost him his administration, not only with respect to his foreign policy but his domestic policy as well, in that the important programs of the Great Society had to be sacrificed to support the war effort. Second, it is not clear that Johnson succeeded ultimately in demonstrating America's will to resist leftist revolution in the third world. The enormous American effort in Southeast Asia never touched the core of the revolution underway for twenty years in Vietnam. The entire effort employed modalities of conflict designed to stop international and conventionally militarized aggression. So while the Johnson administration succeeded in that mode of combat, it failed in countering and even exacerbated the social and economic revolution that was always the crux of the issue in Southeast Asia.

There is a paradox in this; for as we have seen, the Kennedy and Johnson administrations began with a prodigious intellectual effort to anticipate unconventional war. What was lacking, however, was the full acceptance of the implications of Bernard Fall's observations even as the

Johnson administration was undertaking the conventional militarized Americanization of the war in 1965:

> The "kill" aspect, the military aspect, definitely always remain[s] the minor aspect. The political, administrative, ideological aspect is the primary aspect. . . . by its very nature, the insurgency problem is military only in a secondary sense, and political, ideological, and administrative in a primary sense. Once we understand this we will understand more of what is actually going on in Vietnam or in some other places affected by [revolutionary war].[71]

Kennedy may have approached an understanding of this point, but no American president who believed in the necessity of containment and stalemating international communism's advance could act upon such a realization, for it would involve concessions to and acceptance of much of the revolutionary's position. That is to say, one would have to recognize the corruption and repression of a Diem, which was the source and sustenance of much non-Western revolutionary activity.

Failing such a realization or willingness to act upon it, the Johnson administration was committed to the course of escalation and frustration. The upshot was the maiming of Vietnam as well as the spirit of the American people. Insofar as America's conception of world order is maintained by the willingness of the United States, its people, and its leaders to commit its resources to a global effort, then the Vietnam War during the Kennedy and Johnson administrations undercut that willingness. Thus the implementation of stalemate in Vietnam undermined the very will that the commitment was ostensibly to demonstrate.

SAVING THE STALEMATE MACHINE

The Nixon administration entered office with a dual problem. First, the Tet offensive had demonstrated to many, perhaps most, Americans the futility of incremental escalation of and continued American involvement in the war. The beginnings of talks with the North Vietnamese had raised expectations that meaningful negotiations might be possible which could bring to an end the years of frustrating carnage. Moreover, Nixon had during his campaign exploited the cumulating frustrations of the American people to help fashion his marginal victory over Hubert Humphrey. Thus Nixon was confronted with a nebulous, rather inarticulate desire, encouraged by him during the campaign, that the war be ended. If he did not do this or show considerable progress in this direction, his own reelection in 1972 might be endangered.

On the other hand, Nixon maintained the belief that the American right wing remained a potent force. If the ending of the war took on the appearance of what he termed a "bug out," the country and his administration might be ravaged by that McCarthyite segment of public opinion which, of course, he, as much if not more than any American, had nourished and exploited throughout his public career. Therefore the domestic domino was no less important to the Nixon administration than to those of his predecessors. Indeed, Henry Kissinger saw the domestic danger as not unlike the unraveling of Weimar Germany he had experienced as a boy.[72]

The new president's problem in dealing with this fact of political life was complicated by the second dimension of the overall problem confronting his administration. For although Nixon had attacked Johnson's policies in Vietnam, he nevertheless accepted the broad premises upon which they rested. That is to say, he accepted the general notion that the United States must maintain its "special place in the world."[73] Or as Henry Kissinger would argue a decade later:

> As the leader of democratic alliances we had to remember that scores of countries and millions of people relied for their security on our willingness to stand by allies, indeed in our confidence in ourselves. No serious policymaker could allow himself to succumb to the fashionable debunking of "prestige" or "honor" or "credibility." For a great power to abandon a small country to tyranny simply to obtain a respite from our own travail seemed to me—and still seems to me—profoundly immoral and destructive of our efforts to build a new and ultimately more peaceful pattern of international relations.[74]

On the other hand, Nixon and Kissinger were prepared to accept the proposition that "the postwar period in international relations has ended,"[75] and there were new opportunities for "negotiations" especially with the Chinese and the Soviets who were no longer viewed as functionally monolithic. The new situation implied the possibility of reducing somewhat the American global presence. In sum, retrenchment was now a possibility, although retreat was out of the question.

Nixon sought, therefore, to maintain America's global role but to do it in such a manner that what appeared to be opportunities for a stable order could be maximized. At the same time this process of fashioning what he termed a "new strategy for peace" had to be done on the debris of the Vietnam-shattered domestic foreign policy consensus. This constraint dictated the minimalist rhetoric of the Nixon Doctrine. But Nixon and Kissinger knew that rhetoric would not, in itself, save the essential domino—the Nixon presidency. The two dimensions of his foreign policy problem were, therefore, joined in Vietnam: Nixon's own perception of the risks and opportunities in the international system required that he pursue the old objectives of a salient, even dominant American world role, which seemed to imply in turn that Vietnam not appear to be "lost." Simultaneously, however, Americans had to be withdrawn from the swamp in such a manner that Nixon was not cut with either edge of domestic political opinion. The direction of the movement was to be different from that of the Kennedy and Johnson years, but the dangers were the same.[76]

Buying Time

The Nixon administration's effort involved a multitracked process of talking and fighting which the president characterized as the pursuit of "peace with honor." The fighting dominated most of the two and a half years after Nixon's election. There was, however, an important difference from the 1960s. In early June 1969 Nixon met with President Thieu on Midway Island and announced that the United States would begin withdrawing American troops from the South. The withdrawal would continue over the next four years in irregular increments. In the meantime, the scale of violence, especially in the air war, was increased as virtually all target restrictions were removed and reports of American air attacks on civilian targets proliferated. Moreover, a secret air war was opened against North Vietnamese supply areas in Cambodia, the reporting of which by the White House and Defense Department to the Congress and the American people was systematically distorted and covered up so as to hide its existence.

The land war was also expanded before American troop levels were reduced to levels that would be prohibitive of offensive ground action. Most spectacular was the invasion of Cambodia by American and South Vietnamese in the spring of 1970. This was followed by an invasion of southern Laos by South Vietnamese troops with American air support in February 1971. The Cambodian invasion could claim some success in that significant North Vietnamese and Viet Cong supplies were captured. On the other hand, the much-heralded command headquarters for the communist military effort in the South was not found, and large concentrations of communist troops were not located and destroyed.

North Vietnamese and Viet Cong capacity for waging offensive war in the South appeared to have been weakened somewhat by the Communists' Tet casualties and Nixon's actions, but their capacity to continue the war was by no means broken by these efforts. The Communists' reaction during this period of expanded American military activity was like that which they had exercised in the past. When the military pressure increased, they would simply avoid contact as much as possible. It was clear that it was only a matter of time before an active American ground effort would be precluded by reduced American troop levels. It was also apparent that the antiwar sentiment in the United States was undiminished. In fact, the antiwar movement was at its height during the first two years of the Nixon administration, with massive demonstrations in Washington and sometimes violent protest throughout the United States. These protests culminated in the tragic and cathartic events following the Cambodian invasion as four students were shot to death by the Ohio National Guard at Kent State University, followed by an assault on a dormitory at Jackson State University in Mississippi in which two students were killed. Following these events militant antiwar activity did drop off, although there was a notable increase in general antiwar sentiment nationwide. By early and mid-1971 sizeable portions of the American people—in excess of 60 percent—could be found consistently opposed to the war, now believing that it had been a mistake in the first place, and not believing that the Nixon administration was being truthful concerning plans for ending the fighting.

On the other hand, Nixon's expansion of the war did accomplish the end of neutralizing criticism of him from the right insofar as he had taken actions that they had advocated throughout the mid and late 1960s. Furthermore, Nixon allowed ongoing "protective reaction" air strikes against the North and approved the undertaking of a dramatic but fruitless raid on the Son Tay POW camp in North Vietnam. This kind of escapade had marginal impact on the military situation, but as the White House saw it, it was great "theater" and held a feared segment of public opinion at bay.[78]

By roughly the middle of his first term, therefore, Nixon had mollified the right with his willingness to employ and even escalate the level of violence in Vietnam. The costs were enormous as American battle deaths continued to rise, though at a slower rate, toward the 50,000 mark. Vietnamese casualties and refugees increased by hundreds of thousands, and yet another Southeast Asian society and political system—Cambodia—disintegrated under the impact of an expanded war. By 1975 some 700,000 Cambodians had died and more than 250,000 tons of bombs had been dropped. From 1970 to 1975, nearly half the Cambodian population, some 3,389,000 people, had been made homeless by the war; which, to use Nixon's words of July 1, 1970, was waged in order to secure "Cambodia's chances of surviving as a neutral country."[79] Nixon was able, however, to defuse pressure from the left by changing and eventually ending the Selective Service System while initiating aggressive disruptive action against the antiwar left including surveillance, infiltration, and the use of the Justice Department under Attorney General John Mitchell to initiate numerous conspiracy cases against the leadership of the antiwar movement. None of these cases were ever won by the Justice Department. Nevertheless, as long as the antiwar left was tied up in litigation, it was not in the streets. Antiwar sentiment was rising in Congress, but the slowness and incremental nature of congressional action directed against the war gave Nixon room and time for maneuver. Finally Nixon's "middle America" seemed numb and willing to wait. They would not wait forever, however, and 1972 was approaching.

"Peace with Honor"

By the end of 1970 it was not inconceivable that the fighting could remain indefinitely stalemated. American ground forces were approaching a level one-half of that of January 1969, or about 270,000 to 300,000 men. This reduction in American offensive military capability had been offset somewhat by increased air power. Nixon, however, had set in motion a process of withdrawal that would be virtually impossible to stop or reverse in terms of his domestic support. Moreover, continued escalation of American air power was not an indefinitely viable posture, for the North Vietnamese air defense system guaranteed that the number of American prisoners of war would increase.

But there was no certainty as to whether the South Vietnamese could stand without American support. Vietnamization was receiving optimistic evaluations, but vast uncertainty remained. The problem, then, was to extricate the remaining American forces yet leave behind a politico-military framework that would allow the South Vietnamese an opportunity to survive. At a minimum, Nixon would need a "decent interval" between United States withdrawal and a communist takeover in the South. That is, assuming the worst, the "loss" of the Saigon regime, it was essential that it not appear that the United States was responsible. If it could be argued that the good doctor had done all that he could and the patient died anyway, the expected international losses could be minimized. If the death could be delayed until after the 1972 elections, it would not matter domestically. If the patient lived, this would be a bonus from the standpoint of American policy, but it was not essential. All that was essential was that America's international interests and the Nixon administration live.

The obvious way to go about building a real or at least an apparent continuation of stalemate by proxy or at a minimum a decent interval was through the Paris negotiations. The talks, however, had been deadlocked since 1969. The United States was calling for a cease fire in place, a timetable for withdrawal of all foreign forces from the South, and the release of American POWs. Hanoi, on the other hand, refused to acknowledge that it had forces in the South and demanded as a precondition the removal of the Thieu regime in Saigon.[80] In other words, little had changed since Nixon entered office.

In May 1971 Kissinger sought to initiate movement on the diplomatic track in elaborately arranged and protracted secret talks with the North Vietnamese. The American position, in private, was agreement to a deadline for U.S. withdrawal in exchange for the release of American POWs. In public Nixon was dramatically refusing to set any deadline until all POWs had been released. Moreover, the president was emphasizing "mutual withdrawals," but in private Kissinger was ambiguous on this issue. The North Vietnamese did not reject the Kissinger proposal out of hand and continued the secret contacts throughout the summer of 1971. In September, however, they rejected the proposal. The United States responded with further secret proposals, which included having Thieu step down just before new elections were held in the South. The elections were to be supervised by an independent body. Finally, the NLF would be represented in overseeing the elections.

Nixon was now entering the election year with American forces significantly reduced but no peace agreement. To counter anticipated pressure from the left concerning his lack of peace efforts, he made a dramatic television revelation in January 1972 of the secret talks and the American proposals. The Nixon speech opened a round of public and private invective between the United States and the North Vietnamese. Nevertheless, the secret contacts were reestablished even as the North launched an Easter offensive, which succeeded in capturing the northernmost province of South Vietnam and seriously threatening Hue. During the battles that broke out all over South Vietnam, it became clear that the South Vietnamese army was not yet fully able to stand before the North Vietnamese without massive U.S. air support.

Nixon and Kissinger now turned to the use of other secret channels to the North, specifically the Russians. In a secret meeting with Brezhnev in April, Kissinger "produced what probably was the first major turning point in the history of Vietnam negotiations."[81] Kissinger informed Brezhnev that the United States was willing to allow the North Vietnamese to keep in South Vietnam those forces that were there prior to the Easter offensive. At the same time, however, Kissinger linked the offer to a North Vietnamese agreement not to demand the removal of Thieu prior to any agreement. During these negotiations, Nixon's public stance on these questions remained ambiguous. Moreover, the United States throughout all these negotiations had not consulted the South Vietnamese.

In the meantime Nixon decided, despite the upcoming summit meeting with the Russians concerning strategic arms limitations, to punish the North Vietnamese for their spring offensive by resuming massive bombing of the North and, on May 8, 1972, mining Haiphong harbor. It was a serious gamble, for it was conceivable that the Russians would cancel the summit and the excruciating process of negotiating the SALT agreement would be lost. The decision split the administration, but the Russians did not break off their negotiations with the United States. It was clear that their own interests came before those of their socialist brothers in Hanoi, and in fact they might be willing to help their common capitalist adversary out of the Vietnam swamp if the United States could provide needed trade and technology.

During the summit of late May 1972, Kissinger made more concessions to the North Vietnamese concerning political power sharing in the South. The United States was simultaneously pounding the North Vietnamese with the stick of American air power and offering them concessions that very nearly brought the American position in line with that of the North Vietnamese. Only the problem of the survival of the Thieu regime remained, and Kissinger took this up with Zhou Enlai during his secret visit to Beijing in mid-June. Zhou was reluctant to press Hanoi, but according to one report, there were indications that the Chinese passed the word to the North Vietnamese that they should not be so adamant about the removal of Thieu prior to an agreement.[82]

Kissinger was now confronted with the problem of informing Thieu that he had been bargaining over his destiny for the preceding year without consulting him. The meeting was held in mid-August. Kissinger insists that he provided Thieu with a full disclosure of the negotiations and that he "played with the idea" of a diversionary invasion of the North, but asserts that both he and Thieu recognized that this was "a gimmick, not a strategy."[83] Other analysts claim that these talks were a throwback to the end of the Korean War twenty years earlier with Kissinger making extravagant but gossamer promises to Thieu that after Richard Nixon had been reelected it would be a different story. Any concessions that the United States might be making were, he implied, necessary because of the domestic political situation. The United States, he said, "would not hesitate to apply all its power to bring North Vietnam down to its knees,"[84] including the suggestion that Thieu begin preparations for an invasion of the North.

Perhaps Thieu was not "nonplussed" and baffled[85] by all this as some have reported. But even Kissinger concedes that very little was clarified by the negotiations. Confusion, he insists, was the result of diametrically different domestic positions now occupied by Thieu and Nixon: the former needing a continued and open-ended American presence; the latter committed to ending such a commitment. Kissinger now feels that there were unbridgeable cultural gaps between the allies and has tried to shift responsibility for subsequent misunderstanding onto Thieu.[86] Kissinger, for his part, probably intended leaving Thieu in as strong a military position as possible, but he was prepared to go forward with negotiations with Hanoi whether Thieu agreed or not. On the return flight to Washington Kissinger reportedly remarked to his staff: "One thing is for sure: we cannot stand another four years of this. . . . So let's finish it brutally once and for all."[87]

Negotiations proceeded secretly with the North Vietnamese, and it was clear that agreement was within reach as Hanoi accepted the ideas advanced by Kissinger and Nixon through Moscow and Beijing, including acceptance of a continuation, in some form, of the Thieu government.[88] The news now had to be broken to Saigon, and General Alexander Haig was dispatched to tell Thieu who adamantly opposed any arrangement that might lead to a coalition government that might undermine his position. Kissinger, desiring to maintain momentum, decided to press on without Thieu's concurrence, and in October achieved a breakthrough with the North Vietnamese, who nevertheless insisted that the agreements be initialed before the American election. The North Vietnamese, undoubtedly remembering the events of 1954 and 1955, sought to ensure the American commitment, fearing that after the election the Americans might renege. Kissinger agreed, but insisted that he would have to get Saigon's approval first.

Kissinger now flew to Saigon and met with Thieu between October 19 and 23. Thieu's fury was on this occasion unrestrained,[89] and he refused to agree to the arrangements worked out by Kissinger. Kissinger was compelled, therefore, to cancel his planned trip to Hanoi for the signing of the agreement and returned to the United States. However, presidential politics remained paramount. Therefore Kissinger announced on October 26 that "peace is at hand," although he knew that this was simply not the case. If anything, it seemed farther away than ever. In the meantime Hanoi, fearing that it was being used by the Nixon administration for domestic political purposes, announced publicly the terms of the agreement.

Kissinger returned to Paris with a list of South Vietnamese objections, which he read into the record. Kissinger insists that this was done primarily for appearance's sake, but he probably underestimated the North Vietnamese sensitivity to the delay even as he had underestimated Thieu's recalcitrance. By December 1972, the North Vietnamese began to display reluctance to proceed. They suggested changes in the agreement in mid-December, and Kissinger publicly denounced their action as "perfidy." Two days later Nixon ordered "Operation Linebacker II," which included massive bombing of Hanoi and the rest of North Vietnam. William Saxbe, Republican Senator from Ohio and soon to become Nixon's fourth attorney general, guessed, along with many others, that Nixon had "lost his senses."[90] Reports of civilian casualties occupied the front pages of the world's newspapers,[91] but the attacks continued. Marvin and Bernard Kalb report one of their sources who reviewed the situation later as saying:

> Look, we were in an embarrassing situation. Could we suddenly say we'll sign in January what we wouldn't in October? We had to do something. So the bombing began . . . [it] creat[ed] the image of a defeated enemy crawling back to the peace table to accept terms demanded by the U.S. Maybe the bombing had some effect . . . but the B-52's weren't critical.[92]

On January 13, 1973, the North Vietnamese agreed to sign the agreements reached in principle months earlier. Thieu, now satisfied that the North had been seriously weakened and mollified by the American show of force, finally went along, and the negotiations were concluded on January 27, 1973.

Concluding Observations on Leaving Swamps

In reviewing this final phase and termination of direct American combat involvement in Vietnam, one is taken back to 1953 when the United States sought to extricate itself from another Asian war fought to preserve the concept of containment. In both instances, the final agreement confirmed an existing stalemate. In both instances the final agreement was delayed and very nearly precluded because of the actions of America's client. And in both instances American firepower brutally savaged the negotiating adversary partner during the denouement of the bargaining process. In the Vietnamese case this fact is especially tragic, for the Christmas 1972 bombings of Hanoi resulted only in part from anything the North Vietnamese had done. In no small measure, Hanoi was attacked because Henry Kissinger[93] misjudged Thieu's willingness to accept cavalier treatment at Kissinger's hands.

The question of whether the 1972 Christmas bombings could have been avoided raises the question of whether, for that matter, the violence of the preceding four years was necessary. It must have been known that the North Vietnamese would never leave the South. Why should they surrender in negotiations that which they had not been forced to surrender on the battlefield? The negotiation of peace treaties and postwar settlements seldom do more than ratify what has been wrought by the course of battle. If this is the case, then it would follow that Nixon continued fighting for many of the reasons the United States entered the conflict in the first place.

The Nixon administration knew that North Vietnam and the NLF could not be defeated, that they could only be stalemated. But Nixon and Kissinger also believed that if an approximation of the Paris agreements of 1973 had been signed in 1969, the Saigon regime would have fallen quickly, thereby threatening the Nixon administration, the security of which we have since learned was an ultimately all-consuming obsession. The Nixon administration felt it could no more afford to "lose" Vietnam than its predecessors. The survival of the Nixon administration is properly emphasized, we think, because, by their own perception and prescription concerning the international system, many if not most of the conditions of international politics that required a display of will and commitment in 1961 through 1965–1966 were no longer relevant in 1969. The Nixon administration heralded the advent of a new era of negotiations in 1969; why, then, not negotiate in 1969? The answer would seem to lie in Nixon's fear of the domestic consequences of the Viet Cong flag going up over Saigon while he was running for reelection in 1972. For this reason, then, the land and people of Vietnam were pulverized for four more years.

The style of the diplomacy leading to the Paris agreements is revealing. Throughout the process Nixon maintained a public position that was at best ambiguous and frequently contrary to the position adopted in private by Kissinger.[94] To have revealed the positions being set forth by Kissinger would not only have enraged Saigon, which, like the American people, was kept in the dark, it would also have enraged those McCarthyites whom Nixon was so responsible for and yet so afraid of. Nixon was after all bargaining away many of the points over which the war had been stalemated for years. In the end, Thieu was enraged anyway, but his anger could be assuaged with the Christmas bombing of the North and the promise of increased military and economic assistance. The remnants of the McCarthyite segment of American public opinion could not, it was thought, be so easily bought off.

In fairness to the Nixon administration, it should be emphasized that they also feared that the appearance of a "loss" in Vietnam could severely limit their freedom of action in pursuing the other dimensions of the Nixon Doctrine. The opening of relations with China and the negotiation of significant arms control agreements with the Soviets was undoubtedly seen as requiring a good deal of support from the American people. If the potential for a right-wing backlash was as great as the Nixon administration seemed to fear, then a bitter national debate over who "lost" Vietnam had to be avoided if the other pressing business of building Nixon's vision of world order was to go forward. Thus the larger vision of world order could be used to justify the further destruction of

Vietnam, and gave the insurance, if brutally purchased, that Nixon thought he needed.

There may be one additional tragic irony in all of this. In view of the large body of opinion against the war by the middle of the Nixon administration, one wonders whether the potential for the backlash was real, or if real, as substantial as Nixon seemed to imagine. If, as Gelb suggests, domestic opinion had turned decisively against the war, then the much-feared backlash was a figment of the imagination of an administration which, as the Watergate affair demonstrates, was almost paranoid about its public image. To the extent that the four years of war under Richard Nixon were conceived and prosecuted to anticipate a public opinion threat that existed primarily in the mind of Richard Nixon, these were the cruelest years of the war.

Thus, as it began, the direct involvement of the United States in Vietnam ended with Vietnam and the Vietnamese people being used as pawns in a much larger game. There was a new international system to be ordered and maintained. The dynamics of strategic weapons development set in motion by the Cuban missile crisis culminated in the early 1970s in rough strategic parity between the United States and the Soviet Union. The SALT agreements were by and large an effort to institutionalize this parity and make predictable the future growth of strategic arms. The Sino-Soviet split seemed irremediable, and opened up possibilities for a new kind of balance of power diplomacy. Finally, the emergence of new and barely understood transnational economic forces could not be ignored. Tad Szulc reports that during the Paris negotiations "a senior White House official remarked . . . [that] Vietnam was a 'cruel side show' in the Administration's new world wide policies."[95]

For a short while the war in Southeast Asia receded from the American consciousness, replaced by the drama of Nixon trying desperately to save his presidency from the spreading stain of Watergate. (Ironically, many of the Watergate horrors came about as a result of Nixon's efforts to protect his policy in Southeast Asia from domestic dissent.) The military situation remained stalemated throughout 1974. By early 1975, however, the new Ford administration was calling for emergency assistance from Congress as signs of increasing North Vietnamese pressure began to appear. In mid-March, the South Vietnamese undertook a poorly planned and poorly executed withdrawal from the strategic central highlands and thereby initiated massive panic and refugee flights into the Saigon area and the loss of hundreds of millions of dollars' worth of equipment. In the meantime in Cambodia, Communist-led Khmer Rouge forces completely surrounded and cut off the Cambodian capital of Phnom Penh, and on April 17, 1975, the American-backed government surrendered. Four days later President Thieu resigned in Saigon and angrily denounced the United States for reneging on secret promises made by the Nixon administration at the time of the Paris agreements. Thieu (with a sizeable sum of American dollars reportedly on deposit) went into exile in Taiwan.

A week later the surrender of Saigon was negotiated between South Vietnamese officials and the Communists. For the United States, however, the last week of the American presence was marked by the tense withdrawal, often under North Vietnamese fire, of thousands of Americans from Tan Son Nhut Air Base, as South Vietnamese who had associated themselves with and, in some cases, profited from the American war effort desperately sought a way out of the country. By April 29, 1975, the air base had been closed, and a thousand remaining Americans and 5,500 South Vietnamese whose lives were assumed to be in danger had to be evacuated by helicopter from the grounds of the U.S. embassy to aircraft carriers in the South China Sea. In the process yet another four American Marines lost their lives, the body of one being left behind in the frantic last moments of the evacuation.

At home, the long-feared wave of recrimination did not occur. The American people met the final unravelling of South Vietnam with an almost fatalistic detachment and some skepticism concerning the arrival of thousands of South Vietnamese refugees in the United States. Indeed, if there were signs of recrimination they came from the Ford administration, as it tried to shift responsibility for the final collapse of Vietnam to Congress.[96] But even though one additional Southeast Asian domino— Laos—fell and Thailand and the Philippines seemed to wobble noticeably as they announced a reassessment of their relationship with the Asian communist powers in mid-1975, there was no hysteria or, for that matter, outward concern on the part of the American people. After all, the Nixon Doctrine itself was based on a similar reassessment and, even more important, as public opinion analyses during the early 1970s revealed, the American citizenry was not the fickle, belligerent, and vengeful monster prophesied in the conventional wisdom of the foreign policy elite that had managed the cold war. Rather, the American people were in many ways more open to change than the foreign policy community.[97]

NOTES

1. We are indebted for this metaphor to Carl Oglesby, "The Vietnamese Crucible," in Carl Oglesby and Richard Schaull, *Containment and Change* (New York: Macmillan, 1967), p. 3.

2. From John Galloway, ed., *The Kennedys and Vietnam* (New York: Facts on File, 1971), citing speech of June 1, 1956, p. 13. Reprinted by permission.

3. Ibid., pp. 14–15.

4. William Henderson, "South Vietnam Finds Itself," *Foreign Affairs*, Vol. 35 (January 1957), p. 285.

5. George M. Kahin and John W. Lewis, *The United States in Vietnam*, rev. ed. (New York: Delta, 1969), pp. 100–102. An excellent recent history of U.S. involvement in Vietnam is Stanley Karnow's *Vietnam: A History* (New York: Viking, 1983).

6. "Resolution of the Third National Congress of the Vietnam Workers' Party on the Tasks and Line of the Party in the New Stage," quoted in ibid., p. 115.

7. Ibid., p. 119.

8. "1961 Rusk-McNamara Report to Kennedy on South Vietnam," *The Pentagon Papers* (New York: Bantam Books for *The New York Times*, 1971), p. 150. Hereafter cited as *Pentagon Papers*.

9. Ibid.

10. Ibid.

11. Leslie H. Gelb, "The Essential Domino: American Politics and Vietnam," *Foreign Affairs*, Vol. 50 (April 1972), pp. 459–475.

12. Arthur Schlesinger, Jr., *A Thousand Days* (Boston: Houghton Mifflin, 1965), p. 549.

13. Cited in Walter LaFeber, *America, Russia, and the Cold War, 1945–1971*, 2nd ed. (New York: Wiley, 1972), p. 244.

14. See Kahin and Lewis, op. cit., pp. 143–146 and *The Pentagon Papers*, pp. 158–233.

15. CBS Interview of September 2, 1963, *Department of State Bulletin*, Vol. 49, No. 1266 (September 30, 1963), pp. 498–499.

16. Quoted by Kenneth O'Donnell in "LBJ and the Kennedys," *Life*, Vol. 69, No. 6 (August 7, 1970), p. 51.

17. Ibid. (emphasis in the original), pp. 51–52.

18. "McNamara Report to Johnson on the Situation in Saigon in '63," *Pentagon Papers*, pp. 271, 272, 274.

19. Neil Sheehan, "The Covert War and Tokin Gulf: February–August, 1964," quoting the authors of the *Pentagon Papers*, p. 240.

20. "'64 Memo by Joint Chiefs of Staff Discussing Widening of the War," in *Pentagon Papers*, pp. 274–277, esp. p. 277.

21. "Draft Resolution for Congress on Actions in Southeast Asia," in *Pentagon Papers*, pp. 286–288, esp. p. 287.

22. Neil Sheehan, citing authors of the *Pentagon Papers*, p. 240.

23. Anthony Austin, *The President's War* (Philadelphia: Lippincott, 1971), pp. 182–183. See U.S. Congress, Senate Committee on Foreign Relations, *Hearings: The Gulf of Tonkin, the 1964 Incidents*, 90th Congress, 2nd Session, 1968.

24. Austin, op. cit., pp. 182–183. See also Captain Herrick's suggestion that a complete evaluation of the available information be undertaken before the U.S. responded, pp. 205, 292–293.

25. Tom Wicker, *J.F.K. and L.B.J.: The Influence of Personality upon Politics* (Baltimore: Penguin Books, 1972), pp. 224–225.

26. David Halberstam, *The Best and the Brightest* (New York: Random House, 1972), p. 414.

27. Tad Szulc, "Behind the Vietnam Cease-Fire Agreement," *Foreign Policy*, No. 15, (Summer 1974), p. 42.

28. Halberstam, op. cit., pp. 533–534.

29. Neil Sheehan, "The Launching of the Ground War: March–July 1965," quoting *Pentagon Papers*, p. 383.

30. "National Security Action Memorandum 328, April 6, 1965," in *Pentagon Papers*, pp. 442–443.

31. *The New York Times*, August 27, 1966, p. 10.

32. Lyndon B. Johnson, "Pattern for Peace in Southeast Asia," *Department of State Bulletin*, Vol. 41, No. 1348 (April 26, 1965), p. 607.

33. Ibid., p. 607.

34. Ibid., p. 608.

35. "McCone Memo to Top Officials on Effectiveness of the Air War," in *Pentagon Papers*, p. 441.

36. Press Conference of July 28, 1965, in *Public Papers of the Presidents, Lyndon B. Johnson, 1965*, Vol. 2 (Washington, D.C.: U.S. Government Printing Office, 1966), pp. 796 and 797.

37. Sheehan, "Launching of the Ground War," quoting the *Pentagon Papers*, pp. 416–417.

38. McNaughton Memo to Andrew Goodpaster on "Forces Required to Win," in *Pentagon Papers*, pp. 455–456.

39. See Fox Butterfield, "The Buildup: July 1965–September 1966," in *Pentagon Papers*, pp. 459–485.

40. "The Effects of U.S. Bombing on North Vietnam's Ability to Support Military Operations in South Vietnam: Retrospect and Prospect," August 29, 1966, quoted in *Pentagon Papers*, pp. 502–504 and 506–507.

41. Hedrick Smith, "Secretary McNamara's Disenchantment: October 1966–May 1967," in *Pentagon Papers*, pp. 510–541.

42. Ibid., pp. 524–535.

43. U.S. Congress, Senate Committee on the Judiciary, Hearings Before the Subcommittee to Investigate Problems Connected with Refugees and Escapees, *War-Related Problems in Indochina, Part 1, Vietnam*, 92nd Congress, 1st Session, 1971, pp. 1–3.

44. *The New York Times*, February 22, 1974.

45. Arthur Westin and E. W. Pfeiffer, "The Cratering of Indochina," in Herbert F. York, *Arms Control: Readings from Scientific American* (New York: Freeman, 1973), p. 329.

46. Ibid., p. 338.

47. Halberstam, op. cit., p. 633.

48. Ibid., pp. 632–634. McNamara has recently and reluctantly broken with his past practice of silence on the war. In a subpoenaed deposition in early 1984, Mr. McNamara described his growing skepticism concerning American policy: "I did not believe the war could be won militarily," he asserted. By 1965 he claims to have begun doubting the veracity of data on infiltration, casualties and the utility of further escalation. See Charles Mohr, "McNamara on the Record, Reluctantly, on Vietnam," *New York Times*, May 16, 1984, p. A22.

49. E. W. Kenworthy, "The Tet Offensive and the Turnaround," in *Pentagon Papers*, pp. 589–612.

50. See Henry Kissinger, "The Vietnam Negotiations," in *American Foreign Policy: Three Essays* (New York: W. W. Norton, 1969), p. 107.

51. The list of "wise men" comprised a "Who's Who" of U.S. foreign policy. They included General Omar Bradley, McGeorge Bundy, Arthur Dean (Eisenhower's negotiator in Korea), Douglas Dillon, Associate Justice Abe Fortas, former Justice Arthur Goldberg, Henry Cabot Lodge, John J. McCloy, former diplomat Robert Murphy, General Matthew Ridgeway, Maxwell Taylor, former Deputy Defense Secretary Cyrus Vance, and George Ball. The best accounts of the "great reversal" are in *The New York*

Times, March 6, 1969, and March 7, 1969 in stories filed by Hedrick Smith and William Beecher.

52. Johnson, op. cit. p. 609

53. See Arthur Schlesinger, Jr., *The Bitter Heritage: Vietnam and American Democracy, 1941–1966* (Boston: Houghton Mifflin, 1968).

54. Daniel Ellsberg, *Papers on the War* (New York: Simon & Schuster, 1972), pp. 42–135; and Leslie Gelb, "Vietnam: The System Worked," *Foreign Policy,* No. 3 (Summer 1971), pp. 140–167. Gelb's analysis of the war has been expanded in his 1979 book written with the assistance of Richard K. Betts, *The Irony of Vietnam: The System Worked* (Washington, D.C.: Brookings, 1979).

55. Johnson, op. cit., p. 607.

56. Quoted in *Pentagon Papers,* p. 255.

57. Kissinger, op. cit., p. 112.

58. LaFeber, op. cit., p. 255.

59. Arthur Schlesinger, Jr., "The Quagmire Papers (Continued)," *New York Review of Books,* December 16, 1971, p. 41, also cited by Ellsberg, op. cit., p. 124.

60. Lyndon B. Johnson, *Vantage Point* (New York: Holt, Rinehart and Winston, 1971), pp. 151–152.

61. Ibid.

62. Ellsberg, op. cit., pp. 100–127.

63. See Gelb's discussion of this point in "The Essential Domino," pp. 463–466.

64. Ibid., pp. 459–460. See also the assessment of this factor by an important American military historian of the war in Col. Harry Summers, *On Strategy: A Critical Analysis of the Vietnam War* (Novato, CA: Presidio, 1982), esp. pp. 9–80.

65. Ellsberg, op. cit., p. 124.

66. *Pentagon Papers* (original), Vol. IV, pp. 615–616, quoted by Ellsberg, op. cit., p. 124.

67. See the editorial in *The New York Times,* May 15, 1968, and Kahin and Lewis, op. cit., pp. 379–390.

68. Kahin and Lewis, op. cit., pp. 386–388.

69. After the election there were reports that Nixon had communicated through Mrs. Anna Chenault to the South Vietnamese that they should delay their participation until after the election. This could achieve what in fact happened during the last week of the campaign, confusion in the minds of those undecided voters who might have been moving toward Humphrey because of apparent movement toward peace. Presumably the *quid pro quo* from Nixon would have been a promise from Nixon to Saigon that they would get a better "deal" from his administration than from Humphrey's. Theodore H. White, *The Making of the President, 1968* (New York: Atheneum, 1969), pp. 380–381, 383. Much of this speculation was subsequently confirmed by Mrs. Chenault in her memoirs, *The Education of Anna* (New York: Times Books, 1980). See also the review by Robert Shaplan, "A Somewhat Naive Dragon Lady," *The New York Times Book Review,* February 3, 1980, p. 12.

70. A bitterly critical account and analysis of this bombing and all of American policy towards Cambodia is William Shawcross, *Sideshow: Kissinger, Nixon and the Destruction of Cambodia* (New York: Pocket Books, 1979). Kissinger defends himself in *White House Years* (Boston: Little, Brown, 1979), chapters 7 and 12. An account of the extent to which Kissinger wrote portions of his memoirs in response to Shawcross's attack can be found in Wolfgang Saxon, "Kissinger Revised His Book More Than He Reported," *New York Times,* October 31, 1979.

71. Bernard Fall, "The Theory and Practice of Insurgency and Counterinsurgency," *Naval War College Review,* April 1965, reprinted in Mark E. Smith, III, and Claude J.

Johns, Jr., *American Defense Policy*, 2nd ed. (Baltimore: Johns Hopkins University Press, 1968), p. 272.

72. Kissinger, *White House Years*, pp. 229–230. For other indications of the administration's concern about domestic opinion as well as the constraints imposed by the bureaucracy, see pp. 260–261, 282.

73. Richard Nixon, *U.S. Foreign Policy for the 1970's: A New Strategy for Peace* (Washington, D.C.: U.S. Government Printing Office, 1970), p. 2.

74. Kissinger, *White House Years*, pp. 226–235, Kissinger's initial appraisal of the problem before the Nixon administration as it entered office.

75. Nixon, *U.S. Foreign Policy for the 1970's: A New Strategy for Peace*, p. 4.

76. Gelb, "The Essential Domino," pp. 471–472.

77. See Gallup Polls for February through August of 1971 and Gelb, "The Essential Domino," p. 473.

78. Tad Szulc, op. cit., p. 33. Szulc uses this term with respect to the peace talks during 1971 and 1972, but the concept clearly applies here as well.

79. Statistics and Nixon quote cited by Anthony Lewis, "A Successful Operation," *The New York Times*, February 6, 1975. See also Shawcross, *passim*.

80. Szulc, op. cit., p. 25, and Kahin and Lewis, op. cit., pp. 392–405. The following analysis is based primarily on Szulc's essential analysis of the development of the 1973 Vietnam peace agreement, Kissinger's *White House Years* and the highly critical study of Kissinger by Seymour Hersh, *The Price of Power: Kissinger in the White House* (New York: Summit, 1983).

81. Szulc, op. cit., p. 36.

82. Ibid., p. 45.

83. Kissinger, pp. 1321–1324, esp. 1324.

84. Szulc, p. 46.

85. Ibid.

86. Kissinger, pp. 1325–1326. For a less flattering account of these meetings, see Hersh, pp. 570–572.

87. Szulc, p. 47. Kissinger's memoirs are silent on this point.

88. Hersh, op. cit., p. 583.

89. See Hersh's account, pp. 593–595.

90. For a summary of some domestic and foreign press comment see Marvin Kalb and Bernard Kalb, *Kissinger* (Boston: Little, Brown, 1974), pp. 416–417. But it is important to note that the bombing policy was Kissinger's as much as Nixon's. It was a version of the good cop–bad cop routine, wherein a criminal gets brutally harassed by one man and then his partner comes into the interrogation room and offers the dazed man a cigarette and says, "If you cooperate I'll see to it that the despicable first interrogator doesn't return."

91. A less damning account of the bombing—and one favorably cited by Kissinger—is Guenter Lewy, *America in Vietnam* (New York: Oxford University Press, 1978), pp. 413–414.

92. Kalb and Kalb, p. 422.

93. See Hersh, pp. 583–585.

94. It is evident that there *were* serious disagreements between Kissinger and Nixon—largely the result of Nixon's envy of Kissinger's popularity and fears that Kissinger was exercizing too much latitude in the negotiating process. Indeed, as election day approached Nixon—secure in his lead over George McGovern—may have tried to delay the peace treaty until after the election in order to deny to Kissinger the satisfaction of having delivered the peace *and* the election. He seems also to have been

concerned about the appearance of getting an agreement literally hours before the election. For an account of Nixon's ambivalence toward Kissinger and the bizarre, cynical court politics of the Nixon White House, see Hersh, *passim*, but especially, pp. 561–635.

95. Szulc, op. cit., p. 35.

96. See, for example, "CBS News Excerpts," in *Congressional Quarterly Weekly Report*, Vol. 33, No. 17 (April 26, 1975), esp. pp. 853–854.

97. See Murrey Marder, "Public Called Wary on Foreign Policy," *Washington Post*, September 11, 1975, p. A 2; Leslie H. Gelb "Poll-Takers Say Most Americans Oppose Isolationism," *The New York Times*, September 11, 1975, p. 18.

Chapter 10
The Nixon
Doctrine
and Beyond

The Nixon-Kissinger stewardship of foreign policy liquidated the major source of domestic criticism for American foreign policy—Vietnam—but did not relinquish American global commitments, and Vietnam was the logical result of extended commitments. The Nixon Doctrine did not repudiate the premise of American policy since World War II but rather sought not to get caught with the results of the logic of those premises—intervention on a grand scale. Maintaining the means and rebuilding the will to uphold commitments and sustain order while not succumbing to sustained conventional combat intervention was the preoccupation of the Nixon administration. In short, the Nixon Doctrine is not unlike the new look which sought to conserve containment but at a lower cost.

THE NIXON-KISSINGER DOCTRINE:
CONTAINMENT AND MANAGEMENT

The paradoxical nature of the Nixon Doctrine is heightened by the fact that Nixon heralded its promulgation with the assertion that the "postwar period in international relations had ended."[1] Purportedly there were new opportunities for negotiation and the movement of Soviet-American relations to a basis other than the bitter and frequently awesome confrontations that marked the cold war. Yet the president insisted that the United States would not abandon its commitments—commitments incurred during the period of confrontation. There was a new era of international politics, but threats to American interests persisted although the nature of these threats was never clearly delineated.

Moreover, Nixon saw the continued need for the "defense and development of allies and friends."[2] Now, however, the effort would be part of a system of shared responsibilities:

> The United States will participate in the defense and development of allies and friends, but . . . America cannot—and will not—conceive *all* the plans, design *all* the programs, execute *all* the decisions and undertake *all* the

defense of the free nations of the world. We will help where it makes a real difference and is considered in our interest.[3]

Indeed, the concept of "interests" moved to the center of American policy during the Nixon years: "We are not involved in the world because we have commitments; we have commitments because we are involved. Our interests must shape our commitments, rather than the other way around."[4]

But what were American interests? None of Nixon's four major statements on U.S. foreign policy defined these in terms other than in Wilsonian rhetoric conerning a "generation of peace." There was reference to the "creative possibilities of a pluralistic world," but are we to assume that this meant the free play of American and communist ideology with their fundamentally antithetical views of the human condition and potentiality?[5] "We seek a new and stable framework of international relationships," Nixon said.[6]

But the framework that emerged was far more traditional than its Wilsonian rhetoric implied. Nixon foreswore mere balance of power politics as the ultimate form and substance of U.S. foreign policy.[7] But in the absence of the more stable order that his rhetoric referred to and the persistence of perceived threats to American interests, it remained the only prudent course. The policy framework that emerged was designed both to balance and constrain Soviet strategic power but also to pull the Soviets into a detente or easing of tensions within which the Soviets might be schooled in the behavior, expectations, and obligations of great powers.

At least three major elements of the policy framework developed by Nixon and his special assistant for national security affairs and later secretary of state, Henry Kissinger, require close analysis. First, there were direct negotiations with the Soviets to salvage and institutionalize the balance of strategic power between the United States and the Soviet Union that they found when they entered office. Second, there was an historic opening of relations with the People's Republic of China which, when combined with the extraction of the United States from Vietnam, eased the military demands on the United States in Asia. More important, however, Sino-Soviet animosities could be used by the United States to apply diplomatic pressure on the Soviets. Finally, there was to be the notion of detente itself. The Soviets were to be offered recognition of their status as a great power as well as access to American capital, technology, and agricultural assistance if they would in turn relax their revolutionary impulses and support for those in the third world who pursued revolutionary change. At a minimum it was hoped that a relaxation of tensions would allow for minimal strategic arms control.

Strategic Arms Control

The Nixon administration's approach to strategic arms control negotiations with the Soviets was conditioned by two concerns: (1) a perceived deterioration in the strategic balance and (2) the relationship between that balance and what was feared to be declining American political capability. There was concern for stabilizing the arms race and perhaps ultimately even reducing the high levels of strategic arms possessed by the United States and the Soviet Union. The overriding concern of the Nixon administration, however, was that any arms control negotiations and agreements with the Soviets be consistent with and serve the broader strategic concept defined by Henry Kissinger:

> Throughout history the political influence of nations has been roughly correlative to their military power. While states might differ in the moral worth and prestige of their institutions, diplomatic skill could augment but never substitute for military strength. In the final reckoning weakness has invariably tempted aggression and impotence brings abdication of policy in its train. . . . The balance of power, a concept much maligned in American political writing—and rarely used without being preceded by the pejorative "outdated"—has in fact been the precondition of peace. A calculus of power, of course, is only the beginning of policy; it cannot be its sole purpose. The fact remains that without strength even the most elevated purpose risks becoming overwhelmed by the dictates of others.[8]

Thus Kissinger's conception of the relationship between military power and diplomacy remained consistent with what he had set forth during the debate over Eisenhower's new look more than a decade earlier. Furthermore, as in the late 1950s, Kissinger was troubled by the seeming disjunction of military power and political influence in a nuclear age. Finally, the dilemma was seen as being made more complex because its resolution would have to be undertaken by the Nixon administration in a domestic context of intense upheaval and ". . . at a moment when technology, combined with earlier deliberate decisions, was altering the nature of the strategic balance."[9]

The earlier decisions alluded to by Kissinger had been made during the Johnson administration in the mid-1960s. Specifically, then Secretary of Defense Robert McNamara had concluded that the buildup in strategic forces initiated by the Soviet Union in the wake of the Cuban missile crisis made it inevitable that they would achieve a degree of strategic parity with the United States. The Soviet Union, once it had begun to increase its numbers of land-based intercontinental ballistic missiles (ICBMs) and expand its fleet of submarine-launched ballistic missile (SLBM) carrying submarines, would achieve, perhaps within a decade, the capacity to devastate the United States in a nuclear war even if the United States struck the Soviet Union first. Similarly, if the Soviet Union attacked the United States first, the United States would be able to retaliate with devastating effects on Soviet society destroying perhaps one-fourth to one-third of the Soviet population and two-thirds of Soviet industry.

McNamara decided that in the face of this inevitable parity it made little sense to keep expanding the number of ICBMs and SLBMs in the American force structure. McNamara reasoned[10] that once the United States and the Soviet Union had achieved "mutual assured destruction" (MAD) capability, it was wasteful to continue expanding their respective strategic force structures. Accordingly, the United States unilaterally stopped deploying ICBMs and SLBMs after 1967, thereby sustaining a strategic force structure of 1,054 ICBMs and 656 SLBMs as well as several hundred B-52 bombers. Presumably such a step by the United States would offer the Soviets an incentive to halt their force structure expansion and provide a basis for a more stable strategic relationship.

At the same time, however, the Johnson administration, in response to bureaucratic pressures[11] within the defense establishment and political pressures from Congress, went forward with research, development and testing of two new weapons technologies that could serve as hedges against an uncertain future. The first technology was an antiballistic missile (ABM) defense system designed to disable nuclear warheads launched against the United States. The Soviet Union had begun to deploy a limited and, according to American analysis, easily penetrated ABM system around Moscow in the mid-1960s. The pressure to emulate the Soviets grew into what one observer has described as "a wave of ABM hysteria."[12] The Johnson administration responded with a decision to deploy a limited system, although McNamara justified deployment primarily in terms of a defense against what was thought to be an emerging Chinese ICBM capability. The second technological development involved increasing the number of nuclear warheads that each American ICBM and SLBM could launch towards separate targets. These multiple independently targetable reentry vehicles or MIRVs would, therefore, significantly increase the destructive capability of the American strategic forces although the number of missiles or launch vehicles comprising those forces remained fixed at the number which existed in 1967. Thus, for example, a portion of the ICBM fleet—ultimately 550—would carry three MIRVs and some 496 of the SLBMs would be capable of carrying from ten to fourteen warheads.

Either of the new technologies, once incorporated into the Soviet or American force structures, would complicate the accomplishment and maintenance of the strategic stability to which McNamara aspired. ABM was the more immediate problem, however, for if an ABM system could be made to work, then the side deploying the system would be able to remove the threat to its population posed by the other side's strategic forces. In the calculus of deterrence developed in the United States, this could be destabilizing because the retaliatory threat of the non-ABM state would be neutralized leaving it open to blackmail or attack by the side deploying ABM. Moreover, some deterrence theorists and planners feared that the side that saw itself falling behind in the race to develop and deploy an ABM might well decide to use its strategic capability *before* the other side deployed its ABM.

MIRVs were rationalized in the Defense Department in part as a counter to the Soviet ABMs. Thus, it was argued, the deployment of hundreds if not thousands of additional warheads by the United States would allow the United States to overwhelm any ABM system that the Soviets might deploy. On the other hand, if the United States began testing and ultimately deployed MIRVs, was it reasonable to assume that the Soviets could accept a strategic relationship in which they did not also have their own MIRVs? Perhaps, therefore, MIRVs, and thus a further escalation of offensive arms development, could be headed off by an agreement to ban the deployment of ABMs. In fact, the Johnson administration initiated negotiations with the Soviet Union on precisely this point in early 1967 and again at the meeting between President Johnson and Premier Kosygin at Glasboro, New Jersey. The Soviet invasion of Czechoslovakia in early 1968 led to the termination of these initial attempts at strategic arms limitation talks (SALT) and the development of the American ABM system and the testing of MIRVs went forward, leaving to the Nixon administration the decisions concerning their deployment and the future of SALT.

For the Nixon administration, however, the primary question to be addressed was the appearance of a deteriorating strategic balance of forces between the Soviet Union and the United States resulting from the decision by the Johnson administration not to expand the number of American ICBMs and SLBMs even as the Soviet buildup continued. By 1969 the quantitative parity projected by McNamara was fast becoming a reality (see Table 10-1). Notwithstanding the successful flight-test of MIRVs in 1968 which, when deployed, would expand significantly the capability of American launch vehicles, the fixed number of American launchers standing in contrast to a rapidly expanding Soviet force was a concern of Nixon and Kissinger. Moreover, if the numbers of larger Soviet launch vehicles continued to grow significantly beyond the parity point of 1968–1969, and those launchers were subsequently augmented by Soviet MIRVs, then some portion of the American retaliatory capacity might conceivably become vulnerable. Finally, apart from MIRVs, there was little the United States could do to redress the image of a deteriorating quantitative balance except to build more of the smaller (though technologically superior) Minuteman missiles, given the fact that the development of a new American ICBM would take years to develop, test, and deploy.

By early 1969 the Nixon administration was confronted by growing pressure, especially in the Senate, for a unilateral American decision against the deployment of ABMs. Popular opinion in those cities picked in 1967 to be deployment sites for ABMs was running against deployment, and scientific opinion on the feasibility of the system was deeply divided. But Nixon and Kissinger did not want to give up the ABM without some concession from the Russians in return. Thus the Nixon administration, though shifting the deployment of the ABM to defense of ICBM sites (generally located in the less populated areas of the Midwest), announced that the United States would go forward with the system—a decision sustained by a one-vote margin in the Senate when authorization for the system was voted on in August of 1969. The administration had begun, therefore, to regard ABMs and MIRVs as bargaining chips to be used in the upcoming SALT negotiations, which the Russians had agreed to resume in November of 1969.

The Nixon administration's concept of SALT was grounded, therefore, in the view that a stratetic arms control agreement with the Soviets might accomplish a slowing of the momentum of Soviet strategic force expansion and perhaps establish a more predictable and stable strategic relationship with the Soviet Union. Kissinger's negotiating strategy was to offer to limit ABM deployment in exchange for a freeze on further strategic force expansion during the life of the agreement, which was to run for five years. By the time the agreement was completed in 1972, the Soviets had achieved higher force levels than the United States in both ICBMs and SLBMs. But the superior quality of American strategic forces and the very large number of long-range bombers in the American arsenal were viewed as off-setting the quantitative advantages of the Soviet Union. The American advantage with respect to MIRVs was crucial in this accounting, since the ability of the United States to place accurate multiple warheads on its missiles meant that despite the greater number of Soviet missiles allowed under the agreement, the United States retained a significant advantage in the number of more effective warheads.

No less important than the force levels negotiated in the agreement, however, the Nixon administration was able to guarantee that the Soviets would not deploy any more strategic weapons than they had been planning to deploy as of 1972.[13] At the same time, the United States was not required to sacrifice any of its programs directed at offensive force expansion. The Soviets for their part, retained the option to develop

MIRVs in the future and achieved formal recognition by the United States that they had indeed reached a degree of parity with the United States.

TABLE 10-1. Historical Changes in Strategic Forces, 1962–1970

		1962	1963	1964	1965	1966	1967	1968	1969	1970
USA	ICBM	294	424	834	854	904	1054	1054	1054	1054
	SLBM	144	224	416	496	592	656	656	656	656
	Bombers	600	630	630	630	630	600	545	560	400
USSR	ICBM	75	90	190	224	292	570	858	1028	1513
	SLBM	some	107	107	107	107	107	121	196	304
	Bombers	190	190	175	160	155	160	155	145	140

Source: The Military Balance 1975–1976; 1977–1978; 1979–1980; 1980–1981 (London: International Institute for Strategic Studies, 1975, 1977, 1978, 1979, and 1980). Reprinted by permission.

Critics of SALT in the United States insisted that the Soviets had achieved a great deal more as well. Senator Henry Jackson (D., Wash.) quickly became the leader of a large group of Senate critics of SALT who insisted that the agreement confirmed in its freeze on the force structures in place in mid-1972, a substantial Soviet superiority, especially in a class of very large Soviet ICBMs known as the SS-9. Although the agreement on limiting offensive weapons froze the number of SS-9s allowed the Soviets at approximately three hundred, Senator Jackson argued that if and when these large ICBMs were eventually married to accurate MIRVs, they might well make vulnerable the smaller number of American ICBMs. Thus the quantitative advantages in large ICBMs and SLBMs conceded to the Soviets merely institutionalized the appearance of greater Soviet dynamism—a condition that, in the view of Jackson and a growing number of critics in the Congress and among conservative defense analysts, would ultimately be used by the Soviets for their political advantage. Accordingly, Jackson demanded during the Senate debate on the agreements that the administration negotiate equal ceilings on strategic systems as well as pursuing limitations on qualitative developments. The latter objective was already a primary element on the administration's agenda and, together with Jackson's demands, became the core of the next round of negotiations.

A second comprehensive agreement proved impossible to complete as Watergate plagued and truncated the second Nixon term. Gerald Ford was able, however, to initial an agreement with the Russians at Vladivostok in November of 1974, which incorporated the principle of equal ceilings on strategic delivery vehicles (2400) and the number of those vehicles that could be MIRVed (1320). By that time, however, newer technologies developed by the two sides, and Ronald Reagan's conservative challenge to Ford, impinged on the negotiations, leading to a stalemate during the waning months of the Ford administration. SALT II, as it was now being referred to became, therefore, the first item on the agenda of Soviet-American relations during the Carter administration.

In the meantime the SALT process became the most tangible evidence of the Nixon administration's approach to preserving America's preeminent global role in the face of expanding Soviet strategic power and an American public grown ambivalent about an activist global role. SALT became, therefore, a process pursued not because it promised an end to or reversal of the dynamic of strategic arms development and certainly not because it promised any diminution of the American global role. Rather, the process promised a modicum of order and predictability in the ongoing interaction of Soviet and American strategic power.

The Opening to China

The restructuring of political and military order from American hegemony to a kind of duopolistic Soviet-American managed global balance was a continuing process. It required the muting of strident ideological themes so that Soviet-American power and interest could face one another in a context uncluttered by emotionalism. Moreover, to the extent that a Soviet threat persisted, it was to be contained by drawing the Soviets' other rival, China, into a diplomatic and even strategic tripolar relationship. The administration's complex effort assumed that once the American presence on the Asian mainland was reduced, America would be less of an anathema to Beijing than the Soviets were. During the late 1960s, the Soviets became the main enemy to the Chinese. The Soviets, in turn, found the Chinese to be a formidable ideological and diplomatic rival within the communist and third world, with enormous territorial claims against the Soviet Union. Indeed, during the spring and summer of 1969, these territorial claims became a pretext for a series of Sino-Soviet border clashes along the Xinjiang (Sinkiang) province border with the Soviet Union and in the Amur River valley. A buildup of Soviet forces along these areas of the Chinese border undoubtedly deepened the Chinese sense of fear but also strengthened the hand of those within China who desired an opening towards the United States. The Nixon administration's response was in turn an attempt to enlist the Chinese in its structure of world balance.

At the same time, however, improving Soviet-American relations could not help but concern the Chinese. For example, Soviet-American agreement on troop reductions in Europe could release Soviet military forces for the Sino-Soviet border. But insofar as the Chinese became more preoccupied with their northern borders they would be less likely to fish in troubled waters beyond their southern and eastern boundaries. The American burden in Asia might then be transferred to others in the region. Brezhnev's summer 1973 journey to the United States was undoubtedly seen by the Chinese as a measure implicitly directed toward China. The Nixon policy, therefore, was in part to use the great Sino-Soviet dispute to retain American political, economic, and even military access in East, Southeast, and South Asia.[14]

The opening itself was developed over the course of the first two years of the Nixon administration, initially through indirect contacts.[15] On April 21, 1971, the Chinese extended a secret invitation to the United States asking that a personal envoy of the president be sent to Beijing to prepare the way for a formal reestablishment of contact between the United States and the People's Republic. Kissinger made the trip and within a year President Nixon visited China for talks with Mao Zedong and Zhou Enlai. In a communique at the end of the visit the United States affirmed that Taiwan was part of China and acknowledged that the peaceful resolution of the relationship between Taiwan and the People's Republic was a matter that they must decide for themselves. From the Chinese standpoint, however, these statements by the United States were not all that they might have hoped for. Substantively, the issue of American recognition of Taiwan remained, and this meant that from Beijing's perspective the crux of the problem of Sino-American relations also remained.

The Nixon administration, especially once the debilitating effects of Watergate set in, could never respond satisfactorily to this Chinese demand. The political support for full normalization was simply not available to a president fighting for his survival within eighteen months of the visit. Moreover, his successor, Gerald Ford, found himself locked in a bitter struggle for nomination with a representative of the right wing of the Republican party, Ronald Reagan, whose support for Taiwan was unqualified. Thus apart from the significant psychological impact of the initiative, there was always an air of unsubstantiality about the China opening. It was, in a sense, all diplomatic nuance and no substance. But from the administration's perspective this was sufficient:

> Triangular diplomacy, to be effective, must rely on the natural incentives and propensities of the players. It must avoid the impression that one is "using" either of the contenders against the other; otherwise one becomes vulnerable to retaliation or blackmail. The hostility between China and the Soviet Union served our purposes best if we maintained closer relations with each side than they did with each other. The rest could be left to the dynamic of events.[16]

The Difficulties of Detente

The third element of the Nixon administration's foreign policy framework was ostensibly to complement the China opening. If the presidential visit to China was a stick to prod the Russians towards a more accommodating posture, the offer of detente was a carrot offered in reward for the move. Thus as the SALT negotiations proceeded and were ultimately completed in 1972, the United States proffered agricultural sales (which proved disruptive to American food prices), credits, and the prospect of significantly increased trade. The latter inducements could not be delivered by the Nixon administration, however, for those in the Congress suspicious of detente attached conditions to any trade liberalization that made the measures unacceptable to the Soviets. Specifically, Senator Jackson and others in the Senate and House were able to pass amendments to trade legislation that required the Soviets to liberalize Jewish emigration from the Soviet Union, before Moscow could benefit from more U.S. trade. Predictably the Soviets regarded such conditions as interference in their internal affairs and consequently the trade dimension of detente was never fully developed.

On the other hand, Soviet security concerns in Eastern Europe were given grudging recognition by the United States. In part, this was forced on the administration by West German acceptance in 1972 of the Central European status quo as the probably permanent outcome of World War II. All the same, this accommodation was granted reluctantly and incompletely. Something more than echoes of "liberation" and "rollback" lingered in Nixon's actions toward Eastern Europe. Thus the Nixon visit to Rumania in 1969 left the Soviets furious for a year and probably stalled SALT negotiations.[17] And American diplomats continued saying that United States relations with Eastern European countries had nothing to do with the Soviet Union,[18] making it apparent that clear acknowledgment of the Soviet position in Eastern Europe was far from complete. Similarly, funds for Radio Liberty and Radio Free Europe were sought at around $40 million a year. The existence of these organizations undoubtedly reflected bureaucratic politics, but they also suggested a less than complete acceptance of the internal structure of the Soviet empire. More direct evidence of this ongoing American reluctance to accept finally the outcome of World War II was to be found in the conditions the United States would impose on the comprehensive European security agreement sought by the Soviets during the 1970s and partially achieved in 1975, in the Helsinki Accords. Specifically, the United States insisted that Eastern Europe be opened to Western cultural access. Such conditions were clearly unacceptable to a Soviet leadership that crushed the

"Prague spring" and suffered Rumanian eccentricities only as long as Rumanian domestic life remained comfortably neo-Stalinist.

It was where spheres and interests overlapped outside Europe, however, the Soviet-American detente encountered greatest difficulty. For its part, the Nixon administration used American power and diplomacy boldly in order to obviate any speculation that America was developing a "reputation for unsteadiness" or that the United States was becoming in Nixon's words, a "pitiful helpless giant." For example, North Vietnam was bombed and its harbors mined as part of a systematic escalation of violence to force American peace terms on a nominal ally of the Soviet Union and China. The boldness of the act was underscored by the fact that even as their ally was being pummelled, the Soviets and Chinese were being used as interlocutors between Washington and Hanoi.[19]

Again, in May 1975, as the American tragedy of Vietnam was ending, the Ford administration responded to the seizure of the American freighter *Mayaguez* by Cambodia with a dramatic show of force. Air attacks were initiated against Cambodia, and marines were landed on Koh Tang Island in the Gulf of Siam where, incorrectly, it was assumed the American crew was being held. In contrast with the regular resort to diplomatic means when American fishing vessels had been seized, their crews beaten and even shot at off Ecuador, no diplomatic channels were used until after the show of force was completed. It mattered little, however, for the entire incident seemed a useful pretext to demonstrate that the United States would, in Henry Kissinger's words, maintain its "reputation for fierceness."[20]

Perhaps the most dramatic cases of colliding Soviet-American interests occurred in the Middle East. In that area the Soviets were held responsible for disruptions of international order while at the same time the U.S. tried to minimize Soviet influence. The schooling of the Soviet Union in the limitations of influence to be accorded to them by the United States was forceful and frequently undertaken without consultation with or the consent of America's allies, the Congress, and in one instance, the Joint Chiefs of Staff.

In September 1970 American military might was displayed in an impressive effort to force the Russians to withdraw support from the Syrians when they moved tanks into Jordan to help the Palestinians against King Hussein. American troops were mobilized to intervene, but no congressional advice was sought and objections of the Joint Chiefs of Staff, who opposed intervention on both political and military grounds, were overriden. No allies could be found to give American-based C-130's landing rights on their way to the Middle East. But the Russians were warned of "the gravest consequences"[21] if the Syrian tanks did not desist. Kissinger told a tense, frightened Soviet diplomat, "The last time you told me that the Syrians would send no more troops."[22] The Russian minister councilor complained, "We didn't know the Syrians would cross the border, our own military advisers stopped at the border and went no further."[23] Kissinger retorted, "Your client started it, you have to end it."[24]

The episode has been described as another link in the chain of U.S.–Soviet confrontations, and the "management" of the "crisis" has been compared to Cuba.[25] The latter is overdrawn, inasmuch as Cuba involved a direct U.S.–Soviet confrontation. In contrast, the Nixon administration in this instance was instructing the Soviets in how to manage their clients and maintain stability.

> Nixon saw the situation in its broadest implications. Jordan to him was a microscopic spot on the map and yet he viewed it as having far-reaching implications on the world-wide stage and on American relations with the Soviet Union.
> The idea that Soviet-American relations must be viewed as a chain with each link representing a test of the validity of relations as a whole, was . . . uppermost in the President's mind.[26]

Once again in 1973, during the Yom Kippur War, Henry Kissinger pronounced two days after Egyptian and Syrian units moved on Israeli-occupied territory that "we shall resist aggressive foreign policies. Detente cannot survive irresponsibility in the Middle East."[27] The news that the Soviet Union was actively encouraging other Arab states to join the conflict, that Soviet cargo planes were resupplying the Arab belligerents, and that Russian officers were leading Syrian tank columns, again prompted the Nixon administration to point to the delicate linkages of detente. The expansion of trade and technological transfer crucial to the Soviets' pursuit of detente were pegged to their acting responsibly in restraining themselves from an urge to expand influence in the Middle East. American diplomats were given instructions that were unmistakable injunctions for the Soviets to realize the imperatives of detente. As one aide remembered, "We were told to tell the Soviets we hold them responsible for everything the Arabs do."[28]

But American pressure was by no means confined to diplomatic remonstrances. As initial Arab military successes were checked by the Israelis in both the Sinai and on the Golan Heights between Syria and Israel, the Soviets proposed joint Soviet-American diplomatic and military intervention. The United States was prepared to undertake the former but not the latter because Kissinger feared that participation in the joint Soviet-American military force proposed by the Soviets would lead to a reestablishment of a strong Soviet presence in the region. When a United Nations cease-fire did not hold and the Soviet-backed Arab position began to deteriorate rapidly, the Soviets warned Washington that the Soviet Union was prepared unilaterally to prevent an Arab catastrophe. The United States reacted by placing American forces around the globe on alert and sternly warned the Soviets that the introduction of any troops into the area was unacceptable to the United States. The Soviets quickly backed away from the imminent confrontation with the United States; accepted a UN emergency force; and more importantly, acceded to and ultimately lent some support to Kissinger's personal diplomatic effort to establish a cease-fire and develop a basis for some sort of permanent settlement of the Middle Eastern situation.

The Arab members of the Organization of Petroleum Exporting Countries (OPEC) introduced a new sense of urgency into the crisis by imposing an embargo on oil to Europe, Japan, and the United States, and demanding that Arab positions on the Arab-Israeli dispute be adopted in the West. The international oil distribution system ensured that the economic effects of the embargo did not affect any single importer inordinantly. Nonetheless, the Europeans and Japanese, being more dependent upon Middle Eastern oil than the United States, shifted to a more accommodating position vis-à-vis the Arabs and by and large have remained so. By the late 1970s this development would serve to introduce significant strains in the Atlantic alliance.

In the meantime, Kissinger not only succeeded in bringing about a cease-fire and disengagement of Arab and Israeli forces, but through weeks of shuttling back and forth between Arab capitals and Israel in late 1973 and again in the spring of 1974, Kissinger firmly established the United States as the only mediator acceptable to the major parties to the Middle Eastern conflict. The Syrians remained dependent on the Soviets for military assistance but were nonetheless prepared to work with Kissinger in developing the cease-fire and disengagement agreements of June 1974. The Egyptians, having borne the brunt of four wars with Israel, became active and supportive participants in Kissinger's "shuttle" diplomacy. Kissinger's so-called step-by-step approach of dealing with immediate military problems and avoiding the deeper and more contentious issues of the establishment of a Palestinian state ultimately bogged down. In the interim, however, further recourse to military means was avoided; the United States was firmly positioned as interlocutor between Egypt, the largest of the Arab states, and Israel; and perhaps more important from the perspective of the Soviet-American relationship, the United States seized the diplomatic initiative and consigned the Soviets to the sidelines.

By the same token, however, the Soviets were prepared to move in support of anti-American forces in Black Africa when the opportunity presented itself in southern Africa during the latter part of the Ford administration. From the outset of the Nixon administration, American policy had been predicated on the assumption that the Portuguese colonial presence and the white regimes in Rhodesia and South Africa were likely to be permanent fixtures in the region. By 1974, however, the Portuguese presence had collapsed, a black nationalist regime had come to power in Mozambique and civil war among competing nationalist groups raged in Angola. By 1975 a Soviet- and Cuban-backed group had emerged as the likely victor in the Angolan conflict. The Ford administration tried to extend U.S. assistance to competing insurgents, but was blocked by overwhelming congressional votes against any further U.S. assistance to pro-Western Angolan insurgent groups. By early 1976, a Marxist regime was consolidating control of Angola. Meanwhile, Kissinger could only warn the Soviets that the structure of Soviet-American relations was endangered by Soviet abuses of detente.

The Ambiguities of the Nixon-Kissinger Balance

Thus the Nixon administration's effort to define a balance of power managed by means of Soviet-American condominial power, influence, and responsibility was asymmetrical at best; for it prohibited expansion of Soviet power and presence while demanding active Soviet cooperation. Indeed, the Soviets were in some instances faced with the actual diminution of their influence, for in the case of the Middle East, Kissinger's diplomacy was more or less successfully directed at undermining altogether what remained of Soviet influence in the area.

The Kissinger-Nixon policy in Asia was a variation on the theme of responsibility and order played in the Middle East. To no small extent the Vietnam War was an effort to force the Chinese to control their purported clients, the NLF and Hanoi. The Chinese refusal to extend responsible authority south was a significant motivation for the American Vietnam adventure.[29] Under the Nixon administration, this ambition that the Chinese exert a conservative regional influence received some fulfillment. As a key member of the United States team that negotiated with the North Vietnamese, William H. Sullivan, pointed out:

> When President Nixon decided to put the mines into the harbors of North Vietnam on May 8, it produced a situation in which North Vietnam became one hundred per cent dependent upon China for the provision of its equipment. Everything coming from the Soviet Union had to transit Chinese territory. Nothing could go through the waters and come into

Haiphong. . . . This means that China's preoccupation with Soviet encirclement came into play. This means that China's feeling that it would
rather have four Balkanized States in Indochina rather than an Indochina
that was dominated by Hanoi and possibly susceptible to Moscow, came
into play.[30]

And, by early 1974, Chinese Premier Zhou was publicly proclaiming
the end of Chinese assistance to insurgencies in Southeast Asia and was
fretting in public about Soviet influence in North Vietnam and among
Thai insurgents.

A large part of the intellectual framework of this approach to foreign
policy is found in the writings and thoughts of Nixon's and then Ford's
principal adviser, Henry Kissinger. Professor Kissinger's major research
was into the political prerequisites of international stability. To Special
Assistant for National Security Affairs and Secretary of State Kissinger it
remained a universal principle that stability, not peace, is the hallmark of
successful diplomacy.[31] In his view, the greatest contributors to international instability had been revolutionary powers: Napoleonic France
in the nineteenth century, the Soviet Union in the twentieth. Revolutionary powers upset the established norms of governance because
they refuse to accept the "legitimacy" of the international order, based
on familiar, essentially conservative approaches to both international
and domestic political life: order, stability, even hierarchy as the
framework "which promotes social justice and human dignity." Yet now
it appeared that although the "Soviet Union is the greatest menace to
peace," it could also be drawn into the international order. In short,
revolutionary Russia could be instructed to become a status quo power
as Britain was in the nineteenth century and as America has claimed
itself to be in the cold war. As Kissinger explained:

> We are at a point where we can redefine the American position with re-
> spect to the world, where, for whatever reasons, it may be that even the
> Soviet Union has come to a realization of . . . the limits of . . . its ideological
> fervor.[32]

A status quo power can be counted on to respond to the limited, rational
demands of the balance of power. A status quo power can be enlisted in
the worldwide maintenance of order. In either condominium or balance,
the emphasis is to enlist the Soviets in achieving American ambitions,
which, it is argued in good Wilsonian fashion, are in fact the "interests"
of all.

But was all of this an accurate reading of Soviet interests and policy?
Skeptics argued that the Soviets could never accept such a vision. In this

dour view, the Soviets regarded the American pursuit of SALT as but a demonstration that the historical "correlation of forces" was moving against the West and that the West's pursuit of detente was only an admission of the fact. From a Soviet standpoint, detente had the advantage of allowing them to consolidate these gains, but in time they could be expected to continue exploiting the advantages conceded them under SALT I and to redouble their support for revolutionary forces in the third world.[33]

However the Soviets perceived the historical dynamic, they did indeed take advantage of the latitude allowed them under SALT (as did the United States). Moreover, when the opportunity presented itself through a combination of internal developments in southern Africa and an American government distracted by Watergate and an anti-interventionist reaction to Vietnam, the Soviets supported anti-Western forces with military assistance or through their Cuban proxies. In this, however, their behavior was consistent with American action in the Middle East.

Detente was characterized by this fundamental ambiguity: It was heralded by Nixon as a relaxation of tensions tantamount to a new era of international politics. But rhetoric aside, relations with the Soviet Union remained essentially competitive, and when, in time, the competitive essence of the relationship reemerged in the Middle East and in Africa, public disillusionment invariably followed. Moreover, at that juncture those who had been arguing all along that the SALT process was itself pernicious gained new credibility. Finally, when Ford was confronted with a political challenge from the right wing of his own party as he sought nomination in 1976, he felt compelled to move toward the policy positions of his adversaries. In the process, Ford pointedly abjured the use of even the word detente by members of his administration.

THE LIMITS OF TRIANGULAR BALANCE

The long-run vision of the international system that might emerge from the application of the Nixon-Kissinger and then Ford diplomacy was framed in the classic metaphors of diplomatic equilibrium and balance of power. As President Nixon remarked in early 1972, echoing Dr. Kissinger's doctoral thesis:

> We must remember that the only time in the history of the world that we have had any extended periods of peace is when there has been a balance of power. It is when one nation becomes infinitely more powerful in relation to its potential competitor that the danger of war arises. So I believe in

a world in which the United States is powerful. I think it would be a safer world and a better world if we have a strong, healthy United States, Europe, Soviet Union, China and Japan, each balancing the other, an even balance.[34]

The U.S.–Soviet–Chinese dimensions of this vision were, as we have seen, assiduously developed by the president and Kissinger. Europe and Japan on the other hand never achieved comparable status in the "triangular diplomacy" of the Nixon Doctrine. There were other problems as well. The developing world was also conspicuous by its absence in the framework of policy that developed, although—as was evident in Chile and Iran—the United States was prepared to intervene to destroy its ideological adversaries and support those who were prospective surrogates for American power. Moreover, the instruments of force encompassed by this concept of world order were and are increasingly problematic in their applicability. And, finally, there were domestic limits to the entire process.

Europe and Japan

There may be a Europe in the future that can control nuclear weapons and serve as a meaningful balance between the Soviets and America. There might be a nuclear Japan that could do the same. In the meantime, American policy did not push for the independence of Europe; the NATO alliance structure, its commitments, and obligations, stood. The American-European relationship remained essentially one in which the Europeans were dependent on America for their security and open to U.S. economic access. How this political, military, and economic dependence could inspire a separate and credible European pole in the global balance was not explained.

Furthermore, not all Europeans seemed overly anxious to shed their military dependence for more strategic autonomy. Weapons technology is expensive, and the Americans had always been willing, even aggressive merchants. The economies of Europe would be seriously distorted if they had to pay for large standing armies and significant production of military equipment. Indeed, to try and maintain the level of social services provided by most European governments as well as shoulder the added burden of a full defense budget would contribute to already painful European tax levels.

A credible European nuclear deterrent is at least conceivable, for both the French and English possess minimal nuclear systems, but they are somewhat incompatible technologically. More important, such a common defense policy would require that Europe's national forces first be merged and then managed by a political organization representing a "Europe" that does not yet exist. Finally, the thought of Germany with nuclear weapons or strong, more autonomous conventional forces, which would be a highly likely consequence of a military independent Europe, would be enough to give Europeans—East and West—considerable pause.

But even if a nascent Europe with marginal political and strategic independence is emerging, its interests will probably remain narrow and inner-directed, too much so for the foreseeable future for Europe to serve as much more than a regional power. The task of political and economic integration is an immensely complex task. To be sure, many of the prerequisites of a European political economy are already in place, but others—a banking system, a European system of taxation, control of corporations, a European system of social welfare services, and above all, a strong, common political vision—are not present. Moreover, the global economic crisis brought on by the Arab exercise of their "petropower" in late 1973 and early 1974 demonstrated the vulnerability of European political and economic institutions dependent upon external sources for more than 75 percent of their energy needs. One suspects, therefore, that the concerns of Europe will not be Asia or Latin America or the Indian subcontinent, at least not in the sense that a fully dimensionalized balance of power anticipates. The global powers with global interest would still be the Soviet Union and the United States.

Neither could Japan function as an independent and autonomous global power with global interests. Japan's increasingly global economic presence proved even more vulnerable than the Europeans', for in Japan's case more than 90 percent of its oil needs must be met with imports of petroleum from the Persian Gulf. By the mid-1970s, it was apparent, therefore, that previous forecasts of an emerging political and economic East Asian "superstate"[35] required reevaluation. Japan's global military capacity is, to say the least, problematic. A nation that is constitutionally prohibited from using force as an instrument of policy is ill-suited to be a point of countervailing powers to the Soviets, Americans, Europeans, or Chinese. However, the Nixonian vision of a new balance of power sought to alter this situation. Even though Japan's geographical insularity gives it relative security from "conventional" aggression, Japan was increasingly encouraged to expand the definitions of its interest under pressure from the Nixon administration.

The Japanese had relied on the American nuclear umbrella and conformed to the rigid American policy toward mainland China despite much internal opposition and historic interest. When Nixon reversed American policy on China with no prior consultation with the Japanese, it was not only taken as an insult but also read as a humiliating incentive for Japan to elaborate an independent course toward China. A similar shock occurred when the Nixon administration sought unilaterally to force the Japanese to reverse their trading position with America by realigning the value of their currency. The heavy-handed import tariffs, quotas, and embargoes combined with the decline of the dollar as a medium of international liquidity was seen as another indication to the Japanese that they should start to make their own way. American policy, under Nixon, undermined the paternalistic relationship that had evolved from Japan's wartime defeat. The rather brusque treatment of Japan—a country where "face" is a national priority—served, however, to vitiate the surety of the American "nuclear umbrella." As Osgood relates: "Official statements suggest that Japan's nuclear abstention was contingent upon a confidence in the credibility of America's nuclear deterrence, which it no longer automatically takes for granted."[36]

The American effort to draw out the Japanese political and economic presence was designed to present both China and Russia with countervailing power in the Pacific—power that would not be directed against American interest in Asia. The extrusion of Japan could make it considerably less friendly toward the United States, and yet Japan's refusal to be so drawn could involve the Americans more than ever in guaranteeing stability in Asia and the Pacific. The consequence of commitments in Asia, pursued by the encouragement of expanding Japanese power and a new relationship with China was and remains a problematic strategy undertaken in response to the costs of hegemonial power. The alternative of reexamining commitments and responsibilities in Asia seems to have been examined unwillingly if at all.

The Third World

The uncertainties surrounding the position of the third world in the world balance were no less than those relating to Europe and Japan. If, for example, the third world was to be stabilized by American management, then the evidence of the Nixon-Kissinger-Ford years is at best mixed.

In the case of the Indo-Pakistani War of 1971, for example, the policy of great power management under American direction failed in almost every respect. In 1971 India had reversed its policy of nonalignment and signed a mutual assistance treaty with Russia aimed at the Chinese. In response, the Pakistanis and the Chinese became increasingly close; for both now feared the implied expansion of Indian power. It was also a time when the Americans were wooing China into a tripolar relationship. In this context, Pakistan, India's old rival, experienced a massive upheaval in her eastern wing which was one thousand miles from dominant West Pakistan. East Pakistan exploded. An election that voted independence for the East was rescinded and West Pakistani troops started to slaughter East Pakistani civilians in a barely concealed ethnic war. In spite of an attempt to appear neutral, America sent arms to Pakistan, which was a member of the now defunct SEATO. A unified Pakistan was supported by the United States. The rebellion was not considered by the United States as merely an internal affair of Pakistan, but rather in terms of the regional and global balance of power. Although India was inundated with millions of refugees, American aid for refugee relief was little and late. Kissinger, on his way to China, stopped in Delhi and told the Indians that if they moved into Pakistan, China would move on India and that the Americans would not help defend the Indians against the Chinese as they did in the Sino-Indian War of 1962.

Faced with the burden of supporting ten million refugees and tales of horror about the fate of the ethnically kindred people of Bangladesh, the Indians marched against Pakistan. It was India's opportunity to see that its old antagonist would be permanently weakened by a separation of its eastern province. Washington counted on the Soviets to restrain their new Indian clients. However, in spite of America's calculations, the Pakistani-Chinese and Indian-Russian balance served not to inhibit the conflict but to free India to move against Pakistan. The Nixon administration then proceeded to condemn the Indians in the UN for aggression and sent the nuclear carrier *Enterprise* in a barely disguised "tilt" against India. The move failed. India achieved a spectacular military victory capturing seventy thousand West Pakistani troops and secured the independence of Bangladesh and the reduction of Pakistani power on its frontiers.[37]

Protestations by Nixon and Kissinger of their acceptance of "uncertainty or even turmoil . . . in the political flux which is likely to accompany growth"[38] in Africa proved no less problematic. The catalyst for greater American involvement in Africa[39] was the collapse of the Portuguese colonial presence and increasing pressure on the white regimes in Rhodesia and South Africa all within the context of increasing Russian activism in the area. During 1976, internal security within Rhodesia became increasingly tenuous as guerrilla activity expanded markedly. The South Africans, becoming alarmed at the growing threat to their north, proved supportive of an American-British diplomatic initiative in the late summer of 1976. Kissinger sought to replicate his Middle Eastern shuttle diplomacy successes by establishing himself as a mediator between the white regimes and the black governments in the region who were supporting black liberation efforts in Rhodesia. Kissinger tried to develop a framework for a gradual transfer of power from the white Rhodesian regime of Prime Minister Ian Smith to a black majority government. Despite some initial success the initiative eventually died as the Ford administration was defeated for reelection and black resistance to the scope of white control during the proposed transitional period overwhelmed the negotiations in early 1977.

We cannot know, of course, whether a second Ford administration with Henry Kissinger as secretary of state would have proved more successful in southern Africa in resolving the fundamental political and racial issues that rent the region than Kissinger's diplomacy had been earlier in the Middle East. What is clear is that Kissinger's activism and diplomatic virtuosity were brought to bear only after the Soviet-American competition had become salient in the region. Moreover, Kissinger's declaration that American policy was designed to "achieve the great goals of national independence, economic development and racial justice" and that "white South Africa must recognize that the world will continue to insist that the institutionalized separation of the races must end" came only as a previous policy of support for European colonial rule and indifference or, at most, extreme gradualism towards ending white rule in South Africa, was collapsing under the pressures of the black African liberation struggles.

In Chile, the administration was confronted with a constitutionally elected Marxist-socialist government under President Salvador Allende. Because Allende had not received an absolute majority of the presidential vote in September of 1970 (he received a plurality of 36 percent) his election by the Chilean congress was dismissed by Kissinger as a "fluke."[40] It was assumed that because he was a Marxist he would set about the irreversible dismemberment of the Chilean democracy and become a base for communist subversion of the region.[41] Exactly what the United States did about this situation has been a matter of intense debate.[42] Kissinger concedes that the United States attempted to influence votes in the Chilean congress to prevent Allende's election but justifies the action as merely the continuation of the policies of past administrations at the time of the 1964 Chilean elections. More controversial is the extent to which the administration supported the attempts of International Telephone and Telegraph to bring down the government or whether the United States, after Allende's election, encouraged an invisible blockade of Chile through a tightening-up on Export-Import Bank loans and other forms of economic assistance. Money already authorized before Allende's election continued to flow to Chile, but new support from either the United States, private bankers, or international agencies was restricted. On the other hand, the Allende regime's administrative capacity has been called into question as the basis for the development of internal conditions which made the country a poor credit risk for both governmental and nongovernmental financial institutions. It is worth noting, however, that poor administrative performance did not prove a sufficient basis for U.S. support to be withdrawn in other cases where the regimes in question were pro-American, such as the Mobutu regime in Zaire or the succession of American sponsored regimes in South Vietnam.

In any event economic conditions deteriorated within Chile throughout 1971 and 1972, and in September 1973, Allende was overthrown in a violent coup to be replaced by a military junta. Allende was killed—the junta has claimed, by his own hand—and Chilean democracy was aborted. Subsequently the junta's leadership undertook an international campaign of assassination of former officials of the Allende regime, including the car-bomb murder of Orlando Letelier, Allende's foreign minister, as Letelier drove along the streets of Washington, D.C. in 1976.

The character of American involvement in the descent of Chile into right-wing dictatorship remains somewhat obscure. Nonetheless, Kissinger has observed that "presidents of both parties have felt the need for covert operations in the gray area between formal diplomacy and military intervention throughout the postwar period."[43] Presumably, therefore, whatever the role of the United States in Chile, activity in this gray area remained an essential element of the Nixon administration's new framework for international order.[44]

The involvement of the Nixon-Kissinger-Ford administrations with the regime of Shah Mohammed Reza Pahlavi was a continuation of what had developed over the preceding three administrations. The Shah was regarded in Kissinger's words as "a friend of our country and a pillar of stability in a turbulent and vital region."[45] In sum, his regime was viewed as a surrogate for American power in the region and it became the policy of the Nixon administration to provide the Shah with all the military assistance he thought he required for the pursuance of that role. Thus by 1973 the Shah had placed orders, primarily with the United States, which would provide him with almost four hundred modern fighter-bombers, including the F-14 fighter, over six hundred helicopters, more than fifty long-range transport aircraft, as well as maritime patrol aircraft. By 1974–1975, the Shah was placing orders for the most modern United States Navy destroyers, hundreds of armored fighting vehicles, and still more fighter aircraft from the United States. By 1975 the Shah had spent in excess of $15 billion on arms purchases and had proclaimed a security mission for Iran that implied dominance of the region as well as responsibility for maintaining order in the northwestern Indian Ocean.[46]

Internally, the United States provided technical assistance and support for the Shah's secret police, Savak. In return, the United States received permission to establish intelligence sites along the Iran-Soviet border, which provided significant access to Soviet missile testing as well as tactical weapons test ranges. But these benefits were not without their costs, for when OPEC began escalating the price of oil dramatically in 1975, the American dependency on its surrogate proved decisive. Indeed, by the late 1970s allegations had become common that Kissinger had either tacitly accepted or had been blackmailed into accepting the price increases being proposed by America's ostensible ally, the Shah. The oil revenues were clearly necessary to pay for the massive arms imports. Moreover, the threat of closing down American assets in Iran were also available to Tehran. In any event, it is reported that Kissinger refused to support Saudi Arabian attempts to restrain the 1975 price increases.[47]

Thus the pattern of American involvement in the third world and its place in the larger framework developed during the Nixon-Ford years is uneven, but nonetheless, closely related to the larger concern with Soviet-American relations. That is, the countries of the third world remained what they had traditionally been in American postwar policy: objects in a larger game, episodically important, but only insofar as they impinged upon the traditional focus of the Nixon Doctrine. Yet as has so often been the case since World War II, events on the periphery have proved crucial to the development of American policy: Korea in the 1950s, Vietnam in the 1960s, and the Middle East in the 1970s.

The Limits of Force and Diplomacy

A further difficulty of the Nixon approach to a balanced world order was the problem of adapting force as an instrument of that policy. The difficulty with the use of force to maintain a balanced world order in the 1970s was that the consequences of large-scale intervention using conscript personnel had been shown to be unsuccessful and politically intolerable, especially in conflict situations requiring long-term, open-ended, and escalating commitment, such as counterrevolutionary war. Projecting force by symbolic means—the use of nuclear blackmail—has become increasingly unpalatable and problematic, especially with respect to countering revolutionary activity in the third world. Hanoi knew that the United States possessed nuclear weapons, but continued to fight anyway. As Bernard Fall noted some time ago, revolutionary war is essentially a political, not a military phenomenon, and must be dealt with accordingly.[48]

How, then, can the end of stability based on military power be attained? If policy is based on power whose persuasive potential is equated with the implied threat of force, how and at what levels is the force to be employed? The answer of the Nixon administration was that each state has a responsibility for order. Within each region that is not a sphere of influence there would be a balance of power. The Nixonian vision held that access to each region should be open to American power in case stability or balances break down. For such breakdowns, although possibly unimportant in themselves, affect the overall global equilibrium and, most important, the Soviet-American relationship. But the employment of force was recognized to be difficult, so it was deemed best that local powers, such as Iran—with American military assistance which reached perhaps its highest levels during the Nixon-Kissinger years—fend for themselves to enforce stability.

However, the problem remains of what to do in the event that this proves inadequate. The issue was posed succinctly by Earl Ravenal: "The basic question is whether the Nixon Doctrine is an honest policy that will fully fund the worldwide and Asian commitments it proposed to maintain, or whether it conceals a drift toward nuclear defense or an acceptance of greater risk of local defeat."[49] The Nixon administration's effort to incorporate the Chinese into its system of global order suggests that the problem in Asia was mitigated somewhat, at least to the extent that the Nixon administration abjured the close-in containment of the People's Republic. Nevertheless, the dilemma remained, and one cannot escape the inference that the gap between conventional force and the use of nuclear weapons was compressed. Indeed, the nuclear threat seemed the only solution to the quandary of how to keep commitments and keep American ground forces out of ground combat. If forces were to be committed to combat, then they would have to be professionals, and not draftees. But would there be enough of them for *global* commitments?

The Nixon Doctrine was marked by almost impenetrable ambiguity. On the one hand, we have the rhetoric of retrenchment and a "reduced profile," but the implementation of American strategy and diplomacy during the early 1970s suggests that there was no fundamental reduction of American objectives. The Nixon policy seems to have been one of keeping a high degree of policy latitude, especially with respect to the use of nuclear weapons: "[H]aving a full range of options does not mean that we will necessarily limit our response to the level or intensity chosen by an enemy. Potential enemies must know that we will respond to whatever degree is required to protect our interests."[50]

The Nixon-Kissinger variation on John Foster Dulles's theme of nuclear retaliation was fraught with all the problems and dangers of the original doctrine. That the new version could achieve the kind of flexibility appropriate to the world of the 1970s, especially in the face of Soviet-American parity, was nowhere clearly demonstrated. Kissinger himself acknowledged the difficulties of the notion of limited or flexible application of strategic and tactical nuclear weapons.[51] Other experts have commented on the illusory nature of this approach:

> The trouble with this concept is that it rests on faulty assumptions (for example, that civilian casualties and collateral damage can be kept to low levels); it ignores a basic lesson that the leaders of the U.S. Government in all cold war crises have learned—that when faced with a decision to start a nuclear war, almost any other alternative looks better; and it is too risky to serve as the foundation for a preferred strategy.[52]

Domestic Constraints

Finally, there were important domestic implications to the Nixon-Kissinger policies which warrant at least passing mention. First, there was the problem of control. Balance of power politics with shifting alignments was possible in previous centuries when a few men were stewards of foreign policy. Modern states, however, are complex organizations no matter how centralized the foreign policy apparatus might be. As Graham Allison and Morton Halperin have noted, there are inherent bureaucratic interests of the military and other foreign policy bureaucracies that can be reconciled only by compromises.[53] If control were to be achieved by a single will, as in the Kissinger management of the National Security Council, there is little assurance that these practices could continue or be institutionalized by succeeding administrations. Indeed, insofar as Kissinger succeeded in personalizing the formulation and conduct of American diplomacy, he completed the task of enfeebling the State Department begun by Senator Joseph McCarthy more than twenty years earlier. The Kissinger control of foreign policy has proved to be a hard act to follow.

Second, the old diplomacy, on which much of the Nixon-Kissinger approach was based, was secret and insulated from domestic politics. Foreign policy was a game of sovereigns, not nations. The representative of the state achieved glory for his prince and the people were left, until the Napoleonic revolution and the rise of popular sovereignty, to the role of disinterested spectator. Arms were borne by mercenaries. Wars were financed with booty or the spoils of colonial exploration. Military adventure was expensive but had real compensation. Yet in the twentieth century there is little possibility of insulating foreign and domestic politics. As Stanley Hoffmann observes:

> [I]n balance of power diplomacy, national interests were defined in terms that took only small account of domestic politics: secrecy, continuity and

the primacy of foreign affairs were prerequisites. Today . . . [a]ny statesman, however shrewd a negotiator or profound a philosopher of history,
who miscalculates the domestic effects of his moves here or abroad, will be
in trouble.[54]

Nixon and Kissinger sought insulation of themselves and their diplomacy from domestic political constraints. Nixon was quite willing to
use the flash and swirl of foreign affairs to butress his eroding domestic
position. Nevertheless, both he and Kissinger protested efforts to limit
their freedom of maneuver. But if freedom of maneuver requires illegal
surveillance (wire tapping), deceit, and the other distortions of democratic values that were the essence of the Watergate crisis, one is entitled to ask whether a democracy can afford a new balance based on
the old rules.[55]

Summary

Clearly, there are problems with this vision of a newly balanced world
political and military order. Nevertheless, Kissinger's virtuosity in ex-
tricating the United States from Vietnam, SALT, his development and
manipulation of the Soviet-American and Sino-American dimensions of
the balance, and his short-term success with "step-by-step" diplomacy in
the Middle East were significant achievements. At the same time, however, as Kissinger assumed the sole stewardship of American foreign
policy after Nixon's resignation, it was apparent that there were new
forces at work in world politics.[56] The massive transfer of wealth to the
Arabs and a handful of other third world countries resulting from the oil
embargo and escalating prices in 1975 was perhaps the most salient of
these challenges to the prevailing conception of world political reality.
But there were other anomalies: the enormous growth and expansion of
transnationally mobile private economic power—the multinational
corporations—based in the industrialized world, the deep and simultaneous crises of the domestic and international economic systems of the
industrialized world, and the rapid onset of widespread malnutrition and
famine in much of the third world.

Kissinger is reported to have once remarked, "I am not interested in,
nor do I know anything about, the southern portion of the world from the
Pyrenees down."[57] Whether or not the words were actually uttered, the
sentiment expresses the practical effect of Kissinger's world view; indeed it is a fair characterization of the outlook of much of U.S. statecraft
from the onset of the cold war. But new political, military, and economic
realities are increasingly apparent. It is difficult, for instance, to think of
foreign politics as merely a matter of armed force meeting force. Rather,

foreign policy is a mix of domestic and international factors—a close-knit interaction of economies, societies, organizations, and statesmen. And unlike the late 1940s, 1950s, and early 1960s, American foreign economic policy has been something more than an instrument to be used in an overarching political and military confrontation. The American economy, in an interdependent world, has become subject to a gossamer international confidence, and the United States is no longer completely master of its economic and hence political destiny. The Nixon administration's policy of balance to maintain global commitments was shaken by the international effects of domestic politics and international economics in a way that Bismarck or Castlereagh could never have imagined.

THE LIMITS
OF POWER AND POLICY
IN AN INTERDEPENDENT WORLD

In recent years the politico-military and strategic issues so long the preoccupation of American and other statesmen have become increasingly diffused. Instruments of policy such as alliances, threats of military action, and military force have been found increasingly uncertain in their effect and costly in use. Moreover, the formerly dominant sphere of foreign and national security policy is now penetrated by international and transnational economic issues.[58] The breakdown in the international hierarchy of the late 1940s, 1950s and 1960s; the emergent salience of nonsecurity issues; and the problematic applicability of force are the result of this interpretation of security and nonsecurity issues. Understanding the nature of the linkage of politics and economics is critical to how these new phenomena impinged on the traditional notions of force, power, and influence that were central to the Nixon conception of order.

The Collapse of the Bretton Woods System[59]

Economic considerations have occupied a dual position in American foreign policy. At the end of World War II and under the strong influence of the United States, a particular conception of the international economic order was developed and institutionalized at the Bretton Woods Conference in 1944. It was a system that looked to the reconstruction of the world's economy and an institutionalization of conditions amenable to orderly growth and prosperity. Free enterprise, free trade, and the free movement of private capital in accordance with a capitalist conception of economic rationality were to be the basic structural elements of this system. Moreover, it was widely assumed that such an international economic order was absolutely necessary to the establishment and preservation of a stable political and military order commensurate with American national interests.

Thus, the building and maintenance of world economic order, conceived at Bretton Woods, was a primary objective of American foreign policy. At the same time, American foreign economic policy was frequently conceived of in an instrumental manner. American trade and foreign assistance programs (and in the case of East-West relations, their denial) became major instruments of American policy during the 1940s, 1950s, and 1960s. The persistent and growing American balance of payments deficits of these years were not thought of within the context of the Bretton Woods system, as deficits that ultimately would have to be adjusted. Rather, they were seen as simply the price the United States was paying to establish the political and military preconditions of international order. Moreover, it was argued that the American deficits were a kind of international resource in that they provided an international money for a system that was desperately short of liquidity necessary for recovery and growth.

By the mid-1960s, however, this flow of American dollars under changed international conditions, especially in Europe, was no longer viewed as an unalloyed blessing. By the early 1970s, European economies were experiencing inflation in excess of 15 to 20 percent, American corporations were expanding their presence in Europe, and European currencies came under heavy speculative pressure. It was apparent to all that the international supply of dollars ($60 to $100 billion in Europe alone) far exceeded the capacity of the United States to back them with gold.

The Nixon administration's response was initially a policy of benign neglect. During 1969, 1970, and much of 1971 the Nixon administration refused to concede that there was a problem. The Nixon administration's political need as 1972 approached was for a booming domestic economy which required in turn an inflating of the economy.[60] If the Europeans did not want to hold the dollars, they were instructed to spend them on American goods (thereby helping the U.S. balance of payments) or revalue their own currencies upward against the dollar (which would also help the American balance of payments because American goods would then become cheaper vis-à-vis European goods). In short, the Nixon administration told European governments that whether they liked it or not, the dollar and not gold was the basis of the international monetary system. The United States would not change the foreign policy that had made it so, nor would the U.S. government significantly restrain American multinational corporations that were taking advantage of the fact, nor, finally, would the United States significantly deflate its domestic economy (with attendant unemployment in an election year) to soothe European concerns.

In the short run at least, European governments were faced with having to accept the American position. Private holders of dollars were not, however, and began selling dollars for stronger currencies such as the German mark. The upshot was, of course, the threat of more inflation in already inflated economies and, additionally, a further drawdown of American gold reserves. By mid-1971 the dwindling stock of American gold had become intolerable, and Nixon acted by suddenly and without warning ending the convertability of dollars into gold and imposing an import surcharge of 10 percent on foreign goods. Months of speculation followed as the dollar sank on world currency markets, generally to the competitive detriment of other currencies. Finally, in December 1971, at a conference held in Washington at the Smithsonian Institution, the United States officially devalued the dollar, but refused to restore convertability. International economic order was not restored, however, and yet another devaluation occurred in 1972 along with initial European efforts to construct some kind of monetary bloc to protect their own currencies.

By March of 1973, the remnants of the Smithsonian Agreement had vanished. Worldwide inflation and currency speculation continued and by early spring, all governments had retreated from fixed exchange rates—the core of the Bretton Woods system—and were allowing market forces to determine the value of their currencies. Some central bank and private bank intervention was employed to avoid total collapse of the financial structure negotiated at the Smithsonian, but increasingly it was clear that governments and especially the United States were surrendering leadership. Some encouragement could be taken from the fact that there was no return to the nationalistic protectionism of the 1930s. Indeed, steps were taken towards comprehensive reform of the international monetary system. But before the work could be completed, the system was overwhelmed by the international oil crisis growing out of the Yom Kippur War in October of 1973.

The Exercise of "Petropower"

On October 16, 1973, as military events were beginning to turn against the Arabs, the Arab members of the Organization of Petroleum Exporting Countries (OPEC) imposed an embargo on shipments of oil to the United States and other industrialized countries. Simultaneously, OPEC increased the per barrel price of oil such that when added to increases earlier in the year meant that the price of oil increased $2.50 per barrel to

$11.65 per barrel by early 1974. Thus an already disorganized indus-
trialized world economy was confronted with an even more complex
challenge. Apart from the immediate problem of how the vast sums of
money implied in the price increase were going to be recycled from the
industrialized countries to the oil exporters, there were the inflationary
implications of the price increases.

The price of virtually everything produced in the industrialized
world surged dramatically, but oil-dependent industrialized economies
were now confronted with enormous debt stemming from oil import bills
that were now four times higher than they had been a year earlier. Italy,
France, and Britain faced economic chaos; Japan, importing virtually all
of its oil from the Middle East, was faced with a payments deficit. The
United States, because it was less dependent upon OPEC oil imports,
fared somewhat better and, along with the Germans and the Swiss, benefited from the fact that much of the oil wealth surplus now accumulating
in the Middle East was deposited in their banks. The Germans were also
able to handle their oil debts better than their European neighbors because of the strong surplus position they had developed before the crisis.
In fact, the Germans loaned the Italians $2 billion to deal with their
short-term deficit and assumed a more activist role in Common Market
attempts to negotiate with the United States some form of industrialized
world financial response to the crisis. By early 1975 a $6 billion loan
facility had been established within the International Monetary Fund to
aid countries in dealing with their oil debts. However, the immediate
financial crisis was managed primarily by the private banking system of
the industrialized world, which accepted deposits from the oil-pro-
ducing nations and reloaned the money to the oil-importing countries
in the industrialized and third world.

The governments of the West, on the other hand, continued their
desultory pursuit of monetary reform. Apart from ad hoc consultations
among central bankers and marginal interventions in the floating exchange markets, there was no real management of the system. By late
1975 the West Europeans under French and German leadership had
convinced the United States that the prevailing drift in national policies
and lack of international coordination was sufficiently dangerous that a
more systematic effort had to be made to reconstitute international monetary order. The talks culminated in a conference in Jamaica in 1976,
which focused on the issues of international economic management and
monetary reform. That the summit conferences would be so focused is
testament to the new priorities imposed on Western leadership by interdependence.

In the final analysis, however, the Jamaica Conference could not
produce reform of the system. Rather, the participants agreed that float-

ing exchange rates were to remain the central feature of the international monetary system although a return to fixed exchange rates by all countries, or the Europeans regionally, was not precluded. At the same time, multilateral management of the system was furthered insofar as finance ministers and central bankers agreed to consult closely concerning exchange rate developments and interventions in the currency markets. Nonetheless, by the end of the Nixon and Ford administrations all that remained of the old international economic order was a weak consensus that some form of management was a necessity, although leadership toward that goal remained uncertain. The Bretton Woods system had been obliterated,[61] and those who beheld this new and extraordinary set of circumstances could discern no self-evident course for the future. Indeed, the very nature of power and order or the relationship between the two seemed even more problematic than in the past. In something less than a year during 1973 and 1974, the foreign ministries of the developed countries and the politico-military superpowers had to grant new status to a group of "petropowers." The concessions were not always made willingly as some, notably the United States, made threatening noises concerning the use of military force in response to the exercise of economic coercion in the Middle East.[62] In the end, however, the industrialized world turned to the uncertain international financial implications of the dramatic shift in economic power represented by the 1973–1974 oil crisis.

In spite of short-term fears that the transfer of wealth to the oil exporting countries from the industrialized and non–oil exporting developing countries would prove unmanageable, the mid-1970s saw a reasonably orderly adjustment to the problems of recycling and oil debt management throughout the international monetary system.[63] The amounts of money accumulating in the oil exporting countries were indeed impressive. From 1973 to 1974 the current account surpluses of the major oil exporters (Algeria, Indonesia, Iran, Iraq, Kuwait, Libya, Nigeria, Oman, Qatar, Saudi Arabia, the United Arab Emirates, and Venezuela) surged from $6.2 billion to $67.4 billion, with some estimates of projected OPEC financial accumulations in excess of $400 billion by the early 1980s. In contrast, the industrial countries experienced a swing in their current account balances from an $11.1 billion surplus in 1973 to an $11.1 billion deficit in 1974,[64] with no less impressive deficits emerging in the less developed world.

The management of the financial difficulties posed by transfers of this magnitude was facilitated by a number of factors. First, the dramatic increase in the price of oil in addition to stimulating additional international inflation also pushed the international economy into recession, including the first calendar year decline in the volume of the world trade since 1958.[64] The recession led in turn to a reduction in demand for oil in the industrialized world, thereby slowing the growth of exporting countries' surpluses. In fact between 1974 and 1975, the aggregate surpluses on current account of the oil exporting countries dropped from $67.4 billion to $34.7 billion. Simultaneously, the oil exporting countries were initiating substantial development programs which required imports from the industrialized world.[66] In a few instances, notably Iran, these imports included billions of dollars in arms from the United States and Western Europe.

At the same time, more than 90 percent of the oil exporting countries' surplus in 1975 was concentrated in Saudi Arabia, Kuwait, the United Arab Emirates, and Qatar, none of which had the capacity or, given their small size and considerable wealth, the need for massive imports from the industrialized world. During 1974 most of the surplus accruing to these countries was placed in Eurocurrency bank deposits and other short-term government securities where the money was then loaned back out to industrialized and less developed countries to finance their oil deficits. By 1976, however, these same oil exporting countries were diversifying their holdings rapidly with more than half of their investments now being placed in long-term and less liquid investments such as real property and long-term government securities in the industrialized world, especially the United States, Britain, and Germany.[67]

Finally, the immediate financial consequences of the oil crisis were found manageable because the vast network of essentially private international financial institutions proved able to serve as intermediaries in the recycling process. Private banks in the United States, Britain, and elsewhere in Europe became essential brokers in the transfer process by serving as willing receptors of oil exporting countries' investments for relending to the oil importing countries or managers of long-term investment by the oil exporters. Perhaps the most remarkable loan operations had to do with the non–oil exporting third world countries who borrowed heavily in 1974 and 1975 to finance their oil payment deficits. As the world economic recession deepened and industrial activity in the industrialized world slackened, it was this group of primary raw material exporting countries that suffered under the greatest burden of the contraction of world trade. With their earnings thus reduced they were compelled to engage in unprecedented borrowing from private sources in the industrialized world. Indeed, during 1974 and 1975 the non–oil producing, developing countries borrowed more from private sources than they had borrowed from all other sources in any other year prior to 1974.[68]

The worst fears concerning the political and economic consequences of the oil crisis and the emergence of the petropowers were not, therefore, realized. On the other hand, it was clear that the distribution of world political and economic capability had changed significantly as the result of the crisis. By the end of the Nixon-Ford administration this fact was reflected in the increasing status and institutional role accorded the OPEC states, especially Saudi Arabia, in the International Monetary Fund and other international financial institutions. Moreover, OPEC's biannual meetings in which the member states negotiated oil prices assumed an importance and attracted Western media attention previously reserved for Soviet-American summit meetings.

The crisis and its aftermath also underscored the importance that large concentrations of private economic power now played in the world's political economy. Multinational corporations (MNCs) had been a fixture in the international economy since the early 1960s, when American corporations began moving in considerable numbers and with significant economic and political effect into Western Europe. Furthermore, for decades the most common and pervasive form of the American presence of the political economies and even the cultures of the developing world, especially in Latin America, had been the American corporation. And, of course, American interests in the Middle East had always been tied to the fortunes of the international oil cartel, most of which was American. The oil crisis demonstrated that in many instances the MNCs are by no means as autonomous as some had argued and feared. When faced with OPEC and other forms of petropower action, the international oil companies were revealed to be essentially "tax collectors" (who nevertheless took their cut) for the oil producing countries.[69] Finally, there was some evidence that by the mid-1970s many third world countries had begun to approach more systematically—either individually or, in some instances, multilaterally—the problem of balancing, if not actually controlling, the MNCs in their midst.

Nonetheless, an international political economy in which MNCs control tens of billions of dollars and hundreds of subsidiaries throughout the world, and in which much of the world's trade flows among the MNCs, is a rather different world political economy than that envisaged at Bretton Woods. Furthermore, when this vast private activity is undergirded and facilitated by an essentially private international financial system through which hundreds of billions of dollars and other currencies can move for the most part beyond the immediate control of governments, the very concept of international economic management developed in the postwar period becomes questionable. Not only does such activity challenge the international financial instruments of governments, but as the rapidly transmitted inflation of the early 1970s suggests, the management of domestic economies is affected decisively by international economic activity. Indeed, by the end of the Nixon-Ford years the increasing sensitivity and vulnerability of major sectors of American industry to the combination of increasing foreign competition, MNC exploitation of third world labor markets, and raw materials price inflation, was giving rise to demands for protection that threatened the internationalist economic orthodoxy of the post–World War II era.

Finally, a survey of the contemporary political economic system requires a refinement of our conception of the less developed world. In the first place, the onset of worldwide food shortages in the mid-1970s points up the existence of a "fourth world"—a group of nations almost totally dependent upon others for their survival. The combination of low productivity, short-term crop failures due to climate change, and over-population raises the specter of tens of millions starving within the next decade. Indeed, international food and relief experts began to take seriously the prospect of a kind of international system of *triage* in which those peoples who are beyond saving are simply allowed to perish, while limited international resources are directed to those for whom survival seems more likely.[70]

A second group at the bottom of any measure of world power and development are those traditionally thought of as "developing." These are nations that seem able to achieve some growth as measured by traditional economic indices such as GNP. What is less clear, however, is whether this constitutes development in any holistic sense of social, economic, and political development. The answer is not obvious; for, in spite of positive changes in aggregate economic indicators, some observers argue that these changes mask the persistence of enormous social and political inequalities. The latter are frequently viewed as the necessary price that must be paid for economic development. But these inequities can also be seen as the by-product of the "development of underdevelopment" necessary to the preservation of an essentially exploitive relationship between the developed and underdeveloped world, a relationship within which the MNC serves as a kind of autonomous middle man.[71]

The success of the petropowers in exploiting their control of petroleum gave rise to much speculation that other less-developed countries could replicate the petropowers' leap to instant economic and political power.[72] In fact, however, the unique combination of dependence of the industrialized world on petroleum and a mutually perceived threat that could mobilize joint action (in the Middle Eastern case, Israeli military power and the Palestinian question) simply did not exist elsewhere. Moreover, and ironically, the very success of OPEC may have made less likely its replication simply because the greatest burden of debt generated by its action fell on the third world and drove the latter into even greater financial dependency on the private and intergovernmental financial institutions of the industrialized world. Nevertheless, the persistent and militant call during the mid-1970s by the third world for a "new international economic order" embodying a radical redistribution of world wealth and the means whereby that wealth was distributed caused many to worry that the future of the international political economy was unlikely to include much order.[73]

BEYOND THE NIXON DOCTRINE

There were a number of advantages to the Nixon-Kissinger approach to establishing and maintaining world order. First, it represented a breach with fifty years of viewing the Soviet Union as an international leper, an abnormality with interests that were rational only in the context of a perverse dogma. The dogma was still viewed as perverse; the scabrous condition of communism and leftist revolution still existed, but the Russian pariah was seen as recovering if not cleansed. In this sense, therefore, these changes represented an abandonment of the vision of politics epitomized by Dulles, which held international politics as a contest between the forces of light and the forces of darkness. Second, the normalization of relations with China released the United States from a pathological illusion that the People's Republic had been an imperialist or expansionist power. China has been, if anything, the soul of caution, painfully aware of its backwardness and weakness. The rhetoric of "people's war," though interpreted in the West to be the framework for Asian aggression, was always an essentially defensive doctrine of warfare.[74] Third, the ability to deal with great powers as if they are normal and understandable, subject to logic and a calculus of interest and accommodation as well as force, allowed negotiations to proceed on both political and military issues.

Nixon, Kissinger, and Ford sought, with some success, to adjust American policy to what they saw as the new realities of the Soviet-American relationship, especially the conditions and implications of strategic parity. In this Nixon and Kissinger were in fact confronting a reality over which they had little control. A Soviet strategic capacity that is essentially equivalent to the capacity of the United States was a condition that was bound to persist throughout the 1970s. SALT was aimed, therefore, at establishing an accommodation to this situation acceptable to both sides. There was, however, a price: institutionalizing the very bureaucracies, arms development, and deployment dynamic that they sought to restrain. In fashioning a new triangular balance of power incorporating China, Kissinger succeeded in finally suppressing American phobias that his two superiors (Nixon and Ford) had done so much to foster and take advantage of during their political careers. It remains to be seen, however, whether the trilateral balance that Kissinger tried to construct will truly aid the United States in containing Soviet power, or whether the United States will find itself drawn into conflict with the Soviet Union as the Chinese play their new American card in pursuit of their interests.

In the Middle East, Kissinger's tactical virtuosity was at its height as the United States succeeded in projecting itself into the position of mediator between the contending parties. The accomplishment was significant, for it also entailed a diminution of Soviet leverage. It should not be forgotten, however, that in the end this breakthrough could not be exploited beyond the fundamental issue of Israeli security concerns in the face of an Arab demand for recognition of Palestinian rights. Kissinger's shuttle and step-by-step diplomacy could get him no further than a necessary but ultimately insufficient disengagement of the combatants. And perhaps most important of all, American policy during the 1973 Yom Kippur War contributed directly to what may prove to be the most important event of the Nixon presidency, the 1973–1974 oil crisis and its consequences for the world political economy, which still reverberate through the international politics of the 1980s.

For one thing, the Arab oil boycott supplied the coup de grace to a Bretton Woods system then in its death throes. It is important to note that the oil boycott laid bare what many had come to suspect by 1973: American capacity and willingness to manage unilaterally the world's political economy was a thing of the past. In this respect, Nixon's economic policies of mid-1971 started what the Arabs finished in October of 1973. In the immediate wake of the boycott, the Europeans and the Japanese established a pattern of behavior which had emerged spasmodically during the 1960s and would become the norm during the latter 1970s: a decided tendency to pursue their own interests notwithstanding American appeals for unity and joint action, a posture rendered disingenuous if not absurd by American economic nationalism during the years leading up to the oil crisis. Thus as Kissinger tried in the months after the embargo to establish an international energy agency and oil-sharing arrangement, the Europeans and the Japanese, much more dependent on Middle Eastern oil, also went their own way and developed separate arrangements with OPEC. Moreover, it was the Europeans, especially the French, who urged that the United States and the other industrialized powers engage in a formal dialog with the developing nations. The Europeans once again assumed the initiative in moving the United States and the Japanese towards the Jamaica Conference in early 1976.

In fairness it must be said that, by the time that the Nixon administration came to office, management of the international system solely by the United States may no longer have been possible. Parity was, by 1969, a virtual reality, and the Bretton Woods system was already burdened to the breaking point by the international costs associated with the last great but failing effort by the United States to manage and direct events in the third world. But the administration that confronted this situation, though expressing satisfaction with the onset of a new era of international relations—such as in President Nixon's initial State of the World message or Kissinger's conciliatory statement to the third world before the United Nations in 1974[75]—nonetheless, sought to preserve an international order in many respects antithetical to the change its rhetoric welcomed.

NOTES

1. Richard M. Nixon, *U.S. Foreign Policy for the 1970's: A New Strategy for Peace* (Washington, D.C.: U.S. Government Printing Office, 1970), p. 2.
2. Ibid., p. 6
3. Ibid.
4. Ibid., p. 7.
5. See Richard M. Nixon, *U.S. Foreign Policy for the 1970's: Building for Peace* (Washington, D.C.: U.S. Government Printing Office, 1971), p. 6.
6. Ibid.
7. Richard M. Nixon, *U.S. Foreign Policy for the 1970's: Shaping a Durable Peace* (Washington, D.C.: U.S. Government Printing Office, 1973), p. 232.
8. Henry Kissinger, *White House Years* (Boston: Little, Brown and Co., 1979), p. 195.
9. Ibid., p. 196.
10. See W. W. Kaufmann, *The McNamara Strategy* (New York: Harper and Row, 1964) and Robert McNamara, *The Essence of Security* (New York: Harper and Row, 1968).
11. Morton Halperin, "The Decision to Deploy the ABM," *World Politics*, Vol. 25 (October 1972).
12. John Newhouse, *Cold Dawn: The Story of SALT* (New York: Holt, Rinehart and Winston, 1973), p. 101.
13. For estimates of Soviet deployment rates at this time see J. I. Coffey, "The Savor of SALT," *Science and Public Affairs* (May 1973), p. 11.
14. Kissinger, op. cit., pp. 191–192.
15. Ibid., pp. 684–712.
16. Ibid., p. 712.
17. Rowland Evans and Robert Novak, *Nixon in the White House: The Frustration of Power* (New York: Random House, Vintage, 1972), pp. 100–101.
18. See Deputy Secretary of State Kenneth Rush's statements, *The New York Times*, July 10 and July 13, 1973.
19. See Tad Szulc, "Behind the Vietnam Cease-Fire Agreement," *Foreign Policy*, No. 15

(Summer 1974), pp. 21–69 and Seymour Hersh, *The Price of Power* (New York: Summit Books, 1983).

20. William Safire, "Puppet as Prince," *Harper's*, Vol. 250, No. 1498 (March 1975), p. 12.

21. Henry Brandon and David Schoenbrun, "Jordan: The Forgotten Crisis," *Foreign Policy*, No. 10 (Spring 1973), p. 172.

22. Ibid., p. 168

23. Ibid.

24. Ibid.

25. Evans and Novak, op. cit. p. 265.

26. Brandon and Schoenbrun, op. cit., p. 170.

27. *The New York Times*, October 11, 1973.

28. *Newsweek*, October 22, 1973, p. 93.

29. See George Ball's statement in *The New York Times*, February 1, 1966.

30. "Meet the Press," Vol. 17, No. 3 (Sunday, January 28, 1973), Merkle Press, Inc., Washington, D.C.

31. Henry Kissinger, *A World Restored* (Boston: Houghton Mifflin, 1957), p. 1.

32. Text of a background briefing in New Orleans, August 14, 1970, p. 16, cited by David Landau, *Kissinger: The Uses of Power* (Boston: Houghton Mifflin, 1973), p. 128.

33. For an elaboration of this analysis based on an examination of Soviet writings see, R. Judson Mitchell, "A New Brezhnev Doctrine: The Restructuring of International Relations," *World Politics*, Vol. 30, No. 3 (April 1978).

34. *Time*, January 3, 1972.

35. Herman Kahn, *The Emerging Japanese Superstate: Challenge and Response* (Englewood Cliffs, N.J.: Prentice-Hall, 1970).

36. *The New York Times*, February 11, 1975, p. 15. See also his *The Weary and the Wary: U.S. and Japanese Security Policies in Transition* (Baltimore: Johns Hopkins University Press, 1972).

37. See U.S. Congress, Senate Committee on the Judiciary, Subcommittee to Investigate Problems Connected with Refugees and Escapees, *The Tilt: American Views of South Asia*, 93rd Congress, 2nd Session, 1973, p. 183.

38. Nixon, *A New Strategy for Peace*, p. 87.

39. For the background of Kissinger's policies in Africa, see Anthony Lake, *The "Tar Baby" Option: American Policy Toward Southern Rhodesia* (New York: Columbia University Press, 1976).

40. Kissinger, *White House Years*, p. 654.

41. Ibid.

42. See for example Paul E. Sigmund, "The 'Invisible Bloackade' and the Overthrow of Allende," *Foreign Affairs*, Vol. 52, No. 2 (January 1974). See also Elizabeth Farnsworth, "More Than Admitted," and Sigmund, "Less Than Charged," both in *Foreign Policy*, No. 16 (Fall 1974).

43. Kissinger, *White House Years*, p. 658.

44. Ibid., p. 677.

45. Ibid., p. 1258.

46. For a survey of the Shah's military purchases during this period see *Strategic Survey 1973* and *Strategic Survey 1975* (London: International Institute for Strategic Studies, 1974 and 1976).

47. Among the more insistent advocates of this argument has been journalist Jack Anderson. See for example, "How the Oil Mess Got That Way," *Parade Magazine*, August 26, 1979, pp. 4–8. However, among Anderson's quoted sources are James Adkins, U.S. ambassador to Saudi Arabia at this time, and Secretary of the Treasury William Simon.

48. Bernard Fall, "The Theory and Practice of Insurgency and Counterinsurgency," *Naval War College Review*, April 1965.
49. Earl C. Ravenal, "The Nixon Doctrine and Our Asian Commitments," *Foreign Affairs*, Vol. 49 (January 1971), pp. 206–207.
50. Nixon, *Building for Peace*, p. 179. Moreover, as Nixon left office, the full logic of strategic sufficiency came to the fore as the "unthinkable" became thinkable again after more than a decade of suppression. In 1970 and again in 1973 Nixon's first two secretaries of defense could be found saying that "the President has made it perfectly clear that we do not intend to develop counter-force capabilities which the Soviets could construe as having a first strike potential" (Secretary of Defense Melvin Laird, cited in *Congressional Record*, Vol. 116, Pt. 19 (July 29, 1970), 26386; and

> The President has also stated that the numbers, characteristics, and deployments of U.S. strategic forces should be such that the Soviet Union cannot reasonably interpret them as intended to threaten a disarming attack. Such a threat would be inconsistent with the U.S. desire to maintain a stable strategic balance and, thereby, reduce the likelihood of nuclear war. (U.S. Congress, Hearings before the Senate Committee on the Armed Services, *Fiscal Year 1974 Authorization for Military Procurement, Research and Development, Construction Authorization for the Safeguard ABM, and Active Duty and Selected Reserve Strengths*, 93rd Congress, 1st Session, 1973, p. 313.)

But in his "Posture Statement" on the Fiscal Year 1975 Defense Budget, Secretary of Defense James R. Schlesinger stated elliptically:

> Assured destruction must remain an essential ingredient in our overall deterrent strategy. However, under certain hypothetical circumstances, if the use of U.S. strategic capability were required in response to an act of aggression we might well reserve our assured destruction forces so as to deter attacks against the American and other free world cities into the wartime period—what we call intrawar deterrence.
>
> The emphasis in the new retargeting doctrine is to provide a number of options, selectivity, and flexibility, so that our response, regardless of the provocation, is appropriate rather than disproportionate to the provocation. I think that understanding of this will serve to shore up deterrence. (Secretary of Defense James R. Schlesinger, Hearings on *Military Posture and H.R. 12564, Department of Defense Authorization for Appropriations for Fiscal Year 1975*, before House Committee on Armed Services, 93rd Congress, 2nd Session, 1974, p. 14.)

In short, the secretary of defense sought to recoup some of the flexibility lost at the lower end of the spectrum of force by building greater "flexibility" and "options" into the strategic nuclear arsenal of the United States. However, some have suggested that such flexibility already existed due to improvements in American command and control capability allowing for almost unlimited and immediate retargeting of American strategic forces [See John C. Baker, "Flexibility: The Imminent Debate," *Arms Control Today*, Vol. 4, No. 1 (January 1974), p. 2.] Also, it has been argued that the United States has possessed for some time the capacity to attack some Soviet missile silos; hence, any significant increase in U.S. capacity to attack the Soviet ICBM force would of necessity be viewed as provocative by them. [See the colloquy between Morton Halperin and Robert Ellsworth in "Should We Develop Highly Accurate Missiles and Emphasize Military Targets Rather than Cities?" *The Advocates* (Boston: WGBH, February 12, 1974), pp. 28–29, and Herbert Scoville, Jr., "Flexible

MADness," *Foreign Policy*, No. 14 (Spring 1974), pp. 168–170.] The provocativeness of the step proposed by Schlesinger is undoubtedly heightened in the eyes of Soviet defense planners when viewed in conjunction with the accelerated U.S. ASW [antisubmarine warfare] program.

All in all, as Scoville demonstrates (see Scoville, pp. 171–174) it is extremely difficult to conceive of any *strategic* scenario in which increased hard-target killing capability on the part of the United States contributes to strategic deterrence. Indeed, quite the opposite conclusion pushed to the fore: "No matter how often we disclaim it, the development of improved silo-killing missiles must inevitably look to the Russians like an attempt to acquire a firststrike counterforce capability against their ICBMs. Similar Soviet programs for getting high-yield MIRVs have been viewed here in exactly such alarming terms." (see Scoville, p. 170.)

51. Kissinger, *White House Years*, pp. 217–220.
52. Alain C. Enthoven and K. Wayne Smith, "What Forces for NATO? And From Whom?" *Foreign Affairs*, Vol. 48, No. 1 (October 1969), p. 82.
53. Graham Allison, *Essence of Decision* (Boston: Little, Brown and Company, 1971); Morton Halperin, *Bureaucratic Politics and Foreign Policy* (Washington, D.C.: Brookings, 1974).
54. Stanley Hoffmann, "A New Foreign Policy: Is It Possible? Do We Need It?" prepared statement before U.S. Congress, House Committee on Foreign Affairs, Hearings and Symposium Before the Subcommittee on National Security Policy and Scientific Development, *National Security Policy and the Changing World Power Alignment*, 92nd Congress, 2nd Session, 1972, p. 33.
55. For a more extended discussion of the analysis in this section see James A. Nathan and James K. Oliver, *Foreign Policymaking and the American Political System* (Boston: Little, Brown, 1983).
56. Seyom Brown, *New Forces in World Politics* (Washington, D.C.: Brookings, 1974).
57. Gabriel García Márquez, "The Death of Salvador Allende," *Harper's*, Vol. 248, No. 1486 (January–June 1974), p. 46.
58. Richard N. Cooper, "Trade Policy Is Foreign Policy, *Foreign Policy*, No. 9 (Winter 1972–1973).
59. The following section is drawn from Robert Stevens, *A Primer on the Dollar in the World Economy* (New York: Random House, 1972), pp. 142–150, and David P. Calleo and Benjamin M. Rowland, *America and the World Political Economy* (Bloomington, Ind.: University of Indiana Press, 1974), pp. 87–117, and Joan Spero, *The Politics of International Economic Relations* (New York: St. Martin's Press, 1977). Also useful is Robert Solomon, *The International Monetary System, 1945–1976: An Insider's View* (New York: Harper and Row, 1977).
60. See Edward R. Tufte, *Political Control of the Economy* (Princeton: Princeton University Press, 1978), for an analysis of presidential manipulation of the economy in election years.
61. See Robert Triffin, "Jamaica: 'Major Revision' or Fiasco?" In Edward M. Bernstein et al., "Reflections on Jamaica," *Essays in International Finance*, No. 115 (Princeton: International Finance Section, Department of Economics, Princeton University, 1976).
62. "Kissinger on Oil, Food, and Trade," *Business Week*, (January 13, 1975), pp. 66–76.
63. The following discussion, unless otherwise noted, is drawn from: the *Annual Reports* of the International Monetary Fund for 1976 and 1977 (Washington, D.C.: International Monetary Fund, 1977 and 1978 respectively); Thomas D. Willet, "The Oil-Transfer Problem and International Economic Stability," *Essays in International Fi-*

nance, No. 113 (Princeton: International Finance Section, Department of Economics, Princeton University, 1975); Spero, op. cit.; and Raymond Vernon, ed., *The Oil Crisis* (New York: Norton, 1976).

64. *IMF Annual Report, 1977,* p. 14.
65. *IMF Annual Report, 1976,* pp. 9–12.
66. Ibid., pp. 14–15.
67. *IMF Annual Report, 1977,* p. 14, and Willet, *passim.*
68. *IMF Annual Report, 1976,* pp. 20–21.
69. See M. A. Adelman, "Is the Oil Shortage Real?" *Foreign Policy,* No. 9 (Winter 1972–1973), pp. 69–107.
70. Walter Sullivan, "Computer 'Model' of World Sought to Cope with Food Shortage," *The New York Times,* August 10, 1974, pp. 31–46.
71. For a succinct statement of this argument see Osvaldo Sunkel, "Big Business and 'Dependencia': A Latin American View," *Foreign Affairs,* Vol. 50 (April 1972), pp. 517–531; also James D. Cockcroft, Andre Gunder Frank, and Dale L. Johnson, *Dependence and Underdevelopment: Latin America's Political Economy* (Garden City, N.Y.: Doubleday, Anchor, 1972). For a critique of this view, see Benjamin J. Cohen, *The Question of Imperialism: The Political Economy of Dominance and Dependence* (New York: Basic Books, 1973).
72. See the exchange of views, "One, Two, Many OPEC's . . .?" in *Foreign Policy,* No. 14 (Spring 1974), pp. 57–90.
73. Robert Tucker, *The Inequality of Nations* (New York: Basic Books, 1976), *passim.*
74. See Arthur Huck, *The Security of China: Chinese Approaches to Problems of War and Strategy* (New York: Columbia University Press, 1970).
75. "Challenges of Interdependence," Address by Secretary of State Henry A. Kissinger before the Sixth Special Session of the United Nations General Assembly, New York, New York, April 15, 1974 (Washington, D.C.: Department of State, Bureau of Public Affairs, 1974).

Chapter 11
"Commitments in Search of a Roost"

By the late 1970s American foreign policy had become suspended between its cold war past and an interdependent international future of which it had little vision. The new Carter administration avowed a unique sensitivity to this situation. Secretary of State Cyrus Vance and Secretary of Defense Harold Brown publicly acknowledged the inadequacies of the foreign policies of the Democratic administrations they had served during the 1960s. Andrew Young, a civil rights and anti–Vietnam War activist, a close associate of the slain Dr. Martin Luther King, Jr., and an eloquent proponent of a new—sometimes heretical—approach to the third world, was appointed ambassador to the United Nations. The new security adviser, Zbigniew Brzezinski, had written of a new "technotronic age" in international relations that required a diplomacy quite different from the neoclassical approach of his predecessor, Henry Kissinger. Further, he expressed an intent to reduce the visibility of his office in policy formulation in deference to the secretary of state. Finally, the new president was inaugurated proclaiming a commitment to reduce the defense budget significantly, stop the proliferation of nuclear weapons and take steps to eliminate them from the earth, as well as place human rights at the very center of American foreign policy.

Within months, however, even supporters of the administration had begun calling for a clearer sense of direction and priorities among the many but sometimes conflicting objectives.[1] By midterm, "confusion," "incoherence," and "inconsistency" were terms being applied to the administration's actions. And as his reelection campaign began, Carter had to go to the nation, not with an ambitious policy agenda completed, but with a strategic arms control agreement he could not get ratified in the United States Senate, Middle East peace negotiations that had deadlocked after a promising start, and fifty-three American hostages in Iran seemingly irretrievable after an embarrassingly failed rescue attempt and the refusal of America's European and Japanese allies to go through with strong economic and diplomatic sanctions against a revolutionary Iranian regime that had overthrown one of America's closest allies in the Middle East. No less important, relations with the Soviet Union had descended to perhaps their lowest point in more than a decade after the

Soviets invaded Afghanistan in late 1979 and the United States called for—with mixed success—a boycott of the Olympic Games held in Moscow in the summer of 1980. The Afghanistan invasion contributed to the largest peacetime military buildup since the early Kennedy administration with some projections of U.S. military expenditures during the first half of the 1980s running to a trillion dollars. The cold war—so fervently exorcised by part of the Carter foreign policy apparatus for nearly three years yet so feverishly conjured by others—had resurfaced.

INTERDEPENDENCE AND CONTAINMENT

The Carter administration was forced to confront the implications of the two unifying ambitions of postwar U.S. foreign policy. Foremost, of course, has been the attempt to contain Soviet expansion. A necessarily more elusive but no less avidly pursued policy has been the attempt, as Carter's special assistant for national security affairs, Zbigniew Brzezinski, put it, "to make the world congenial to ourselves" and "to prevent America from being lonely."[2] In order to escape from solitude and to confine Soviet influence, few places have been immune from American concern. Throughout the cold war, formal guarantees were issued to over forty countries. But it was clear, after the Korean War, that America's security perimeter was defined not merely by treaty but also by events. The Soviets' involvement in all this was viewed in more sophisticated terms than in the past. It was understood that they did not instigate every coup, insurrection or international disturbance. Still, there has always been a central policy tenet that the Soviet Union gleaned profit from upheaval. The consistent positing of a cosmology— variously labeled "domino theory," "linkage," or the "spreading arc of crisis"—implied, at the least, the necessity for unfailing American vigilance lest there begin a changing rhythm of history. For in any retreat, there might be a gathering of miscalculations about American determination. Ultimately, then, the nuclear card itself might have to be played through inadvertence or as a desperate signal of American will.

But resort to an overtly threatening posture dependent upon American strategic superiority was an option of limited credibility. In fact, strategic superiority was a thing of the past and the Carter administration could initially find no alternative to the strategic arms limitations process initiated by the Nixon administration. Furthermore, the resort to lower levels of military capability as a response to revolutionary instability was deemed no less inappropriate in view of the Vietnam experience. Moreover, it was little solace to the many members of the Carter administration who had criticized the Nixon and Ford administrations that they were now compelled to confront dilemmas that emerged and were, in some measure, exacerbated by those earlier administrations. The strategic arms limitations approach to the problems of strategic parity had been shaped by Carter's predecessors. The constraints—both political and material—on the use of force had been established in the preceding decade as had the decline of American economic hegemony. And American dependence on regional surrogates such as the Shah of Iran was the result of the Nixon-Kissinger-Ford pursuit of stability in the third world without a substantial American military presence or capability. Nonetheless, it seemed that the worst fears of those who argued for the necessity of preserving some relationship between force and diplomacy (lest policy paralysis result from their divorce)[3] were met at the threshold of the Carter administration.

"Interdependence" as Policy

The response of the Carter administration to these problems was frequently ambivalent; at worst, almost inexplicably incoherent and unpredictable. Much of this inconsistency can be traced to contending and ultimately irreconcilable policy perspectives within the Carter foreign policy establishment.

One part of the administration sought to make a virtue of the dilemmas presented by the apparently limited utility of American military capability. Proponents of the position argued that the growing interdependence of the international system provided unique opportunities for the United States. These new conditions meant, for example, that economic transactions and issues within the industrialized world and between the West and the third world now defined the crucial arenas of world politics. The cold war Soviet-American confrontation was, therefore, decreasingly relevant. If ideological questions remained important, they were not the old issues of Soviet communism versus American capitalism. The new issues concerned the third world's aspirations for national dignity and a greater measure of autonomy in its relationship with the industrialized West. The third world recognized that the relationship is necessary, because its aspirations for development required access to Western capital, technology, markets, and technical assistance. It was argued by many in the departments of State and Treasury, and with particular force by Andrew Young, Carter's United Nations ambassador, that in such a world, the United States possessed an enormously varied, appropriate, and readily applied set of economic and technical instrumentalities.[4]

In contrast, the Soviets had little to offer. Their influence on the development of an international economic order for the industrialized West was nonexistent. Moreover, Soviet influence on the more volatile conditions of the third world was greatest where revolutionary conflict was underway. Young—who was appointed to the UN post because of his presumed sensitivity for and appeal to the non-West—and others argued that the United States should be less supportive of its traditional antirevolutionary clients and more responsive to the aspirations of those seeking change. Where violent change implied inordinate Soviet influence, such as in southern Africa, then American policy should anticipate those circumstances through diplomatic efforts designed to facilitate the emergence of change-oriented, nationalistic, but pragmatic regimes. In some instances this might require deferring to the United Nations or the diplomacy of other Western allies, such as the successful British mediation of the revolutionary situation in Zimbabwe in 1979–1980. In other cases, such as Nicaragua in 1978 and 1979, this approach would require at least a passive U.S. stance even though a former U.S. client, Anastasio Somoza, was threatened with ouster. In either case, it was argued, the United States would be well positioned to advance its interests in the postrevolutionary situation. Indeed, Young was prepared to assert publicly, to the administration's embarrassment, the heretical position that Soviet intervention in Africa or elsewhere via its Cuban surrogates need not be regarded as necessarily a bad thing if it contributed to the termination of revolutionary turmoil and the onset of circumstances in which the need for Western development assistance came to preoccupy a particular third world country's foreign policy, as in Angola, or in the Nicaraguan revolutionary government's initial turn to the United States rather than Cuba for assistance.

As the outset, therefore, some within the Carter administration seemed to accept the end of the cold war pronounced by Nixon in 1969 and baptized in Helsinki as the great given of contemporary history. The problem in formulating policy in a "post cold war environment," as Leslie Gelb, then at the State Department's Bureau of Politico-Military Affairs, explained in 1977, was that "fewer and fewer things had to do with the Soviet-American connection."[5] The question of how to proceed with Soviet-American relations since outstanding issues were seen as either settled or marginal to the larger course of history (a history which did not include an especially bright prospect for the Russians), was uncertain. Nonetheless, American capabilities in such an environment were far superior to those of the Soviet Union. Though the context of foreign policy would likely prove constraining for the old means and ends of American policy, there was considerable reason to believe that a new set of means and ends commensurate with these changed conditions could prosper.

Brzezinski Speaks
to Realpolitik . . . and Interdependence

On the other hand, there was in the Carter administration another conception of the appropriate American response to these new conditions, a
position forcefully articulated and advanced by Carter's special assistant
for national security affairs, Zbigniew Brzezinski. Carter came to office
with little background in foreign policy save his participation in the
Trilateral Commission, a collection of political, economic, and academic
notables from throughout the industrialized world (the United States,
Canada, Western Europe, and Japan) under the leadership of David
Rockefeller. The commission's executive director during Carter's association with it had been Brzezinski. Moreover, his secretary of state, Cyrus
Vance, was usually heralded as more of a technician in negotiations
than a conceptualizer. Thus whatever coherent view of the world that
eventually emerged in the Carter administration would be heavily, even primarily, influenced by Brzezinski. He was, after all, as
Carter explained, "the eyes through which I view the world."[6]

Brzezinski's views were not, at least superficially, totally inconsistent with the arguments advanced by those who saw an interdependent world potentially more responsive to American diplomacy than
Soviet power. The world had entered a "technotronic age," according to
Brzezinski, one in which "technology and electronics—particularly in
the area of computers and communications" were now the dominant
shapers of domestic and international society.[7] Simultaneously, "[g]lobal
politics are becoming egalitarian rather than libertarian, with demands
from more politically activated masses focusing predominantly on material equality than on spiritual or legal liberty."[8]

There were in these conditions great dangers for the United States,
especially if it adopted what Brzezinski called a "siege mentality," setting itself intransigently against these conditions and especially demands for greater equality. Preferable, said Brzezinski in an essay published during the bicentennial year, was

> . . . an America that is cooperatively engaged in shaping new global rela-
> tions, both despite and because of the rising global egalitarian passions. . . .
> America still provides to most people in the world the most attractive social
> *condition* (even if not the *model*) and that remains America's special
> strength. The Soviet Union is not even a rival in this respect. But that
> strength can only be applied if American foreign policy is sympathetically
> sensitive to the significant shift in global emphasis toward a value
> [egalitarianism] which has not been central to the American experience.
> This need not entail an embrace of egalitarianism as the supreme vir-

tue. . . . But it does imply a policy that does not ignore (nor reciprocate with doctrinal hostility) the global pressures for reform of existing international arrangements.[9]

At the same time, however, Brzezinski departed from the interdependence perspective in that he persisted in the more traditional American preoccupation with the Soviet Union and especially its presence in Eastern Europe. But he took great pains to distinguish his outlook and methods from those of previous eight years. On the eve of the signing of the Helsinki accords, for example, when Carter was but a distant gleam in his eye, Brzezinski gave a remarkably candid assessment of his differences with the "Ford-Kissinger approach" to detente "which seeks to perpetuate the status quo" in Europe "with all that entails."[10] For Brzezinski, the whole purpose of Helsinki and the latter years of Kissinger's tenure was ill-conceived and ahistorical:

> . . . the anachronistic division of Europe . . . is the source of instability. If we contribute to its legitimation in the form of some security declaration, we are not contributing to European security but to its opposite.[11]

Brzezinski's plan for the future of the Soviet Union was as fissiparous as it was for Eastern Europe. As he confessed to a Radio Free Europe interrogator:

> . . . realistic encouragement of pluralism via nationalism and separatism may be our best answer to the Soviet challenge on the ideological front . . . [A]fter the disappearance of the communist state, a combination of residual socialism and internationalsim would mitigate the power-oriented ambitions of extreme Russian nationalism. . . .[12]

For President Carter's soon-to-be-appointed national security advisor, the Soviets could be treated in a fundamentally different fashion from the status finally accorded to them by Kissinger and Ford. To Brzezinski, the Soviets' internal regime could be publicly questioned and loudly proclaimed illegitimate, irrelevant, and even pernicious to the tide of progress sweeping the globe. A "truly *comprehensive* [emphasis his] detente" would be "a challenge to [the Soviet Union's] legitimacy and thus . . . their very existence, and I must say their fears [would be] justified."[13] Carter echoed this theme when he told members of the Magazine Publishers Association:

> My own inclination . . . is to aggressively challenge . . . the Soviet Union and others for influence in areas of the world that we feel are crucial to us now or potentially crucial in 15 or 20 years from now.[14]

All this could not help but abrade the Soviets at their most irritable spots. When Carter visited Poland and Rumania early in his administration, Brzezinski was not unaware of the implications, "[I]t was," he explained, "a gesture which underlines our interests in pluralism in Eastern Europe."[15] Brzezinski elaborated Carter's reversal of American accession to Helsinki in his address to the Foreign Policy Association on December 20, 1978: " . . . We do not believe that our relations with Eastern Europe should be subordinate to our relationship with Moscow. . . ."[16] It was not widely noticed, but in his first budget request, Carter asked for a doubling of broadcast capability of Radio Free Europe and Radio Liberty. VOA broadcasts to the Soviet Union were increased by 25 percent.[17]

Brzezinski (as well as many of those he brought to the National Security Council) was not, therefore, insensitive to either the constrained condition of American military power or the complex interdependence that contributed to that condition. Furthermore, he seemed to accept that the emerging new age of world politics was potentially more amenable to a reformed American view of world order and new American instrumentalities (largely political and economic, but also American ideals in the form of an almost militant emphasis on human rights) than it was to Soviet power and policy. Brzezinski, however, was not prepared more or less to ignore Soviet power and international presence. Soviet strategic power had to be checked as a necessary condition of world order, but presumably this could be achieved by arms control agreements and the continued mobilization of American technological sophistication and superiority. Even more important, Brzezinski was prepared to engage—not merely coexist with—Soviets within the context of the new interdependence, using American advantages and leverage to contribute to Soviet difficulties internally and especially within their East European empire.

Here, then, was a crucial difference, not only in Brzezinski's position with respect to many of his colleagues within the Carter administration, but compared with his Republican predecessors as well. A Soviet Union beset by internal weakness and dubious prospects for long-term successful participation in the new era of world politics was not to be merely accepted as a kind of struggling junior partner. Rather, wherever possible its problems and difficulties were to be exacerbated. Its need for Western capital and technology was not to be approached as an opportunity to pull it gradually into a moderating web of detente but as a vulnerability to be exploited so as to hasten its decline. Soviet sensitivity to Chinese potential on its Asian border was not to be subtly and carefully manipulated through diplomatic maneuver, but rather prodded and even inflamed through indirect and direct military assistance to the Chinese.

The ambivalence and indecision that many observers have attributed to the Carter years can be traced in considerable measure to these warring policy perspectives within the Carter administration. The media often explained things in terms of an intense personal and institutional clash between, on the one hand, Brzezinski and his National Security Council staff, and on the other hand Secretary of State Vance and his department, a clash culminating in Vance's resignation in early 1980. Though there were clearly elements of such a struggle permeating Carter administration policy, it is important to recognize that the two men represented subtly but consequentially different views of the world, American interests, the specific options available, and the means to be used.[18] Furthermore, to the extent that American policy in the late 1970s can be seen as having drifted towards the pole represented by Brzezinski, that outcome was made more likely by the president's desire to make human rights a centerpiece of his foreign policy.

Human Rights

In his inaugural address, Carter told the American people and the world: "Because we are free we can never be indifferent to the fate of human beings elsewhere . . . our commitment to human rights must be absolute." In March of 1977, he told the United Nations: "No member of the United Nations can claim that the mistreatment of its citizens is solely its own business."[19] Nonetheless, the specific meaning and application of the policy remained unclear and, upon examination, proves problematical.

The NSC spent innumerable hours in 1977 and 1978 attempting to assess what human rights means to Islamic, Latin, and Oriental societies. One participant at these meetings despaired: "It's a hard problem for a bureaucracy to come to grips with. It's a hard subject for people to discuss collectively."[20] Early on, the Carter administration discovered that if it is difficult to discuss what constitutes human rights with people of the same cultural-political-ethnic backgrounds, it is downright confounding to discuss the matter of judicial torture and wholesale murder with representatives of other cultures that are often in revolutionary contexts.

The problem of cultural variability of human rights as an absolute principle of foreign policy stems from the necessarily indiscriminate nature of an absolute commitment to human rights. To most people educated in Judeo-Christian principles, humans have rights. If, then, their rights are violated and abused, how is one to express concern? If one manifests concern wherever there are abuses, then one must be prepared to identify an enormous array of circumstances and activities that are, by most Americans' standards, obnoxious. But what, then, is one to *do*? Dealing with the problem implies a willingness to intervene in some fashion in the internal affairs of another society. Presumably, one should be prepared to chastise and even dispatch leadership if the abuses are gross enough. But also, if one's policy is to have significant moral force, its application would have to be consistent. But should moral opprobrium and intervention be directed at the Saudis, South Koreans, or the Shah of Iran? Were the Chinese to be the object of moral condemnation even as the Carter administration sought to complete a *de facto* alliance with the Chinese to contain the Soviets?

One could, in theory at least, rank one's interests from the most important to the least important, trading lesser interests to safeguard the more serious. But how can one rank or differentiate the objects of great and absolute principles? Does sacrificing some segment of a principle weaken it altogether? One can compromise competing interests, but compromising with morality is a visible sin. The policy now seems to have been foredoomed, whether it was an "absolute principle" of foreign policy as Carter proclaimed, or "absolute in principle but flexible in application" as one of the president's NSC assistants explained to one of the present authors.[21]

The American public's sentiment that Carter perceived and sought to respond to with his pronouncements concerning human rights is, nonetheless, difficult to exaggerate and easy to underestimate. But among some Europeans and the Soviets, there was incomprehension and even hostility to Carter's concern for those who suffered abridgment of liberty or dignity. Among the Germans especially, there were fears that open letters to dissidents in the Soviet Union and the reception of Soviet exiles in the White House would jeopardize a decade of detente. Carter found it "surprising" that the Soviets would have an "adverse reaction." His policy had, he would in time confess, "provided a greater obstacle to . . . common goals, like SALT, than I had anticipated."[22]

If Carter had not suspected that the Soviets would be taken aback by his professions of sympathy for Soviet dissidents, his national security adviser might have pointed to the words that he and his associate, Samuel Huntington, authored as early as 1962. The main source of danger to the stability of the Soviet political system, wrote Brzezinski and Huntington, is

> any decline in the ideological and political monopoly of the ruling party. If tomorrow the Soviet Union were to open its frontiers to foreign books,

newspapers and criticism of the system, the effect could be politically dramatic. . . .[23]

But as we have seen, such a politically dramatic effect was, for Brzezinski, the most desirable of outcomes for American policy in the complexly interdependent world confronting the United States. Thus Carter's emphasis on human rights vis-à-vis the Soviet Union was congruent with Brzezinski's conception of American policy. At the same time, however, this convergence of views merely underscored the traditional foci of American policy in the late 1970s. That is, notwithstanding much rhetoric and some policy initiatives that reflected awareness of interdependence, there was in the moralistic thrust of Carter's human rights emphasis a throwback to the globalism of Truman and even beyond that, to Wilson. To the extent that this moralism came into focus with Brzezinski's approach to the new age through continued confrontation with the Soviet Union, this moralism was subject to becoming indistinguishable from NSC-68. In the short run, these irreconciled tensions between interdependence and containment complicated an already deteriorating Soviet-American relationship. In the longer run, they were reflected in most other aspects of the Carter administration's foreign policy as well.

CARTER AND THE WORLD

The context of Soviet-American relations for the Carter administration was considerably more complicated than that confronting the last Democratic president who assumed office after a Republican ascendancy. John Kennedy found the cold war oppressively in place in 1961. Indeed, he all but exulted in the challenge to American purpose presented by that stony prospect. Jimmy Carter, on the other hand, inherited a relationship still in the process of redefinition following the radical changes accompanying America's post-Vietnam retrenchment and the Soviet Union's achievement of strategic parity with the United States. SALT negotiations were moving forward, but Soviet-American consensus on relations beyond arms control was lacking. Furthermore, American domestic support for either SALT or more importantly, detente, was extremely fragile. In addition, there was the now chronic dependence on Middle Eastern oil and the nagging sense that that region was once again headed for war unless the diplomatic momentum of the period after the 1973 war could be regained. But notwithstanding the desire of many in the Carter administration to refocus American diplomacy on these and other interdependence issues, the Soviet-American nexus could not be displaced.

There seemed to be a general desire for better Soviet-American relations and especially an extension of the SALT process, but there was also an undercurrent of skepticism as to whether the detente atmosphere of the early 1970s could be regenerated or was even worth the effort. Continuing Soviet activism in Africa made it clear that they entertained a different conception of detente than the United States. Furthermore, there was growing concern about the balance of Soviet-American military capability, as critics of SALT and the balance of forces in Central Europe warned ominously of Soviet superiority within a decade, a superiority that would surely be used to extract advantages from the United States. Such criticism was especially intense in the Senate where, of course, any SALT II treaty would have to be ratified and could be blocked by a coalition of conservative Democrats and Republicans numbering only thirty-four—a number deemed well within the grasp of Senator Jackson, who was regarded as the leader of the anti-SALT and antidetente forces in the Senate. Apart from whatever uncertainties, ambivalence, or conflicting policy approaches there were in the Carter administration, these domestic political factors served as powerful and active constraints on the development of Carter's policies.

SALT

There were, as we have seen, important differences in perspective coexisting within the new administration. On the question of strategic arms control, however, there was a degree of consensus—the Carter administration wanted to move rapidly to conclude a SALT II agreement. Such a step was consistent with the president's oft-repeated desire for arms reductions and defense expenditure cuts. Like Kissinger and Nixon before him, SALT seemed the only readily available means to limit Soviet force structure expansion. In addition, the SALT I agreement was due to expire in October of 1977. Finally, the Ford administration had left behind fifty pages of draft treaty text already agreed to by the Soviets. In fact, it was widely believed that the only issues left to negotiate were problems associated with the Soviets' newly developed "Backfire" bomber—thought by some in the West to possess strategic capability—and the Americans' cruise missiles which, because of technological developments since Vladivostok, could now be deployed in considerable numbers on virtually any air, land, or sea-based platform. They might also be easily deployed by the United States in Europe or transferred to the West Europeans for their own use. Finally, their small size presented significant verification problems given their easy concealment.

By late March the administration was prepared to reopen negotiations on SALT II.[24] However, when Secretary of State Vance met with the Soviets in Moscow, the United States proposed a much more far-ranging agreement than had been negotiated within the Vladivostok guidelines. The Vladivostok guidelines placed equal ceilings on strategic delivery vehicles and MIRVed launchers at the relatively high levels already programmed by or acceptable to the Soviet and American military establishments. In contrast, the new Carter comprehensive package called for significant cuts in total forces and MIRVed launchers, but also proposed ceilings on MIRVed ICBM launchers that would have cut deeply into the muscle of Soviet forces. The Carter administration's proposal has been judged to have been a major departure in the strategic arms limitations process.[25] For the first time a proposal was advanced that would have meant significant reductions in the capability of both sides as well as limiting the modernization of strategic arsenals. The Soviet Union, however, brusquely dismissed the plan, charging that with its proposed deep cuts in ICBM numbers, the proposal was designed to extract unilateral advantage for the United States, since it was precisely by means of ICBM numbers and the size of Soviet warheads that the Soviet Union had achieved strategic parity with the United States. The Soviets insisted that negotiations return to the framework developed during the preceding five years.

In May the United States brought forth another suggestion that sought to break the new impasse that had emerged. First the United States would accept a treaty to run until 1985, based on the Vladivostok ceilings as a starting point, though the United States made it clear that it would pursue lower levels. Second, the two sides would develop a protocol to the treaty that would run for three years and cover all the systems and issues, such as cruise missiles, Backfire bombers, limits on new ICBMs such as mobile ICBMs, and qualitative restraints which the two sides could not negotiate into the treaty itself. Finally, a set of mutually agreed principles would be negotiated to apply to subsequent talks; in effect, agreeing in advance on the agenda for SALT III. It was recognized that the October deadline was not likely to be met, but the two sides agreed to observe the ceilings imposed under the 1972 agreement, and proceeded with what would prove to be a laborious 2½-year process of negotiations culminating in a treaty and protocol signed by presidents Carter and Brezhnev at Vienna on June 18, 1979.

The treaty signed at Vienna was in fact much closer to the American comprehensive package than might have been expected in March of 1977. The overall ceilings were higher than those desired by the United States: 2250 strategic delivery vehicles, 1320 of which could be MIRVed. However, subceilings on MIRVed ICBMs and SLBMs were agreed to, and many of the issues that had been thought likely to be

included in the protocol for subsequent negotiations (such as modernization controls, new ICBM developments, and qualitative limits, e.g.,
limits on the number of warheads that could be deployed on MIRVed
launch vehicles) were actually incorporated into the treaty. Only some of
the issues involving the cruise missile and the Backfire bomber remained outside the treaty but within the protocol or other understandings incorporated under the Vienna package.

Yet when the treaty and protocol were submitted to the Senate for
ratification in the summer of 1979, it was clear that the treaty was in deep
trouble. Notwithstanding an elaborate public relations campaign undertaken by the Carter administration, the hearings before the Senate
Foreign Relations Committee revealed substantial opposition to the
agreements. Objections included the familiar arguments that SALT II,
like SALT I before it, did nothing to eliminate the Soviet lead in large
ICBMs; doubts about whether the United States could verify key provisions of the treaty in view of the loss of intelligence facilities resulting
from the fall of the Shah's regime in Iran in early 1979; and concern that
acceptance of the treaty would lull the American people into com-
placency about what many senators saw as the growing threat of Soviet
strategic superiority.

The administration responded to these questions on the treaty. But
in the course of the hearings and debate, it was revealed by the administration that intelligence data suggested the presence in Cuba of about
twenty-six hundred Soviet combat troops with their equipment. Even
staunch supporters of SALT II demanded that the president do something about the situation, although it was generally known that Soviet
troops had been on the island for the preceding seventeen years, and it
was not clear how a brigade of fewer than three thousand men with no
amphibious transport constituted a threat to the United States. The fact
that such an issue could command such attention, bring the treaty ratification process to a virtual halt, and require a presidential address to the
nation was an indication that far more than a strategic arms control
agreement was being debated in the United States in late 1979.

The Final Decline of Detente

Signs of trouble were apparent at the very outset of the Carter administration, as the Soviets complained privately and then publicly about the
human rights policy of the administration. The president professed not
to be concerned and wrote a sympathetic letter to the most well-known
Soviet dissident, Andrei Sakharov. The week before the Moscow meeting in which the comprehensive SALT II package was to be presented,
however, Brezhnev complained that the tone and thrust of the adminis-

tration's policies constituted interference in Soviet internal affairs. The Soviet rejection of the administration's SALT package was undoubtedly based on objections to the proposal's contents, especially when they seemed to deviate so markedly from what had been negotiated previously. Nonetheless, the atmosphere surrounding a deteriorating detente had clearly not improved with the arrival of the new administration.

In the meantime, events in Africa continued as an irritant in Soviet-American relations. In February 1977, a Marxist regime seized control of Ethiopia and, while seeking assistance from the Russians, undertook full scale war against Somalia over the latter's territorial claims in the Ogaden region of Ethiopia. The Soviets were initially in a difficult position, for they had previously supported the Somalis, but by the fall of the year the Soviets had aligned themselves with the Ethiopians and had begun providing military assistance, including the dispatch of thousands of Cuban troops. Earlier, in March, both Fidel Castro and then Soviet President Podgorny had visited the southern African "front-line states" and Castro visited Ethiopia and Somalia as well. Also in March, Zaire's resource rich Shaba province was invaded by a rebel group operating out of Angola. The invasion was turned back after the insertion of some fifteen hundred Moroccan troops and additional U.S. military assistance.

By early 1978, however, relations had become even more strained, not only regarding Africa but also with respect to Carter's human rights policy. Early in the year the United States and the Soviet Union exchanged warnings concerning each other's actions, with the Soviets asserting that the U.S. attitude on arms control and other issues was unhelpful, and the United States responding that Soviet actions in Africa threatened relations. In May yet another invasion of Zaire was launched from Angola, with the president charging that Cubans were involved. The United States responded with an airlift of French, Belgian, and Moroccan troops, and by June the situation was once again calm. Simultaneously, however, the Soviets had placed on trial a number of prominent dissidents, all of whom were convicted and sentenced to prison terms. Congress passed joint resolutions deploring the trials as Carter announced that Soviet-American exchange programs would be reevaluated and the sale of high technology to the Soviet Union would receive closer scrutiny and be subjected to tighter controls than in the past. In mid-July 1978, as two American newspapermen were being convicted of having libeled Soviet television and ordered to pay fines, the president canceled the sale of computer equipment to the Soviet Union.

Undoubtedly even more alarming from a Soviet perspective, however, was the culmination of the American-Chinese rapprochment begun by Nixon. In late May, after Soviet attempts to improve relations with the

Chinese had broken down, Brzezinski visited China to discuss SALT and normalization. Upon his return to Washington, the sale of technology (in this case infra-red scanning equipment) previously denied the Russians was approved for the Chinese. Throughout the remainder of the year, a parade of high U.S. officials went to China to discuss scientific exchanges and assistance, energy, and agriculture. Finally, in December 1978, after the Chinese had provided assurances to the United States concerning the future status of Taiwan, normal diplomatic relations were established and official ties with Taiwan broken, including the mutual defense treaty between the United States and Taiwan. By early spring of 1979 Deputy Prime Minister Deng Xiaoping visited Washington to sign scientific and cultural agreements but, more provocatively from a Soviet standpoint, issued stern lectures to American audiences concerning the threat posed by Soviet imperialism and "hegemonism."

Midway through Carter's term, therefore, there was little left of the detente, save trade in grain, that the Nixon administration had sought to construct. The demise of detente was well underway by the time Carter came to the White House, but by mid-1978 he was warning the Soviets in language reminiscent of an earlier time: "The Soviet Union can choose either confrontation or cooperation. The United States is prepared to meet either choice."[26] In fact very little remained except the common interest in a SALT agreement. Against a backdrop of increasingly cool relations along virtually every other dimension of contact, the last details of the treaty were worked out in early 1979 and the treaty submitted to the Senate at mid-year. By that time, however, SALT had become the last salient vestige and symbol of a policy of detente that was—in the minds of many, perhaps a majority, in the Senate—a thoroughly discredited approach to dealing with Soviet power. Moreover, for many of these same skeptics and opponents of SALT and detente, the debate and ratification vote were nothing less than a vote on the Carter administration itself.

The domestic reaction against Carter's stewardship of American policy set in almost immediately upon his assuming office. Carter had, of course, come to the presidency promising to reduce defense spending and he immediately cut the Ford defense budget by about $2.8 billion. He also announced, however, that he wanted to reevaluate the need for procuring the new B-1 strategic bomber, which was nearing completion of its development. His appointment of Paul Warnke, a noted advocate of detente and arms control as his chief SALT negotiator, also provoked the more hard-line critics of American policy. But perhaps even more important was the president's apparent willingness to adopt a restrained posture towards Soviet policy in Africa, even as Ambassador Young articulated in forceful language his heretical views concerning the character of third world revolutionary activity.

In addition, Carter's seeming inconsistencies lent support to the growing impression among those who wanted a harder and more uncompromising line towards the Soviet Union, that this president was not the man for the job. Thus in early 1978, after urging the West Europeans to accept deployment of the enhanced radiation or neutron bomb, Carter reversed course and deferred a production decision. For those Europeans, such as Chancellor Helmut Schmidt in West Germany, who had expended considerable political capital building support for the weapon, the reversal was a rude shock. For those in the United States who wanted to see a buildup of U.S. military capability, the decision was very nearly outrageous, especially when combined with what were deemed by them to be overly limited increases in defense spending by the United States. Moreover, Carter even took the unusual step in August of 1978 of vetoing a Defense Department appropriation authorization bill when Congress included in it funds for a nuclear-powered aircraft carrier that the president had not requested.

The severing of relations with Taiwan necessary for the reestablishment of normal relations with the People's Republic and the playing of the China card against the Russians further incensed conservative critics of the administration. Conservatives and long-time supporters of Nationalist China refused to accept the president's rationale that the step was but the culmination of Richard Nixon's geopolitical balancing of Soviet power. No less galling to most conservatives was Carter's advocacy, signing, and active support in the Senate for treaties to return the Panama Canal Zone back to the sovereignty of Panama. The United States retained operating rights over the canal and as the result of understandings and reservations to the agreements increased its security access to the canal; but to its opponents, the treaties were a giveaway of what Republican presidential hopeful Ronald Reagan insisted upon calling "our canal." Here again, the president's view—that the treaty was the fulfillment of a diplomatic initiative originally undertaken in the Johnson administration, pursued by his Republican successors, and, in any event, was essential to establishing a more sensitive and responsive relationship with Latin America—was to no avail.

The Camp David Summit:
An Ambiguous Breakthrough

President Carter was able to deflect, for a time, this building resentment with his temporarily successful mediation of the Egyptian-Israeli peace-making process at Camp David in late 1978. But even here, the initiative was not the president's and the results proved far less certain than the president's rhetoric at the signing of the agreements suggested.

There was initially, in the Middle East, an attempt by the Carter administration to draw the Soviets into the negotiating process between Israel and its neighbors. The negotiating framework proposed was multilateral negotiations in Geneva co-chaired by the United States and the Soviet Union. The Carter administration reasoned that no settlement would be lasting if the Soviets could always act the role of spoiler. The explicit tone of Kissinger's policy, which was designed to expel the Soviets from the Middle East, would, therefore, be reshaped. The melody that the Carter administration now whistled beckoned the Soviets back into the region in an effort to make their would-be proxies and clients in the Arab world—especially the Syrians, Libyans, and the Palestine Liberation Organization—more susceptible to an accord. But the lyrics of the song did not speak of any rewards to the Soviets apart from those of the psyche: mere acknowledgment of some residual Russian interests and influence by the Americans, who would continue to hold most of the cards. In sum, as in the early Nixon years, the Soviets were once again called to be of assistance in their own containment.

The astonishing announcement and subsequent trip of President Anwar Sadat of Egypt to Jerusalem in November 1977 for the purpose of opening a direct dialogue between Egypt and Israel, unhinged American policy. Sadat, fearing precisely a superpower designed and imposed settlement, moved to establish a negotiating process in which he would have maximum control of the agenda, minimum Soviet involvement, and, by encouraging American intermediation, the benefit of whatever credits he had accumulated in Washington following his dramatic ouster of the Soviets in 1972 and his generally pro-American stance since the 1973 war and Kissinger's shuttle diplomacy. Sadat would thereby represent not only his own interests, but if successful, would seize leadership of the Arab camp. In the meantime, the rest of the Arab world reacted with dismay and hostility as the largest Arab state set out on its own, ostensibly in pursuit of common interests, but initially proposing a permanent end to Egyptian-Israeli hostilities and hence, though Sadat would deny it repeatedly, pursuing a separate peace with Israel.

The Soviets would be pushed not only away from center stage but almost out of the theater. Sadat, was, however, perilously poised, extending himself like some over-aged trapeze artist to an initially confused and even indifferent American assistant. The Carter administration, like much of the rest of the world, was knocked off stride by Sadat's initiative. Their planning had all reflected a great-power solution. But Sadat initiative had its advantages—Soviet displacement—and its desired effect:

the road toward a Middle East settlement via Geneva and Soviet participation was abandoned.

The American grip was breathtakingly late. But once in hand, a new "island of stability"—at a cost of up to $10 billion in economic and military assistance to Egypt—was to be established. There were other diplomatic costs, however, for in supporting what other Arab states regarded as treasonous behavior on Sadat's part, American diplomatic credibility in the region was diminished. Apparently, however, the Carter administration reasoned that if by using the opportunity presented by Sadat's boldness, a settlement could be reached; the rest of the Arabs, the Palestinians, and even the Russians, confronted with a *fait accompli*, would in time accept.

After months of negotiations between Sadat and Israeli Prime Minister Menachem Begin produced no diplomatic breakthroughs, however, President Carter in early September 1978, convened a tripartite summit at Camp David, Maryland.[27] For eight days between September 5 and 13, the president, with the assistance of Secretary of State Vance, served as a personal mediator trying to narrow differences for an Egyptian-Israeli peace treaty and what came to be known as a "Framework for Peace in the Middle East" within which detailed negotiations on the Palestinian issue might proceed. As always, the issue of Palestinian rights proved most difficult and very nearly led to the collapse of the talks. In the final analysis, however, President Carter's persistence won a compromise on the Palestinian issue with which Sadat and Begin could live: (1) provisions for the establishment of some form of elected self-governing Palestinian authority, (2) withdrawal of the Israeli occupation forces on the West Bank, and (3) negotiations concerning the final status of whatever Palestianian political entity was eventually formed out of the West Bank and Gaza.

Leaving aside the drama surrounding the negotiations and the fanfare with which the peace treaty and "framework for peace" were announced, it is important to underscore that nothing final concerning the Palestinian question was settled at Camp David. Rather it was at most an attempt to get serious negotiations under way. Apart from whatever short-term domestic benefits accrued to President Carter, the ultimate success of the Camp David process would depend on the diplomatic follow-up to the summit.

Moreover, though the Camp David improvisation was masterful and courageous, it was also expensive and fraught with dangers. For by excluding the Russians yet again in an area of traditional concern to them, it pinned the most radical Middle Eastern groups and states closer than ever to the Soviets. It is also not unlikely that the Soviets' worst fears concerning the Carter administration's acceptance of the Soviet Union's new international status were confirmed by the diplomatic maneuvering in 1977–1978. The reaction was summarized by State Department Soviet expert Marshall Shulman in October of 1979:

> The action of President Sadat in going to Jerusalem and the development of a bilateral negotiations between Egypt and Israel has had the practical effect of excluding the Soviet Union from effective participation in the negotiating process. They bear this very resentfully and have spoken of it quite sharply many times. . . . It clearly is the situation that the Soviet position in the Middle East has deteriorated compared to what it was. That has been the outcome of diplomatic efforts on our part.[28]

But if the Soviets had been shoved aside once again, American diplomacy, as in 1973 and 1974, proved insufficient in itself to bring about a resolution of the Arab-Israeli dispute. Carter, like Kissinger before him, found it easier to get agreement and action by Israel and Egypt concerning territorial questions associated with their bilateral peace treaty, such as Israeli withdrawal from most of the Sinai still held by the Israelis after the 1973–1974 round of negotiations, return of oil producing facilities in the Sinai and the Red Sea to the Egyptians, return of the Gaza area with its large Palestinian refugee population to Egyptian sovereignty, and the reestablishment of normal diplomatic relations between Cairo and Tel Aviv. But on the central question of a Palestinian homeland and its political status, there was little progress.

The framework for negotiating some measure of Palestinian autonomy developed at Camp David proved to be a point of diplomatic contention rather than an agreed agenda for action. Notwithstanding more or less constant American intermediation as well as direct Egyptian-Israeli talks throughout 1979 and early 1980, agreement proved elusive. Indeed, the Begin government, in the face of increasingly militant West Bank Palestinian reaction to the Camp David accords and continuous Jewish selttement in previously Arab areas, reaffirmed and expanded its support of Jewish settlement by groups of Jewish militants who denied any legitimate Arab rights on the West Bank. By mid-1980, open clashes between West Bank Arabs and these Jewish militants were becoming commonplace, and disagreements within the Begin government concerning settlement policy and the negotiations had broken into the open. Foreign Minister Moshe Dayan and Defense Minister Ezer Weizmann—both regarded as moderates on the Palestine question—resigned from the Begin government. Israeli-Egyptian talks stalemated, agreed deadlines for beginning the autonomy process passed, and with the stalemate, the Carter administration was confronted with the possibility that the West Europeans were about to launch their own diplomatic initiative for a resolution of the Middle East situation. Such a move would further emphasize the disarray in the alliance and the lack of European confidence in Carter's leadership. It was also widely assumed that given European dependence upon Arab oil and the West European contention that no lasting settlement could be reached without Palestinian participation in negotiations, whatever proposals the Europeans might advance would likely be far more pro-Palestinian than could be acceptable to a Carter administration facing a difficult presidential election season.

Thus as Carter's reelection effort began, what he had hoped could be advanced as decisive proof of his diplomatic skill—a genuine Middle East peace—seemed as far away as ever. He now found himself positioned between two weakening and hence, inflexible partners within the region: the Begin government, torn internally by reaction to its West Bank settlement policy and the raging Israeli inflation fed in large measure by military spending; and Sadat, who found himself more and more isolated as he and his American benefactors proved unable to deliver the diplomatic breakthrough assumed to have been inherent in Sadat's courageous Jerusalem pilgrimage and the Camp David process. Furthermore, the entire structure of American policy was now being subjected to pressure from a new quarter: the West Europeans, concerned about their own economic interests in the region and the seeming inability of American diplomacy to protect those interests.

A return to Egyptian-Israeli belligerence seemed unlikely. The removal of Egyptian military capability from any potential Arab military coalition and the realignment of the Egyptians with the United States was an important, even fundamental change in the Middle Eastern strategic situation. Moreover, war between Iraq and Iran and military confrontation between Syria and Jordan at the end of 1980 further underscored the Moslem world's inability to unite to meet the Israeli nemesis. But Carter's rhetoric after Camp David seemed to promise much more than the continued isolation of the Soviets from the region and ambiguous geopolitical shifts in the Middle Eastern strategic equation. Furthermore, the uncertanties rather than accomplishments were underscored by the caveat that nearly everyone attached to analysis of the Camp David process: Consolidation of what had been achieved and progress within the Camp David process depended largely on Sadat's retention of power in Egypt—a condition that could prove increasingly problematical unless the Camp David process yielded both the international and internal developmental benefits foreseen and promised by Sadat when he undertook his momentous 1977 trip to Jerusalem.

One could not be sure that the Camp David framework was itself sufficient. For even if a major breakthrough in Egyptian-Israeli negotiations could be achieved, it was always unclear how the Palestinians and Arab states were to be incorporated into the agreement. In this respect the initial position of the Carter administration in 1977 may have made more sense. For in its diplomatic overtures to the Palestinians and its apparent commitment to multilateral negotiations that would have included Palestinian representation at Geneva in some form, Carter was developing a framework that might have been more readily perceived as legitimate by all parties in the region. The Camp David process, in addition to cutting the Soviets out of the action, seemed to preclude this necessary contact with the Palestinians and other Arabs—with the exception of King Hussein of Jordan who refused to attend.

Finally, in addition to the Palestinian homeland/autonomy question, there remained the issue of Jerusalem's status. That Jerusalem should be again free of Israeli control seemed crucial to the Saudi Arabians and all other Arab states. However, the Saudis' aspirations seemed unlikely to be fulfilled as the Israeli Knesset passed legislation in mid-1980 to make Jerusalem the permanent capital of Israel. Moreover, as these and other issues (such as outstanding territorial issues regarding Jordan, Syria and even Lebanon) dragged on, no one in the Carter administration (or among his political adversaries) could offer ideas as to the next step. And, of course, the longer the impasse persisted, the more likely it became that Arab West Bank militancy would continue to develop in the direction of more of the violence that had emerged by the end of the 1970s. Indeed, by mid-1980, the specter of PLO *and* extremist Israeli nationalist terrorism appeared as Arab attacks on Israeli settlements elicited extremist Israeli retaliations in the form of attacks on West Bank Arab leaders. If such violence escalated the United States could find itself caught between Camp David's rhetorical support for the Palestinians and the Israeli need to suppress the violence. Moreover, such instability could provide opportunities for increased Russian influence. The signing of a twenty-year friendship treaty by Syrian President Hafez Assad and the Russians in late 1980, for example, provided access for the Russians. The Soviet Union, it seemed, almost like some adolescent Romeo, was available to any client who would accept its advances.

Nicaragua and Iran

Whatever domestic political respite Carter received for undertaking this tactically impressive act of summit diplomacy was brief, for long-standing American clients on opposite sides of the world were toppling. In 1978 and 1979, in Nicaragua Anastasio Somoza's regime grudgingly and then violently gave way before a coalition of Marxist revolutionaries, the Sandinista National Liberation Front, in coalition with a broad-based collection of opposition groups within the country. The American posture was to push Somoza towards a mediated settlement. The effort failed and after another six months of fighting, the Somoza regime collapsed in mid-1979, with the Carter administration moving quickly to recognize the new revolutionary government and support with economic assistance its efforts to achieve economic viability.

The reluctance to support Somoza represented something of a departure in American policy in Latin America. But though it conformed to the policy approach preferred by interdependence advocates, it was distrubing to traditionalists. The collapse of the twenty-five year American investment in Iran was even more dramatic evidence, for those longing for the more simple era of pre-Vietnam and pre-parity American hegemony, of the bankruptcy of the Carter administration's foreign policy.

Throughout 1978 what had been assumed to be the unshakeable regime of Shah Mohammed Reza Pahlavi and, hence, the surrogate for American interests in the Persian Gulf area, slowly disintegrated in the face of increasingly violent demonstrations and rioting. Beneath the religious rhetoric concerning the immorality of the modernization programs pursued by the Shah was deep and intense resentment of a regime that was perceived as illegitimate and only the extension and instrument of American control. By the fall, the religious leader, the Ayatollah Ruhollah Khomeini, exiled from Iran for fifteen years, was calling from Paris for demonstrations to bring down the Shah and for the institution of an Islamic Republic that would expel the United States and its influence. Strikes shut down the oil industry in November, and by the end of the year virtually all sectors of the economy were paralyzed in response to the Ayatollah's urging. By early January 1979 the Shah was expressing his willingness to take a "vacation" once a new government appointed by him was in power. Within a week the United States government—after considering a coup d'état[29]—endorsed his leaving, and on January 16 the Shah departed on a desultory journey that would take him to Egypt, Morocco, the Bahamas, Mexico, Panama, and finally Egypt again, in search of a place of exile. In the meantime, the Ayatollah returned to Tehran and despite the existence of a civilian government, he and his Revolutionary Council assumed power.

Within Iran months of revolutionary turmoil ensued as the religious militants consolidated their control of the revolution and, in the face of rebellions among Kurds, Baluchis, and other ethnic minorities, prepared for parliamentary elections and the promulgation of an Islamic constitution. American policy at this juncture was ambivalent. There did seem to be a willingness on the part of the Carter administration to wait for a subsiding of the revolutionary disorder and in the interim try to work with whatever government emerged while maintaining contact with presumably the most pro-American elements on the Iranian scene. Thus, for example, in early October the Defense Department announced that it was resuming the shipment of spare parts for American aircraft previously sold to the Shah.

This American search for a moderate center proved to be a profound misunderstanding of what was occurring within Iran. The religious hierarchy with its deep hatred and resentment of the Shah and his American benefactors was in control of the revolution despite the presence of a government that seemed to give the impression of working towards more normal relations with the United States. The magnitude of this misunderstanding of the internal situation in Iran became dramatically apparent in late October when President Carter, reportedly yielding to pressure from former Secretary of State Henry Kissinger and David Rockefeller, admitted the Shah to the United States for cancer treatment.

The effect inside Iran was electric. On November 4, militant students seized the U.S. embassy in Tehran and made hostages of some sixty Americans in the embassy compound. They would be released, the militants told the world through the hundreds of media representatives that converged to cover the seizure and the massive demonstrations that accompanied it, only if the Shah and the wealth he had taken from Iran were returned. Subsequently, the militants released the women and black hostages, but insisted that the remainder would be held until their demands were met or the Ayatollah ordered otherwise. The Ayatollah, however, gave full support to the militants and threatened to put the hostages on trial.

With the Ayatollah and his militant Revolutionary Council now in control, the Carter administration found it virtually impossible to carry out negotiations. A United Nations Security Council resolution and International Court of Justice ruling that the seizure was illegal, and demanding the immediate release of the hostages, were obtained. Moreover, a United Nations mediation attempt was undertaken under the secretary general's auspice even as some economic and diplomatic sanctions were being applied. None of the efforts gained anything, however, but the Islamic Republic's defiance and a reiteration of the demands for the Shah's return. Finally on April 24–25 (to the dismay of Secretary of State Cyrus Vance, who was trying to negotiate even more stringent economic sanctions with the Common Market countries and Japan against Iran—a condition of which was that the United States would not use force), Carter ordered a rescue attempt involving helicopters, C-130 aircraft, and commandoes from a special antiterrorist unit. The rescue attempt failed disastrously as equipment failures at the desert strike base led to a decision to abort the mission, followed by the collision of a helicopter and a C-130 aircraft. Eight crewmen died, their bodies then ghoulishly displayed by the Iranians. The United States government and people could only wonder in frustrated consternation what, if any, instruments of power could now be brought to bear.

Apart from the collapse of the Pahlavi regime itself, what outraged conservatives in the United States was the seeming reluctance and then inept use of American military power by Carter in support of the Shah and afterward. Whether military capability was relevant to the crisis is an issue to which we will turn below. However, Carter's performance during the crisis was noteworthy for its apparent indecisiveness. When the crisis broke, the president was not prepared to extend unequivocal support to a man he had earlier toasted as an "island of stability" and for the remarkable "respect and admiration and love which your people give to you." In fact, he mixed public statements of support with ambivalence concerning the positioning of a naval task force in the region. Later, Carter sent the task force, but when the Shah suggested his own withdrawal, the administration seemed to encourage him. Finally, of course, there was the embarrassing failure of the rescue mission itself. For those who had come to question the president's leadership it was the quintessential example of what one proponent of using military force in the region called an "America in decline."[30] The president, however, as his poll ratings declined, asserted that matters were now under "better control" and returned to the campaign activities he had earlier forsworn until the hostages were returned.

Another Decade . . . Another Doctrine

By the end of the decade, therefore, policies that the president liked to characterize as involving "a combination of adequate American strength, of quiet self-restraint in the use of it, of a refusal to believe in the inevitability of war and of a patient and persistent development of all the peaceful alternatives . . ."[31] were being rejected by a vocal and increasingly influential segment of the policy establishment. Indeed, that organ of the establishment, Foreign Affairs, gave the lead article of its retrospective evaluation of 1979 to a critic who judged Carter foreign policy to have been a "failure" burdened by its "self-inflicted wounds."[32] Moreover, as the decade turned into an election year, the president was confronted by poll after poll which showed diminishing popular confidence in his foreign policy leadership and the likelihood that if the election had been held in mid-1980, he would have lost to his Republican adversary.

Confronted with these political facts the president had already begun to move toward his critics' position. As it became apparent, for example, that the SALT treaty was in trouble, Mr. Carter expressed a willingness to increase defense spending at both the conventional and strategic levels. Furthermore, when in November, the U.S. embassy in Tehran was seized, the president, while rejecting the immediate use of force, increased the American naval presence in the Indian Ocean and began planning a permanent military presence in the region. By early 1980 more than twenty naval vessels, including two aircraft carriers, were stationed in the Arabian Sea. However, it was not the hostage crisis or the travails of SALT alone that led to the crystallization of a new posture on the part of the Carter administration. Rather, on December 26, 1979, the Soviet Union launched an invasion by upwards of eighty thousand men into Afghanistan in support of a pro-Soviet coup directed against a Marxist regime whose leader, Hafizullah Amin, was proving both unable to control an Islamic insurgency but also pursuing an increasingly independent line from that preferred by Moscow. By December 27, Amin was dead and it was apparent within the next few weeks that the Soviets intended to stay in Afghanistan in force until a pro-Soviet regime was firmly in place. The reaction in Washington recalled the deep days of crisis in the five years after World War II.

The SALT treaty was withdrawn by the president. Though there were ritual references to the need to pass the treaty, the administration's rhetoric was now predominantly that of confrontation. The last remnant of detente was to be consigned to the attic, its presence too embarrassing for a president who now asserted that the United States "... must pay whatever price is required to remain the strongest nation in the world."[33] Just before the Afghanistan invasion, the secretary of defense had warned, "We must decide now whether we intend to remain the strongest nation in the world. Or we must accept now that we will let ourselves slip into inferiority, into a position of weakness in a harsh world where principles unsupported by power are victimized, and that we will become a nation with more of a past than a future."[34] Afterwards, in his State of the Union Address, Carter claimed that in "a world of major power confrontation . . . We have a new will at home to do what is required to keep us the strongest nation on earth."[35] What was "required" in Carter's view was a defense budget some 5 percent larger than the previous year and proposed future spending on defense that would lead to about 5 percent per year through the middle of the decade.[36]

No less important, the security interests and commitments to which these resources were to be committed had now grown. There remained, of course, the traditional European and Asian commitments which, in the president's words, "would be automatically triggered." Now, how-ever, there was the Persian Gulf and its oil:

> The denial of these oil supplies—to us or to others—would threaten our security and provoke an economic crisis greater than that of the Great Depression 50 years ago, with a fundamental change in the way we live.
>   Twin threats to the flow of oil—from regional instability and now potentially from the Soviet Union—require that we firmly defend our vital interests when threatened.[37]

Accordingly, the administration established a rapid deployment force to be capable, when fully developed at mid-decade, to move anywhere from a few ships to as many as a hundred thousand men anywhere in the world, but especially into the Persian Gulf region. Much of their equip-ment was to be pre-positioned on storage ships permanently stationed in the Indian Ocean. The troops, if and when needed, would be rapidly deployed by air into bases, access to which was to be negotiated with countries in the region. Finally in the fall of 1980, as war raged between Iraq and Iran at the head of the Persian Gulf, the Carter administration responded to a Saudi Arabian request for aid by deploying an AWACS air defense aircraft and ground support personnel in Saudi Arabia. In addi-tion, the American naval presence in the Persian Gulf itself was in-creased. A Carter Doctrine was born and bapitized.

Nor was the buildup to be concentrated solely on the Persian Gulf. Modernization of NATO was to proceed, including the introduction of a new main battle tank for U.S. forces, a new fighter aircraft, the F-16, and an expansion of the ability of NATO to launch nuclear weapons against the Soviet Union in the form of a new Pershing II missile to be supple-mented by ground launched cruise missiles. Strategically, the MX mis-sile, a mobile ICBM with three times the number of warheads and throwweight and twice the accuracy of the Minuteman III, and the new Trident SLBM and submarines would all be fully deployed by the end of the decade, giving the United States the capacity to threaten the Soviets ICBMs where some 70 percent of their deliverable warheads were de-ployed in 1980. Talk of "nuclear war fighting" and "victory" in a nuclear war became commonplace. Subsequently, a new American targeting doctrine was announced which officially confirmed the intention of the United States to attack hardened Soviet targets. Finally, and perhaps most ominously from a Soviet standpoint, observers of the evening news were treated to the extraordinary sight at midyear of a Chinese Communist defense official standing shoulder-to-shoulder with an American secre-tary of defense in the halls of the Pentagon and announcing that the

United States would begin the sale of "nonlethal" military hardware to the Chinese. Combat equipment, the Chinese official noted, would not be made available "at this time."

FACING THE LIMITS

In its initial formulation, therefore, the Carter Doctrine had about it the kind of open-ended and globalist character contained in the first of the many cold war doctrines. In Southwest Asia the pledge as well as the region to which it was directed were filled with uncertainties. "You are not alone," Brzezinski told refugees at the Khyber Pass in early 1980. Facing Soviet-occupied Afghanistan with an automatic weapon in hand, he exhorted, "You will go back to your villages and your mosques. Your cause is just. God is on your side."[38] The Almighty, the Americans, and the disaffected Afghan mountain people might form a league against atheistic Southwest Asian communism. But neither the petropowers nor the middle-range powers of Europe or even Pakistan were eager to be enlisted in the new crusade. All the more reason to be grimly steadfast. For as a stern Brzezinski lectured television audiences during the latter half of 1980, Southwest Asia was now regarded as of no less strategic importance than had been Europe and East Asia during the early cold war years:

> I think it is important to remember that since WWII there first emerged the central strategic zone of Western Europe. The second central strategic zone for us was the Far East. In both places we have permanently stationed American forces. The third central strategic zone is southwest Asia, the Persian Gulf. . . . Iran, Turkey, to some extent Pakistan, Afghanistan as a buffer were the protective shield. That shield is now being pierced. As a consequence, our friends in the region and our vital interest in the third central strategic zone are beginning to be threatened. This is why this is becoming a strategic problem.[39]

Though Brzezinski recognized the need for using a different mix of foreign policy instruments in this new central strategic zone than had been employed elsewhere, America's buildup of military capability was the primary evidence of its new commitment. Moreover Brzezinski predicted that American involvement in the region would be prolonged, stretching for at least two or three decades into the future.[40] Thus the hard ground of confrontation stretched toward a horizon beyond vision. And if Brzezinski's rhetoric on the Afghan border is translated into policy, then rollback and liberation may be conjoined with the newly invigorated nuclear threat. Carter and Brzezinski seemed to have found John Foster Dulles three hundred miles from the Indian Ocean.

The Limits of Military Instruments

One reason that the Carter administration turned towards a reemphasis of security policy was the fear that the visible presence of American firepower was fast becoming about as welcome and as valuable as a Susan B. Anthony dollar: A discounted coin of uncertain value would have to be either withdrawn from circulation or given special emphasis. This was clearly the case in the long Iranian ordeal, when American arms seemed irrelevant and when American promoted reform seemed a proximate (but certainly, in fact, not the only) cause of the Shah's collapse. As the one who once warmed the Peacock Throne flew off to exile, a pivotal assumption of at least the Kissinger years was challenged: American clients, no matter how well stocked militarily, could not be counted to remain semiautonomous agents of American interests. They could even become a foreign policy nemesis.

A defining characteristic of the Iranian crisis was the hesitance of American policy makers to use force or even to broach the subject openly. The gestures of support that were offered seemed out of a comic opera. A carrier force was ordered to the Persian Gulf from Subic Bay in the Philippines and then, after barely reaching the Straits of Malacca, directed to steam around in a desultory fashion. Equally frustrating was the fact that some of the United States' most dependable European clients refused to allow their NATO air bases to be used as staging areas for even a rescue squadron for the evacuation of American personnel.

American reluctance to use force and the unwillingness of its allies to even contemplate abetting its efforts is not understandable merely in terms of military incapacity. It can neither be simply attributed to a frayed post-Vietnam consensus or explained by a fear of Soviet intervention. A comprehensive explanation for American restrained, albeit clumsy, behavior must also include the realization that, quite simply, nobody in or outside the Carter administration could see what bearing force had to the political, religious, and social tensions tearing at the Pahlavi regime. Even if a quick strike team had entered Iran, no one could offer a reasonable scenario of what they might accomplish once they had arrived. In early 1978, as Iran sank into chaos, Secretary of Defense Brown despondently ruminated: "We are as yet unsure of the utility of U.S. military power in Persian Gulf contingencies."[41]

The Enlistment of Economic Interdependence

In part, in response to the obvious uncertainty concerning the relevance of military responses and the unmanageable elements of Carter's human rights campaigns, the administration turned to economic coercion. Perhaps, it was felt, economic preponderance could do what armies and threats could not. Ironically, however, this use, or misuse, of economic power came at the nadir of America's relative economic strength in this century. That is to say, the Carter administration had been unsuccessful in leading the industrialized world to the establishment of a comprehensive new international economic order. Much had been made of the initial attempt of the Carter administration to promote a series of economic summit conferences among the industrialized powers to coordinate their domestic economic policies. This reflected acceptance of the fact that these economies were now inextricably linked but also vulnerable to one another. Within months, however, it had become apparent that none of the industrialized powers were prepared to accept readily the kind of political risks that such coordination implied.

In the United States, for example, the Carter administration was confronted with a number of powerful economic interests demanding protection from, not an increase in, interdependence. The automobile industry—both management and labor—the steel industry, and portions of the home appliance industry were all pressuring the Carter administration to impose new quotas or tariffs to protect them from Japanese and European competition. The Europeans and Japanese, in turn, were critical of the inability or unwillingness of the United States to move decisively against its domestic inflation and thereby restore confidence in the dollar. And, of course, suffusing all of this international economic anxiety was the persistent vulnerability of developed and developing economies alike to rising prices for their energy imports from OPEC.

In short, interdependence had served to emphasize the conflicting needs and vulnerabilities of those caught in its web. This suggested in turn the need for sensitive and systematic coordination of policies. But for a Carter administration increasingly preoccupied with the Soviet-American and Iranian crises, a traditional emphasis on using economic relationships as instruments of coercion gradually assumed dominance. The irony of this was doubly intense because the administration had come to office rejecting such an approach to economic interdependence. Moreover, those officials responsible for the attempted enlistment of economic interdependence as an instrumentality of American confrontation with the Soviet Union and Iran, had been, in some instances, among the most forceful proponents of a new and more cooperative approach to managing interdependence before they assumed public office. Now, however, they were called upon to design and administer a kind of economic cold war. In truth, as many of them understood, economic warfare was more a symbol of pique and a sop to domestic critics on the right than a realistic instrument to affect events.

In the case of the Soviet Union, it was argued that even if a cut-off of wheat, high technology, or phosphates hurt Americans as much as it did the Soviets, it was all for the better. For any step that involved a trivial cost to the United States would be treated unseriously by the Russians. Yet there were almost no specific commodities for which the United States was the most important supplier. In dollar terms, most American exports to the Soviet Union were agricultural. Even if the Russians could not find enough grain on the open market, there was little reason to believe they would not be able to survive the contretemps. In the end, they would obtain most of the grains they need from others or simply do without. And, there was no evidence that European, Japanese, and Latin American suppliers and creditors would treat the Soviets in any manner other than business-as-usual.

If a convincing argument could be made that the Soviet Union and Eastern Europe had reached a point of strategic vulnerability vis-à-vis technological imports from the West, it still remained unclear how or whether such a vulnerability could be manipulated. Restraining credits would, at best, reduce the subsidy Western governments give their business to export to the Soviet Union. Tighter controls—if obtainable—would only increase the cost to the Russians of their own modernization. It would neither prevent it nor significantly retard it. And, attempts to restrict exports of some oil and gas equipment and technology would, at best, reduce the energy generating capacity of the Soviet Union, and perhaps give a kind of ironic incentive to any Russian urge to increase their stake in the Middle East. Further, a cutback on United States or European oil-related technology might leave Eastern Europe without Russian oil supplies and would force Soviet bloc countries to import more oil from OPEC, thereby further undermining Eastern Europe's hard currency-credit reserves as well as drawing down scarce financial resources necessary to purchase Western technology.

In the Iranian case, as well, there were important questions concerning the American use of economic leverage unanswered by an administration attempting to substitute economic warfare for military coercion. Clearly the boycott of Iranian oil was an effort to prevent Iran from blackmailing the United States over the hostages. But the application of financial pressure on Iran, begun with a freeze on Iranian financial assets in the West, could not be effective unless the rest of the industrialized world was enlisted in the American designed and led economic warfare. At the onset of the crisis with Iran, reports circulated that the

Europeans might participate in limited measures, including even a slowing of trade with the Iranians. But they were reluctant to go much further. The Japanese were accused by American officials of moving with "unseemingly haste" to buy on the spot market Iranian oil previously intended for the United States. The government of Masayoshi Ohira, having narrowly survived a parliamentary crisis during the fall of 1979, resisted having the almost totally import-dependent Japanese economy drafted into the American economic war against Iran. With about 15 percent of Japanese daily imports coming from Iran (in early 1980), Japanese sensitivity was or should have been predictable. Moreover, since the Japanese had been the primary target of the Ford and Carter administrations' attempts to get the rest of the industrialized world to relent in its export pressure on the American market, one suspects that there were not all that many American credits left in Tokyo. Moreover, disruption of the overall United States–Japanese economic relations seems scarcely worth the gains of economic warfare. Indeed, one wonders whether at some point American pressures on the Japanese to act against their economic self-interests, presaged by the "Nixon shocks" of the early 1970s, does not risk setting off a syndrome of Japanese hostility similar to that of the interwar period.

The Europeans Resist Conscription

The Carter administration's almost frantic attempts to fashion a new doctrine incorporating some combination of military and economic instruments raised a final and disturbing set of questions concerning the traditional core of American policy—the Atlantic community. The cold war, after all, had begun because of the fate of Europe and had been centered there for the most past. Throughout the period of European economic reconstruction, American ends and means had been ultimately—though sometimes reluctantly—accepted by the Europeans. By the late 1970s, however, European leaders, especially in the largest countries of the European community, were often brutal in their rejection and defiance of American leadership. Only with respect to the military dimensions of the alliance was there acceptance of American conceptions. But as the SALT process moved through the 1970s, there was an undercurrent of European worry that the United States' strategic concerns were ultimately not their own. By the onset of the 1980s, the Europeans had insisted upon and won from the Carter administration an American commitment to place in Europe a new generation of intermediate range nuclear weapons that could threaten the Soviet Union from Europe. Presumably this would counter the Soviets new tactical theater nuclear weapons, especially the SS-20 missile. It was understood that this step would complicate subsequent strategic arms limitations talks and negotiations concerning force reductions in Central Europe. But in the late 1970s there seemed to be diminishing prospect that such negotiations would lead to significant results in any event. In the larger sense, however, the nagging fear persisted that at some point American strategic concerns and policy would be decoupled from Europe's.

On other matters the decoupling seemed already to have occurred, largely at European initiative. Thus the American attempt to conscript the Europeans into economic warfare against the Iranians and diplomatic isolation of the Russians was met with resistance and then outright defiance. Slowly and painfully throughout early 1980 the Common Market countries and Japan negotiated a series of economic sanctions that they might bring to bear on Iran. Perhaps in fear that unless they participated in some form of economic warfare, the Americans would attempt what, from a European perspective, would be a dangerously provacative use of military force in a region upon which they were vitally dependent for oil. But after the United States attempted precisely such an intervention, even this rationale for cooperation vanished. The British government of Prime Minister Margaret Thatcher could not command the support of even its own Conservative party, and the common European-Japanese position disintegrated. An independent European initiative on the Middle East was discussed within the European Community. The French lectured the new American secretary of state, Edmund Muskie, about the lack of coordination of diplomacy within the alliance and then, with studied cynicism, undertook their own announced summit with the Russians.

Reports circulated that throughout Europe there was a mixture of condescension and despair concerning the Carter administration's leadership capacity and the prospect of submitting the leadership of the alliance to the winner of a Carter-Reagan presidential contest. An American reporter in Europe felt that the European mood was captured by a French satirical magazine which portrayed the differences between the likely American presidential contestants in terms of cross-sectional views of Reagan's and Carter's heads showing the former as empty and latter containing only a small peanut.

European concern and skepticism about the wisdom and constancy of American diplomacy was not new. The 1970s, however, saw somewhat greater willingness and capacity to articulate policies often in conflict with those of the United States. Certainly one would not view the institutional mechanisms of the European Community as being equal to the task of fashioning and sustaining a truly "European" diplomacy. At the same time, however, coordinated and coherent alliance policy on anything except perhaps elements of security policy, seemed a thing of the past. Even here difficulties seemed likely to multiply, especially if the major European states—France, Great Britain, and Germany—set out on some form of quasi-coordinated military cooperation involving the British and French nuclear forces coupled with cruise missile technology. Finally, if the decline of American economic and diplomatic preponderance and the arrested state of development of European-wide institutions is not reversed, then it is not inconceivable that the larger European political economies might well feel compelled to seek their independent resolution of the tensions of interdependence.

CONCLUSION

One by one, the means by which the Carter administration had, at first, wished to turn aside from the cold war proved vulnerable to the apparent immutability of the Soviet-American contest and the doctrines and commitments that have surrounded that conflict. By the beginning of 1980, the Soviet Union—once placed in an equivalent situation with other global issues—reemerged as the pivotal focus of the Carter administration. With the Afghan crisis, an even more expansive series of undertakings was contemplated and formal overtures were tendered to an embarrassingly coquettish constellation and would-be satrapies in the Persian Gulf region. It could not be argued that Oman, Yemen, or Somalia were outposts of liberal values. But the cold war quandary of aligning with regimes of low repute and military advantage had, after all, been customary to just about everyone but Carter and some of his younger State Department advisers. Perhaps, after Afghanistan, the reproduction of personal animus in Soviet-American relations made it easier to yield scruple to necessity. Moreover, tired critics of an undifferentiated definition of American interests seemed to have spent their energies as cold war policy routines, shaped in an era when American power had been little contested, reappeared. It seemed reasonably clear that early advocates of interdependence and world order policies no longer controlled much of the Carter administration's image of international reality. On the other hand, it was by no means clear whether the attempt to marry somehow the more traditional conception of American interests with the ambiguous conditions of contemporary interdependence could serve as a guide for policy either.

In the tenth century, foreign ambassadors used to be called to Constantinople in order that they might be impressed with the military splendor of an enervated empire. There were, as Harold Nicholson once described, interminable reviews at which the same troops emerging from one of the gates and entering by another, came round and round again carrying different kinds of armour. In order to dazzle . . . [by] glamour and mystery, mechanical devices caused the lions on the steps of [the Emperor's] throne to roar terribly.[42]

By 1980, one had the feeling that the American empire, like that of Byzantium, was also largely held together with smoke and mirrors. Not that firepower was unavailable—rather, the real question was whether any volume or type of coercion could now service extended American commitments.

NOTES

1. See for example Stanley Hoffmann's two essays: "The Hell of Good Intentions," *Foreign Policy*, No. 29 (Winter 1977–78), pp. 3–26 and "A View from At Home: The Perils of Incoherence," *Foreign Affairs, America and the World 1978*, Vol. 57, No. 3, pp. 463–491.
2. See his interview with James Reston, *New York Times*, December 31, 1978 and again in the *New York Times*, March 30, 1980.
3. See, for example, Henry Kissinger, *White House Years* (Boston: Little, Brown and Co., 1979), esp. pp. 54–70 and 195–225; also Robert Tucker, "America in Decline: The Foreign Policy of Maturity," *Foreign Affairs, America and the World 1979*, Vol. 58, No. 3, pp. 449–484 and "A New International Order?" *Commentary*, Vol. 59 (February 1975).
4. Among the many analyses of the sort outlined here see Robert O. Keohane and Joseph Nye, Jr., *Power and Interdependence: World Politics in Transition* (Boston: Little Brown, 1977); C. Fred Bergsten and Lawrence Krause, eds., *World Politics and International Economics* (Washington, D.C.: Brookings, 1975); Seyom Brown, *New Forces in World Politics* (Washington, D.C.: Brookings, 1974) and Brown, "The Changing Essence of Power," *Foreign Affairs*, Vol. 51 (January 1973); Richard Cooper, *The Economics of Interdependence* (New York: McGraw-Hill, 1968); and Ed Morse, *Modernization and the Transformation of International Relations* (New York: Free Press, 1976). Nye, Bergsten, Cooper, and Morse all became part of the Carter administration.
5. Leslie Gelb, cited by *U.S. News and World Report*, January 20, 1980, p. 24.
6. Cited by James Wooten, "Here Comes Zbig," *Esquire*, November 1979, p. 120.
7. Zbigniew Brzezinski, *Between Two Ages: America's Role in the Technotronic Era* (New York: Penguin Books, 1970), p. 9.
8. Brzezinski, "America in A Hostile World," *Foreign Policy*, No. 23 (Summer 1976), p. 65.
9. Ibid.

10. From a remarkably revealing interview in March of 1975, found in G. R. Urban, ed., *Detente* (New York: Universe Books, 1976), p. 263.
11. Ibid.
12. Ibid., pp. 278–279.
13. Ibid., p. 264.
14. Cited by Joseph Kraft, *Washington Post*, June 17, 1977.
15. Speech of November 21, 1977, Department of State, Bureau of Public Affairs, Washington, D.C., 1977.
16. Ibid.
17. *New York Times*, March 23, 1977.
18. See, for example, Vance's Harvard Commencement Address on June 5, 1980 in *New York Times*, June 6, 1980, p. A12.
19. "Human Rights: Selected Documents," No. 5 (Washington, D.C.: Department of State, Bureau of Public Affairs, n.d.).
20. Elizabeth Drew, "Reporter at Large: Human Rights," *The New Yorker*, July 18, 1977, p. 54.
21. For similar comments see ibid, *passim*.
22. Ibid., p. 56.
23. Zbigniew Brzezinski and Samuel Huntington, *Political Power: USA/USSR* (New York: Viking, 1964), p. 424.
24. Excellent surveys of the development of the Carter administration's SALT II positions and the negotiations themselves can be found in Strobe Talbot, *Endgame: The Inside Story of SALT II* (New York: Harper and Row, 1979), and Thomas W. Wolfe, *The SALT Experience* (Cambridge, Mass.: Ballinger Publishing Co., 1979). Useful documentary sources are Roger P. Labrie, ed., *SALT Handbook: Key Documents and Issues 1972–1979* (Washington, D.C.: American Enterprise Institute, 1979) and U.S., Department of State, *SALT II Agreement*, Selected Documents No. 12A (Washington, D.C.: Bureau of Public Affairs, June 1979).
25. Wolfe, op. cit., pp. 222–223.
26. Presidential address to the graduating class at the United States Naval Academy, June 7, 1978, *New York Times*, June 8, 1978.
27. For a review of the Camp David Summit and American policy during this period see, John C. Campbell, "The Middle East: The Burden of Empire," *Foreign Affairs, America and the World 1978*, pp. 613–632. Documentary materials may be found in U.S., Department of State, *The Camp David Summit, September 1978* (Washington, D.C.: Bureau of Public Affairs, 1978).
28. Testimony given at a hearing before the Subcommittee on Europe and the Middle East of the Committee on Foreign Affairs, House of Representatives, 96th Congress, 1st Session, October 16, 1979.
29. See the article by the former American ambassador William H. Sullivan, "Dateline Iran: The Road Not Taken," *Foreign Policy*, No. 40 (Fall 1980), pp. 175–186.
30. Tucker, "America in Decline," op. cit.
31. Address at the United States Naval Academy, op. cit.
32. Tucker, op. cit., pp. 468ff.
33. State of the Union Message, *New York Times*, January 22, 1980.
34. *New York Times*, December 14, 1979.
35. State of the Union Message, op. cit.
36. See U.S. Department of Defense, *FY 1981 DOD Report* (Washington, D.C.: Government Printing Office, 1980).
37. State of the Union Message, op. cit.

38. CBS Sunday Night News, February 4, 1980. See also *Washington Post,* February 4, 1980. Brzezinski's more studied analysis of this event was revealed in an interview with television commentator Bill Moyers: "Bill Moyers' Journal: A Conversation with Zbigniew Brzezinski," Public Broadcasting System, November 16, 1980.

39. "National Security Adviser Brzezinski Interviewed on 'Issues and Answers,'" *Department of State Bulletin,* Vol. 80, No. 2039 (June 1980), p. 49.

40. *McNeil/Lehrer Report,* Public Broadcasting System, October 15, 1980.

41. *Washington Post,* January 27, 1978.

42. Harold Nicholson, *The Evolution of Diplomacy* (New York: Collier Brooks, 1954), p. 41.

Chapter 12
The New
Cold War

The constancy of American foreign policy is striking. After forty years of practicing variations of containment, U.S. foreign policy has assumed the unconscious deliberation of a sleepwalker. The goal of American policy in the cold war, a congenial world order, has always implied both the constraint and the contraction of Soviet power. Debates have persisted concerning the most appropriate means for constraining Soviet power. But, with the exception of a brief period at the onset of the Carter administration, the Soviet Union has remained the singular focus of American foreign policy since the end of World War II.

In perhaps no other administration since the end of World War II has this fixation with the Soviet Union been so exclusively central to American foreign policy than during the Reagan administration. Ronald Reagan's world view and that of his closest advisers reflect not just an aversion to the Soviet Union but a loathing of its history and institutions. It is not surprising, therefore, that Soviet-American confrontation, both bilateral and wherever major crisis and instability was manifest in the world, should displace virtually all other concerns during the early Reagan administration.

In this chapter, we shall trace the dimensions of the deterioration in Soviet-American relations during the early Reagan years. In the following chapter, attention will focus on the effects of the Reagan administration's preoccupation with the Soviet Union on the major crisis areas of the Middle East and Central America. In addition, we shall examine the consequences and implications of this resurgence of traditional cold war perspectives and concerns for the elements of interdependence that assumed new importance in the 1970s as well as U.S. relations with its allies in Europe and Asia.

CONTAINMENT AND THE CITY
ON THE HILL

The Reagan administration's view of the struggle between the United States and the Soviet Union was layered with the historic sense of American exceptionalism. Jefferson had called the United States a new Zion. Its seal should be a portrait of Moses leading his people, in the dark, to the promised land guided by a pillar of light. Woodrow Wilson held with evangelical certainty that if the American experiment were adopted globally, war would be vanquished from the planet. Consistent with these views, Mr. Reagan told an audience in 1976 that the "Anglo-American ideology" is "nothing short of a heavenly gift of humanity. I have long believed that God placed this land here to send people of a special kind . . . [we] have a rendezvous with destiny."[1] If America is a new chosen land, the Soviet Union is its moral antithesis. "I believe," Reagan told an audience in Orlando, Florida, in 1983, the Soviet Union "is another sad bizarre chapter in human history whose last pages are now being written . . . [it is] the focus of evil in the modern world."[2] The Soviet Union was "an evil force that would extinguish the light we've been tending for 6,000 years."[3]

In the Reagan team's analysis it was clear that it was both the nature of the Soviet system and its external behavior that drove America and Russia into opposition. According to the leading White House Kremlinologist, Harvard Professor Richard Pipes, the result would eventually be war—unless the Soviets abandoned communism.[4] Pipes's logic was echoed by Mr. Reagan: "every Soviet leader from the beginning has proclaimed that Communism can only succeed if it is a one world Communist State. . . . [They] are going to aid social revolutions until the whole world has been liberated to Communism. . . ."[5] Little wonder, then, that other foreign policy considerations were obliged to give way to the pre-eminent issue of Soviet power. As Secretary of State Alexander Haig explained: "Moscow is the greatest source of insecurity today. Let us be plain about it. Soviet promotion of violence as an instrument of policy constitutes the greatest danger to the world."[6]

Observers and critics of the Reagan administration derided its simplistic tone and asserted that it was nostalgia for an imagined lost era of American virtue and power. This rhetoric was, it was suggested, either unserious, irrelevant, or distorting propaganda in support of a vast defense expansion and a contraction of domestic spending in the midst of the hardest economic times since the mid-1930s.[7] A jaded Washington press corps, for instance, was known to break up over the president's handling of foreign policy details in press conferences.[8] His grasp of recent American foreign policy was often hopelessly garbled as displayed in his muddled recounting of America's involvement in Vietnam. Characteristically, his recollection of events conveniently maximized communist and minimized American responsibility for the catastrophe which followed. The result was that the Reagan team's ideology had "no ideological force," declared political psychologist James David Barber. "His [Reagan's] philosophy is 'the little-house on the prairie' and his data base is the airline magazine and daily horoscope."[9]

Even if Mr. Reagan were no sage in foreign policy, the direction of the Reagan administration demonstrated almost Cartesian rigor in the linkage of its assumptions and its actions. In a maintaining struggle between the city on the hill and an aberrant anti-Christ, moral and programmatic choices narrow. Little wonder the search was for the means to "prevail" in the struggle with evil. As Thomas Reed, White House foreign policy adviser, put it: "We believe the free world can prevail. . . . Prevailing with pride is the primary objective. . . . When vital interests are at stake there is nothing wrong with winning."[10] To confound and defeat the Soviets, not to accommodate them, was the Reagan administration objective, for as Pipes put it, "Russian imperialism must end."[11]

Since the Reagan administration felt that American defense had been bested by a maximum Russian effort during the detente years of the 1970s, there was little incentive, save a nervous public, to begin arms control negotiations with the Soviets. As the Reagan administration's second secretary of state, George Schultz, put it: "Arms control has not been—cannot be—the dominant subject of dialogue with the Soviets."[12] Negotiations with the Soviets were to proceed on the basis of what the president understood as "linkage":

> . . . In any talks, there has to be linkage. I don't think we can sit there and talk about some agreement on weapons and ignore what they're doing with regard to intervening in other countries, taking over other countries. It has all got to be part of the same package. If we're going to have good relations, then it must be based on conduct different from what they've done in the past.[13]

A diplomacy directed at the adjustment of specific differences between the United States and the Soviet Union or the working out of a framework for interaction in areas of mutual interest and danger was not, therefore, envisioned as the basis of the superpower relationship. Instead the focus was to be, as it had been at the onset of the cold war, the very structure of international relations and the legitimacy of the Soviet regime and its hegemony in Central Europe. Secretary of State Shultz put matters bluntly in early 1984 when he declared in a statement at the Stockholm Conference on European Security with Soviet Foreign Minister Andrei Gromyko present, that the United States "does not recognize the legitimacy of the artificially imposed division of Europe" and regarded the division as the source of all insecurity on the continent.[14] Predictably, therefore, foreign policy in the early 1980s reverted to the rhetorical stridency and emphasis on confrontational testing of will and strength that was commonplace in the decades before detente in the 1970s.

FACING DOWN THE EVIL EMPIRE

During the 1980 campaign, Ronald Reagan had hammered away at the purported weakness, uncertainty, and allegedly dangerous inadequacies of the Carter administration's foreign and defense policies. Yet, as had happened in 1952, 1960, and 1968, the new administration accepted most of the defense policy premises left to it by its predecessors.[15] Thus Secretary of Defense Caspar Weinberger argued upon assuming office that the central problem was that the Carter administration had not been willing to provide the military resources required by U.S. commitments:

> The principal shortcoming of the defense budget we inherited is not so much that it omitted critical programs entirely in order to fully fund others, but rather that it failed to provide full funding for many programs it conceded were necessary but felt unable to afford.[16]

Accordingly, the new administration moved rapidly to take advantage of the congressional consensus in favor of defense spending increases that had been swept into office with Mr. Reagan.

In a series of budget requests beginning in March of 1981, the Reagan administration advanced Five-Year Defense Plans which increased the total spending authority available to the Defense Department between 1982 and 1988, from the $1,276.1 billion requested by the Carter administration to $1,768.1 billion. Modernization programs had been requested by the Carter administration for intercontinental ballistic missiles, Trident submarines, air-launched cruise missiles, and a new generation of land-based missiles in Western Europe—the Pershing IIs—and ground-launched cruise missiles. The Reagan administration supported these programs and revived the B-1 strategic bomber, more tactical fighters, new U.S. continental antibomber defenses, as well as significant expansion of the U.S. Navy to a planned level of six hundred ships including at least three new large-decked nuclear-powered aircraft carriers.[17] But none of these programs attracted more attention and controversy than the administration's proposals for modernizing America's strategic retaliatory capability.

The Pursuit of Strategic Superiority

Conservative critics of the Carter administration maintained that while the United States had been focusing on developing detente and strategic arms control agreements, the Soviet Union had undertaken a massive buildup of its strategic and conventional military forces and had acquired the capacity for the global projection of its military power.[18] All of this contributed to a condition of American military inferiority, the most important element of which was Soviet strategic superiority. The number, size and accuracy of Soviet ICBMs and SLBMs and their warheads had opened a "window of vulnerability" for American land-based strategic forces which the Soviets would exploit politically if not militarily.

Between 1973 and 1983, the Soviets developed and deployed three new strategic missiles, all capable of carrying highly accurate multiple warheads. Members of the Reagan administration, many drawn from the Committee on the Present Danger, argued that this gave the Soviet Union the theoretical ability to eliminate U.S. ICBMs with a small percentage of their ICBMs and would leave a U.S. president with a choice of horribles. The first was that the U.S. submarine-launched missiles, not accurate enough to destroy hardened Russian military targets, as well as U.S. bombers, could massively retaliate against the Soviets perhaps killing half the Russian population. But this would incite near certain Russian retribution with their remaining ICBMs and SLBMs. The Soviet Union would be annihilated as a society . . . and so would the United States. The second alternative, given worst-case assumptions about Soviet intentions and capabilities, was just as unthinkable. With only its missiles gone and several million dead, a U.S. president could sue for an unfavorable accommodation. The United States could be Red, or dead, or both.

Critics of these scenarios were not hesitant to point out the "static" nature of this argument. Weapons never fired before in anger, timed with a choreography as carefully calibrated as a Swiss watch, over terrain never before overflown by missiles, causing casualties the United States has never before experienced, unprecedented disruption of civil and political life, uncertainties as to whether the initial Soviet strike was truly limited or merely the opening shots of an unrestricted frenzy—all of these unanswered questions seemed to make the argument tendentious.

Yet, the Soviets did possess a hypothetical capability, a "fact" that was repeated endlessly by critics of the Carter administration and detente.[19] Moreover, the chief spokesman for the Committee on the Present Danger and, subsequently, a member of the Reagan team, Paul Nitze despairingly asserted that the Soviets had embarked on a civil defense program and because their industry and population were more dispersed than that of the United States, any American riposte for a precise Soviet nuclear blow aimed at U.S. missiles would be "just to level a number of Soviet cities with the anticipation that most of ours would then be destroyed."[20]

> Unfortunately . . . neither negotiations nor unilateral restraint have oper-
> ated to dissuade Soviet leaders from seeking a nuclear war winning
> capability—or from the view that with such a capability they could effec-
> tively use pressure tactics to get their way in a crisis.[21]

In the end, therefore, that perceived danger was more political than
military. Insofar as the Soviets possessed strategic superiority, however
theoretical, then in crises of the magnitude of the Cuban missile crisis,
the American president rather than the Soviet leader would be subject to
nuclear blackmail. Khrushchev had backed down because he was confronted with American nuclear superiority as well as conventional
superiority in the Caribbean; could an American president in
Khrushchev's position in some future confrontation do otherwise? The
need, it was argued throughout the mid and late 1970s by Nitze and
other conservative defense analysts, was for the United States to develop
forces and strategies which were the mirror image of those they attributed to the Soviets.[22]

Notwithstanding the speculative and abstract character of these
charges and fears, the Carter administration had taken a number of steps
in response to them. There were monies and plans for civil defense,
augmented command control capability, increased hardening of U.S.
missiles, and plans for a large, extremely accurate mobile missile, the
MX. Most important, however, was the formulation of an American
strategy for the controlled use of nuclear weapons. In 1977, Carter's
secretary of defense, Harold Brown, ordered a review of U.S. strategic
targeting policy. The results were adumbrated in his posture statement
in early 1979, and on July 25, President Carter signed Presidential
Directive 59 (PD59), which codified the new approach to nuclear war.[23]

Carter defense specialists found that nuclear emergency procedures
were sluggish and confused. Moreover, even if the United States had a
viable second strike capability, the White House was subject to "decapi-
tation," i.e., the destruction in an initial nuclear exchange of responsible
political authority. No negotiations could take place. There would be no
coordination with field commanders. In case of a nuclear strike, the
United States would most probably respond in a "spasm." Indeed, the
Carter administration began to agree with Nitze's observations that
Soviet civil defense ought to be taken seriously. For, if the Soviet civil
defense measures were as good as touted, even a deliberate attempt to
kill as many Russians as possible in a second strike—merely for retaliation—might result in fewer than 25 million casualties. This would
be well short of the 100 million figure which had been the bureaucratic
definition of "unacceptable damage" since 1963.[24]

Among the results of this analysis was for the Carter defense planners to advance hard targeting programs such as the submarine-launched Trident II and a decision to build the biggest missile allowed by SALT II, the MX. However, both systems were designed to counter Soviet warhead accuracy in that the Trident II was submarine based and the MX was mobile. Another outcome was that PD59 contained options for a variety of nuclear strikes in an attempt to minimize damage by destroying Soviet missiles, limit casualties and ensure negotiations before Armageddon was unavoidable. Paradoxically, however, according to leaked versions of PD59, there was the premise that Soviet leadership would be an explicit target of nuclear weapons.[25]

Secretary of Defense Brown tried to soften public explanations of the new doctrine. As Brown told a Naval War College audience: "Nothing in the policy contemplates that nuclear war can be a deliberate instrument. But we cannot afford to risk that the Soviet leadership might entertain [that] illusion. . . ."[26] For his part, Brown expressed skepticism concerning the concept of limited or controlled nuclear war. Rather the new strategy was to provide the president with options allowing a "countervailing" capacity if the Soviets initiated the kind of escalating nuclear blackmail feared by Nitze and the others soon to occupy positions of authority.

Thus PD59 was a bureaucratic and political instrument as well as a statement of national strategy. In this former sense, its aim was to respond to the political attack of the Republican right by embracing part of their analysis but offering a more restrained remedy. As national strategy, PD59 was evolutionary. The United States had possessed silo-breaking Minuteman missiles since the mid-1970s and, indeed, the whole SALT process with its acceptance of heavier and more numerous Soviet missiles had been predicated on confidence that whatever U.S. warheads lacked in yield, they more than made up in their superior accuracy and larger numbers. As for accepting "war fighting" strategies, the notion had been explicitly articulated by then Secretary of Defense James Schlesinger in the mid-1970s.

Thus, other than reinstituting the B-1 bomber, the first steps of the Reagan administration were only slightly to the right of the center of the road constructed by its predecessors. The furor caused by Reagan's campaign criticism of the basing mode for the MX may have created an appearance of radical new departures in strategic forces, but in time, Reagan would recommend deploying no more MXs than proposed by Carter. Furthermore, in the short run, the Reagan administration rejected a number of "quick fix" proposals for closing the so-called "window of vulnerability" advanced by the more strident of his advisers. Parity, it seemed, would remain a reality well into the 1980s.

At the same time, however, the declaratory posture of the United States concerning the use of strategic weapons did shift. Whereas PD59 advocated a countervailing strategy designed to deny the Soviets certain limited war options, the Defense Department's Defense Guidance for 1983–1984 demanded strategic capacity which "should deterrence fail and strategic nuclear war with the U.S.S.R. occur, the United States must prevail and be able to force the Soviet Union to seek earliest termination of hostilities on terms favorable to the United States."[27] The objective of PD59 could be seen as employing limited war-fighting capability in the service of the traditional objectives of mutual deterrence, albeit with ambiguous effects on the stability of the relationship. Although Secretary of Defense Weinberger argued that the Reagan administration's pursuit of the capability to prevail was consistent with these traditional strategic objectives, the notion of "prevailing" seemed to suggest more. War-fighting capability was no longer something one possessed in order primarily to *threaten* one's adversary in the interests of deterrence; now it was capability to be *used* in a strategic exchange so that the war might be ended "on terms favorable to the United States."[28] In the deepest sense, therefore, the evolving consensus formalized by Carter's PD59 could be seen to have masked tension between advocates of stable deterrence and war fighting. Whereas previously the proponents of stable deterrence could be said to have been dominant, strategic posture was now tilting towards war fighting.[29]

Domestic reaction to this new rhetoric was frightened and forceful. Widespread editorial and popular demands for a reinvigoration of the arms control process surged during 1981 and 1982 and a nationwide movement for a verifiable bilateral freeze on the production of nuclear weapons peaked. Moreover, as the Reagan administration sought to develop an alternative basing mode for the MX missile, it found that its staunchest Western and Rocky Mountain-state defenders in the House and Senate were not prepared to support its deployment if it meant new and environmentally disruptive bases in their states. The Mormon Church came out in opposition to the new system and the Catholic bishops after long and careful study advanced pastoral guidance which challenged not only the MX but the moral basis of the administration's strategic posture.[30] Against this backdrop of rising public concern and public opinion polls showing majority support of a freeze, resolutions favoring a nuclear freeze were introduced in both houses of Congress. A modified and weakened resolution passed the House but to the relief of the administration was defeated in the Republican-controlled Senate.

In the meantime, the administration had been forced to back away from its declared opposition to arms control and enter into what it termed Strategic Arms Reductions Talks, or START, in pursuit of what it called "deep reductions" in the superpowers' strategic arsenals.[31] The immediate objective, Mr. Reagan stated, in May of 1982, was a cut in the number of warheads deployed by the two sides on missiles. Furthermore, no more than 2500 of the remaining 5000 warheads could be deployed on ICBMs which, in combination with submarine-launched missiles, would be limited to 850 missiles. In the longer term, missile throw-weights would also be equalized.

Inasmuch as the Soviets had rejected a similar proposal some five years earlier when advanced by the Carter administration, it should not have been surprising that they rejected it once again. Because such proposals for deep reductions required them to reduce their ICBMs far more significantly than the United States, the Soviets maintained that Reagan's START proposal was in fact directed at disarming the Soviets (their ICBMs) while allowing itself to retain the large numbers of warheads that it had deployed on long-range strategic bombers, the latter not being included in the original START proposal. Though talks continued throughout the latter half of 1982 and into 1983, no progress was evident as the Reagan administration held, with some modifications, to its call for deep reductions and the Soviets insisted on an agreement in conformity with the more marginal and incremental reductions worked out under the SALT II agreement.

Finding MX a Home

Although both sides announced their intention to abide by the limits agreed upon in SALT II while START negotiations proceeded, both continued weapons development allowed under the moribund treaty. Mr. Reagan's ridiculing and rejection of the Carter administration's mobile mode for basing the new MX missile made it incumbent that his administration come up with a new basing scheme that would ensure the invulnerability of the new ICBMs. After months of study and internal debate, the administration proposed basing 100 missiles in a tightly packed configuration or "dense pack."[32] The theoretical basis of the proposal was that if the Soviets tried to attack the new missile field, the blast effects of hundreds of warheads detonating on and over the missile field would be so great that incoming warheads would be destroyed or their flight paths sufficiently disrupted that the accuracies needed to destroy the heavily hardened and densely clustered MX missile silos could not be achieved. This "fratricide" effect would purportedly allow enough MX missiles to survive that the United States could then mount a highly accurate retaliatory strike against the remaining Soviet ICBMs.

Unfortunately for Mr. Reagan, his advisers could convince few but themselves of the feasibility of the proposal. With the chairman of the

Joint Chiefs of Staff testifying that a majority of the chiefs were skeptical of the proposal, the Congress rejected it and directed the president to come up with a new basing mode by March of 1983.[33] The president responded by appointing a commission of former Department of Defense secretaries and strategic planners under the direction of former National Security Adviser General Brent Scowcroft. On April 11, 1983, the Scowcroft Commission delivered a report which, in its effort to be all things to all sides of the strategic debate, gave Mr. Reagan his MX missiles while undercutting assertions of "windows of vulnerability" and nuclear war fighting.[34]

The commission concluded that although the ICBM leg of the strategic triad was increasingly vulnerable, U.S. strategic capability as a whole was adequate to the task of deterring a first strike against the United States. Moreover, rather than base U.S. strategic posture on warfighting capability, the commission reaffirmed the notion of stable deterrence as the only sound basis for the Soviet–U.S. strategic relationship. Concerning the future of the ICBM, however, the commission both supported and departed from the administration's position. On the one hand, it argued for the limited deployment of the MX in existing Minuteman silos as an incentive to the Soviets to continue negotiations and maintain the flexibility of the ICBM leg of the triad. At the same time, the commission urged that this step be viewed as transitional, for it also proposed that the United States develop a new, much smaller, mobile, but single warhead missile as the ultimate means for modernizing the ICBM force while maintaining a stable balance with the Soviets. The hope behind the new missile—immediately christened "Midgetman"—was that by moving away from strategic arsenals deploying many large missiles armed with multiple and highly accurate warheads, neither side could credibly threaten a first strike against the other. Insofar as the fear of a first strike diminished, and thus the need to contemplate a pre-emptive strike of one's own, the entire relationship could become far more stable.

The MX had survived for the time being, but none of the problems that had plagued strategic policy throughout the late 1970s had been resolved. Notwithstanding congressional approval of funds for the procurement of the first MX missiles in late 1983, the basing of the missile remained problematic. The vulnerability problems were made more acute for now the commission and the administration proposed deploying the new missile in the same supposedly vulnerable silos that had caused concern in the first place. Inasmuch as the MX would mount far more warheads than the older Minuteman (ten as opposed to three), it became an even more attractive target for the Soviets contemplating the need to eliminate the bulk of U.S. war-fighting capability quickly in the event of a nuclear war. Indeed, given the purported vulnerability of these highly accurate warheads, the only plausible use for the MX was as a first strike weapon—unless, of course, the Minuteman silos in which the MX was now to be deployed were *not* vulnerable to a first strike. But if this were the case it was unclear why one needed the MX at all if one's objective was stable deterrence. No less perplexing was the problem of how to get the Soviets to accept the idea of completely restructured ICBM arsenals built around a new missile (which neither the Soviets nor the United States possessed) and requiring the Soviets to eliminate their existing ICBM capability—the kind of proposal they had already rejected twice within five years.

"Star Wars"

The situation was not promising; it seemed as though the paradigm of strategic stability based on deterrence and arms control that had dominated American strategic thinking during the 1960s and 1970s was bankrupt. And in fact this was exactly what Mr. Reagan suggested in a speech on March 23, 1983.[35] In closing an appeal for support of his arms buildup, the president offered the American people a "vision" which provided, in his view, a way out of the paradox of "deterrence of aggression through the promise of retaliation[;] [t]his approach to stability through offensive threat." Rather than "rely on the specter of retaliation, on mutual threat," the president urged "that we embark on a program to counter the awesome Soviet missile threat with measures that are defensive."[36] Mr. Reagan offered no details for his defensive system, but it was clear to most observers that what he had in mind was a resurrection of the idea of ballistic missile defense that had been ostensibly severely restricted in the 1972 treaty on antiballistic missile defenses because of its potentially destablizing effects.

The new technologies that the president seemed to have in mind were to be based in space rather than around U.S. ICBM sites although the latter were certainly not excluded. The president was apparently persuaded that the more than $50 billion[37] that the United States had invested in the development of military space applications since 1958 was on the verge of paying off with a new generation of weapons. The effort under the Reagan administration had been impressive: the Defense Department's space budget had grown from $6.4 billion in fiscal year 1982 (when it was larger than the National Aeronautical and Space Administration's budget of $5.9 billion, almost 25 percent of which was for military applications) to more than $14 billion in fiscal year 1984 when the military applications of NASA's budget were included. By 1988 one projection of the Defense Department's space applications budget was as high as $20 billion while civilian programs would be spending more than $4 billion. Moreover, in September of 1982, the Air Force had established an independent Space Command responsible for coordinating and developing space applications for the new technologies.

U.S. programs were not designed to be exclusively reactive. Though defensive applications were under study, General Robert T. Marsh, the commander of the Air Force Systems Command, made it clear in 1982 that "we should move into war-fighting capabilities, space-to-space, space-to-ground."[38] And consistent with its strategic posture, the administration's 1984–1988 Five Year Defense Guidance admonished the development of capabilities to "wage war effectively" and "vigorously pursue" technological applications that would allow the U.S. to "project force in and from space."[39] The Air Force, echoing Mr. Reagan's rhetoric, called for "space superiority" so as to ensure that the United States would "prevail" in any conflict.[40]

These preparations for "space combat" as the Air Force put it, left many questions concerning the president's notion of "defensive" systems and a stable future. The immediate objective of all this spending was the development of an antisatellite capability superior to that which the Soviets could develop. On the horizon, however, were laser and particle-beam applications which proponents saw as justification for the president's optimism. But would such applications (assuming that they would work, an assumption that many scientists and engineers rejected) ensure the hoped for era of stability? Many analysts thought not; rather, the prospect was for extending the strategic arms race into yet another dimension where stability and arms control could become even more problematic.[41]

The president acknowledged that "defensive systems have limitations and raise certain problems and ambiguities. If paired with offensive systems, they can be viewed as fostering an aggressive policy; and no one wants that." But was the president proposing that the United States eliminate its offensive systems, i.e., its triad of ICBMs, SLBMs, and bombers? In fact, of course, the United States was modernizing and expanding its offensive capability for the 1990s and beyond. Furthermore, the defense establishment's programs for space emphasized war-fighting applications. And finally, it was clear that the administration had no intention of restraining the development of such ambiguous developments through existing or future arms control arrangements. Indeed, the 1984–1988 Defense Guidance stated categorically that the United States "must insure that treaties and agreements do not foreclose opportunities to develop these capabilities" notwithstanding the conclusion of the Arms Control and Disarmament Agency (ACDA) in 1979 that "The deployment by both sides of highly capable ASAT [antisatellite weapons] systems could have an adverse effect on the stability of the strategic nuclear and regional balances."[42] In the final analysis, therefore, it is difficult to see how the Reagan vision of the future differs from his image of the present: security was to be achieved through an assertion of American strategic superiority. But it was no less difficult to see how such a vision escaped the dilemmas of the present where both superiority and security prove so elusive and ambiguous.

DEADLOCK IN EUROPE?

This pattern of Soviet and American arms buildup, deadlocked negotiations, and uncertain prospects was paralleled throughout 1982 and 1983 along a second dimension of the superpowers' expanding nuclear arsenals: theater nuclear forces in Europe. Europeans had always hoped that the defense of Europe would mean an early use of nuclear weapons at the strategic level. For this and other reasons American urgings that the Europeans make better use of their resources and prepare NATO for a realistic and practical ground defense never became a European priority. In addition, the destructive implications of another war in Europe and the presumed added costs to their economies associated with larger European conventional capability seemed daunting. Thus for all the seven thousand nuclear warheads as well as three hundred thousand U.S. servicemen and women in Europe, it was always hoped, by Europeans, that the forces would be a deterrent: an awesome symbol of American commitment. If the worst were to come, they would cause an early recourse by the United States to its strategic arsenal. In Henry Kissinger's words, "the bombs would fly over European heads." Europeans desired deterrence but feared defense.[43] When, in 1979, Kissinger challenged these assumptions of an automatic and early U.S. response to a Soviet attack, it was as if he had made a rude noise in church.[44]

The loss of superiority at the strategic level implied in the Vladivostok agreements and the introduction in the late 1970s of a new Soviet intermediate range missile in Europe, pointed to an impending "Eurostrategic" balance tipped, many feared, towards the Soviets. The Soviets were always considered to have superior numbers of men and equipment on the ground in Europe, but this could be offset by U.S. theater nuclear superiority. Now many European military planners began to fret about the validity of America's NATO guarantee as both theater and strategic nuclear superiority became questionable. As Kissinger recalled, strategic superiority used to be "magic words which had a profoundly reassuring effect."[45] By late 1977, such utterances were not congruent with appearances.

Especially ominous was the Soviets' new SS-20. In 1977 the Soviets began deploying what were to become more than 300 (240 in Europe) powerful, MIRVed, mobile, and reloadable nuclear weapons capable of hitting any spot in Europe. Then German Chancellor Helmut Schmidt worried that the Carter administration, preoccupied with SALT, would ignore these new Soviet weapons in any arms control deal. Hence, in London, in October 1977, Schmidt called for "equivalence" not only at the strategic level but also in Europe as well. A strategic arms accord, he said, would "magnify the significance of the disparities between East and West in tactical nuclear and conventional weapons."[46] The Carter administration, having fumbled issues of trade and deployment of the neutron bomb, was anxious to rise to Schmidt's call.

By late 1979 NATO ratified a plan, inspired by German-American coordination, for the Europeans to host and share the cost of 572 new American missiles. One hundred and eight were to be Pershing IIs— mobile ballistic missiles capable of being MIRVed and with accuracies of about thirty meters—based in West Germany. Their range was variously reported as approaching or reaching Moscow. The missiles' flight time to these targets was under ten minutes which transformed them in Soviet eyes into strategic first strike weapons. The other 474 missiles were ground-launched cruise missiles (GLCM) to be based in Britain, Italy, Belgium and West Germany. Slow and sub-sonic, they were considered by arms controllers and the Soviets as less destabilizing.

The December 1979 NATO decision was two tracked in that it offered to negotiate reductions of theater nuclear systems with NATO deploying the American systems if negotiations failed. Yet many Europeans, and especially Germans, were troubled by Pershing IIs, for, aimed at Soviet command centers, they became part of a U.S. war-fighting strategy. Moreover, although mobile, Pershing IIs were vulnerable to Soviet counterforce strikes. If the United States and Soviet Union found themselves in a confrontation on the brink of war, the West German–based Pershing IIs would become a necessary target for a preemptive Soviet strike which might not involve U.S. strategic systems based in the continental United States.[47]

As the December 1983 deployment date approached, European public distemper was brought into the streets. Throughout 1983 hundreds of thousands of antinuclear activists demonstrated in West Germany, France, Britain and Holland. The antinuclear group captured the British Labor party and, by 1983, were the dominant voice in the German Social Democratic party. The Reagan administration's rhetoric was unhelpful to the European policy elites now trying to contain the public protests. Eugene Rostow, Reagan's first director of ACDA, testified in confirmation hearings, "It may be that a brilliant light will strike [our] officials. . . . But I do not know anybody with whom I have talked on this problem who knows what it is we want to negotiate about; what kind of measure we want."[48] President Reagan compounded the anxiety when he seconded Secretary of State Haig's Senate Foreign Relations confirmation testimony by musing in public that "you could have the exchange of tactical weapons against troops in the field without it bringing either of the major powers to pushing the button."[49]

In mid-November of 1981 President Reagan tried to neutralize emerging European discontent by a "zero-option" arms reduction proposal. The United States would not deploy the 572 Pershings and cruise missiles if the Soviets would dismantle 600 of their comparable systems including all their SS-20s. But the proposal seemed a nonstarter as an arms control proposition. The Soviets were asked to give up their systems already in place for U.S. weapons which, if there were enough European public pressure, might not be deployed in any case. The Reagan initiative was, therefore, an invitation to the Soviets to apply pressure to European governments and publics.

Negotiations were begun in late November of 1981, but these Intermediate Nuclear Forces (INF) talks quickly stalemated. As the deployment deadline approached, the Soviets advanced a proposal which would have them reduce their SS-20s to numbers roughly equal to the missiles or warheads deployed by the British and French in their national nuclear arsenals (162 launchers, mostly in submarines). The United States, Britain, and France rejected the idea arguing that these systems were not under the control of NATO and were, therefore, not subject to U.S.–Soviet negotiations. Earlier it had been revealed that the U.S. and Soviet negotiators had, in July of 1982, in private conversations informally developed a proposed reduction of Soviet systems to between 50 and 100 in return for a similar U.S. deployment. Both the Soviet Union and the United States had, however, quickly and unequivocally rejected the proposal.[50]

In the case of the Soviet Union it was speculated that the terminal illness of Leonid Brezhnev had perhaps paralyzed the Soviet decision-making process. In Washington it seemed that there was simply no desire for an agreement. Eugene Rostow had carried the proposal to Washington for his chief negotiator, Paul Nitze. Both men, as founders of the Committee on the Present Danger, had impeccable cold war credentials but in Rostow's case his association with the proposal was rumored to have contributed to his dismissal from the administration in January of 1983. Mr. Nitze escaped rebuke probably because the administration feared that the public might view the administration as not being serious about the INF talks.[51] The Reagan administration did propose unspecified reductions in missile levels as a compromise, but throughout 1983 the primary focus of the INF exercise seemed increasingly in line with the observations of a high-level State Department official that "what this negotiation is all about . . . [is] whether we or the Russians are more convincing to the Europeans, and whether the Europeans will back new American missile deployments or will block them"[52]

ECONOMIC CONFRONTATION AND CONTAINMENT

However uncertain its ultimate effect, the first and essential element of the Reagan administration's confrontation of Soviet power involved the expansion of American strategic capability vis-à-vis the Soviet Union. But when William Clark, President Reagan's second national security adviser, stated in late 1982, that "with an active national security policy, we might one day convince the Soviet Union to turn inward,"[53] it was understood that the instruments of that active policy involved more than military capability. Economic instruments and the economic relations of America's allies were to be mobilized as well in the service of an American conceived and coordinated assault on the Soviet economy. The objective was to "force our principle adversary . . . to bear the brunt of its economic shortcomings."[54] Policy proved more difficult to formulate and implement, however, than rhetoric.

The assertion that the Soviet Union is a ramshackle economic and social misfit, out-moded and ill-suited for modernity and, therefore, vulnerable to economic warfare, is hardly novel and extends back to at least the Truman administration. Moreover, in 1978, President Carter, in the face of disagreement within his administration, had expanded the list of restricted exports—mostly in technology intensive products—in response to the jailing of two prominent Soviet dissidents. Similarly, U.S. grain exports to the Soviets—once considered an integral part of the detente process and inextricably linked to SALT in the Nixon years—were restricted by Mr. Carter in early 1980 following the invasion of Afghanistan.

Economic warfare under the Reagan administration also deeply divided the President's advisers and many of the subsequent fits, starts and reversals can be ascribed to the division between the Pentagon, National Security Council staff, and some at the Department of Commerce, on the one hand favoring sanctions, and others at Commerce and the State Department opposing trade embargos on the other. Roughly this same bureaucratic alignment had fought over the export of computers in the Carter years. Now the greatest clamor was centered on the Reagan administration's attempt to stop the export, by American and West European companies, of pipeline construction equipment to the Soviet Union and the reciprocal Russian export of natural gas via pipeline to Western Europe. The whole European gas line project involved investments exceeding $250 billion and included potential sales of U.S. products or U.S. products licensed to foreign subsidiaries in drilling, exploration, pipe laying and manufacturing. The arrangement, scheduled for completion in 1985, would supply 30 percent of Western Europe's natural gas requirements. From some $3.8 billion (1982 dollars) up to $10 billion a year of hard currency for at least twenty-five years would be remitted to the Russians.[55] Part of the Reagan administration's concern was that Europe would become overly dependent on Soviet energy supplies and, therefore, more pliant to Soviet pressure. Another element motivating the Reagan administration was the obvious economic benefits the arrangement would bring to a foreign exchange deficient Soviet economy.

But the pipeline would supply only 5 percent of the overall energy requirements of Europe.[56] Further, at a time of record unemployment, the pipeline project promised perhaps six hundred thousand jobs to European workers. The incentive for the Soviets to halt shipments, short of war, was not apparent to Europeans. And the attempt to halt American licensees based in Europe was a legal nightmare. American subsidiaries could be sued abroad or even nationalized for failure of contract compliance even as the parent companies were placed under legal restraint, sequesterings, and fines in the United States for failure to comply with the Reagan administration's restrictions. Moreover, the U.S. makers of pipe-laying equipment were some of those hardest hit by recession in the United States. Substitutes were available abroad especially from Japanese firms that were eager to take over U.S. contracts. Finally, in October 1982, the Reagan administration, fulfilling a compaign promise to American farmers, had resumed negotiations to sell up to 23 million metric tons of wheat to the Soviets. Predictably, the Europeans viewed Reagan's animus against the pipeline as hypocritical; indeed, the policy proved more disruptive to America's relations with its allies than it did to Soviet economic prospects.

By November 1982 the Reagan administration, largely as the result of new Secretary of State George Schultz's diplomacy, had scuttled away from most of the sanctions and by August 1983 virtually all the inhibitions on pipeline sales were canceled. But a symbol of European discontent was French President François Mitterand's refusal to take Mr.

Reagan's phone call intended to outline his November 13, 1982, capitulation on the issue.[57]

The Reagan decision on grain and ultimately, the pipeline, was consistent with most analysis of the effect of economic warfare: it seldom works. As F. H. Sanderson, former director of the State Department's Office of Food Policy, has argued, embargos are "more likely to *strengthen* the Soviets since scarce foreign exchange . . . could . . . be spent on high technology imports . . . [and] the Soviets . . . take measures to conserve grain by raising the prices of livestock products and by increasing feeding efficiencies."[58] The Soviets may have spent an additional $4 billion in Canadian and Argentinean markets, but they hardly suffered as much as U.S. farmers. Moreover, their hard currency oil export receipts rose 40 percent in the same period. Within the Kremlin, many of President Yuri Andropov's advisers apparently suggested that there was no reason for the Russians to renew a grain pact with the United States after all this. A new pact would slacken the incentive for Russian agricultural reform and help Reagan electorally.[59] Nonetheless, in the summer of 1983, a new treaty obliging the Russians to purchase some nine million tons of wheat a year was signed.

Thus a policy of economic denial was reduced to an aspiration confronting stubborn domestic and international complexity. U.S. students of the Soviet economy concluded that even if denial were successful, that is, if there were no seepage from alternative suppliers, the Soviet Union was sufficiently autarchic to withstand the pressure. The Soviet economy was in a period of slower growth, but according to a CIA report, only 5 percent of Soviet GNP was involved in international trade.[60] The West was utterly different. Any effort at economic warfare confronted the real monetary interdependence of the West. European and some American banks have loaned $77 billion to Soviet bloc countries since 1970. Sanctions invite default which, in turn, would expose several of the biggest German banks to possible collapse, since West Germany held up to 30 percent of all Eastern debt.[61] Hence, when President Reagan imposed economic sanctions on Poland in October 1981, in the wake of the imposition of martial law within that country, the administration was in the anomalous position of forbidding new loans to reschedule a huge Polish debt while authorizing the U.S. Treasury to cover payments due to European banks.[62] Finally, historic experience demonstrated a Soviet capacity to shift priorities. The security imperative in Soviet society has always overridden alternatives in consumption and production. The Soviets could, as they put it, "storm" a problem. The process might not be cost-effective and the outcome something less than elegant in Western eyes, but in the short run it was usually, from a Soviet perspective, acceptable. And they had not yet shown a willingness to forsake military interests, no matter what the cost.[63]

INTO THE DEEP FREEZE

In the Soviet Union the cumulative effect of Mr. Reagan's rhetoric as well as the realities of the anticipated strategic buildup, deadlocked arms control negotiations and, with the single exception of grain sales, economic warfare produced anger, frustration, threats of a new arms race and the promise that if relations continued to deteriorate, "New rules of the game will apply."[64] Yet, in mid-1983, more optimistic observers could find some reason to hope: arms control negotiations were still underway with proposals, however laden with propaganda content, still being advanced. Moreover, Andropov was reported in early 1983 to be maintaining an open mind concerning the future of Soviet-American relations.[65] By year's end, however, there was little room for optimism.

On the night of September 1, 1983, a Korean Air Lines Boeing 747 on a flight from the United States to South Korea with 269 people aboard, including a member of the United States House of Representatives and 60 other Americans, inexplicably strayed off course and over Soviet territory at the Kamchatka Peninsula and Sakhalin Island. This area contains perhaps the most sensitive and important ballistic missile test facilities in the Soviet Union and was being used, as Flight 007 strayed off course, for the testing of new ICBMs—tests which were being closely monitored by the United States including the presence in the area of U.S. reconnaissance aircraft. The Soviets maintain that they attempted to contact the 747's pilot, and when that failed, shot the aircraft down with the loss of all on board.

Why and how the airliner got so far off course; whether and in what manner the Soviet air defense forces tried to contact the airliner or visually identified it as such; whether the Korean pilot realized that he was lost; whether Western intelligence officials knew the airliner was in the area and tried to contact it—were all questions that begged for a clear answer given the total loss of life and the failure to recover the 747's flight recorder. What was deafeningly apparent, however, was the reaction of the Reagan administration to the event as the president demanded, "What can be the scope of legitimate mutual discourse with a state whose values permit such atrocities. And what are we to make of a regime which establishes one set of standards for itself and another for the rest of humankind."[66]

The Soviet Union—historically sensitive to the verge of paranoia concerning espionage—maintained that the KAL flight was on a spy mission, refused to respond to Soviet efforts to contact it, and behaved evasively when approached by Soviet interceptor aircraft. The United States called for a meeting of the U.N. Security Council where it played tape recordings of the Soviet pilots closing in for what was characterized by the United States as a massacre. Days later the United States would concede that further analysis of the Soviet pilot's communications perhaps supported the Soviet contention that warning shots had been fired and that the Korean pilot had turned off a device on the aircraft which automatically identifies it as a civilian airliner. But there was little if any room for the diplomatic management of the crisis.

As the president denounced the Soviet Union for the "terroristic act" and "atrocity," the governors of New York and New Jersey announced that they could not guarantee the safety of Foreign Minister Andrei Gromyko if he landed in the New York area for the fall session of the United Nations. Although the United States government had previously responded vigorously to interference by state and local officials in the conduct of foreign affairs, the White House and the State Department refused to reverse the governors in this case, offering instead the use of a military base for the arrival of the Soviet diplomat. The administration's response was viewed by diplomatic and legal experts as remarkable; for if it did not violate the letter, it certainly violated the spirit of the 1947 treaty entered into by the United States which guaranteed that "the Federal, state and local authorities of the United States shall not impose any impediments to transit" of U.N. representatives.[67] Gromyko refused to attend the U.N. session and the decibel level of mutual recriminations began approaching that of the most grim days of the cold war in the late 1940s and early 1950s.

As year's end approached, members of the State Department ruminated "off the record" whether the administration had perhaps not mishandled the KAL incident given the Soviet reaction.[68] The Soviets, speaking through no less an authority than Mr. Andropov, observed, "Even if someone had any illusions as to the possible evolution for the better in the policy of the present American Administration, the latest developments have finally dispelled them."[69] A former State Department official summarized the dilemma confronting the United States and the Soviet Union:

> What is happening is that both sides now believe that their own propaganda about the other is coming true. The President is convinced more than ever that the Russians cannot be trusted, and the Kremlin is just as convinced that they cannot do business with Reagan.[70]

The KAL incident was not in itself as critical as the other dimensions of Soviet-American relations surveyed in this chapter. The stability of the strategic relationship, the balance of forces in Europe, even economic relations were all questions of greater import than Soviet motives in the downing of the KAL aircraft. Most fundamental, however, was the question of whether the United States was prepared to accept the Soviet Union as a great power with legitimate interests and security concerns. Mr. Reagan's immediate reaction to the KAL incident seemed to confirm the thrust of his rhetoric both before and after assuming the presidency: He was not prepared to accept the Soviet Union as an equal with legitimate security concerns, a view bluntly confirmed by Secretary of State Schultz in Stockholm in early 1984.

Thus the Reagan administration in its direct dealings with the Soviet Union continued to operate within a framework of assumptions established in the earliest and darkest days of the cold war: that the Soviet leaders only understand and respond positively to manifestations of toughness in the West and, when so confronted, they are compelled to modify their illegitimate regime in the face of the frustration of their aggressive foreign policy designs. But as one experienced observer of Soviet politics and foreign affairs, Seweryn Bialer, noted in early 1984, the Soviet reaction to this posture on the part of the Reagan administration has not been one of intimidation; rather:

> President Reagan's rhetoric has badly shaken the self-esteem and patriotic pride of the Soviet political elites. The administration's self-righteous moralistic tone, its reduction of Soviet achievements to crimes by international outlaws from an "evil empire"—such language stunned and humiliated the Soviet leaders, especially since it followed so suddenly a decade of the greatest mutual civility in the history of Soviet-American relations.[71]

Moreover, having been denied the "status they thought had been conceded once and for all by Reagan's predecessors, not to speak of America's allies," their inclination is not to seek appeasement of the United States, but instead,

> a rekindled sense of insecurity fires an angry and defiant response, a desire to lash out, to reassert self-esteem, to restore the diminished respect of others. Such an attitude must surely make us reconsider our confident expectation that Soviet pragmatists will continue to be content with policies of "low risk" and "low cost."[72]

This prospect was especially worrying in view of the deterioration of relations and testing of wills that developed elsewhere in the world of the early 1980s. In addition, the position of the United States was made no stronger by the weakening of its relations with its traditional allies in

Europe and its apparent insensitivity to the complex forces at work in other regions and the world's political economy.

NOTES

1. Cited by Helene von Damm, *Sincerely Ronald Reagan* (New York: Berkley, 1981), p. 88.
2. *New York Times*, 9 March 1983, p. A18.
3. Commencement Address at the United States Military Academy, West Point, New York, 27 May 1983.
4. *Baltimore Sun*, 19 March 1981, p. 4.
5. *New York Times*, 2 January 1981, p. 1.
6. Speech to the American Society of Newspaper Editors, 24 April 1981, in Department of Defense, *Selected Statements*, May 1981, p. 13.
7. Thomas Hughes, "Up From Reaganism," *Foreign Policy*, No. 44 (Fall 1981), pp. 3–24.
8. *Washington Post*, 8 May 1983, p. A27.
9. *New York Times*, 8 September 1980, p. 19.
10. Richard Halloran, "After Detente, the Goal Is to Prevail," *New York Times*, 23 September 1982, p. B16.
11. *Baltimore Sun*, op. cit.
12. *Washington Post*, 16 June 1983, p. 1.
13. Interview in *U.S. News and World Report*, 19 January 1981. See also Reagan's press conference of 6 November 1980.
14. Quoted in Bernard Gwertzman, "Shultz Echoing Reagan, Invites Russians to New Talks With U.S.," *New York Times*, 18 January 1984, p. A4.
15. See, for example, Secretary of Defense Caspar Weinberger's press conference of 18 August 1983, Department of Defense, *Selected Statements*, September 1983, p. 7.
16. U.S. Senate, Hearings before the Committee on the Budget, *First Concurrent Resolution on the Budget, FY1981, The Administration's Defense Program*, Vol. I, 97th Congress, 1st Session, 1981, p. 121.
17. For a detailed review of the Reagan administration's defense budget requests, see W. W. Kaufmann, "The Defense Budget" in *Setting National Priorities: The 1984 Budget*, ed. by Joseph A. Pechman (Washington, D.C.: Brookings, 1983), pp. 39–79.
18. See Department of Defense, *Annual Report to Congress, FY1983* (Washington, D.C.: U.S. Government Printing Office, 1982), pp. II-4 – II-7. The secretary of defense's comparisons of Soviet and U.S. military investment are controversial and regarded by many experts as misleading. See, for example, Franklyn Holzman, "Soviet Military Spending: Assessing the Numbers Game," *International Security*, 6 (Spring 1982), pp. 78–101.
19. Department of Defense, *Soviet Military Power, 1983* (Washington, D.C.: U.S. Government Printing Office, 1983), pp. 13–15. For a careful critique of the contention that the Soviets possess a "first strike" capability see Albert Carnesale and Charles Glaser, "ICBM Vulnerability: The Cures Are Worse Than the Disease," *International Security*, Vol. 7 (Summer 1982), pp. 70–85; McGeorge Bundy, "Maintaining Stable Deterrence," *International Security*, Vol. 3 (Winter 1978–1979), pp. 5–16; and Spurgeon M. Keeny and Wolfgang Panofsky, "MAD vs. NUTS: The Mutual Hostage Relationship of the Superpowers," *Foreign Affairs*, Vol. 60 (Winter 1981–82), pp. 287–304.

20. Paul H. Nitze, "Assuring Strategic Stability in an Era of Detente," *Foreign Affairs*, 54 (January 1976), p. 222.
21. Ibid., p. 232.
22. See, for example, Colin S. Gray, "Nuclear Strategy: A Case for a Theory of Victory," *International Security*, 4 (Summer 1979), pp. 54–87.
23. Walter Slocombe, "The Countervailing Strategy," *International Security*, 5 (Spring 1981), p. 21.
24. Thomas Power, "Choosing a Strategy for World War III," *The Atlantic Monthly* (November 1982), p. 96.
25. Ibid, p. 104.
26. Quoted in Robert Scheer, *With Enough Shovels* (New York: Random House, 1983), p. 11.
27. See Richard Halloran, "New Weinberger Directive Refines Military Policy, *New York Times*, 22 March 1983, p. A18 and Leslie Gelb, "Is the Nuclear Threat Manageable?" *New York Times Magazine*, 4 March 1984, p. 29.
28. See the exchange between Weinberger and Theodore Draper in *The New York Review of Books*, 18 August 1983, pp. 27–33.
29. For development of this argument, see Leon V. Sigal, "Tilting Toward War-Fighting: The Scowcroft Commission and the Future of Deterrence," *Arms Control Today*, 13 (September 1983), pp. 2–4, 8.
30. For the text of the bishop's letter and a review of its development see Jim Castelli, *The Bishops and the Bomb: Waging Peace in a Nuclear Age* (New York: Doubleday, 1983).
31. For the text of the administration's START concept see *Survival*, 24 (1982), p. 231.
32. See President Reagan's address of 22 November 1982 in *New York Times*, 23 November 1982, pp. 1, 13–14.
33. Richard Halloran, "3 of 5 Joint Chiefs Asked Delay on MX," *New York Times*, 9 December 1982, p. 1 and Steven R. Weisman, "Reagan Gives Way, Agrees to Freeze on Money for MX," *New York Times*, 15 December 1982, p. 1.
34. The text of the Commission on Strategic Forces' report is available in *Survival*, 25 (July–August 1983), pp. 177–186.
35. Ronald Reagan, "Peace and National Security," Address to the Nation, March 23, 1983, Current Policy No. 472 (Washington: Bureau of Public Affairs, Department of State, 1983).
36. Ibid., p. 7.
37. The following budgetary data were taken from Center for Defense Information, "Militarizing the Last Frontier: The Space Weapons Race," *The Defense Monitor*, 12 (1983), p. 2.
38. Quoted in ibid., p. 1.
39. Ibid.
40. Ibid.
41. See, for example, David Andelman, "Space Wars," *Foreign Policy*, No. 44 (Fall 1981), pp. 94–106 and *Arms Control Today*, 13 (December 1983). The latter source contains an excellent bibliography on space-based weapons and technologies.
42. "Militarizing the Last Frontier," p. 1.
43. See Henry Kissinger, "NATO: The Next Thirty Years," *Survival*, 21 (November–December 1979), pp. 264–268.
44. In fact Kissinger had little more than echoed sentiments—and doubts—expressed on both sides of the Atlantic for some time. See, for example, Helmut Schmidt's views expressed in 1962 in his *Defense or Retaliation* (New York: Praeger, 1962), esp. p.

103. Even earlier, of course, in the 1950s, Charles de Gaulle had infuriated Americans by bluntly suggesting that the Americans would never be willing to exchange New York for the Louvre.

45. Kissinger, "The Future of NATO," *The Washington Quarterly*, 2 (Autumn 1979), p. 4.

46. Schmidt, "The 1977 Alastair Buchan Memorial Lecture," *Survival*, 20 (January–February 1978), pp. 2–10.

47. Richard H. Ullman, "The Euromissile Mire," *Foreign Policy*, No. 50 (Spring 1983), pp. 46–47.

48. U.S. Senate, Hearings before the Committee on Foreign Relations, *Nomination of Eugene V. Rostow to Director, Arms Control and Disarmament Agency*, 97th Congress, 1st Session, 1981, p. 45.

49. Remarks to a group of national news editors, October 1981, and cited by I. M. Destler, "The Evolution of Reagan Foreign Policy," in Fred Greenstein, ed., *The Reagan Presidency: An Early Assessment* (Baltimore: Johns Hopkins University Press, 1983), p. 144.

50. See Bernard Gwertzman, "U.S. Aide Reached Arms Agreement Later Ruled Out," *New York Times*, 16 January 1983, p. 1.

51. See ibid. and Gwertzman, "Rostow Defends Arms Agreement Disowned by U.S.," *New York Times*, 17 January 1983, p. 1 and Leslie H. Gelb, "An Arms Negotiator Determined to Get His Way," *New York Times*, 2 February 1983, p. 1.

52. Quoted in Gelb, "Missile Plan: Plea to Allies," *New York Times*, 31 March 1983, p. 1.

53. Halloran, "After Detente . . . ," op. cit.

54. Cited in Louis J. Walinsky, "The Case for Economic Denial," *Foreign Affairs*, 61 (Winter 1982–1983), p. 272.

55. See Jonathan Stern, "Specters and Pipe Dreams," *Foreign Policy*, No. 48 (Fall 1982), p. 23.

56. Josef Joffee, "Europe and America: The Politics of Resentment," *Foreign Affairs*, 61 (1982), p. 570.

57. In "Sanctions Call Too Late, Mitterand Says," *Washington Post*, 27 November 1982, p. A21.

58. Sanderson, "The Uses of Food Power," *The Brookings Review* (Summer 1983), pp. 4–5.

59. See *Washington Post*, 30 July 1983, p. 1. The article by Dusko Doder confirms private conversations with Soviet authorities by one of the authors in Moscow in July 1981.

60. *New York Times*, 9 January 1983, p. 16.

61. Mark J. Ellyne, "East-West Debt and the Trade Debate Reconsidered," *SAIS Review*, 3 (Fall 1983), pp. 203–218.

62. For a more skeptical view see Jerry F. Hough, *The Polish Crisis: American Policy Options* (Washington: Brookings, 1982).

63. See Myron Rush, "The Soviet Buildup and the Coming Succession," *International Security*, 5 (Spring 1981), p. 169.

64. Leslie H. Gelb, "Moscow Angrily Settles Back to Await the End of the Reagan Era," *New York Times*, 30 March 1983, p. A16. See also the lengthy report on the Soviet leadership's mood by Seweryn Bialer, "Danger in Moscow," *New York Review of Books*, 16 February 1984, pp. 6–10.

65. Ibid.

66. "Soviets Hit as Terrorists," *Baltimore Sun*, 3 September 1983, p. 1.

67. Bernard Gwertzman, "U.S. Officials See Crisis with Soviet Lasting Into 1984," *New York Times*, 19 September 1983, pp. 1 and 8.

68. Ibid.

69.   "Text of Soviet Statement on Relations with the U.S.," *New York Times*, 29 September 1983, p. A14.
70.   Gwertzman, "Crisis with Soviet Lasting Into 1984," p. 8.
71.   Bialer, op. cit., p. 6.
72.   Ibid.

Chapter 13
Hawks on an
Unsteady Perch

If bilateral U.S.–Soviet strategic, economic and diplomatic relations were locked in the extremities of a renascent cold war, Mr. Reagan's conception of global confrontation with communism was prosecuted with all the assertiveness and activism of 1960s style interventionism on the periphery. In Latin America and the Middle East, conflict was understood to be the result of the Soviets and their clients pushing forward the perimeters of communist world empire. In these cases, which, along with the deterioration of Soviet-American relations, came to dominate U.S. foreign policy by 1983, the administration's response was proclaimed in the rhetoric of Truman and Dulles and implemented with the instruments of Kennedy and Johnson.

"GOING TO THE SOURCE"
IN LATIN AMERICA

Not since the presidency of John Kennedy had an administration so involved itself economically and militarily in the western hemisphere. Part of the Reagan administration's concern, also borne by Kennedy, was preoccupation with Fidel Castro. Reagan's closest advisers were convinced that pressure on Cuba would ameliorate instability in the hemisphere. Hence, they were prepared, they said, to strike directly at Cuba if Castro did not reverse his policies. Speaking on February 17, 1981, Secretary of State Haig said: "Cuban activity has reached a peak that is no longer acceptable in this hemisphere . . . [I]t is our intention to deal with this matter at its source."[1] Wayne Smith, chief of the U.S. interests section in Havana from 1979 to 1982, recalled: "[B]lockade, surgical air strikes, invasion . . . no option was excluded." As a portent of the administration's intent, armed Cuban exiles reopened training camps in Florida and began launching raids.[2]

The Reagan administration's concern had several dimensions. One was the intrinsic and growing interest of the United States in its neighboring region's instabilities. Second, the problem seemed manageable. Central American interests were less hypothetical than those in

Southeast Asia a generation earlier. They offered a seemingly manageable opportunity for the United States to turn back at acceptable costs what the Reagan administration gauged was a tide of declining U.S. influence. And, third, since the world view of the Reagan administration was steeped in nostalgia for the golden period of foreign policy—the Truman Doctrine and Marshall Plan era—the same rationales prevailed: the shadow of Soviet power in a world in which symbols of influence were as important as the substance of Soviet power, especially in a world of nuclear weapons. A challenge to any part of the fabric of American commitments threatened the whole cloth. Nearby disorder was threatening not because of dependence on Central American coffee and bananas; rather, there was concern about the demonstration effect of a successful revolution, supported by Castro, elsewhere in the hemisphere. And, more fundamentally, disorder was thought potentially damaging to the extended formal and informal U.S. guarantees issued worldwide since the beginning of the cold war. As Haig explained:

> We must demonstrate to everyone—the Russians, our allies, the Third World—that we can win, that we can be successful. We must move decisively and quickly to turn things around in the world or be nibbled to death by the Soviets.[3]

To be sure, the Reagan administration's fixation with Latin America was part of an evolution begun under the Carter administration.[4] When the besieged right-wing government of El Salvador came under pressure from guerrilla forces, the Carter administration, five days before leaving office, decided to give the Salvadorans military assistance. It was known that El Salvador was one of the most oligarchic, repressive regimes in the world. A civil war had begun in earnest there in 1979 and government-backed para-military death squads were "disappearing" people at the rate of some ten thousand a year. The United States conceded that at least thirty thousand had been killed between 1979 and 1982, the great majority by the right-wing death squads. The bodies were found on the side of roads or in ditches with their thumbs wired behind them. There was not one conviction—even when American labor leaders and churchwomen were murdered. Indeed, an investigation of the nuns' murder conducted for the United States by former Federal Judge Harold E. Tyler, concluded that authorities in the Salvadoran government had tried to cover up the crime.[5]

The Reagan administration was determined, however, not to do in El Salvador what U.S. Ambassador to the United Nations Jeane Kirkpatrick, the leading analyst of the region in the Reagan administration, claimed the Carter administration had done in Nicaragua:

"bring down the Somoza regime."[6] Mrs. Kirkpatrick had charged that the "State Department deprived the Somoza regime of legitimacy not only by repeated condemnations for human rights violations . . . but also by negotiating with the opposition."[7] El Salvador was clearly going to be a different story during the Reagan years. It was going to be saved from Soviet-Cuban-Nicaraguan revolution.

The attention to Latin America was spread across a broad spectrum of problems. The bankrupt Mexican economy, with over $80 billion of debt owed mostly to U.S. banks, had to be rescued by some fancy footwork involving innovations of the Treasury, the Federal Reserve, and private banks. Brazil and Argentina carried similar debt burdens necessitating renegotiations of interest payments with private banks and International Monetary Fund intervention—a triumph of necessity over the market ideology of the Reagan camp. In the Caribbean, a huge aid package directed to desperate Caribbean economies was pushed through Congress. But it was all accompanied by tub thumping and anti-communist jeers reminiscent of the heyday of American power.

More pointedly there was a display of military support for counterrevolution. In Honduras, ex-Somoza supporters and other anti-Sandinista groups were marshalled to harass the Nicaraguan government. The anti-Sandinista movement numbers reached ten to fifteen thousand by mid-1983. There was an attempt to make Honduras a secure redoubt for this "covert" venture. Huge airstrips were cut and massive amounts of military materiel and men were brought to Honduras in August of 1983 in Operation Big Pine II. One hundred fifty million dollars of electronic intelligence equipment powerful enough to reach "anywhere" and to hear "anything" was put into place. The Honduran navy of five hundred men and eight coastal patrol craft exercised with an unusual armada of American ships: two carriers, thirty-two other combatants and the battleship *New Jersey* were sent up and down the Atlantic and Pacific coasts of Nicaragua. The operation involved more than thirty-seven thousand U.S. naval personnel and six thousand American troops lifted in by C-5As and other transports. In late 1983, it was announced that Big Pine II would be followed in mid-1984 by Big Pine III and in early 1984 the administration announced that up to twelve hundred American military personnel would be permanently stationed in Honduras.

These exercises were both a practice run at testing the U.S. capability of blockading Nicaragua and an attempt to intimidate the Nicaraguan government, Castro, and even the Russians. As Dr. Fred C. Ikle, undersecretary for policy in the Department of Defense, proclaimed, "Let me make this clear to you, we do not seek a military defeat for our friends. We do not seek a military stalemate. We seek victory for the forces of democracy."[8] The pursuit of victory over Nicaragua with American-backed rebels operating out of Honduras and Costa Rica, and escalating conflict between Salvadoran rebels and the Salvadoran government, threatened to engulf the whole area in strife. Moreover, by defining the region as "vital" and the stakes as critical, the promise of maximum involvement seemed ineluctable.[9]

Thus during his first thirty-six months in office, most foreign policy instruments, save direct combat, were called into service by Mr. Reagan. Even a massive radio station was established to beam its signal at Cuba fourteen hours a day. Presumably, as in the Old Testament, the sound of loud instruments and the movement of many soldiers could smash high walls and smite enemies. From October 25 to 27, 1983, however, the Reagan administration moved dramatically beyond propaganda and overt and covert aid as more than six thousand Marines, Army Rangers, and Navy personnel invaded Grenada ostensibily to protect the lives of some one thousand Americans, many of them attending medical school on the island.

A bloody coup had taken place earlier in the month leading to the displacement of one Marxist regime by another more radical group with ill-defined lines of authority. Political instability led, in turn, to the small eastern Caribbean neighbors of Grenada with, it appears, some American encouragement, to invite the Americans to act. This political uncertainty and the invitation provided the pretext for the invasion which encountered somewhat stiffer resistance than expected from some seven to eight hundred Cubans and several hundred Grenadians. As resistance crumbled and some ten thousand mostly small arms along with captured documents outlining Cuban and Russian military assistance were put on display, the administration's rationale shifted to an emphasis on the political and strategic importance of the invasion. For months the administration had been pointing out the "threat" posed by the construction of a ten thousand-foot runway on the island, dismissing the claims of Grenada and the British construction company building the facility that the runway was to improve the prospects of tourism on the island. Captured arms, documents, and the presence of more Cubans than anticipated allowed the administration to portray Grenada as a nascent communist base for the support of insurgency and instability throughout the region. The invasion itself could only be read by the Soviets, Cubans, and Nicaraguans with anxiety, a clearly desirable outcome for an administration that had been straining for almost three years to reestablish an American reputation for toughness and a willingness to use force.

Apart from the tiny eastern Caribbean states that had invited the United States to invade their neighbor, however, there was no other support in Latin America for the act. Hemispheric and international legal norms were seen as violated.[10] Even El Salvador condemned the act in the Organization of American States echoing the concern throughout the region that the step marked a return to the days of gunboat diplomacy and Yankee intervention. In the United Nations, support was predictably absent from the third world, but also from some unpredictable quarters as America's European allies deserted the United States on the issue. Especially in Britain, the Reagan administration's invasion of a Commonwealth country against the express wishes of the Thatcher government proved embarrassing. Not only had British opinion been ignored, but the invasion occurred at precisely the moment when the first U.S. cruise missiles were being moved to their bases in Britain in the face of large antinuclear and anti-American demonstrations. For Mrs. Thatcher, indeed, for all European governments scheduled to receive the missiles, trying to convince their parliaments and people that the United States was a restrained, dependable, and predictable ally willing to consult with and be guided by the advice of its allies, the Grenadian invasion precedent would be difficult to explain away.[11]

At home there was ambivalence as well. On the one hand, there was, as is common in times of crisis, a surge of support for the president, if not initially for the invasion itself. As the captured documents and arms were displayed and grateful American students were paraded before the television cameras, public and congressional support for the invasion coalesced. Undoubtedly of assistance to the administration in this regard was the inability of the press to cover the fighting itself as the administration refused to allow the press into the combat zone until the fighting was virtually over. Thus, unlike Vietnam, Americans were subjected to the official version of events with no alternative accounts being available. Most Americans seemed to support this action by the administration. Perhaps, the idea of a clearcut American "win" after decades of confusing and frustrating global engagement—with all the ambiguity being reported and accentuated by the press—was at least momentarily more important than the larger implications of the administration's manipulation of the flow of information. In any event, the Reagan administration enjoyed a surge of support in the days immediately after the invasion. Whether Mr. Reagan could translate this applause into long-term support for his foreign policy remained, however, in doubt.

The basis of this uncertainty lay in the fact that the Grenada melodrama was played out against a backdrop of public and even governmental ambivalence concerning virtually every other element of American policy. Regarding Central America, only one-third of those polled in mid-1983 supported Mr. Reagan's approach to the region's problems with 64 percent of the general public refusing to countenance U.S. combat forces in Central America; 56 percent of an elite sample concurred.[12]

Moreover, this opposition could be found within the government as well, especially within the upper levels of the military. The post-Vietnam leadership of the military, reflecting their Vietnam experience, proved to be more cautious than much of the civilian leadership in Mr. Reagan's national security establishment.[13] Thus both Army chiefs of staff under Mr. Reagan warned that they were not prepared to fight another war by increments or without the full support of the American people. A book by Colonel Harry Summers, Jr., *On Strategy*, assessing the Vietnam War and emphasizing these points, became a Pentagon best seller and obligatory reading at military staff colleges.[14] Retiring Army Chief of Staff General Edward C. Meyer seemed to summarize the concern when, in an interview in mid-1983, he observed: "There will have to be a consensus within the United States populace that what we are doing is sufficiently important that American soldiers go to war. You can't send soldiers off to war without having the support of the American people."[15]

Such public support could be generated after the fact in the case of Grenada and within the military as well if they were allowed, as they were in the Grenada operation, to control the flow of information to the American public. But it was not clear how this situation could be replicated on the much larger scale of Nicaragua, El Salvador,[16] or in that most complicated and dangerous region, the Middle East.

THE MIDDLE EAST

Since the mid-1970s two problems, one new and the other old, had beset American foreign policy in the Middle East. The Arab-Israeli dispute had dominated the region since before the Second World War, but by the late 1970s, policy makers were no less preoccupied with the vulnerability of the industrialized world's access to the Persian Gulf region's oil supplies. In the latter case, the threat was twofold: first, there was the potential for supply cut-offs and embargoes on the part of the producers of the oil and second, the possibility that the Soviet Union might gain strategic dominance in the region and thereby threaten to strangle the West. Predictably, it was the latter possibility that seemed of most concern to the Reagan administration. Indeed, the Arab-Israeli and all other conflicts in the region were initially viewed largely in terms of Soviet expansionism thereby shifting somewhat the focus of policy attention away from the indigenous sources of conflict, the priority concern of the late 1970s. Nevertheless, the persistence of these local dynamics forced the Reagan administration back to reliance upon the negotiating framework established by Henry Kissinger and Jimmy Carter. But when the Camp David process deadlocked and then collapsed under the burdens of continuing PLO and Syrian intransigence on the question of Israel's right to exist, the tough and uncompromising policies of the Begin government, and Anwar Sadat's assassination, the Reagan administration stumbled towards what virtually all postwar administrations had sought to avoid: direct U.S. military involvement in the byzantine and bloody conflicts of the region.

The Gulf

In 1977 a CIA report projected that the Soviets would suffer an oil shortage by the early 1980s. The result, they warned, would be a covetous Soviet view of the Persian Gulf oil fields. After the catastrophic collapse of America's Iranian surrogate and the Soviet invasion of Afghanistan, a prospect inspiring real dread seemed imminent. The Soviets, it was feared at the time, in a pincers movement, could fall upon Iran, caught in a paroxysm of revolutionary upheaval and still bound to a Soviet defense treaty dating from 1921. With Afghanistan and Iran in tow and its Syrian, Iraqi, and Southern Yemeni clients in lock step, the pressure on the Saudis and the rest of the conservative Gulf states would become excruciating and ultimately irresistible. The Straits of Hormuz could be closed and the Soviets, for a minimum military investment, given their presumed local military superiority and overall strategic equality, could bring the West to terms while capturing the two largest known reserves of oil for themselves.

The Carter administration answer to the threat was the anemic Rapid Deployment Force (RDF) and loud warnings. Carter defense planners estimated that the United States could bring twenty thousand troops to Iran in a month. In that time, they could be facing five times as many Soviet soldiers. The calculation discounted a probable Soviet shortage of tactical air cover and hence vulnerability to U.S. carrier-based air power, the burdens on existing Soviet military lift capacity, and long passages through some of the most treacherous and arid terrain in the world. The scenario also discounted local opposition and deflated Soviet readiness requirements. Nonetheless, defense planners and analysts brooded apocalyptic visions in public: The Soviets seemed on the verge of offering the West a choice between political-economic disaster or the use of atomic weapons.[17]

By 1983 the Pentagon disclosed that ten times as many men could be deployed to the Persian Gulf in thirty days, and by the end of the 1980s, the administration planned to augment the RDF to 440,000. But there would be a price—itself a matter of debate. The additional strategic lift and hardware costs, exclusive of manpower costs, according to the Congressional Budget Office, would approach $100 billion.[18] Even larger was the 1983 cost estimate of a long-time defense planner and analyst, MIT's W.W. Kaufmann. A minimum force to defend the Gulf, he wrote, would require two aircraft carriers, fifty escort vessels, sixty amphibious ships, nine divisions and thirty-six aircraft squadrons. The total cost would exceed $500 billion.[19]

Yet none of these conditions, feared or evident in 1979 and 1980, had occurred by 1983. Indeed they seemed more distant. The Soviets were not poised at the straits as they were mired in a bloody and seemingly interminable war of occupation in Afghanistan. Western analysts believed that the Soviets would need twice the force levels they had committed (105,000 by early 1983) to do better against fierce and embarrassing resistance. The Soviets, through the United Nations, by May of 1983, had in fact worked out the terms of a withdrawal which was rejected by the United States. The Reagan administration was content to let the Soviets twist while, in the words of veteran observer Selig Harrison, "the U.S. fought to the last Afghan,"[20] while piously deploring Soviet brutality including the alleged use of chemical warfare.

Meanwhile Secretary of Defense Caspar Weinberger continued to emphasize the Soviet oil imperative. "We think it very likely," he declared on September 24, 1981, the Russians will invade Iran when they "soon run short of energy supplies."[21] But in a report released in the summer of 1981, the CIA projected that the Soviets would continue to be an exporter of oil for the foreseeable future. Furthermore, Soviet oil surpluses by 1983 were substantial with more than one-half million barrels a day being offered on the spot market at prices consistently lower than the OPEC benchmark price.[22]

The RDF had also been rationalized on the belief that Persian Gulf oil would remain an indispensable ingredient of world politics. Though European and Japanese dependence remained significant, the decade of oil dictates from the Gulf—indeed, the peak of OPEC power—may well have passed. During the 1970s the economies of the countries of the Organization for Economic Cooperation and Development grew at about 2.3 percent, while oil consumption rose at less than .2 percent per year. A breakout from global recession might change these figures somewhat, but over the next decade, world-wide demand for oil is expected to rise by no more than 1 percent per year. The drop led to speculation that OPEC might never again regain its 1970s vitality or essential position in world markets.[23]

Notwithstanding these changed conditions, the Defense Department was not forsaking an opportunity to parley the aftershock of successive oil crises and Soviet miscalculation into a luxury train, capable of carrying every military service to new procurement levels even as the Korean crisis had thirty years earlier. As Mr. Weinberger, in his 1983 annual report to Congress wrote, Southwest Asia "poses some special problems requiring us to develop unique solutions. . . . [H]owever the majority of our rapid deployment programs enhance our overall combat capability even though they may have *originally* been developed *primarily* for S.W.A."[24]

It was a bizarre truth that the great reversal of Arabian fortune did not inform U.S. defense policy. The RDF was invented to protect the economies of the West. Yet the world's economic recovery was put at risk by the cost of the armada. The projected deficits in the American budget, resulting largely from Reagan tax cuts and defense spending, were larger in the aggregate than all previous annual deficits in the history of the United States combined. For an administration much taken with the wizardry of markets, the enormous undertaking to shore up a decaying cartel was almost inexplicable. It was never mysterious why preparations should be made to prevent the West from being economically strangled. By 1983, however, some of the marks on the developed world's collective throat appeared to be self-inflicted.

The truth that Weinberger dared not speak, but one implied by the president on October 1, 1981, was that the most likely contingency the United States thought it might face was an Iran-type dissolution of Saudi Arabia or a cutoff of Gulf oil resulting from an expansion of the Iran-Iraq War. An RDF could conceivably be of use in the latter case. But with respect to the Saudi contingency, the techniques of regime stabilization had eluded a generation of U.S. policy officials. The means contemplated for getting U.S. troops to the area did not seem to augment the region's stability. In fact, it would undercut the position of conservative leaders by identifying them with the United States. Thus highly visible joint exercises and cooperative efforts with conservative regimes in the region became embarrassments and devoid of enthusiasm. The RDF, and not the Soviets, was greatest threat to the region remarked United Arab Emirates President Sheik Zayed bin Sultan al-Nahiyan in June of 1981.[25] Moreover, how the United States might occupy and operate one hundred thousand square miles of oil fields, major oil terminals and a portfolio of $100 billion in investments in the West with the RDF has never been articulated.

The Arab-Israeli Conflict

Military instrumentalities became central to the Reagan administration's approach to the Arab-Israeli dispute as well. Here again, the perception that the Soviet Union was the ultimate source of the conflict within the region was crucial to the administration's understanding of American objectives. Although the local sources of conflict and the expansionist policies of the Begin government in Israel forced the administration to focus for a time on the indigenous causes of instability, the confrontation of American and Soviet influence had come to dominate the American image of Middle Eastern reality by 1984.

Initially, the administration sought to pursue the development of what Secretary of State Haig termed a "strategic consensus"[26] directed against Soviet influence and power in the region even as the United States lent its support to the on-going Camp David process of negotiations between Israel and Egypt. By the time Mr. Reagan took the oath of office, however, the Camp David process was already in deep trouble. Though negotiations concerning the return of all Egyptian territory in the Sinai were proceeding reasonably well and were consummated in April of 1982 with the withdrawal of the Israelis from Egyptian territory, the discussions of Palestinian autonomy on the West Bank and in Gaza were deadlocked. In the meantime, conditions within the region began deteriorating rapidly as Israeli-backed Christian and Syrian-backed Muslim forces in Lebanon escalated their fighting to the most intense levels since 1976. By late April, the Israeli Air Force was launching air strikes into southern Lebanon and the Syrians were moving surface-to-air missiles (SAMs) into the Bekaa Valley leading the Israelis to threaten military action against the Syrians unless the SAMs were removed. U.S. diplomatic intervention via special envoy Philip C. Habib's shuttling between Israel and the Arab countries throughout the summer was instrumental in avoiding major fighting although Israeli attacks in Lebanon continued, including a strike against PLO positions in Beirut which resulted in three hundred dead and eight hundred injured.

The pursuit of an anti-Soviet strategic consensus continued throughout this hardening of regional animosities. This policy included an administration plan to sell the Saudi Arabians equipment to upgrade their F-15 fighter aircraft as well as provide them with five Airborne Warning and Control System (AWACs) aircraft. At the same time, the administration sought an agreement on strategic cooperation with the Israelis including some joint maneuvers, medical stockpiling in Israel, and joint security planning. As anti-Soviet measures such steps might appear reasonable, but within the deteriorating regional context, the regional actors—the Israelis and the Arabs—could be expected to react skeptically. The regional antagonists quite predictably viewed each American move in terms of its effect on their conflicts and the regional balance. Accordingly, they attended their own agendas and not that of the Americans.

In the case of the Israelis, Syrians, and the PLO this activity focused on the strategic situation in Lebanon where the Syrians and PLO were seeking to consolidate their control. Israeli strategic concerns extended to the entire Arab world as was dramatically evident on June 8, 1981, when Israeli forces bombed and destroyed an Iraqi nuclear reactor which the Israelis contended was on the threshold of providing the Iraqis with nuclear weapons. The raid and the Israelis' contemptuous rejection of the condemnation which followed underscored both the toughness of the Begin government but also its relative strategic freedom in the wake of the Camp David agreement with Egypt. Freed from military concerns on its Egyptian flank, the full weight of Israeli military superiority could be turned on the rest of the Arab world. Furthermore, if the Reagan administration hoped that the Camp David process might restrain Israeli belligerence and cool the regional conflict, those hopes were dashed when, on October 6, 1981, Egyptian President Sadat was assassinated by Moslem fundamentalists thereby removing an essential actor in the negotiating process. And if the Reagan administration believed that the agreement on strategic cooperation could constrain the Israelis, it was jolted yet again, for two weeks after signing the agreement with Prime Minister Begin, the Israelis extended Israeli law to the Golan Heights captured from the Syrians in 1967, a move widely viewed in the Arab world as tantamount to annexation. Although the United States suspended the agreement with Israel, the Saudis extended their full support to Syria even as the Israelis attacked the United States for treating them, in Begin's words, as a "vassal state."

With diplomatic efforts frozen the Israelis, Syrians, and PLO slid towards war. In April and May Israeli aircraft attacked PLO positions in Beirut and the PLO shelled Israeli settlements in northern Israel. On June 6 the sixth Arab-Israeli war began with thirty thousand Israeli ground troops invading Lebanon and moving within a week to positions around Beirut, cutting off in the process some seven thousand PLO and two thousand Syrian troops, as the Israelis laid siege to the city.[27] In their march north Israeli forces inflicted significant casualties on the Syrians including the destruction of seventy-nine Syrian MiG-21 and MiG-23 aircraft and nineteen SAM sites. Only one Israeli aircraft was lost in this embarrassing defeat of Soviet military hardware. But this would not result in the decline of Soviet influence for within a year Syrian forces were completely replenished by the Soviets and buttressed by the presence of between five and seven thousand Soviet military personnel training the Syrians or actually operating their new and more effective air defense system.

The extent of American knowledge of Israeli intentions is disputed. Former Secretary of State Haig denies that the Israelis had informed him of their intention to move north. Israeli sources insist, however, that months before the attack, Washington was informed of Israel's intention to invade Lebanon.[28] In any event, Israeli actions demonstrate clearly that Begin and Defense Minister Ariel Sharon were seeking the elimination of the PLO, a decisive defeat of Syria, and a responsive regime in Beirut. By mid-August and after massive air and artillery attacks on Beirut itself, all sides accepted an American proposal for the insertion of a small multinational peace-keeping force (MNF) comprising U.S., French, and Italian troops which would supervise the withdrawal of Syrian and PLO forces. As the last of the PLO and Syrian troops left Beirut, President Reagan launched his own peace plan for the region.[29] On September 1 he proposed "self government" for the Palestinians on the West Bank of the Jordan River "in association with Jordan" as well as a freeze on further Israeli settlements on the occupied West Bank. Jerusalem was to be an undivided city with final political arrangements to be negotiated. Although Arab leaders in a meeting in Fez, Morocco[30] as well as Jewish leaders outside Israel found the proposal, if not entirely acceptable, at least useful as a point of departure for future negotiations, the Israeli cabinet rejected it outright. Indeed, four days after the Reagan proposal was announced, Israel allocated funds for three new settlements on the West Bank and began planning seven more.

In Lebanon, the peace-keeping force had begun withdrawing on September 10. Four days later Bashir Gemayel, the newly elected, right-wing, Israeli-backed phalangist Christian president of Lebanon, was assassinated, and the Israelis moved their troops into and took control of central Beirut. By September 18 reports began to appear of hundreds of Palestinian civilians being massacred by Christian militia allowed into refugee camps in south Beirut by the Israelis. In the midst of international outrage, the multinational force was hastily reinserted (supplemented by about one hundred British personnel) with the Israelis withdrawing from Beirut by the end of September.

American policy now focused on negotiating a withdrawal of Israeli and Syrian troops from Lebanon while supporting the government of Lebanon, now under the presidency of Amin Gemayel, Bashir Gemayel's brother. The latter task was complicated by the fact that Gemayel, like his brother, was seen as representing but one faction of the fractured Lebanese political setting. The government's political base was narrow and its political control did not extend much beyond the embattled Beirut suburbs. Insofar as the United States was identified with Gemayel, the Americans inevitably became participants in the Lebanese civil conflict rather than being viewed as neutral peace keepers. Throughout the winter of 1982–1983 and the spring of 1983, the United States Marines comprising the U.S. contingent of the MNF had to contend, therefore, not only with the extremely testy Israelis but also the contending militias in and around the city. In April of 1983 the American embassy was bombed

and destroyed by terrorists weeks before Secretary of State Shultz finally negotiated an agreement in principle on the ultimate withdrawal of
troops. But it was the steady increase in casualties suffered by the Israelis as well as eroding Israeli domestic support for the government's
policy that led to their decision to withdraw to more secure southern
Lebanon in September rather than any agreement. Ironically, by that time
the Americans were encouraging them to remain in the Beirut area to
serve as a stabilizing force.

With the Israelis gone, fighting intensified between the Lebanese
Army, which sought to reoccupy the areas vacated by the Israelis, and
the Syrian-supported militias. Furthermore, the sixteen hundred U.S.
Marines stationed around the difficult-to-defend Beirut airport as well as
the French elements of the MNF were attacked with greater frequency
and effect. By the fall, a large U.S. naval force consisting of two aircraft
carriers, the battleship *New Jersey* and more than thirty other ships had
been assembled off the Lebanese coast and sporadically turned its
firepower on the militia in the hills above the airport in support of the
Marines but also the Lebanese army. By late summer, support of the
Gemayel government—reportedly over the opposition of the Joint
Chiefs of Staff who feared retaliation—had become a rationale for the
use of U.S. firepower equal to that of protecting the marines. Yet none of
this could prevent another successful terrorist attack on the American
presence, this time a building at Beirut airport in which hundreds of
marine and naval personnel were sleeping on the night of October 23.
(Almost simultaneously a French barracks area was hit as well.) Two
hundred forty-one Americans died in the huge truck-bomb explosion
detonated by a lone terrorist suicide who raced his vehicle into the
courtyard of the multistory building used by the Marines for a barracks.
As the names of the dead were released in newspapers and newscasts,
the American people underwent a kind of macabre *déjà vu* as they
contemplated the prospect of American involvement in a Lebanese civil
war ten years after their painful exit from Vietnam.[31]

The Reagan administration seemed unable, however, to convince
the public or a frustrated Congress, which had granted an eighteen-month
mandate for American participation in the MNF, that exit from Lebanon was in the immediate future. Rather, the president warned of a
"force"—the Soviet Union through its Syrian surrogates—poised to take
over the region and the international repercussions of a withdrawal
of American forces. In the wake of the October 23 tragedy, a full-scale
review[32] of American policy was completed with a decision being taken
to reinvigorate the strategic cooperation arrangement with the Israelis
and force the Syrians out of Lebanon. Reportedly the administration had

virtually given up hope that moderate Arab leaders could any longer influence the Syrians, if they ever could.

In Lebanon itself, the administration tied itself to the fate of the Gemayel regime with the U.S. Navy providing episodic support of the Lebanese Army's attempts to reassert government control over strategic points around Beirut. Gemayel refused, however, to broaden the base of his government with the result that by February of 1984 Druse and Shiite Moslem forces, heavily supported by the Syrians, launched an all out assault on government forces. As the fighting escalated, the Italians and British announced that they would be withdrawing their forces in the MNF. The Reagan administration followed suit and announced, "The Marines are being deployed 2⅓ to 3 miles to the west," i.e., off-shore, a move, they insisted, that had been planned for weeks—even as they attacked those in Congress who were proposing such a step as wanting to "surrender."[33] The naval task force would remain in the area until sometime in 1985, however, supporting the Lebanese government. What precisely the Americans would support was problematical, for as Mr. Reagan was insisting that the Lebanese Army had been transformed into a viable military force, it disintegrated, losing key positions south of the city and control of West Beirut, leaving the beleaguered Marines almost totally surrounded at their Beirut airport base. By late February the Marines began their withdrawal as the secretary of state for the first time conceded that American policy in Lebanon had failed. The president and vice president seemed to disagree with the secretary of state, however, with Vice President George Bush asserting that most of America's objectives had been accomplished. Mr. Reagan went so far as to hint in a news conference on Februray 23, 1984, that the Marines might be sent back into Lebanon "if they could improve the possibility of carrying out their mission"—though the mission remained as unclear to most Americans as ever.[34]

Thus in the Middle East as in Latin America, the Reagan administration's preoccupation with the Soviet-American struggle came to dominate the American approach to regional conflicts. It was no more obvious, however, how facing down the Soviets globally would resolve the centuries-old sectarian agony of Lebanon, decades of Arab-Israeli conflict, or the Moslem world's struggle between on-rushing modernity and Moslem fundamentalism than it would alleviate Central American social upheaval. But a president convinced of the special mission of America and the great evil embodied in its Soviet antagonist seemed certain that a massive military buildup at all levels and the vigorous prosecution of strategic confrontation with the Soviet Union could result in the comprehensive peace that had escaped all of his predecessors.

A WORLD ELSEWHERE

In view of the administration's preference, even insistence, on American activism in dealing with the new cold war which resulted from the deterioration of Soviet-American relations at the center and confrontation on the periphery, it is not surprising that American initiatives were asserted elsewhere as well. Thus with respect to the world political economy and emergent new conditions in Europe, Africa, and Asia, U.S. perspectives and priorities were much in evidence throughout the early 1980s.

Global Preoccupations and Regional Politics

The Reagan administration's preoccupation with the vestiges of the pre-detente world, the Soviet Union, and its presumed clients tended to dominate its approach to regional politics. Thus in Asia and Africa as in Latin America and the Middle East the focus of the administration's policy was never focused primarily on the dynamics of the region. Almost always the source of regional instability was presumed to be the external influence of the Soviet Union. Even when the Soviet Union could not be construed to be at work—as in the China-Taiwan dispute—the president could not seem to disentangle his approach and policy from what he assumed were the constraints of past commitments. Insofar as he was unable to do so opportunities for an increase in Soviet influence were perhaps increased. More important in the long run, however, was that this cold war focus—both old and new cold wars—diverted attention from what many observers were coming to view as the far more significant consequences for American interests of the economic development of the region.[35]

Mr. Reagan's ambivalence concerning the triangular diplomacy of the 1970s was, of course, in evidence even before he assumed office. Throughout the late 1970s and as a candidate, Reagan insisted that notwithstanding the normalization of relations with the Beijing government, some kind of "official" relationships with Taiwan should be maintained. Mr. Reagan's strident anti-Soviet rhetoric and rearmament received applause on the mainland but his insistence on selling arms to both Beijing and Taiwan was regarded by the Chinese as unacceptable. Not until the administration was intent upon consolidating its anti-Soviet position vis-à-vis the Polish crisis, did it accept most of the Chinese position concerning a reduction and eventual elimination of arms sales to Taiwan. Not coincidentally, it would seem, the Chinese were applying pressure of their own as they played European, Japanese, and American business suitors against one another as they all sought to benefit from the post-Mao modernization of the potentially massive Chinese internal economy.

Finally, the Chinese always have available the "Russian card" to play against the Reagan administration. Thus hints of, and real improvements in, Sino-Soviet relations of the sort that seemed to develop in 1983 even as Sino-American relations deadlocked over the Taiwan and arms sales issues, constituted a useful stick with which to pod the Americans towards policies more responsive to Chinese interests. In the final analysis, however, it may be unrealistic to expect that Sino-American relations can ever move much beyond the kind of difficult pseudoalliance that had emerged by the 1980s. By the early 1980s it was evident to military analysts that it would take decades before China could develop a full range of military capability beyond self-defense. China's utility as a military make-weight was, therefore, dubious. In the meantime, it was evident that political-economic issues had begun to displace strategic priorities in the Sino-American relationship. Thus throughout 1983, the question of U.S. quotas on Chinese textile imports and limits on high technology sales to China tended to dominate the agenda of Sino-American relations, superseding at times even the Taiwan issue.[36]

That Sino-American relations or, for that matter, U.S. relations with the entire region, might come to be a reflection of U.S.–Japanese relations is not happenstance. Obviously the fate of the Ferdinand Marcos regime in the Philippines, which began to totter in the wake of the suspicious assassination of opposition leader Benigno Aquino, while being closely guarded by government security forces as he sought to return to the Philippines from the United States, was central to American interests. No less important was the continuing deadlock on the Korean peninsula. However, the emergence of Singapore, Hong Kong, Taiwan, and South Korea as newly industrialized countries could prove more significant as their low-cost steel production and light manufacturing encroached upon the American market. If, as seems possible, China follows the lead of these countries, economic developments will likely prove far more consequential for the future of U.S. relations with the region than whether the Japanese assume more of the American defense burden— a major concern of the Reagan administration—or whether Soviet naval forces operate out of Cam Rahn Bay in Vietnam. Unfortunately, as Chalmers Johnson pointed out in early 1984:

> American policy toward the region, although displaying a deceptive and superficial competence, is based largely on premises that are a decade or more out of date. A majority of the senior governmental officials concerned

with East Asia are specialists in Asian communism; and with some important exceptions, they all suffer to varying degrees from the tunnel vision that long immersion in communist affairs produces. The need for a regional or even global political-economy perspective is only beginning to be recognized.[37]

In Africa, the focus of the administration's policy was, as in the Carter administration, on the south. However, rather than attempt to pressure the South Africans into a resolution of conflict along their northern borders and with respect to Angola over Namibia, the administration chose to pursue a policy of "constructive engagement" emphasizing inducements to the South Africans including warmer relations and even relaxation of restrictions on economic contacts. In return, the administration assumed that the South Africans could be eased toward a resolution of regional conflicts with their black neighbors as well as a liberalization of their internal apartheid policies.[38] Moreover, from the administration's perspective, the overriding problem in the region was Cuban influence and presence in Angola; therefore, any resolution of regional conflicts centering on Namibia and Angola were to be predicated on Cuban withdrawal.

The South Africans (like the Gemayel regime in Beirut), understanding that this U.S. concern for the global confrontation with Soviet power transformed the Americans into their patrons in the region, showed little willingness to adopt a more pliant posture. Indeed, South African attacks in Angola were increased as well as into Mozambique, from which guerrillas of the black opposition African National Congress were operating to greater effect in South Africa during the 1980s. Early 1984 did see some progress on regional security arrangements between the South Africans and their neighbors as the latter were forced to confront superior South African military capability. Furthermore, all parties needed a respite from armed conflict if their own internal development needs were to be met.

In the longer run, however, it is not clear how American policy will accomplish its twin objectives of regional stability and internal liberalization in South Africa. Insofar as South African policy continues to be based on a combination of military power and diplomatic delay with respect to its neighbors while emphasizing the communist threat to the region and itself, the Reagan administration seemed unable to serve as anything more than a guarantor of South African interests. As in the Middle East, however, this American association with the status quo weakens its credibility as a mediator of the region's disputes, a position belatedly but carefully constructed during the latter 1970s. Moreover, to the extent that the region's disputes remain unresolved and South Africa's regime remains based on apartheid and under intensifying black assault from within, the opportunity for the realization of the administration's great nightmare—growing Soviet influence—increases.

American Economic Recovery and the World Economy

Apart from the Reagan administration's abortive attempt to enlist the Europeans in its economic warfare against the Soviet Union, international economic policy receded from the position of prominence it had occupied during the 1970s. In part this was due to the declining fortunes of OPEC noted above. As the exercise of petropower proved more constrained than feared in the mid- and late 1970s, the broader concern with international economic interdependence lost much of its urgency. The international political economy of the early 1980s was dominated by the consequences of the intense politicizing of international economy in the 1970s: global economic depression, massive debt problems in the third world and Eastern Europe which threatened the international financial system, aggravated global poverty, and a lingering concern about the security of energy supplies. But by the 1980s such issues were no longer dominating the headlines; it was as though they had become routine.

No less important, perhaps, was the attitude and approach of the Reagan administration. Rather than regard these problems of international political economy as largely the result of conditions of interdependence which must be actively managed internationally, the administration viewed them as the result of *American* economic distress. It followed, therefore, that international economic difficulties, whether they afflicted the industrialized or developing nations, were best attacked through the reinvigoration of the American economy. The theme was set forth explicitly in the president's 1982 *Economic Report:*

> The successful implementation of policies to control inflation and restore vigorous real growth in the United States will have a profound and favorable impact on the rest of the world. . . . More generally, the Administration's approach to international economic issues is based on the same principles which underlie its domestic programs: a belief in the superiority of market solutions to economic problems and an emphasis on private economic activity as the engine of noninflationary growth.[39]

The principles of international coordination of economic policies received deference in the summit conferences of the major industrial powers at Versailles and Williamsburg in 1982 and 1983.[40] It was clear, however, that the United States was not prepared to make concessions to the Europeans and Canadians on those issues that concerned them most, i.e., high American interest rates that were pulling money out of their stagnant economies, if it meant weakening in any way what the administration regarded as an instrument of its domestic recovery program. Insofar as the American economy was perceived as the engine of global recovery by the administration, then American priorities would become the priorities of the industrialized world, notwithstanding the difficult accommodation to a more multilateral perspective during the 1970s.

The same policy held with respect to the developing world.[41] At the summit meeting of leaders from twenty-two industrialized and developing countries in October of 1981 in Cancun, Mexico, Mr. Reagan repeated the message that he had delivered at the meeting of the International Monetary Fund the month before. Development would occur, the president asserted, when the third world was opened up to the "magic of the marketplace" and the American economy was fully recovered. The latter was the essential precondition for eliminating poverty in the third world, but in the meantime these countries could prepare the way by reducing government controls on their own economies and opening themselves up to more outside investment.[42]

"We did not waste time on unrealistic rhetoric or unattainable objectives" Mr. Reagan noted upon his return from Cancun.[43] Thus the third world's call, during the 1970s, for a new international economic order was laid to rest by the administration. Nor were significant increases in foreign aid forthcoming for the poorest of the poor. Aid levels for Africa were maintained at the levels which had been granted in the late 1970s, but for a region beset with staggering debt—$65 billion in 1983 vs. $5 billion in 1970—and with virtually no prospect for growth during the 1980s,[44] such aid levels would prove increasingly inadequate. The administration was prepared to ask for significant aid levels, but it was for the Caribbean basin countries—especially El Salvador—Turkey, Israel, and Egypt, countries undoubtedly afflicted with poverty, but whose primary qualification for American attention was their strategic importance.

By early 1984 the American economy had clearly entered a period of recovery, but the benefits that the administration had assured the other members of the international economy would accrue to them were only dimly apparent. Whereas the United States was expecting growth of about 4 to 4.5 percent, Japan had experienced something over 3 percent and the Europeans had barely topped 1 percent. Moreover, although unemployment appeared to be dropping in the United States to levels near those that had existed at the onset of the recession, European unemployment rates were at the highest levels since the Second World War and showed no evidence of declining. Finally, the rate of recovery in the industrialized world offered little prospect of relief for the developing countries. The World Bank projected that the modest rates of recovery in evidence by the mid-1980s left an "outlook for many developing countries [that] is somber."[45]

Apart from the improving employment picture in North America and the diminished rate of inflation brought on by the recession itself, most of the international economic problems of the late 1970s remained firmly rooted in the mid-1980s. Very high U.S. interest rates—the result of the U.S. Federal Reserve's concern about a resurgence of inflation stemming from the enormous deficits built up by the Reagan administration as the result of its tax cuts in 1981 and its defense expenditures—had attracted a flow of dollars from abroad throughout the recovery thereby keeping the dollar strong. Europeans, undoubtedly conveniently ignoring many of their own domestic economic rigidities, placed much of the blame for their sluggish "recovery" on these high rates. In addition, European, Japanese, and American trade was increasingly afflicted by protectionism as all parties resorted to more and more bilateral arrangements, such as quotas, to manage their trade relations. By the mid-1980s, one observer estimated that the percentage of "managed" trade in what was ostensibly a free trading world had reached 30 to 40 percent and seemed likely to increase. "It remains an open—and valid—question," OECD trade expert Sylvia Ostry observed in early 1984, "whether creeping protectionism can just continue to creep or whether slow erosion, on reaching some invisible and unpredictable threshold, will abruptly transform the world trading system."[46]

The combination of the second oil shock in 1980, resultant global recession, and dramatic increases in real interest rates had led to another transformation of the system that was hardly creeping and held the possibility of a dramatic and catastrophic collapse of the international financial structure: the international debt crisis. As the price of oil and money soared and their economies collapsed into recession, a number of newly industrializing countries in the third world, several Eastern European countries, and virtually all less developed countries found their debt burden escalating dramatically. Whereas total outstanding debt had stood at $130.1 billion in 1973 this amount had increased to $614.2 billion by the end of 1982 with more than $100 billion of it owed to American banks. Latin American countries accounted for more than half of the total. By the end of 1982, the IMF estimated that the debt was equivalent to 246 percent of the annual export earnings of the non-oil-producing countries of Latin America. Argentina, for example, had an average debt in 1983 as a percent of its export of goods and services of 424 percent, Brazil stood at 359 percent, Chile 290 percent, and the oil-producing countries of Mexico and Venezuela stood at 275 percent and 196 percent respectively.[47] The entire structure of international banking seemed threatened and Mr. Reagan's recovery seemed to offer little solace. In fact, the high interest rates that seemed an inevitable part of the recovery exacerbated the problem.

As in the case of the oil crises that had brought on the debt crisis, *ad hoc* initiatives followed by an increasing degree of multilateral management emerged as the systemic response. Inasmuch as most of the debt was held by private banks, bank debt restructuring increased dramatically, especially during 1983 when some twenty countries negotiated refinancing, rescheduling, or deferment of debt totaling more than $59.2 billion. The previous year had seen six countries restructure $9.5 billion.[48] Simultaneously, official creditors, working closely with the IMF and the Bank for International Settlements, worked together within the so-called "Paris Club" to restructure debt resulting from various bilateral and multilateral foreign aid arrangements. Significantly, the IMF did not come to this process of private and official debt restructuring as a mere supplicant. In most instances, the Fund refused to offer its loan guarantee facility and its services as an agent for planning and administering the often "brutal" domestic adjustment programs in the debtor countries unless the private banks cooperated through the extension of more credit.[49] Even the Reagan administration was compelled in the end to pressure Congress into increasing the American government's participation in the Fund's exercise in international regulation—an ironic outcome for an administration ideologically committed to diminishing regulation of all kind and reliance on the market.

It would, of course, be a mistake to conclude from these developments either that the international system had once again "dodged the bullet" of international economic catastrophe by resorting to increased centralized, if *ad hoc*, management of the system or that the Reagan administration had accepted the process. Rather, it seemed likely that the debt-restructuring process would become a recurring crisis in that most of the arrangements worked out in 1982 and 1983 were scheduled to end by the end of the decade. Further, the Reagan administration's tenacious adherence to its "America first" approach to international economic recovery and policy suggested that the support of the IMF initiatives to deal with the debt crisis were at most pragmatic concessions in the face of undeniable international economic realities that were inexplicable and unmanageable within the confines of their market ideology.

CONCLUSION

In his advocacy of his domestic economic program, Mr. Reagan sought to reverse what he understood to be fifty years of ill-conceived social activism. In his most central foreign policy conceptions and actions of the early 1980s, it is evident that he sought a no less radical reversal or redirection of America's international relations away from what he regarded as the failed policies of accommodation and detente developed during the 1970s. In its intensely conflictive and bipolar view of international structure, the Reagan world view was not unlike that of Dean Acheson and Paul Nitze in NSC-68. Reagan's emphasis on strength, even superiority, as the basis of negotiations was the idiom of that early strategy for prosecuting the cold war. Mr. Reagan frequently indicated a desire to break out of what he felt was a debilitating "Vietnam syndrome"which overemphasized international complexity and limits on American power and thereby enfeebled American will. The anti-Soviet military buildup and economic warfare as well as the exercises of military power in the Caribbean and the Middle East, all within a framework of strident and moralistic rhetorical attacks on the Soviet Union and the legitimacy of its political and social order, became, therefore, the instrumentalities of this renewed American nationalism and activism. A softening of the rhetoric appeared as the president prepared for his reelection effort in early 1984,[50] but nothing in the policy framework put in place during the preceding three years was changed.

But this posture also included an often explicit denial of developments of the Vietnam era which, as we have seen, involved a great deal more than the defeat of American power in Southeast Asia. No less important were the onset of strategic parity; the emergence of new political economic forces as American postwar hegemony declined; a new configuration of political and economic capability in both East Asia and Europe; and an intensification of nationalism which tended to lend primacy to local forces and conditions in understanding instability in the third world. Notwithstanding their subordination to the superpower focus of the Reagan administration's renewed cold war, these forces and conditions retain their capacity to shape international politics and frustrate a foreign policy which ignores them.

NOTES

1. Cited by Wayne S. Smith, "U.S. Policy: The Worst Alternative Syndrome," *SAIS Review*, 3 (Summer–Fall 1983), p. 17.

2. Ibid., pp. 17 and 18.
3. *New York Times*, 4 March 1982, p. 4. Haig was quoted by an unnamed aide.
4. Thomas O. Enders, "Revolution, Reconciliation, and Reform," *SAIS Review*, 3 (Summer–Fall), p. 3. For reference to internal Carter administration attitudes see Abraham F. Lowenthal, "Ronald Reagan and Latin America: Coping with Hegemony in Decline," in Kenneth Oye, et al., *Eagle Defiant: U.S. Foreign Policy in the 1980s* (Boston: Little, Brown, 1983), pp. 312 – 316.
5. For a disucssion of the numbers killed by the death squads see Charles Mohr, "Salvador and Vietnam," *New York Times*, 10 August 1983, p. A8. For the report of the Salvadoran government cover-up of the churchwomen's death, see Raymond Bonner, "Cover-Up Charged in Death of Nuns," *New York Times*, 16 February 1984, p. A3.
6. Kirkpatrick, "U.S. Security and Latin America," *Commentary*, 71 (January 1981), p. 36.
7. Ibid.
8. "Central America Military Victory Called Necessity," *Washington Post*, 13 September 1983, p. A12.
9. For example, see Weinberger's statement of 6 September 1983 in Panama in *Washington Post*, 7 September 1983. The move to support the Salvadoran government and topple the Sandinistas was a boon to the CIA operations directorate. Almost every covert agent "riffed" in the 1970s—over 600 under retirement age—returned. The operations budget was doubled and was augmented by separate arm and drug enforcement intelligence units. *Washington Post*, 23 August 1983, p. A6.
10. On the legality of the American action, see the exchange between Abram Chayes and Eugene Rostow in *New York Times*, 15 November 1983, p. A35.
11. See the interview with Prime Minister Thatcher in *New York Times*, 22 January 1984.
12. *New York Times*, 1 July 1983, p. A1.
13. See two reports by Richard Halloran, "Vietnam Consequence: Quiet From the Military," *New York Times*, 2 May 1983, p. A16 and "For New Commanders, A Key Word is Caution," *New York Times*, 16 November 1983, p. A22.
14. *On Strategy* (Novato, CA: Presidio Press, 1982).
15. Halloran, "U.S. Army Chief Opposes Sending Forces to Aid El Salvador," *New York Times*, 10 June 1983, p. A9.
16. Michael Barone, "The Polls and Central America," *Washington Post*, 25 August 1983, p. A21.
17. Kenneth Waltz, "The Rapid Deployment Force," *International Security*, 5 (Spring 1981), pp. 49–74 and Robert Tucker, *The Purposes of American Power* (New York: Praeger, 1981), esp. pp. 69–114.
18. Congressional Budget Office, *Rapid Deployment Force: Policy and Budgetary Implications*) Washington, D.C.: Congressional Budget Office, 1983), pp. xvi ff.
19. Kaufmann, "The Defense Budget," in J.A. Pechman, ed., *Setting National Priorities, 1984* (Washington: Brookings, 1983), p. 67.
20. Harrison, "A Breakthrough in Afghanistan?" *Foreign Policy*, 51 (Summer 1983), pp. 3–26.
21. *Washington Post*, 25 September 1981, p. 10.
22. Jonathan Stern, "The USSR and Eastern Europe," in Joan Pearce, ed., *The Third Oil Shock: The Effects of Lower Price* (London: Routledge and Kegan Paul, 1983), pp. 60–72.
23. See Edward Morse, "An Overview: Gains, Costs and Dilemmas," in Pearce, op. cit., pp. 1–31 and Albert Bressard in "Oil Exporting Countries," p. 41. For a different view concerning OPEC's future, see Bijan Mossavor-Rhmani, "The OPEC Multiplier," *Foreign Policy*, 52 (Fall 1983), pp. 136–148.

24. Emphasis added; Weinberger, *Annual Report to the Congress, Department of Defense, FY1984* (Washington, D.C.: U.S. Government Printing Office, 1983), p. 191.
25. See the "Chronology 1981," in *Foreign Affairs—America and the World, 1981*, 60 (1982), p. 734.
26. See Christopher Van Hollen, "Don't Engulf the Gulf," *Foreign Affairs*, Vol. 59 (Summer 1981), p. 1067 *passim* and Stephen S. Rosenfeld, "Testing the Hard Line," *America and the World 1982–Foreign Affairs*, Vol. 61 (1982), p. 499.
27. For a brief overview of the war see International Institute for Strategic Studies, *Strategic Survey, 1982–1983* (London: IISS, 1983), pp. 64–78.
28. See "Sharon Misled Cabinet on Beirut Advance," *The Jerusalem Post*, January 29–February 4, 1984, p. 2.
29. "A New Opportunity for Peace in the Middle East," Current Policy No. 417 (Washington, D.C.: Department of State, 1982).
30. See the partial text of the Fez summit communique in *The Times* (London), 11 September 1982.
31. See the survey "The Marine Tragedy: An Inquiry Into Causes and Responsibility," *New York Times*, 11 December 1983, pp. 49–52.
32. For an account of this policy review and an overview of Middle East policy during the early Reagan administration, see Bernard Gwertzman, "Reagan Turns to Israel," *New York Times Magazine*, 27 November 1983, pp. 62–65, 82–88.
33. See Secretary of Defense Weinberger's description of the "redeployment" in Lou Cannon and John Goshko, "Troop Move Timetable Is Uncertain," *Washington Post*, 10 February 1984, pp. 1 and 23. This attack by Reagan included an attack of Speaker of the House Tip O'Neill *after* the Reagan administration had arrived at an internal decision to withdraw.
34. "President's News Conference on Foreign and Domestic Issues," *New York Times*, 23 February 1984, p. A12 and an interview with pollster Louis Harris of American opinion on Lebanon on "Morning Edition," National Public Radio, 23 February 1984. See also the Gallup Poll results reported in Steven Weisman, "President Asserts Marines in Beirut Still Have a Role," *New York Times*, 23 February 1984, p. A13.
35. For good overviews of regional developments in Asia from which this discussion is drawn, see Banning Garret, "China Policy and the Constraints of Triangular Logic," in Oye, op. cit., pp. 237–271; Chalmers Johnson, "East Asia: Another Year of Living Dangerously," *America and the World, 1983—Foreign Affairs*, 62 (1984), pp. 721–745, and Stephen P. Gibert, "Reagan's Asian Policy: The Past is Prologue," *Asian Perspective*, 7 (Spring-Summer 1983), pp. 51–72.
36. Johnson, op. cit., p. 734.
37. Ibid., p. 745.
38. For an elaboration of "constructive engagement" by its chief architect and subsequently assistant secretary of state for Africa in the Reagan administration, Chester Crocker, see "South Africa: Strategy for Change," *Foreign Affairs*, 59 (Winter 1980–1981), pp. 323–351. Useful critiques and overviews of the Reagan administration's policy in Africa are: Jennifer Seymour Whitaker, "Africa Beset," in *America and the World, 1983—Foreign Affairs*, 62 (1984), pp. 746–776, and Donald Rothchild and John Ravenhill, "From Carter to Reagan: The Global Perspective on Africa Become Ascendant," in Oye, op. cit., pp. 337 –365.
39. Council of Economic Advisers, *Annual Report, 1982* (Washington, D.C.: U.S. Government Printing Office, 1982), p. 167 and cited in Benjamin Cohen's overview of the administration's international economic policy, "An Explosion in the Kitchen? Economic Relations with Other Advanced Industrial States," in Oye, op. cit., pp. 105–130.

For a useful survey of the effects of this policy see Sylvia Ostry, "The World Economy in 1983: Marking Time," *America and the World, 1983*, pp. 533 – 560.

40. See the communiques of the Versailles and Williamsburg summits in *New York Times*, 7 June 1982 and 31 May 1983 respectively.

41. Richard E. Feinberg, "Reagonomics and the Third World," in Oye, op. cit., pp. 131–165.

42. The IMF speech can be found in *New York Times*, 30 September 1981, p. D22 and the president's assessment of the Cancun summit in *New York Times*, 25 October 1981, pp. 1 and 12.

43. "Text of Reagan's Statement on Cancun Talks," *New York Times,* 25 October 1981, p. 12.

44. Indeed, the World Bank projected in 1983 that Africa was likely to experience per capita incomes by the end of the decade lower than those of the 1960s. See World Bank, *World Development Report 1983* (Washington, D.C.: World Bank, 1983), passim.

45. Ibid., p.39.

46. Ostry, op. cit., p. 548.

47. See ibid, pp. 549–551 and E. Brau et al., *Recent Multilateral Debt Restructurings with Official and Bank Creditors,* Occasional Paper No. 25 (Washington, D.C.: International Monetary Fund, 1983). For the background of the Latin American situation see Pedro-Pablo Kuczynski, "Latin American Debt," *Foreign Affairs*, 61 (Winter 1982–1983), pp. 344–364 and Kuczynski, "Latin American Debt: Act Two," *Foreign Affairs*, 61 (Fall 1983), pp. 17–38.

48. Brau, op. cit., Table 8, p. 22.

49. See ibid, pp. 9–10, 13–14, and 23–24. The characterization of the Fund's "adjustment" arrangements as "brutal" is Ostry's, op. cit., p. 551. On the Fund's leverage on the entire restructuring process, see Ostry, pp. 551–552.

50. See "Transcript of Reagan's Speech on Soviet-American Relations," *New York Times*, 17 January 1984, p. A8.

Chapter 14
Conclusion

By the late 1940s it had become clear that world politics could never again be of episodic significance to the United States. Indeed, because of America's emergency as a great power, the Soviet presence in Europe, and the impact of nuclear weapons, foreign affairs would become very nearly transcendent. It was realized that there was more to international political life than Soviet-American relations. But since only the Russians and the Americans possessed both nuclear weapons and the semblance of a coherent foreign policy design reaching far beyond their respective frontiers, it was not illogical to suggest that their antagonistic relationship was central and gave a bipolar structure to international society. The notion implied, in the words of one of the patriarchs of contemporary international studies, a "worldwide balance of which the United States and the Soviet Union are the main weights, placed on opposite scales."[1] The ancient balance of power in Europe and the politics of the Near and Far East "shared the fate of the general European system. They have become functions of the new worldwide balance, mere 'theaters' where the power contest between the two great protagonists is fought out."[2]

AMERICAN POWER AND
THE DYNAMICS OF THE COLD WAR

This portrayal of a cosmic struggle found resonance in NSC-68. Here it was explained how total were the stakes, how irrelevant the specific day-to-day issues, how consuming the struggle, and how brutally the battle must be fought:

> What is new, what makes the continuing crisis, is the polarization of power which now inescapably confronts [a] slave society with the free. . . . The assault . . . is world wide, and in the context of the present polarization of power a defeat . . . anywhere is a defeat everywhere. . . .[3]

If there were to be negotiations, they would have to occur well past the mid-1950s—and then, the report concluded, they should be only a means for recording a favorable outcome for American power, not accommodating Soviet interests. Hence, American objectives were to

> . . . promote the gradual retraction of Soviet power. . . . To encourage the development . . . of the national life of groups evidencing the ability . . . to achieve and maintain national independence . . . [and to] promote . . . the emergence of satellite countries as entities independent of the USSR.[4]

In short, the description was of a world divided by a Manichean struggle in which the Soviet Union had few if any legitimate interests. The only means of obviating the contest was to gain the upper hand and then demand a withdrawal by the Soviet Union to a position of such reduced circumstances that the Soviet Union, no matter what its ultimate designs, would be forever limited in its means.

Technically, the American strategy was less incongruent with international and Soviet-American reality than it is now. That is, the Soviet Union was, by all accounts, a relatively weak although highly militarized society with limited means beyond those in place by 1948. In fact, for much of the postwar period, the world described by planners and professors was neither militarily equilibrated nor was it balanced in any other way. The Soviets, from the late 1940s to the mid-1960s, could pose no realistic military threat to the United States. At the end of World War II, although the Soviets had the largest armed force in the world, less than 50 percent of their transport was motorized, the rest was drawn by man and horse. And in 1962, at the time of the Cuban missile crisis, the Russians had few operational ICBMs, and they may well have been vulnerable to an American first strike. It is true that the Soviets could threaten Europe, probe at the frontiers of their empire, and, in that sense, hold those areas hostage. But there was always a ramshackle bluster attendant to each Soviet performance that belied the fears in American military planning documents and academic descriptions regarding the dimensions of the Soviet challenge.

The Soviets were, therefore, a massive, potential counterweight, largely isolated from international politics. To some extent their exclusion was self-imposed. Just as much, it was a product of the heroic scale of the American engagement in world affairs. Zbigniew Brzezinski's characterization of most of the years of the cold war rings true:

> more than a million American troops stationed on some 400 major and almost 300 minor United States military bases scattered all over the globe. [There were] more than forty-two nations tied to the United States by security pacts, American military missions training the officers and troops of many other national armies, and the approximately two hundred thousand United States civilian government employees in foreign posts all makes for striking analogies to the great classical imperial systems.[5]

This position of preeminence was basically unchanged until the 1970s. Yet most of the cold war was also marked by the growing complexity of international society as this American hegemony gradually deteriorated. And once American hegemony was lost and bipolarity became a more empirical portrait, those earlier strategies constructed around the hegemonial reality became less plausible.

A DECLINING PROSPECT FOR ORDER?

For the first twenty years there was a series of intense but, from an American standpoint, manageable spasms of change that undulated over global politics. Middle range powers gained access to nuclear weapons, but whatever form the professions of independence the nascent nuclear powers of Europe, China, and Israel took, their weapons inventories were no threat to the United States. On the contrary, they were almost invariably targeted on the Soviet Union.

In the former colonial areas, nationalist upheavals were as common as Marxist rhetoric, but if America's European associates were embarrassed by a declining capacity to monopolize the profit and politics of third world states, America hardly suffered from the process of decolonization. Although uncomfortable with both nationalism and collectivist ideologies, American business nonetheless moved with alacrity to fill the opportunities presented by rising demands for modernization and diminished European vigor. By the mid-1970s, notwithstanding a spurt of Soviet activity in the late 1950s and occasional abortive efforts on the Europeans to retain vestiges of the past, decolonization was complete. And nowhere in what was now called the third world were American and Western capital and technology unwelcomed; at worst, conditions were attached. When it mattered—in providing the means for international liquidity, managerial techniques, technology, or arms—American goods and services still had a leg up on the rest. The world had been, in Brzezinski's words, "filled by the more pervasive but less tangible [than military power] influence of American economic presence and innovation. . . ."[6]

By the 1970s, then, the reach of the United States—even its access—was no less and perhaps as great as at any time in the postwar era. However, the capacity to control events and determine outcomes had, nevertheless, been vitiated. In part, this resulted from circumstances over which the United States had little control. In other respects, the diminution of American hegemony has resulted from the playing-out—sometimes in an unforeseen manner and with unintended consequences—of policies consciously set in motion by the United States at the height of its international preeminence.

Perhaps the most fundamental change to affect the structure and dynamics of world politics in the 1970s has been the emergence of real Soviet military power that approximates the image of its power that existed in the early cold war years. Whereas its power was more hypothetical and potential than real and immediate in the late 1940s, 1950s, and most of the 1960s, by those early standards of the cold war, the Soviet Union is now a great power. It has a flexible nuclear capability, competent conventional arms, and adequate logistics, if not to sustain a global presence at great distance from the Soviet Union, then at least sufficient to complicate such a projection of power by the United States. Moreover, through the employment of proxies and surrogates such as the Cubans or East Germans, the Soviets can now conjure a more favorable correlation of forces, which, in the view of some Western observers, allows for the development of their own global presence.[7]

Short of preemptive war, the United States had few if any means available to it to prevent the Soviet Union achieving strategic parity. But the loss of nuclear supremacy has meant that American foreign and national security policies predicated on the threat or use of military force have become more problematic when applied to the Soviet Union. Though retaining a measure of deterrent utility and perhaps defensive efficacy should deterrence fail, nuclear weapons are hard to relate to any other purposeful activity. Few objectives really seem worth the costs associated with carrying out a nuclear threat. But a policy so poised seems loud, dangerous, and, ultimately, paralyzed.[8]

Nor are the constraints on the use of force confined to the domain of nuclear weapons. If there are observers to write a century or so hence, they may well record the 1970s and 1980s a watershed in the history of weapons. Innovations in weapons technology have allowed for miniaturization and the exponential multiplication of missile warheads deliverable with near perfect accuracy and thus the capacity to extirpate any target, once acquired. Consequently technological change may have doomed any serious attempt to monitor nuclear or conventional weapons stocks, fix the number of nuclear warheads, control the dispersion of inventories, and, equally distressing, may have eroded the functional distinction between the effects of nuclear and conventional weapons.

Then, too, there is the revolutionary increase in the defense capacity of conventional weapons inspired by the advent of precision guided, "one shot–one kill" weapons.[9] When these weapons spread to less advanced countries, the coercive capabilities of even superpowers against the weak will be constrained. Any future military planner contemplating military intervention will have to consider putting ships, planes, even tanks and armored personnel carriers at the risk of being disabled by foot soldiers toting simple, cheap, precision-guided weapons.

Finally, American policy must operate within an international system in which this diffusion of military capability encompasses nuclear as well as conventional weapons. In not many years, states that have abutted one another in hostility for years will gain access to nuclear weapons. Yet their technical ability to manage any meaningful control or viable command of these weapons, even in peacetime, may not be as extensive as the explosive power they can project into a territory that is the locus of ancient hatreds. Of those states that arms control experts expect to have viable nuclear delivery systems by 1990, many are in the third world and perhaps as many as seven have direct interest in the future of the Persian Gulf–Indian Ocean area. Insofar as antagonistic neighbors have had some tendency to bloody one another, it is not hard to understand why most observers are not hopeful about the future of a proliferated world.

Some have argued, however, that an extended "domino effect" of future conflict implicit in these arguments was discredited by the experience of the United States in Vietnam. But the example may be poorly chosen. For Vietnam's effects could be isolated, it could be argued, because of an eccentric confluence of events and circumstances: a domestic political paralysis in the United States and an international stalemate produced by the emerging triangular Sino-Soviet-American relationship and Soviet-American strategic parity. But what of an international environment in which—as may be the case now—diplomacy has fallen into low repute among the most significant actors, and military technology has begun to proliferate? Moreover, to the extent that the idea that peace is indivisible has prevailed, the notion itself has probably constrained interstate violence. Ironically, however, success in isolating Vietnam, not to mention a succession of Mideast wars, the Indo-Pakistani War, or the Sino-Vietnamese War, may have called into question the understanding that peace is a seamless web. War, especially in the non-West, may now be becoming more comfortably contemplated.

Of course, one cannot be sure. Some suggest, for example, that even if proliferation occurs it need not follow that war is inevitable between nuclear armed neighbors within a region. Or, if conflict occurs, it need not follow that it will be comprehensive and inevitably implicate the United States and the Soviet Union. Thus it may well be that deterrence dynamics will come to dominate the relationships of the *nouveau* nuclear powers and their relations with the superpowers even as deterrence has come to define so much of mutual superpower affairs.[10] But even if the latter condition does come about, other global interdependencies seem likely to ensure persistent vulnerabilities, tension, and conflict. And these are conditions likely to implicate the United States given the magnitude of its international economic involvement and dependency.

This is especially ironic, for if there was one set of conditions that the United States thought it could control after World War II, it was international economic interaction within the Western world. Weapons diffusion may have proceeded with unforeseen consequences in spite of an American attempt to use arms transfers as an instrument of policy. However, American initiative and resources for international economic reconstruction after World War II constituted a virtual monopoly. Presumably, therefore, an American vision would obtain.

In a sense it has. American policy was conceived within a context of economic ideas that held that if the economies of Western Europe and Japan could be reconstructed within an interdependent framework of monetary stability and free trade, both prosperity and peace would result. The benefits of interdependece, it was hoped, would constrain the nationalism that had ripped the world system to shreds during the first half of the twentieth century. Moreover, American planners believed that prosperity based on such interdependence was a necessary condition for the containment of Soviet power and the world economic growth necessary for the development of the third world.

The Bretton Woods system, Marshall Plan, and the dependencies of the third world on the industrial West for capital and markets are in a sense the fulfillment of the vision. On the other hand, the United States has not been able to escape the implications of this interdependence. For the decline of American strategic hegemony has been paralleled by the decline of its economic hegemony as well. The rise of European and Japanese centers of economic and, hence, political power—in part by American design—impinges on American freedom of diplomatic maneuver internationally and, no less painfully, penetrates American society through economic competition that threatens formerly secure markets and jobs. Similarly, formerly pliant energy producers in the third world whipsawed the industrialized world's economy through the exercise of a kind of economic power unimagined at the dawn of the cold war. In short, the United States and the rest of the world have come to realize what Jean-Jacques Rousseau knew: that interdependence and propinquity are as likely to produce conflict as peace.

Although the international politics of the late twentieth century does not therefore conform to a vision of an exclusively American century, the United States is, nevertheless, in a position of considerable potential leverage on the future. American resource scarcities and economic and military dependencies are linked to the financial, technological, investment, and security dependencies of others including America's adversaries. The sheer size and scope of America's military capability and economy and their centrality to the security of both the industrialized and the less developed world ensures that, as Helmut Schmidt once put it, "it is hard to achieve anything fundamental without the cooperation of the United States."[11] There are now others in international politics whose cooperation is no less essential, but, in a word, the United States, though no longer a hegemonial power, remains, nonetheless, a preponderant power.

The United States finds itself, therefore, at that point where most of the vulnerabilities and interdependencies of the rest of the world intersect. That position means that the United States will likely incur significant and probably increasing costs in its foreign and national security policies. But it also means that the United States is a necessary participant if successful international adjustment to the difficulties of interdependence is to come about. Dictating outcomes—a capability that the United States fleetingly possessed after World War II—is no longer within American grasp. But to the extent that very little that is creative can be done without it, the United States retains considerable capacity to influence and shape the relationships that will determine its international position and fortunes. As a power to be reckoned with and as a compelling voice, it could revert to some of the traditions of mediation and arbitration that characterized American diplomacy in the early twentieth century. This would require a retreat from a sense of American mission and exceptionalism; a return to some diplomatic formalism, tolerance, and patience; and the forswearing of the short-term advantages that sometimes accrue to the manipulation of national security issues and fears in domestic politics. But real American security could be enhanced. And that alone should give sufficient warrant to the effort.

THE ROAD TAKEN?

As the United States entered the 1980s, however, first the Carter and then the Reagan administrations persisted in defining American interests in the same way as administrations that preceded them: in terms of an American-inspired international order. That order, it has been believed, is held together by power—not an equilibrium of power, but an overall position of preeminence. Beyond a rational worry about the sum of deliverable warheads, alliances, and the distribution of bases, there continues to be the overarching concern with a psychological intangible: the malevolent intentions of the Soviet Union to feed on international chaos and the questioned capability of Americans to face the worst and stay the course. Hence, traditional criteria of evaluating interests such as geography, raw materials, markets, and armaments are placed alongside considerations of image, perceptions, prestige and credibility at home and abroad. The result is to blur distinctions between one American interest and another. For the means to case the "shadow of power," as Acheson once put it, has come to imply that American steadfastness must seem convincing on virtually a global scale. It is not surprising, therefore, that American interests remain in undiminished and undifferentiated definition or that the United States still concerns itself with the internal social structure and stability of states that have little tangible relationship to American security.

Brzezinski's words as he left office could have been spoken by Reagan, Dulles, Eisenhower, Rusk, McNamara, or Truman without hesitation over anything but syntax. Power, he suggested, "has to be sustained, cultivated and, when need be, applied so that others find it credible." "[O]ur willingness to cooperate with the Soviets," he warned, "must be carefully balanced with our willingness to compete assertively."[12] Similarly, when a Zbigniew Brzezinski, Walter Mondale, or Ronald Reagan publicly polishes old commitments lest any hint of tarnished doubt remain and adds new commitments in the Middle East or Central America there is always a sense that, whatever understandings there might have been as "new global political and economic arrangements . . . reflect new realities," the American response is fundamentally unchanged. American commitments remain extended like one of those financial empires of Billy Sol Estes, Bernard Cornfeld, or the Hunt brothers—offering ever new and shiny prospectuses, and living in dread of the auditors. The alternative of reexamining the structure and assumptions and techniques used to buttress the enterprise goes untried, lest the attention itself seem to lead to a panic which neither the United States nor its associates could withstand.

An especially deep pathos attached to the Carter administration. This was an administration, it will be recalled, that came to office proclaiming new perspectives and sensitivities to the international position of the United States—a "post–cold war internationalism."[13] Moreover, the American electorate, though undoubtedly skeptical, seemed, nonetheless, tolerant of an attempt to develop policies predicated on new perspectives and a sensitivity to a changed international environment. The 1976 Carter campaign, lest we forget, was based on an underscoring of its proclaimed differences from its predecessors who, especially in the figure of Henry Kissinger, represented the old approach to the world—and the electorate chose Carter, not Ford and Kissinger.

The Carter administration had, therefore, great opportunities. It could have used a moral appeal to ask Americans to contribute generously to a soothing of North-South issues instead of letting the issue become, by 1980, a battering ram for the left and right. It could have used the Kissinger legacy of a resurgence of diplomacy and attempted to sustain a sensible dialogue with the Soviet Union rather than attacking its legitimacy through the human rights issue. At home the nature of American commitments and interests might have been debated instead of insisting that all were equivalent and beyond reexamination.

Carter could have dealt with the revolutionary third world in terms other than simply a Soviet-Cuban cabal. There were, of course, some steps in this direction in Central America and southern Africa. But Carter's contribution to the trivial question of Soviet troops in Cuba was a half-hearted compromise that pointed to the nub of the administration's problem: Carter conceded that there was no security threat in troops that had been stationed in Cuba for over seventeen years. Yet at the same time he gave in to pressures to make parallel military arrangements with the Chinese, to examine yet again the question of bludgeoning the Soviets with economic weapons only marginally at America's disposal, and reopened the lid on a repertoire of military responses that have proved problematic and whose relevance to contemporary conditions seems more distant than ever. All this was *before* the Afghanistan crisis begot the Carter Doctrine that threatened to seal Soviet-American relations at the frigid plateau to which they had been diving since the Ford administration abandoned detente in the face of Ronald Reagan's thunder from the right.

Cuba, SALT, and Afghanistan became the vehicles for moving off the fence. No longer could the Carter administration contend that it would keep the interests and commitments of an imperial power and point to the logic and requirements of interdependence at the same time. That issue had been settled. The United States would dampen the rhetoric of human rights, redistributive equality, and arms control and would yield to the language of military superiority.

Of course, these shifts towards a renewed cold war internationalism could be rationalized as necessary tactical adjustments in the face of the domestic political threat posed by Ronald Reagan. The outcome of the Brzezinski-Vance conflict and the defense budgets advanced by the Carter administration as it was leaving office argue against such an interpretation, however. In any event, if the recrudescence of cold war internationalism was merely an electoral tactic, it failed and ideologically committed cold war internationalists ascended to power in the early 1980s. Ambivalence was replaced by passionate and simple conviction that an increase in the availability of military instruments and the assertion of activist will on a global scale could reverse the erosion of American primacy. The world was not understood to be structured around the complexities of liberal, post–cold war internationalism. Indeed, such arguments were seen as but manifestations of a "Vietnam syndrome"; its victims laden with guilt and denigrating the utility of military power not because international politics had changed but because they had lost their courage along with the war.

But if the Reagan administration's cold war internationalist assertion that the international system encompassed a simple bipolar world politics and gave to coercion a new centrality, it did not mean that force had found a new utility. Although the Grenada invasion seemed to substantiate the efficacy of force, the administration's failure in Lebanon, the bloody stalemate in Central America, and the onset of a new cold war in Soviet-American relations pointed to a more ambiguous conclusion. Force and diplomacy are two different tracks; sometimes they parallel one another; sometimes one leads into the other. But, as Averell Harriman once observed, "Nobody negotiates while being beaten on the head." The act of giving such a thrashing may serve short-term or even domestic interests, but it involves costs that successful and sustained diplomatic relations might have avoided. Force is diplomacy's nemesis; it serves best when it stands mutely behind a negotiator.

Yet in much American thought on international relations and strategic studies, and in much current political discussion, coercion and diplomacy have become synonymous. Force, even nuclear war, it is widely held, are instruments capable of a kind of choreography in which the manipulation of threats of violence and the use of violence itself in dealing with crisis has been defined as statecraft. Let us recall, however, that a diplomacy of violence has been tested and found wanting. Not the least, because Americans became aware of the difficulties in rearranging their domestic institutions to meet the needs of a diplomacy of force, or, for that matter, imposing democratic institutions on others by dint of firepower. Yet, the drum marshalling another attempt to fashion an American-designed world order has been beaten ever more forcefully in recent years. "Never," George Kennan despaired recently,

> since World War II has there been so far-reaching a militarization of thought and discourse in the capital. An unsuspecting stranger, plunged into its midst, could only conclude that the last hope of peaceful, nonmilitary solutions had been exhausted—that from now on only weapons, however used, could count. . . . We are now in the danger zone. I can think of no instance in modern history where such a breakdown of political communication and such a triumph of unstrained military suspicions as now marks Soviet-American relations has not led, in the end, to armed conflict.[14]

How such force and conflict could be made relevant to the task of world order in the contemporary environment has not yet been explained. Force could, to be sure, serve to inhibit the Soviets from embarking on a course of precipitous military action against states with whom Americans have associated themselves by reason of treaty, trade, or sentiment. Beyond that, however, military power has not staved off revolutionary change. The spread of collectivist ideologies antithetical to liberal procedural values has proceeded. Nor has military power seemed very relevant to a policy designed to promote human rights. And, finally, military power has seemed only tangentially, and perhaps even harmfully, to touch upon the increasing salience of international economic issues.

The relevance of military power is most apparent if the world is portrayed as anarchical and encompassing a zero-sum, bipolar Soviet-American relationship a struggle for supremacy between "an evil empire" and "the last and best hope of mankind."

But this was an unabashed call for the refutation of compromise and the adjustment of differences—the essence of diplomacy. With the abandonment of the diplomatic enterprise, however, only force remains. But if the irrelevance of diplomacy is coupled with generalized conditions inhospitable to American power, then the United States could realize its worst fears: expensively armed with inappropriate instruments but still vulnerable to careening events.

NOTES

1. Hans J. Morgenthau, *Politics Among Nations*, 1st ed. (New York: Knopf, 1949), p. 149.
2. Ibid.
3. NSC-68, p. 51.
4. Ibid., p. 62.
5. Zbigniew Brzezinski, *Between Two Ages: America's Role in the Technotronic Era* (New York: Viking, 1970), p. 34.
6. Ibid., p. 35.
7. Donald Zagoria, "New Soviet Alliances," *Foreign Affairs*, Vol. 57, No. 4 (Spring 1979), p. 738.
8. This is not to say that there are not many who assert that a rational and credible strategy of nuclear weapons use against the Soviet Union cannot be developed. For example, see: Colin Gray, "Nuclear Strategy: A Case for a Theory of Victory," *International Security*, Vol. 4, No. 1 (Summer 1979), pp. 54–87, and Gray and Keith Payne, "Victory is Possible," *Foreign Policy*, No. 39 (Summer 1980), pp. 14–27. For a more restrained view of the utility of force see, Robert J. Art, "To What Ends Military Power?" *International Security*, Vol. 4, No. 4 (Spring 1980), pp. 3–35 and Robert McNamara's recent denial of any political utility for nuclear weapons: "The Military Role of Nuclear Weapons," *Foreign Affairs*, Vol. 62 (Fall 1983), pp. 59–80.
9. James F. Digby, "Precision-Guided Weapons," *Adelphi Papers*, No. 118 (London:

International Institute for Strategic Studies, 1975) and Richard Burt, "New Weapons Technologies: Debate and Directions," *Adelphi Papers*, No. 126 (London: International Institute for Strategic Studies, 1976).

10. For an elaboration of this projection, see John J. Weltman, "Nuclear Devolution and World Order," *World Politics*, Vol. 32, No. 2 (January 1980), pp. 169–193.

11. *New York Times*, August 25, 1974.

12. See Richard Burt, "Brzezinski Calls Democrats Soft Toward Moscow," *New York Times*, November 30, 1980, and Michael Getler, "A Balanced Foreign Policy 'Much Needed,' Brzezinski Says," *Washington Post*, November 30, 1980.

13. See pp. 11–12, in the Introduction, for an elaboration of this notion.

14. *New York Times*, "Op Ed," February 1, 1978.

Index